A Concise Dictionary
of the Bible
and Its Reception

A Concise Dictionary
of the Bible
and Its Reception

JOHN F. A. SAWYER

WJK WESTMINSTER
JOHN KNOX PRESS
LOUISVILLE · KENTUCKY

Westminster John Knox Press
Louisville, Kentucky

09 10 11 12 13 14 15 16 17 18—10 9 8 7 6 5 4 3 2 1

Book design by Sharon Adams
Cover design by designpointinc.com

Library of Congress Cataloging-in-Publication Data

Sawyer, John F. A.
  A concise dictionary of the Bible and its reception / John F. A. Sawyer.—1st ed.
      p. cm.
  Includes bibliographical references (p.   ).
  ISBN 978-0-664-22338-0 (alk. paper)
  1. Bible—Dictionaries.   2. Bible—Reader response criticism—History—
Dictionaries.   I. Title.
  BS440.S29 2009
  220.3—dc22   2008022820

In memory of

Norman Porteous (1898–2003) and James Barr (1924–2006)

תנצב"ה

Contents

rida), and other individuals rather less obvious like Virgil and Seneca; and on major religious traditions (Jewish interpretation, Muslim interpretation, Orthodox interpretation) as well as minor (Anabaptists, the Baha'i Faith, Christian Science). Other topics include geographical areas (African interpretation, Asian interpretation, North American interpretation), chronological periods (Patristic interpretation, Medieval interpretation, Reformation), and philosophical or other movements (atheism, existentialism, hasidism, mysticism, romanticism, womanism, Zionism). There is ample discussion of matters like ethics, law, medicine, politics, popular culture, preaching, and war and peace, both in separate entries and in the articles on biblical books and themes. Much of the dictionary is devoted to literature and the arts, and in most cases there is one general survey article and separate articles on representative examples: for instance, one general article on art and architecture, and separate entries on selected artists (Blake, Chagall, Doré, Michelangelo, Rouault, Titian), as well as special cases such as Byzantine art, catacombs, Chartres Cathedral, and the Sistine Chapel. The same applies to literature, music, and drama.

An important feature of the dictionary is the lavish use of biblical references in almost every article, with an index at the end to enable readers to trace the afterlives of a particular verse or passage through the dictionary. Numerous cross-references are intended to make the work more homogeneous and user-friendly, and a good many brief definitions are included (aretalogy, catena, calque, glossolalia, *quadriga*), although even there

some reception history is included where appropriate. Many Hebrew and Greek terms are provided in transliteration (Heb. *mishkan*, "tabernacle"; Gk. *doxa*, "glory"), as are the usual Hebrew, Greek, and Arabic equivalents in the case of proper names common to Judaism, Christianity, and Islam: thus Abraham (Heb. *Avraham*; Arab. *Ibrahim*), Jerusalem (Heb. *Yerushalayim*, Arab. *Al-Quds*), Jesus (Heb. *Yeshua*; Gk. *Iesous*, Arab. *'Isa*), Solomon (Heb. *Shlomo*; Arab. *Suleiman*). A brief bibliography contains a selection of well-known and widely used dictionaries, encyclopedias, and the like, and some useful Web sites, for further reference. Quotations are from the RSV (1973) unless otherwise indicated.

It has been a pleasure to work on this project, and I hope that its readers will find it helpful, informative, and enjoyable. I am grateful to Philip Law and Donald McKim of Westminster John Knox for their patience, enthusiasm, and helpful advice and to the production team, especially Dan Braden. Of the many friends, colleagues, and relatives to whom I gladly record my gratitude for help and encouragement along the way, I will mention only my two professors, Norman Porteous and James Barr, who at New College Edinburgh in 1959 infected me with a passion for the Hebrew Bible from which I have never recovered and to whose memory I dedicate this volume; and, in another special category, my two sons, Alexander and Joseph, for their undeserved support and comments—not only on musical matters and popular culture.

John Sawyer
Perugia

a matter of course and in some cases somewhat reluctantly, the biblical allusions in works that they study. But modern biblical specialists have focused on ancient history and the quest for the original meaning of the text to the exclusion of its fascinating and often profoundly significant afterlives. The situation began to change in 1990 with the publication of Richard Coggins and Leslie Houlden's pioneering interdisciplinary *Dictionary of Biblical Interpretation* (rev. ed. 2003), which has articles on the Bible in art, the Bible in music, Marxist interpretation, the metaphysical poets, and the like. In the following year a valuable little book was published, *The Bible and Its Readers* (ed. Wim Beuken, Sean Freyne, and Anton Weiler), and in 1992 came another interdisciplinary reference book, David Jeffrey's *Dictionary of Biblical Tradition in English Literature*. Now as we enter the third millennium, biblical scholars are regularly publishing works on reception history like Yvonne Sherwood's *A Biblical Text and Its Afterlives: The Survival of Jonah in Western Culture* (2000), and Judith Kovacs and Chris Rowland's study, *Revelation: The Apocalypse of Jesus Christ* (2004) for the new Blackwell Bible Commentary Series. It is against this background that the present *Concise Dictionary of the Bible and Its Reception*, the product of half a century of *wirkungsgeschichtliche* biblical research, was conceived.

The Bible on its own is an enormous field, creating the need for multivolume dictionaries and encyclopedias, and I am well aware that the task of producing a one-volume dictionary to cover both the Bible and its reception would seem nearly impossible. But to quote the late Robert Carroll, "That's no reason for giving up." It just means that the result cannot be as perfect or as comprehensive as one would have liked, but I am confident that, for the most part, I have allowed the Bible and a very large and representative selection of its readers—poets, preachers, painters, sculptors, and musicians—to speak for themselves in a convenient and readable form. I have tried to include at least a brief discussion of everything important and relevant. What that means depends to some extent on who I am, what I have devoted my life to, and where I am at the moment, and I make no apology for any bias there may be toward Scottish Presbyterianism, the Hebrew Bible, and Renaissance Italy. But I have made every effort to allow the individual voices of other readers, ancient, medieval, and modern, worldwide, to be heard as clearly and as accurately as possible.

All the articles on the *Bible* are written with the emphasis on reception history, although important historical-critical issues are also referred to. The books of the Bible, the Apocrypha, the Pseudepigrapha, and some other texts (*Gospel of Thomas*, Qur'an) have their own entries, as do most of the main biblical characters, images, and events, all with reference to their role in Judaism, Christianity, and, where relevant, Islam, as well as in literature, music, art, film, and elsewhere. Some famous passages like the Akedah and the Sermon on the Mount have their own entries, as have many liturgical texts like the Kaddish, Dies Irae, and Magnificat. There are articles on relevant ancient languages (Arabic, Greek, Hebrew), cities (Babylon, Jerusalem, Rome), the versions (Septuagint, Vulgate, Authorized Version), types of Bible (Children's Bibles, Curious Bibles, Family Bibles), and also on book production, literacy, manuscripts, Masoretes, and the like. Scholarly tools and approaches (form criticism, oral tradition, reader response, semantics, structuralism, textual criticism) have their own entries as have many important biblical scholars (Jerome, Rashi, Calvin, Gunkel, Bultmann).

The other part of the project, *its reception*, involved identifying individuals and areas where the Bible has played a significant role. There are entries on preachers (Charles Spurgeon, Martin Luther King), hymn writers (John Newton, Isaac Watts, Charles Wesley), poets (Judah Halevi, Milton, Blake), philosophers (Maimonides, Kierkegaard, Der-

Introduction

What people believe the Bible means has often been more significant than what it originally meant. The tradition that Moses wrote the Pentateuch, for example, is more relevant to understanding its structure, meaning, and authority than the fact that he did not. The virgin (Gk. *parthenos*) in Matthew's version of the Immanuel prophecy (1:23) has had infinitely more impact on Western culture than the young woman (Heb. *'almah*) of the original Isaiah (7:14). The famous soprano aria in Handel's *Messiah* beginning "I know that my Redeemer liveth" has inspired and enchanted millions mainly because it has very little to do with the original passage in Job, which is very difficult and probably had nothing to do with life after death (Job 19:25); and the timeless beauty of Leonardo's *Last Supper* or a Raphael *Madonna* is due, partly, to the obvious cultural and topographical anachronisms. It can also be fascinating and valuable to reconstruct what the world was like in the ancient Near East, and how the teachings and prophecies of the Bible were originally understood by their earliest listeners or readers. Nor need such research be the exclusive preserve of archaeologists and historical critics. Postcolonial commentators, for instance, have sought to recover the original Asiatic face of Jesus, long submerged under white Eurocentric prejudice, and liberation theologians have identified important parallels between eighth-century B.C.E. Israel and contemporary worlds of peasant poverty and social injustice.

The study of postbiblical readings and artistic representations is known as reception history or *Wirkungsgeschichte*, that is, the history of the effect the Bible has had on its readers. It involves research into how the Bible was used by great thinkers like Augustine, Maimonides, Luther, Milton, Blake, and Kierkegaard, and what role it has played in the history of Judaism and Christianity, as well as in other aspects of human culture from Gnosticism to the Enlightenment, from the Renaissance to Rastafarianism. It also involves collecting and analyzing the many meanings that each text has had in different contexts, in a way that often gives us new insights into the language and imagery of the Bible. What better way to appreciate the dynamics of the extraordinary story of the Akedah (Gen. 22), for example, or the parable of the Prodigal Son (Luke 15) than by comparing and contrasting some of the ways in which they have been interpreted in literature and art?

The value of such research seems obvious, and yet until recently little room was left for it in biblical commentaries and dictionaries. Art historians and literary critics, as well as theologians, church historians, and others, discuss, as

Abbreviations

Akk.	Akkadian
ANET	Ancient Near Eastern Texts Relating to the Old Testament
Ant.	Josephus, *Antiquities*
Arab.	Arabic
Aram.	Aramaic
AV	(King James) Authorized Version
Egyp.	Egyptian
ET	English translation
Gk.	Greek
Heb.	Hebrew
JB	Jerusalem Bible
JPS	Jewish Publication Society Version
Lat.	Latin
LXX	Septuagint
ms(s)	manuscript(s)
MT	Masoretic Text
NAB	New American Bible
NEB	New English Bible
NIV	New International Version
NJB	New Jerusalem Bible
NRSV	New Revised Standard Version
NT	New Testament
OT	Old Testament
REB	Revised English Bible
RSV	Revised Standard Version
Tg	Targum
Ugar.	Ugaritic
Vg	Vulgate

APOCRYPHA AND PSEUDEPIGRAPHA

Esd.	Esdras
Jub.	*Jubilees*
Jdt.	Judith
Macc.	Maccabees
Sir.	Sirach (Ecclesiasticus)
T. Ab.	*Testament of Abraham*
T. Asher	*Testament of Asher*
T. Gad	*Testament of Gad*
T. Job	*Testament of Job*
T. Levi	*Testament of Levi*
Tob.	Tobit
Wis.	Wisdom of Solomon

RABBINIC LITERATURE

References to the Mishnah (*m.*) and Palestinian Talmud (Yerushalmi) (*y.*) are in the form *Sanhedrin* 10:1 (tractate title, chapter, paragraph).
References to the Babylonian Talmud (Bavli) (*b.*) are in the form *Hagigah* 14b (tractate title, page number).
References to *Midrash Rabbah* are in the form *Gen. Rab.* 60.3 (book title, *Rabbah*, chapter, paragraph).

Aaron (Heb. *Aharon*; Arab. *Haroun*). Brother of *Moses and *Miriam, Aaron plays a significant role in the story of the exodus (cf. Mic. 6:4). He stands by Moses in most of his dealings with the *pharaoh and in the battle against the Amalekites. At *Sinai he and his sons are anointed priests of the *tabernacle, and, like the high priest in the *temple at Jerusalem, who traced his ancestry back to Aaron, he is given unique authority to enter the Holy of Holies once a year, on the Day of Atonement (Lev. 16). Aaron courageously makes atonement for his people when they are threatened by destruction after Korah's rebellion (Num. 16). There was rivalry between the two brothers (Num. 12), and in the story of the *golden calf Aaron is represented as setting up an alternative cult (Exod. 32). Universally interpreted as synonymous with utter corruption and idolatry (e.g., Deut. 9:16, 21; Ps. 106:19; Acts 7:41), the story probably reflects opposition between rival Israelite hierarchies, the one later based in Jerusalem and the other at Bethel or Samaria in the north (cf. 1 Kgs. 12:25–33; Hos. 4:5–6; Mic. 1:6–7).

Tradition raised Aaron to a level equal to that of Moses (Mic. 6:4; Sir. 45:6); indeed, for *Hillel he represented peace and love in language never applied to Moses (*m. Abot* 1:12). The image in Ps. 133 of "precious oil" running down Aaron's beard onto his breastplate, where the twelve tribes of Israel were represented, was interpreted as referring to his role as peacemaker. From NT times, like *Melchizedek, Aaron points toward Christ the great High Priest (Heb. 5:4; 7:11). For George *Herbert and others his vestments symbolized the inner spiritual qualities required of a priest, while for *Calvin "Aaron and his sons" smacked more of Roman apostolic succession. In Christian iconography Aaron's rod, which miraculously bore fruit (Num. 17), prefigures the virgin birth, while in D. H. Lawrence's novel *Aaron's Rod* (1922) the same biblical symbol is applied to sexual and artistic liberation. Arnold Schönberg's unfinished opera *Moses und Aron*

(1930–32) provides a rare opportunity for the characters of Aaron and his brother to be developed in a powerful and dramatic way.

Abel (Heb. *Hebel*; Arab. *Habil*). Brother of *Cain, the first martyr (*1 Enoch* 22:7; Matt. 23:35; Luke 11:51) and paragon of faith (Heb. 11:4). He is also the first righteous man (cf. 1 John 3:12), and one ancient Jewish text represents him as seated on a throne judging all creation, because the righteous should be judged by a righteous man, not by God (*T. Ab.* 13). Patristic and medieval Christian interpretations follow the same line, as does *Milton, who associates him with Christ. In Christian *liturgy and iconography his offering, which was acceptable to God (Gen. 4:4), along with those of *Abraham and *Melchizedek, is a type of the eucharistic sacrifice. The rabbis speculated on the reasons for Abel's murder, the murder weapon, and problems associated with his burial, while "the voice of Abel's blood crying from the ground" has prompted many writers, including *Coleridge, *Byron, and Shelley, to focus on the psychology of guilt.

Abraham (or Abram; Heb. *Avraham*; Arab. *Ibrahim*). The first of the three patriarchs, Abraham, *Isaac, and *Jacob, spiritual ancestor of Judaism, Christianity, and Islam. He was called by God to leave his family in Ur of the Chaldeans and journey to *Canaan, where he and his family were buried. God's *covenant (or "promise"; cf. Luke 1:55, 73) with Abraham, according to which their descendants would settle there and spread throughout the world bringing blessing to all the families of the earth (Gen. 12), was sealed by the rite of *circumcision that he instituted (Gen. 17). Of the many stories told of him in Gen. 11–25, by far the most familiar and widely used in the traditions of all three world religions is the *Akedah. But the biblical accounts of his relationship with his wife *Sarah, his concubine *Hagar, and his nephew *Lot, his visit to Salem (*Jerusalem) in the days of *Melchizedek, and his intercession for the doomed people of *Sodom, all play a significant role too.

For Christians from Paul (Rom. 4) to *Luther and *Kierkegaard, Abraham is the archetype of the man of faith. In the *Qur'an he is the "Friend of God," a man of pure faith (Arab. *hanif*), the first to submit completely to his will and thus the first Muslim (3:60; 4:124). In Jewish prayer God is addressed as the "Shield of Abraham" (Gen. 15:1) in the first blessing of the *Amidah; and in the parable of Lazarus and the Rich Man, "Abraham's bosom" signifies the peaceful repose of the righteous after death (Luke 16:19–21; see *Lazarus 2). In music Abraham appears in the refrain at the end of the *Dies Irae, *Quam olim Abrahae promisisti*, "As you once promised to Abraham," as well as in the *Magnificat, the *Benedictus, and an 18th-century English hymn beginning "The God of Abraham praise." In addition to many paintings of Sarah, Hagar, the destruction of Sodom and Gomorrah, and the Akedah, the visit of the three angels to Abraham (Gen. 18) has been a favorite subject for artists, including *Ghiberti, *Raphael, *Rembrandt, *Turner, and *Chagall.

In the light of modern archaeology scholars have sought to reveal historical events and conditions behind the biblical narrative. The names of some of the characters in the story, such as Amraphel and Tidal in Gen. 14, have been compared to names occurring in ancient Babylonian and Hittite texts of the 18th century B.C.E., while some of the legal practices recounted in the narrative, such as marriage customs, seem to be mirrored in legal documents found at Nuzi, *Mari, and other cities from about the same period. Abraham's connections with centers of Davidic influence such as Hebron (Gen. 23) and Jerusalem (Gen. 14:18–20; 22) probably reflect conditions centuries later, and it is more than likely that his unique role in biblical tradition was strengthened and modified as the beliefs and practices of Israel took shape over a period of many centuries.

Abraham, Testament of. See *Testament of Abraham*.

Abravanel, Isaac (1437–1508). Jewish statesman and exegete. Born in Lisbon, he was forced to leave home with all the other Jews in 1496 and died in Venice. He wrote commentaries on the *Pentateuch, the Prophets, and *Daniel. Despite anti-Christian *apologetic in much of his work and the fact that his commentary on *Isaiah was placed on the Index, he was influenced by Christian writers including *Jerome, *Augustine, and *Thomas Aquinas, and his works were translated into Latin and widely consulted by non-Jewish Renaissance scholars.

Absalom. *David's third son, who rebelled against his father and died, hanging by his hair from a tree, while trying to escape from his pursuers (2 Sam. 13–18). According to ancient Jewish tradition, the crime against his father was so serious that he was one of the few Jews who have no share in the world to come. The church fathers used him as an illustration of human sinfulness, while medieval writers for the most part marveled at Absalom's physical beauty and the appropriateness of the mode of his death. Political interpretations of the story, like those of Cranmer, *Tyndale, and *Dryden, were common in 16th- and 17th-century England. David's grief on hearing the news of his son's death, expressed so poignantly in the verse "O my son Absalom, my son, my son Absalom! would God I had died for thee, O Absalom, my son my son!" (2 Sam. 18:33 AV), has moved many modern writers, including Walter Scott, Thomas Hardy, and Alan Paton in his *Cry, the Beloved*

Country (1948). *Faulkner's *Absalom, Absalom!* (1936) makes clever use of other parts of the biblical story as well, including Absalom's killing of his half-brother Amnon for raping his sister Tamar.

Acrostic.   In an acrostic poem the first letters of each line make up some kind of recognizable sequence. In a number of examples in the Hebrew Bible the sequence is alphabetical. These include nine *Psalms (e.g., 34; 111; 119), the poem "In praise of the virtuous woman" at the end of *Proverbs (31:10–31), and most of *Lamentations (Lam. 1–4). The function in some cases was no doubt to display the writer's literary expertise or to facilitate memorizing, but in other contexts it was probably intended to suggest that everything, from A to Z, had been said on the subject of the poem.

Acts of Andrew.   An apocryphal work, probably from the 3rd century, recounting the travels of the apostle and his imprisonment and martyrdom in Patras in Greece. It survives only in fragments, but an extended epitome is given by Gregory of Tours (6th century). See *Andrew.

Acts of John.   An apocryphal work, known already to Clement of Alexandria, which contains the apostle's memories of Jesus, including his own detailed account of the *transfiguration and the *passion, as well as some information about his later life and martyrdom in Ephesus. It also contains the beautiful "Hymn of Jesus" arranged for chorus and orchestra by Gustav Holst (1917).

Acts of Paul.   An apocryphal work comprising the *Martyrdom of Paul*, the *Acts of Paul and Thecla*, and the *Third Letter of Paul to the Corinthians*. Written probably in the 2nd century, it adds many details to the biblical sources that have been influential in Christian literature and the iconography of Paul. These include the description of Paul as "bald and bandy-legged," references to the role of Nero, and a remarkable account of the virgin *Thecla's conversion on hearing him preach, and her miraculous survival, first when thrown to wild beasts and then when her mother tries to have her burned on a pyre.

Acts of Peter.   An apocryphal 2nd-century Greek text containing a popular account of the martyrdom of Peter, in which the famous *Quo Vadis?* scene appears for the first time, as well as the description of Peter's crucifixion upside down.

Acts of Pilate.   An apocryphal work appearing in some mss as the first half of the *Gospel of Nicodemus*. Written probably in the 5th or 6th century, it tells of the trial, death, and resurrection of Jesus, adding to the canonical account such details as the bowing of the Roman standards to Jesus and the names of Pilate's wife (Procla) (cf. Matt. 27:19) and the two robbers crucified with him (Gestas and Demas).

Acts of the Apostles.   *Luke's account of the origin and growth of the church from the final parting of Jesus from his disciples in Jerusalem (*Ascension) and the coming of the Holy Spirit at *Pentecost, to the arrival of *Paul in *Rome. Most of the first half of Acts is set in *Jerusalem and recounts the role of *Peter and *John in the regrouping of the disciples, the martyrdom of *Stephen, the conversion of Saul on the road to Damascus, the martyrdom of *James, and the imprisonment and miraculous release of Peter. The second half is devoted to the missionary journeys of *Paul to Asia Minor, Greece, and Rome accompanied by Barnabas, John, Simeon, Silas, Timothy, and others, perhaps including Luke himself (Col. 4:14). After *Irenaeus, who cites Acts frequently as evidence for the unity of the apostolic tradition, the first writers to focus on Acts as Scripture were *Ephrem and John *Chrysostom (c. 400), who defends its importance for what it says about the Holy Spirit, followed later by *Bede and *Rabanus Maurus. Not until the 12th century is Acts treated in the same way as the other books of the Bible, and not until the Reformation do full-scale commentaries, like those of *Calvin and *Grotius, become common. *Luther described Acts as a commentary on Paul's letters, proving with historical examples that justification is by faith alone.

*Historical criticism in the 18th and 19th centuries cast doubts on the historicity of Luke's account of Christian origins, and questions raised about the author's political and theological aims. F. C. *Baur argued that it was an attempt to reconcile two conflicting elements in the early church, a Judaizing party represented by Peter and a pro-Gentile lobby led by Paul. Others argued that it was primarily addressed to the Roman authorities, designed to convince them that Christianity was not going to cause any trouble. Twentieth-century theologians like *Bultmann saw in Luke–Acts a shift from an early eschatological *kerygma about the imminent end of the world to a continuation of the biblical narrative of God's mighty acts, while social scientists look for evidence in Acts for the earliest stages in community organization and growth.

Dissident or minority groups within the church have found in Acts scriptural authority for an egalitarian form of Christianity ("having all things in common," 2:44), women priests (21:9), house churches (12:12–18; 16:11–15), and the charismatic movement. A number of imaginative apocryphal works are modeled on the biblical book: *Acts of Paul and Thecla, *Acts of Peter, *Acts of Thomas, and *Acts of Pilate, some of which contain interesting material cited by feminists and others as evidence for alternative forms of early Christianity.

The most complete representation of Acts in art, including scenes showing the stoning of Stephen, the death of Ananias, and the conversion of Paul, is the series of ten tapestries designed by *Raphael for the *Sistine Chapel and now in the Vatican Picture Gallery. Many passages from Acts are set to music in Mendelssohn's oratorio *Paul* (1836) and *Elgar's *The Apostles* (1902–3).

Acts of Thomas. A 3rd-century gnostic work, probably originally composed in Edessa in *Syriac, that contains an account of some of the legends about *Thomas (Mar Thoma), including his journey to India, and the beautiful Hymn of the Pearl (108–13). It also recommends poverty, chastity, and even celibacy in marriage.

Adam. The first human being, created out of the soil of the earth (Heb. *adamah*) according to Gen. 2. In Hebrew *adam* is the collective noun for "human beings, humankind," male and female (Gen. 1:26–27), so that *ben adam* ("son of man") means "a human being, a person." It is also a proper name, "Adam," and when "man" (*ish*) and "woman" (*isha*) are formed later in the story, this becomes the name of the first male ancestor of the human race, consort of *Eve. The Greeks interpreted the four letters of his name in Greek as referring to the four points of the compass. The biblical story of his behavior in the garden of *Eden, first obedient to God's will, then independent of it, provided Christians from Paul on with a scriptural model of fallen humanity, paving the way for the coming of Christ as the "second Adam" to redeem them (1 Cor. 15:22). The concept of two Adams, an earthly, human one and a heavenly, ideal or primeval one, is well known in Jewish tradition too, starting with *Philo and culminating in traditions about the shining heavenly garments of Adam and Eve, and the mystical notion of the "Perfect Man." In Jewish tradition the angels advise God to refrain from putting human beings into the world because of the evil that is bound to result. The church fathers speculated on how Adam's sin was transmitted to the rest of the human race, while later speculation focused on whether he was a historical character, and whether he had a navel. The image of Adam in Christian literature and iconography is often one of weakness and sorrow, as in the 15th-century Easter hymn "Adam lay y-bounden" and *Piero della Francesca's *Legend of the True Cross* in Arezzo, although better known is *Michelangelo's painting of the creation story where the fingers of God and Adam are almost touching. See *Life of Adam and Eve*.

Adam and Eve, Books of. See *Life of Adam and Eve*.

Adam, Testament of. See *Testament of Adam*.

Advent. The ecclesiastical season of approximately three weeks (four Sundays) leading up to *Christmas. Advent lectionaries focus on the second coming of Christ (*Parousia) (Matt. 3:1–12; 24:37–44; Rom. 13:11–14) and the day of judgment (Isa. 2:1–5, 2 Pet. 3:8–14) as well as generally on the dawn of a messianic age in which the language of *Isaiah predominates (Isa. 9:2–7, 11:1–9; 35:1–10; 40:1–11; 54:1–10). There are also many musical settings of verses from Isaiah, notably the "O Antiphons" popularized in the hymn "O Come, O Come Immanuel," and the popular medieval chant *Rorate coeli* (Isa. 45:8), originally interpreted as referring to the virgin birth and still current in a modern version beginning "Rain down justice."

Aetiology. An explanation of why things are as they are. Many biblical stories, especially in the book of *Genesis,

contain aetiological elements explaining, for example, the origin of words like *isha*, "woman" (Gen. 2:23), or names like Isaac (17:17–19) and Bethel (28:17–19). Others describe the origin of natural phenomena like the rainbow (9:12–17), ancient customs like the *Passover rituals (Exod. 13), and territorial claims such as the right of Abraham's descendants to settle in the promised land (Gen. 15:18–21). Technically the function of such aetiologies is to answer questions about ancient tradition (e.g., "What mean these stones?" Josh. 4:21 AV), but frequently they function as a literary device designed to make a political or theological claim. The identification of a narrative as primarily aetiological, from the appearance of such phrases as "to this day," may imply that it does not recount historical fact, but this does not apply in every case.

African American interpretation. Forcibly imported from a predominantly oral culture into one that was in almost every respect alien to them, the African slaves in America at first had little direct contact with the Bible. It was not until the appearance of the evangelical preachers of the late 18th century that they began to learn about it and make it their own. They found it easy to identify with the Hebrew slaves and their hope that one day they would cross over the Jordan to the promised land, and to believe in a Savior who showed how suffering and death can lead to new life. Their distinctive retelling and appropriation of the biblical stories can be seen in spirituals like "Go down, Moses," "Joshua fit the battle of Jericho," "Balm in Gilead," and "Were you there when they crucified my Lord?" as well as in much of 19th- and 20th-century American literature from the poetry of the black slave Phillis Wheatley (c. 1753–85) and Stowe's *Uncle Tom's Cabin* (1852), to Alice Walker's *The Color Purple* (1982) and Toni Morrison's *Beloved* (1987).

The Bible provided the language and imagery of the rhetoric that was eventually, under the leadership of twentieth-century political activists like Martin Luther *King Jr., to win black Americans equal rights. Favorite texts included the eighth-century prophets' calls for social justice (e.g., Amos 5:21–24) and passages declaring that "all are one in Christ Jesus" (Gal. 3:26–28; Acts 10:34–36). More recently the existence in many parts of the United States of predominantly black congregations, however, many of them Pentecostal and mostly led by academically well qualified preachers and pastors, may mean the end of distinctive African American interpretations of the Bible, for so long dominated by racial and socioeconomic questions, and an approach in most respects indistinguishable from that of many white American Christians. See *African interpretation; *North American interpretation; *Slavery; *Womanism.

African interpretation. An approach to biblical interpretation that reassesses the role of Africa in the Bible and Christianity, and challenges the white Greco-Roman tradition that has been superimposed on Western Christianity for much of its history. There has been some discussion of whether the term "Africa" is itself a European construct bringing together disparate cultures, and to what extent diaspora African interpretations, especially from America and the West Indies, are included. An increasing number of publications such as *The Bible in Africa* (ed. Gerald West and Musa Dube, 2000) demonstrate a growing consensus among African scholars and general readers of the Bible. The European setting of the biblical stories, as portrayed in Christian iconography down the centuries and more recently in film, is questioned on the grounds that Europe plays a very minor role in the biblical account of Christian origins and the chief biblical characters were Afro-Asians, not white Europeans. Some of the church fathers were Africans, including *Tertullian and *Augustine of Hippo, but they wrote in

Latin and did not deliberately address the indigenous population.

Afrocentric readings of the text focus on references to Africa throughout the Bible, from the location of the garden of *Eden (Gen. 2:13) and African involvement in the exodus story (Num. 12:1), to the Holy Family's journey to Egypt (Matt. 2:13–20), Simon of Cyrene, the African who helped Jesus in the *Passion Narrative (Matt. 27:32), and the Ethiopian eunuch (Acts 8). Special significance is perceived in Ps. 68:31 ("let Ethiopia hasten to stretch out her hands to God"), and other passages where Africa has a share in some of the great prophetic visions of the Bible (Isa. 11:11; 18:1–2). Modern definitions of "black" that include people of African and Asian origin extend the number of blacks in the Bible from a few individuals like *Nimrod the son of Cush, the *Queen of Sheba, and the prophet *Zephaniah (1:1) to almost everyone, including Jesus. This is also reflected in black Madonna icons familiar in parts of North Africa and Eastern Europe. A striking example of the influence of African interpretation on some modern translations of the Bible can be seen in the *Song of Songs where the traditional "I am black but comely" (AV) has become "I am black and beautiful (NRSV) (1:5). The role of divination in some African cultures has also contributed to African readings of Scripture, and political readings of the Bible are naturally popular in postcolonial Africa. See *Rastafarianism.

Aggadah (Heb. "story, anecdotage"). Aggadah (or haggadah) and *halakkah are the two chief categories of material in rabbinic exegetical literature. Aggadah consists of stories and legends on all manner of topics, historical, astronomical, medical, etc., often containing profound philosophical and ethical insights on which most of the theology of rabbinic Judaism is based. Much of this type of material is contained in *midrash and has an exegetical function, but aggadah also accounts for a large proportion of the *Talmud as well. Only a small proportion of the midrash is halakkic. Typical examples of aggadah would be stories about the angels trying to persuade God not to create humankind and not to give Israel the Torah, or about the patriarchs studying Talmud, or the child who was destroyed by fire because he was found reading the first chapter of *Ezekiel, or the four rabbis who entered paradise. The *Passover Haggadah contains aggadic material filling out the story of the exodus.

Agnus Dei (Lat. "O Lamb of God [that takest away the sins of the world]"). The first words of an ancient Christian prayer derived from John 1:29 (cf. Isa. 53:7), the fifth and final part of the Roman *Mass since the 7th century. It also plays a role in other liturgies as an independent anthem and there is a well-known setting for eight-part choir by Samuel Barber (1967).

Ahikar (or Ahiqar; Arab. *Loqman*). "The Story of Ahikar" is an Aramaic text found in a 6th–5th-century B.C.E. papyrus at *Elephantine, and surviving also in a number of translations, especially Syriac, Arabic, and Armenian. It tells how Ahikar, a wise political leader in the government of the Assyrian king *Sennacherib (cf. Tob. 14:10), is condemned to death on forged evidence but survives in hiding to be ultimately reinstated by the king with great honor. The story is similar to that of *Tobit, and his "Teachings" or "Parables," which make up a significant part of the book, have parallels in the Bible (Ps. 141:4; 2 Tim. 4:17) and the Qur'an (31:17).

Akedah (or *Aqedah*). Of all the biblical traditions about *Abraham, *Isaac, and *Jacob, "the binding (Heb. *akedah*) of Isaac" is the most influential (Gen. 22). It was originally perhaps an aetiological legend explaining the change of ritual practice from human *sacrifice to animal

sacrifice, and claiming ancient patriarchal authority for the site of Solomon's temple at Jerusalem. But in its canonical *context, and as it is interpreted in many later contexts as well, it is interpreted as the supreme test of Abraham's faith. At an early stage in the history of its interpretation the focus shifted from Abraham to his victim: the fate of Isaac who survived was contrasted with that of the martyrs who did not, or according to some, like the poets Ephraim of Bonn (1132–1200), writing at the time of a crusader massacre, and the war poet Wilfred Owen (1893–1918), Isaac actually died (Gen. 22:4). Both Abraham's meritorious act and the atoning "blood of Isaac" or "the ashes of Isaac" figure in Jewish prayer (see Shalom Spiegel, *The Last Trial*, 1967).

Christian *typology identified Isaac with Christ, the wood on his back, for example, foreshadowing Christ bearing the cross on his way to Calvary. In art the image of Abraham preparing to slay his son with a knife appears, in widely differing versions, from early *synagogue decoration (*Dura Europos, 3rd century; Beth Alpha, 6th century) and the Renaissance artists *Ghiberti, *Raphael, *Caravaggio, and *Rembrandt, down to *Blake and *Chagall. There is a reference to the Akedah in the Qur'an (37:101–7), though interpreters locate the event at Mecca and identify the son as Ishmael rather than Isaac. Modern interpreters have seen it is a parable of the agony of a man forced to choose between religious faith and ethics (*Kierkegaard, *Fear and Trembling*), or used it as a vehicle for protest against war (Wilfred Owen; *Britten, *War Requiem*). In some post-Holocaust readings, such as that of the Israeli poet Amir Gilboa (1917–84) and the Oscar-winning film *La Vita è bella* (*Life Is Beautiful*, 1997), it is the father who dies, not the son.

Akiba (or *Aqiba*) (c. 50–132 C.E.). Great Jewish rabbi in the period from the destruction of the *temple in 70 C.E. to the

Bar Kokhba Revolt, when it is said he died a martyr's death with the words of the *Shema on his lips (Deut. 6:4) (b. Berakot 61b). There are references to a "*Mishnah of Rabbi Akiba" (m. Sanhedrin 3:4), and among the many sayings attributed to him are that "the tradition (masora) is a fence round the Torah (m. Abot 3:14), "all is foreseen but freedom of choice is given" (Abot 3:16), and "all the world is not worth the day on which the *Song of Songs was written" (m. Yadayim 3:5). Of the "four who entered paradise" on a mystical journey (cf. 2 Cor. 12), he alone returned unscathed (b. Hagigah 14b).

Albright, William Foxwell (1891–1971).

Semitic philologist and biblical archaeologist. Son of a Methodist missionary, Albright taught himself Hebrew and Assyrian at an early age and won a scholarship to study Modern Hebrew and Arabic in Palestine, where he became director of the American School of Oriental Research in Jerusalem. He excavated a number of important sites, including Tell Beit Mirsim and Bethel. His overriding concern was to use archaeological evidence to throw light on the origin and meaning of the Bible. His influence on specialists and the general public alike was immense, both through his teaching at Johns Hopkins University in Baltimore, Maryland, where his former students include John Bright, Frank Moore Cross, T. O. Lambdin, Raymond *Brown, and a host of other illustrious biblical scholars, and through his publications, of which the most widely read are From the Stone Age to Christianity: Monotheism and the Historical Process (1940) and The Archaeology of Palestine (1949).

Alexandria (modern Iskenderun).

Founded by Alexander the Great in 331 B.C.E. on the Mediterranean coast of Egypt, Alexandria soon became a major center of Greek learning. Under the Ptolemies a famous library and an inter-national research center known as the "Museum" were established there, and the first Greek translation of the Hebrew Bible, the *Septuagint, was produced for use in the large Greek-speaking Jewish community. Alexandria was the second city in the Roman Empire after *Rome. Alexandrian scholarship influenced Jewish writers, especially *Philo, and both Christian and rabbinic exegetical methods. Under the leadership of *Clement, *Origen, and *Cyril, distinctive Alexandrian traditions of biblical interpretation emerged, characterized by the belief that texts have other senses beside their *literal meaning and the regular, some would say excessive, use of allegory and *typology. See *Allegorical interpretation.

All Saints' Day.

The feast celebrating all the Christian saints, observed in the East on the first Sunday after Pentecost, and in the West since the 8th century on November 1. Many families also count their own loved ones among the saints in heaven and lay flowers on their graves. Scripture passages prescribed to be read on All Saints' Day include a hymn from *Sirach (44:1, 10–15), the Beatitudes (Matt. 5:1–12), John's vision of "a great multitude that no one can number . . . clothed in white robes with palm branches in their hands" (Rev. 7:9), and a promise that the faithful too will one day see God as he is (1 John 3:1–3). Among the most popular hymns for the day are "For all the saints who from their labours rest," set to music by *Vaughan Williams, and John *Newton's "Glorious things of thee are spoken," based on Ps. 87 and Isa. 33:20–21, and normally sung to *Haydn's "Austrian melody." In many countries, especially in the English-speaking world, All Saints' Day is preceded by a pagan celebration with little direct connection known as Halloween ("All Hallows Eve").

Allegorical interpretation.

A method of interpretation by which

meanings other than the *literal meaning of a text are sought. It was applied, especially to ancient or sacred texts, throughout the Hellenistic world, and provided a means whereby interpreters could find deeper spiritual or moral meanings in such texts, while at the same time making them relevant to their own situation. The method also provided a means of solving problems with the literal meaning of many passages of Scripture, for instance, descriptions of God in human form, and laws without any obvious rational explanation. One of its commonest uses was in *apologetic or polemical discourse, often directed by Christians against Jews and gnostics. Despite the widespread use of allegory in the rabbinic exegetical literature, Christian writers frequently accuse Jews of seeing only the literal or surface meaning of Scripture and being incapable of grasping its deeper, allegorical truth. It is true that the rabbis, like the Antiochene fathers, were more cautious in their use of allegory and had a greater respect for the literal meaning of the text than *Philo, but their rejection of Christian interpretations of Scripture arose more from its christological content than its allegorical method.

It was developed most extensively among the scholars of *Alexandria, notably Philo and *Origen, so that an Alexandrian school of allegorical interpretation evolved to be challenged by more literal and historical approaches to biblical exegesis practiced elsewhere, particularly at *Antioch from the 4th century.

There are some allegories in the Bible (Ezek. 17:2; 24:3 RSV), and some passages have been regularly interpreted allegorically, notably "the allegory of old age" (Eccl. 12:1–7) and the *Song of Songs, interpreted by the rabbis as an allegory of God's love for Israel, and by Christians, notably *Bernard of Clairvaux, as an allegory of Christ's love for his church. An early Christian example, used to give scriptural authority to the method, is Paul's allegorical interpretation of the story of the sons of *Sarah and

*Hagar in Gal. 4:21–31, according to which Hagar stands for the *Sinai *covenant, *law, and *slavery, while Sarah is *Jerusalem above and freedom: "So then," Paul concludes, "we are not children of the slave, but of the free woman." Elsewhere Paul draws a distinction between the letter of Scripture and the spirit (Rom. 2:29; 2 Cor. 3:6). Origen identifies three levels of meaning corresponding to the body, soul, and spirit of a human being: the obvious literal meaning of the text (its body), its moral application to everyday life (its soul), and its hidden, theological meaning (its spirit).

In the Latin West, particularly under the influence of *Jerome and *Isidore, allegory comes to be understood as the dominant method whereby believers can arrive at the true, mystical meaning of Scripture. Medieval scholars like *Nicholas of Lyra, influenced perhaps by Jewish exegetical methods, further refined the method and distinguished four levels of meaning: the literal meaning and three deeper, nonliteral senses known as allegorical, moral, and anagogical, the last being concerned to find future or mystical insights in the text. The influence of this approach to understanding Scripture can be seen in the conventional structure of sermons, meditations, and other literature throughout the Middle Ages.

The Reformers and humanists, and the succeeding two centuries of *higher critics, biblical archaeologists, and Semitic philologists, rejected allegorical interpretation as arbitrary, artificial, and farfetched, confident that the literal meaning of the text and the author's intention were sufficient goals for biblical exegesis. More recently disillusionment with the historical-critical quest for a single original meaning, along with a new appreciation of the fact that texts can and do have more than one meaning, has led to a reassessment of the value of allegorical interpretations, ancient, medieval, and modern. Origen's concern was to make sense of the ancient texts to which he devoted his life but which seemed to him to be at times superficial, irrational, or irrelevant, and in this he provided subsequent biblical scholarship with a model only now perhaps fully appreciated.

Alleluia. Latin form of Heb. *halleluyah*, "Praise the Lord." Apart from the *Psalms, where it appears 20 times (104–6; 110–18; 134–35; 145–50), it occurs in the Bible only in Tobit (13:22) and Revelation (19:1, 3, 4, 6), where it is sung by the saints in heaven. It is always sung at masses, especially before the reading of the Gospel, except during Lent in the Western tradition. See *Hallel.

Allusion. One of the most striking features of biblical literature, however diverse its contents and literary genres, is the frequent occurrence of allusions, where one text apparently refers indirectly to another. This was already noted and exploited by the ancient exegetes: one of the chief rabbinic principles of interpretation (*middot*) was to interpret one passage by reference to another. In modern times strict historical-critical criteria for establishing the date and authorship of texts precluded this exegetical method in many cases, on the grounds that an author could not have been aware of texts written after his death: Isa. 1:10 (8th century B.C.E.) cannot be explained by reference to Ezek. 16:49 (6th century B.C.E.). More recent literary approaches, less concerned with date and authorship and taking the text of the Hebrew Bible as a single literary corpus, are rediscovering allusiveness as a vital hermeneutical tool. Deliberate allusions to the OT in the NT, as well as exact *quotations, have the additional function of highlighting the sense of continuity and fulfillment in the Christian Bible.

Alpha and Omega (Gk. *A* and *Ω*). The first and last letters of the Greek alphabet, used as a name for God: "I am Alpha and Omega, the beginning and end, the first and the last" (Rev. 22:13; cf. 1:8; Isa. 44:1; 48:12). They are frequent in Christian art from the 3rd century, often combined with the monogram *Chi-Rho and the *Tau cross (see Taw). A Latin version of the name appears in the 14th-century Christmas carol "In dulci jubilo": *Matris in gremio / Alpha es et O*, "on a mother's lap, you are Alpha and O." In Jewish tradition the three letters of the Hebrew word *'emet*, "Truth," one of the names of God, are the first (*aleph*), middle (*mem*), and last (*taw*) in the alphabet, and have been interpreted in a similar way.

Alphabet. The alphabetical script from which the Hebrew, Greek, and Roman writing systems derive was invented in the mid-2nd millennium B.C.E. and is first documented in inscriptions from the *Sinai peninsula. It was almost certainly a development from a small selection of Egyptian *hieroglyphics, and is a far simpler and more efficient writing system than both it and the equally widespread *cuneiform system invented in Mesopotamia. An alphabetical text from *Ugarit of the 14th century B.C.E. seems to prove that the order of the letters was fixed from the beginning so that the 22 Hebrew letters and 24 Greek letters could also function as numerals (*aleph/alpha* = 1; *beth/beta* = 2; *yodh/iota* = 10; etc.). The total numerical value of words and names could then be calculated (see *Gematria) and alphabetical *acrostics designed. The tradition that God created the world by using letters of the alphabet arose partly from a belief in its divine origin and partly from its significance as a symbol of cosmic order.

Ambrose (c. 339–397). Bishop of Milan and, with *Jerome, *Augustine, and *Gregory the Great, one of the four Doctors of the Latin Church. He had a good knowledge of Greek language and literature, typical of the aristocratic elite of his day, and his biblical interpretation is characterized by a preference for moral readings of the text, often allegorical like those of *Philo and *Origen. He quotes Philo so extensively that he has been described as a "Christian Philo." He wrote studies of Genesis (*In Hexaemeron*), Samuel, Psalms, the Minor Prophets, Luke, and Acts, and recommended the book of Isaiah to his protégé Augustine as reading in preparation for *baptism.

American interpretation.   See *African American interpretation; *Liberation theology; *North American interpretation.

Amidah (Heb. "standing"). One of the three most important ancient prayers in the Jewish liturgy, so called because worshipers stand up to recite it. It is discussed already in the *Mishnah (*Berakhot* 4:1), where it is referred to simply as "the Prayer" (*ha-tefillah*). Also known as the "Eighteen" (Heb. *shmonesreh*), it consisted originally of eighteen benedictions. To these was added a nineteenth, referring to heretics (Heb. *birkat ha-minim*) and thought by some to have been aimed at Christians. The first three blessings are about history (from the time of *Abraham to the coming of a redeemer), the resurrection of the dead, and Isaiah's vision of heaven ("Holy, holy, holy . . ." Isa. 6:3); the last three are a prayer for the return of God's presence to a rebuilt *temple, a general thanksgiving, and a prayer for peace. The middle section includes prayers for repentance, forgiveness, healing, the redemption of the Jewish people, and the coming of the *Messiah.

Amos, book of. One of the twelve Minor Prophets containing bitter attacks on organized religion and social injustice in Israel, laced with warnings of imminent judgment, although the possibility of repentance (5:6) and future restoration (9:11–15) is also proclaimed. Amos comes from Tekoa near Bethlehem in Judah and refers to Jerusalem at the beginning and end of the book, but the main part of his preaching is addressed to Samaria in the north, and the one autobiographical reference is located at Bethel (7:10–17). He claims to be a simple herdsman, not a professional prophet, although his knowledge of international affairs and his sophisticated literary style somewhat belie this. His famous words, "I am no prophet nor a prophet's son" (7:14), have made him since *Jerome into a model of the untutored man of faith, owing everything to divine inspiration.

Scholars place the origin of much of the book in an 8th-century B.C.E. context in which impending Assyrian invasions, culminating in the destruction of Samaria in 721, give his prophecies, including his radical interpretation of the *Day of the Lord (5:18–20), particular poignancy. Cited prominently in Acts (7:42–43; 15:16–17), there are important commentaries on Amos by Jerome and *Ambrose. In many contexts Amos is the archetypal prophet of doom, and 19th-century Protestant scholarship saw in him the founder of the prophetic tradition of ethical monotheism and a powerful challenge to traditional ritualism (4:4–5; 5:21–25; 8:1–3). Twentieth-century *liberation theologians interpreted his calls for social justice and "righteousness like an ever-flowing stream" (5:24) against a background of peasant poverty similar in some respects to the situation addressed by them in the developing world.

Anabaptists. A European Reformation movement so called because they rejected infant *baptism. Like the mainstream reformers of the 16th century, they believed Scripture to be the sole *authority, but preferred their own lay interpretations to those of established biblical scholars. They were denounced by *Luther, *Zwingli, and *Calvin, and persecuted by both Protestants and

Catholics. Modern Anabaptist groups include the Amish, Hutterite, and Mennonite communities in North America and elsewhere. They had a supersessionist view of the OT and made extensive use of the *Apocrypha.

Anachronism. A type of historical error common in ancient literature, and first identified in Renaissance times. Biblical anachronisms include passing references to the camel as a domestic animal in Gen. 38:10 and damask in Amos 3:12 (MT). Genesis 12:6 ("The Canaanite was then in the land") is one of the most often quoted anachronisms that casts doubt on the Mosaic authorship of the Pentateuch. Passages in Isaiah and other 8th-century prophets that presuppose the destruction of Jerusalem and the Babylonian exile in the 6th century constitute another frequent type of anachronism arising from traditional beliefs about the authorship of biblical texts. Attempts to deal with anachronisms range from textual emendation to claims that the prophets had supernatural powers. Recent commentators, less concerned with historicity, see instead in such cases a valid literary device for making ancient stories come alive in a contemporary context, rather than historical errors. Charming anachronisms occur also in art, where, for example, *Mary is depicted in medieval European dress, reading the Bible in Latin.

Analogy. A resemblance or parallelism between things otherwise different. By analogy language and imagery about animals and plants, for example, can be applied to human experience in the form of metaphors (Gen. 16:12; Amos 4:1), similes (Ps. 42:1; Isa. 42:14), and parables (Judg. 9:7–15). Language cannot function without analogy. The rabbis identified analogy (Heb. *gezerah shavah*) as a fundamental hermeneutical principle in talmudic law, and philosophers and theologians have constantly debated the nature and adequacy of human analogies employed in language about God, since God is incomparable (Isa. 40:18; 55:8–9) and human knowledge imperfect (1 Cor. 13:9–12). *Thomas Aquinas even questioned whether we can say anything at all about God in human language. Analogy plays a crucial role in modern sociohistorical reconstructions of "how things were" in the ancient world: hence the *liberation theologians' reading of the 8th-century prophets in the context of Latin American politics, and the analysis of first-century messianic or *millenarian movements in the light of better-documented contemporary examples.

Andrew (Gk. *Andreas*). One of the twelve apostles. With his brother *Peter, he left his nets and followed Jesus to become a "fisher of men" (Mark 1:16–18). According to John's Gospel he was on his own when he first found Jesus and went to tell his brother (1:35–42). For this reason he is known in the Eastern church as the "first called" (Gk. *Protokletos*). Numerous legends, recorded in the apocryphal *Acts of Andrew, *Eusebius, and several medieval texts, stress his strength and courage (cf. Gk. *andreios,* "manly") and trace his missionary journeys from Greece and Asia Minor (including Byzantium) north to Russia and beyond. According to tradition he died a martyr in Achaea (Greece), was crucified on an X-shaped cross, and became patron saint of Greece, Russia, Scotland, and a number of other countries where his relics are venerated.

Andrew of St. Victor (d. 1175). Biblical commentator. He was a canon at the Abbey of St. Victor in Paris until he returned to England between 1161 and 1163 as abbot of the Victorine Abbey of Wigmore in Herefordshire. He wrote commentaries on the first eight books of the Bible, the Prophets, Proverbs, and Ecclesiastes that anticipate modern biblical criticism in their concern for the literal/historical meaning of the text. He had some knowledge of Hebrew (though not of Greek) and the Jewish sources, partly from his conversations with Jews in Paris, but mainly at secondhand from *Jerome. He recommended the Jewish interpretation of the *Immanuel prophecy in Isa. 7:14.

Angel. In biblical usage the term has two distinct meanings. In a few contexts it refers to God himself, as in the case of his appearance in human form to Hagar (Gen. 16), Moses (Exod. 3), and Gideon (Judg. 6). Elsewhere there is a clear separation between God and his angels, who are known as "*sons of God," that is, "members of the heavenly court" (Gen. 6; Job 1–2). The ambiguous theological relationship between God and these other divine beings is reflected in such passages as Ps. 8:5 and the application of the term "Son of God" to Jesus (Mark 1:1; 15:39). In many passages angels are sent or commissioned by God, hence the Greek term *angelos*, "messenger" (Heb. *mal'ak*), and in the later books of the Bible four of them are given personal names, *Michael (Dan. 12:1; Rev. 12:7), *Gabriel (Dan. 8:16; Luke 1:19), *Raphael (Tobit), and Uriel (2 Esd. 4:1). A highly developed angelology appears already in the writings of *Philo and in the books of *Enoch and *Jubilees.

In Christian tradition angels play a key role from creation (Job 38:7; cf. Gen. 1:26; 3:22) to the Gospels (Mark 1:13; John 20:12) and Revelation. From Ezekiel's cherubim (1:5) and Isaiah's seraphim (6:2) are derived traditions about their winged appearance, and from Paul (Eph. 1:21; Col. 1:16) the notion that they are organized in celestial hierarchies. "Fallen angels" come from Gen. 6, and Lucifer in particular from Isa. 14. Patristic and medieval theologians speculated at great length on the form and nature of angels, and they appear very frequently in the literature, art, and music of all periods, as well as in the *liturgy, where, for example, the

*Sanctus (Isa. 6:3) is sung "together with angels, archangels, and all the company of heaven."

Angelico, Fra (Beato) (c. 1400–1455). Fra Giovanni of Fiesole, Renaissance artist and Dominican friar, was known as "Angelico" on account of the religious devotion evident in all his works. His paintings include a series of 50 frescoes on NT themes in the convent of San Marco in Florence, many of them, like the *Annunciation* and *Noli me tangere*, very well known, the *Coronation of the Virgin* in the Louvre, and scenes from the lives of Stephen and Lawrence in the Vatican.

Annunciation. The appearance of the angel *Gabriel to *Mary with the news that she is going to conceive and become the mother of Jesus. The words used (Luke 1:31) recall other biblical annunciations such as those announcing the forthcoming birth of Isaac (Gen. 18:10), Samson (Judg. 13), and John the Baptist (Luke 1:13). In Matthew it is to Joseph that the angel appears, and the story is presented as a fulfillment of the *Immanuel prophecy in Isa. 7:14 ("Behold a virgin shall conceive . . . ," LXX). The Feast of the Annunciation, celebrated nine months before Christmas, has held an important place in the Christian calendar since ancient times, and provided the church with the opening words of the *Ave Maria, "Hail Mary," as well as the inspiration for many familiar hymns and carols such as *Angelus ad Virginem*.

The annunciation is one of the most familiar scenes in Christian iconography of all periods, from a 5th-century mosaic in the Church of Santa Maria Maggiore in Rome and numerous medieval examples, to famous paintings by Fra *Angelico, *Leonardo da Vinci, El *Greco, and Dante Gabriel Rossetti. In many of these the words of Isa. 7:14 appear, as cited in Matthew. Many also contain apocryphal symbols like the dove of the Holy Spirit and the lily of virginity. Among the many readings of the story in literature must be mentioned *Donne's *La Corona*, Rossetti's *Ave*, and parodies in *Chaucer's *The Miller's Tale* and Pope's *The Rape of the Lock*. Modern interpreters of the story compare it to the story of Danae, virgin mother of Perseus, and similar myths from other cultures.

Anthem. English term derived from Gk. *antiphonos* but nowadays applied to any musical composition sung by the choir at public worship. Most often it is a setting of biblical words, especially a psalm or a canticle. Among the most famous English anthems are Purcell's "Bell anthem" (Phil. 4:4–7), Handel's coronation anthem "Zadok the High Priest" (1 Kgs. 1:39–48), Elgar's "Great is the Lord" (Ps. 48), and Vaughan Williams's "O taste and see" (Ps. 34:8). See *Antiphon.

Anthropology. One of the social sciences invented in the 19th century to investigate the social structures and beliefs of preindustrial societies. At first the application of anthropological data to the Bible introduced the notion that Hebrew religion, as recorded in the Bible, developed from a primitive, animistic stage when people believed in spirits through a polytheistic phase to monotheism. Theories about nomadism were crudely applied to some of the patriarchal stories so that, for example, scholars argued that the Hebrews had a totemistic view of sacrifice (W. R. Smith) and could not distinguish clearly between an individual and his or her group (T. H. Robinson). More recent studies, informed by the structuralism of Claude Lévi-Strauss, have completely undermined such generalizations about the Hebrew mind and seek instead to explain biblical laws and rituals in terms of symbolism and social structure. Thus the laws separating clean from unclean in Leviticus represent a worldview with ethical and ecological implications, and the biblical sacrifice system divides the world into recognized spheres in a way that gives society stability and order (Mary Douglas). Biblical *prophecy has been analyzed afresh in the light of new research on the phenomenon of ecstasy and social responses to it (R. R. Wilson), and the history of early Israel revolutionized by the application of theories of cultural materialism (N. K. *Gottwald), and by studies of the impact of technological advances, economic factors, and urbanization (N. P. Lemche).

Anthropomorphism. The application of human language and images to God or other nonhuman creatures and objects. The ban on all idols and graven images in the Law (Exod. 20:4–5) and the Prophets (Isa. 40) demanded a generally negative attitude toward divine anthropomorphism, but there are many references in the Bible to the "hand of God," "his outstretched arm," and the like, as well as passages where he is depicted as walking in the garden (Gen. 3:8), grieving over human sin (Gen. 6:6), crying out like a mighty warrior or a woman in labor (Isa. 42:13–14), and losing his temper (Isa. 54:8). To remove these or explain them away, ancient Greek and Aramaic versions of the Hebrew Bible systematically translate "the arm of God" by "the power of God" and substitute terms like "the *Word" (Memra) or the "Presence" (*Shekinah) for the name of God in such contexts. The increasing appearance of *angels in many ancient Jewish texts is another example of anti-anthropomorphism. Despite the efforts of theologians and philosophers, notably *Maimonides, biblical anthropomorphism survived and developed both in Judaism and Christianity, as can be seen in rabbinic descriptions of God studying Torah or putting on phylacteries, and centuries of Christian iconography in which God the Father is almost as familiar in human form as his Son.

Antichrist. The term itself appears only in the *Johannine Letters, where it refers to one who "denies the Father and the Son" (1 John 2:22), especially "the deceiver" (2 John 7) who was to come in the last days (1 John 2:18). There are numerous other references, however, to a cosmic adversary of God, identified from early times with the antichrist: for example, "Gog and his forces" (Ezek. 39:11), the "man of sin" (2 Thess. 2:2–10), "Belial" (*Jub.* 1:20; 15:33), the "beast" (Rev. 13:18; 19–20; cf. Dan. 7), and especially *Satan (Mark 8:33; Rev. 20:2). In all periods of church history the name "antichrist" has been applied to historical figures, from Emperor Nero in the 1st century and the heretic Arius in the 4th, to "the Jew" and "the Turk" during the Crusades, the pope from the Reformation onward, and Napoleon, Hitler, Stalin, and other world leaders in modern times. There is a *Signorelli fresco in Orvieto cathedral depicting the Antichrist as a grotesque mirror image of Christ, and a famous *Cranach woodcut of c. 1526 showing the pope as the antichrist.

Antioch (modern Antakya, Turkey). Capital of the Roman province of Syria and third-largest city in the Roman Empire after *Rome and *Alexandria. It had a substantial Jewish community and from the evidence of *Acts also a strong Christian presence from the beginning. By the end of the 1st century its bishop, *Ignatius (d. 107), was an important authority in the church, and at the end of the 4th century, under the leadership of *Theodore of Mopsuestia and John *Chrysostom, the patriarchate of Antioch rivaled that of Alexandria. Thereafter the role of Constantinople and Jerusalem in Eastern Orthodoxy and of Edessa in the Syriac-speaking churches eclipsed Antioch.

The Antiochene school of biblical interpretation, of which Theodore was the most important exponent and for which he was condemned by the Second Council of Constantinople in 553, was characterized by a concern for the plain meaning of the text and the consequent rejection of many traditional christological interpretations of the OT, adopted by the more influential Alexandrian school. The Antiochenes did, however, leave room in their approach for what they called *theoria,* "vision," apparent in some texts such as Isa. 53 and Zech. 9:8–12. By means of this a prophet saw beyond the plain meaning of what he wrote for its original context, to a messianic reality, a fuller meaning (*sensus plenior*), waiting for Jesus and the early church to explain.

Antiphon (Gk. *antiphonos,* "answering sound"). Originally a refrain consisting of a few verses of Scripture, sung before and after a psalm or canticle, but later applied to independent compositions. Popular examples are the seven Isaianic "O Antiphons" (*O Adonai, O Radix Jesse, O Clavis David . . . O Emmanuel*), which are the basis of the Advent hymn "O come, O come Immanuel," and the four "Antiphons of the Blessed Virgin Mary," including *Salve Regina* and *Regina Coeli.* See *Anthem.

Anti-Semitism. Prejudice against Jews became a major difficulty in Christian interpretation of Scripture. There were naturally from the beginning many points of disagreement between Jews and Christians on the meaning of Scripture, particularly in passages interpreted christologically and passages where there were significant differences between the Hebrew text used by the Jews and the Greek translations used by the church. There have been few periods in church history, however, when Jews and Christians have discussed their respective interpretations dispassionately. A negative, often hostile attitude toward the Jews was justified by reference to two types of scriptural authority:

the prophets' own denunciations of their people and the notorious verse in the Passion Narrative where the Jews themselves claim responsibility for Christ's death (Matt. 27:25).

Many of the church fathers, including *Justin, *Tertullian, *Augustine, and John *Chrysostom, interpreted passages originally addressed by the prophets to the citizens of ancient Judah or Jerusalem as Christian polemic against the Jews of their own day. It was their own fault that their temple at Jerusalem had been destroyed and their country taken away from them (Isa. 3:8); they are blind and stubborn (Isa. 6:9–11); their hands are full of blood (Isa. 1:15). Their literal interpretation of the text was frequently condemned, and the 2nd-century Christian heretic *Marcion even attempted to have the entire OT removed from the canon as the work of an evil Jewish god.

*Luther wrote a treatise on "The Jews and Their Lies" despite his respect for the original Hebrew text, and Hitler's Nazi campaign to destroy the Jews included an effort to "de-Judaize" the Bible. Jews were officially demonized by the church and suffered repeated persecution and attempts at forcible conversion. These attitudes were represented in Christian art by the evil expressions on the faces of Christ's Jewish tormentors, and by the figure of *Synagoga caeca*, "Blind Synagogue," carrying the broken tablets of the law and a broken staff (Isa. 3:1), and perpetuated in literature, drama, and the liturgy down to the present. Public pronouncements by the churches, most of them since World War II, have gone some way toward combating Christian anti-Semitism in the West. See *Reproaches.

Apocalypse of Baruch.   See *Baruch, books of.

Apocalypse of John.   See *Revelation, book of.

Apocalypse of Moses.   See *Life of Adam and Eve.

Apocalypse of Paul.   An important apocryphal work written probably in the 4th century C.E. Intended to fill in details missing from 2 Cor. 12:2, it gives Paul's own account of his journey to paradise, where he meets Enoch, *Elijah, and others, and witnesses the fate of the wicked as well as the righteous, described in lurid detail, which proved immensely influential in subsequent Christian tradition. It is quoted by *Dante (*Inferno* 2.28) and alluded to in *Poussin's *Ecstasy of St. Paul* (1649–50, Louvre).

Apocalypse of Peter.   An apocryphal work of the 2nd century C.E. In it *Peter recounts what he saw on his journey to heaven, at times indulging in grotesque descriptions of the torments allotted to men and women guilty of immorality in this world.

Apocalypse of Thomas.   An apocryphal work, composed probably in Latin in the 5th century, it survives in several Anglo-Saxon versions. Probably *Manichean in origin, it describes how it will be on the last six days before the end of the world.

Apocalyptic.   The term, derived from the word *apocalypse,* may be defined as "resembling the book of Revelation," and is applied in the first instance to a group of Jewish texts written between c. 200 B.C.E. and c. 100 C.E. These include *Daniel, 2 *Esdras, *Enoch, *Jubilees, *Assumption of Moses, Ascension of Isaiah, *Testaments of the Twelve Patriarchs, and the book of *Revelation itself. The apocryphal *Apocalypse of Peter, of Paul,* and *of Thomas* are Christian examples from a slightly later period. By extension the term is also applied to a number of biblical texts, most commonly

Isa. 24–27, Ezek. 38–39, Joel, Zech. 12–14, Matt. 24–25, Mark 13, Luke 21, 1 Cor. 15, 1 Thess. 4, and 2 Peter. Common to all these texts is a worldview according to which the problems of this world are too great and too complicated to be capable of any human solution: only supernatural knowledge about the workings of the heavens, the process of world history, and the possibility of life after death could give human existence meaning and purpose. The more catastrophic the present plight of the community became, the more elaborate became the language and images of Jewish apocalyptic: it was during the Maccabean persecution of the Jews under Antiochus IV Epiphanes between 167 and 164 B.C.E. that Daniel was written, and in the shadow of the destruction of Jerusalem in 70 C.E. that the book of Revelation was most probably composed. It was then that the chief characteristics of Jewish apocalyptic literature began to crystallize: angelology, demonology, complex symbolism (numbers, metals, beasts, horns), patterns in history and astronomy, the resurrection of the dead, and the day of judgment.

Its origins are to be found in two sets of biblical passages: in the one, the secrets of human history are revealed to prophets given a glimpse into the heavenly court (Isa. 6; cf. Jer. 23:18; 1 Kgs. 22). Prophecies about the *Day of the Lord also had a role in the development of apocalyptic traditions about the day of judgment and the end of the world. The other strand in the apocalyptic tradition can be traced to passages in which secret knowledge is revealed through dreams to certain gifted individuals with special wisdom like Joseph (Gen. 40–41) and Daniel (Dan. 1–2). The notion that apocalyptic literature was the preserve of the few, too difficult and too dangerous for ordinary people, is reflected in rabbinic restrictions on the reading of Ezek. 1, frequently citing Sir. 3:21–22, and cautionary tales about the fate of individuals caught up in apocalyptic visionary experiences. Modern scholarship has vacillated between the theory that apocalyptic was primarily a literary genre, unrelated to mystical experience and written for political or propagandist purposes (e.g., to claim divine authority for the violent and unequivocal rejection of social injustice), and the view that, like the better documented examples from later Jewish and Christian history, it belongs firmly within the *mystical tradition, no less of a challenge to contemporary regimes and institutions, but driven by genuine religious experience.

Whatever its origin, the afterlife of Jewish apocalyptic, especially the Apocalypse of John itself, is long and fascinating. Recent research has demonstrated the influence of *Jubilees* on the Qumran community and of *1 Enoch* on early Christianity. Visions of the open heaven (Mark 1:10; John 1:51; Revelation) and journeys to heaven by Jesus (Acts 1) and Paul (2 Cor. 12:1–4), as well as Moses, Elijah, Isaiah, Muhammad, and countless mystics down the centuries, represent a central and lasting theme in Western religious tradition, directly derived from the apocalyptic tradition. Attempts to apply apocalyptic tradition to contemporary history were made by *Joachim of Fiore (c. 1132–1202), Isaac *Newton, and many others. Apocalyptic *eschatology, central to early Christianity and surviving in Montanism and other sects long after it had been condemned by the church, surfaced again among the *Anabaptists and other Protestant groups in the Reformation, and survives to this day in a variety of *millenarian sects. *The Last Judgment* is the title of oratorios by Spohr (1835) and *Elgar (unfinished). Twentieth-century apocalyptic works include D. H. Lawrence's essay *Apocalypse* (1931), T. S. Eliot's *The Waste Land* (1922), Messiaen's *Quattuor pour la Fin du Temps* (1940), and the film *Apocalypse Now* (1979). See *Mysticism; *Revelation, book of.

Apocrypha, New Testament. A collection of writings, mostly from the first three centuries C.E. and similar in form to the canonical Gospels and Acts, but of sectarian origin. The main extant Gospels are the *Gospel of Thomas, *Gospel of Peter, *Protoevangelium of James, *Gospel of Pseudo-Matthew, *Gospel of Nicodemus, *Infancy Gospel of Thomas, and the *Arabic Infancy Gospel. A Gospel according to the Hebrews is quoted by *Origen and *Jerome and the Gospel of the Egyptians by *Clement of Alexandria but have not survived, nor has the Gospel of Bartholemew, mentioned by Jerome, unless it is included in a work entitled the Questions of Bartholemew, which is extant in a number of mss. Apocryphal Acts include the *Acts of Andrew, *Acts of John, *Acts of Paul (including the Acts of Paul and Thecla), *Acts of Peter, and *Acts of Thomas. Of these only the Acts of Thomas has survived intact. The *Acts of Pilate appears in several mss as the first half of the *Gospel of Nicodemus. There are also apocryphal letters, notably Paul's Epistle to the Laodiceans and the correspondence between *Paul and *Seneca, and apocalyptic works including the *Apocalypse of Paul, *Apocalypse of Peter, and *Apocalypse of Thomas. None of these writings ever acquired the same status in Western and Eastern Orthodox tradition as the OT Apocrypha, and some were explicitly rejected as heretical by church leaders. But numerous popular details in traditional accounts of the lives of *Mary, Anna (Mary's mother), Peter, Paul, and Thomas, for example, as well as of Jesus himself, as represented in medieval literature and iconography, are recorded first in the NT Apocrypha. English editions are by M. R. James (1924); Edgar Hennecke, Wilhelm Schneemelcher, and R. McL. Wilson (1963–65); and J. K. Elliott (1993). See *Apocrypha, Old Testament; *Golden Legend.

Apocrypha, Old Testament. The books not in the Hebrew Bible but included in the OT *canon by the early church. They are also referred to as "ecclesiastical" (as opposed to Jewish) and "deuterocanonical." The following list comprises all the works considered apocryphal by one or more Christian traditions (cf. NRSV): *Wisdom of Solomon, *Sirach (Ecclesiasticus or Wisdom of Jesus ben Sira), *Baruch, *Tobit, *Judith, 1–4 *Maccabees, 1 and 2 *Esdras (= 3 and 4 Ezra), Additions to *Esther, Additions to *Daniel (= Prayer of *Azariah, *Song of the Three Children, *Susanna, Bel and the Dragon), and the Prayer of *Manasseh. Already *Jerome had doubts about the Apocrypha, but it was *Luther and *Calvin who finally separated them from the rest of Scripture, and most Protestant Bibles now omit them altogether. Most of the Apocrypha are pieces of Hellenistic Jewish literature, originally written in Greek between 200 B.C.E. and 70 C.E. Although never part of the Hebrew Bible, some remained part of Jewish tradition, particularly Sirach, Judith, Tobit, and Maccabees. The language and images of the Apocrypha have played a significant role in the history and development of Christian tradition, from "Let us now praise famous men" (Sir. 44) in the *liturgy, to famous pictorial, literary, and musical representations of "Tobias and the angel," "Judith and Holofernes," and "Susanna and the Elders." The first modern English edition of the Apocrypha was by R. H. Charles (1913). See also *Genesis Apocryphon; *Pseudepigrapha.

Apologetic. A technical term used to describe speeches or writings produced in defense of one's beliefs and practices. Examples of Jewish apologetic, written to defend Judaism against Hellenistic questions and criticisms, include the Letter of *Aristeas and the writings of *Philo of Alexandria and *Josephus. Philo's allegorical interpretations of Jewish law, designed to give rational meaning to ancient, often bizarre customs, had an obvious apologetic function. Another example is the typological, often far-fetched use of Jewish Scripture by the early church, to give authority to contemporary Christianity over against rab-

binic tradition. Second-century Christian apologists include the Athenian philosophers *Aristides and *Athenagoras, and *Justin Martyr, *Tatian, and *Tertullian, who wrote in Latin. They sought to defend Christianity from accusations of *atheism, incest, cannibalism, and the like, and demonstrate to emperors and the educated pagan public in general its common ground with the philosophies of Plato and the Stoics, if not its superiority to them. A number of biblical texts about the Canaanites (Joshua–Judges) and the Romans (Acts) have apologetic elements in them that readers from later generations must take into account.

Apostles. A frequent name, from NT times, for the twelve disciples, "sent forth" (Gk. *apostello*, "to send forth") by Jesus as his representatives. They were originally Simon *Peter, *Andrew, *James the son of Zebedee, *John his brother, *Philip, *Bartholomew, *Thomas, *Matthew, James the son of Alphaeus, Thaddaeus, Simon the Cananean, and *Judas Iscariot (Matt. 10:2–4). After the death of Judas, Matthias was appointed by lot in his place (Acts 1:21–26). "The apostle" in Christian discourse is usually *Paul, although in Eastern Orthodox tradition the "Thirteenth Apostle" is *Constantine. The doctrine of the apostolic succession, on which, for example, the unique claims of the papacy are based, derives its authority from the original Twelve, in particular Peter, first bishop of Rome, and some famous churches are dedicated to them in Moscow, Thessalonica, Rome, Venice, and elsewhere, as well as a mountain range not far from Cape Town.

Apostolic Fathers. A title given since the 17th century to Christian writers living in the century or so between the end of the NT period (c. 95 C.E.) and the beginning of the patristic period (c. 150 C.E.). They include *Clement of Rome, *Ignatius, *Hermas, Polycarp, *Papias, the authors of the *Letter of *Barnabas*, *Letter to Diognetus*, and the *Didache*, and in some editions the martyrdoms of Clement, Ignatius, and Polycarp. For them the collection of Christian writings that began to be called the "New Testament" by the end of the 2nd century was not yet established. Their use of the Jewish Scriptures in Greek to authorize Christian beliefs, practices, and institutions is interesting. Their importance within the early church can be seen in that some of them, notably Clement, Hermas, and Barnabas, appear in early mss of the Bible.

Aqedah. See *Akedah.

Aquila (c. 130 C.E.). Author of a Greek version of the Hebrew Bible, intended to replace the LXX, which had come to be monopolized by Christians. He came from Pontus in Asia Minor and, as a convert from Christianity to Judaism, is known in the rabbinic literature as "Aquila the Proselyte." His translation adheres very closely to the Hebrew original, for which it was praised by *Origen and *Jerome. See also *Hexapla, *Septuagint.

Aquinas. See *Thomas Aquinas.

Arabia. In biblical times the area covered by modern Saudi Arabia was the home of Midianites, Nabateans, Mineans, and other bedouin groupings in the north, and the kingdoms of Saba (Sheba), Qataban, Ma'in, and Hadramawt in the south. The "Arabs" mentioned in the Bible (cf. Heb. *arabah*, "desert") are normally the people living on the south and east frontiers of Judah. "Arabia" where Paul went (Gal. 1) was northwest Arabia, known as Arabia Petraea after its capital Petra (Heb. *Sela*) and incorporated into the Roman Empire in 106. Evidence for trading links with southern Arabia and the East provides a historical background for the story of the *Queen of Sheba's visit to Jerusalem (1 Kgs. 10). Modern scholarship from the 18th century has focused on northwest Arabia as the home of Moses' father-in-law, a Midianite priest at the mountain of God (Exod. 2–3). The occurrence in a 13th-century B.C.E. Egyptian text of a place name similar to "YHWH" lends some support to this. Data collected from bedouin tribes has frequently been applied to biblical phenomena such as the gods of the *patriarchs, the *Passover, and *prophecy.

The Arabic language has played a significant role in biblical interpretation. *Jerome (c. 400) says he used Arabic as well as Hebrew and Syriac for his translation of the book of Job, and close relations between Jews and Arabs in medieval Egypt and Mesopotamia led to the beginnings of comparative Semitic philology and Hebrew *linguistics. Serious *etymologizing began in the 18th century mostly on the basis of Arabic, a language notorious for the many different meanings almost every word can have. From the 7th century C.E. Arabic superseded Coptic and Syriac as the everyday language of Christians, and some Arabic Christian mss have survived, including one of *Tatian's *Diatessaron and several of 4 Ezra (2 Esdras) and the *Testament of Abraham. There are also many important medieval Arabic translations of Classical Greek scientific, medical, and philosophical texts.

Arabic Infancy Gospel.

Arabic Infancy Gospel. An apocryphal text composed in *Syriac, probably in the 6th century C.E., and later translated into Arabic. Dependent on earlier apocryphal works, especially the *Protoevangelium of James and *Gospel of Thomas, it contains popular stories about the nativity, the flight into Egypt, and the miracles performed by Jesus when he was a child. Some of these appear regularly in medieval Christian tradition and the *Qur'an.

Aramaic.

Aramaic. The language of ancient Syria (Heb. *Aram*) spoken by the Jews in Palestine and Babylonia throughout the Second Temple period (c. 500 B.C.E.–70 C.E.). Parts of the Hebrew Bible (Ezra 4:8–6:18; 7:12–26; Dan. 2:4b–7:28) are written in Aramaic, and from the time of Ezra (c. 400 B.C.E.) the Jewish Scriptures were translated into Aramaic (see *Targum). Aramaic influence is evident in Biblical Hebrew and in NT Greek, where some of the words of Jesus have been preserved in Aramaic (Mark 5:41). It was written in the same script as Hebrew and to outsiders was often confused with Hebrew. The Babylonian *Talmud and the medieval *Zohar are written in Aramaic, as are some popular ancient prayers still recited in Jewish worship (see *Kaddish). In addition to Jewish Aramaic, other dialects include *Samaritan and *Syriac.

Archaeology.

Archaeology. Archaeology can be said to have dominated biblical research during most of the 19th and 20th centuries. It was seen as a modern scientific method for getting back to how things actually were in ancient times. Napoleon's invasion of *Egypt in 1798 inaugurated two centuries of astonishing archaeological discoveries throughout the Middle East, starting with the explorations of his own engineers in Egypt and *Palestine. Since then excavations throughout the Middle East have revealed a bewildering quantity of data on ancient Near Eastern cultures, with the result that biblical history was interpreted almost exclusively against the background of our growing knowledge of the ancient Near East, rather than as literature in its own right. Names like Tutankhamen, Hammurabi, Amarna, *Mari, Lachish, and *Qumran became as familiar to several generations of students of the Bible as many parts of the biblical narrative itself, if not more so.

Archaeology occasionally adds extrabiblical evidence to the biblical narrative, as in the case of *Sennacherib's own account of his siege of *Jerusalem in 701

B.C.E. (cf. 2 Kgs. 18:13–20:11) and the Cyrus Cylinder (2 Chr. 36:22–23). But too much collusion between archaeology and biblical research led to errors in both. Archaeological evidence was sometimes forced to fit the biblical stories, as in the case of the walls of Jericho (Josh. 6) and "Solomon's stables" at Megiddo (1 Kgs. 9:15–19); while the nuances of the biblical texts, most of which have no direct connection with any archaeological evidence, were neglected. Archaeological discoveries are often accidental and arbitrary, like the spectacular finds at *Ras Shamra (1928), *Nag Hammadi (1945) and Qumran (1947; see *Dead Sea Scrolls), and can easily play a role in biblical interpretation that is out of proportion to their intrinsic importance. National boundaries also affect the progress of archaeological work; for example, in the State of Israel after 1948 enormous resources were devoted to excavating sites identified as biblical. Expeditions in search of Noah's ark, and attempts to reconstruct conditions in the age of the patriarchs or to determine the route of the exodus will no doubt continue, but scholars in both fields have developed much more refined techniques, and are now on the whole more skeptical about the potential of archaeology to answer our questions.

Archaism. The deliberate use of an ancient linguistic or literary form for stylistic effect, whether to give a touch of realism to the speech of elderly people in the presence of the younger generation, like Boaz and Naomi in the book of Ruth, or to make the poetry of an ancient figure like Moses (Exod. 15) or Deborah (Judg. 4) sound authentic. Given the difficulty in dating Biblical Hebrew, it is not always possible to determine whether an ancient form is an indication of an early date of composition or an archaism. Archaizing factors certainly operated in the decision of the hierarchy at *Jerusalem to retain *Hebrew for religious discourse in the face of pressure to change to *Aramaic (Neh. 13:23–27). The same applies to the unique continuing use of the Old Hebrew script by the *Samaritans, and the Western church's retention of *Latin as their sacred language, worldwide, for over 1,500 years.

Aretalogy. Derived from the Greek word for "virtue" (*arete*), the term is applied to Egyptian and Hellenistic texts in which the virtues of a deity or a miracle worker are enumerated for liturgical use or with a propagandist purpose. Examples from the OT include poems in which Wisdom sings her own praises (Prov. 8:22–31; Sir. 24:1–22), and NT scholars have suggested that some of the discourses in John's Gospel (6:25–65; 10:1–39) and some of the apocryphal Acts may owe something to pre-Christian aretalogies.

Aristeas, Letter of. A Jewish *pseudepigraphical document purporting to be by an official at the court of Ptolemy II Philadelphus (285–247 B.C.E.). It is an *apologetic work, written in Greek in *Alexandria sometime after 200 B.C.E., and contains the famous legend of the miraculous origin of the *Septuagint as well as some interesting, often *allegorical interpretations of Jewish law that anticipate *Philo.

Aristides. Second-century Athenian philosopher and Christian apologist (see *Apologetic). According to *Eusebius and *Jerome his Apology was addressed to the Emperor Hadrian. In it he argues that Christianity is superior to religions that worship the planets (Chaldean), deities with human failings (Greek), animals (Egyptian), and angels (Jewish), and that Christians are characterized by their knowledge of God and love for their fellow human beings.

Ark of the covenant. Ancient Israel's most sacred object, described twice in great detail in the *Sinai narrative (Exod. 25; 37). Literally a "box, chest" (Lat. *arca*; Heb. *aron)*, the ark was designed by the legendary craftsman Bezalel and contained the tablets of the law. Its lid, known as the "mercy seat" (Heb. *kapporet)*, functioned as a kind of throne from which God spoke to Israel from between two winged cherubim of gold. It was housed in the *tabernacle on Israel's journeys through the wilderness, and plays a powerful role in the legends surrounding the settlement of the twelve tribes in Canaan, in particular in their struggles with the Philistines. It was ceremoniously brought into *Jerusalem by King *David, and then by *Solomon into the inner sanctuary (the Holy of Holies) of his *temple. Last referred to by *Jeremiah (3:16; cf. 2 Macc. 2:4–8), it was lost in the destruction of the temple by the Babylonians in 586 B.C.E., and has been the subject of legends, like the Holy Grail, down to the blockbuster Steven Spielberg film *Raiders of the Lost Ark* (1981).

In Christian interpretations its mediating function and its role in priestly atonement rituals (Lev. 16; Heb. 9) made it a popular type of Christ and the church. As the container or bearer of the *Word of God, it was also an appropriate type of *Mary. Fanciful artistic representations of the ark appear in paintings of the *Plague at Ashdod* and the *Destruction of Dagon's Temple* (1 Sam. 5–6) by *Poussin, *The Return of the Ark from Captivity* (Ps. 132) by Sebastien Bourdin, and *David Dancing before the ark* (2 Sam. 6) by Luca Giordano. There have also been scholarly attempts to identify the materials and techniques used, and to trace its origin to cult objects attested among bedouin tribes in modern *Arabia.

Armageddon. The Greek form is derived from the Hebrew place name Megiddo, which was the scene of many battles from the victory of Thutmose III over an Asiatic army and Israel's triumph over the Canaanites celebrated in the Song of Deborah (Judg. 4–5), to General Allenby's victory over the Ottoman forces in 1917. It was also the scene of the death of Josiah in 609 B.C.E. (2 Kgs. 23:29–30; 1 Esd. 1:29). From Zech. 12:11 and Rev. 16:16 it came to symbolize the final cosmic struggle between good and evil envisaged by *Ezekiel, *Daniel, and other *apocalyptic writers; and in the language of 20th-century film, music, and political discourse it is a byword for global catastrophe.

Armenia. Known in ancient times as Urartu, a name related to Ararat (Gen. 8:4; 2 Kgs. 19:37), Armenia was situated in an isolated mountainous region east of Turkey, and c. 300 was the first nation to convert to Christianity. Independent of orthodox Christian doctrine, Armenian scholars, notably Mesrop, produced their own Armenian Bible, originally translated from the *Peshitta. There are Armenian versions of 2 *Esdras, 3 *Maccabees, *Testaments of the Twelve Patriarchs*, and several other noncanonical books. Despite repeated persecution under Persians, Arabs, Turks, and Russians, the Armenians have retained their own language, literature, and religion both in their own country and in the diaspora.

Art and architecture. Artists and artwork in general are rarely praised in the Bible, Bezalel and the building and decorating of the *tabernacle in the wilderness (Exod. 31:2; 36–40) and *Solomon's *temple and palace (1 Kgs. 6–7) being conspicuous exceptions. Skilled craftsmen are ridiculed (Isa. 44:9–20; Wis. 15:7–17) and things of great beauty like the *golden calf (Exod. 32), the bronze serpent (Num. 21:9; John 3:14), and the city of Tyre (Ezek. 28:11–19) are enthusiastically destroyed. While archaeological evidence of Egyptian painting, Philistine pottery, and Assyrian ivory work illustrate the artistic achievement of its neighbors, Israel chose to discourage artwork, mainly on the basis of the second commandment, which applies only to naturalistic art (Exod. 20:4–6), at times also for socioeconomic reasons that go further (Amos 3:15; 6:4). Orthodox Jewish and Islamic traditions have on the whole followed this pattern with the result that *synagogue and mosque decoration is limited to geometric patterns and calligraphy. Again there are exceptions, like the *Dura Europos frescoes (3rd century C.E.), the mosaic floor of the Beth Alpha synagogue (6th century), a number of medieval illustrated Bible mss and *Passover Haggadahs, and many modern examples, including *Chagall's *Tribes of Israel* windows in the Hadassah Synagogue in Jerusalem. But it was Christianity, more open to Greek and other cultural influences, that broke with the biblical tradition and exploited art and architecture to the full to celebrate and communicate their beliefs.

Among the earliest examples are illustrations in the *catacombs and on *sarcophagi of Daniel in the lion's den, *Abraham and *Isaac, *Jonah and the whale, and the Good Shepherd. Before Christianity became the state religion under *Constantine, biblical characters were often depicted in the guise of Orpheus, Apollo, Hermes, or the like to conceal that they were Christian. This is probably why the crucifixion, too obviously Christian, does not appear until later. From the 5th century on, illustrated mss become increasingly common (e.g., the 6th-century Rossano Gospels; 9th-century Utrecht Psalter) as well as *Byzantine iconography and the mosaic decoration of churches (6th-century San Vitale, Ravenna), the choice of scene very often determined by liturgical considerations. The Middle Ages saw the emergence of the Gothic cathedral with its intricate iconographical schemes in stone and stained glass (*Chartres) and still more elaborately designed Bibles like the *Bible Moralisée* and the *Speculum humanae salvationis*.

The rediscovery of classical humanism led to the *Renaissance in Italy and the introduction into Christian art of a new realism that enabled artists to depict even the most familar biblical scenes more subtly and often more poignantly, beginning with *Cimabue, *Giotto, *Masaccio, and *Fra Angelico, and culminating in the great masters of the Cinquecento *Leonardo da Vinci, *Raphael, and *Michelangelo. Their influence on the Reformation and Counter-Reformation can be seen in many of their great successors, including *Tintoretto in Italy, *Dürer and *Grünewald in Germany, *Rembrandt and *Rubens in Holland, and El *Greco in Spain. Edward *Hick's primitive paintings of the *Peaceable Kingdom* and William *Blake's visionary art and the other *Romantics bring us into the 19th century, where there are some rare biblical works by the *Pre-Raphaelites and the French Impressionists, but also some famous Bible illustrators like Gustave *Doré. Influential 20th-century examples include Salvador *Dali's famous *Crucifixion*, a marvelous *Madonna and Child* by the English sculptor Henry Moore (1943), and Graham Sutherland's *Christ the King* tapestry in Coventry Cathedral (1962). The effect of world wars on artists' interpretation of the Bible is evident in the works of *Chagall and Stanley *Spencer, while the paintings of the peasant artists of Solentiname in Nicaragua beautifully illustrate *liberation theology in art.

Ascension.   A miraculous ascent into heaven. Two OT characters are described explicitly as having been taken up into heaven, Enoch (Gen. 5:24) and *Elijah (2 Kgs. 2), and the ascension of *Isaiah is recounted in the *Pseudepigrapha. In these cases the ascension marks the end of an earthly life, for others, including *Paul (2 Cor. 12), Jewish mystics (see *Kabbalah), and the Prophet Muhammad (Sura 17), it is a journey into heaven from which they return. It is in the first sense that the term is applied to Christ, who was "taken up into heaven" (Mark 16:19; Luke 24:51) from the Mount of Olives, forty days after the resurrection (Acts 1:1–12). His eternal presence in heaven guarantees that humanity can never again be separated from God (1 Tim. 3:16; Eph. 2:4–6), while his place on earth is taken by the Holy Spirit (John 16:7; Acts 2).

The Feast of the Ascension has been celebrated, often with the singing of Ps. 47 ("God is gone up with a shout"; cf. 68:4), in most Christian traditions since the 4th century. Representations in art since c. 400 C.E. often give prominence to the cloud and show angels carrying Jesus, while the astonished disciples, usually with the Virgin Mary among them, gaze upward. Well-known examples include paintings by *Giotto (c. 1306), *Tintoretto (1579–81), and *Rembrandt (1636).

Ascension of Isaiah. See *Martyrdom and Ascension of Isaiah.*

Aseneth. See *Joseph and Aseneth.*

Asian interpretation. From the 16th century Christian *missionaries began to translate the Bible into the languages of Asia, but the process was one-sided and resulted in little if any Asian interpretation. Increased contacts between European and Asian scholars in the 19th and 20th centuries, however, produced some notable commentators on Scripture, including the Hindus Rammohun Roy and Mahatma Gandhi, and the Indian *Muslim Sayyed Ahmad Khan. Asian readers of the Bible noted with approval, for example, that as a sacred text it is more unitarian than trinitarian and that Jesus is more Asiatic than British. The second half of the 20th century saw a marked increase in the number of scholars from India, Japan, Korea, Hong Kong, and other parts of Asia studying Semitic languages, biblical archaeology, Israelite history, Christian origins, and the like, in the United States, Europe, and Israel, although initially few of them allowed much Asian culture to intrude into their scholarship.

Since the 1970s many Asian writers influenced by *liberation theology, *feminism, and *postcolonialism have sought to create new approaches designed to throw off Western models superimposed by the colonial powers and to read the Bible in an Asian cultural context. One notable example is the critical reading of biblical texts about the oppressed and marginalized in *Exodus, the 8th-century prophets, and the Gospels, in reference to the *Minjung* in Korea or the *Dalit* in India. Another is the Asian interpretation of passages where both gender and ethnicity are involved, like the stories of the Samaritan (John 4:5–30) and Syro-Phoenician women (Mark 7:24–30), in which cultural details are given a radical new emphasis. The pioneering work of R. S. Sugirtharajah (Sri Lanka), C.-S. Song (Taiwan), Kim Yong Bok (Korea), Aruna Gnanadason (India), Kwok Pui-Lan (Hong Kong), and others, together with the publication since 1987 of the *Asia Journal of Theology* and several important regional periodicals, confirm the start of a new chapter in the history of biblical interpretation.

Assumption of Moses. See *Testament of Moses.*

Assumption of the Virgin Mary. The belief that after her death or *Dormition* ("falling asleep") *Mary was "assumed into heavenly glory," where she was crowned Queen of Heaven. The Feast of the Assumption on August 15 (Ital. *Ferragosto*) has been celebrated in some form since the 4th century, when the earliest evidence for the belief appears in apocryphal works attributed to John the evangelist. Scriptural authority was found in passages about the raising of "the root of Jesse" (Isa. 11:10), the bride "fair as the moon, bright as the sun" (Song 6:10), the enthronement of *Bathsheba (1 Kgs. 2:19), and the *ark (another type of the Virgin Mary) accompanying the Lord to his resting place (Ps. 132:8). It was made a dogma of the Catholic Church by Pope Pius XII in 1950.

There are many representations of the assumption in art and architecture, of which paintings by *Titian (1516–18), El *Greco (1577), and *Rubens (1626) are outstanding examples. The apostle *Thomas appears in some well-known paintings of the assumption, receiving the Virgin's girdle. It is the name of the capital of Paraguay (Spanish Asunción) and a popular Catholic personal name worldwide (cf. Ital. *Assunta*; Polish *Assumpta*).

Assyria (Heb. Ashur). The northern region of Mesopotamia (modern Iraq) where a powerful empire was based from c. 900 B.C.E. to the fall of its capital Nineveh (near modern Mosul) in 612 B.C.E. In 663 Assyria invaded Egypt and destroyed Thebes (Nah. 3:8). Assyrian is an East *Semitic language written in *cuneiform on clay tablets. The king of Assyria figures prominently in the Bible, both as the rod with which God in his anger punishes a disobedient Israel (Isa. 10:5) and the feared enemy from which God miraculously rescues *Jerusalem (Isa. 36–37). In later prophecy (Isa. 40–66; Jeremiah; Ezekiel) the Assyrians' role is for the most part taken over by the Babylonians, though the fall of Nineveh is gloatingly celebrated (*Nahum), and they are remembered as the enemy that can be forgiven if they repent (*Jonah).

Archaeological evidence from the sites of great cities at Ashur, Nineveh, Nimrud, and elsewhere include the Black Obelisk of Shalmaneser III showing a picture of Jehu, king of Judah, paying him tribute; dramatic illustrations of *Sennacherib's siege of Lachish in 701 B.C.E. (2 Chr. 32:9); and numerous cuneiform inscriptions containing contemporary records of events like the invasion of Tiglath-pileser III (2 Kgs. 15:29), the fall of Samaria, and the deportation of its inhabitants in 721 B.C.E.

(2 Kgs. 18:9–11). The salvation of Jerusalem in 701 B.C.E. (Isa. 36–37), however, has a different explanation in the Assyrian records from that in the Bible (but cf. 2 Kgs. 18:13–16). Among many other documents discovered in the palace libraries of ancient Assyria are copies of a type of treaty between a king and a vassal, similar in style and structure to the treaty (or *covenant) made between God and Israel at Sinai.

The Assyrian Church, in the Middle East, the United States, and elsewhere, traces its origins to the disciple *Thomas, who according to legend traveled as far as India, and to Bishop Nestorius, who was condemned as a heretic at the Council of Ephesus in 431 C.E. It retains the *Syriac language in its liturgy and has no connection with the ancient Assyrians.

Astruc, Jean (1684–1766). Physician and amateur Hebraist, author of a pioneering study of the book of *Genesis (*Conjectures*, 1753) in which he identified distinct sources used by *Moses, partly on the basis of their use of the divine names Elohim (E) and YHWH (J, from French *Jahve*). His work was translated into German (1782) and English (1836), and his theories were later refined into what came to be known as the *Documentary Hypothesis.

Athanasius (c. 296–373). Bishop of Alexandria from 328 and influential champion of orthodoxy at a time when the Greek Church was defining its doctrines at the Councils of Nicea (325), Alexandria (362), and Constantinople (381). His most celebrated theological works are his treatise *On the Incarnation* and his *Life of Antony*. All his writings contain frequent references to the Bible, but his mystical exegesis of Scripture, which owes much to *Origen and was written with pastoral concerns in mind, can best be seen in his *Festal Letters* (329–73), which include an allegorical interpretation of the *Song of Songs in celebration of Easter, and his *Letter to Marcellinus on How to Read the Psalms.* He also used Scripture for dogmatic purposes, as can be seen in his famous interpretations of Prov. 8:22–23 and Phil. 2:5–7 in his speeches against the Arians (*Contra Arianos* 339–59).

Atheism.   The denial of the existence of God or gods. The term was applied in the ancient world to Socrates as well as to Christians because they did not believe in the gods of a state religion, although they did not deny the existence of a supreme deity (Gk. *ho theos*, "the god"). Similarly in the Bible the existence of all other gods apart from YHWH is occasionally explicitly denied (Deut. 4:35; 32:39; Isa. 45; 1 Cor. 8:1), while the belief that no god of any kind exists is dismissed as due to wickedness (Ps. 10:4) or folly (Pss. 14:1; 53:1). In modern usage the term is generally applied to the belief that statements about God are meaningless (logical positivism) or capable of a human or scientific explanation (humanism, materialism). In Christian usage it often also covers those who believe in a transcendent power of some kind, but reject all miracles and divine intervention on the biblical model (*deism, pantheism).

The application of atheistic principles to the Bible goes back to the great 17th-century rationalist *Spinoza, whose pantheism led to his excommunication from the Jewish community, but opened the way to the *historical-critical methods of *Reimarus, *Strauss, *Schweitzer, and others. Many scholarly attempts to find a rational explanation for the miracles at the Red Sea, the battle of Jericho, even the resurrection, were motivated by similar concerns. But it was through the influence of *existentialism and Marxism that atheism can be said to have made a major contribution to biblical studies. *Bultmann, Bonhoeffer, and others found in existentialism a way to challenge traditional dogmatic theology and make sense of biblical texts without the notion of a creator God outside human experience. In post-Holocaust Europe and the United States, Jewish writers like Elie *Wiesel who believed they had witnessed the "death of God" in Auschwitz also began to read the Bible in a radically new way, while in the developing world *liberation theologians discovered in the materialist ideology of Marxism the hermeneutical key to a new understanding of the prophets' calls for social justice and their vision of a new age to be fought for in this world rather than the next. See *Marx, Karl.

Athenagoras.   Second-century Athenian philosopher and Christian apologist. In his *Supplicatio pro Christianis,* addressed to Emperor Marcus Aurelius and his son Commodus (c. 177), he cites Euripides, Plato, Aristotle, and the OT prophets (Isa. 44:6; 66:1) to prove the truth of Christian claims that God is three in one, and vigorously defends Christianity against accusations of *atheism, incest, and cannibalism. A treatise on the resurrection of the dead has also been attributed to him. See *Apologetic.

Attributes.   Symbols traditionally associated with biblical characters and saints in art, literature, and music. Many of these are derived from the Bible, like David's harp (1 Sam. 16 AV), Tobit's dog (Tob. 11:4), John the Baptist's camel-hair garment (Matt. 3:4), and a palm branch in the hands of the martyrs (Rev. 7:9). Many are postbiblical, like Isaiah's saw, a symbol of his martyrdom (see *Martyrdom and Ascension of Isaiah*; cf. Heb. 11:37), and the four creatures from Rev. 4 (cf. Ezek. 1) traditionally associated with the *evangelists. Along with the saints' attributes like Jerome's lion, Catherine's wheel, and the iron grill of St. Lawrence, these became a fundamental part of the language of Christian iconography without which it is virtually unintelligible. In the 16th and 17th centuries, with the invention of *printing, a number of important collections of such *symbols or *emblems were published.

Audience.

Those who hear the spoken word, and whose knowledge and presuppositions are taken into account, to a greater or lesser extent, by the speaker. In some cases a clearly described audience is addressed in anger ("you rulers of Sodom," Isa. 1:10; "you cows of Bashan," Amos 4:1) or in gentle words of encouragement ("fear not, Jacob my servant [collective]," Jer. 30:10; "my little children," Gal. 4:3). In most cases, however, the original audience is unknown, but it is agreed that oral tradition played an important role at least in the early stages, and studies of Hebrew *poetry have revealed to what extent its use of conventional structures and techniques was designed to help the audience appreciate what is being said. Later the audiences of Scripture read in the vernacular at public worship, with or without an accompanying exegetical homily, often played a crucial role in the history of interpretation, and studies of the dynamics of audience participation, in a postcolonial context for example, prove just how crucial it can be. See also *Reader-response criticism.

Augustine

of Hippo (354–430). Greatest of the four Doctors of the Latin Church. Born in North Africa, his mother Monica, a devout Christian, had her child anointed as a catechumen in the Catholic Church, but Augustine considered Christianity intellectually inferior to philosophy and the rhetorical career he was pursuing. For over a decade he embraced *Manicheism. After doubts about the truth of Manichean teaching and exposure to *Ambrose's interpretation of Scripture, Augustine underwent a spiritual crisis that culminated in a divinely inspired discovery of Rom. 13:13–14 (*Confessions* 8). He was baptized by Ambrose, bishop of Milan, in 387, and

returned to Africa, where he was bishop of Hippo from 396 to his death.

He was a prolific writer and brilliant defender of orthodoxy against the Manichean, Donatist, and Pelagian heresies, and his influence on the subsequent history of Christian doctrine, especially his views on evil, *baptism, women, and the Jews, was immense. In addition to his *Confessions* (397), which is a classic of world literature, and *The City of God* (413–26), a monumental exposition of the Christian philosophy of history, his works include many sermons, letters, philosophical dialogues, and a large treatise *On the Trinity* (399–41). Under the influence of *Ambrose and *Jerome, he made constant use of the Bible, searching for its inner, spiritual, or allegorical meaning and applying this to the contemporary church (see *Allegorical interpretation). Unlike Jerome he made no attempt to get back to the Hebrew original, and included the Greek *Apocrypha in his *canon.

Authority.

Since most of Scripture can be, and has been, read and interpreted in different ways, the question of who has the authority to declare that one interpretation is true and another false has been crucial from the beginning. Disputes such as that between *Athanasius and Arius on the meaning of Prov. 8:22 ("begotten" or "created"?) or between Christians and Jews over the meaning of Isa. 7:14 ("young woman" or "virgin"?) were settled by the authority of the church, often supported by military and economic might; and the Arians, Jews, and other dissident voices were simply silenced. It was assumed that the authority of the church's official biblical interpreters, many of them bishops, was sufficient, and an ecclesiastical consensus evolved in the West, based mainly on the *Vulgate and expressed from time to time in the pronouncements of the pope and the General Councils of the church.

It was against this tradition that the Reformers reacted, arguing that the

Bible itself is an authority, if not the only authority (*sola scriptura*), and that people ought to be able to read it for themselves in their own language. At the same time *Renaissance scholarship, encouraging critical analysis and the study of the original languages, began to have an effect on the study of the Bible, which reached a crisis point in the *Enlightenment and 19th-century *historical criticism. Scholars now claimed to have a new authority, which challenged not only the authority of the church but also the authority of Scripture, since they had proved that much of the Bible is not historically true. Finally the new authority of the historical critics was challenged on literary-critical grounds as barely doing justice to the subtleties of the text, and new notions of authority were sought in *Marxism, *existentialism, *feminism, *postmodernism, and the like. One hopes that this has opened the way for constructive dialogue between the church, the scholars, and the people on the meaning(s) of the Bible, yesterday, today and tomorrow. See *Pontifical Biblical Commission; *Reformation.

Authorized Version (King James).

The most widely used and influential English *translation of the Bible. Begun in 1604 and published with King James's approval in 1611, the AV was reliant on 16th-century English versions, particularly *Tyndale and the *Geneva Bible, but among the 54 scholarly contributors were a number of experts in Hebrew and Greek. Criticized at first for its use of uncouth and obsolete expressions, it eventually became a major influence on the development of English syntax and vocabulary, not only in the *liturgy but in all types of political and social discourse. No attempt was made to render Hebrew poetic structure into English, but thanks to the AV many beautiful *Semitisms were adopted, like "all flesh is grass" (Isa. 40:6) and "the LORD lift up his countenance upon thee" (Num. 6:26).

Authorship. Virtually nothing is known about the authors of the books of the Bible. It is generally agreed that *Paul wrote most of the letters attributed to him and we know something about him both from *Acts and the letters themselves, but that is an exception. Probably partly because of the belief that in some sense God must be the author of "the *Word of God," the human agents involved in the production of the Bible have disappeared without a trace. In their place tradition attributed the first five books to *Moses, the Former Prophets to Samuel (Judges and 1 and 2 Samuel) and *Jeremiah (1 and 2 Kings), the five books of Psalms to *David*, and Proverbs, Ecclesiastes, Song of Songs, and Wisdom to *Solomon. The process continues into the NT, where four of the twelve disciples have books attributed to them (Matthew, John, Peter, and James), and into the apocryphal literature as well, which includes the *Gospels of Thomas, Mary, Judas, Nicodemus* and others. There are in addition the so-called OT *Pseudepigrapha such as the books of *Enoch*, *Testaments of the Twelve Patriarchs*, and *Apocalypse of Baruch*, and numerous other works like *Pseudo-Philo, Pseudo-Dionysius, and Pseudo-Isidore, where the false attribution is overtly acknowledged.

Outside Orthodox Judaism and some forms of Christian *fundamentalism, few today believe these traditions about authorship to be historical. But in some cases they may have an important literary and theological function. The Mosaic authorship of the *Pentateuch, for example, invites us on the one hand to appreciate that in Judaism it is believed to be the most ancient, most precious, and most authoritative part of Scripture, and on the other to approach it as a single literary work, a prophet's vision of how things will be in God's world and his people's role in it. Similarly the Solomonic authorship of Ecclesiastes gives it a valuable literary context in which to interpret passages like 2:20–21 and 11:9. The historical critics posited a variety of anonymous authors for separate literary units or sources, such as the *Yahwist, the Priestly writer, Proto-Matthew, and the like, but initially neglected the idea of an actual "author." More recently, the notion of authors, living and writing in real situations at every stage in the literary process, has become more widespread. See *Reader-response criticism; *Redaction Criticism.

Ave Maria (Lat. "Hail Mary"). The popular prayer addressed to the Virgin *Mary, based on the words of the archangel *Gabriel at the *annunciation (Luke 1:28) and Elizabeth at the *visitation (1:42), and a very popular part of Western Christian worship, both private and public, since the Middle Ages. Greek and Slavonic versions, beginning "Mother of God and Virgin, hail," are popular in the Eastern Orthodox Churches, but less so. Among the most famous musical settings of the Ave Maria are those of *Mozart, *Verdi, and Gounod. *Schubert's popular *Ave Maria* (1825), on the other hand, is a setting of a German translation of Ellen's prayer from Scott's *Lady of the Lake* (1810).

Azariah, Prayer of. An apocryphal addition to the book of *Daniel, attributed to Azariah, one of Daniel's companions also known as Abednego (Dan. 1:7). See *Song of the Three Children.

Baal. Canaanite deity, known mainly from the *Ugaritic texts (c. 1400–1200 B.C.E.) and polemical references in the Hebrew Bible (e.g., 1 Kgs. 17). The name, like Bel in Babylonian (Isa. 46:1), means "lord." His continuing struggle with the forces of evil personified as "Death," "Sea," "Flood," "Leviathan," etc., provided important language and imagery used to describe YHWH (e.g., Pss. 74; 93; Isa. 27:1), though his relationship with the rest of the Canaanite pantheon, especially his father El, his powerful sister

Anat, and the goddess Astarte, distanced him from Yahwism (cf. Exod. 32; 1 Kgs. 12). Later identified with other pagan deities, the name appears in the "abomination of desolation" (a wordplay on *Baal Shamayim*, "Lord of heaven") in Dan. 8 and in one of the names of *Satan, Beelzebub, "Lord of the flies" (Mark 3:22 AV). References to Baal as the epitome of apostasy or paganism are frequent in *Milton and *Blake, while the phrase "priests of Baal" is scathingly applied to clergy in the writings of Hawthorne, Tennyson, and others.

Babel, tower of. Symbol of human arrogance and subsequent divine retribution, resulting in the world's many mutually unintelligible languages (Gen. 11). The city with a huge tower reaching up to heaven was probably inspired by ancient Babylonian architecture, and its name, which originally meant "gate of god," was given a Hebrew etymology from the verb *balal*, "confuse." Ancient Jewish commentators identified *Nimrod, founder of *Babylon (Gen. 10:8–10), as the architect of the tower of Babel, and he subsequently plays a major role in interpretations of the story. Christians, including *Augustine, contrast the story with *Pentecost when Christ's humility once again united the diverse languages (Acts 2). *Dante begins his tour of Inferno in a cacophony of *diverse lingue*, and medieval readings of the story increasingly focus on the origins and nature of language. Thomas More suggested that the evil of Babel would be undone if *Latin became the universal language; and the Reformers used *Nimrod as a symbol of tyranny, bent on obstructing the translation of Scripture into the vernacular. Modern studies of language use the symbol too, as in Friedrich Delitzsch's *Babel und Bibel* (1902; ET 1903) and George Steiner's *After Babel* (1998). Babel is frequently alluded to in literature of all kinds. There are some well-known artistic representations of the tower, notably two by Pieter *Brueghel the Elder (one with Nimrod, one without), and one by the 20th-century artist M. C. Escher. "Nimrod" is also the title of the best-known of *Elgar's *Enigma Variations* (1899).

Babylon (Heb. *babel*).   Ancient city in southern Mesopotamia (Iraq), capital of two mighty empires, one under Hammurabi and his successors (18th–16th centuries B.C.E.), and the other under Nebuchadnezzar, Nabonidus, and Belshazzar (6th century B.C.E.). Jerusalem was destroyed by the Babylonians in 586 B.C.E. and the Jews exiled in Babylon until it was conquered by Cyrus the Great in 538 B.C.E., and subsequently "Babylon" and the "Babylonian exile [or captivity]" became much used symbols of oppression and idolatry in *prophecy (Isa. 14), *poetry (Ps. 137), and *apocalyptic (Dan. 2–5). In Revelation "Babylon" is identified with *Rome, which will be cast down in the last days (14; 18; 19). For *Augustine and the church fathers the two cities, Jerusalem and Babylon, regularly represent good and evil, freedom and oppression, love of God and love of the world, heaven and hell. The exile of popes and cardinals to Avignon in the 14th century was compared by contemporaries to the "Babylonian captivity." In the 16th century the Reformers, especially *Luther, applied the term to the tyranny of the Church of Rome, and in the 17th century the Puritans applied it to the Anglican Church. F. Scott Fitzgerald's "Babylon Revisited" and Jorge Luis Borges's "The Lottery of Babylon" are 20th-century examples of its application, while the "whore of Babylon" (Rev. 17 AV) figures frequently in all periods of literature and is a major archetype in the works of William *Blake.

*Cuneiform documents discovered in modern times on the site of ancient Babylon and the cities under its imperial control include the Epic of Gilgamesh and other significant parallels to the *Genesis stories, ritual texts from a New Year Festival that contain language similar in many respects to that of some of the *Psalms (Pss. 74; 93; 95–100), and archives and administrative documents relating to Nebuchadnezzar's destruction of Jerusalem in 586 and the conditions of the Judean exiles in Babylon. These provide important background to many other parts of the Hebrew Bible as well, in particular Isa. 13–14, 34–35, and 40–66, and most of *Jeremiah and *Ezekiel. The fall of Babylon in 538 is surrounded with legends, richly documented in ancient Babylonian, Persian, and Greek literature as well as the Bible (e.g., Isa. 47; Jer. 50–51), and dramatically represented in paintings by John Martin (1789–1854), an oratorio by Spohr (1842), and *Walton's cantata *Belshazzar's Feast* (1931).

Bach, Johann Sebastian (1685–1750). One of the greatest organists and composers of all time. His compositions include works for organ, other keyboard instruments, chamber ensembles, orchestra, and choir. Most of his church music, including the St. *Matthew Passion*, *St. John Passion*, B Minor *Mass, *Magnificat, Christmas Oratorio, six motets, and the majority of his 200 church cantatas, was composed while he was music director at St. Thomas's Church in Leipzig from 1723 till his death. A devout Lutheran, Bach put great emphasis in his music on interpreting biblical texts and themes, often in *Luther's translation. His sublime setting of the *Sanctus in the B Minor Mass, for example, is based on the number six (e.g., six voice parts, recurring sixths), which reflects the six-winged seraphim in Isa. 6:3. His works transcend denominational divisions and, apart from his popular settings of hymns and chorales that appear in many hymnbooks, are played today probably more outside the context of worship than in it.

Baha'ism.   The Baha'i faith evolved out of Babism, a Shi'ite religious movement founded by the Iranian Ali Muhammad Shirazi, known as the *Bab*, "Gate" (1819–50). His contemporary Mirza Huseyn Ali Nuri, known as *Baha'u'llah*, "the Glory of God" (1817–92), founded a new and independent "religion of the book." Modernist from a Muslim perspective and in many respects parallel to 19th-century European liberalism, it teaches the oneness of God and the harmony of all peoples, in particular the unity of all faiths and respect for the sacred Scriptures of all the major world religions. The numerous sacred texts "revealed" to the Bab and Baha'u'llah, which are in Arabic and Persian, make frequent reference to the *Qur'an and Muslim tradition but also to the *Bible, and subsequent Baha'i leaders have made much use of the Bible in their missionary activities. Baha'i writings have been translated into many languages, and Baha'is see themselves as having a special role in interfaith dialogue worldwide.

Balaam. A prophet from Transjordan, hired by Israel's enemies to curse God's people (Num. 22–24). He was possessed by the spirit of God, however, and uttered a series of beautiful prophecies, including "How fair are your tents, O Jacob," and "A star shall come out of Jacob." According to some, the prophet shown pointing to a star in a 2nd–3rd century catacomb painting of the Madonna and Child is Balaam (Num. 24:17), and in medieval Christian tradition he is included among the prophets who foretold the birth of Christ. Despite this, he is remembered as an unattractive character, a mercenary soothsayer (Deut. 23:4–5), who incited Israel to immorality (2 Pet. 2:12–16; Rev. 2:14), and according to rabbinic tradition had no share in the world to come (*m. Abot* 5:19). For Jews Balaam became an antitype of Moses and, in some medieval polemical texts, a prototype of Jesus. Balaam's ass, who saw what human eyes could not see (Num. 22:23), also became proverbial and is the subject of a number of paintings, including one by *Rembrandt

(1626). A badly damaged 8th-century B.C.E. Aramaic inscription on the wall of a house at Tell Deir Alla in Jordan refers to him.

Baptism. The rite by which Christians are admitted into the church. Various rites involving the use of water to wash or purify were practiced in ancient Israel (Lev. 11:32) and at Qumran. The disciples were commanded to go into the world to baptize all nations (Matt. 28:19), and Acts tells how Philip baptized a convert (Acts 8:3). Scriptural authority for the use of the Trinitarian formula was sought in Matt. 28:19 (but see Acts 2:38; 10:48), and for infant baptism in passages like Acts 16:33 and comparisons with the Jewish rite of *circumcision. The meaning of baptism was explained and elaborated by reference to the Red Sea event (1 Cor. 10:2–11), the flood (1 Pet. 3:20–21), and passages about washing (Isa. 1:16) and "the wells of salvation" (Isa. 12:3; cf. John 4). The link between "water and the Spirit" appears not only in the Gospel account of the baptism of Jesus by John the Baptist, but also in Ezek. 36:25–26 and John 3:5. For Paul baptism was being buried with Christ so as to participate in his resurrection (Rom. 6:4; Col. 2:12). "Baptism with fire" (Matt. 3:11) was interpreted both as spiritual cleansing in "the refiner's fire" (cf. Mal. 3:2) and as martyrdom (cf. Rev. 7:14). In William *Blake's *Jerusalem* furnaces of affliction are transformed into "fountains of living waters flowing from the Humanity Divine." In Melville's *Moby Dick* Captain Ahab baptizes his harpoon barbs in the name of the devil. The scene of Christ's baptism, with the heavens open and the Holy Spirit descending on him like a dove, is very frequent in Christian art from the 3rd century. Memorable examples are the dome mosaics at Daphne and Osios Loukas in Greece, and paintings by *Giotto in Padua and *Piero della Francesca in the National Gallery, London. Others can be seen in specially designed baptisteries like those in Ravenna and San Giovanni Laterano in Rome.

Barnabas. A Cypriot Jewish convert to Christianity and companion of *Paul, mentioned several times in Acts, sometimes in association with Mark (cf. Col. 4:10). An apocryphal text known as the *Letter of Barnabas*, dated c. 100, is included with other NT writings in the Codex Sinaiticus. Barnabas was venerated as an apostle by the church, especially in England and Tuscany, and is sometimes represented in Christian iconography holding Mark's Gospel. Because he was mistaken for Jupiter (Acts 14) he was believed to have a majestic appearance. The *Gospel of Barnabas* is a 15th-century text, written in Italian by a Christian convert to Islam.

Barr, James (1924–2006). Scottish theologian and biblical scholar. The publication of his *Semantics of Biblical Language* (1961), in which he identified errors such as "etymologizing" and the "root fallacy" in much contemporary writing on biblical language and interpretation, marked a turning point in modern scholarship (see *Root meaning). His subsequent works, in particular *The Bible in the Modern World* (1973), *Fundamentalism* (1981), *The Concept of Biblical Theology* (1999), and *The Scope and Authority of the Bible* (2nd ed. 2002), continue to challenge current assumptions about the biblical text, the Hebrew language, and the relationship between language and thought.

Barth, Karl (1886–1968). Swiss Protestant theologian. He taught in Germany from 1921 till 1935, when his opposition to Hitler led to his enforced return to Basel, where he remained till his death. His commentary on *Romans (1919; ET 1933), written while he was still a pastor, broke new ground in its insistence that the Bible is divine as well as human and a contemporary text of theological significance, whatever its origins in the ancient world. His writings, not least the monumental *Church Dogmatics* (1932–59; ET 1936–62), are filled with bold and frequently original interpretations of the biblical text. Labeled "precritical" by some critics and "postcritical" by others, Barth has no consistent method of biblical *exegesis, at times accepting the results of modern *source criticism, while at others working with the canonical text as it stands. Often he assumes that the christological interpretation of a text, sometimes involving elaborate allegorizing, is its "only legitimate sense."

Barthes, Roland (1915–80). French critic and literary theorist. His brilliant semiological, structuralist, and later poststructuralist analysis of literary texts, notably Jacob's struggle with the angel (Gen. 32:22–32), influenced all postmodern approaches to biblical interpretation. His most important publications are *Mythologies* (1957), *S/Z* (ET 1974), and *Image-music-text* (ET 1977).

Bartholomew. One of the twelve *apostles, traditionally identified with *Nathanael. No details of his life are given in the Bible but, according to *Eusebius, he took the Gospel of Matthew to India, and there are traditions that he brought Christianity to Baku in Azerbaijan, where he was martyred by being flayed alive. In art he is represented with a knife, symbol of his martyrdom, and often, as in *Michelangelo's *Last Judgment* (1534–41), holding his own skin in one hand. He plays an important role in Francis Bacon's short story *The New Atlantis* (1626), and his Feast Day in August is the setting for Ben Jonson's comedy *Bartholomew Fair* (1614). The Gospel of Bartholomew is mentioned by Jerome but has not survived, unless as part of an apocryphal work known as the *Questions of Bartholomew* in which, among other things, he asks Jesus about the devil, death, and the descent into hell and Mary tells the apostles about the *annunciation.

Baruch, books of. Four works purporting to have been written by *Jeremiah's secretary (Jer. 32; 36). The first of these, probably from the 2nd century B.C.E., is in the *Apocrypha as an addition to Jeremiah, and parts of it have been widely used in the church, especially 3:36–37. *Second Baruch*, known today as the *Syriac Apocalypse of Baruch*, is a Jewish work composed, like *4 Ezra* and the *Letter of Barnabas*, in the first part of the 2nd century. *Third* and *4 Baruch* are Christian works from about the same period or a little later. *Third Baruch* is known to scholars as the *Greek Apocalypse of Baruch*. A third character from the book of Jeremiah, Abimelech the Ethiopian (cf. Jer. 38), appears in *4 Baruch*, which gave the book a special significance in the Ethiopian Church.

Basil of Caesarea (c. 329–379). Basil the Great, one of the three "Cappadocian Fathers." He studied at Constantinople and Athens before becoming priest and eventually bishop of Caesarea in succession to *Eusebius c. 370. His sermons, including nine on the *Hexaemeron and seventeen on the Psalms, are characterized by sophisticated exegetical method, influenced by *Origen, but critical of an overly allegorical approach. His Liturgy and his Monastic Rule are still used in the Greek Orthodox Church today.

Bat Qol. Rabbinic Hebrew term for the heavenly voice, by which God communicated with humanity when the age of *prophecy ended. In a famous rabbinic debate recorded in the *Talmud, the opinion of Rabbi Eliezer ben Hyrcanus was rejected despite a Bat Qol intervening in his favor (*b. Baba Metziah* 59b). In the Gospels it was a Bat Qol that

was heard at Christ's *baptism (Mark 1:11), *transfiguration (Mark 9:7), and *passion (John 12:28).

Bathsheba. Wife of Uriah the Hittite, seduced by King *David, who then had her husband killed (2 Sam. 11–12). Bathsheba subsequently became the mother of *Solomon (Matt. 1:6). Patristic and rabbinic commentators saw the hand of *Satan in the story. Others, including modern feminist interpreters, focused on the resourcefulness and determination of Bathsheba in ensuring that Solomon succeeded his father as king (1 Kgs. 1–2). Some ancient and medieval Christian exegesis saw in her a type of the *Law, liberated from Jewish literalism (Uriah) and married to the spirit of Christ. In the 1951 Hollywood film *David and Bathsheba*, and in Christian iconography generally, she represents the perils of carnal desires. Recent cultural studies use Bathsheba in critiques of the "male gaze." Like *Susanna she provided an opportunity for religious artists to paint the nude female form, though *Rembrandt's painting in the Louvre of Bathsheba receiving a letter from David is a beautiful exception.

Baur, Ferdinand Christian (1792–1860). German theologian and NT critic. He applied thoroughgoing historical-critical methods to the NT, including what he called *Tendenzkritik*, that is, getting behind the text to the aims and motives of the writer. NT research is thus primarily concerned with factions and tensions in early church history. He concluded that only four of the Pauline epistles are genuine and dated Luke–Acts and the *Catholic Letters to the second century. His pioneering work on the life of Jesus was developed by his students, especially D. F. *Strauss.

Bavli (Heb. "Babylonian"). The Babylonian *Talmud.

Beatitudes. Proverbial sayings beginning "Blessed (Lat. *beati*) are those who
. . .," especially the sayings of Jesus at the
beginning of the *Sermon on the Mount
(Matt. 5:3–10; Luke 6:20–23). The word
"blessed" (Heb. *barukh*) implies "blessed
by God," but in many cases (e.g., Psalms
and Proverbs) the word (Heb. *ashre,* Gk.
makarios) is not passive and might be better translated "happy," without the
notion of divine reward. The Beatitudes
have been interpreted as celebrations of
God's goodness to the needy, as the first
part of a series of ethical pronouncements on the perfection of Christ's followers, either in this world or the next
(Matt. 5:48), and as a list of principles on
which the new Christian community
was founded alluding to Isaiah (Isa.
61:1–3). In the *Dead Sea Scrolls beatitudes appear to represent wisdom-type
characteristics of a pious or happy life
(4Q 525) and are connected with a messianic figure (4Q 521). Luke's version of
the Beatitudes more explicitly offers
comfort to the poor and hungry, albeit
in the world to come (Luke 5:20; cf.
4:18–19). In Catholic tradition, represented by *Thomas Aquinas and *Dante,
for example, the eight Beatitudes in
Matthew are used as a framework for
spiritual training, while the Reformers
sought to apply them as ethical rules for
Christians to live by. They appear in both
Catholic and Anglican lectionaries on
*All Saints Day.

Bede, the Venerable (c. 673–735).
English monk, biblical scholar, and historian, known as the "father of English History" on account of his unique *Historia
Ecclesiastica* (731). He studied Hebrew,
Classical Greek, astronomy, and medicine, and his works include studies of
physical science, chronology, and grammar as well as lives of the saints, hymns,
and homilies. Influenced by the church
fathers, especially *Augustine, *Jerome,
and *Ambrose, he wrote commentaries on many biblical books (including
Genesis, Exodus, Samuel, Kings, Ezekiel,

Nehemiah, Song of Songs, Tobit, Mark,
Luke, Acts, and Revelation), and trans-
lated the Gospel of John into Anglo-
Saxon.

Behemoth. A creature mentioned
along with *Leviathan in Job 40–41,
where some commentators have identified two natural animals, usually the
hippopotamus and the crocodile, that
Job is called upon to admire. Leviathan
elsewhere is a mythical monster (Isa.
27:1; cf. Job 3:8), and in postbiblical literature this is how both creatures, always
mentioned together, are interpreted
(*1 Enoch* 60:8; 2 Esd. 6:49–52; cf. Ps.
50:10). In the *Talmud the two engage in
a titanic fight to the death, a land monster against a sea monster, on the day of
judgment, and the righteous will be
invited to a banquet to feast on their
flesh (*b. Baba Batra* 74b–75a). Thomas
*Hobbes's second and less well known
work on the causes of the English civil
wars is entitled *Behemoth.*

Bel and the Dragon. One of the
additions to the book of *Daniel (Dan.
14), not in the Hebrew Bible. Probably
written, like the canonical book, in
Hebrew or Aramaic in the 2nd century
B.C.E., it contains two stories of Daniel's
heroic struggle against Babylonian idolatry. One of these contains a popular
variation on the lion's den story in which
the prophet *Habakkuk miraculously
rescues Daniel by bringing him food, a
scene frequently represented in Christian iconography.

Bellini, Giovanni (c. 1430–1516).
Italian painter. Initially trained by his
father and influenced by *Mantegna, his
brother-in-law, Bellini soon surpassed all
before him and became the greatest
Venetian painter of his day, having a for-
mative influence on his pupils *Titian,
Giorgione, and others. His paintings,
which are mostly deeply religious and

thoughtful compositions, include several different treatments of *Christ's Agony in the Garden*, the *Lamentation over the Dead Christ*, the *Pietà*, and the *Dead Christ Supported by Angels*, as well as numerous Madonnas in Rome, Florence, Milan, London, Berlin, Paris, New York, and elsewhere. Bellini's famous San Giobbe altarpiece in Venice, showing the Virgin and Child flanked by Job, St. Sebastian, St. Francis, and others (1487), is a rare composition, as are his late paintings of the *Drunkenness of Noah* (Gen. 9) (c. 1515) and the apocryphal *Preaching of St. Mark in Alexandria* (1504–7).

Benedicite (Lat. "Bless [the Lord]!"). Latin title for the *canticle in the *Song of the Three Children (35–68).

Benedictus (Lat. "Blessed") **1.** The words "Blessed is he that cometh in the name of the Lord" applied to the entry of Christ into Jerusalem (Matt. 21:9; cf. Ps. 118:26), and sung with the *Hosanna as part of the *Sanctus in the Roman Catholic *Mass.

Bernard of Clairvaux (1090–1153). Cistercian monk and one of the most charismatic and influential religious figures of 12th-century Europe. His 86 sermons on the first three chapters of the *Song of Songs are a commentary as much on the devotional life of the monks to whom they were originally addressed as on the biblical text, but all his writings are steeped in biblical language and imagery. Applying traditional methods of exegesis that go back to *Origen, Bernard distinguished three levels of interpretation: on the first level the Song literally contains the words addressed by King Solomon to his bride; on the second it is an allegory of the love between Christ and the church; on the third it is a moral composition containing practical instruction on how to live the Christian life. Unlike most previous Christian interpreters, however, Bernard often highlighted the literal meaning of the text, so that human desires and passions aroused among his monastic congregations through the physical imagery of the poem, might be channeled toward union with Christ.

Beza, Theodore (1519–1605).   French theologian and author of the first critical edition of the NT (1565). At the age of 29 he renounced Catholicism and left France to join the Protestant Church in Switzerland. From 1558 he was a colleague of *Calvin in Geneva. His works include a drama, *The Sacrifice of Abraham*, an important annotated Latin translation of the NT (1556), and a *Life of Calvin* (1564). His name is best known for the Codex Bezae, an important 5th-century ms of the Gospels and Acts that he discovered in Lyons and presented to Cambridge University in 1581.

Bible.   Derived from the Greek word *biblia*, "books," the term is used to describe the sacred texts of Judaism and Christianity. The Jewish Bible is written almost entirely in *Hebrew (parts of *Ezra and *Daniel are in *Aramaic), and is in three parts: the Law (Heb. *Torah*, "the Five Books of Moses"); the Prophets (Heb. *Nevi'im*), and the Writings (Heb. *Ketuvim*). Known in Hebrew as the *Tanakh*, an acronym from the initials of its three parts, it is referred to already in the prologue to *Sirach c. 130 B.C.E. (cf. Luke 24:44). The oldest complete ms is the St. Petersburg Codex (Codex Leningradensis) dated 1008 C.E., although much earlier mss of large parts of the Hebrew Bible are among the *Dead Sea Scrolls. Printed editions of the *rabbinic Bible date from the early 16th century.

The Christian Bible contains all the books of the Hebrew Bible, but in a different order and supplemented by the addition of a number of other books known as the OT *Apocrypha and the New Testament. It is in two parts. The OT is in three sections with the narrative and historical books first (Genesis–Maccabees), poetry and *Wisdom literature next (Job, Psalms, Proverbs, Ecclesiastes, Song of Solomon, Wisdom of Solomon, Sirach), and the Prophets last (including Daniel), leading into the NT, seen as the fulfillment of OT prophecy: four Gospels, Acts, Letters of Paul, Hebrews, James, Peter, John, Jude, and Revelation. Some of these books were rejected as apocryphal at the time of the *Reformation but remain part of the Catholic and Orthodox *canon. The earliest mss of the Christian Bible are in Greek, Latin, and Syriac and date from the 4th and 5th centuries C.E.

Bible Moralisée. A pictorial commentary on the Bible, composed in Paris in the first half of the 13th century. It consists of over 5,000 illustrations with accompanying commentary, arranged in columns alongside each biblical story. Elaborate use is made of *typology and other conventional interpretations. See also *Biblia Pauperum*.

Bible Societies. At a time of major expansion in missionary activity worldwide in the 18th and 19th centuries, the British and Foreign Bible Society (1804) and the American Bible Society (1816) were established to improve methods of translating and distributing the Bible. In 1947 several societies agreed to work together worldwide as the United Bible Societies with their own periodical, *The Bible Translator,* and close links with the evangelical Summer Institute of Linguistics, where many distinguished linguists, notably Eugene Nida and Kenneth Pike, ensured the highest standards in linguistic theory and practice. By 2000 the Bible or parts of it had been translated into over 2,000 different languages. See also *Missionaries.

Biblia Pauperum (Lat. "Bible of the poor"). The title of this mediaeval pictorial commentary on the NT probably refers to its popularity among poor preachers in late medieval Europe. The earliest mss are of Dutch and German origin, and from the 15th-century printed editions become common. It normally covers 40 events in the life of Christ, from the *Annunciation to Christ giving the crown of eternal life to the church. The elaborate design of each page consists of three scenes, one in the center illustrating the event itself and an OT scene on either side, all accompanied by explanatory texts above and below. The central scene is framed by four appropriate biblical texts, each with a portrait of its author. The "*Annunciation" scene, for example, is flanked by "Eve and the Serpent" (Gen. 3:14) and "Gideon's Fleece" (Judg. 6:36–38), and framed by Isaiah (7:14), David (Ps. 71:6), Ezekiel (44:2), and Jeremiah (31:22). The exegetical material follows closely the conventions used in contemporary architecture and stained-glass representations of the same scenes, in the cathedrals of Rheims, *Chartres, and elsewhere.

Biblical criticism. The general term for modern approaches to the study of the Bible informed by the insights and challenges of the *Enlightenment. From ancient times Jewish and Christian scholars had raised critical questions on such matters as the relationship between the Greek version of the text and the original Hebrew (*Jerome), the age of Methuselah (*Augustine), and the unity of the book of Isaiah (*Ibn Ezra). What was new in 18th-century Europe was the spirit of free inquiry, unchecked by religious dogma both inside the church and outside it. The Mosaic authorship of the *Pentateuch was questioned with new rigor (*Astruc), the character of David fiercely criticized (*Voltaire), and the historicity of the resurrection rejected (*Reimarus). A crucial element in 19th- and 20th-century biblical scholarship was the discovery of archaeological data from Egypt, Mesopotamia, Palestine, and elsewhere that encouraged the view that the only legitimate goal for modern biblical research was "the original meaning of the text" and "how things actually were" when it was written.

Biblical criticism itself soon disintegrated into discrete disciplines. OT criticism and NT criticism went their separate ways as the unity of the Christian Bible could no longer be defended. A distinction was drawn between lower criticism, which was concerned with textual matters, and higher criticism, dealing with date, authorship, and other *historical-critical questions. Twentieth-century biblical scholars further defined their methods as *form criticism, *source criticism, *redaction criticism, etc., while biblical scholarship in the 1990s was characterized by an emphasis on literary, sociopolitical, and psychological approaches, disillusionment with traditional biblical criticism, and a new awareness of the value of "precritical" readings of the text. See *Reception history.

Biblical theology.

All Christian theology claims to be biblical in the sense of officially acknowledging scriptural authority. But the relationship between the Bible and theology is complex, and the term *biblical theology* often implies criticism of theological systems that pay too little attention to what the Bible and modern biblical scholarship are saying. The first attempt to define biblical theology as distinct from dogmatic theology was made by the German scholar J. P. Gabler in 1787. Nineteenth-century biblical scholarship focused more on ancient Israelite religion and Christian origins than on theology, and it was not until World War I and the publication of Karl *Barth's commentary on *Romans* (1919) that biblical theology was taken seriously. Since then there have been numerous OT theologies (e.g., Walther Eichrodt, Gerhard von *Rad), NT theologies (e.g., Rudolf *Bultmann), and theological dictionaries of the Bible (e.g., Gerhard Kittel and Gerhard Friedrich).

Many of these were based on generalizations about the "Hebrew mind" and the distinctiveness of biblical thought in its ancient context, inconsistencies between biblical *salvation history and what actually happened, christological interpretations of texts written centuries before Christ, and other controversial assumptions unacceptable to many. Tensions between the historian's approach to the text and that of the believer or theologian remain, as do doubts as to whether a single unitary "biblical theology," drawing on all the many diverse parts of the OT and NT, will ever be possible. Recent literary approaches to the text of the Bible as a whole, the recognition that texts have many valid meanings, not just one, and a new appreciation of the importance of reader response, prepare the way for new ways of tackling the biblical theology problem. See *Reader-response criticism.

Black theology.

Among the first academic studies of black theology were James Hal Cone's *Black Theology and Black Power* (1969) and *A Black Theology of Liberation* (1970), published soon after the assassination of Martin Luther King Jr. in 1968. They contain, on the one hand, a challenge to white hegemony in Western theology, and, on the other, an attempt to contextualize Christian theology in the experience of blacks in America and elsewhere. Resources for black theology were readily available, much of it in oral form, in African American spirituals, protest songs, and sermons, born of generations of slavery and oppression. It was fuelled also by a new awareness among theologians, including *liberation theologians and *feminists, of the relevance of the contemporary experience of believers to theology if it was to be, in Karl Barth's words, "a function of the Church." At the same time the imperialistic notion of "indigenizing" Christianity was challenged by African theologians like John Mbiti who argued instead that the Bible is already at home in Africa, waiting to be articulated in the words and images of African religious experience. Thanks to a significant increase in the number of black scholars and the development of *postcolonial criticism worldwide, the role of black theology in biblical studies is likely to expand in the future. See *African interpretation; *African American interpretation; *Context.

Blake, William (1757–1827). English poet, artist, and visionary. Most of his many works are religious in content and characterized by deep personal experience and a powerful imagination, which posed a challenge to the rational climate and ecclesiastical conventions of his day. His writings, from the *Songs of Innocence* (1789), *The Marriage of Heaven and Hell* (1791), and *Songs of Experience* (1794), to *Milton* (1904), which contains the famous hymn "Jerusalem" (set to music by Hubert Parry), the great allegorical poem *Jerusalem* (1808–18), and the unfinished *Everlasting Gospel,* contain some of the most original interpretations of the Bible. The same is true of his numerous paintings and engravings, which include *Nebuchadnezzar, Elijah, The Elohim Creating Adam, The Ancient of Days, Jacob's Dream, The Last Judgment,* and his twenty-one brilliant *Illustrations to the Book of Job* (1820–26).

Bloch, Ernest (1880–1959). Swiss composer. He studied music in Brussels, Frankfurt, and Munich and then, after living for a few years in Paris, was appointed professor of music aesthetics at Geneva in 1911. In 1917 he moved to the United States, where his compositions won him international acclaim, and apart from a brief period of retirement in Geneva (1930–38), he spent the rest of his life in America. Although not a practicing Jew, he was proud of his Jewish origins, which inform much of his music including his settings of three psalms (22; 114; 137) for solo voice and orchestra (1912–14), *Schlomo* (Solomon) for cello and orchestra, inspired by the book of Ecclesiastes (1916), and a choral setting of the liturgy entitled *Avodath Ha-Kodesh* ("Sacred Service") (1930–33), including the hymn *Adon Olam*, the *Shema, and many passages from the Hebrew Bible (e.g., Num. 24:5; Ps. 19:14; 24:7; Prov. 3:18).

Blood. The Biblical Hebrew word for "blood" (*dam*) is associated most often with murder (e.g., Gen. 4:10; 9:4–6) and the slaughter of animals (e.g., Deut. 12). The shedding of blood in *sacrifice denotes giving up a life for a life by which atonement can be achieved (cf. Lev. 17:11), and blood rituals to seal a *covenant mean death to whoever breaks it (cf. Exod. 24; cf. Gen. 15; Jer. 34:18–20). The awful power of blood is also seen in its efficacy in warding off the "destroying angel" in the *Passover story (Exod. 12:23), and in the very strict prohibition, in Jewish law to this day, against eating or drinking it (Deut. 12). To have "blood on one's hands" means to be guilty of murder (e.g., Isa. 1:15), and the biblical idiom "flesh and blood" signifies human frailty (e.g., 1 Cor. 15:50). It is never a source of life or a bond between kin.

Christian traditions about "the blood of Christ" draw on all these scriptural precursors, especially the ritual of sacrificing the Passover lamb (e.g., 1 Cor. 5:7; Heb. 9:12–23), but add the notion of drinking Jesus' sacred blood in the *Eucharist. Much is made of the blood-grape-wine symbolism in Christian art and literature from the "true vine" saying in John 15:1 to the bizarre images of Christ being crushed in a cross-like winepress (cf. Isa. 63:3), his blood pouring into a chalice beneath. Another popular Christian image, still in some evangelical hymnbooks, is that of being washed in the blood of the Lamb (cf. Rev. 7:14).

Bonaventure (Giovanni di Fidanza) (c. 1217–1274). Italian Franciscan. Born in Tuscany, he studied in Paris, where he was influenced by the works of Peter Lombard and *Hugh of St. Victor. In 1257 he was appointed minister general of the Franciscan Order. His writings include popular and influential commentaries on Luke, John, and Ecclesiastes, as well as the mystical *Itinerarium Mentis in Deum* ("Journey of the Mind into God"), and a biography of Francis of Assisi (1263). He believed, like Hugh, that the Bible mirrors the "Book of Nature" (Ps. 19; Rom. 1:20), and likened it to the love of Christ, analyzing the exegetical process in terms of its breadth, length, depth, and height (Eph. 3:18).

Books and book production.

Books in the Bible, such as the "book of the covenant" (Exod. 24:7), the "book of the law" (Neh. 8), the "book of truth" (Dan. 10:21), and the "book of life" (Rev. 20:12–15), were scrolls similar in construction to the handwritten Isaiah Scroll A, discovered at Qumran in 1947. This is made of seventeen strips of leather stitched together, seven and a half meters long, and is the oldest complete biblical ms in existence. The prophets' words were sometimes written on scrolls (Jer. 36). Ezekiel was instructed to eat a scroll (Ezek. 3; cf. Rev. 10:9) and a flying scroll figures in Zechariah (Zech. 5). Such scrolls were sealed, with up to seven seals (Rev. 5–6; 8).

By the 2nd century C.E. the scroll had been almost universally superseded by the more convenient *codex, a book more like modern books made up of pages bound at the spine. Most surviving mss of the Bible are in codex form, although in Jewish practice scrolls (Heb. *megillot) of the Torah and other biblical texts are used for liturgical purposes up to the present day. The invention of *printing in the 15th century had a significant impact on the dissemination of the Reformers' ideas, not least vernacular translations of the Bible which often became for them the main, if not the only, Christian symbol. *Rabbinic Bibles

were among the earliest printed books, while the 20-plus volumes of the Talmud stand as a written authority equal to the Hebrew Bible. (See *Manuscripts)

The belief that alongside the Bible, the "Book of Nature" is another means of divine self-revelation goes back to biblical texts like Ps. 19 and Rom. 1:20. The early medieval Jewish "Book of Creation" (*sefer yetzirah*) reads alphabetical and numerical patterns in the divine process of *creation. In the words of *Hugh of St. Victor (12th century), "this whole visible world is like a book written by the finger of God," a view taken up by *Bonaventure and later by *Dante, who, at the end of *Paradiso,* pictures the two books, the Bible and the Book of Nature, as bound in a single volume. Other liturgical books that have played an important role in Christian tradition are the Roman Missal, which contains the text of the *Mass; the Breviary, containing the words of the Daily Office for priests and religious; the medieval Books of Hours, mainly produced for lay devotion and often richly illustrated; and the Anglican Book of Common Prayer (1550, rev. 1662).

Booths, Feast of. See *Tabernacles, Feast of.

Bosch, Hieronymus (c. 1450–1516). Dutch painter. He was brought up in a strongly religious environment, and rarely if ever left his native town, 's Hertogenbosch, from which he got his name. The subjects of all his paintings are religious or moralistic, often handled with a vivid and nightmarish imagination, probably inspired by contemporary sermons and a widespread belief that the end of the world was imminent. Typical is *The Hay Wain,* a triptych based on the text "All flesh is grass" (Isa. 40:6–8), showing a progression from *Eden on the left, through this world symbolized by a wagonload of hay surrounded by grasping human figures, to one of his

famous depictions of hell on the right. There are two other similar triptychs, *The Garden of Earthly Delights* and *The Last Judgment*, and his paintings of the *passion, no less grotesque, include an *Ecce Homo* (1490), *Crowning with Thorns* (1495–1500), and *Christ Carrying the Cross* (1515–16).

Brahms, Johannes (1833–97). German composer. After earning a living by playing in taverns, saloons, and other places in Hamburg, in 1862 he settled in Vienna, where he devoted his life to composing, mainly orchestral works, of which the four symphonies and four concertos are his most popular, and chamber music. The words of his greatest choral work, the *German Requiem* (1866–69) are taken from the Bible, in Luther's translation, and include "All flesh doth perish as the grass" (Isa. 40:6), "I will comfort you as a mother's love doth comfort" (Isa. 66:13), and "O Death where is thy sting" (1 Cor. 15:55). One of his last works, the *Vier ernste Gesänge* ("Four Serious Songs"; 1896) are settings of passages from Ecclesiastes (3:19–22; 4:1–3), Sirach (41:1–2), and 1 Corinthians (13:1–3, 12–13).

Britten, (Edward) Benjamin (1913–1976). English composer and cofounder of the Aldeburgh Festival in 1948. In addition to operas (e.g., *Peter Grimes*, *Death in Venice*), a few orchestral works (*Young Person's Guide to the Orchestra*), and some chamber music, most of Britten's compositions were inspired by words. They include settings of poems by John *Donne, William *Blake, W. H. Auden (*Hymn to St. Cecilia*), and Christopher Smart (*Rejoice in the Lamb*); five canticles; *Noye's Fludde* (a children's opera); *St. Nicholas*; and a *Cantata Misericordium*. Of his three church parables, two are retellings of well-known biblical stories, *The Burning Fiery Furnace* and *The Prodigal Son*. His *War Requiem*, composed for the consecration of the rebuilt Coventry Cathedral in 1962, combines the tradi-

tional text of the Latin *Mass (e.g., *Sanctus, *Dies Irae, Libera me) with the words of Wilfred Owen, notably his radical interpretation of the "Sacrifice of Isaac" (Gen. 22).

Brown,   Raymond   Edward (1928–1998). American Catholic priest and biblical scholar. A student of *Albright, he taught for many years at Union Theological Seminary in New York. In his numerous publications, from *The Sensus Plenior of Scripture* (1955) and studies of *Daniel* (1962) and *Deuteronomy* (1965), to his better known and enormously influential two-volume commentary on *John* (1966, 1970), *The Critical Meaning of the Bible* (1981), and his *Introduction to the NT* (1997), he sought to reconcile modern historical-critical scholarship with Catholic tradition. He served twice on the *Pontifical Biblical Commission and wrote authoritatively on the Virgin Birth, the resurrection, the apostles, and many other topics. He was coeditor of the popular *Jerome Bible Commentary* (1968; rev. 1992).

Bruckner, Anton (1824–96). Austrian composer. In 1855 he was appointed cathedral organist in Linz and in 1868 professor at the Vienna Conservatory, where he spent the rest of his life. Strongly influenced by Wagner, his romantic symphonies were eventually successful, but he is also much admired for his religious music, which includes several masses, a *Te Deum, settings of five psalms (notably 150), and many motets, such as *Os Justi* (Ps. 37:30–31) and *Christus Factus est* (Phil. 2:8–9).

Brueghel, Pieter the Elder (c. 1525–69). Dutch painter. He traveled in France and Italy, but worked for most of his life in Antwerp, where he associated with influential printers and humanist scholars. Influenced by *Bosch but with a sense of humor evident in *Big Fish Eat*

Little Fish (1557) and *Dulle Griet* ("Mad Meg," 1562), his greatest religious paintings include the *Triumph of Death* (1562), the *Fall of the Rebel Angels* (Rev. 12:3–9), and the *Tower of Babel* (1563). His most famous scenes from the Gospels are the two snow scenes, *The Census at Bethlehem* (1566) and the *Massacre of the Innocents* (1565–66), and an extraordinary picture of a public execution showing *Christ Carrying the Cross* (1564) in the middle, surrounded by crowds of ordinary people.

Buber, Martin (1878–1965). Austrian Jewish existentialist philosopher. Born in Vienna, educated in Vienna, Leipzig, Berlin, and Zurich, Buber taught at the University of Frankfurt until forced to leave Nazi Germany in 1938. He was professor of social philosophy at the Hebrew University, Jerusalem, from then until 1951. He was a lifelong Zionist, though his *Zionism was more romantic and cultural than political, and his friendship with its founder, Theodor Herzl, was shortlived. His most widely known and influential works are *I and Thou* (1923; ET 1937) and *Tales of the Hasidim* (2 vols. ET 1947; see *Hasidism). With his friend Franz *Rosenzweig, Buber produced an innovative German translation of the Hebrew Bible (1925–61), rendering YHWH by "the Present One," for example, and *qadosh* by the active "hallowing" rather than "holy" (cf. *Scripture and Translation*, 1936; ET 1994). In his many writings on the Bible he maintained a healthy skepticism toward much historical-critical scholarship, favoring instead a literary approach in which he emphasized the importance of such features as intertextuality and orality, and sought to make biblical traditions speak afresh to contemporary faith. His publications on biblical topics include *Kingship of God* (1932; ET 1967), *Moses* (1946), *The Prophetic Faith* (1940; ET 1949), and *Biblical Humanism* (1968).

Bucer, Martin (1491–1551). Protestant reformer. He spent most of his career in Strasbourg, where he influenced *Calvin. Under the influence of *Erasmus, his biblical scholarship, evident notably in his commentary on the *Psalms* (1529), was characterized by an emphasis on the literal meaning of the text, and he drew heavily on medieval Hebrew sources. Bucer sought to resolve the tension between the two Testaments and to apply Scripture to contemporary moral and political issues.

Bultmann, Rudolf Karl (1884–1976). German Protestant theologian and NT scholar. As NT professor at Marburg (1921–51) he applied form-critical methods to the Gospels and concluded that little could be known of the historical Jesus, though his faith in Christ was never in doubt. He also focused on Hellenistic elements in the language and theology of the NT, which he argued had to be demythologized to make them comprehensible today. His rewriting of the *kerygma owed much to 20th-century existentialist philosophy, and his many critics argued that the language of ancient myth and poetry can be understood without the need for such drastic reinterpretation. His most influential works were a commentary on *John* (1941; ET 1971), *Theology of the NT* (1948–53; ET 1952–55), *History and Eschatology* (1957), *Jesus Christ and Mythology* (1958), and his contribution to *Kerygma and Myth* (1953). Some of his sermons were published in 1956 (ET 1960) and an important collection of his essays as *Faith and Understanding* (1969).

Bunyan, John (1628–88). English Nonconformist writer and preacher. Prosecuted more than once by the royalists, he wrote some of his best-known works in jail. Of little education apart from his own study of the Bible, he wrote a number of evangelical works, including *Some Gospel Truths Opened* (an attack on Quakerism, 1656), *Christian Behaviour*

(1663), *The Holy City* (1665), *The Resurrection of the Dead* (1665), and the autobiographical *Grace Abounding* (1666). His masterpiece, *The Pilgrim's Progress*, was written in two parts, the first in prison in 1673 and published in 1678, and the second in 1684. Combining homeliness and directness with a highly original application of biblical language and imagery, it tells the story of Christian's progress from the "city of destruction" (Isa. 19:18) to "the city of God" (Ps. 46:4) by way of "the Valley of the Shadow of Death" (Ps. 23:4), "Beulah" (Isa. 62:4), and other allusions that, largely thanks to Bunyan, have become part of the English language.

Buxtorf, Johann (1564–1629). Hebrew scholar. As professor of Hebrew at the University of Basel, he vigorously promoted the study of rabbinic and medieval Hebrew, Aramaic, Syriac, and even Yiddish, alongside Biblical Hebrew, by publishing grammars and dictionaries as well as his own edition of the *rabbinic Bible. His *Synagoga judaica* (1604), a study of Jewish faith and practice, was reprinted many times (between 1680 and 1989) and twice translated into English (1657; 1748), and his *Lexicon chaldaicum, talmudicum et rabbinicum* (edited by his son in 1639) was reprinted in 1977.

Byrd, William (1543–1623). English Catholic composer. Prosecuted several times for recusancy but always favored by Queen Elizabeth, Byrd was probably the greatest of the Tudor composers. He wrote three masses, numerous anthems, and settings of Psalms as well as miscellaneous music for strings and keyboard. His over 300 motets are choral settings of biblical passages, many of them of great historical, political, and exegetical interest.

Byron, Lord George Gordon (1788–1824). English poet. From an early acquaintance with Isaac Nathan, a Jewish singer and composer, he acquired a lifelong interest in the OT, in particular the human drama in the stories of Jephthah, Saul, Job, and others. For Nathan he wrote *Hebrew Melodies* (1815–16), including *Sennacherib* ("The Assyrian came down like a wolf on the fold"), which in turn was the inspiration for a piece by the Russian composer Mussorgsky (1867). Later, after he had left England, he produced an extraordinary, blasphemous biblical poem entitled *Cain: A Mystery* (1821).

Byzantine art and architecture. The art and architecture of the Eastern Roman Empire, with its capital at Constantinople (Byzantium), from the reign of *Constantine (312–337) to the Turkish conquest in 1453. The style and splendor of the early period are still evident in magnificent 6th- and 7th-century buildings in Rome, Ravenna, Thessalonica, Jerusalem, and elsewhere, as well as Istanbul itself. After the iconoclastic controversy, which officially banned images from 724 to 843, the Byzantine tradition flourished for another six centuries, and indeed continued in Russia and other Orthodox Christian countries long after the fall of Constantinople. Typical are the rich mosaic decorations designed both to beautify the building and to educate the illiterate. These were done according to strictly controlled conventions, determining, for example, in what part of the church building each biblical or liturgical subject should be placed: the Pantocrator in the dome and the Virgin in the apse with the apostles lined up below her. How they should be represented was also fixed; for example, because one of the functions of the mosaic was to encourage devotion, venerated characters like Jesus, Mary, and the saints had to be depicted facing the worshiper, while Christ's tormentors and traitors like Judas were shown only in profile or turned away. Despite such rigid conventions, however, which applied to wall paintings as well, artists sometimes achieved a remarkable degree of realism or tenderness as in the mosaic series depicting the life of the Virgin in the Kaariye Mosque (formerly the Church of Christ in Chora) in Istanbul (14th century), and an unusually dynamic painting of the *nativity in the Peribleptos Church at Mistra in southern Greece (c. 1400).

Byzantine art on a smaller scale can be seen in early ivory work like the 4th-century Brescia casket depicting the Good Shepherd, Jonah and the whale, Susanna and the elders, and other biblical scenes, and a splendid throne in Ravenna with scenes from the life of Joseph as foreshadowing the life of Christ (6th century). There are also some exquisite illuminated mss such as the *Vienna Genesis* and the *Rabbula Gospels,* both from the 6th-century, and some very beautiful book covers made of ivory, silver, or enamel, depicting a variety of biblical scenes of which the *annunciation, the *visitation, and the women at the tomb are among the most frequent. The long history of the *icon, the most enduring and widespread Byzantine art form, reached its high point in the centuries immediately following the end of the iconoclastic controversy, and has continued largely unchanged in the Eastern Orthodox Churches to this day.

Cadbury, Henry Joel (1883–1974). American Quaker scholar and activist. He was professor of divinity at Harvard (1934–54) and winner of the Nobel Peace Prize in 1947. He wrote the first account in English of *form criticism and made substantial contributions to NT scholarship, challenging many widespread assumptions, for example, that Luke was a doctor, that we can know much about the historical Jesus, and that a modern faith can be found in the Gospels. His works include *The Making of Luke–Acts* (1927), *The Peril of Modernizing Jesus* (1937), and *The Book of Acts in History* (1955).

Cain (Heb. *qain*, lit. "smith"; Arab. *Kabil*). The first son of Adam and Eve (Gen. 4). Cain, who was a tiller of the soil, murdered his brother, *Abel, a shepherd. He denies the crime ("Am I my brother's keeper?") and is condemned to an itinerant life, "a fugitive and a vagabond in the earth," both identified and protected by the "mark of Cain." He built the first city, named after his son Enoch, and among his descendants are the inventors of musical instruments and metalworking. In the NT he is associated with *Satan (1 John 3:12) and wicked behavior in general (Jude 11); while in Jewish tradition he is spawned by the devil, associates with the "angel of death," and is responsible for bringing violence and robbery into urban life. *Augustine saw him as a symbol of the "city of man" pitted against the "city of God." Cain appears frequently in literature in connection with brothers and fratricide: a 14th-century political lyric credits him with founding an order of friars. *Dante names the lowest part of hell after him, and in art he is traditionally contrasted with Abel, a type of Christ "the good shepherd." In 18th- and 19th-century writing, including *Coleridge's *The Wanderings of Cain* (1798) and *Byron's *Cain: A Mystery* (1821), Cain was romanticized as a visionary wanderer, estranged from society, and this is how he appears in much modern literature.

Cairo Genizah. In many Jewish communities sacred mss too worn or damaged to be used were stored in a special room in the synagogue known as a *genizah.* The most famous genizah is the one in the Ben Ezra Synagogue in Cairo, which contained 200,000 medieval mss in Hebrew, Aramaic, and other languages, three-quarters of which were brought to Cambridge in 1897 by Solomon Schechter. They contain valuable evidence for early Jewish lectionaries and the textual tradition of the Hebrew Bible, as well as Hebrew mss of *Sirach and the *Damascus Document* (see

*Dead Sea Scrolls), some *Karaite mss, and many other texts.

Calmet, Augustin (1672–1757).

French Benedictine scholar, noted for his influential 26-volume commentary on the Bible, the first Roman Catholic commentary in French (1707–16), and his biblical dictionary (1720–21), which became popular in an English translation (9th ed., 1847). Calmet's work was rarely original but his reference works are invaluable as a means of ready access to patristic and medieval comments on the biblical text.

Calque. A linguistic term for semantic borrowing that results, for example, in a Greek word with a Hebrew *meaning. See *Loanwords; *Semitisms.

Calvary. The hill outside Jerusalem where Christ was crucified. It is the Latin translation of words for "skull" in Hebrew, Aramaic (*Golgotha*, Matt. 27:33), and Greek (*kranion*, Luke 23:33). *Origen refers to a tradition that Adam's skull was buried there. Latin writers since *Augustine and *Isidore connect it with *calvus*, "bald," and explain it by reference to Christ's tormentors pulling out his hair (cf. Isa. 50:6; 53:7). Since the time of *Constantine, Calvary has been identified as a rocky hillock now inside the Church of the Holy Sepulchre (cf. John 19:41–42), although some favor another site outside the present city walls, identified as Calvary in the 19th century by General C. G. Gordon of Khartoum.

Calvin, John (1509–64). French theologian and reformer. Forced to flee from France, he championed Protestantism first briefly in Basel and Strasbourg, and then from 1541 in Geneva, where he founded a College of Pastors and Doctors, a Court of Discipline, and a theological academy. His doctrine of Scripture, presented in book 1 of his *Institutes of the Christian Religion* (2nd ed. 1539), states that the Bible is the sole authority of the church (*sola scriptura*), as understood by believers through the working of the Holy Spirit in their hearts. To get at the true meaning of Scripture behind layers of Catholic tradition, it had to be studied in the original languages, but to ensure that every believer could have access to it, it also had to be made available in the vernacular.

Calvin wrote commentaries on most of the OT, excluding the *Apocrypha, and the whole NT, apart from Revelation. Explicitly concerned to get as close as possible to the plain meaning of the text, Calvin reconstructs ancient cultic contexts for some of the Psalms and rejects many christological interpretations of OT texts. Typological readings of the literal sense of the text were possible, however, since God was already uniquely active in the work of the OT writers. While for *Luther "the word of the Lord abideth for ever" in Isa. 40:8 refers directly to Christian Scripture, for Calvin its significance is more general in that it "comprehends the whole Gospel in a few words." His respect for the text as both ancient literature and contemporary Scripture resonates with some *postmodern approaches to the Bible.

Canaan. The biblical name for the land promised to Abraham (Gen. 12) and conquered by Joshua (Josh. 14), possibly derived, like "Phoenicia," from a word for "red dye." Contemporary Egyptian and Mesopotamian references locate Canaan in Syria, Phoenicia, and Palestine, although the citizens of *Ugarit did not consider themselves part of Canaan. Biblical references to Canaan depict it as a "land flowing with milk and honey"; but the Canaanites (or Amorites) who dwelt in great cities (Deut. 1:28), equipped with "chariots of iron" (e.g., Judg. 4) and worshiping idols of *Baal and other pagan deities, were to be utterly destroyed (Deut. 20:17). Modern archaeology identi-

fies the Canaanites with the inhabitants of Bronze Age Palestine, and broadly confirms the biblical picture of a prosperous urban culture, influenced by the Egyptian, Hittite, and Babylonian empires and finally destroyed by foreign invasions. Despite efforts to dissociate the Canaanite race from the Hebrews (Gen. 10), Biblical Hebrew and the language of Canaan belong to the same Northwest Semitic language group (cf. Isa. 19:18), and the abiding influence of Canaanite mythology and literary tradition, reconstructed mainly from the discoveries at Ugarit, can be clearly seen in such passages as Isa. 27:1, the Song of Deborah (Judg. 5), and Pss. 29 and 48.

Canon. An authoritative list of books used as a "rule, standard" (Gk. *kanon*), and, in Jewish and Christian tradition, believed to be sacred. The earliest mention of the Jewish canon of Scripture, the Hebrew Bible, in more or less its final form, appears in the prologue to the apocryphal book of *Sirach in c. 130 B.C.E. in a reference to "the law, the prophets, and the rest of the books." There were still disputes about the canonicity of some of the books in the third part of the Hebrew Bible among the rabbis (e.g., *Song of Songs), and discoveries of mss of Sirach, *Enoch, and other noncanonical texts at Qumran and elsewhere confirm that the Hebrew canon was not finally fixed for all varieties of Judaism before the 2nd century C.E. Later attempts were made to ensure that the number of books in the canon corresponded to the 22 letters of the Hebrew *alphabet. Surviving mss of the Greek Bible contain the *Apocrypha and follow a different order (Law–Writings–Prophets). Though these mss are Christian in origin, it is likely that they represent an alternative form of the Jewish canon, either earlier than the Hebrew canon or from a nonrabbinic variety of Judaism.

The earliest Christian preachers and writers cited Jewish Scripture in Greek, and there are several references to "the

law and the prophets" in the NT (e.g., Matt. 7:12; Rom. 3:21). It was not until late in the 2nd century that the four Gospels and the Letters of Paul were added to the canon. The first efforts of the church to establish a Christian canon of Scripture were in response to the attempt by the heretic *Marcion to rid Christianity of all Jewish elements, including all of what was later known as the OT. One of the earliest lists, the *Muratorian Canon (c. 190 C.E.), has the apocryphal Wisdom of Solomon and the pseudepigraphical *Apocalypse of Peter in it, but not Hebrews, James, or 1 and 2 Peter. Not until the 4th century is there a specific list with all the books of the NT as the canon. Decisions at the ecumenical councils of the church in the 4th and 5th centuries determined the canon of Scripture for the Western and Eastern Orthodox Churches, while the Armenian, Coptic, and Ethiopian Churches continued to count *Jubilees*, *1 Enoch*, and other works as canonical.

*Jerome consistently referred to the Hebrew Bible in working on his Latin version of the Bible (c. 391–406) and to Aramaic for *Tobit and *Judith. For the other deuterocanonical works employed by the church, he preferred the *Theodotion version of the *Septuagint. *Luther and the Reformers would extend this respect for the Hebrew canon by excluding the Apocrypha from the Christian canon. Today Catholic, Anglican, and Orthodox Bibles contain the Apocrypha, while Protestant Bibles omit it. A notable innovator in the history of the Christian canon was Emanuel *Swedenborg (an early influence on William *Blake), who excluded Job, Proverbs, and all the *Epistles from his canon. Today current interest in the apocryphal and pseudepigraphical books and the alternative forms of Christian theology they represent is not uncommon, as are demands for readings from T. S. *Eliot, Khalil Gibran, African literature, or the like in public worship.

Canonical criticism. An approach to the study of the Bible that focuses on the canonical text of whole books and of the Bible, seen as a sacred text. The method is associated with attempts by Brevard Childs (*Biblical Theology in Crisis*, 1970), J. A. Sanders (*Canon and Community*, 1984), and other American Christian scholars to resolve the tension between the role of Scripture in the church and the results of modern *literary criticism and *archaeology. Thus the authorship, date, and original meaning of separate literary units (e.g., *JEDP, *Deutero-Isaiah), though historically important, is less relevant to preachers and practicing Christians than the meaning of the final form of the text (*Pentateuch, book of Isaiah), which is what the church canonized. While there is common ground between canonical criticism and some modern and postmodern literary methods, a crucial difference concerns the problem of defining the *canon (Jewish, Catholic, Protestant, Orthodox?) and the privileging of one stage in the complex history of the text.

Canticle. A song or prayer taken from the Bible (excluding Psalms) for liturgical use. In the Eastern Orthodox tradition there are 9, while in the Catholic Breviary there are over 40, including the songs of Moses (Exod. 15; Deut. 32), Hannah (1 Sam. 2), Habakkuk (Hab. 3), Isaiah (12; 26:1–21), Jonah (2), and the Three Children (apocryphal addition to Daniel), the prayer of Hezekiah (Isa. 38), and the NT canticles in Luke 1–2. It is also applied to the *Jubilate (Ps. 100) and the *Te Deum.

Canticles. A traditional English title for the *Song of Songs, derived from Lat. *Canticum Canticorum*.

Caravaggio, Michelangelo Merisi da (1573–1610). Greatest 17th-century Italian painter. His paintings are remarkable for their crude realism, drawn from street life in Rome, for which he was much criticized during his lifetime. In 1606 he killed a man and had to flee from Rome. His masterpieces include the *Sacrifice of Isaac, Judith Beheading Holofernes,* a *Life of St. Matthew* cycle, *Conversion of St. Paul, Crucifixion of St. Peter,* and two striking Madonnas (one with the infant Jesus' foot helping the Virgin to stamp on the serpent's head), all in Rome, *Supper at Emmaus* in London, and *Decollation of John the Baptist* in Malta. His influence can be seen on later European religious art, particularly in the works of Velazquez and *Rembrandt.

Catacombs. Underground Jewish and early Christian cemeteries, especially in and around *Rome, where the dry tufa rock made elaborate tunneling relatively easy. From the 5th century martyrs' relics began to be transferred to safer locations within the city walls, and the catacombs were neglected until the 16th century when archaeological study began, culminating in the publication of G. B. de' Rossi's massive three-volume *Roma Sottoterranea* (1863–77). Among numerous frescoes, mostly of poor quality, often badly damaged, and difficult to date, are representations of Christian symbols like the Good Shepherd, loaves and fishes, *Ichthys and *Chi-Rho, and scenes from the OT and the NT, particularly Jonah and the whale, Daniel in the lions' den, Moses striking the rock, the raising of Lazarus, the Samaritan woman at the well, and the marriage at Cana.

Catena (Lat. "chain"). A type of biblical commentary in which each text is followed by a series or chain of comments by previous commentators, thus providing easy access to the works of different authors. The earliest date from the later patristic period and the most famous is *Thomas Aquinas's "Catena aurea" on the four Gospels (13th century). See *Scholia.

Catholic Letters. The term, applied first by *Eusebius, to a miscellaneous group of letters, so called because they are addressed to a general or catholic readership (unlike the Pauline Letters). Nowadays they normally comprise James, 1 and 2 Peter, 1, 2, and 3 John, and Jude, although 2 and 3 John are addressed to individuals. They mostly have a distinctly Jewish tone and were at first of disputed canonicity. Some add *Hebrews to the list in view of its Jewish idiom and non-Pauline authorship. Their presence in the NT canon provides evidence for diversity in the early church.

Catholic modernism. A movement within the Roman Catholic Church toward the end of the 19th century dedicated to bringing traditional belief into a closer relationship with modern science and philosophy. Its leaders, working for the most part independently in France (*Loisy, Blondel), England (von Hugel, Tyrrell), and Italy (Fogazzaro), embraced the results of biblical criticism but, in contrast to liberal Protestant scholars like Harnack, used them to show that Christianity had been a growing and developing tradition from the start, whatever the precise historical nature of its origins in the 1st century. Catholic modernism was condemned by Pope Pius X in 1907, but its aims and methods were later vindicated in *Divino afflante spiritu* (1943) and the Second Vatican Council (1962–65).

Chagall, Marc (1887–1985). Russian-born Jewish artist who spent most of his life in France. He is perhaps best known for his series of stained-glass windows in the synagogue at the Hadassah Medical Center near Jerusalem, depicting the *Twelve Tribes of Israel* as portrayed in the blessings of Jacob (Gen. 49) and Moses (Deut. 33) (1960). He also designed memorial windows for the cathedrals of Metz, Reims, and Chichester, and tapestries in the Knesset, Jerusalem, illustrating the *Creation, Exodus,* and *Entry into Jerusalem.* His many biblical paintings and lithographs, most of them in the Musée National Message Biblique Marc Chagall at Cimiez near Nice, include representations of creation, the Abraham story, the Song of Songs, and a powerful series on Job, strongly influenced by the *Holocaust.

Chapter and verse divisions. The meaning of a text is affected by the way in which its literary context is divided into phrases, verses, and larger units. The most ancient biblical mss, such as those found among the *Dead Sea Scrolls, had no standardized system for doing this, pauses in the text being still largely a matter of oral tradition. As the written text of ancient Scripture diverged from the vernacular, and at the same time became more authoritative, punctuation systems were invented. The Hebrew Bible was divided into paragraphs and the Torah into 54 weekly portions (*sidrot* or *parashot*), still followed in synagogue worship. Chapter divisions and numbered verses date from the printed Hebrew Bibles of the 15th century. Ancient Christian mss of the Greek Bible marked divisions into chapters, but these were not standardized before the 13th century, when the modern system was introduced into the *Vulgate and later applied to Hebrew, Greek, and other Bibles. The numbered verse divisions in most modern Bibles date from the 16th century and do not always reflect the most widely accepted meaning of the text.

Chariot. See *Merkavah mysticism.

Chartres Cathedral. Masterpiece of French Gothic architecture consecrated in 1260. Much influenced by the innovative design of Abbot Suger of St. Denis near Paris, its decoration, external and internal, in stone and stained glass, contains numerous examples of medieval biblical interpretation. The magnificent sculptural program on the west end of the building, known as the Royal Portal, depicts, above the central door, Christ in glory surrounded by the four beasts representing the evangelists (Rev. 4:7), with the incarnation and ascension above the doors on either side. Around them are scenes from the NT and the Apocrypha, the twenty-four elders of the Apocalypse, the twelve apostles flanked by Elijah and Enoch, angels, and many other motifs, including the seasons, the signs of the zodiac, and a selection of Greek philosophers. The north and south porches are equally rich in sculptural allusions to the Bible, while the many magnificent stained-glass windows include illustrations of the good Samaritan (referring to *Bede's commentary), the prodigal son, the Joseph story, the four evangelists on the shoulders of the four *Major Prophets, and a famous *Jesse tree (Isa. 11:1–2). The rood screen inside, built in the 16th–18th centuries, has over 40 scenes from the lives of the Virgin and Christ.

Chaucer, Geoffrey (c. 1345–1400).

English Christian poet, contemporary of John *Wycliffe. He enjoyed royal patronage and traveled widely in Europe. He was influenced by French and Italian writers, especially Boccaccio, but all his works, whatever their theme, exhibit a mature familiarity with the Bible and the biblical commentaries of *Augustine, *Jerome, *Nicholas of Lyra, *Bernard of Clairvaux, the *Glossa ordinaria, and others. The Canterbury Tales describes an act of group penitence in which pilgrims journey from the worldly city of London to the "new Jerusalem" in Canterbury, and many parts of the poem are built around biblical texts, concluding with the Parson's sermon on Jer. 6:6.

Children's Bibles. Since biblical times it has been an obligation on all

Jewish parents to teach their sons *Torah (Deut. 6:7), and in the *Talmud this is further defined to include the teaching of Hebrew and restrictions on the reading of certain passages of Scripture considered unsuitable for children (e.g., Ezek. 1; Lev. 18). In Christian tradition one of the results of the Reformation was that Sunday schools were set up and special efforts made to teach children Scripture. It was not until the 19th century, however, that consideration was given to designing special texts for children's use. An illustrated Child's Bible Reader was published in 1898, and Walter de la Mare's very popular Stories from the Bible in 1929. By the end of the 20th century, there were innumerable publications of all kinds, including many designed for use in religious education syllabuses in schools, from single storybooks about Noah, Moses, David, Jonah, Jesus, and the like for younger children, to substantial Bible dictionaries, atlases of the Bible, and other reference works for older age-groups. There have been several attempts to produce a special translation of the Bible into language considered suitable for children at various stages in their development, such as the International Children's Bible, New Century Version (1986).

Chi-Rho. Chi (Gk. X) and Rho (Gk. P) are the first two letters of the Greek word Christos, "Christ." The monogram ☧ has been one of the commonest Christian symbols since the 2nd century, and especially after *Constantine put it on the standard of the Roman army. See *Alpha and Omega; *Ichthys.

Christian Science. A faith-healing movement founded in the 19th century by the American Calvinist Mary Baker Eddy (1821–1910). Her book Science and Health with Key to the Scriptures (1875), which is still in print, advocates a "spiritual literal" way of reading the Bible, opposed both to liberal and fundamen-

talist approaches. Challenging tradition at many levels, she occasionally used the feminine pronoun for God and began her version of the *Lord's Prayer with "Our Father-Mother God." Today biblical study is central to the movement, which has "Churches of Christ Scientist" in many parts of the English-speaking world and parts of Germany. Begun in 1908, their leading publication, the newspaper *Christian Science Monitor*, has a wide circulation.

Christmas. The Christian festival celebrating the birth of Christ. From the 4th century C.E. it was celebrated on December 25, probably to counter an ancient Roman festival of *Sol invictus* ("the unconquered sun") on that day. Before that, and still in the Eastern tradition, the main winter festival was on January 6, originally commemorating Christ's baptism and later the *nativity and coming of the *magi. In the Western Church the festival was influenced by Roman customs (the Saturnalia), Greek and Latin traditions about St. Nicholas, patron saint of children (Santa Claus), and the Druids (mistletoe); and because of its pagan associations, celebrations were officially restrained until the 13th century, when Francis of Assisi invented the institution of placing a crib (Lat. *presepium*) in churches at Christmas time. From then, with a few puritanical exceptions, Christians of all denominations have celebrated Christmas with great enthusiasm. Since the 19th century, the German custom of decorating a Christmas tree has become very popular worldwide.

Alongside the reading of the Gospel accounts of the nativity in Matthew and Luke and of the incarnation in John, many texts from the OT were interpreted as referring to the Christmas story, including Isa. 1:3; 9:1–7; 52:7–10; 60:1–9; 62:1–5; Hag. 2:7; Sir. 24:1–2, 8–12; and parts of Pss. 95, 97, and 99. No festival has inspired more music, not least the disproportionate number of Christmas carols, which include lullabies, odes to Jesus, calls to come to Bethlehem and celebrate, hymns of praise, and countless other variations on the theme. A modern version of the original Franciscan interpretation was Band Aid's Feed the World lyric "Do they know it's Christmas time at all?" (1984).

Christology. The study of the person of Christ, in particular the notion of *incarnation, the relationship between his divine and human natures, and his role in the *Trinity. The first stage in the history of Christology was concerned with the interpretation and definition, for the most part in Greek, of the various titles given to Jesus in the NT, especially Christ (= *Messiah), *Son of God, *Son of Man, *Lord (Gk. *kyrios*), and *Wisdom (= the Word), together with events in his life as recounted in the Gospels. The emergence of alternative doctrines during the 2nd and 3rd centuries, challenging the true humanity of Christ (Docetism), for example, or his true divinity (Arianism), or the union of the two natures in one person (Nestorianism), prompted the Ecumenical Councils of the 4th and 5th centuries to formulate the creeds.

From the beginning scriptural authority was sought in the Greek or Latin OT as much as the NT: thus Isa. 42:1 describes his baptism, 53:8 the mystery of the incarnation (*generationem* in the active sense of the term), 53:9 his sinlessness, and 66:7 his preexistence. The meaning of Prov. 8:22 depended on whether the interpreter believed that Christ, the Wisdom of God, was "created" (Arius) or "begotten" (*Athanasius). Modern Christologies, like those of *Schleiermacher, Bonhoeffer, and Schillebeeckx, owe more to psychology, philosophy, and politics than to Scripture, while specifically NT Christologies vacillate between discussions of the meaning of Christ's titles and the quest for a historical Jesus.

Chronicles, book(s) of. The last book(s) in the third part of the Hebrew

Bible, known in the earliest Greek mss as *ta paralipomena*, "the things left over." It consists of a retelling of the history of the world down to the edict of Cyrus, which encouraged the Jews to return from exile in Babylon and rebuild the temple in Jerusalem. For the most part it repeats material from Genesis, Exodus, Numbers, Joshua, Ezra–Nehemiah, and especially Samuel–Kings, but presents it all in a distinctive form with clear aims and interests reflecting the period in which it was written, probably the 4th century B.C.E. Some parts of the tradition are conspicuous by their absence, like most of the Saul story (cf. 1 Chr. 10) and the infamous David and Bathsheba episode (2 Sam. 11–12), while others like the Manasseh and Josiah stories are dramatically altered. Possibly composed by the same author as *Ezra and *Nehemiah, Chronicles puts *Jerusalem, rather than *Sinai, at the center of Jewish life, and attributes to *David the detailed plans for *Solomon's *temple. Always somewhat marginal to liturgical tradition, Chronicles has nevertheless left its mark on *Kabbalah (1 Chr. 29:11) and a Christian *liturgy for martyrs (2 Chr. 24:18–22). In modern times there has been much scholarly interest in Chronicles as representative of an early stage in the history of biblical interpretation.

Chronology.
Most biblical narratives, especially but not exclusively in the Pentateuch, Prophets, and Gospels, are set in a chronological framework denoted by reference to an elaborate genealogy (Gen. 10; 1 Chr. 1–8; Matt. 1), a person's age (Gen. 25; Deut. 34), the length of a king's reign (2 Kgs. 15; 16; 17; 18), or a specific historical event (Isa. 6:1; Amos 1:1; Luke 3:1). The theological motive behind this is to emphasize the role of divine intervention in human history, but the historical implications of biblical chronology are problematic, partly because there are discrepancies within it, and partly because it is often hard, if not impossible, to relate it to

what is known of ancient Near Eastern history (e.g., Herod the Great died in 4 B.C.E.). There is also a problem of conflicting chronologies in the Samaritan tradition, the *Dead Sea Scrolls, and the book of *Jubilees. The schematic nature of the system is evident in the recurrence of the number 40, interpreted as the length of one generation, and other round numbers, notably 480 years from the exodus to the foundation of the temple (1 Kgs. 6:1).

There has been much discussion of biblical chronology down the ages from the rabbinic *Seder Olam Rabbah, *Eusebius, and *Bede to Archbishop *Ussher, who calculated the date of creation as 4004 B.C.E. Much of modern scholarship, informed by *archaeology and the other sciences, has been dominated by chronological questions such as the date of the exodus and the dating of texts, often at the expense of other exegetical issues. *Millenarian sects too in every age have based their calculations about the end of the world on the Bible, especially *Daniel and *Revelation.

Chrysostom, John
(c. 347–407). Syrian theologian and world-famous orator (hence *chrysostomos*, "golden-mouthed"). His homilies on Genesis, Isaiah, Psalms, Matthew, John, Romans, Galatians, Corinthians, Ephesians, Timothy, and Titus, delivered in Antioch, established his reputation as one of the greatest biblical exegetes, noted for his preference for a more literal reading of the text as opposed to the Alexandrian *allegorical tradition. In 398 he was appointed bishop of Constantinople, but his moralizing tone displeased Empress Eudoxia, who, despite his popularity, banished him from Constantinople. He is remembered in the Liturgy of St. Chrysostom, still used in many languages throughout the Orthodox Church, and in his famous contribution, derived from Matt. 18:20, to Cranmer's *Book of Common Prayer*, "Almighty God . . . who dost promise that when two or

three are gathered together in thy name. . . ."

Church. The Biblical Greek word for church, *ekklesia*, "assembly" (cf. 1 Kgs. 8:14, 65), from the beginning dissociated the Gentile Christian community from the much more frequent and typically Jewish Greek *synagogue, as does the appropriation of the phrases "Israel of God" (Gal. 6:16) and "a chosen race, a royal priesthood, a holy nation" (1 Pet. 2:9). Jesus' own blessing of the new institution and its first leader is described in Matt. 16:18, although many doubt its authenticity. It was the church that fixed the *canon of Scripture and determined the correct method of using and interpreting it in homilies, commentaries, and other works, although theological and political disputes led to the division of the church into Western (Roman) Catholic, Orthodox, Syrian, Armenian, and other varieties of Christianity. Heterodox interpreters like the gnostics, the Montanists, and the Arians were disposed of and it was not until the individual voices of *Hus, *Wycliffe, *Luther, and other Reformers could not be silenced that alternative interpretations gained widespread acceptance. Modern scholarship at first challenged the church's traditional reading of the Bible, questioning such fundamental matters as the Mosaic authorship of the *Pentateuch and the historicity of the Gospels, to such a degree that the gap between the church's teaching and biblical scholarship seemed to be virtually unbridgeable. Recent scholars have given more serious attention to the insights of traditional Christian interpretation, as preserved in the *liturgy and theology of the church, alongside historical-critical issues.

Cimabue (c. 1240–1302). Florentine painter and teacher of *Giotto. The St. John mosaic in the apse of Pisa Cathedral is the only work certainly by him, but the influence of his naturalistic style, signaling the first move away from Byzantine formalism, can be seen in the works attributed to him, especially the Santa Trinità Madonna in the Uffizi, the portrait of St. Francis at Assisi, and the great Crucifix in Santa Croce, Florence, which was almost totally destroyed in the 1966 flood.

Circumcision. Ancient Jewish initiation rite for males in which the foreskin is removed. Known as *brit mila* ("the covenant of circumcision") in Hebrew, its biblical origins are traced to *Abraham (Gen. 17), *Moses (Lev. 12:3), and Joshua (Josh. 5:2–7), and its power appears in the story of how Moses' wife saved him from death by circumcising their son (Exod. 4:24–26). Non-Jewish enemies of Israel like the Philistines were known as the "uncircumcised." In the early church the rite of *baptism and the desire to separate the "new Israel" from the "old" led eventually to the abandonment of the rite in Christian tradition, despite the efforts of Peter and others to retain it (Gal. 2). Its theological significance as a sign of the covenant between God and Israel (Gen. 17) and the notion of circumcision of the heart (Deut. 30:6; Jer. 4:4) provided Christian interpreters and some modern radical Jewish feminists with biblical authority to interpret the rite metaphorically. The circumcision of Christ is rarely depicted in Christian art: *Mantegna's triptych, where it is confused with the presentation at the temple, is a conspicuous exception. Christ's blood shed at circumcision is one of the Seven Sorrows of Mary, and some medieval representations of the instruments of the *passion include the knife. From medieval times the circumcision of Christ has been celebrated in both Eastern and Western Christianity on January 1.

Claude Lorraine (1600–1682). French landscape painter. Born in

Lorraine (his real name was Claude Gellée), he spent most of his life in Italy, where he worked with *Poussin. A number of his landscapes are devoted to biblical topics, chosen by the churchmen who commissioned them. A pair showing the marriage of *Isaac and *Rebekah (Gen. 24) and the departure of the *Queen of Sheba (1 Kgs. 10), for example, was commissioned by Cardinal Pamphili, who later left the priesthood in disgrace to get married. Others include the expulsion of *Hagar (Gen. 21), *Jacob and the angel (Gen. 32), the finding of *Moses (Exod. 2), the worship of the *golden calf (Exod. 32), and the cave of Adullam (1 Sam. 22). Toward the end of his life he painted a famous version of the *Noli me tangere scene (John 20:17), with the morning light over Jerusalem in the background (1681).

Clement of Alexandria (c. 150–215).
Theologian and teacher at *Alexandria (where a teenage *Origen may have been among his pupils), until forced by persecution to flee to Palestine in 202. In his writings, some concerned with debating gnostic teachers and others with how Christians should relate to the larger society, he makes great use of Scripture, citing the OT as frequently as the NT. Much influenced, directly or indirectly, by *Philo's writings, his approach to the Bible is always logical and concerned with symbolic or *allegorical meanings. His chief works are the *Paedagogus* ("The Teacher"), the *Protrepticus* ("The Persuader"), and *Stromateis* ("Miscellanies").

Clement of Rome (died c. 101).
Bishop of Rome and first of the *Apostolic Fathers. His first letter to the Corinthians (*1 Clement*), written c. 96, played an important part in the development of Christian doctrine, and was sometimes read in church along with Scripture. In it he frequently cites the OT, which he interprets, "through the Holy Spirit," as applying directly to the church

in his own day: e.g., Isa. 60:17 refers to "bishops" (LXX *episkopous*). *Second Clement*, the earliest extant Christian homily, is probably not by Clement, and various other apocryphal legends about him are recorded in the much later Clementine literature.

Codex.
A ms in the form of a book with pages bound at the spine. Codices gradually replaced scrolls in the first centuries C.E. apart from liturgical uses. See *Books and book production; *Manuscripts.

Cognitive dissonance.
A theory derived from social psychology that focuses on the human tendency to rationalize perceived discrepancies or inconsistencies between, for example, belief and practice or between prophecy and fulfillment. It may be used to explain some aspects of biblical tradition—or its interpretation—as attempts by religious groups, like the early Christians or the followers of Shabbetai Zvi, to respond to the apparent failure of their *messiah, or the fact that the world did not end when they prophesied that it would. The interpretation of the Jews' rejection of Christ as a punishment (Isa. 6:9–10; cf. Matt. 13:14–15) rather than a mystery, and of the death of Christ as a means of redemption (Heb. 9:15) rather than a failure, may be seen as examples of dissonance resolution. Other examples might include the emphasis on the enormous number of believers from all over the world to confirm the truth of the gospel (Isa. 60; cf. Matt. 2:11; Rev. 21:25–26), the spiritual interpretation of the first beatitude (Matt. 5:3; cf. Luke 6:20), and medieval Christian metaphorical readings of such passages as Isa. 2:4.

Colenso, John William (1814–83).
Bishop of Natal, South Africa. His tireless struggle for peace and justice for the Zulus and his controversial views on the

Bible, particularly concerning historicity and ethics, led to his excommunication and the appointment of another bishop in his place, but he held on to his position by appealing to the Privy Council. As well as a pioneering Zulu translation of the NT and a Zulu-English dictionary (1861), he published a commentary on Romans (1861) and seven volumes on the Pentateuch and Joshua (1862–79). His views on the dating of the Pentateuch sources won the appreciation of *Wellhausen and his suggestion of a "Deuteronomistic history" (Joshua–Kings) anticipated *Noth.

Coleridge, Samuel Taylor (1772–1834). English poet, friend of Wordsworth, and important influence on 19th-century Anglicanism. He studied biblical criticism in Germany and brought German philosophical ideas to England. A romantic, critical of rationalism and "mechanical philosophy," he advocated an approach to the Bible inspired by faith and imagination, but argued strongly against literalism and the infallibility of Scripture. His main contribution to biblical interpretation is to be found in his *Confessions of an Inquiring Spirit* (1840) and his most famous poems are "The Rime of the Ancient Mariner" and "Kubla Khan."

Colossians, Letter to. The seventh of the Pauline Epistles, purporting to have been written by Paul in prison (4:10, 18) in Rome or perhaps Ephesus. Addressed to the church at Colossae in Phrygia, 100 miles east of Ephesus, the letter deals with two main issues: the challenge of some new "philosophy or empty deceit" (2:8), and the personal circumstances of the slave Onesimus (chap. 4; cf. *Philemon). The letter, especially the passage about Christ as "the image of the invisible God, the firstborn of all creation" (1:15; cf. John 1), played a critical role in the early development of *Christology. *Marcion and others used Colossians as a scriptural weapon

against Judaism. Medieval writers including *Thomas Aquinas focused on 2:8 in debates about the role of philosophy in theological speculation. *Calvin and other Reformers found in Colossians scriptural authority for polemic against Catholic ritualism (2:17), the worship of saints (2:18), monasticism (2:23), and the apostolic succession (1:1). For stylistic reasons modern scholars question its Pauline authorship, or suggest that it was revised by a later writer, possibly Timothy. There has also been extensive discussion of the "Colossian heresy," probably a mixture of gnostic (2:3, 8) and Jewish (2:11–16) elements.

Comedy. The Aristotelian definition of comedy as a literary form that represents ordinary people in everyday situations, as opposed to the ideal worlds of classical tragedy, has no biblical application. But comedy in the sense of writing intended to make the reader laugh has been discussed in relation to a number of biblical texts. They include Elijah's mocking of the priests of Baal ("perhaps he is asleep," 1 Kgs. 18:27), the picture of idolators praying to a block of wood that they also use to fuel their fire (Isa. 44), and Abraham's rather irreverent argument with God over the fate of Sodom (Gen. 18), immediately preceded and followed by the laughter of Abraham and Sarah at the birth of their son Isaac (Heb. *yitzhaq*, "laughs," Gen. 17:17; 18:12, 13, 15; 21:6). Delight at an unexpected or incongruous happy ending (Ruth 3:8; Esth. 5:14–7:10; Ps. 126:1–2) is another example, and gloating laughter at the fate of a defeated enemy (Pss. 2:4; 37:13) must be mentioned too. The boisterous humor in the way Noah's wife, the cuckold Joseph (cf. Matt. 1:19), the shepherds at Christ's birth, the ox and the ass, and other characters are represented in Christian iconography and medieval *mystery plays illustrates the role of comedy in the history of biblical interpretation. Comedy also plays an important part in rabbinic tradition, and the Jewish sense of humor, accustomed down the ages to coping with adversity, is legendary.

Commentary, biblical. A literary genre intended to explain or elucidate the biblical text. Its origins can be traced to the exegetical and critical notes, known as *scholia*, written in the margin of Greek and Latin mss from the 3rd century B.C.E. on. Among the first to write commentaries of this type were Aristarchus (c. 216–144 B.C.E.), head of the library at *Alexandria, and Didymus (1st century B.C.E.), who wrote commentaries on virtually all the great classical authors. The earliest Jewish commentaries on the Bible were discovered at Qumran (see *Pesher), although there is a sense in which the books of *Chronicles and the NT can be described as commentaries on earlier biblical texts. Greek, Aramaic, and Syriac translations are also in varying degrees commentaries on the Bible.

The commentary genre proper, consisting of verse-by-verse interpretations of the text, emerges in the extensive Jewish *midrash literature and the numerous commentaries of the church fathers from the 2nd century C.E. on. The earliest known Christian commentary is that of the gnostic Heracleon on the Gospel of John. Since then there have been countless commentaries, Jewish and Christian, from almost every period. Of these *Midrash Rabbah* and the medieval commentaries of *Rashi, *Ibn Ezra, and others are the most widely used Jewish commentaries, printed in *rabbinic Bibles. Among the most influential patristic and medieval Christian commentaries are those of *Augustine, *Jerome, *Gregory the Great, *Rabanus Maurus, and *Thomas Aquinas. In the 16th century *Luther and *Calvin stand out, and in the 17th Cornelius Lapide, Hugo *Grotius, and Matthew *Poole (1669–76). Since the 18th century, commentaries on the whole Bible like those of Matthew *Henry (1706–10) and Augustin *Calmet (1707–16) have been influential, as have single-volume commentaries like Peake's (1919; rev. ed. 1962) and series like the International Critical Commentary, Old Testament Library, New Century Bible, and Anchor Bible commentaries, while the influence of *Gunkel's commentary on Genesis, *Duhm's on Isaiah, and *Barth's on Romans are striking examples of the impact the genre can make upon the history of Christianity.

Community. The role of community as a factor in determining the origin and meaning of a text can be illustrated in all periods of biblical interpretation, but has been given new prominence in the context of modern social anthropological research. Studies like John G. Gager's *Kingdom and Community* (1975), Philip F. Esler's *Community and Gospel in Luke–Acts* (1987), David C. Verner's *The Household of God* (1981), and Wayne Meeks's *The First Urban Christians* (1983) switch the emphasis away from the quest for the original words of individual authors to "schools" or "sects" or other sociopolitical groupings. Such studies also signal a move away from individualistic interpretations characteristic of many Protestant writers from *Luther to *Bultmann, to an approach more in line with traditional Roman Catholic exegesis where the authority of a community (e.g., the church) plays a crucial role. Current scholarly interest in the role of the "guild" of professional scholars and other "readerly communities" in determining the contents of biblical commentaries is a *postmodern example (see *Reader-response criticism).

Comparative philology. A branch of modern *linguistics concerned with comparisons and interactions between languages, normally those shown to belong to one language group or family. It has been a major factor in the study of Biblical Hebrew since medieval times, mainly because of its superficial similarity in numerous respects to other *Semitic languages. Hebrew *shalom* and Arab. *salam*, "peace," illustrate the kind of phonological, structural, and semantic correspondences that exist between two Semitic languages. *Isidore of Seville's *Etymologiae*, *Saadia's Hebrew-Arabic dictionary, and Brian Walton's *Biblia Sacra Polyglotta* (1657) are early examples, but it was in the 18th century that the Semitic language family was first defined, and comparative philology became integral to Hebrew Bible scholarship. Arabic was thought to be the key to understanding problematical Hebrew words, especially those that appear only once in the Bible (*hapax legomena*). Later the discovery and decipherment of Babylonian, Assyrian, Epigraphic South Arabian, *Ugaritic, and other ancient *Semitic languages, as well as Egyptian, a Hamitic language in the wider Afro-Asiatic (Hamito-Semitic) language group, provided still more comparative data. The abuse of such material was exposed by James *Barr in *The Semantics of Biblical Language* (1961), who presented numerous examples of what he called "*etymologizing" or the "root fallacy" (see *Root meaning) from standard dictionaries and theological writings. Another damaging consequence of too much reliance on comparative philology was the neglect of the rabbinic evidence, which is historically closer to Biblical Hebrew than most of the other Semitic languages, and can make possible a higher degree of subtlety in semantic definition.

Computers. The advent of the high-speed computer has had far-reaching effects on biblical interpretation. Accurate word counts and sophisticated search techniques facilitate the collection and analysis of data from texts in any language; and significant morphological evidence, scarcely available before computers, can be readily extracted, for example, the absence of imperatives in Leviticus. Sophisticated computer-generated *concordances can achieve a degree of accuracy and subtlety inconceivable to Mandelkern, Cruden, or Hatch and Redpath. Commentators with an interest in how the Bible has been interpreted in Christian *art and architecture now have easy access to relevant resources on the Internet.

Concordance. A reference work in which all the passages where a given word occurs are listed or quoted in part. The earliest was a concordance of the Latin Vulgate by Hugo of St. Cher, assisted by 500 Dominicans, published in 1230, and the first Hebrew concordance was that of Nathan of Arles, printed in Venice in 1523. The widely used concordance of Solomon Mandelkern was first printed in Leipzig in 1896 (7th ed. 1967). An ambitious Israeli project to compile a full concordance and lexicon of Biblical Hebrew (1957–58) is unfinished, and has been superseded by computer-generated analytical linguistic concordances. Hatch and Redpath's famous two-volume *Concordance to the Septuagint* was published in 1892–97. Various NT concordances have been compiled, most notably the one produced in Münster under the direction of Kurt Aland (1975–83). Most widely used of all concordances, among Protestants especially, is that of Alexander Cruden on the English Bible, first published in 1737, and still in print. Electronic editions of the text with word-count and search facilities will soon no doubt make the traditional concordance superfluous.

Constantine the Great (d. 337). Roman emperor. He succeeded his father in 306 and defeated his rival Massentius at the battle of the Milvian Bridge near Rome in 312. Said to have seen a cross of light in the sky during the battle with the words *IN HOC SIGNO VINCE*, "in this sign conquer," he proceeded immediately to bring together the Christian church and the secular state. He adopted the *Chi-Rho symbol for his imperial military banners and ended religious persecution in the empire by the so-called Edict of Milan (313). He defeated and executed another rival, Licinius, in 324 and made Byzantium his new capital, renamed Constantinople in 330. He also presided over the Council of Nicea (325), decreed that Sunday should be a public holiday, and generously funded church building throughout the empire. He is venerated as a saint in the Eastern Orthodox Church, where he is known as the "Thirteenth Apostle." See *Cross; *IHS.

Context. The context of a word or passage, that is, the literary framework(s) in which it is set and the sociohistorical setting(s) in which it is read, is of the utmost importance in the analysis of its meaning. The same word or passage may have different meanings in different contexts. For example, Heb. *kabod* means "glory" in descriptions of a deity (Isa. 6), but "honor, respect" in social instructions (Prov. 3:35); and Jephthah (Judg. 11) is interpreted as a paragon of virtue and faith in some contexts (Heb. 11:32) but as a cruel ignorant fool in others (*Midrash Gen. Rab.* 60:3). The form critics' concern to define the original *Sitz im Leben* of a literary genre was an early example from modern literary criticism, while the linguistic theorists' terms "universe of discourse," "context of situation," and the like further define aspects of context. Finally the postmodern focus on *reader response and the plurality of meaning completes the shift of emphasis away from the original text in its original context to later contextualizations in the history of culture.

Corinthians, Letters to. Written by Paul in Ephesus between 50 and 54 C.E., these two letters, placed immediately after Romans, contain a unique insight both into one of the most vibrant and cosmopolitan of the young churches, and into the private life and thought of Paul himself. Among the many issues raised by the Corinthian situation to which Paul addresses himself in his first letter to them are sexual relationships (1 Cor. 7), worship (including the Eucharist, 1 Cor. 11), the gifts of the Spirit ("the greatest of these is love," 1 Cor. 12–13), and the resurrection of the dead (1 Cor. 15). In the second letter Paul tells how he triumphed over suffering and persecution (2 Cor. 1–6) in an attempt to comfort and inspire his readers, and gives a unique description of his "*ascension to the third heaven" (12:1–3).

The Corinthian correspondence were among the first NT books to be included in the canon (even by Marcion), and notable commentaries were written by *Origen, *Thomas Aquinas, *Erasmus, and *Calvin, to which John *Chrysostom's 44 homilies must be added. A clue to Paul's exegetical method is contained in the rejection of the literal interpretation of Deut. 25:4 in 1 Cor. 9:9, while the Alexandrian school of predominantly *allegorical interpretation found their scriptural authority in 2 Cor. 3:3, a favorite also of *Luther. Scholars since the 18th century have questioned the literary unity of 2 Corinthians, noting in particular a contrast in the author's tone as between chaps. 1–9 and 10–13, and debated the nature of the opposition to Paul at Corinth (Jewish or gnostic?). First Cor. 11:2–16 and 14:33–36 have been at the center of feminist critiques of Paul. The notion of Christ as the "second Adam" and the images of death and resurrection in 1 Cor. 15 have played a significant role in literature (*Milton) and music (*Handel's *Messiah*; *Brahms's *German Requiem*).

Covenant. The Hebrew word *berit*, translated "covenant," in everyday language refers to a political agreement or treaty between two parties (e.g., 1 Kgs. 5:12; [MT 26]). In the Bible it is a theological term frequently applied to the relationship between God and Israel, expressed either as an everlasting promise to *Abraham and his descendants (Gen. 15) and to King *David (2 Sam. 23:5), or as a conditional agreement binding on both parties (Exod. 19:5; Deut. 29). In Jewish tradition the rite of *circumcision is understood as a sign of the covenant (cf. Gen. 17) and known as *berit milah* "covenant of circumcision," and the Sinai covenant (Exod. 19–Num. 10; cf. Deuteronomy) is the basis of all Jewish law. Evidence from ancient *Hittite and *Assyrian vassal treaties suggests that the biblical writers consciously applied legal concepts and formulations (e.g., a historical introduction preceding the basic stipulations) to their understanding of their laws and their relationship to God (Exod. 20:2–17; Deuteronomy).

The terms of the agreement, voluntarily entered into at *Sinai, are known collectively as the "book of the covenant" (Exod. 24:7), and the wooden chest in which they were contained as "the *ark of the covenant" (Exod. 25:16). Prosperity is interpreted as a reward for keeping the covenant, disasters as the result of breaking it (Deut. 28). Out of suffering came a belief in divine compassion capable of changing people's hearts (Deut. 30:6–8), renewing the everlasting covenant (Isa. 54), and making a new covenant that all can keep (Jer. 31:31–34). The Greek translation *diatheke* (Lat. *testamentum*), follows this emphasis and provides the background for the NT theology of an unconditional "new covenant" or "promise," made by Christ (Mark 14:24; 1 Cor. 11:25; Heb. 7–8).

Coverdale, Miles (c. 1488–1568). First translator of the complete Bible into English. He knew no Hebrew or Greek, and worked in Hamburg alongside *Tyndale, and in Antwerp with *Luther's German Bible, the Zurich Bible, and the *Vulgate. His translation published first in 1535 and then as the officially commissioned "Great Bible" in 1539, is characterized by the beauty of its language, which left its mark on subsequent English translations. His version of the Psalms is still used in the Anglican 1662 Prayer Book.

Cowper, William (1731–1800). English poet and hymn writer. Troubled for most of his life by bouts of melancholy and religious delusions, he collaborated with the ex–slave trader and Calvinist John *Newton in the production of the *Olney Hymns* (1779). His greatest work is *The Task* (1785), but some of his hymns also became very popular and contain memorable uses of Scripture such as "Can a woman's tender care / Cease toward the child she bare?" (Isa. 49:15).

Cranach, Lucas (1472–1553). German painter. After working for a short period in Vienna, he moved to Wittenberg, where he designed woodcuts for printed editions of the Bible and other Reformation writings, and painted portraits of *Luther and *Melanchthon. In addition to paintings of paradise, Adam and Eve, Samson, Judith, and Salome, Cranach chose to paint several scenes from the Gospels, less often depicted, including *Rest on the Flight into Egypt* (1504), *Christ Blessing the Children* (Mark 10:14; 1540s), and *Christ and the Adulteress* (John 8:3–11; 1532), as well as the apocryphal *Annunciation to Joiachim* (1516–18).

Creation. The Bible begins with an account of the creation of heaven and earth (Gen. 1), and ends with the vision of "a new heaven and a new earth" (Rev. 21). Hebrew *bara*, "create," means to impose order upon "formlessness," "the deep," and the "waters" (Gen. 1:2; cf. Wis. 11:17), rather than producing something out of nothing (*creatio ex nihilo*), although later Jewish and Christian interpreters of Gen. 1, in the light of passages like Prov. 8:22, 2 Macc. 7:28, and John 1, argued that Gen. 1:1 proclaims a prior, independent act of creation before the scene described in v. 2. Effortless creation by a word or command appears in Egyptian mythology and in the Qur'an (6:72; 40:70). Elsewhere there are colorful accounts of a battle between God and mythical personifications of the powers of chaos (e.g., Pss. 74:12–17; 89; 93), closely parallel to myths common in ancient Canaan and Babylon. The exodus of Israel from slavery in Egypt is described as an act of "creation" (Isa. 51:9–10; cf. 43:15), and "create" is also the word used to describe the operation of divine forgiveness on a guilty heart (Ps. 51:10). The creation of human beings "in the *image of God" is described in Gen. 1:26–31, and elaborated in the story of Adam and Eve in Gen. 2–3 (cf. 3:22). The rabbinic belief that angels assisted at the creation of human beings, and even raised objections, arises from the plural in Gen. 1:26 ("Let us make man in our image").

The notion of "Wisdom" as the sole agent of divine creation (Prov. 8:30) was later applied to the Torah (Sir. 24) and the "word of God" made flesh in Christ (Gk. *logos*; John 1). Among recurring intellectual and theological problems raised by the biblical accounts of creation, one might mention the question of who created the primeval chaos if Gen. 1:2 describes how things were before creation, and the obvious inconsistencies between the two biblical creation stories in Gen. 1–3. The Arian claim that Christ was a created human being like everyone else was answered by the church fathers in the *creeds ("begotten not made"). "Creationists" who claim that the biblical account, which among other things dates the creation of the world to 4004 B.C.E., is to be understood more or less literally have to explain the evidence of modern science for the age of the earth and the celestial bodies. In art, literature, and music the creation story has played a central role: among the best-known examples are works by *Michelangelo and William *Blake and *Milton's *Paradise Lost*, parts of which, along with passages from Genesis and Psalms, form the basis of *Haydn's enchanting oratorio *Creation*. See *Leviathan; *Word of God.

Creed. A formula in which believers enunciate their beliefs, usually in a ritual or devotional context. In Judaism the *Shema functions as a kind of creed, while *Maimonides' *Ten Principles*, each beginning "I believe with perfect faith . . . ," is a more elaborate creedal formulation, printed in Jewish prayer books but without the same liturgical importance. In Islam the equivalent is the *Shahadah* ("There is no god but God and Muhammad is his prophet"), an essential part of Muslim prayer, and frequently displayed in Arabic in Muslim communities, as on the national flag of Saudi Arabia.

In Christianity, by contrast, the creeds are more detailed and have played a much more central role from their formulation in the 4th and 5th centuries down to the present day. Most Christians are accustomed to regularly reciting the Apostles' Creed as a major part of public worship, and acceptance of every detail of its ancient formulation, albeit in modern vernacular translation, is essential to being a communicant member of the church. The creed (Lat. *Credo*) has been an integral part of the Roman Mass since the Middle Ages, and today is sung, between the *Sanctus and the *Agnus Dei, wherever the Latin *Mass is sung in secular concert halls as well as churches. The Trinitarian structure comes from the Bible (Matt. 28:19) as does much of the language: from "I believe" (Mark 9:24), "maker of heaven and earth" (Gen. 14:19, 22), and the life, death, and resurrection of Christ, to "baptism for the remission of sins" (Mark 1:4 AV), "the resurrection of the dead" (Matt. 22:31), and "the world to come" (Mark 10:30). But it also owes much to the concerns of patristic theologians, who introduced unbiblical terms like "of one substance" (Gk. *homoousios*), "incarnate, catholic, and apostolic," without which they could not have countered the Nestorians, Arians, and other ancient theological heresies.

Cross. An instrument of torture on which criminals were impaled in public view. It was used by the Persians, Carthaginians, and Romans, though not by the Greeks, as a particularly painful and humiliating form of capital punishment. All four Gospels agree that Christ died on a cross, and already in the Pauline Letters the "cross of Christ" (1 Cor. 1:17; Gal. 6:12, 14) has symbolic significance. In Christian iconography, however, the cross did not become an important symbol until the time of *Constantine, who, in the light of his experience at the Milvian Bridge ("in this sign conquer"), initiated the search for the true cross in Jerusalem in an attempt to discover a unifying symbol for the empire he had inherited. The success of Constantine's policy can be illustrated by the elaborate medieval "Legend of the True Cross," which traces the wood of the cross back to the garden of Eden and the visit of the Queen of Sheba to Jerusalem (exquisitely depicted in a series of frescoes by Piero della Francesca in the Church of San Francesco, Arezzo), together with the role of relics of the cross during the Crusades and the universal association of the cross with Christianity. Since Constantine crosses, crucifixes, and crossing oneself became integral to Christian tradition, as are apocryphal stories about the crucifixion of *Peter (upside down) and *Andrew (on a saltire). In Christian art the *Jesse tree (Isa. 11:1), as well as the winepress in which Christ suffers (Isa. 63:3), can be transformed into crosses, and more recently female figures on the cross, such as Edwina Sandys's sculpture *Christa* (1975) and the pop star Madonna (2007), explicitly involve women in the crucifixion as a symbol of suffering and redemption. See *Stations of the Cross; *Taw.

Cross-cultural interpretation. A method of reading the Bible in which a conscious effort is made to overcome the strangeness or remoteness of texts written in a cultural context different from that of the reader. Although applicable to some of the critical methods of modern Western scholarship, the term is more commonly applied to comparative studies of concepts and stories as between the Bible and Hindu, Chinese, Japanese, African, Native American traditions or the like, in addition to more familiar ancient Near Eastern parallels. The result can be to discover hitherto unnoticed meanings or nuances in the text, as well as enabling non-Western readers to appropriate texts for centuries monopolized by the West. See *Asian interpretation; *Postcolonialism.

Crucifixion.   See *Cross; *Passion.

Cultic interpretation.   A method of interpretation based on the assumption that a text had its origin or was regularly used in a cultic context, and that to understand it that context has to be reconstructed. The annual celebration of the *Passover in ancient Israel no doubt influenced the telling of the exodus story (e.g., Exod. 12; Deut. 16). But with some obvious exceptions (e.g., the scapegoat ritual), few details are known of ancient Israelite worship apart from what can be deduced from the texts themselves. Most of the *Psalms, so far as we know liturgical texts from the beginning, cannot be placed with any confidence in a precise cultic setting: only the most general indications are occasionally available, e.g., Sabbath (92), thanksgiving ceremony (100), coronation (110). One of the most influential examples of a cultic interpretation is the Scandinavian *Myth and ritual school's theory of an annual enthronement ritual, best documented in Babylon but surviving in several psalms (74; 89; 93; 95–100) and elsewhere (Isa. 51:9–10), in which the Deity defeats a series of mythical monsters and is pro-claimed king ("The Lord reigns!").

It has also been suggested that the abrupt change from lament to thanks-giving in some psalms (e.g., 22:22) is due to the intervention of a cultic official responding to the lament with a "salva-tion oracle" of some kind: the oracle is no longer present in the text of the psalm but may survive in passages like Isa. 41:14–20, 43:1–7 and 44:1–8. The associa-tion of prophets with sanctuaries (e.g., Isa. 6; Ezek. 1:3; Amos 7:10–13) and the appearance of psalms or psalm-like pas-sages in the prophetic literature (e.g., Jonah 2; Hab. 3) suggested that a cultic interpretation of many other biblical texts might be appropriate. Recent schol-ars have increasingly turned their atten-tion to better documented cultic settings of Second Temple Judaism and the ways in which the biblical text was under-stood in that context: for example, Jonah on Yom Kippur, Song of Songs at Passover, Ecclesiastes at Sukkot. The church's use of Scripture in the lec-tionary as an important stage in the his-tory of interpretation is another example of cultic interpretation.

Cultural relativism.   The view that perceptions of the world and expressions of belief are so closely determined by the cultural context in which they were formed that it is difficult if not impossi-ble for those outside that context to understand them. For example, biblical accounts of God, miracles, angels, devils, heaven, and hell were written in a world so different from our own, not necessar-ily more primitive or intellectually infe-rior, but so vastly different, that they can have little or no meaning today. Likewise biblical teaching about women, slaves, homosexuality, war, capital punishment, and numerous other issues belongs to a different world and cannot be relevant today. While some have attempted to reinterpret the Bible in new ways, to read it cross-culturally, to rewrite it in modern language, to demythologize it, or the

like, others have pointed to the rich his-tory of the Bible in literature, art, and music as evidence that, despite modern science and rationalism, the human imagination has not changed so radically as to find it impossible to make sense of the myths and beliefs of ancient cultures.

Cuneiform.   A writing system most commonly used on clay tablets, employ-ing "wedge-shaped" characters (Lat. *cuneus*, "wedge"). The earliest cunei-form script was invented by the Sumeri-ans c. 3000 B.C.E., and adopted by the Hittites, Babylonians, Assyrians, and most other ancient Near Eastern cultures (apart from Egypt) until it was replaced by various forms of the Syro-Phoenician alphabetic script, including Aramaic and Greek, by c. 300 B.C.E. Special *cuneiform *alphabets were invented at *Ugarit (c. 1500 B.C.E.) and much later, indepen-dently, by the Persians.

Curious Bibles.   Bibles memorable either because of the unusual format in which they were published or because of some printing error or error in transla-tion. The first category includes minia-ture Bibles known as "Thumb Bibles," one of the smallest measuring 40 x 30 mm (Glasgow, 1806). A Bible in which the books are printed in alphabetical order (Acts–Zephaniah) was published by Tyndale House Publishers in 1988 and another in chronological order (e.g., Job before Abraham) by Harvest House in 1999. Famous misprints appear in the so-called "Adulterous Bible" of 1631 ("not" omitted in Exod. 20:14) and the "Wife-hater Bible" of 1810 ("wife" for "life" in Luke 14:26). Curious transla-tions occur in the "Breeches Bible" of 1560 (Gen. 3:7) and the "Treacle Bible" of 1535 (Jer. 8:22).

Cyril (826–69) and **Methodius** (c. 815–85).   Known as the "Apostles of the Slavs," the two brothers were responsi-

David (Arab. *Dawood*). One of the most colorful and important biblical characters, son of Jesse, a shepherd boy, musician, conqueror of Jerusalem, the Lord's anointed, father of *Solomon, and founder of the royal dynasty from which the *Messiah was to come. The earliest interpretation of the David stories is in 1 Chronicles, where he is already idealized by, for example, the omission of any reference to his adultery with Bathsheba and the addition of a dream in which he receives the plans for the temple to be built by his son. His skill as a musician and his authorship of the Psalms are part of the same development, culminating in an apocryphal psalm in which he is compared to Orpheus (Ps. 151 [LXX]).

The church fathers saw in David a type of Christ, at times resorting to bizarre allegorization to cope with his shortcomings (e.g., Bathsheba is the Law and Uriah the Jewish people). David has been a favorite subject for artists from 3rd-century Christian *catacomb paintings and medieval illustrated Psalters, to statues by *Donatello, *Michelangelo, and Bernini, and representations of the two favorite scenes from his life, the beheading of Goliath (*Caravaggio, *Raphael, *Titian) and the Bathsheba affair (*Rembrandt, *Rubens, *Blake, Cézanne). In Christian iconography he is normally represented with a crown and a harp, and, as the ancestor of Christ, in the widely used image of the *Jesse tree (Isa. 11:1). The so-called Star of David (Heb. *magen david*, "shield of David") has been a popular Jewish symbol since the 19th century.

The figure of King David has inspired a host of writers: as a model of the man of faith (*Nicholas of Lyra, *Calvin, John *Donne), as scriptural authority for the divine right of kings (the Arthurian legend, Marvell, Dryden), and for homosexuality (Melville, D. H. Lawrence, Gide). Other examples include J. M. Barrie, *The Boy David*; Christopher Fry, *A Sleep of Prisoners*; William *Faulkner, *Absalom, Absalom!*; and Joseph Heller, *God Knows*. Eighteenth-century rationalist critics of Christianity, including *Voltaire, high-lighted his moral failings (2 Sam. 11) and his bloodthirstiness (2 Sam. 12:31; Ps. 137:9). Modern scholars have questioned the historicity of biblical stories about David, including parts of the "Succession Narrative" (2 Sam. 9–20; 1 Kgs. 1–2). On the other hand, archaeology has provided some material evidence for a degree of peace and prosperity under a successful central government in Palestine during the 10th century B.C.E., the period in which the reigns of David and Solomon are traditionally dated.

Day of the Lord (Heb. *yom YHWH*). A powerful biblical image first used by the prophets to express their belief that the present age would end in a spectacular act of divine intervention "on that day" (Isa. 2:6–22; Amos 5:18–20; Joel). In some contexts the scene is one of meteorological and astronomical catastrophe, while in others it is, like "the day of Midian" (Isa. 9), a military one in which Israel's God defeats their enemies. Of particular significance are those texts in which the day is celebrated by some cultic enactment, perhaps culminating in the enthronement of YHWH and the recited formula "The LORD is king" (Pss. 93, 96–99). The more intense the believers' faith in the power of God to redeem, the more eschatological the concept becomes and the nearer it comes to a belief in the final end of human history and the day of judgment (Dan. 12). Already in the LXX the related phrase "the latter days" (Isa. 2) is translated "the last days," and by NT times the belief that the coming of Christ signaled the end of the present age gave the *Day of the Lord (= Christ) a special eschatological meaning. The Christian appropriation of the image continues in many popular settings of the medieval *Dies Irae hymn.

Dead Sea Scrolls. A collection of about 800 mss, many of them fragmentary, in Hebrew, Aramaic, and Greek, discovered between 1947 and 1962 in caves on the west side of the Dead Sea. The bulk of these were found in the vicinity of a monastic settlement at Qumran, occupied for over 200 years by a Jewish sect, probably the Essenes, until its destruction in 70 C.E. Most of them, like the *Community Rule*, the *Damascus Document*, the *Temple Scroll*, and biblical commentaries (see *Pesher), are sectarian and provide valuable evidence for the study of varieties of ancient Judaism, including Christianity, and the ways in which Scripture was interpreted. The community was led by the "Teacher of Righteousness" and was preparing for the end of the world by adhering strictly to all the commandments contained in the Law. About one quarter of the Scrolls are copies of all the books of the Hebrew Bible (except Esther and Nehemiah), together with apocryphal or pseudepigraphical works like *Tobit, *Jubilees, *1 Enoch, and the *Genesis Apocryphon. Among them is the beautiful Isaiah Scroll A, 7.34 meters long, on display in Jerusalem. The texts, written without *pointing, are 1,000 years earlier than most previously known Hebrew mss of the Bible. The publication of all the scrolls, delayed for many years by a variety of personal and political factors, was finally completed in the 1990s, and the *Biblia Qumranica*, a complete edition of the biblical mss, is currently being published.

Deborah. Prophet and judge of Israel. Her role in Barak's victory over the Canaanites and their "900 iron chariots," under the command of Sisera, is first recounted in prose (Judg. 4), then celebrated in verse in the famous Song of Deborah (Judg. 5). The same is true of the supporting role of Jael, who lured the defeated Sisera into her tent and drove a tent peg through his head. The poem ends with the poignant scene of Sisera's wealthy mother and her ladies standing at the window waiting in vain for their menfolk to return. It has all the characteristics of ancient Hebrew *poetry, and archaeologists have used the references to Taanach and Megiddo (5:19) and other details to confirm its antiquity. In the Jewish lectionary it is the *haftarah prescribed to be read on the same Sabbath as Exod. 15, the Song of the Sea.

The appropriateness of the name Deborah (Heb. "bee") has been interpreted in various ways (cf. Deut. 7:20, Sir. 11:3). She is said to be the "wife of Lappidoth" (Heb. *eshet lappidot*, Judg. 4:4), about whom nothing is known but who is identified by the rabbis with Barak; it has also been suggested, however, that the phrase means "woman of fire." Ancient and medieval Christian commentators found both Deborah and the ancient poem difficult to handle, but since the 18th century her achievements have been fully recognized in such works as Handel's oratorio *Deborah* (1733), Alfred Ford's pageant *Jael and Sisera: A Woman's Rights Drama* (1872), and Ildebrando Pizzetti's *Debora e Jaele* (1922), of which Sisera is the tragic hero.

Decalogue. The Ten Commandments revealed on two tablets of stone to Moses at Sinai. The two versions of the Decalogue (Exod. 20; Deut. 5) give us an insight into an early stage in the history of their interpretation: for example, the Exodus version of the fourth commandment gives it a theological interpretation (Exod. 20:11), the Deuteronomy version a humanitarian one (Deut. 5:15). Known in rabbinic tradition as the "Ten Words" (cf. Gk. *deka logoi*), they are sometimes compared to the ten words by which God created the world (Gen. 1). The first of the ten is a historical statement by God in which he refers to the exodus from Egypt as a motive for obeying the commandments, and modern scholars have suggested a parallel with ancient Hittite and Assyrian vassal treaty formulations: "whereas I have . . . thou shalt not . . ." The imperatives read more like religious and moral instructions (cf. Prov. 1–9; 22:17–24) than laws, and have been compared to the "commandments" of Jonadab, founder of an ancient religious sect (Jer. 35:6–7). The prohibition of idols and the worship of other gods, and the ban on working every seventh day, are unique in the ancient world, and gave this religious community its distinctive character.

The influence of the Ten Commandments worldwide on ethical teaching, aided by its compact structure and direct style, is incalculable: they have often been an integral part of Jewish and Christian worship and are frequently represented in *art and architecture. The interpretation of individual commandments, however, varies: for example, the Sabbath commandment as applied to Sunday in some Christian communities; "thou shalt not kill (AV, RSV; "murder" NRSV; cf. Heb.) in relation to war or capital punishment.The tenth commandment, especially in the Deuteronomy version (5:21), is the only one concerned with a state of mind rather than an action, and has been prominent in internalizing interpretations such as those of Jesus (Matt. 5:27). In Christian reckoning, unlike the Jewish, the first commandment is two verses long ("I am the Lord . . . thou shalt have no other gods . . ."). Catholics and Lutherans include the ban on idols in the first commandment, and divide the last one in two to retain the number ten.

Deism.   The belief that knowledge of God can be attained through reason or natural theology. For 17th- and 18th-century English deists such as Lord Herbert (George *Herbert's brother), Alexander Pope, and John Locke, the biblical revelation had little or no meaning, and critical attacks on traditional beliefs about prophecy and fulfillment, miracles, and the divinity of Christ, by them and their contemporaries *Voltaire, Rousseau, Kant, and others, paved the way for the historical-critical approaches of F. C. *Baur and *Reimarus.

Delacroix, Eugène   (1798–1963). French painter. The shocking realism of the *Barque of Dante in Hell* (1822) made his name as a rebel against the neat pallid paintings of many of his contemporaries and a champion of *romanticism. He was involved in politics all his life, and his works include many studies of historical and literary themes, like *Liberty Leading the People* (1830), *Attila and the Hordes Overrunning Italy* (1847), and *Hamlet and Horatio in the Graveyard* (1843). Among his biblical paintings are the *Expulsion from Paradise* (1853), the *Raising of Lazarus* (John 11; 1850), and the *Good Samaritan* (Luke 10; 1850). Toward the end of his life he completed the decoration of the Saints-Anges Chapel in the Church of St. Sulpice in Paris with *St. Michael Defeating the Devil* (Rev. 12) on the ceiling, *Jacob and the Angel* (Gen. 32) on one wall, and *Heliodorus Driven from the Temple* (2 Macc. 3) on the other, an achievement for which he has been likened to *Michelangelo.

Demythologization.   The process by which texts, like the NT, written in the context of a thought world remote from our own, are reinterpreted or rewritten in such a way as to make them intelligible. Modern writers, notably Rudolf *Bultmann, often influenced by the existentialist philosophy of Martin *Heidegger and others, sought to demythologize such ancient traditions as the creation story and the concepts of heaven and hell, miracles, and the resurrection of the dead. The influence of this approach on historical criticism was profound, but since the application of socioanthropological and literary techniques to the meaning and function of myth, demythologization has become less popular and less necessary.

Derash   (pronounced *Drash*). The nonliteral or applied meaning of a text according to traditional Jewish exegetical method. It is the opposite of *peshat, the plain or literal meaning, and illustrates the fact that for the rabbis, as also for the church fathers, texts had more than one meaning. See also *Jewish interpretation; *Midrash.

Derrida, Jacques (1930–2004).

French philosopher. Mainly self-taught, he studied briefly in Paris and Harvard, and taught philosophy at the Sorbonne (1960–64) and the École Normale Supérieure (1964–84) in Paris, where he worked with *Ricoeur and especially *Levinas, whom he greatly admired. In 1986 he moved to the United States, where he was professor or visiting professor at a number of universities and honored by many more. Derrida advocated a deconstructionist approach to reading that challenges dominant Western notions of authority, and celebrates the limitless potential of the text to interact with different readers in different ways. His three first and most influential works, all originally published in 1967, are *Speech and Phenomena* (ET 1973), *Of Grammatology* (ET 1976), and *Writing and Difference* (ET 1978). See *Hermeneutics; *Postmodernism.

Deutero-Isaiah.

Modern term for Isa. 40–55, recognized since the time of *Ibn Ezra as radically different from Isa. 1–39, and believed by scholars to have been written, like the *Deuteronomistic History, during the Babylonian exile. See *Isaiah, book of.

Deuteronomistic History.

The history of Israel from the end of the wilderness period to the Babylonian exile, as told in the books of Joshua, Judges, Samuel, and Kings. It is so called by modern scholars, notably Martin *Noth, because of recurring stylistic and structural similarities to the book of Deuteronomy, and if it is a literary unity, it must have been written after the release of Jehoiachin, king of Judah, from prison in the 37th year of the exile (i.e., 560 B.C.E.), as this is the last event described (2 Kgs. 25:27).

Deuteronomy, book of (Heb.

Devarim "words," Deut. 1:1). The fifth book of Moses, so called because it is a second version of the Law (Gk. *deuteros nomos*; cf. Deut. 17:18). It contains the words addressed by Moses, just before he died, to all Israel assembled on the hills overlooking the promised land (Deut. 34). The first part (chaps. 1–11) exhorts them to remember what the Lord has done for them, and contains a version of the *Decalogue (Deut. 5) and the first part of the *Shema (6:4–9; 11:13–21). The second part is a law code (chaps. 12–26) repeating and reinterpreting many of the laws given in Exodus, Leviticus, and Numbers; and the third part (chaps. 27–34) is a kind of appendix consisting of instructions on keeping the laws, lists of blessings and curses, two poems known as the Song of Moses (chap. 32) and the Blessing of Moses (chap. 33), and an account of his death (chap. 34). The directness of the style of address ("you who are here today . . ."), and the theology of Deuteronomy, which includes explicit monotheism (4:35, 39; 32:39; cf. Isa. 45), a distinctive view of Israel's role in history (Deut. 28), and the notion of a covenant written on the heart (30:6; cf. Jer. 31:31), have ensured a central role for Deuteronomic tradition in both Judaism and Christianity. It is often quoted in the Gospels, Paul, and Acts.

Modern scholars have questioned the Mosaic authorship of Deuteronomy and suggested that it was the "book of the law" discovered in the temple at Jerusalem during the reign of the 7th-century B.C.E. reformer Josiah (2 Kgs. 22). Apparent references to the Babylonian exile (30:1–5), parallels with *Deutero-Isaiah, and its relationship to the *Deuteronomistic History make it more likely that, in its present form at least, it was written several generations later. The last days of Moses (Deut. 34) are represented in art by Signorelli (in the *Sistine Chapel), *Blake, and *Chagall. They also feature in a hymn by Isaac *Watts, "There is a land of pure delight" (1706), and in Martin Luther *King Jr.'s Memphis address the day before he was assassinated in 1968.

Devil. English form of Gk. *diabolos*, "slanderer, accuser," which is the regular Greek translation of Heb. *satan* (cf. Job 1–2; Zech. 3:1). Never much more than a member of God's heavenly court in the Hebrew Bible, this figure assumes a much more threatening role in Greek literature (1 Pet. 5:8; Eph. 6:11; Matt. 4). In the Apocalypse he is identified with the dragon, the primeval serpent, and *Satan (Rev. 20:2; cf. Ps. 74:13–14; Isa. 27:1); and elsewhere he is known as Beelzebub (Mark 3:22) and Lucifer (Isa. 14:12 Vg). His origin in the universe was explained by reference to a fall from heaven, described, for example, in Gen. 6:1–4 and Isa. 14:12 (cf. Milton's *Paradise Lost*), although in the course of time he was also identified with the serpent in the garden of Eden.

In Christian art devils are represented as frightening monsters, often black-skinned, as in the paintings of *Bosch and *Brueghel. Two other famous examples are *Grünewald's *Temptation of St. Antony* and *Dürer's engraving *The Knight, Death, and the Devil* (1513). In literature the devil appears as Mephistopheles in the German legend of Faust, and as Apollyon in John *Bunyan's *Pilgrim's Progress*. The French Revolution turned the devil into a heroic rebel against tyranny, as he is in works by *Blake, *Byron, and Shelley, while the world wars of the 20th century reawakened interest in the devil on the part of authors like C. S. Lewis, Charles Williams, and Dorothy L. Sayers.

Dialogue. A literary form in which questions and answers or alternative points of view can conveniently be expressed, as in the dialogues of Plato and many of Cicero's philosophical works. Others include Egyptian and Babylonian dialogues (*ANET*, pp. 405–7; 437–40) and many of Aesop's fables. The book of *Job employs the form of a dialogue, although it is for the most part made up of independent speeches, and the dialogue structure is largely artificial.

Diatessaron (Gk. "through four"). A *harmony of the four Gospels written, probably in *Syriac, by *Tatian c. 160 C.E., and first referred to by *Eusebius. A few fragments survive, an Armenian translation of a commentary on it by *Ephrem the Syrian (4th century) and a 10th-century Arabic translation. It testifies to the importance of the four Gospels already in the 2nd century C.E.

Dickinson, Emily (1862–1932). American poet and recluse. Brought up in Protestant New England, she abandoned "the dry wine" of Calvinist logic for a post-Christian religiosity, but her many poems, well over 1,000 published after her death, are full of scriptural language and imagery. Described by one biographer as "daughter of prophecy," she brought a rare freshness, originality, and intensity into her reading of many texts.

Dictionaries and encyclopedias. The scribes of ancient Egypt and Mesopotamia compiled word lists, including bilingual vocabularies, and from the 5th century B.C.E. Greek scholars were producing glossaries of difficult words and phrases in such authors as Homer. These activities were developed and refined in Hellenistic Alexandria. Later *Eusebius, *Jerome, *Isidore of Seville, and others compiled works containing systematically arranged material on words, names, and other biblical topics. The earliest dictionaries of Hebrew are *Saadiya's *Agron* and Ibn Janah's

Book of Roots, both composed in the 10th century. Until late in the 20th century, *comparative philology dominated modern Hebrew dictionaries from the polyglot lexica of Schindler (1612) and Castellus (1669) to the enormously influential dictionary of *Gesenius (1810–12), published in many editions and several English translations, notably that of Brown, Driver, and Briggs (BDB), first published in 1891 and still in print. The new Sheffield *Dictionary of Classical Hebrew* (1990–) for the first time moves away from the comparative method and incorporates all the extant ancient extrabiblical material, including the *Dead Sea Scrolls. Eliezer Ben Yehudah's *Dictionary of Ancient and Modern Hebrew* (in Hebrew) (1908–) cites examples from all periods of Hebrew literature. Among modern NT Greek dictionaries, which include the evidence of the papyri, the most significant is that of Walter Bauer (1928), which has appeared in many editions and English translations by Arndt and Gingrich (1957), Aland (1988), and Danker (2000). Louw and Nida's NT lexicon (1988) is arranged according to semantic domains.

Numerous biblical wordbooks and dictionaries were compiled in medieval Europe, mostly in Latin, but the modern era began with R. *Simon, *Le Grand Dictionnnaire de la Bible* (1693), published at about the same time as G. Bartolocci's polemical *Bibliotheca magna rabbinica* (Rome, 1683) and Pierre Bayle's pioneering *Dictionnaire historique et critique* (Paris, 1695–97). It was followed soon after by that of Auguste *Calmet (1719), which was translated several times into English in Britain (1797) and the United States (1832). Since then many multivolume biblical dictionaries and encyclopedias have been published in the English-speaking world, of which perhaps the best known are J. Hastings (1898–1904; a new edition is currently in progress), the *Interpreter's Dictionary of the Bible* (1962; a new edition is in progress) and the magisterial *Anchor Bible Dictionary* (6 vols. 1992). Other significant examples are the French *Dictionnaire de la Bible* (5 vols. 1905–12; with supplements 1928–), the Spanish *Enciclopedia de la Biblia* (1963–65; Italian translation 1969–71), and the Hebrew *Entziklopedia miqra'it* (1950–82). A twentieth-century phenomenon was the appearance of "theological dictionaries" like those of Kittel and Friedrich (NT 1932–79; ET 1964–76), Botterweck, Ringgren, et al. (OT, 1970-; ET 1977–), and Jenni and Westermann (OT, 1971–76; ET 1997), widely used, but criticized as being based on questionable assumptions concerning the relationship between language and thought.

Didache (Gk. "teaching"). A short manual of Christian teaching on morals and church practice, dating from the late 1st or early 2nd century C.E. The ethical part is in the form of a homily, probably of Jewish origin, contrasting the way of life and the way of death (chaps. 1–6) (cf. Prov. 2; Matt. 7:13–14), while a second part deals with worship and church organization (*Did.* 7–15). It ends with an eschatological warning reminiscent of Matt. 24 or Mark 13 (*Did.* 16). Frequently referred to by the church fathers and even considered canonical by some it survives in only one Greek ms dated 1056.

Dies Irae (Lat. "the day of wrath"). Thirteenth-century Latin hymn based on Zeph. 1:15–16, 1 Thess. 4:16, 2 Pet. 3:7, and other passages, sung at Requiem Masses until 1969 and in one of several English versions as a hymn ("Day of wrath and doom impending"). Written in the first person singular, the original plainsong has been used by numerous composers, but it is best known to modern audiences in spine-chilling settings in the Requiems of *Mozart, *Verdi, Berlioz, *Britten, and others. The Polish composer *Penderecki dedicated his *Dies Irae* to the victims of Auschwitz. There are also popular settings by Fauré and Andrew Lloyd Webber of the concluding prayer on its own, beginning *Pie Jesu* ("O sweet Lord Jesus").

Dilthey, Wilhelm (1833–1911). German philosopher and historian of ideas. Editor of the works of Kant and biographer of *Schleiermacher, he stressed the fundamental differences between the "human sciences" and the "natural sciences," and placed life and lived experience at the center of his hermeneutics. His appreciation of the need to understand the socioeconomic context in which language and religion operate influenced *Buber, Troeltsch, *Heidegger, *Gadamer, and many others.

Dinah. Daughter of Jacob and Leah (Gen. 30:21). The distasteful story of the "rape of Dinah" by a Canaanite named Shechem, and her two brothers' murderous revenge, is told in Gen. 34. Modern scholars have interpreted the story as Judean polemic against the northern kingdom, of which Shechem was the early capital. The role of Simeon and Levi also recalls the golden calf episode where the Levites are commended as executioners (Exod. 32:25–29, cf. Deut. 32:8–11), although Jacob on his deathbed curses his sons' violence and wantonness (Gen. 49:3–7). According to the *Talmud Dinah later became Job's wife (*b. Baba Batra* 16b), while in *Targum Jonathan she is sent away by her father to protect her from her brothers' anger and with divine assistance reaches Egypt, where she becomes the mother of Aseneth, wife of *Joseph. In modern literature she is the heroine of a poem by Zachary Boyd (in *Zion's Flowers*, 1855) and more recently a novel by Anita Diamant, *The Red Tent* (1998).

Disciples, the twelve. See *Apostles.

Dittography. In *textual criticism the term for a scribal error in which a let-ter, a group of letters, or even a whole line is accidentally written twice. In the famous Isaiah Scroll A from Qumran, a whole verse (38:19) is repeated twice, presumably by mistake, although it cannot be finally proved that the repetition was not the original author's intention.

Diversity. The notion that within the Bible there are many different, conflicting traditions, and that any attempt at a unified *biblical theology must take account of this. One of the main challenges of 18th- and 19th-century *biblical criticism was the identification of diversity in the style, composition and theology of the books of the Bible. Separate sources like JEDP, 1, 2, and 3 Isaiah, Q, and Proto-Mark were isolated, each with its own distinctive style, content, and original context, as were distinct literary genres like *law, narrative, *Wisdom literature, liturgical poetry, and the like. Theological diversity can be seen in conflicting notions of *creation, as between Gen. 1:1–2 (cf. Wis. 11:17) and John 1 (cf. Prov. 8:22; 2 Macc. 7:28). Late-20th-century literary and social-scientific approaches sought to recover the intellectual unity of the Pentateuch, Isaiah, the Gospels, and the rest of biblical literature, which had played such an important role in the precritical history of interpretation.

Divino afflante spiritu. The encyclical letter of Pius XII issued in 1943 on the fiftieth anniversary of *Providentissimus Deus*, which condemned the abuse of new methods of biblical scholarship. It acknowledges the importance of *archaeology and the *historical-critical method in establishing the literal meaning, while at the same time recommending to interpreters the spiritual or figurative sense of Scripture.

Documentary Hypothesis. The theory, associated above all with the name of the brilliant German Protestant scholar Julius *Wellhausen, that the *Pentateuch is composed of four sources known by their initials as JEDP. The first two sources were already identified by the 18th-century French doctor *Astruc, who noted stylistic consistency in the use of the *names of God, Elohim (E) in Gen. 1–2:4a, for example, and YHWH (J) in Gen. 2:4b–3:24. A Deuteronomic source (D) and a Priestly source (P) were later identified, and the chronological sequence JEDP established, where J is the most ancient, possibly reflecting the time of David, and P the latest, datable to the Babylonian exile or later. The style, theology, and historical context of each were carefully analyzed, and subsequently refinements included subdivisions such as P^1, P^2, etc., additional sources identified such as a Kenite source (K) and a Holiness source (H), and a redactor (R) responsible for the final stage in the process. Valuable literary and historical insights were undoubtedly achieved by the application of this hypothesis to the Pentateuch, but in many cases the method was applied too mechanically and the nuances of the text as a whole obscured.

Dodd, C. H. (1884–1973).

English NT scholar, author of many influential works, notably *The Meaning of Paul for Today* (1920), *The Founder of Christianity* (1970), *Gospel and Law* (1951), and *The Interpretation of the Fourth Gospel* (1953). A brilliantly original thinker with a background in Classical and Hellenistic Greek, he coined the famous phrase "realized eschatology," introduced the word *kerygma into NT theology, and pioneered a new method of interpreting the parables by reference to their situation in the life of Jesus (in, e.g., *Parables of the Kingdom*, 1935).

Dominicans.

The Order of Preachers (OP), also known as Blackfriars, founded by the Spanish priest St. Dominic in 1216. By their devotion to learning and preaching, Dominicans like the Jewish convert Pablo Cristiani, who opposed *Nahmanides, and the notorious Torquemada, played a prominent role in the Inquisition, from which their name acquired the meaning "the Lord's watchdogs" (*Domini cani*). Their study of Hebrew was employed in a sustained campaign to convert the Jews, including the practice of "compulsory sermons" preached to captive Jewish audiences in Rome, Florence, and elsewhere. Institutions like the École biblique in Jerusalem, however, have made a significant contribution to learning worldwide, including philosophy and biblical studies. Among the most famous Dominican saints are Peter Martyr, *Thomas Aquinas, Albertus Magnus, and Catherine of Siena, while radicals include Savonarola (1452–98) and Giordano Bruno (1548–1600), both burned at the stake, and Bartolomé de las Casas, champion of social justice for Native Americans (1484–1566).

Donatello, Donato di Niccolò

(c. 1386–1466). Florentine sculptor. Founder of modern sculpture in the sense that he separated statues from architecture, he is best known for his bronze figure of David, and statues of Habakkuk, John the Baptist, Mary Magdalene, and Judith and Holofernes. His relief of Herod presented with the head of John the Baptist is brilliantly innovative in technique and perspective.

Donne, John

(1572–1631). English poet. Born into a Catholic family, he converted to Protestantism after a long period of religious questioning during which he compared his own situation to that of Paul and Augustine, and for the last ten years of his life served as Dean of St. Paul's in London. His works, mostly published after his death, include both secular erotic poems and "divine poems," all intensely personal and often passionate compositions, filled with biblical language and imagery. In his sermons and essays he shows a special interest in Genesis and Exodus as well as Job, Psalms, and Proverbs.

Doré, Gustave (1832–83). French artist and book illustrator. Among Doré's many publications are illustrated editions of works by Rabelais, *Dante, *Shakespeare, *Milton, Tennyson, and other English writers; fairy tales; and a very popular and influential illustrated Bible (including the Apocrypha) published in French (1866), English (1866–70), and German (1876–77). Well over 200 illustrations were also published separately in abridged editions of the Bible and displayed at exhibitions in London (where Doré lived for some time), Chicago, and elsewhere.

Douay-Reims Bible. English version of the Bible produced by a group of Oxford Catholics in the English College at Douay in Flanders. The NT was completed in Reims in 1582, and the OT back in Douay in 1609. The translation was made from the *Vulgate, not the original languages, and retained much of the original Latin in a rather literal and artifical English style. It nonetheless had considerable influence on the *Authorized Version (1611) and was used by English-speaking Catholics for over three hundred years.

Doxology. One of a number of liturgical formulae ascribing *glory (Gk. *doxa*) to God, as at the end of Pss. 41, 72, 89, and 106. In some Christian traditions the singing of Psalms is followed by what is known as the "lesser doxology," derived from passages like Rom. 16:27 and Phil. 4:20, but influenced no doubt also by the Trinitarian formula at the end of Matthew's Gospel.

Drama. At the time of the *Reformation *mystery plays were banned in En-

gland and elsewhere in Europe. There was one interesting exception in England entitled *The Chaos of the Word*, a puppet show depicting Abraham and Isaac, Jonah and the whale, the fall of Nineveh, and other biblical scenes in the 1620s and 1630s. The famous *Passion Play* at Oberammergau in Germany, performed there since 1634 till the present day, is another exception. But otherwise biblical drama virtually ceased. There was a revival in the 20th century with works such as Christopher Fry's *The Firstborn*, about Moses and the exodus, written in 1946 as news of the Nazi genocide began to emerge, and the church parables of Benjamin *Britten in the 1960s. These were followed by television dramas like Dennis Potter's celebrated *Son of Man* (1969) and some successful musical productions for the stage, including *Jesus Christ Superstar* (1970) and *Joseph and the Amazing Technicolor Dreamcoat* (1968, 1972). But in comparison with television and the cinema, the theater now seems no longer the appropriate place for biblical drama. See *Film; *Passion plays.

Dryden, John (1631–1700). English poet, playwright, and translator. As poet laureate from 1668 through 1688 and a convert to Catholicism in 1685, he wrote satirical and didactic plays, essays, and poems, some, like *Absalom and Achitophel* (1681), with a clear political subtext. His later years were devoted to translating Virgil, Juvenal, and other classical writers, and his paraphrases of Chaucer, Ovid, and Boccaccio were among his most successful works.

Dual Torah. A modern term for Jewish Scripture, designed to emphasize the role of the *Oral Torah in traditional Judaism, in particular *Talmud and *Midrash, as equal in antiquity and authority to the written *Torah.

Duhm, Bernhard (1847–1928). German OT scholar. His commentaries, especially those on Isaiah and Jeremiah, and his work on the prophets had a profound influence on subsequent biblical studies. His reading of the prophets as poets and political theologians, motivated by religious and ethical idealism, in many ways anticipated some of the insights of late-20th-century scholarship, though it is for his division of *Isaiah into three parts and the identification of the four *Servant Songs that he is probably best remembered.

Dura Europos.   Syrian town on the Euphrates, occupied by the Romans from 165 to 257 C.E., when it was captured by the Persians and abandoned. The 3rd-century synagogue contains an important series of wall paintings illustrating 58 scenes from the Hebrew Bible, including the *Akedah, the exodus, the façade of the Second Temple, and Ezekiel's vision of the valley of the dry bones (National Museum, Damascus). There are also significant remains of a 3rd-century Christian house church, also with wall paintings (Yale University).

Dürer, Albrecht (1471–1528).   German painter and engraver. His popular series of woodcuts illustrating the *Apocalypse* (1498) was the first book published by an artist. His other series are the *Life of the Virgin* (1501–11) and three illustrations of the *Passion* (1498–1510; 1509–11; 1507–12), and among his numerous single prints are the *Prodigal Son, Adam and Eve,* and *St. Jerome.* He traveled to Venice and the Netherlands, where he met *Erasmus, and he admired *Luther although they never met. His brilliant craftsmanship, prodigious output, and the astonishing narrative detail of his illustrations, combined with the ease with which his works could be printed and disseminated throughout Reformation Europe, made his work a milestone in the history of Christian iconography. See *Icon.

E.   One of the literary sources of the Pentateuch, so called by *Astruc because it uses the name Elohim. See *Documentary Hypothesis.

Early catholicism.   A term (Ger. *Frühkatholizismus)* used by Ernst Troeltsch and others to describe the stage of hierarchical institutionalization that followed the apostolic age. Usually implying a decline from a period of simplicity and charismatic spontaneity, the term is applied to the writings of *Ignatius of Antioch and *Clement of Rome as well as to Luke–Acts, 1 and 2 Timothy, Ephesians, and 2 Peter.

Easter (Lat. *Pascha).*   The Feast of the Resurrection, the church's oldest and most important festival, preceded by forty days' fasting (*Lent) and a week of special ceremonies (*Holy Week). Its Latin name and its date are derived from the Jewish *Passover (Heb. *pesach;* cf. Matt. 26; Mark 14; Luke 22; John 13), but, as in the case of Christmas, its original pagan associations are evident in the nature symbolism of some of its carols ("Now the green blade riseth"), Easter eggs, and possibly the name Easter itself, derived, according to the Venerable *Bede, from the Anglo-Saxon spring goddess Eostre. In many traditions the feast begins on Saturday, with fireworks and the reckless lighting of candles. Scriptural passages given special prominence in paschal lectionaries include Gen. 22, Exod. 15, Isa. 12, 54, 55, Ezek. 36, and Pss. 16, 30, 42, 51, 117; while of the numerous musical compositions inspired by the festival Bach's *Easter Oratorio* (1725) and Rimsky-Korsakov's *Russian Easter* (1884) are two of the best known. See *Resurrection.

Ebenezer.   The place where the ark of the covenant was captured by the Philistines (1 Sam. 4–5) but later a famous victory over them, commemorated by Samuel with a monument called "the stone of help" (Heb. *eben 'ezer*, 1 Sam. 7:12). The name signifying defeat followed by victory, captured the imagination of an 18th-century hymn writer ("Come, thou fount of every blessing"), while another popular hymn ("What a friend we have in Jesus") is usually sung to a 19th-century Welsh tune called *Ebenezer*. The embittered miser Ebenezer Scrooge is the main character in Charles Dickens's novel *A Christmas Carol* (1843).

Ebla (Tell Mardikh).   One of the largest archaeological sites in Syria, excavated since 1964. It reached its greatest size for about 200 years in the mid-3rd millennium B.C.E., ending in its destruction by Sargon of Akkad c. 2300. About 4,000 cuneiform texts, many of them in a *Semitic language in some respects similar to *Ugaritic and Hebrew, the rest in Sumerian, contain information about the history and religion of the earliest Semitic urban culture outside Mesopotamia. The value of the Ebla discoveries for biblical research was at first greatly exaggerated.

Ecce Homo (Lat. "Behold the man!"). The words used by Pilate when he presented Jesus to the Jews, bound, scourged, and wearing a crown of thorns and a purple robe (John 19:5). In the Middle Ages it came to signify the true humanity of Christ as the "man of sorrows" (Isa. 53:3) and the *Ecce Homo* scene is frequent in art (*Bosch, *Dürer, *Titian, *Rubens, and many others) and literature from *Milton's *Samson Agonistes* ("Behold him in this state calamitous") to Nietzsche's ironic use of the term as the title of his autobiography (1888).

Ecclesiastes (Heb. *Qohelet*).   Controversial from the beginning, by the end of the 1st century C.E. it was accepted as

canonical by the rabbis, including Akiba, partly because it was attributed, along with Proverbs, the Song of Songs, and Wisdom, to Solomon. It purports to be the teaching given by the aging Solomon to his son (11:12). In the Jewish lectionary it is prescribed to be read at the Feast of *Tabernacles, its pessimism intended as a restraint on excessive rejoicing. Others place the emphasis of the book on the call to "rejoice in your youth" (11:9; cf. 2:24), and there is also a positive recommendation to live every day as if it was your last (9:10). In Jerome's interpretation, it was a condemnation of all worldly pursuits and a call to "fear God and keep his commandments" (12:13). Otherwise unpredictable tragedy and death undermine all traditional religious teaching (chaps. 1–3; 9:11–12), though the possibility of life after death is mentioned (11:9). Many scholars from *Gregory the Great, *Ibn Ezra, and *Bonaventure down to modern times recognize different voices in Ecclesiastes such as those of an Epicurean (2:24; 9:9–10), a conventional wisdom teacher (12:9–11), and a Hasidic commentator (12:11–13). Since *Maimonides and *Luther the Solomonic authorship of the whole book has been questioned. Aramaisms and other late Hebrew idioms suggest that the book was written sometime during the 3rd century B.C.E. at the earliest.

The popularity of the book, not least in Hebrew literature, can be seen in the number of phrases that became part of everyday speech: "Vanity of vanities"; "for everything there is a season"; "under the sun"; "eat, drink, and be merry"; "cast your bread upon the waters"; "of making many books there is no end." *Vanitas Vanitatum et omnia Vanitas* (1:2) is the refrain of a macaronic (partly in Latin, partly in English) poem by William Dunbar (c. 1500). The parable of the ruined house (12:3–7), with which the teaching of Qohelet ends (like Prov. 1–9 and the *Sermon on the Mount), frequently interpreted as an allegory of old age, is one of the best-known passages in the Bible. Nineteenth-century commentators found Stoic and Epicurean influences in the book and condemned it as unchristian, but George Bernard Shaw frequently cited "my friend Koheleth" with approval. Pete Seeger set to music 3:1–8 in a popular 1960s song, "Turn! turn! turn!"

Ecclesiasticus.   See *Sirach.

Ecology.   The biblical teaching that places human beings at the center of the universe (Gen. 1:26–31) and praises a God of history, repeatedly dissociated from the nature gods of Israel's neighbors, has been blamed for human destruction of the environment. The command to human beings to "subdue the earth and have dominion . . . over every living creature" (Gen. 1:28) contains unmistakably violent language, and provided Christians with scriptural authority to conquer and colonize. A life devoted to "tilling the soil" is perceived as a curse (Gen. 3:17–19). Apocalyptic images of the pollution and destruction of the earth (Isa. 24:4–6) show scant regard for the natural world and look toward a new heaven and a new earth quite unlike this one, without the sea, for example (Rev. 21:1). Modern ecologists, searching for counterexamples in the Bible, have found in the flood story a moral imperative to preserve biodiversity, and in the Sabbatical legislation (Lev. 25) a demand to treat both the land and its inhabitants with respect. The prophets' urgent calls for justice for the poor and needy are given new meaning in the context of 20th-century ecofeminism, and the less familiar biblical notion of a loving God, interacting with the world's changing patterns and situations like a woman in labor (Isa. 42:14; cf. John 16:20–21) or a mother with child (Isa. 66:13; cf. Luke 13:34), is given a new emphasis.

Eden.   The garden where the story of Adam and Eve is located (Gen. 2–3). Translated into Latin as *paradisus*, "paradise" (cf. Gk. *paradeisos*), it became a universal symbol of primeval bliss, applied to all kinds of situations from return to the promised land after exile (Isa. 51:3) to life after death (Luke 23:43). In Jewish parlance the "garden of Eden" (Heb. *gan 'eden*) is the usual term for "heaven," and expulsion or exclusion from Eden is used as a metaphor for coming judgment (Ezek. 31; Joel 2:3). In Christian art pictures of Christ the Good Shepherd seated in a garden, such as those in 5th- and 6th-century mosaics in Ravenna, may be inspired by biblical images of Eden, influenced in some cases by those of the "peaceable kingdom" in Isa. 11. Hieronymus *Bosch's *Garden of Earthly Delights* is perhaps the most famous representation in art, as are those of *Dante and *Milton in literature. Christian writers have frequently tended to depict Eden in spiritual terms (*Augustine, Duns Scotus, *Blake), while in Muslim tradition it includes physical bliss as well (Qur'an 37:40–45). Others have given it a political meaning, applied to Britain (Marvell, *Dryden) and the newly discovered America (Drayton, Morton).

Edersheim, Alfred (1825–89).   Austrian theologian and NT scholar. Brought up as a Jew in Vienna, Edersheim was well versed in Hebrew and rabbinic studies, and his most popular work, the 2-volume *Life and Times of Jesus the Messiah* (1883), made a significant contribution to 19th-century understanding of the Jewish context of early Christianity. His approach to the Gospels was uncritical, however, and his work has had little influence on subsequent biblical interpretation.

Education.   There is virtually no direct evidence for the educational methods and institutions in ancient Israel, but the repeated injunctions to "tell your son . . ." (Exod. 10:2; 13:8, 14; Deut. 6:20–25), the use of mnemonics in education (Deut. 6:4–9), and summons to "remember," "hear," "listen," and the like, especially in the book of Deuteronomy, indicate that education was given a high priority. Traditions about the wisdom of Solomon (1 Kgs. 3–4), the scribes of Hezekiah (Prov. 25:1), and the like, together with interesting parallels between parts of Proverbs (1–9; 22:17–24:22) and the Instruction literature of ancient Egypt and Babylon, suggest that aims and methods were similar, in the royal establishment at least. It is likely that the prophets were educated men and women despite protests that they were not (Amos 7:14), and there are references to skilled "scribes" (Ps. 45:1; Jer. 36:32; Ezra–Nehemiah; Sir. 38:24–39:11), although the earliest reference to a "school" is in Sir. 51:23, dated c. 180 B.C.E.

In the 1st century C.E. there were already rabbis or "teachers" in many Jewish communities and over 400 *synagogues, also known as schools (Heb. bet midrash, lit. "house of study"), in Jerusalem alone. Jesus was a teacher as were his disciples after him (Matt. 28:20); and the leader of the Qumran community was known as the "Teacher of Righteousness." Paul studied under Rabbi Gamaliel (Acts 22:3). Jewish education focused on Hebrew and the Torah, although some advocated the study of Greek literature, and there is evidence that some Jewish writers (including Paul) were schooled in classical rhetoric. In the church, particularly since the Reformation, educational factors have been crucial in the history of the Bible, from the imperative to translate the Bible into the vernacular and make it intelligible to as many people as possible, to using it as the primary authority in determining the moral and theological content of the curriculum.

Edwards, Jonathan (1703–58). American philosopher and theologian. A Calvinist caught up in the New England revivalist movement known as the "Great Awakening," though at the same time fascinated by the Enlightenment writers, he appeals to the authority of Scripture even in his most philosophical writings. His view of Scripture as a collection of "symbolical representations" and "spiritual truths" in some ways anticipated *postmodern readings of the Bible.

Egypt. The role of Egypt in the Bible is well known, especially in the stories of Abraham (Gen. 12), Joseph (Gen. 37–50), and the exodus (Exod. 1–12). The journey of the Holy Family to Egypt in fulfillment of a prophecy (Matt. 2:12–20; cf. Hos. 11:1) carries the tradition into the NT. In the vast corpus of Egyptian literature from c. 3000 B.C.E. to the Hellenistic period, no reference to the exodus or the plagues has yet been discovered, though the name "Israel" appears on a late 13th-century B.C.E. Egyptian inscription found in Palestine. Some interesting parallels with the Bible, such as the "Song of the Harpist" (cf. Eccl. 11:9) and the "Thirty Sayings of Amenemope" (cf. Prov. 22:17–24:22), confirm biblical traditions about Egyptian influences (e.g., 1 Kgs. 3:1). Most often Egypt symbolizes oppression (Exod. 20:2; Deut. 4:20; Rev. 11:8), and many prophecies of judgment are addressed to it (e.g., Jer. 46; cf. Isa. 31). Isaiah 19:24–25 is a conspicuous exception due probably to the presence of a thriving Jewish community there from the time of the Babylonian exile (see *Elephantine Papyri). The Hellenistic Jewish community received official recognition from the Ptolemies, and a Greek version of the Torah was produced there (c. 250 B.C.E.; see *Septuagint). The influence of Alexandrian scholarship on the development of early Christianity was immense. See *Hieroglyphics.

Eighth-century prophets. The general term for those prophetic writings considered, especially by many Protestant scholars, to contain the high point of OT moral and theological teaching. They are normally understood to comprise Amos, Hosea, Micah, and Isaiah, excluding those passages (e.g., Amos 9:11–15) and chapters (e.g., Isa. 40–55) dated to a later period; though according to 2 Kgs. 14:25 Jonah belongs there as well, and in the canonical book of the twelve Minor Prophets, Joel and Obadiah are grouped with the 8th-century prophets too.

Eisegesis.   The derogatory term for a type of interpretation involving reading into a text, often for doctrinal or political reasons, a meaning different from its original *meaning. Doubt about the possibility of establishing an "original meaning," and modern interest in *reception history and the plurality of meanings that a text can have, have rendered the term virtually obsolete.

Election.   The central biblical notion that God chose a people to serve his purposes in the world. The term occurs in Deuteronomy and especially in Isa. 40–55, where it is applied to Israel as God's Servant (41:8–9; 42:1; 44:1–2). Moses and David, as representatives of their people, are also "chosen" (Pss. 106:23; 89:3). The story of election begins with the call of Abraham (Gen. 12), although the term itself does not occur there, and continues into the NT, where Christ (Luke 23:35; 1 Pet. 2:4), the apostles (Acts 1:2; Rom. 16:13), and followers of Christ in general (Eph. 1:4) are said to have been "chosen." The problem raised by the existence of the church and the Jewish people, both "chosen" by God, is discussed by Paul in Rom. 9–11. Christian theologians, especially in the Protestant tradition, have used the biblical traditions about election as an appropriate means of placing the emphasis on the divine initiative, unmerited grace, and predestination. Election has been a central issue in definitions of Jewish identity, and until very modern times seen as the greatest of many acts of divine intervention in the history of the Jews, though rabbinic tradition often stresses Israel's part in securing divine election: other nations did not accept the Torah when it was offered to them (*Midrash Exod. Rab*. 27:9).

Elephantine Papyri.   Fifth-century B.C.E. Aramaic documents discovered in 1904–8 on the island site of an ancient Jewish colony in Upper Egypt. They provide valuable evidence for religious beliefs and practices there, including a copy of a letter sent to Jerusalem by the priests requesting permission to rebuild their temple, and a reference to the goddess Anathbethel, apparently worshiped there alongside YHWH. Today Elephantine (Heb. *yeb*) is in the city of Aswan (Gk. *Syene*), and it has been conjectured that there may be a reference to the Jewish colony in Isa. 49:12, reading *sweniyim* with Qumran Isaiah Scroll A for MT *sinim*.

Elgar, Edward (1857–1934).   English composer. Self-taught son of a Worcester music dealer and organist, he played bassoon, violin, and organ and composed an early version of *The Wand of Youth* suite at the age of 12. In 1889 he married and moved to London, where he composed all his greatest works and was honored with an Elgar Festival and a knighthood in 1904. He is best known today for his first *Pomp and Circumstance March* traditionally played at the Last Night of the Proms in London, and for "Nimrod" from the *Enigma Variations*, frequently played at national funerals and memorial services, and also for his three symphonies, a violin concerto, and very popular cello concerto. But he also composed settings of liturgical music, including a *Te Deum and *Benedictus, and three deeply religious choral works, the *Dream of Gerontius* (1900) and the two first parts of a great Wagnerian trilogy, *The Apostles* (1902–3), *The Kingdom* (1901–6), and *The Last Judgment* (unfinished), tracing the epic story from the call of the apostles to the coming of the antichrist at the end of time. The *Dream* is a setting of words by Cardinal Newman, and contains many memorable allusions to the Bible, especially the Psalms, but the other two oratorios are based on a selection of familiar texts taken directly from the Bible. The *Apostles* includes the Beatitudes, the resurrection, the ascension, and especially the stories of Judas Iscariot and Mary Magdalene. The *Kingdom* finds its inspiration mainly in Acts 1–4, although Mary's wonderful aria "The sun goeth down" near the end of part 4 comes from Ecclesiastes (1:5).

Elijah (Gk. *Elias*; Arab. *Ilyas*). Greatest of the biblical prophets after Moses (1 Kgs. 17–2 Kgs. 2:12; Sir. 48:1–11), known also as "the Tishbite." The biblical account presents him as a miracle worker and powerful opponent of Baal worship ("Is he asleep?" 1 Kgs. 18) and social injustice (Naboth's vineyard, 1 Kgs. 21) during the reign of Ahab and Jezebel. His experience of God in a cave ("the still small voice," 1 Kgs. 19) and his ascent to heaven in a whirlwind (2 Kgs. 2) mark him out as unique, and this is reflected in his special role in subsequent Jewish and Christian tradition. He is the prophet who will prepare the world for the "day of the LORD" (Mal. 4:5; cf. Luke 1:17), identified or confused with John the Baptist (Matt. 16:14); and appears with Moses at the *transfiguration (Mark 9). In Jewish literature he intervenes in the lives of fortunate individuals (cf. Sir. 48:11) to rescue or encourage them and to solve their intellectual problems. The Baal Shem Tov is said to have had a lengthy meeting with him (see *Hasidism). In Christian art the most frequent scene represented is that of the ascent of Elijah to heaven with chariot and horses, but the stories of the widow's cruse, the bringing of her dead child back to life, the massacre of the prophets of Baal on Mount Carmel, and the transfiguration are regularly portrayed too, especially in the Orthodox Church. *Mendelssohn's *Elijah* (1846) contains some impressive musical settings of biblical texts from Kings, Isaiah, and Psalms. In literature the stories of Elijah, as in Milton's *Paradise Lost*, are frequently interpreted as prefiguring the life of Christ. For William *Blake, "He is the spirit of prophecy, the ever apparent Elias."

Eliot, T. S. (Thomas Stearns) (1888–1965). American-born British poet and dramatist. His earlier works, notably *The Waste Land* (1923) and *The Hollow Men* (1925), were cynical and defeatist. After his conversion to Anglo-Catholicism in 1927, he wrote in a very different, more sacramental vein and produced works like *Ash Wednesday* (1930), *Murder in the Cathedral* (1935), and *Four Quartets* (1944), for which he is perhaps best known today. He treated the Bible as a sacred text rather than a piece of literature, and uses it frequently alongside *Dante, John of the Cross, the Bhagavadgita, and countless other allusions.

Elisha. Prophet and disciple of Elijah, he is remembered for his role in masterminding the overthrow of Ahab and Jezebel at the hands of Jehu (2 Kgs. 9–10), but also for his acts of compassion, some of them miraculous. His example is quoted by Jesus (Luke 4:27). After his death, his bones were able to bring the dead back to life (2 Kgs. 13:21; cf. Sir. 48:12–14). In art he is often represented as bald (2 Kgs. 2:23) and often with Elijah's mantle (2:13–14). Individual incidents in his life are regularly illustrated including the incident with the two bears (2:23; *Tiepolo), the multiplication of the loaves (4:38–44; *Tintoretto), and the cure of *Naaman from *leprosy (chap. 5; Vasari), but neither in art nor literature did he ever rival his great master.

Elizabeth. Husband of Zacharias and mother of John the Baptist (Luke 1).

Mary visited her in her house, traditionally believed to have been in the village of Ain Karem near Jerusalem, where Elizabeth uttered the words "Blessed art thou among women . . ." and Mary sang the *Magnificat, both important elements in the liturgy (see *Visitation). She is represented in Christian art as an elderly woman, in scenes illustrating the life of John the Baptist (e.g., *Ghirlandaio) and the Marian cycle, but also in the *Holy Family* (e.g., *Raphael) and the *Flight of St. Elizabeth with the Infant St. John*, especially in Orthodox iconography. In literature she does not play a prominent role.

Elohist. The author of the E source, coined by *Astruc to facilitate discussion of its style and content. See *Pentateuch.

Emblem. In art history an image employed to illustrate a motto or epigram, frequently drawn from the Bible. Emblems range from symbols or attributes like the branch of the *Jesse tree in the hands of King David's descendants (Isa. 11:1) and Mary Magdalene's jar of priceless ointment (John 12:3), to elaborate, often bizarre illustrations of biblical topics like the "beautiful feet of him that bringeth good tidings" (Isa. 52:7 AV). The earliest collection of these was Andrea Alciati's *Emblematum Liber* (Augsburg, 1531), but the most influential is Cesare Ripa's *Iconologia* (1593). A valuable and accessible modern collection of 16th- and 17th-century examples, with an index of biblical references, is Henkel-Schöne, *Emblemata* (Stüttgart, 1976).

Enlightenment (Ger. *Aufklärung*; Heb. *Haskalah*). A predominantly 18th-century European movement, associated with *Spinoza, *Hobbes, Locke, *Herder, Kant, *Voltaire, Hume, and others, that stressed the individual's intellectual freedom, challenged the fundamental beliefs and authority of religion, and signaled the dawn of modernity. In relation to the Bible, questions were raised about the existence and nature of God, the historicity of miracles, the morality of some of the biblical stories, and the like. New methods of biblical interpretation increasingly focused on such matters as authorship, style, sources, date and place of composition, and historicity, and, despite the efforts of Christian scholars like Bishop *Lowth and Jewish reformers like Moses *Mendelssohn, separated the academic study of the Bible from dogmatic theology and from the continuing life of the church. The archaeological evidence from Palestine, Egypt, and Mesopotamia that came to light in abundance during the 19th and 20th centuries ensured that the *historical-critical method, which took root in Enlightenment Europe, dominated the study of the Bible until late in the 20th century, at the expense of subtler literary, rhetorical, and social-scientific approaches.

***Enoch*, books of.** A collection of diverse Jewish literature attributed to the mysterious antediluvian character Enoch (Gen. 5:24), dating from the 3rd century B.C.E. to the 5th or 6th century C.E. *First Enoch*, known as *Ethiopic Enoch* because it first came to light in mss discovered in Ethiopia, consists of five separate works of which the first two, the *Book of Watchers* (chaps. 1–36) and the *Parables* or *Similitudes* (chaps. 37–71), are the longest and most important. *First Enoch* certainly had a significant influence on early Christian doctrines of the son of man, the messianic kingdom, the resurrection of the dead, and eschatology in general. Fragments of *1 Enoch* in Aramaic were discovered among the *Dead Sea Scrolls, and it also influenced the state literature of Ethiopia. The main part of *2 Enoch* (*The Secrets of Enoch*), or *Slavonic Enoch*, originally written in Greek or Hebrew, tells of Enoch's journey through the seven heavens, and ends with the birth and ascension of his descendant *Melchizedek. *Third Enoch* is a Hebrew work in the Jewish mystical tradition, probably from the 5th or 6th century C.E., that describes the journey of a certain Rabbi Ishmael to heaven, where he saw God's chariot and encountered the archangel Metatron.

Ephesians, Letter to. Paul's letter from prison (4:1; 6:20) to what was to become an important center of Christianity at Ephesus in Asia Minor, home of Aquila and Priscilla, and location of one of the great ecumenical councils in 431 C.E. Though similar to Colossians in much of what it says (e.g., cf. 5:21–32 and Col. 3:18–25), there are stylistic and linguistic problems, noted already by *Erasmus, which throw doubt on whether it was actually written by Paul. It was considered a genuine Pauline letter by *Clement, *Marcion, and others, and has been part of the NT *canon since the 2nd century C.E., though its references to gnosis and its cosmic Christology made it a favorite with gnostics too. *Thomas Aquinas, *Luther, and *Calvin all make constant use of Ephesians, especially the recurring notion of an increasingly institutionalized universal church as the "fullness" (Gk. *pleroma*) and heavenly body of Christ (1:20–23). The marriage imagery of Christ and the church as his bride (Eph. 5:22–32) has formed Roman Catholic theories of liturgical priesthood from the Middle Ages to Benedict XVI. The blessing in 1:3–14 (a Christian prayer in Jewish form), and the appeals to "speak the truth in love," "let not the sun go down upon your wrath," and "put on the whole armor of God" are some of the best known parts of the legacy of Ephesians to Christian liturgical and literary tradition.

Ephrem the Syrian (306–373 C.E.). Christian poet-theologian. His works, which are in *Syriac, mostly in verse, and always inspired by Scripture, include theological and exegetical writings as well as hymns. His commentaries on Genesis and Exodus show that he followed the Antiochene literal method of *exegesis, for the most part avoiding allegorization. He was widely admired during his lifetime, and many of his works were translated into Armenian, Greek, Latin, and Slavonic. His liturgical writings greatly influenced the development of Greek and Syriac hymnography.

Epigraphy. The study of inscriptions. There are a relatively small number of Hebrew and Aramaic inscriptions from ancient Israel (e.g., the Siloam inscription, Lachish Ostraca), in contrast to the vast number of inscriptions, particularly those in Greek, Aramaic, Hebrew, and Latin, from synagogues, tombs, and graffiti, in the Hellenistic world and the Roman Empire. As providing firm contemporary evidence for social, political, and religious conditions in the ancient world, the importance of epigraphy has become increasingly appreciated: for example, *synagogue inscriptions have demonstrated the senior role played by women in many Jewish religious institutions (cf. Rom. 16:1–16), while tomb inscriptions and graffiti tell us what languages people spoke in ancient Rome and Palestine.

Epiphany (Gk. "manifestation"). Since the 4th century, one of the three great annual festivals of the church, along with Easter and Pentecost. Celebrated on January 6, it originally commemorated Christ's baptism and later also his nativity, and in the Eastern tradition is still associated with other manifestations of Christ's divine power including the wedding at Cana in Galilee (John 2:1–11). In the West it became a separate festival, twelve days after Christmas, commemorating the adoration of the *magi and the manifestation of God to the world. Epiphany lectionaries include Isa. 9:1–2 (cf. Matt. 4:12–16) and Isa. 60:1–6, Ps. 71, and Eph. 3:1–6 as well as the Gospel narrative itself (Matt. 2:1–12).

Epistles. The traditional term for the 21 NT "letters" attributed to the apostles Paul, James, Peter, John, and Jude. Of these probably not all are genuine letters in the sense of having been written by someone actually intending to send them to a specific audience. Ephesians and Hebrews read more like theological treatises, with an epistolary framework added at the beginning and/or end. Recent evidence suggests, however, that most of the NT letters are similar in important stylistic features to a form of pseudonymous letter written by ancient philosophers, with the aim of recommending an ideal teacher as a model to be imitated. In Christian usage the "Epistle" denotes one of three readings from Scripture read aloud at public worship, and may include Acts and Revelation. See *Pastoral Epistles.

Erasmus, Desiderius (c. 1466–1536). Dutch humanist and scholar. Ordained priest in 1492, he was critical of scholasticism and the church in general, but did not advocate dividing Christendom as Luther did. In addition to his many theological writings, some of them satirical, his major work was a critical edition of the Greek text of the NT, published alongside the Vulgate and a new Latin translation by himself, with critical *Annotations* (1516). This was eventually published in the *Complutension Polyglot Bible* (1522). Influenced by Neoplatonism and the church fathers, of whose works he published critical editions, he believed that the text has a spiritual as well as a literal meaning, and maintained that scholarship must not be divorced from the life of ordinary Christians for whom he saw the need for a vernacular translation of Scripture.

Esau. The hirsute son of Isaac and Rebekah, who forfeited his birthright to his twin brother Jacob "for a mess of pottage" (Gen. 25:29–34) and was tricked out of his father's blessing by Jacob (Gen. 27). He was ancestor of the Edomites (Gen. 36), his red hair alluded to both in the name Edom itself (Heb. *adom*, "red") and in the Edomite hill country Seir (Heb. *sa'ir*, "hairy"). No doubt the biblical legends of sibling rivalry reflect Israel's hostile relations with their neighbors (cf. Jer. 49:7–22; Obadiah; Sir. 50:26), although according to one ancient tradition Mount Sinai was in Edom (Deut. 33:2–3, Judg. 5:4).

In rabbinic tradition Esau is a hunter and a murderer, and "has no share in the world to come" (*b. Sanhedrin* 101b). He and his descendants were identified with Rome and later with the church, and there is even a legend that he tried to remove the mark of his circumcision (*b. Sanhedrin* 44a; cf. 1 Macc. 1:15). Christian tradition from Paul (Rom. 9:14) and Augustine on is no less sympathetic, identifying the "sons of Esau" with unbelievers in general, including in particular, ironically, the Jews. William *Blake, influenced by *Swedenborg, is a rare exception who, in the light of Isaac's blessing of Esau (Gen. 27:38–40), reverses the destinies of the two peoples, even in Isa. 34, and identifies Esau with the "hairy youth" from France who inspired the American Revolution (*America*, 1793).

Eschatology. Language and imagery concerning the end of the world, the resurrection of the dead, and the day of judgment. In the Hebrew Bible it is only in Daniel that the notion is explicit (Dan. 12), but many other passages were given an eschatological interpretation from the 2nd century B.C.E. on by most varieties of Judaism, including the Qumran community, Christianity, and rabbinic Judaism. The *Sadducees were an exception (Matt. 22:23). This process, probably due to Persian influence and perhaps also to the phenomenon of martyrdom (cf. 2 Macc. 7), is evident already in the LXX, where Hebrew phrases meaning "in days to come" (NRSV) are translated "in the last days" (Isa. 2:2; cf. AV), and in the Jewish *apocalyptic literature.

Eschatology is a major theme in the NT expressed in the images of the imminent coming of the Son of Man (Matt. 16:28), the kingdom of God (Matt. 6:10), and the end of the world (Mark 13). NT writers believed that Jesus was the *Messiah and that they were already living in the messianic age: the kingdom of God had been established on earth and they were preparing for a new heaven and a new earth heralded by the second coming (Gk. *parousia*) of the Son of Man (Mark 13). The messianic age (Heb. *yeme ha-mashiah*), foretold by the prophets and characterized by peace and justice, is a this-worldly aspect of Jewish eschatology as opposed to the world to come (*ha-olam ha-ba*). The belief that one day in the future all that is wrong with this world will be put right, if not in this world then in the next, has given human beings—Jews, Christians, and Muslims—the will to survive in times of crisis and suffering. Calculations of the precise time when the end was to come, based on numbers and symbols in Daniel, Revelation, and other apocalyptic texts, are common in *millenarian sects.

Esdras, books of.   First and 2 Esdras are two apocryphal books attributed to the priest and scribe Ezra (Gk. *Esdras*). In the Vulgate they are entitled 3 and 4 Ezra, the biblical books Ezra and Nehemiah being referred to there as 1 and 2 Ezra. First Esdras (3 Ezra) was written originally in Greek probably in the early 2nd century B.C.E., and retells the history of the Jews, already recounted in Chronicles, Ezra, and Nehemiah, from Josiah's reformation to Ezra's reforms, with the main emphasis on the period of restoration after the exile and the achievements of Zerubbabel in particular. It was used by Josephus and quoted frequently by the church fathers. But thrown out of the canon by Luther, it has been neglected by modern scholars with some notable exceptions, including Hugo *Grotius, C. C. Torrey, and more recently Giovanni Garbini, who argued for its priority over

Ezra–Nehemiah. Second Esdras (4 Ezra) is a Jewish apocalyptic work (chaps. 3–14) from a later period, probably c. 100 C.E., with parallels in 2 *Baruch, 1 *Enoch, and similar texts, and may have been written originally in Hebrew or Aramaic. There are Christian elements in an introductory section (e.g., 2:42–48) loosely attached to the apocalypse proper (chaps. 3–14), which comprises Ezra's seven visions culminating in a vision of the Messiah rising from the depths of the sea (chap. 13).

Essenes.   A Jewish sect mentioned by *Josephus and *Philo, but not in the NT or rabbinic literature. According to Josephus, they were more akin to the Pharisees than the Sadducees in their beliefs, but lived in ascetic communities where they had no wives, servants, or personal possessions, but had everything in common (cf. Acts 2:44). Many have suggested that members of the Qumran community were Essenes, but any direct connection between them and John the Baptist or Jesus is unlikely.

Esther, book of.   The Megillah, "scroll" read at the Jewish festival of *Purim and located among the *Ketuvim in the Hebrew Bible. It comes last of the narrative books, after Nehemiah, in the Christian OT. It tells how Queen Esther rescued her people and her cousin Mordecai from persecution in a foreign land, by pleading with her husband, the Persian king Ahasuerus (Xerxes), and ensuring that the wicked Haman was hanged on the gallows he had prepared for Mordecai. The book is unique in the Bible in that it makes no mention of God, the patriarchs, the exodus, or the prophets, although the Greek version rectifies this anomaly with a number of apocryphal additions to the Hebrew text, printed in Catholic and Orthodox Bibles. Esther is not cited in the NT, and there is no trace of it among the *Dead Sea Scrolls. *Josephus treats it as canonical, the Mishnah has a tractate devoted to it (*Megillah*), and there is an important midrash on it (*Esther Rabbah*) as well as two targumim, of which *Targum Sheni*, "the second Targum" (9th century), became very popular. *Maimonides valued Esther next after the Pentateuch.

The church fathers make little reference to Esther, and apart from works by *Rabanus Maurus (836) and *Nicholas of Lyra (14th century), little attention is paid to the book until the modern period, when scholarly questions about its Mesopotamian background and the like are discussed (e.g., Mordecai = Marduk; Esther = Ishtar). *Feminist interpreters of the story focus on the reversal of a woman's powerlessness at a Persian court as a paradigm of hope for the powerless Jew in the Diaspora. Christians have traditionally seen in her a type of Christian salvation, as in Michelangelo's *Sistine Chapel fresco, and also a type of the Virgin Mary, as in a number of medieval lyrics. There is an Esther series by Filippino Lippi, while a number of artists, including *Tintoretto, *Signorelli, and *Rembrandt, found in the story a pretext for painting sumptuous scenes of oriental luxury. Esther was the inspiration for oratorios by *Handel (c. 1720) and Dittersdorf (1773), and a drama by Racine (1689). She also figures in Browning's masterpiece *The Ring and the Book* (1868–69) and Tennyson's poem "The Princess."

Ethics. Ethics in the Hebrew Bible is first of all a matter of keeping the commandments, revealed at Sinai. According to rabbinic reckoning, worked out in the *Oral Torah, there are 613 of them, divided into positive and negative, ethical and religious, time-bound and not time-bound, and the like. They can be interpreted in many ways, but their authority was not questioned. The role of the Decalogue, particularly nos. 5–10, is fundamental to Jewish ethics and indeed to Western ethical teaching in general. Universal moral imperatives also appear in the story of *Noah, and in a number of other passages where biblical cosmology has ethical implications: thus it is wrong to kill or maltreat even the poorest person as that would be an insult to the Creator (Prov. 17:5) since all are made "in the image of God" (Gen. 9:6). The prophets' juxtaposition of ethical teaching and creation imagery appears to make the same point (e.g., Amos 5:4–15).

The Christian use of Scripture in ethical teaching can be traced back to Jesus, who points to "the law and the prophets" as his authority in the Sermon on the Mount (Matt. 5:17). He frequently illustrates this in his use of the Law (Decalogue; Lev. 19:18) to teach personal morality (Matt. 19:19), and the Prophets (esp. Isaiah) for his social ethics (Luke 4:18–19). His emphasis on motivation (Matt. 5:21–48) goes back to the tenth commandment (Deut. 5:21), and his commandment to "love your enemy" (Matt. 5:44) has its background in the pragmatism of Proverbs (24:17–18). The invidious contrast often made between "OT ethics" and "NT ethics" is based on too much stress on passages about vengeance and the brutal administration of justice, by God and humans, in the OT, and a misunderstanding of the continuity of Scripture from the Torah to the Gospels. The Jewish work *Pirqe Abot*, "The Sayings of the Fathers," is often known by its Christian title, "Ethics of the Fathers." Postmodern writers have called for the ethical interpretation of Scripture, that is, an awareness of the ethical motives and implications that are involved in every reading of the text.

Ethiopia (Heb. *Cush*). In the Bible a country south of Egypt, properly known as Nubia. Modern Ethiopia is situated in what was once the kingdom of Sabaea (Heb. *sheba*; cf. Isa. 43:3), and traditions about the Queen of Sheba and her son Menelek have played a significant part in the history of Ethiopia. Also known as Cush and often bracketed with Egypt in biblical tradition, Ethiopia plays a distinctive role in prophecy (e.g., Isa. 18; Jer. 13:23), and an Ethiopian is said to have come to Jerusalem to worship (Acts 8:26–40). Old Ethiopic or Ge'ez, the language of the Ethiopian Church, and its modern form Amharic are Semitic, and a number of important pseudepigraphical texts, including *Jubilees* and *1 Enoch*, are best known in Ge'ez versions. A very ancient form of Judaism survives in modern Ethiopia in the Beta Israel, known to outsiders as the Falashas, who emigrated to Israel from the 1970s till 1993. See *Rastafarianism.

Etymologizing. A method of determining and defining the meaning of a word or name by reference to its etymology. Well-known biblical examples include the etymological explanations given for the names Eve (Gen. 3:20), Moses (Exod. 2:10), and Jesus (Matt. 1:21). The method is widely used in rabbinic and patristic literature, and influential works like *Isidore of Seville's very popular *Etymologiae* and David *Kimhi's *Book of Roots* show how it continued and developed into the Middle Ages. In the 17th and 18th centuries biblical scholars further expanded the study of comparative Semitic philology in polyglot Bibles, dictionaries, and grammars, while in the 19th and 20th centuries archaeological discoveries in Egypt, Mesopotamia, Syria, and elsewhere added hitherto unknown *Semitic languages like Babylonian and *Ugaritic to the data regularly used in defining Hebrew words. Dictionaries giving prominence to etymological data became the norm, and students of the Bible regularly studied Arabic, Ugaritic, and other Semitic languages. Not until the publication of James Barr's *Semantics of Biblical Language* in 1961 was the priority given to etymology seriously questioned. The etymology of a word may or may not be significant in the way in which it is used in particular contexts; for example, the author of Isa. 49:15 may

have wished to observe that the Hebrew for "compassion" is derived from a word *rehem*, "womb" (cf. Malta from Semitic *melita*, "escape," Acts 28:1). But without contextual evidence it is not legitimate to assume that the *root meaning can be identified with the true meaning or the literal meaning.

Eucharist. A term derived from the Greek for "thanksgiving" (1 Cor. 14:16), applied since the 2nd century C.E. to the main Christian sacrament, also known as the *Last Supper, the Lord's Supper, Communion, and, in the Roman Catholic tradition, *Mass. Its Jewish origin in the *Passover meals and blessings over bread and wine is obscured by the Christian nomenclature. The "eucharistic words" are derived from the Gospels (Matt. 26:27; Mark 14:23; Luke 22:17–19) and Paul (1 Cor. 11:24), and the account of Jesus' feeding of the multitudes may have been influenced by early liturgical practice (Matt 15:16; Mark 8:6).

Euphemism. An alternative way of speaking to avoid words or phrases considered to have obscene or dangerous associations. The word "know" (Heb. *yada'*) is sometimes a euphemism for sexual intercourse (Gen. 4:1), as is "feet" for private parts (1 Sam. 24:3; Isa. 6:2). The Hebrew for "Curse God and die!" in Job 2:8 literally means "Bless God and die!" The name for Israel's God "YHWH" was too sacred to pronounce and various euphemisms were used in its place, including "the Lord" (Heb. *Adonai*) and "the Name" (Heb. *ha-shem*) in the Hebrew Bible (Lev. 24:11) and "the Holy One Blessed Be He" (Heb. *ha-qadosh barukh hu*) in the rabbinic literature. See *Tetragrammaton.

Eusebius of Caesarea (c. 264–340). Palestinian theologian and scholar, known as the "Father of Church History." His *Ecclesiastical History,* the work for which he is best known, contains much valuable evidence on the first three centuries of Christianity. He also wrote an interesting study of biblical topography (*Onomasticon*), a collection of quotations from pagan authors used to prove the truth of Christianity (*Praeparatio Evangelica*), and a large-scale apologetic work intended to prove the truth of Christian interpretations of Jewish Scripture (*Demonstratio evangelica*). He wrote commentaries on Isaiah and Psalms, and devised the first synoptic system known as the "Eusebian canons" for studying parallels in the Gospels.

Evangelical interpretation. The term "evangelical" (lit. "gospel-based," from Gk. *euangelion*, "gospel") has been applied generally since the Reformation to Protestant churches characterized by a strongly held belief in the sole authority of Scripture, individual salvation, and the importance of preaching, accompanied by a suspicion of liberalism, ritualism, and Roman Catholicism. As other Protestant movements developed, institutions like the Evangelical Alliance in England (1846), the Evangelical Union in Scotland (1843), and the Deutsche Evangelische Kirche (1945) emerged to preserve the evangelical tradition. Major contributions of evangelical scholars to biblical interpretation have been in biblical *archaeology (W. F. *Albright, A. R. Millard) and in the field of language and linguistics (E. A. Nida, T. Muraoka). Although they reject many of the conclusions of modern critical scholarship, their challenge to the source critics' fragmentation of the text and their consequent holistic approach to biblical literature, as well as their belief in its timeless relevance, have been vindicated in some respects by recent literary and social-scientific methodologies. See *Fundamentalism.

Evangelists. The term means "preachers of the *gospel," and is applied to Philip in Acts 21:8, but later especially

to the authors of the four canonical *Gospels, two of them, Matthew and John, among the original twelve disciples, the other two, Mark and Luke, sometimes included in the place of two lesser known figures. They are represented with Christ in a 4th-century catacomb in Rome, and in many illuminated mss at the beginning of their Gospels. From as early as *Irenaeus (late 2nd century) they were identified with the four creatures in Rev. 4 (cf. Ezek. 1:5–10): Mark as the lion, Luke as the bull, Matthew as the man, and John as the eagle, and this is how they are frequently represented in art from the 4th century at the latest. The term is often used of preachers in general, and Isaiah's famous verse beginning "How beautiful are the feet?" (52:7) was applied to them already by Paul (Rom. 10:15).

Eve (Heb. *hava*; Arab. *hawa*). The first woman according to the biblical creation story, formed from the side of Adam and named Eve because she became "the mother of all human life." Through her conversation with the serpent and her subsequent act of disobedience in taking the forbidden fruit and leading her husband astray, she was responsible for evil, suffering, and death in the world, starting with her own labor pains and subjection to male domination (Sir. 25:24; 1 Tim. 2:8–15). Rabbinic tradition made sexist jokes about the reasons why she was created out of Adam's side, and connected her name with an Aramaic word for "serpent" (*hivya*; Gen. 3:20 Tg Neofiti margin).

In Christian art the serpent frequently has the features of a woman, in some cases identical with Eve. Christian tradition also contrasts Eve, a virgin before the fall, with the Virgin Mary, who then transforms her curse into a blessing, stamps on the serpent's head with her heel, and assumes Eve's title "mother of all living." In Latin *Eva* is the reverse of *Ave*, Gabriel's greeting to Mary (Luke 1:28). Milton's more sympathetic depiction of Eve in *Paradise Lost*, which focuses on her loving relationship with Adam, her natural fallibility, and subsequent penitence and magnanimity, influenced Haydn in his musical version of the story (*Creation*, 1798) as well as many modern writers including Elizabeth Barrett Browning and Christina Rossetti. Recent feminist interpreters appreciate Eve's role as the one who takes the initiative in the story and leads humankind to freedom and fulfillment, a view beautifully expressed by Robert Frost in "Never again would birds' song be the same" (1923) and Archibald MacLeish in "Songs for Eve" (1954).

Exegesis. The process of interpreting or explaining the *meaning of a text and making it relevant in a contemporary *context. Exegetical methods, many of them devised by the *Alexandrian scholars two or three centuries before Christ, were applied to Jewish Scripture by *Philo, the Qumran community, the early Christians, the church fathers, and the rabbis. These included etymology, allegory, and analogy, and the distinction between the literal meaning of a text and its nonliteral or allegorical meaning was clearly established. Translation into Aramaic, Greek, and later Syriac, Latin, Coptic, and other vernaculars provided another method of exegesis, ranging from quite literal to free and creative as in the case of some of the Aramaic *Targumim. Mystical exegetes, especially in the medieval period, used still more elaborate conventions to reveal hidden meanings in the text. The authority of the church's official exegetes, like *Augustine and *Thomas Aquinas, was rejected by the Reformers in favor of the individual's direct engagement with the text and a doctrine of the "inner testimony of the Holy Spirit." Exegetical preaching came to be a special feature of Protestant tradition. In the 18th and 19th centuries traditional methods of exegesis were challenged by modern biblical criticism. In the 20th century Catholic

authorities moved toward a compromise with critical scholarship while Protestant leaders like *Barth and *Bultmann placed exegesis right at the center of their theology.

Exile (Heb. *galut*). The biblical period between the destruction of Jerusalem in 586 B.C.E. (2 Kgs. 25) and the Edict of Cyrus in 538 permitting the Jews to return to Jerusalem (2 Chr. 36), known as the "Babylonian exile" or "captivity," was a watershed in the history of the Jews, reflected in the widespread modern concept of "postexilic Judaism." Jeremiah's letter to the exiles (Jer. 29; cf. 2 Kgs. 25:27–30) suggests that conditions in Babylon were in fact not too bad, and many Jews chose to remain there to form what was to become a major Diaspora community. It was also a period of radical rethinking and reinterpretation evident not only in the books of Jeremiah and Ezekiel, but also, if the insights of modern scholarship are to be believed, in the Deuteronomic tradition (Deuteronomy–2 Kings) and Deutero-Isaiah (Isa. 40–55). Yet for many it was a time of despair (Lamentations) and nostalgia (Ps. 137), comparable to Israel's time in Egypt (Isa. 43:14–21). After the destruction of the Second Temple at Jerusalem in 70 C.E., exile came to be the primary symbol for suffering and alienation from God, and hope of return an integral part of biblical and Jewish tradition (Isa. 35:8–10; Amos 9:13–15). Medieval Jewish mystics in the diaspora made much of the concept of the exile of God or his Presence (*Shekinah). Christian writers from Augustine to John Bunyan used the image figuratively to describe their plight in this world, as pilgrims in exile journeying hopefully back toward the new Jerusalem and the promised land. In a famous treatise (1520) Luther wrote of the "Babylonian Captivity" of the Church at Rome, and Verdi's famous chorus of the Hebrew slaves in Babylon (*Nabucco*) has frequently been sung in situations of political exile, literal or metaphorical.

Existentialism. A modern philosophical movement, derived from *Kierkegaard's analysis of the freedom, the *Angst* ("fear, anxiety"), and the "leap of faith" of individual human beings like himself, and opposed to all abstract and objective systems of thought, including traditional theology. It was rejected by orthodox theologians like *Barth and officially condemned by a papal encyclical in 1950, but became popular in Europe after World War I in the works of *Buber, *Heidegger, Sartre, and others. It influenced biblical scholars, particularly *Bultmann, who argued that it is the subjective encounter of the individual with God that is important rather than the historicity of the Gospel stories. Subsequent writers on *reader-response criticism and other aspects of the reading process, including *Levinas, *Gadamer, and *Derrida, acknowledge their debt to existentialism but introduce ethical and sociopolitical issues neglected by the existentialists.

Exodus, book of (Heb. *shemot*, "names," Exod. 1:1). The second of the Five Books of Moses, it tells of the miraculous escape of the Hebrew slaves, led by Moses, from Egypt (chaps. 1–18) and their arrival at Sinai where they receive the Torah (chaps. 19–24) and instructions for building the tabernacle (chaps. 25–40). The book is one of the most popular in the Bible, containing the stories of *Moses in the bulrushes, the burning bush, the plagues of Egypt, the *Passover, the parting of the Red Sea, water from the rock, manna in the wilderness, the Ten Commandments, the *covenant, and the *golden calf. The exodus itself is frequently alluded to throughout the Bible as an act of "creation" (Isa. 43:15), comparable to the creation of heaven and earth and accompanied by spectacular natural phenomena including the plagues and the parting of the Red Sea. The Jewish Feast of Passover (Exod. 12; Deut. 16) is an ancient annual family celebration of the exodus, and the *Aggadah records many of the traditions that have grown up around the event down the centuries, especially its association with the coming of the Messiah and the return to Jerusalem. The giving of the Law at Sinai is commemorated at Shavuot (*Pentecost).

Christian tradition applied the exodus imagery to Christ's death (Luke 9:31) and to *baptism (*Tertullian, *Ambrose). It was the subject of a 2nd-century B.C.E. Greek drama by an Alexandrian poet known as Ezekiel, and a large part of the apocryphal Wisdom of Solomon is a graphic elaboration of the story (Wis. 10–19), as is the Old English Caedmonian poem *Exodus* (8th century). The Exodus themes of oppression, desert, sea, and pilgrimage have played a central role in Christian literature from *Dante and *Calvin to the Pilgrim fathers and *African Americans. Representations of the Exodus story in art are numerous, from the 3rd-century Dura Europos synagogue and the 5th-century churches of Santa Maria Maggiore and Santa Sabina in Rome, to paintings by Veronese, *Tintoretto, and especially *Poussin. Cecil B. DeMille's three and a half hour film epic *The Ten Commandments* (1956) remains one of the most ambitious versions of the story. Leon Uris's thriller (1958) and its film version (1960) about the struggle to create the State of Israel in 1947 is entitled *Exodus* after the symbolic name of the ship in which the refugees from Nazi Europe traveled.

There are no references to the exodus in the Egyptian records, and modern attempts to reconstruct what actually happened have got little farther than possibly identifying the king in question on the basis of two place names (Exod. 1:11), and rerouting the biblical story on the assumption that the term "Red Sea" (Heb. *yam suph*) would be more accurately translated "Reed Sea," a reference to a lake in the Nile Delta. The narrative contains many ancient elements, including the Song of the Sea (Exod. 15), the Decalogue (chap. 20), and intriguing details of Moses' relations with the Midianites (chaps. 2–3; 18). The impact of liturgical practice can probably be detected in some places, for example, Solomon's temple (chaps. 25–27; cf. 1 Kgs. 6–7), the Bethel sanctuary (Exod. 32; cf. 1 Kgs. 12:25–33), and the high priesthood in the Second Temple (Exod. 28; cf. Zech. 9:16). Feminist commentators have rediscovered the role of women, especially *Miriam, in the book of Exodus, and for *liberation theologians the story has provided a scriptural model for revolution especially in the light of evidence that "Hebrew" (cf. Akk. *habiru*; Egyp. *'aperiw*) originally meant "marginalized."

Eyck, Jan van (c. 1389–1441). Greatest Flemish artist of the 15th century. His paintings, of which the mysterious Arnolfini Marriage in the National Gallery, London, is perhaps his best known, are characterized by meticulous detail and perfection of the oil technique. His other works, all completed during the last ten years of his life, include the *Adoration of the Lamb* and *Annunciation* on the Ghent altar, and a number of unusual treatments of the Virgin Mary in Berlin, Dresden, Antwerp, and Washington, DC, the last of which incorporates illustrations of Samson and Delilah and David and Goliath.

Eyewitness. Claims made by Isaiah (Isa. 6), Peter (2 Pet. 1:16), Paul (2 Cor. 12:1–4), John of Patmos (Rev. 1; 21:1), and others to be eyewitnesses (Gk. *autoptai*) are intended as proof of the authority and reliability of their testimony. This is often enhanced by giving circumstantial details like the place (Rev. 1:9), date (Isa. 6:1), or time of day (Jer. 42:7), or stressing that more than one person was involved (Luke 1:2). In modern scholarship, where historical accuracy was crucial and the reliability of the biblical narratives submitted to the closest possible scrutiny, the identification of an eyewitness account was seen as an important achievement. On the basis of some of the vivid detail in several biblical narratives, for example, the Succession Narrative (2 Sam. 9–10; 1 Kgs. 1–2) and Luke's Gospel, scholars have argued that they are eyewitness accounts or at least owe much to eyewitnesses of the events described. More recent approaches to such texts place the emphasis on more complex literary, political, and theological factors.

Ezekiel, book of. Third of the *Major Prophets, Ezekiel contains some of the best-known and at the same time most bizarre texts in the Bible. There were rabbinic restrictions on reading Ezek. 1, for example, and the Gog and Magog prophecies in chaps. 38–39 have fuelled the imaginings of *millenarians in all ages. The prophet eats a scroll (chaps. 2–3), digs a hole through the wall of his house (chap. 12), and describes how he is lifted up and transported from place to place by the Spirit (chap. 11). Ezekiel also contains the vision of the dry bones (chap. 37) and the life-giving water flowing from the temple (chap. 47). The book clearly reflects the political and religious turmoil brought about by the destruction of Jerusalem in 586 B.C.E., and, according to the introduction (1:1–3), was written in Babylonia (Chaldea) soon after. It is divided into three parts: judgment on Judah and Jerusalem (chaps. 1–24), judgment on Judah's enemies (chaps. 25–39), and the vision of a new temple (chaps. 40–48). The first two parts are written in colorful, at times lurid language, exploiting a wide variety of literary forms, images, and traditions (e.g., proverbs, lamentations, the harlot, the shepherd, the mountain, Noah, Daniel, Job, Sodom). The final vision is written for the most part in the style of an architect's report, describing in detail the dimensions and materials of the new temple, massively fortified to ensure it will never again be contaminated by ritual impurity, and controlled by the Zadokite priests.

The impact of the book on early Jewish tradition can be appreciated in the reference in Sir. 49:8, the 1st-century B.C.E. *Ezekiel Apocryphon*, extant in fragments, and the 1st-century C.E. *Lives of the Prophets*, which tells of Ezekiel's martyrdom in Babylonia. The vision of the chariot in chap. 1 provided the scriptural basis for the *Merkabah tradition of Jewish mysticism, and the origin of the synagogue is sometimes traced to a meeting of elders in Ezekiel's house (14) and the possible reference to a "little sanctuary" (11:16 AV). There is also an important series of wall paintings illustrating the valley of dry bones in the *Dura Europos synagogue (3rd century C.E.).

In the NT the image of the good shepherd (John 10) and the concept of a new heart (2 Cor. 3:3) are Ezekiel's (chaps. 34; 36), and the book of Revelation is deeply indebted to Ezekiel. In the patristic period scriptural authority for nonliteral exegesis was found in Ezekiel's scroll "written within and without" (2:10 AV), and the closed door (*porta clausa*) in 44:2 became a popular type of the Virgin Mary in medieval art and literature. There are commentaries on the temple vision by Richard of St. Victor (1175) and *Nicholas of Lyra (14th century). Calvin's commentary on chaps. 1–20 focused on Ezekiel's theocentricity, and 19th-century liberals found an appealing individualism in the book (chap. 18). *Dante, *Milton, and *Blake all draw constantly on the language and imagery of Ezekiel. In Christian art there are many illustrations of the four living creatures in Ezek. 1:10 (cf. Rev. 4), representing the four *evangelists, and an elaborate symbolic representation of the wheel within a wheel (Ezek. 1:15–21) by Fra *Angelico. The best-known representations of the prophet himself are those of *Raphael (c. 1517, Florence) and *Michelangelo (*Sistine Chapel).

Ezra, book of. One of the *Ketuvim or Writings in the Hebrew Bible, closely associated with *Nehemiah and the books of *Chronicles of which it is a continuation (2 Chr. 36:22–23=Ezra 1:1–4). In the Vulgate it is known as 1 Ezra (see *Esdras, books of). The book covers the period from Cyrus (550–529 B.C.E.) to Artaxerxes I (465–424) or more likely Artaxerxes II (404–358), and tells how, after initial setbacks under Jeshua and Zerubbabel (cf. *Haggai), Ezra, a priest and scribe acting on Persian authority, led his people back to Jerusalem. In addition to the narrative, it contains an archive of official documents written in Aramaic (4:8–6:18), a formal prayer of confession by Ezra (chap. 9), and two lists of names, one purporting to be of those who returned with Jeshua and Zerubbabel (chap. 2), and the other of all those who had married foreign wives (10:18–44). The story is continued in the book of Nehemiah.

Ezra is regarded in Judaism as equal to Moses as an authority on the Torah, and one of the "men of the Great Synagogue," at the very start of the rabbinic tradition (*m. Abot* 1:1). A curious verse in the Qur'an compares his status in Judaism as "son of God" to that of Jesus in Christianity (9:30). The rabbis credit him with having the Torah rewritten in the new Aramaic script and dividing it up into weekly portions for Sabbath readings. *Spinoza and other pioneers of modern biblical criticism believed he may actually have been the author of the "Five Books of Moses" as we have them. It has also been suggested by historical critics that Nehemiah came to Jerusalem first, under Artaxerxes I in 445 B.C.E. (Neh. 2:1), and Ezra later, under Artaxerxes II in 398 (Ezra 7:7), the biblical Artaxerxes being a conflation of the two kings and priority having been given to Ezra.

Faith. In the Hebrew Bible faith in God generally means trust and commitment, expressed in an act of obedience like that of Abraham (Gen. 15:6; cf. Heb. 11). Thus according to a talmudic tradition the Torah is founded on the principle that "the righteous shall live by faith

[Heb. *emunah*]" (Hab. 2:4; *b. Makkot* 24a). For NT writers faith (Gk. *pistis*) is itself an act of commitment and obedience to Christ as the divine Lord and Savior, and defined as "the assurance of things hoped for and the evidence of things not seen" (Heb. 11:1). In some contexts *pistis tou Christou* (lit. "the faith of Christ") could be interpreted as "the faithfulness of Christ" rather than "faith in Christ" (Acts 24:24). Paul's interpretation of the Abraham story (Rom. 4) stressed the notion of "justification by faith" rather than works of the law (Rom. 3:19–28), which led to anti-Jewish polemic, and later to the Protestant individualistic emphasis on "faith alone" (*sola fide*). Christian theologians, notably *Augustine, Anselm, and *Thomas Aquinas, defined faith as the fundamental Christian experience, relating it to reason, emotion, and the doctrine of the church as a "faith community." Modern challenges to the truth of faith statements and critical analysis of what kind of rational arguments can be presented to support them had a major impact on the interpretation of the Bible. See *Biblical criticism.

Fall.   In Christian tradition the descent from the original bliss and perfection of *Eden, brought about by the disobedience of *Adam and *Eve (Gen. 3). This interpretation of the story, which places the responsibility for sin and death on Eve, had important consequences for Christian attitudes to women (Sir. 25:24; 1 Tim. 2:13–14). It also provided Christian theologians, notably *Augustine, with scriptural authority for the doctrine of *original sin, inherited by all subsequent generations of humankind, and set against the grace of Christ as a "second Adam" (Rom. 5:18–21; 1 Cor. 15:21–22). There are no references to this doctrine in the Hebrew Bible, and in Jewish tradition the disobedience of Adam and Eve is not normally understood to have permanently corrupted the human race, although there are some exceptions (Job 4:18–19; 2 Esd. 3:5–8).

The ultimate origin of evil is sometimes explained as due to the "fall" of an angel from heaven, as in Luke 10:18–19 (cf. Isa. 14:12–15).

Both Jewish and Christian writers from *Philo and *Paul to the *kabbalists described prelapsarian ("before the fall") conditions in great detail: the snake had four legs (cf. Gen. 3:14); human beings were immortal; the primeval human being (*adam kadmon*) was incorporeal, both male and female, the source of cosmic light and a mystical link between heaven and earth. Modern readings of Gen. 3, anticipated by rabbinic legend, *Irenaeus, and others, recognize the theme of discovery whereby naïve, naked, and innocent beings became truly human, with free will, the ability to think for themselves, and the propensity to suffer and die. Nineteenth-century writers like Shelley (*Prometheus Unbound*) understood the fall of *Satan as progress. The paradoxical formula *felix culpa*, "happy guilt," in a part of the Easter liturgy associated with *Ambrose (4th century), focuses on the fact that the joy of redemption could not have been experienced if there had been no fall, and the 15th-century carol *Adam lay ybounden* contains the words "Blessed be the time, the apple taken was." Among the best-known artistic representations of the fall are those of Hugo van der Goes, Hieronymus *Bosch, *Michelangelo, *Raphael, and, very different from the rest, *Rembrandt.

Family Bibles.   A specially produced printed Bible in which a Christian family record of births, baptisms, conversions, marriages, and deaths can be inscribed, thereby symbolizing their involvement in and commitment to the history of God's people. The custom goes back to the Reformation, when printed vernacular Bibles became affordable and people were encouraged to read and study it as part of daily devotion. Veneration of the "Good Book" increased, especially among 17th-century Puritans and 18th–19th-century evangelicals, and special items of furniture were designed on which the Family Bible could be displayed. See *Icon.

Faulkner, William (1897–1962).

American novelist, born in Oxford, Mississippi, and awarded the Nobel Prize for Literature in 1949. His novels, especially *Light in August* (1932) and *Absalom, Absalom* (1936), are heavily influenced by the language and imagery of the Bible, and his "Bible Belt" background is also evident in recurring allusions to the Adam tradition in his handling of the problem of evil.

Feminism.

The application of a modern feminist critique to the Bible and biblical interpretation began with Elizabeth Cady Stanton's *Woman's Bible* (1895–98), but feminist interpreters made little impact before Mary Daly, *Beyond God the Father* (1973); Phyllis Trible, *God and the Rhetoric of Sexuality* (1978) and *Texts of Terror* (1984); Elisabeth Schüssler Fiorenza, *In Memory of Her* (1983); Rosemary Radford Ruether, *Sexism and God-Talk* (1983); and the *Women's Bible Commentary* (1992, rev. 1998). The insights of feminist interpretation, which go beyond issues of sexual equality, have contributed much to modern biblical research. There is now a heightened awareness of the meaning of passages like Gen. 1:27, traditionally translated "God created man in his own image," more accurately translated "God created human beings . . . male and female." New questions are asked about the role of women in many biblical stories, not only named ones like *Eve, *Sarah, *Miriam, *Deborah, *Ruth, *Hannah, and *Judith, but also the unnamed victims of male cruelty like *Jephthah's daughter (Judg. 11), the Levite's concubine (Judg. 19–20), and the Samaritan woman (John 4). The use of almost pornographic female imagery in scenes of idolatry, humiliation, and destruction (e.g., Isa. 3–4; 47; Ezek. 23) is seen in a new light. Passages where the significance of female images has been traditionally overshadowed by male imagery are reassessed, as in the "daughter of Zion" passages running alongside the "Servant of the Lord" poems in Isaiah, and the rare biblical descriptions of God as a mother (Deut. 32:18; Ps. 131; Isa. 42:14; 49:14–15; 66:13; Luke 13:34). Scriptural authority is also discovered for women's participation in worship (Miriam, Exod. 15:21; Hannah, 1 Sam. 2; Mary, Luke 2) and leadership (Miriam, Mic. 6:4; Deborah, Judg. 4–5; Mary, Mark 16:6; cf. Rom. 16). See *Sexuality; *Womanism.

Film.

The global, multibillion dollar film industry has found, throughout the first hundred years of its history, that biblical stories interpreted on the big screen can be huge and instant box office successes, far surpassing printed versions or paintings in art galleries or sculptures, frescoes, and stained-glass windows in buildings like *Chartres Cathedral and the *Sistine Chapel. Cecil B. DeMille's *Ten Commandments* (1956), cleverly designed to appeal to both Jewish and Christian audiences, and *The Greatest Story Ever Told* (1965) are two obvious examples. Star-studded casts ensured that *Sodom and Gomorrah* (1962), *Moses the Lawgiver* (1975), *Samson and Delilah* (1949), *David and Bathsheba* (1951), *Solomon and Sheba* (1959), *Esther and the King* (1960), and many other biblical stories reached a wider audience than was ever possible before.

Alongside the Hollywood blockbusters many subtler attempts have been made to find new ways of telling familiar stories. Some, like the Marxist Pasolini's *Gospel according to St. Matthew* (Ital. *Vangelo secondo Matteo*, 1964), seek to reconstruct the original sociopolitical setting as faithfully as possible; while others, like Mel Gibson's more recent and more controversial *The Passion of the Christ* (2004), are filled with allusions to traditional iconography, liturgy, and theology intended to involve the believer as much as possible in the action. Both films were given official approval by the Vatican. Another technique is to set the story in a modern context as in *Christ Recrucified* (1969) and *Jesus in Montreal* (1989). No less successful subversive reinterpretations of the biblical narrative include *Monty Python's Life of Brian* (1979) and Kazantzakis's *The Last Temptation of Christ* (1988, based on his 1960 novel).

Some interpreters find significant allusions to biblical themes and images in films viewed by others as secular or amenable to an entirely different interpretation. In the science fiction *Matrix* trilogy (1999–2003), for example, the hero Neo, known as "The One," who is to save the world, suffers, dies, and rises again, supported by the heroine, whose name is Trinity, but not everyone is convinced that a Christian message is intended. Studies by biblically aware writers of the Western classic *Shane* (1952), *One Flew over the Cuckoo's Nest* (1975), *Blade Runner* (1982), *Terminator II: Judgment Day* (1991), and many other films in which biblical themes are less explicit, are now very common and add a new dimension to biblical studies. Isolated biblical phrases can be given new meaning by their use both as titles like *And a Still Small Voice* (1918), *East of Eden* (1955), *The Seventh Seal* (Rev. 8:1; 1957), and *My Brother's Keeper* (1995), and within the narrative of the film as in Oliver Stone's *Platoon* (1986), set in Vietnam, which opens with Eccl. 11:9 ("Rejoice young man . . .").

Flesh (Heb. *basar*; Gk. *sarx*). The ordinary meaning of the term is "meat" (Judg. 6:19–21 RSV). It is also applied to the human body (Gen. 2:23), and in biblical English, reflecting Hebrew usage, frequently refers to humanity in general: e.g., "all flesh is grass" (Isa. 40:6; cf. Gen. 6); "the Word became flesh" (John 1). In such contexts it is often associated with frailty (Job 10:4; Ps. 78:39), sinfulness (Rom. 7:5) and death (Rom. 8:5–6), and opposed to "the spirit" (Gal. 6:8). This negative view of the flesh, despite the incarnation, has flourished in various forms of Christian asceticism and puritanism down to the present day. The biblical usage survives in everyday expressions like "sins of the flesh" (Col. 2:11) and "the spirit is willing but the flesh is weak" (Matt. 26:41), as well as in some memorable musical settings of Isa. 40:6, especially Handel's *Messiah* and Brahms's *German Requiem*.

Flood (Heb. *mabbul*). The flood story begins with God's grief that the human race had become corrupt and his decision to destroy them, permitting only *Noah and his family to survive in a wooden vessel known as the ark (Gen. 6:5–9:17). The story ends with the return of the dove with an olive branch in its beak and God's unbreakable promise to Noah, sealed by the appearance in the sky of the first rainbow. This is the focus of one of the earliest references to the story in Isa. 54. Early Christians saw in the flood a type of salvation through water in baptism (1 Pet. 3:20–21), while later writers interpreted the ark as a prefiguration of the Virgin Mary carrying in her womb the sole survivor of the corrupt human race.

The flood is a fertile image in literature, notably Byron's *Heaven and Earth* (1821), based on *1 Enoch* as much as Genesis; Herman Melville's, *Moby Dick* (1851), George Eliot's *The Mill on the Floss* (1860), and D. H. Lawrence's *The Rainbow* (1915). There are early illustrations of the flood story in the Vienna Genesis (6th century) and the Ashburnham Pentateuch (6th or 7th century). Better known are the frescoes of *Michelangelo (*Sistine Chapel) and Uccello (Santa Maria Novella, Florence). The York and Chester *miracle plays contain lively interpretations of the story, while 20th-century staged versions include a musical play by Stravinsky (1962) and *Britten's *Noyes Fludde* (1958). There are some interesting parallels with the Gilgamesh Epic from ancient Mesopotamia and other primeval flood stories from many parts of the world. Despite the efforts of modern archaeologists, no traces of the biblical flood have yet been found, and the discovery of fossilized remains of creatures far more ancient than the biblical chronology would allow, led to fierce controversies between science and Christian traditionalists.

Florilegium. An anthology or collection of texts, selected for dogmatic, spiritual, or ethical purposes as well as historical or biographical. Patristic florilegia are particularly frequent and include selections from the writings of *Origen, *Augustine, *Gregory the Great, and others. Selections of biblical texts known as *Testimonia have been found at Qumran and were probably also used by NT writers. Cyprian's *Testimonia* (3rd century) is the oldest surviving Christian example. Later biblical anthologies range from the popular and widely used *Liber scintillarum* ("Book of Sparks") of the 8th century to Oliver Cromwell's *Soldier's Pocket Bible* (1643). See *Catena.

Folklore. Early folklore-based studies of the biblical stories, like those of *Gunkel and J. G. Frazer, tended to assume that their origin should be sought in preliterate, primitive, and superstitious societies. Subsequent studies of folktales in many societies, ancient and modern, by structural anthropologists like Claude Lévi-Strauss (*Anthropologie structurale* 1958; ET 1963) and others, showed that oral traditions are more complex and often have a clear political, religious, or ethical function. Works like Vladimir Propp's *The Morphology of the Folktale* (1928; ET 1958) and more recently Susan Niditch, *Folklore and the Hebrew Bible* (1993), show how, for example, stock characters like the trickster, the wise woman, and the hero operate in folktales, and apply such folkloristic insights to the biblical stories of Jacob, Deborah, David, and others. See *Oral tradition.

Form criticism. A method of studying the Bible by isolating distinct literary "forms" (Ger. *Gattungen*) or "genres," each with its own specific setting in life (*Sitz im Leben*), for example, in worship, education, law, politics, and entertainment. *Gunkel's work on the Psalms, which he analyzed as hymns, thanksgivings, laments, wisdom psalms, and the like, was an early and influential example. Form-critical studies by Martin Dibelius (*From Tradition to Gospel*, 1919; ET 1934), Rudolf *Bultmann (*History of the Synoptic Tradition*, 1921; ET 1963), Vincent Taylor (*Formation of the Gospel Tradition*, 1933), and other NT scholars identified paradigms (models for preachers, e.g., Mark 12:13–17), miracle stories, sayings, historical narratives, baptismal formulae, and the like, each with its own setting and function in the early church. While the method undoubtedly provided ancient historians with important data for reconstructing conditions in the ancient world, too much emphasis on isolated passages or pericopes often led to the fragmentation of the text and the neglect of larger literary units. See also *Redaction criticism.

Franciscans. Religious order (OFM) founded by Francis of Assisi in 1209. Originally devoted to a life of complete poverty, the practical demands of the order as it expanded over the years produced differing interpretations of the rules, and divisions that were not reunited until 1897. The Poor Clares are the Second Franciscan order, founded for women by Francis and his friend Clare in 1219, and the Capuchins are an austere offshoot of the Franciscan Order founded in 1529. There is also an Anglican Society of St. Francis. Popular preachers and missionaries, although never as learned as the *Dominicans and *Jesuits, they were given custody of the holy sites in Jerusalem in 1324, and contributed to the history of biblical interpretation by their emphasis on poverty in the *nativity scene and the development of the *Stations of the Cross in the liturgy. Franciscan scholars, from the 13th–14th centuries, include *Bonaventure, Roger Bacon, Duns Scotus, Raymond Lull, and William of Ockham.

Freemasonry. A secret society for the promotion of brotherly love and morality, founded probably in the Middle Ages and firmly established in Europe and the United States since the 18th century. Condemned as heretical by both Catholicism and Orthodoxy, masons have frequently been associated with Jews and become like them the target of anti-Semitism. They use the Bible, especially the OT, as one of several "Volumes of Sacred Law," with special emphasis on descriptions of the temple at Jerusalem and characters associated with it like *Melchizedek, Zerubbabel, *Haggai, and, in the higher orders, Hiram-Abiff, a craftsman (cf. 2 Chr. 2:13) murdered, according to Masonic tradition, when the building of the temple was completed. The Masonic rituals contain many biblical terms such as I AM THAT I AM (Exod. 3:14), Immanuel (Isa. 7:14), Jachin and Boaz (1 Kgs. 7:21) and Shibboleth (Judg. 12:6), as well as some derived from Jewish tradition, including Sanhedrin, *Kabbalah, and Sefiroth.

Freud, Sigmund (1856–1939). Austrian neurologist and founder of psychoanalysis. Among his most important works are *The Interpretation of Dreams* (1900; ET 1953), *Totem and Tabu* (1913; ET 1955), *Ego and Id* (1923; ET 1961) and his cynical critique of religion, *The Future of an Illusion* (1927; ET 1928). Brought up in a Jewish family although a self-confessed atheist, he knew the Hebrew Bible and refers to it frequently in his writings. In *Moses and Monotheism* (1939), his only extended study of the Bible, he argues that Moses imposed Egyptian monotheism on the Israelites and was subsequently murdered by them, which helps to explain not only

some features of Israelite religious belief and practice but also the mystery surrounding his burial. Freud applied his methods to interpreting Greek myths, notably the Oedipus story, rather than the Bible and left the psychoanalytical interpretation of the Bible to his followers, especially *Jung and Jacques Lacan.

Fulfillment. The completion of a process that begins with a prophecy foretelling the future. For biblical writers it was an article of faith that God is always true to his word (Deut. 18; Isa. 55:10–11) and the prophecy-fulfillment pattern, albeit an artificial one, gives history a structure (on Josh. 6:26 cf. 1 Kgs. 16:34; on 1 Kgs. 13:1–10 cf. 2 Kgs. 16:23). Many of the great biblical prophecies of the 8th–6th centuries B.C.E. are predictions of forthcoming disasters as well as visions of a future messianic age of justice and peace. Later communities, including the Qumran sect and the first Christians, believed that some of these prophecies had been, or were shortly to be, fulfilled in their own lifetime, and sought to find detailed correspondences between Scripture and contemporary events (e.g., Isa. 4:12–17). Jesus himself claimed to have come to fulfill the Law and the Prophets (Matt. 5:17), and his followers believed he was the *Messiah foretold in many biblical passages. Other Jews rejected these interpretations of Scripture, and controversy has continued ever since, both between Jews and Christians, and among Christians of different persuasions.

Fundamentalism. The term applied to a variety of conservative religious beliefs, especially Christian and Jewish, characterized by, among other things, the conviction that the Bible is free from any kind of human error, historical, scientific, ethical, or theological. Fundamentalists reject the discoveries of modern *archaeology, biblical criticism, and science where they appear to contradict Scripture, as in the case of *Wellhausen's *documentary hypothesis and Darwin's theory of evolution. Territorial claims derived by some ultraorthodox Jews from passages in Genesis and Deuteronomy, ethical principles derived from some of the laws in Leviticus, and the like are often referred to as fundamentalist readings of Scripture, though perhaps "literalistic," "conservative," or "precritical" would be more accurate.

Gabriel (Arab. *Jibril*). An angel mentioned by name in Daniel (8:16; 9:21) and in Luke, where he announces the coming birth of John the Baptist (1:11) and Jesus (1:31). In the Pseudepigrapha, notably *1 Enoch*, and the rabbinic literature he is active in many spheres, including the creation of Adam (*b. Hagigah* 12a), the burial of Moses (Deut. 34:6 Tg), and the last judgment (*1 Enoch* 54:6), and eventually dominates all other angels as the archangel Gabriel. In Muslim tradition he is believed to have dictated the *Qur'an* to Muhammad. In Tasso's *Gerusalemme Liberata* Gabriel is sent by God to urge the crusaders to attack Jerusalem, but in Christian tradition he is most often associated with the *annunciation as in Peter Abelard's hymn "To Gabriel of the Annunciation" and the carols "Gabriel's message does away / Satan's curse and Satan's sway," and "The Angel Gabriel from God." He plays a major role in Milton's *Paradise Lost*, and no doubt Thomas Hardy had him in mind in *Far from the Madding Crowd* (1874) when he named Bathsheba Everdene's loyal friend and eventual husband Gabriel Oak.

Gadamer, Hans-Georg (1900–2002). German philosopher. Studied with *Heidegger, Otto, and *Bultmann at Marburg and was appointed professor of philosophy at Heidelberg in 1949, where he spent the rest of his life. His notion that as readers of a text we participate in the history of its effect (*Wirkungsgeschichte*) and to understand it there has to be a "fusion of horizons" has been widely used not only in philosophical hermeneutics but in literary criticism, theology, and the social sciences. His major work is *Truth and Method* (1960; rev. ET 1989). See *Hermeneutics.

Galatians, Letter to. One of the earliest Christian documents, written by Paul possibly before the Council of Jerusalem in 49 C.E. (Acts 15) and comparable to *Romans in its impact on subsequent history and theology. It is addressed to Christian communities founded by Paul in the Roman province of Galatia, which included parts of ancient Phrygia, Pisidia, and Lycaonia and the cities of Pisidian Antioch, Iconium, Lystra, and Derbe (Acts 13–14; 16). It may be that the term Galatia in Acts does not always refer to the Roman province but to a region inhabited by Gauls since the 3rd century B.C.E., and visited by Paul after Derbe and Lystra (Acts 16:6; cf. 18:23). The letter is concerned with a bitter dispute over the question of to what extent Christians have to observe Jewish practices, in particular circumcision. In some of his most passionate rhetoric Paul curses his opponents (Gal. 1:8–9), condemns their foolishness (3:1), and points to his own personal experience of Christ in one of his longer autobiographical narratives (chaps. 2–3). He argues that Christians living in the Spirit have been, like him, "crucified with Christ" (2:19–20), redeemed (3:13), adopted (4:4), baptized (3:27), and "justified by faith" (3:6–8, 24), and are free from slavery (chap. 4) and are living in a "new creation" (6:13).

Prominent in the legacy of the letter to subsequent generations down to this day are the words "There is neither Jew nor Greek, bond nor free, male nor female" (3:28; cf. Col. 3:11), the image of true sons crying "Abba, Father" (4:6), the allegory of Hagar and Sarah (4:21–31), the "fruit of the Spirit" (5:22), and the proverb "You reap whatever you sow"

(6:7 NRSV). Galatians was a favorite text for *Marcion in his efforts to de-Judaize Christianity. Important commentaries were written by *Chrysostom, *Jerome, and *Augustine. *Luther identified himself with the Paul of Gal. 1–2, believing he was above the authority of Peter at Antioch and thereby above Peter's successors in Rome. F. C. *Baur's study of Galatians, which highlighted and over-simplified the split between Jewish and gentile Christianity (1831), dominated NT scholarship for a century, despite J. B. Lightfoot's classic commentary (1865) and some subtler studies of Christian origins. Paul's first four letters, Romans, 1 and 2 Corinthians, and Galatians, which may have been the earliest collection circulated among churches, represent the core of his teaching.

Galilei, Galileo (1564–1642). Italian astronomer and mathematician. His calculations and discoveries, particularly concerning the solar system, led him into conflict with the Roman church, which condemned him in 1616 and again in 1633. He nonetheless argued in his *Dialogue Concerning the Two Chief World Systems* (1632) and elsewhere that since God created both nature and revelation, science and the Bible cannot contradict one another provided each is properly understood. He advocated a nonliteral method of biblical interpretation for which he claimed the authority of *Augustine, and pointed out that many parts of the Bible have nothing to say on matters of faith. But it was not until 1992 that Pope John Paul II rescinded the Roman Catholic condemnation of Galileo.

Gamaliel. Rabban Gamaliel the Elder, probably the son of Hillel, was a member of the Sanhedrin and Paul's teacher in Jerusalem (Acts 22:3). "Held in honor by all the people" according to the author of Acts (5:34), and hence "Rabban," not just "Rabbi," it was said

that when he died, "the respect for the Torah ceased and purity and abstinence died at the same time" (*m. Sotah* 9:15).

Garden of Eden. See *Eden.

Gattungsgeschichte. See *Form criticism.

Gay and lesbian interpretation. Approaches to biblical interpretation informed by modern attitudes to same-sex relationships and new theories about the social and cultural organization of gender and sexuality in the ancient world. Examples include attempts to interpret relationships such as those between Ruth and Naomi, David and Jonathan, and Jesus and the Beloved Disciple as having an erotic dimension, and the condemnation of homosexual practices in Leviticus (Lev. 18:22; 20:13) and Paul (Rom. 1:26–27; 1 Cor. 6:9) as reflecting ancient hierarchical views on gender boundaries or referring more to specific cultural phenomena such as cultic prostitution or Greco-Roman pederasty than to homosexuality in general. Others interpret the Sodom story (Gen. 18–19) as having more to do with social justice in general (cf. Ezek. 16:49) than with homosexual practices, which are in fact very rarely referred to in the Bible. Members of the gay community in Israel have noticed that the words *kol ge yinnase*, "every valley shall be exalted," in Isa. 40:4 can also be translated out of context as "any gay person can get married."

Gematria. An arithmetical method of expounding the meaning of words and numbers, based on the numerical values of the letters of the Hebrew and Greek alphabets. In Hebrew the eight consonants of the name of Emperor Nero (*nrwn qysr*), for example, add up to 666, the number of the "beast" (Rev. 13:18). Gematria is used to explain why

Abraham had 318 "trained men" (Gen. 14:14), why the disciples caught 153 fish (John 21:10), and why 14 is so important in the genealogy of Jesus (Matt. 1:1). The method was of little significance in the rabbinic literature, but taken more seriously in some varieties of Jewish *mysticism. Today several computer-assisted gematria programs are available on the Internet.

Genealogy. A list of names designed to trace the ancestry, not only of priests (Num. 3) and kings (1 Chr. 2–4) where dynastic succession was an issue, but also of the human race (Gen. 10–11) and, in particular, the people of Israel and their neighbors (Gen. 25; 36). Genealogies can be used to make important social and political points: Canaan is descended from Ham along with Egypt and Babylon, rather than Israel's ancestor Shem (Gen. 10:6–20); the foreign blood in King David's veins is concealed by the omission of Ruth the Moabitess from his family tree (1 Chr. 2–4). Two of the Gospels contain genealogies of Jesus: one includes four women and a strong emphasis on his Davidic lineage (Matt. 1:1–17), the other appears to place more stress on his descent from Adam and his oneness with all humanity (Luke 3:23–38). See also *Jesse tree.

Genesis, book of (Heb. *Bereshit*, "in the beginning," Gen. 1:1). The first of the Five Books of Moses. It tells the story of the origins of the universe, from the first appearance of human beings on earth to the point where the people of God, descended from the patriarchs Abraham, Isaac, Jacob, and his twelve sons, are settled in Egypt on the eve of the exodus. The book acts as an introduction to the whole Bible in that many of the stories contain promises to be fulfilled and other themes to which later books, from Exodus, Psalms, and Isaiah to Paul and Revelation, make frequent reference. Many also have an aetiological compo-

nent explaining why, for example, the seventh day of the week is a day of rest, why women suffer pain in childbirth, how Beer-sheba and Bethel got their names, and why the Jews made their home in Canaan. But this does not obscure the intricate, often profound psychological, social, and religious issues raised by many of the stories, such as the garden of *Eden and the *Akedah, in their own right. The history of the book's influence on world literature and culture in general is probably unique, profoundly affecting not only literature (*Milton, William *Blake, Thomas *Mann), art (*Michelangelo, Hieronymus *Bosch), and music (*Haydn's *Creation*, *Britten's *Noyes Fludde*, Rice and Webber's *Joseph and the Amazing Technicolor Dreamcoat*), but also philosophy (*Kierkegaard), mysticism (*Zohar), science (*Galileo, *Newton), *linguistics (Semitic/Hamitic), and ethics (Schwartz, *The Curse of Cain*). Notable commentaries on Genesis are those by *Augustine, *Basil, *Bede, *Pico della Mirandola, *Luther, *Calvin, *Gunkel, von *Rad, and Westermann.

Apart from Jacob's lengthy poetic prophecy concerning his sons (Gen. 49), the book of Genesis consists almost entirely of prose narrative in which we may distinguish broadly between two types: the mythical stories of *creation and the *flood, where the context is global and the main character the Deity (Gen. 1–11), and which have interesting parallels in ancient Sumerian and Babylonian cultic literature; and the patriarchal legends in which the focus is on the lives of men and women whose relationship to actual historical events has been much discussed, as has the question of the authorship, date, and sources of the narrative. See *Pentateuch.

Genesis Apocryphon. An apocryphal version of stories from Genesis, preserved in Aramaic in a badly damaged ms from Qumran, (see *Dead Sea Scrolls), dated late 1st century B.C.E. or early 1st century C.E. The best-preserved section retells some of the stories about Abraham and Sarah (Gen. 12–15), much of it in Abraham's own words, but there are other fragments, including one about the miraculous birth of Noah, recounted by his father Lamech, who, suspecting his wife of unfaithfulness (cf. Gen. 6:2), consults his father Methuselah, who in turn journeys to paradise to consult Enoch (Gen. 5:21–32). The text has parallels in *Jubilees and other Jewish writings and provides valuable insights into late Second Temple period biblical interpretation.

Geneva Bible. English translation of the Bible, published in Geneva in 1560 for Protestants in exile. Based on Tyndale's version and crammed with radical comments, for example, identifying Rome as the antichrist and the "monks, friars, archbishops, cardinals . . . and all who forsake Christ" with the locusts in Rev. 9:3, it became very popular in England, although it never received the authority of the *Authorized Version. It is also known as the "Breeches Bible" on account of its translation of the garments made by Adam and Eve (Gen. 3:7).

Genizah. See *Cairo Genizah; *Synagogue.

Genre. A term applied to categories of literature such as letter, sermon, novel, epic, and myth, each with its own form, character, and purpose that provide an important key to interpretation. Parts of Proverbs (1–9; 22:17–24:22) and Ecclesiastes, for example, belong to a genre known as "royal instruction," well documented in ancient Egypt and Babylon. There is often scholarly disagreement, however, about genre, as in the case of the book of Jonah, which according to some is a comic novella characterized by humor and irony, while to others it is a prophetic legend with significant parallels in the Elijah and Jeremiah traditions.

Gentile (Heb. *goy*). The Hebrew term is used in the Bible for all the nations of the world, including Israel (*goy tzaddiq* "a righteous nation," Exod. 19:6; Isa. 26:2) and the descendants of Abraham (Gen. 17:3–6), but most often it refers to foreign, non-Jewish nations (Deut. 4:27; Ps. 2:1 AV). The English term comes from the *Vulgate, which distinguishes between nations in general (*gentes*) and non-Jews in particular (*gentiles*; John 12:20 Vg; 1 Cor. 12:13), and this is the meaning the word "Gentile," like *goy*, eventually acquired. Biblical attitudes to Gentiles and proselytizing range from generosity (*Ruth; Zech. 8:22–23) to suspicion and hostility (Neh. 13:23–27). An outer court in Herod's temple was known as the Court of the Gentiles beyond which it was forbidden for non-Jews to go. The early church, especially Paul, for the most part directed its activities toward the Gentiles, rejecting Jewish religious practices and abandoning the Hebrew language. Modern translations, however, discard the exclusive interpretation of phrases like "a light to the nations" (Isa. 49:6; cf. 42:1–6; AV "gentiles") in line with the inclusive words of the aged Simeon: "a light to lighten the Gentiles, and the glory of thy people Israel" (Luke 2:32 AV). The Holocaust Memorial in Jerusalem has a garden dedicated to the "Righteous among the Gentiles."

Gersonides. The common name of Levi ben Gershon (1288–1344), French philosopher, exegete, and astronomer. Heavily influenced by Aristotle, his most important work was the six-part philosophical *Wars of the Lord*. He also wrote a number of biblical commentaries characterized by a concern to derive moral lessons from the text and to find rational explanations for miracles. He rejects the view that Gen. 1 describes creation out of nothing and argues that Joshua telling the sun to stand still simply meant ensuring that the enemy was defeated in one day (Josh. 10:12–14).

Gesenius, Heinrich Friedrich Wilhelm (1786–1842). Hebrew lexicographer and grammarian. As professor of theology at Halle he published the first edition of his Hebrew-German lexicon in two volumes (1808, 1812), which was soon translated into English, supplemented by the *Thesaurus philologicus criticus* (1829–53). In the Brown, Driver, and Briggs edition (BDB) it is still widely used, as is his Hebrew grammar, first published in 1813, revised by Emil Kautzsch (1909) and translated into English by A. E. Cowley (1910).

Ghiberti, Lorenzo (1378–1455). Florentine sculptor. Most of his life was devoted to the making of two sets of bronze doors for the baptistery at Florence. The first, completed in 1424, shows scenes from the life of Christ, including the adoration of the magi, Peter walking on the water, and Pilate washing his hands, and is somewhat stylized; while the second, completed in 1452, illustrating the OT, is a Renaissance masterpiece of originality, powerful realism, and perspective showing the influence of Masaccio, Brunelleschi, and Donatello. It shows scenes from the stories of Adam and Eve, Cain and Abel, Noah, Abraham, Jacob, and Joseph from Genesis as well as Solomon and the Queen of Sheba. There is also an early *Sacrifice of Isaac* (1401), which won him his first commission against the competition of Brunelleschi.

Ghirlandaio, Domenico (1449–94). Italian painter. Son of a Florentine goldsmith, he began his career as a painter in 1480 and worked almost exclusively in Florence, where *Michelangelo was his apprentice. Among his best-known works on biblical subjects, noted for their sensitive treatment of human expression and attention to background detail, are *Christ Calling Peter and Andrew* in the *Sistine Chapel (1481); his rich, crowded *Adoration of the Magi* in the Ospedale degli Innocenti, Florence (1488); two fine series of frescoes in Santa Maria Novella, Florence, showing scenes from the lives of Mary and John the Baptist (1486–90); and the *Visitation of the Virgin* (1491) in the Louvre.

Gideon (Jerubbaal). One of the judges of Israel (Judg. 6–8), after Samson probably the best known. He is remembered for the victory of his 300 men, with trumpets and torches in the night, over a vast Midianite horde (Isa. 9:2–4), and listed in Heb. 11 with others who "through faith conquered kingdoms." The story contains a number of other incidents, including his encounter with an angel, the miraculous fleece, his desecration of a pagan altar, the lapping test by which the 300 were selected, the brutal punishment of Succoth and Penuel, his refusal to accept an invitation to become king of Israel, and the tale of his ill-fated son Abimelech, who did become king for a short period.

In ancient and medieval art and literature Gideon was compared to Christ the victorious warrior, while the victory of the cross over paganism was seen in the number 300 (= *tau*; see *Gematria). Likewise the fleece, miraculously impregnated with the divine dew, was a frequent type of the Virgin Mary (cf. Isa. 45:8). The Reformers by contrast saw Gideon as a model leader, not least as an iconoclast, and various writers made comparisons with Oliver Cromwell, who like Gideon refused the crown. Calvin saw him as a flawed hero, and many writers since have debated the self-doubt of a man who would not act without first seeing signs of divine power, and also his apparent involvement in pagan religion, something already criticized in ancient rabbinic sources. He figures in many contexts, from Andrew Marvell's *The First Anniversary* in praise of Cromwell (1654) to the "Gideon Bibles" placed in hotel bedrooms since 1908 and Paddy Chayevsky's Broadway comedy *Gideon*

(1961). There is a painting of the "Battle of Gideon against the Midianites" by Nicolas Poussin in the Vatican (1625–26).

Giotto di Bodone (c. 1266–1377). Italian artist generally considered to be the first to move away from rigid Byzantine conventions toward a more realistic representation of people and events. His works, most notably the great cycles of frescoes in the Arena chapel, Padua, and the Basilica of St. Francis at Assisi, the *Ognissanti Madonna* in the Uffizi, and the striking *Navicella* mosaic formerly in St. Peter's, Rome (known now only through copies), had a decisive influence on later Renaissance artists, including *Michelangelo, who made copies of them. The Padua frescoes include a *Life of Christ* in which there are some particularly innovative and moving scenes.

Gloria (in excelsis Deo) (Lat. "Glory to God in the highest"). An early Christian hymn, beginning with the song of the angels (Luke 2:14), sung immediately after the *Kyrie in the Roman Catholic *Mass, and at the conclusion of Communion in the Anglican tradition. It is also known as the "Angelic Hymn" or the "Greater *Doxology," to distinguish it from the Trinitarian "Lesser Doxology" beginning *Gloria Patri*, "Glory be to the Father" (cf. Rev. 5:13; Matt. 28:19), sung at the end of Psalms in Christian tradition since the 4th century.

Glory. A biblical concept referring to how believers experience the presence of God. The chief Hebrew term for "glory" (*kabod*) in relation to humans can also be translated "honor," a quality that commands awe and respect (Prov. 3:16; cf. Exod. 20:12). God's glory is described most graphically at Sinai (Exod. 24) and in the temple at Jerusalem (1 Kgs. 8:11; Ezek. 10), but can be experienced also in the wonders of nature (Isa. 6:3; Ps. 8). The NT Greek equivalent (*doxa*) is applied to Solomon (Matt. 6:29) and to the Son of God (John 1). Christ's *transfiguration recalls Sinai (Luke 9:28–36), but his glory is revealed uniquely in his death and resurrection (Heb. 2:9–10) and shared by his followers (2 Cor. 4:17; Eph. 3:13). In the language of worship glory has naturally always had a central role, starting with the Psalms, where it is very frequent, and then within the Christian tradition in the *Gloria, various doxologies, and elsewhere. In art the concept was represented by a halo, applied to Roman emperors and from the 5th century C.E. to Christ, the Virgin Mary, and the saints. Medieval artists sometimes enclosed the whole body in an oval shape known as a *mandorla* (Ital. "almond"), while others used rays of light in less stereotyped forms to represent glory. See *Shekinah.

Glossa ordinaria. The standard medieval commentary on the Bible, completed at Laon and Auxerre by the mid-12th century. It is a vast compilation of material from patristic and early medieval sources, especially *Isidore of Seville and *Rabanus Maurus, and was one of the main sources used by designers of the great French cathedrals at *Chartres, Rheims, Bourges, and elsewhere. Arranged, like the *Talmud and *Rabbinic Bibles, with a short biblical text on each page accompanied by extensive commentary, it contains both brief scholarly comments and lengthy speculative, often symbolic interpretations, always seeking to ensure that no subtle or hidden meaning is missed. Thus by the use of number symbolism the dimensions of Noah's ark (Gen. 6:14–16) are given christological significance: 30 is the age of Jesus, 10 refers to the Decalogue, and 300 is the numerical value of the Greek letter *tau*, "which clearly indicates a cross." See *Gematria.

Glossolalia. The phenomenon of "speaking in tongues" listed by Paul as one of the gifts of the Spirit along with the gift of "the interpretation of tongues" (1 Cor. 12:10). It has been connected by many with the miracle of Pentecost when the tower of Babel story is reversed (Acts 2:1–13), and is still practiced in some forms of Christianity, notably Pentecostalism. Although well-documented in forms of shamanism and spirit possession in various parts of the world, there is as yet little agreement on the linguistic process involved. Its ritual function, however, seems to be to inspire belief in something beyond human understanding, not unlike the role of Latin, Sanskrit, and Arabic in worship, where unintelligibility is perceived by the faithful to be a virtue.

Gnosticism.   Derived from the Greek word *gnosis*, "knowledge," Gnosticism most commonly refers to a complex religious movement associated particularly with the names of two 2nd-century C.E. Alexandrian theologians, Valentinus, who spent most of his life teaching in Rome, and Basilides. Their opponents, notably *Irenaeus of Lyons, *Clement of Alexandria, *Tertullian of Carthage, and Hippolytus of Rome, provided much of what was known about their teaching until discoveries of Coptic codices containing gnostic texts. The most important collection was discovered in 1945–46 at Nag Hammadi in Upper Egypt. Influenced by Platonic and Pythagorean philosophy, and probably also by *Zoroastrianism and early Jewish *mysticism, gnostic interpreters understood the biblical creator God, or Demiurge as they called him, to be working on a lower level than the supreme unknowable Source of all Being. Christ the Savior was a divine being sent to give humanity the *gnosis* by which they might escape from this evil material world, and he was never required to live and die as a real human being. The human race was then divided between the "spiritual," who achieved this special knowledge and in whom there was a divine spark, and the "fleshly," who could not escape from the material world. With the exception of Genesis interpretation found in the mythological texts and the excerpts from a commentary on John by the Valentinian Heracleon found in Origen's commentary, the biblical commentaries of these teachers have not survived.

Christian orthodoxy took shape in the patristic period to some extent as a reaction against some of these ideas. But more recently some of the gnostic literature, such as the *Gospel of Judas*, has been seen as source material for an interesting and important stage in the history of Christianity. Ben Sira (c. 180 B.C.E.) discouraged meddling in "matters too great for human understanding" (Sir. 3:21–25), and the rabbis explicitly warned against the dangers of too much speculation on the meaning of Gen. 1 (*m. Hagigah* 2:1), but there was never the same anti-gnostic polemic in Judaism, and elements in the medieval *Kabbalah could be described as gnostic. Gnostic concepts can be found in John's Gospel (3:13; 6:62–63), Paul occasionally uses gnostic terminology such as *pleroma*, "fullness" (Col. 1:19; 2:9), and Clement of Alexandria actually uses the term of himself and his teaching.

God, gods.   For historical reasons there is more than one Hebrew word for "god, deity." *Elohim* is the most general. It is the plural form of the rarer *Eloah* (frequent in Job), from which Arab. *Allah* (*Al-Ilah*, "the God") is derived, and is used of Adam and Eve (Gen. 3:5) and divine beings in general (Ps. 8:5), as well as being the commonest term for Israel's God. A third frequent term is *El*. This was originally the name of *Baal's father in the Canaanite pantheon, and occurs in a number of ancient formulas like "God Most High" (*El Elyon*, Gen. 14:20), "Almighty God" (*El Shaddai*, 17:1), and "Everlasting God" (*El Olam*, 21:33), as well as in proper names (Bethel, Elijah, Michael). Like the English word *God* (with a capital), these three words are used as personal names of Israel's God, who is also referred to by his sacred personal name YHWH (see *Tetragrammaton). In most other languages, including LXX and NT Greek, there is only one word for "god."

YHWH is a central character in most of the biblical narratives, and YHWH's actual words are recorded at length at Sinai, in the prophetic books, in Job, and elsewhere, and he is often addressed directly, especially in the Psalms. Only the book of Esther makes no reference to God. Introduced as omnipotent creator of heaven and earth, overcoming the powers of chaos by his word (Gen. 1), his involvement in human history is described in the Hebrew Bible down to the restoration of the Jews in the Diaspora (2 Chr. 36:22–23), and according to the Christian Bible, until the creation of a new heaven and new earth (Rev. 21–22). The story of the biblical God is predominantly one of decisive, often violent intervention in human affairs, albeit usually to punish wickedness and rescue the oppressed, but the images of God as shepherd (Ps. 23; Isa. 40:11), loving father (Isa. 63:16; Gal. 4:6), and devoted mother (Isa. 66:13; Ps. 131:2) are there as well.

In Jewish art the "hand of God" appears in some early mosaics and in the frescoes from *Dura Europos, despite the ban on images, and elaborate kabbalistic diagrams trace the interaction among the ten emanations (*sefirot*) that make communication between God and humanity possible. In Christian art from around the 7th century God is represented with increasing frequency as the "Ancient of Days" (Dan. 7), an old man with a beard, despite the clear statement that both male and female were created "in the image of God" (Gen. 1:27). *Rembrandt's depiction of the prodigal son's father, whose tender, and clearly female, right hand has been much discussed, attempts to set that right.

His existence and that of other gods is rarely questioned, except by a fool (Ps. 14:1), although explicit *monotheism, which became a central tenet of Judaism, Christianity, and Islam, has its origins in the Bible. The worship of *Baal and the gods of Israel's idolatrous neighbors is repeatedly condemned, and single-minded devotion to YHWH demanded (Exod. 20:2–6; Deut. 6:4–5; Matt. 22:37). The terrifying sense of the holiness of God, expressed in terms of fire, clouds, thunder, earthquakes, and the like (Exod. 19; 1 Kgs. 19), led to the strictest ritual legislation (Lev. 10:2) as well as the euphemistic description of God's presence in the world in terms of his *Name, *Glory, *Shekinah, *Word (*Memra*), *Wisdom, and the like. This prepared the way for the Christian doctrines of the divinity of Christ, as the "Word made flesh," and the *Trinity.

Golden calf. The idol made by the Israelites at Sinai under *Aaron's leadership while *Moses was absent (Exod. 32; Deut. 9), and by Jeroboam at Bethel and Dan after the death of Solomon (1 Kgs. 12). Both traditions probably reflect ancient cultic practice in which YHWH was represented as a young bull or as riding on one like the Canaanite deity *Baal. The incident at Sinai is frequently quoted in Jewish and Christian tradition, and recounted twice in the Qur'an (7:148–54; 20:83–98). Moses' violent suppression of a rebellious people was cited with approval by Macchiavelli and some of the Reformers, including Knox and *Calvin. In 1933 Bonhoeffer used the story in a sermon to highlight the conflict between two conceptions of religion, as does Schönberg's opera *Moses und Aron* composed around the same time. In literature the golden calf is most often a symbol of wealth or materialism. The incident is a popular subject with artists, as in the Utrecht Psalter, where it illustrates Ps. 81:9–10, and in works by *Raphael, *Tintoretto, *Poussin, and William *Blake. There is also Cecil B. DeMille's memorable version in *The Ten Commandments* (1956).

Golden Legend. One of the most famous and widely read books of the

Middle Ages. Originally entitled *Legenda Sanctorum*, it is a collection of biblical, apocryphal, and hagiographical legends arranged to follow the liturgical year, with a strong homiletical purpose, rather than any historical interest. Composed in 13th-century Italy by the *Dominican Jacobus de Voragine, its influence on medieval *mystery plays, iconography, and cathedral architecture can hardly be overestimated. In the 16th century it was condemned as superstitious and unreliable, and virtually disappeared until 19th-century romantics rediscovered it. It survives in over 500 mss, in several languages and editions. An English version was printed by Caxton in 1483 and again by William Morris in 1892.

Golem.   Derived originally from Ps. 139:16, where it is translated "unformed substance" (RSV) or "embryo" (JB), and discussed in the Talmud in relation to the creation of Adam, the golem later became the subject of legends about a Frankenstein-like being created by magic out of clay or wood, but who got out of control and had to be destroyed. The best-known of these is that of Rabbi Judah Löw ben Bezalel in 16th-century Prague. There have been several novels about the golem, an opera, a ballet, a film, and an orchestral suite. In Yiddish the term most often just means a stupid person.

Good Friday (Gk. "Great Friday"). The Friday of Holy Week on which the crucifixion is commemorated by the Veneration of the Cross, a three-hour Devotion from noon to 3 p.m. (Luke 23:44) and in many traditions, including that of the Franciscans in Jerusalem, a symbolic procession along the Via Dolorosa marked in churches by the 14 *Stations of the Cross. Readings prescribed for the day, in addition to the *Passion Narrative (usually John 18–19), often include Exod. 12:1–11 and Heb. 10:11–25, to which should be added the

*Reproaches (Lat. *Improperia*), sung during the Veneration of the Cross, and the *Seven Words of the Savior on the Cross. Meditation on the passion down the centuries frequently erupted into violent *anti-Semitism, and it was not until some years after World War II that notorious Good Friday prayers for the "faithless Jews" (Lat. *perfidis judaeis*), "Jews, Turks, and Infidels and Heretics" or the like, were modified. By contrast the themes of Wagner's "Good Friday Music" from act 3 of *Parsifal* (1882) are suffering, compassion, and redemption.

Good Samaritan. The usual title given to the parable of the man who fell among thieves on his way from Jerusalem to Jericho and was eventually rescued by a passing *Samaritan. In its original context (Luke 10) it is given by Jesus as an answer to the question "Who is my neighbor?" and focuses both on the self-righteousness of the two "neighbors" who "passed by on the other side," and on the breaking down of the traditional barrier between Jews and Samaritans (John 4:9). Early writers, including *Origen, *Augustine, and *Bede, interpreted the parable as an *allegory in which Christ is the Samaritan who delivers Adam (humankind) from evil, admits him into the inn (the church) and will come again (*Parousia). By contrast, in some early artistic representations, including a fresco in Sant'Angelo in Formis (near Capua), Christ is the victim and the Samaritan is an angel. From the 16th century there are a number of paintings of the subject including those of Jacopo Bassano, *Rembrandt, *Delacroix, and Van Gogh. In modern parlance "Samaritan" has come to be synonymous with giving a helping hand, not least in the telephone counseling service of that name founded by Chad Varah in 1953.

Gospel.   The Old English translation of Lat. *evangelium* (Gk. *euangelion*), "good news." The Greek term is used of the *preaching of Christ (Mark 1:14–15), and then later applied to the telling of the story of his life, death, and resurrection, probably first orally and then in written accounts. Of these the Gospels attributed to Matthew, Mark, Luke, and John were by the end of the 2nd century understood to be unique and accepted as canonical. They constitute the most sacred part of Christian Scripture, equivalent to the Torah in Judaism. Variations in the accounts of the four Gospels, and between the three *Synoptics and the Fourth Gospel, have done little to undermine their authority. Two of the earliest illustrated mss of the Gospels are preserved in Corpus Christi College, Cambridge, and Rossano Cathedral, Calabria. There are a number of *apocryphal Gospels, which contain a wide variety of material not in the canonical four, some of it gnostic in origin. See *Evangelists; *Synoptic problem.

Gospel of Nicodemus.

An apocryphal work of the 5th or 6th century, comprising two separate texts. The first tells of Jesus' trial, death, and resurrection (see *Acts of Pilate), and the second describes his descent into the underworld (cf. Ps. 16:10; 1 Pet. 3:19). It had a major influence on medieval literature and iconography. See *Harrowing of Hell.

Gospel of Peter.

One of the earliest of the NT apocryphal texts, dating probably to the 2nd century C.E. and extant only in fragments. It recounts the Passion Narrative, for the most part keeping close to the canonical Gospels, but changes the cry of dereliction on the cross to "My power, O power, why have you forsaken me?" and tells how soldiers saw the risen Jesus actually coming out of the sepulcher, supported by two angels whose heads reached to heaven.

Gospel of Philip.

A 2nd- or 3rd-century Gnostic work discovered at *Nag Hammadi in the same Coptic codex as the *Gospel of Thomas. It contains no continuous narrative despite its title, but is a series of reflections on the way to salvation, the sacraments, especially marriage, and other topics. A reference to intimate relations between Jesus and Mary Magdalene is sometimes cited in connection with modern fiction such as Kazantzakis's *The Last Temptation of Christ* (ET 1960) and Dan Brown's *Da Vinci Code* (2003).

Gospel of Pseudo-Matthew.

An apocryphal text, composed probably in the 8th century. It tells the story of the *nativity, adding a number of details not in the canonical accounts of Matthew and Luke, such as the role of the ox and the ass who adore Jesus as devoutly as the shepherds and the wise men (cf. Isa. 1:3).

Gospel of Thomas.

An apocryphal work known from some 3rd-century Greek papyrus fragments and a 4th-century Coptic version found at *Nag Hammadi. It consists of 114 sayings of Jesus, some variants of those in the canonical Gospels, others quite different, clearly influenced by gnostic theology. Its significance as an independent source for his *ipsissima verba is doubtful.

Gottwald, Norman K.

(1926–). American Protestant scholar whose application of modern social-scientific theory to the study of the Bible, particularly in his magisterial work *The Tribes of Yahweh: A Sociology of the Religion of Liberated Israel* (1979), had a profound impact on all subsequent treatments of the history of Israel. The wider implications of his interest in *Marxist theory and *liberation theology have been developed in his own subsequent writings, in particular, *The Hebrew Bible: A Socio-Literary Introduction* (1985) and *The Hebrew Bible in Its Social World and in Ours* (1993), but also in the many responses to his work both in social history and in *postmodern literary theory, *ideological criticism, and *hermeneutics.

Grace. The concept of a gracious and merciful deity (Heb. *hanun we-rahum*, Pss. 111:4; 112:4; 145:8; Isa. 30:19; Joel 2:13; Jonah 4:2; cf. Exod. 34:6), who intervenes on behalf of those in need, not because they deserve it but just because he loves them (Deut. 7:7; 9:4–6), is present throughout the Bible. Although the term *charis*, "grace," is never used of God in the Greek OT, Paul uses it very frequently for the divine initiative revealed in Christ, without which human salvation is not possible (Rom. 3:21–25). The belief that divine grace is a "free gift" (Lat. *gratia*) from God, and cannot be earned or deserved, is fundamental to Pauline and much subsequent Christian theology (Rom. 5:15). The church owes its existence to the grace of God (2 Cor. 4:15), and the "Grace of the Lord Jesus Christ" became a central element in Christian social and liturgical discourse at an early stage.

The theological ramifications of this doctrine concerning free will, original sin, predestination, the significance of infant baptism, and the belief that without the means of grace supplied by the one true church there can be no salvation, led inevitably to bitter theological disputes, as between *Pelagius and *Augustine in the 5th century, the Reformers and the Anabaptists in the 16th, and between the church and the rest of the world in every age. The notion that "while we were yet sinners, Christ died for us" (Rom. 5:8), however, is central to the Christian gospel and has inspired humility and gratitude in many famous writings, including John Bunyan's autobiographical *Grace Abounding to the Chief of Sinners* (1666) and John Newton's hymn "Amazing Grace" (1764).

Grammar. Important differences between the grammatical systems of Semitic languages, in particular, Biblical Hebrew and Aramaic, and those of Indo-European languages have been much discussed in relation to the translation of the OT into Greek, Latin, and the other languages of Western Christendom. A functional overlap between the present and future tenses in the Hebrew verb system, for example, fundamentally affected Christian interpretations of such verses as Exod. 3:14, where the Greek has "I am the one who is," an impossible rendering of the Hebrew. Generalizations about "the Hebrew mind" based on such evidence, however, should be avoided. The absence of a neuter gender in Hebrew means that the "spirit of God" (*ruah elohim*) in the OT appears occasionally to be female (Gen. 1:2). In both Hebrew and Greek "wisdom" is feminine, and this may have been one factor in the choice of the Greek masculine *logos*, "word," as applied to Christ in John 1 (cf. Prov. 8:22–31; Sir. 24:8).

Greco, El (Domenikos Theotokopoulos, 1541–1614). Spanish painter. After some training in his native Crete, he traveled to Italy, where he came under the influence of *Titian, *Tintoretto, and *Michelangelo (who, according to El Greco, "didn't know how to paint"), and then, for unknown reasons, to Toledo in Spain, where he spent the rest of his life. His first work was a series of huge paintings for the Church of S. Domingo el Antiguo, in particular the *Assumption*, now in Chicago, and the *Trinity*, in the Prado, Madrid. Among his other works the *Crucifixion* and the *Resurrection* are also in the Prado, while the *Purification of the Temple* and *Christ's Agony in Gethsemane* are both in the National Gallery, London.

Greek. Classical Greek is the language in which the works of Homer, Plato, Aristotle, and the other authors of ancient Greece were written. After the victories of Alexander the Great, Hellenistic Greek or *Koine Greek became the dominant language of education, literature, and commerce from Spain to Persia until eventually superseded by Latin in the West and Syriac and Arabic in the East. It was the language of the Jews in Egypt, where the first Greek translation of the Bible was produced in the 3rd century B.C.E. (see *Septuagint), and the works of *Philo of Alexandria and *Josephus are in Greek, as are the NT and most of the *Apocrypha. The role of Greek language and thought in the early history of Christian doctrine, which was first formulated in Greek, cannot be overestimated, and the presence of numerous Greek *loanwords in Latin, Syriac, Coptic, etc., is an indication of its profound influence on subsequent Christian tradition. The history of Christian Bible translation and exegesis, including the Vulgate and the AV, is likewise dominated by the LXX, a crucial factor in twenty centuries of conflict between Christians and Jews on the meaning of many biblical texts.

Gregory of Nazianzus (329–89).

One of the three Cappadocian Fathers, known as "the Theologian." He studied with Basil in Athens, and, after some years as a monk, became a powerful preacher and eventually bishop of Constantinople during the council there in 381. He wrote a commentary on Ezekiel that is now lost, but his considerable exegetical skills are evident from the numerous readings of scriptural texts in his "Five Theological Orations." Familiar with both Origen and the rhetorical methods of Plato and Aristotle, he appreciated the value of close attention to grammar, syntax, and context, in a way that anticipates some modern literary criticism.

Gregory of Nyssa (c. 335–95). One of

the three Cappadocian Fathers and brother of Basil the Great. Trained in Greek philosophy, he championed

Nicene orthodoxy at the Council of Constantinople in 381, as well as in a number of theological treatises and his famous *Catechetical Orations*. His exegetical works, which include a life of Moses, a commentary on the *Hexaemeron*, and homilies on Psalms, Ecclesiastes, the Song of Songs, the Lord's Prayer, and the Beatitudes, are influenced by *Philo and *Origen, but also inspired by the Pauline belief in the role of the Holy Spirit in the interpretive process (1 Cor. 2:10; 2 Cor. 3:6).

Gregory the Great (c. 540–604).

Born in Rome, unanimously elected pope in 590, Gregory was an outstanding administrator, responsible for reorganizing public worship (including "Gregorian" chants), evangelizing England, and reforming the church's attitude to the Jews and slavery. Most of his writings are exegetical and include homilies on the Gospels and commentaries on Job, Ezekiel, Song of Songs, and 1 Kings. He popularized Origen's system of fourfold exegesis according to which the literal or historical sense was the foundation on which nonliteral senses were built (see *Quadriga). Largely as a result of the huge popularity of Gregory's writings, this method became universal throughout the Middle Ages.

Grotius, Hugo (1583–1645). Dutch

theologian and lawyer. Imprisoned for life in 1619 for supporting the Arminian heresy, he escaped to Paris two years later. Arguably the founder both of international law and of modern Christian *apologetics, he published works on the laws of *peace and war (1624) and *The Truth of the Christian Religion* (1627), the latter translated into many languages, including Arabic, Persian, and Chinese. His *Annotations* on the Bible (1641–46) combine a passion for philology with a simple faith in Scripture and a commitment to the ethical purpose of *exegesis, and contain a wealth of material from the classical writers and Jewish literature, as well as the church fathers. His tragedy *Adamus Exsul* (1601) was known to *Milton.

Gunkel, Hermann (1862–1932).

German Protestant biblical scholar. He studied at Göttingen and was professor at Berlin (1894–1907), Giessen (1907–20), and Halle (1920–27). His contributions to the study of the Bible were pioneering and wide-ranging. In *Genesis* (ET 1997) he introduced a new critical methodology into the study and use both of Babylonian parallels and of folklore and oral tradition, while in *Psalms* (ET 1998) his *form-critical approach (*Gattungsgeschichte*), with its concern for the original situational context (*Sitz im Leben*) of each psalm, brought a new precision into the field. He also wrote on the "Religio-historical Interpretation of the NT" (1903). A giant in the world of *historical criticism, he nonetheless, unlike many of those before him and those that followed, always retained a keen interest in the religious meaning of the text.

Gutiérrez, Gustavo (1928–). Peru-

vian priest, professor of theology in the Catholic University in Lima, and one of the founders of *liberation theology. His interpretations of Scripture, informed by careful biblical scholarship, the conviction that the Bible is intended to address the current situation, and an avowed bias in favor of victims of social injustice, are often original as well as challenging. His writings, especially *A Theology of Liberation* (ET 1973), *The Power of the Poor in History* (ET 1983), and *On Job: God-Talk and the Suffering of the Innocent* (1987), have been hugely influential.

Habakkuk (Gk. *Ambakoum*). One of

the twelve Minor Prophets who lived apparently shortly before Judah was invaded by the Babylonians ("Chaldeans," 1:6). He interprets this imminent national disaster as divine punishment on the wicked, but concludes with a hymn of thanksgiving, celebrating the cosmic might of YHWH and the salvation of his people (chap. 3). An early Hebrew commentary (*pesher) turned up among the *Dead Sea Scrolls, in which the Chaldeans are interpreted as the Kittim, that is, the Romans.

He is remembered especially for his statement "The just shall live by his faith" (2:4), cited twice by Paul (Rom. 1:17; Gal. 3:11) and in the Talmud as the basis of the whole Torah (*b. Makkot* 24a). In Christian art he is noted for a reference to the ox and the ass in the Greek version of 3:2 ("between two animals"), and for his miraculous, though apocryphal, mercy dash to Daniel in the lion's den (Dan. 14:33). There is a terra-cotta statue of *Habakkuk and the Angel* (1655) by Gianlorenzo Bernini in the Vatican. There are important christological commentaries by *Cyril of Alexandria, *Augustine, and *Jerome, as well as those of *Luther and *Calvin that oppose them.

Haftarah. The reading from the

Prophets that follows the reading from the Torah in synagogue worship. The practice may go back to ancient times (Acts 13:15), though the Jewish lectionaries in use today cannot be dated much before the early Middle Ages. Isaiah accounts for about a quarter of them, including the seven "Consolation" readings taken from chaps. 40–63 that are prescribed to be read on the seven Sabbaths following the Fast of the Ninth of Ab. It has been observed that passages containing language and images with strong Christian associations have been deliberately avoided (e.g., Isa. 7:14; 42:1–4; 53; 61:1–4). The reading from the Isaiah scroll (61:1–2) that Jesus preaches on in a Nazareth synagogue (Luke 4:16–30) is not in any extant Jewish *lectionary.

Hagar. Abraham's Egyptian concu-

bine and mother of his first son, Ishmael. When Isaac was born, a jealous Sarah made Abraham send Hagar into the wilderness, where an angel protected her and promised her that her son would become the father of a great nation (Gen. 16). Hagarites or Hagarenes are mentioned elsewhere (1 Chr. 5; Ps. 83:6). She is usually depicted as a foreign slave, an Egyptian according to some, contrasted with Abraham's true wife, and in Christian tradition thus symbolizes old versus new (Gal. 4), earthly versus heavenly (*Augustine), spiritual versus carnal (*Thomas Aquinas). In Muslim tradition, by contrast, she is mother of Abraham's preferred son, and her miraculous survival in the desert is ritually reenacted every year at the Hajj in Mecca. Arabic *muhajirun*, "refugees" (Qur'an 9:118), especially those who emigrated with Muhammad from Mecca to Medina in 622 C.E. (cf. Hijrah; Lat. *Hegira*), and medieval Gk. *agarenoi*, "saracens," may be related. Among many paintings of Hagar's story are those of *Rubens, *Tiepolo, *Poussin, and *Claude Lorraine, while modern writers, including William *Blake, are also sympathetic.

Haggadah. See   *Aggadah   or *Passover Haggadah.

Haggai. One of the twelve Minor Prophets associated, along with Zechariah and Malachi, with the rebuilding of the temple under Darius the Great in 521–515 B.C.E. (Ezra 5:1; 6:14). The short book comprises several speeches designed to inspire the builders to complete their work, including the prediction that the "treasures of all nations" will come to Jerusalem and the glory of the Second Temple will be greater than that of the First (2:7–9). The book ends with a messianic prophecy addressed to Zerubbabel (2:20–23), which makes Haggai a suitable authority for the author of Hebrews to quote (12:25–29), while the coming of "the desire of all nations" (Hag. 2:7 AV) is applied by many Christian writers to the coming of Christ. There is

also the account of a discussion between Haggai and the priests on ritual contamination (2:10–19), which led the rabbis to see him as a legal authority as well as a prophet, and therefore a bridge between the age of prophecy, which ceased with these three prophets, and the age of rabbinic Judaism.

Hagiographa.   See *Ketuvim.

Hail Mary.   See *Ave Maria.

Halakhah (Heb. "procedure, law"). One of the two chief categories of rabbinic literature, concerned with law and practice as opposed to *aggadah, which is concerned with theology and belief. The only halakhic *midrashim are the commentaries on Exodus (*Mekhilta*), Leviticus (*Sifra*), Numbers (*Sifra*), and Deuteronomy (*Sifre*); the rest are aggadic. Halakhah is to be found mainly in the *Mishnah and *Talmud, supplemented by the medieval commentaries and codes, and by the decisions of rabbis and rabbinic courts down to the present. Typical examples would be halakhic definitions of "work" in the Sabbath commandment (Exod. 23:12) and detailed interpretations of the law never to eat milk and meat at the same meal (23:19). It has now come to be equated with Jewish law, and decisions on halakhah, its sources and methods of interpretation, its relevance to the 21st century, its application to women, and its role in modern science, medical ethics. and the like, determine the course of Judaism in all its varieties.

Hallel (Heb. "Praise!"). The joyful singing of Pss. 113–118 on the three major Jewish festivals, *Passover, *Pentecost, and *Tabernacles. Hallel is also recited at *Hanukkah but not at *Purim. Four of the six "Hallel Psalms" begin or end with the words *hallelu yah* ("Praise the LORD!") and all six contain frequently cited verses including "Not unto us, O LORD . . ." (115:1 AV), "Precious in the sight of the LORD . . ." (116:15), "the stone which the builders rejected . . ." (118:22), and "Blessed is he that cometh . . ." (118:26). At Passover they are sung at the end of the Seder in the home, and it is probable that the reference to the disciples "singing hymns" after the *Last Supper (Matt. 26:30; Mark 14:26) refers to the Hallel Psalms. See *Alleluia.

Ham.   Youngest of Noah's three sons. Noah's curse on Ham's descendants, especially the blacks, has been quoted as scriptural authority for *slavery (Gen. 9:20–27). See *Semitic Languages; Shem.

Handel, George Frederick (1685–1759).   German-English composer. Studied music and played organ, violin, and harpsichord, first in Halle where he was born, then in Hamburg. After traveling in Italy, he was appointed Kapellmeister to the elector of Hanover in 1709, but soon after left for England, where he lived till his death. In addition to his *Roman Vespers* (1707), a *Te Deum and a Jubilate to celebrate the peace of Utrecht (1713), and a number of *anthems, most of his many oratorios are on biblical themes. They include treatments of biblical characters—Esther, Deborah, Saul, Samson, Joseph and his brothers, Belshazzar, Joshua, Judas Maccabeus, Susanna, Solomon, and Jephthah, as well as *La Resurrezione* (1733), *Israel in Egypt* (1739), and *Messiah* (1742). These often throw light on the 18th-century English political and theological scene as in the case of Charles Jennens's libretto for *Messiah*, in which he makes use of numerous, often unexpected texts from the OT to prove the truth of the Gospel as the fulfillment of prophecy against rationalist opponents of Christian orthodoxy.

Hannah.   Mother of the prophet Samuel (1 Sam. 1–2). At first unable to

have a child, she prayed to the Lord, vowing to dedicate her son to the temple at Shiloh. Her prayer was answered and Samuel joined Eli the priest at Shiloh. Hannah's Song of Thanksgiving was the inspiration for the *Magnificat (Luke 1:46–55), and considered by the rabbis to be the model prayer (*b. Berakhot* 3a–b). The story of Hannah is the *Haftarah for Rosh Hashanah.

Hanukkah.   The minor Jewish festival celebrated on 25th Kislev to commemorate the victories of Judas Maccabeus and the rededication (Heb. *hanukkah*) of the temple after its desecration by the forces of Antiochus, king of Syria (168–163 B.C.E.). The story is told in 1 and 2 Maccabees and the festival referred to in John 10:22. The legend of the miraculous jar of oil that survived the destruction and fueled the temple lamp (Heb. *menorah*) for eight days with only enough oil for one, is told in the Talmud (*b. Shabbat* 21b), and remembered in the use of a special eight-branched candelabrum known as a *hanukkiyah* throughout the eight days of the festival, which is also known as the Feast of Lights. Eight daily readings are taken from Num. 7–8:4.

Harmonizing.   The process whereby divergent traditions, for example, between one Gospel and another, are explained or removed to produce a unified literary whole. An early example is Tatian's *Diatessaron*, and there are medieval Gospel harmonies, some of which are dependent on Tatian, as well as modern ones, including Dorothy L. Sayers's *The Man Born to Be King* (1943), and the film *King of Kings* (1961). Others, starting with *Irenaeus (2nd century C.E.), argued that fourfoldness was as necessary a part of the Gospel tradition as the four corners of the earth.

Harrowing of hell.   A popular English term for the descent of Christ into hell during which he breaks open the doors of hell, routs Satan and his evil spirits, and leads the righteous, beginning with Adam, to paradise. It was inspired by a passage in the apocryphal *Gospel of Nicodemus*, which was popular in the Middle Ages, but draws also on a verse from the Psalms, "Thou shalt not leave my soul in hell" (Ps. 16:10 AV), quoted in Acts 2:27, and 1 Pet. 3:19, as well as other passages (Ps. 68:17–18; Isa. 24:21–22; John 5:25; Eph. 4:8–10), and the *creed ("he descended into hell"). In Eastern Orthodox iconography it is an integral part of the resurrection (Gk. *anastasis*), and a very familiar scene in church frescoes throughout Greece and Eastern Europe. In the West it is dramatically portrayed in representations of the resurrection or the last judgment by *Donatello, *Bellini, *Dürer, *Cranach, *Tintoretto, and others, and in some of the medieval English *mystery plays. In literature it figures prominently in the 14th-century poem *Piers Plowman*, but rarely after the Reformation, a modern exception being Charles Williams's allegorical novel *Descent into Hell* (1937).

Hasidism.   A radical religious movement founded in Poland by Israel ben Eliezer (c. 1700–1760), known as *Baal Shem Tov*, "Master of the Divine Name" (or the *Besht*). He was not a rabbi himself and met with fierce opposition from Orthodoxy, led especially by Elijah, Gaon of Vilna (1720–97), but among his followers were powerful religious personalities (rebbes) who founded dynasties like the Satmarers, the Bratslavers, and, best-known today outside New York and Israel, the Lubavitchers. The name is derived from the biblical word *hasid* "godly, faithful, kind" (Pss. 32:6; 149:5), also used of God (Ps. 145:17). A group of "Hasideans" is mentioned in connection with the Maccabean revolt in the 2nd century B.C.E. (1 Macc. 2:42–48), and in the Middle Ages a unique group of Jewish ascetics was known as the *haside ashkenaz*, "saints of Germany,"

whose mystical prayer, known as the "Hymn of Glory," found its way into the Jewish Daily Prayerbook.

Dissatisfied with the existing institutions and strongly influenced by 16th-century Lurianic *mysticism, the Hasidim encouraged ordinary people to engage in zealous private prayer and to reflect on the cosmic significance of every action: "the upper world moves in response to the lower world" (*Zohar 1:164a). The homilies, teachings, and anecdotes of the Hasidic masters, encompassing a wide variety of diverse beliefs and practices, were at first transmitted by word of mouth, but eventually collected in several thousand volumes. The Hasidic literature contains homiletical, often mystical comments on the Bible on every page, whose contemporary interest and lasting value have been appreciated by many modern writers, notably *Buber (*Tales of the Hasidim*, 2 vols., ET 1947–48) and *Heschel (*A Passion for Truth*, 1973).

Haskalah   (Heb. "Enlightenment"). The Jewish movement originating in 18th-century Germany with the aim of encouraging and enabling Jews to take their place in Western society by opening their minds to secular learning. Key developments in the movement were Moses *Mendelssohn's translation of the Hebrew Bible into German, with a modern commentary, and the emergence of Reform Judaism and Neo-Orthodoxy. See *Enlightenment.

Haydn, Franz Joseph (1732–1809). Austrian composer. Born in Vienna he was Kapellmeister at the court of Count Eszterhazy in Hungary (1761–90), where he composed most of his 104 symphonies, almost 80 string quartets, and 14 masses, including a *Rorate* Mass (Isa. 45:8 Vg). His cantatas and oratorios include a *Stabat Mater* (1767), *The Return of Tobias* (1777), and *The Seven Last Words* (1796). Haydn's enchanting oratorio *Creation* (1798) is based on a poetic rendering of verses from Genesis and Milton's *Paradise Lost*. The introduction representing chaos, the chorus "The heavens are telling" (Ps. 19), and Adam and Eve's duet "Graceful consort" near the end are examples of Haydn's skill as a biblical exegete.

Hebrew. The language in which most of the Hebrew Bible (OT) was originally written. Hebrew is a *Semitic language, related to *Aramaic, Arabic, Ethiopic, Egyptian, Coptic, and other members of the Afro-Asiatic language group, with which it shares many characteristics that distinguish it from *Greek, *Latin, and other Indo-European languages. It is written from right to left in an *alphabetical script. It was the chief spoken language of ancient Israel and Judah until the Babylonian exile by which time it had been superseded by *Aramaic, although in religious contexts it has continued to be used by the Jews, who refer to it as "the sacred language," until the present day. As well as the Hebrew Bible and a relatively small number of inscriptions from ancient Israel such as the Gezer calendar (9th century B.C.E.), the Siloam inscription (8th century B.C.E.) and the Lachish ostraca (6th century B.C.E.), the *Dead Sea Scrolls and much of the rabbinic literature (including the *Mishnah and the *Midrash) are in Hebrew. Medieval Jewish commentators on the Hebrew Bible like *Rashi, *Ibn Ezra, and *Kimhi also wrote in Hebrew, thereby sometimes avoiding errors caused by the difficulties of *translation into a non-Semitic language. The revival of Hebrew among leading European Jews in the 18th century and its adoption as the official language of the State of Israel in the 20th have had interesting implications for the *semantics of Biblical Hebrew.

Hebrews, Letter to the. Cited by *Clement of Rome (1st century) and first ascribed to Paul by *Clement of Alexandria (2nd century), this letter is consid-ered by many (including Luther), for stylistic and theological reasons, to have been written by Apollos of Alexandria (Acts 18:24), perhaps to the Corinthians. Consisting in the main of exegetical discussion of Hebrew Scripture, the letter seeks to demonstrate the superiority of Christianity to all other varieties of Judaism: Christ is more than an angel, the new covenant supersedes the old, Christ's atoning sacrifice is once and for all, while sacrifice at the temple has to be repeated annually. The mysterious figure of *Melchizedek, not elsewhere mentioned in the NT but important in subsequent Christian tradition, is given a significant christological role in Hebrews. Notable commentaries on Hebrews were written by John *Chrysostom, *Theodore of Mopsuestia, *Luther, *Calvin, and the "Christian socialist" F. D. Maurice (1853).

Heidegger, Martin (1889–1976). German philosopher. After studying Catholic theology at Freiburg, he switched to the philosophy faculty, studying the phenomenology of Edmund Husserl. Heidegger's reformulation of metaphysics focused on the human experience of existing. He became professor of philosophy first at Marburg (1923–28) and then at Freiburg, where he openly declared his support for Hitler (1928–45). Influenced by *Augustine, *Luther, and *Kierkegaard, Heidegger's famous notion of "the hermeneutical circle" emphasizes the prior understanding of the subject that shapes the inquiry, because "we always construct our activities in an understanding of Being." Although he did not himself like the label "existentialist," his influence on Sartre, *Gadamer, *Ricoeur, *Bultmann, and others has been profound, despite the very difficult and obscure style of his major work *Being and Time* (1927; ET 1962). Heidegger's later writings focused on poetic experience and thought, which initiated a shift in biblical *hermeneutics toward such poetic speech as Jesus' parables.

Hellenism. The influence of *Greek language and culture especially in Asia Minor, Syria, and Egypt, from the time of Alexander the Great (356–323 B.C.E.) to the 1st century C.E. Hellenistic cities like *Antioch and *Alexandria became powerful centers of commerce and culture often at the expense of indigenous cultures, although some Eastern cultures including Judaism survived in Greek-speaking forms. The Jews of Egypt knew little Hebrew or Aramaic by the end of the 2nd century C.E. as the prologue to Sirach illustrates, and the Hebrew Scriptures were translated into Greek (*Septuagint), while other notable Jewish literary works were written in Greek, including the *Wisdom of Solomon, the works of *Philo, *Josephus, and the NT. The effect of translating Hebrew, a Semitic language, into Greek, an Indo-European language, was significant, if at times overstated by modern scholars, and ultimately contributed to the schism between the Jews for whom Hebrew remained the "sacred language," and the Christians who made a point of translating their sacred texts into other languages. See also *Koine *Greek.

Henry, Matthew (1662–1714). Presbyterian minister at Chester in the north of England, and author of the very popular *Exposition of the Old and New Testaments* (1708–10), an elegant and convenient compendium of influential Christian exegetical tradition, still in print as *Matthew Henry's Commentary on the Whole Bible*.

Herbert, George (1593–1633). Poet, orator, and musician. He was ordained at the age of 37 and spent the last few years of his short life as parish priest near Salisbury. His poems, which are all devotional, were published posthumously in a collection entitled *The Temple* (1633) and had a widespread influence on later poets. His handling of biblical language and imagery is subtle and profound as in his interpretation of Ps. 23 in the popular hymn beginning "The God of love my shepherd is."

Herder, Johann Gottfried (1744–1803). German critic and preacher. He was a prolific writer whose works include *The Spirit of Hebrew Poetry* (1782–83; ET 1933), a commentary on Revelation, important and influential writings on Genesis, the Song of Songs, and the NT, and his most famous *Reflections on the Philosophy of the History of Mankind* (1784–91; ET 1880). A student of Kant and admirer of *Spinoza, Herder rejected mystical and allegorical interpretations of the Bible, seeking to understand it as *poetry ("among the Hebrews history itself is properly poetry"), but against the rationalists he believed in the power of the Bible to speak God's word to the human condition.

Hermas. "*Apostolic Father" and author of an early Christian work entitled *The Shepherd*. Similar in some respects to *Dante's *Divina Commedia*, this contains the teaching of a freed slave who had been guilty of false dealing, rejected by his family, and who now, having repented, experiences heavenly visions and divine forgiveness. Twelve *Mandates* ("Believe that God is one. . . . Fear God and keep his commandments . . .") are preceded by five visions in which Hermas is guided first by a woman he loves, now dead, and then by the "angel of repentance" in the garb of a shepherd. The work concludes with ten *Similitudes* or *Parables* ("an elm and a vine . . . a willow tree . . . a tower"), each interpreted by the angel. The author was identified by *Origen as the Hermas greeted by Paul in his Letter to the Romans (16:14), but he probably lived early in the 2nd century. The work was cited as scriptural by some (*Irenaeus, *Clement of Alexandria, *Origen) until the 4th century and continued to be much quoted until the Middle Ages.

Hermeneutics. The theory of interpretation (Gk. *hermeneuo*, "interpret"). The problem of understanding texts written centuries ago, often in another language, was appreciated in ancient times, and Hellenistic scholarship, followed by the rabbis and church fathers, developed methods and rules of interpretation. Hermeneutics as a modern science began with *Schleiermacher (1768–1834) and was developed by *Dilthey (1833–1911) and, in particular, *Heidegger (1889–1976), whose existentialist thinking, especially on the role of presuppositions in the reading and understanding process, influenced many, notably *Gadamer, *Ricoeur, and *Bultmann. Others like *Barth considered these developments to be an illegitimate and dangerous misuse of the text. *Demythologization, *reader-response criticism, the plurality of meaning, the ethics of reading, and even *biblical theology are key issues in modern hermeneutics.

Heschel, Abraham Joshua (1907–72). Born in Warsaw, the son of a *Hasidic rebbe, he studied at the liberal Jewish seminary in Berlin until forced to leave Nazi Europe first for London, then the United States, where he was professor of Jewish ethics and mysticism at the conservative Jewish Theological Seminary, New York, from 1945 until his death. His writings, the best-known and most influential of which are *God in Search of Man: A Philosophy of Judaism* (1955) and *The Prophets* (1962), combine modern philosophical concepts with traditional Hasidic *mysticism. His most original contribution to biblical studies was his description of the divine pathos, shared by the prophets in their passion for social justice. Heschel was active in the civil rights movement and the Vietnam War protests, in addition to serving as a Jewish representative at the Second Vatican Council.

Hexaemeron. A Greek term referring to the "Six Days" of the creation story in Gen. 1, and used as the title of several patristic commentaries on the passage, notably those of *Ambrose, *Basil, and *Gregory of Nyssa.

Hexapla. *Origen's most important work of biblical scholarship, in which he demonstrated the need to establish the correct text of Scripture, in Hebrew and in Greek, as a prerequisite for good biblical *exegesis. It contained the Hebrew text itself, a Greek transliteration of the Hebrew, and four Greek versions, those of *Aquila, *Symmachus, *Septuagint, and *Theodotion, in six parallel columns. The fifth column, containing the LXX, complete with a system of signs indicating differences between the Hebrew and Greek texts, was considered the most valuable by Christian scholars and frequently printed on its own. A *Syriac version of the Greek text of the Hexapla, known as the Syro-Hexaplar, was made in the 7th century. The original, a work that would have filled 40 codices, probably never copied in its entirety, survives only in fragments.

Hexateuch. The first six books of the Bible, the *Pentateuch plus *Joshua, considered by *Wellhausen and others, notably von *Rad, for structural and stylistic reasons to be a single literary unit.

Hezekiah. King of Judah (715–687 B.C.E.). During his reign the northern kingdom was destroyed by the Assyrians, but Jerusalem, alone of all the cities of Judah, survived (2 Kgs. 18–20). The role of Isaiah in his reign, the miraculous defeat of *Sennacherib, his illness, and the Babylonian embassy to Jerusalem are also recounted with variations in the book of Isaiah (36–39; cf. 2 Chr. 29–32). Modern scholars, citing Sennacherib's own account and a reference in 2 Kgs. 18:13–16, to Hezekiah giving the Assyrians gold and silver treasures from the temple, offer a different explanation for

Sennacherib's decision to leave Jerusalem alone in 701. But he is remembered as a good king who destroyed the bronze serpent and reformed Judean religion, as well as providing Jerusalem with a new supply of water (known today as Hezekiah's tunnel; 2 Kgs. 20:20). Rabbinic sources suggest that the *Immanuel prophecy (Isa. 7:14) refers to him, despite chronological difficulties, and attribute to him not only parts of Proverbs (cf. Prov. 25:1) but also Isaiah, Ecclesiastes, and the Song of Songs. In Christian tradition Hezekiah's prayer on recovery from sickness (Isa. 38) is included among the *Canticles, and he also figures among the ancestors of Christ (Matt. 1:9) on the ceiling of the *Sistine Chapel.

Hicks, Edward (1780–1849). Quaker preacher-artist best known for his pictorial interpretations of "The Peaceable Kingdom" (Isa. 11:1–9) of which he painted nearly 100 versions highlighting different motifs, such as the branch, the little child, the great lion, peace, and liberty. In several he depicts, in the background, the signing of the 1681 peace treaty between the Native Americans and William Penn.

Hieroglyphics. Literally "sacred marks," commonly applied to the writing system of ancient Egypt. Most of the signs are stylized pictures of birds, animals, parts of the body, and the like, but they stand for letters and syllables so that their meaning may or may not have anything to do with what they represent visually. Thus a duck is the sign for the word for "son" (Egyp. *sa*). But the system can be used to good effect in art. The word for "truth, justice," for example, is written as a feather (*ma'at*) and can be weighed against the heart (*yeb*) on the scales of justice in the afterlife (cf. Prov. 21:2), and worn on the headdress of the goddess Ma'at, who holds in one hand "long life" (*ankh*) and in the other a scepter symbolizing wealth and dignity

(*was*) (cf. Prov. 3:16). The decipherment of the Egyptian hieroglyphic writing system, thanks to the discovery in 1799 of the Rosetta Stone, on which an inscription dated 196 B.C.E. is written in Egyptian and Greek, was published by the young French scholar Champollion in 1824.

Higher criticism. See *Historical criticism.

Hilary of Poitiers (c. 312–67). French bishop and most respected Latin theologian of his age. He wrote a treatise on the *Trinity against the Arians that earned him the title "*Athanasius of the West," and commentaries on the Psalms and Matthew that show the influence of *Origen.

Hillel. Greatest Jewish teacher in Palestine in the 1st century B.C.E., listed with *Shammai in the *Sayings of the Fathers* as the last of the "pairs" before rabbinic authority passed to his descendants, who included Rabban Gamaliel (*m. Abot* 1:12–15). To Hillel is attributed a set of seven exegetical rules or "principles" (*middot*) by which the Torah is expounded. The school of Hillel was considered more liberal and lenient in its interpretation of the law than the school of Shammai, and Hillel himself is remembered chiefly for his version of the Golden Rule: "What is hateful to you, do not do to your fellow human being" (*b. Shabbat* 31a).

Historical criticism. Although not without precursors in ancient and medieval times, the historical-critical method, involving *archaeology and the study of recently deciphered ancient Near Eastern texts, took center stage in the study of the Bible at the time of the European *Enlightenment. For three centuries biblical scholarship was dominated by historical questions concerning date, sources, authorship, and ancient origins to the point where a commentary on Genesis might well contain more information on ancient Canaan, Babylonia, and Egypt than on the meaning of the biblical stories themselves. Historical criticism challenged naive credulity about biblical narratives and brought the study of the Bible into the modern world; but at the same time, by dismissing as "late" or uncritical the centuries of traditional biblical interpretation in literature, art, music, and the like, it drove a wedge between the Bible and its use in the discourse of religious believers. Current "postcritical" approaches, while acknowledging the value of historical criticism, challenge the assumption that the original meaning of the text is necessarily the primary goal of biblical scholarship, and seek to analyze the final form of the text, and the history of its impact on generations of readers (*Wirkungsgeschichte). See *Literary criticism.

Hittites. An Indo-European people who ruled over much of what is now modern Turkey c. 1650–1200 B.C.E. and at their strongest conquered Aleppo in Syria and fought an inconclusive battle with the Egyptians in 1300 B.C.E. There are probably some Hittite *loanwords in Hebrew (e.g., qova, "helmet"), and Hittite documents reveal parallels with the biblical literature, including a prayer beginning "Let the mountains be leveled before you" (cf. Isa. 40:3–4). But the term "Hittite" applied to the people who sold land to Abraham (Gen. 23) and the ill-fated Uriah (2 Sam. 11–12) most probably refers to one of many ethnic groups living in pre-Israelite Canaan about which nothing is known (cf. Gen. 15:19–21).

Hobbes, Thomas (1588–1679). English political philosopher. His writings, including his best-known work *Leviathan* (1651), show him to have been a thoughtful and critical biblical exegete. He used anachronisms (e.g., Gen. 12:6)

to disprove the Mosaic authorship of the Pentateuch and considered the book of Job more a treatise on wealth and wickedness than history. He developed a powerful sociopolitical interpretation of the "kingdom of God" in the Bible.

Holistic interpretation. A modern approach to reading the Bible that focuses on complete literary units, such as the *Pentateuch or the book of *Isaiah, rather than seeking to identify separate "forms" or "sources," each with its own separate history. It is thus similar to *redaction criticism but more akin to normal *literary criticism in its interest in plot, character, meaning, *reader response, and the like. In biblical studies, where the whole unit is believed by readers to be canonical or sacred, the method has particular significance and is an integral part of other approaches including *ideological criticism and *reception history.

Holocaust. Originally a technical term for a type of sacrifice in which the victim was totally burned (Gk. *holokaustos*), now applied to the devastation caused by a nuclear explosion and, especially, by the Nazi killing of six million Jews during World War II. Responses to the Nazi Holocaust (also known as "Auschwitz" from its most infamous site or the "Shoah" from a Hebrew word for "devastation") range from attempts to find biblical explanations or comfort in the binding of Isaac, the Suffering Servant, the book of Job, and the notion of God hiding his face (Isa. 45:15) (Eliezer Berkovits), to the notion of a complete rupture in history that makes the reading of the biblical accounts of God's mighty acts no longer possible (Richard L. Rubenstein, Emil Fackenheim). Jewish writers who have attempted to read the Bible in new ways after the Holocaust include the novelists Eli *Wiesel and Primo Levi, and the poets Amir Gilboa and Yehuda Amichai. In art *Chagall and others have transformed the Christian symbol of the crucifixion to represent Jewish suffering, while some Christian writers have suggested ways of interpreting the Bible, especially the *Passion Narratives, both to give new emphasis to the Jewishness of Jesus and to acknowledge Christian guilt in the centuries of anti-Judaism that culminated in the Holocaust.

Holy Week. The week preceding Easter marked, since the 4th century at the latest, by devotion to the *passion of Christ. Beginning with *Palm Sunday, the reenactment of the final events of the gospel narrative progressed through *Maundy Thursday, *Good Friday, and Holy Saturday to *Easter Sunday, and sometimes include liturgical drama as well as special prayers and readings such as Lamentations and the *Servant Songs from Isa. 42–53. In some traditions all paintings and crucifixes are covered.

Homilies. Homilies and sermons are part of the history of biblical interpretation and, alongside commentaries, important collections have been made from the patristic period to the present day. Of these the homilies of John *Chrysostom and *Augustine are of particular interest, as are the 86 mystical sermons of *Bernard of Clairvaux on the Song of Songs and John *Wycliffe's biblical expositions on the eve of the Reformation. Thanks to the invention of *printing, a vast number of sermons by *Luther and *Calvin were published in the 16th century as were the Church of England's two *Books of Homilies* (1547, 1563), which were for use in the absence of a priest or curate or as models for inexperienced preachers. Many of John Wesley's 40,000 sermons were published in the 18th century, and those of the Baptist Charles *Spurgeon and Cardinal John Henry Newman in the 19th. Influential 20th-century collections include those of *Barth and *Bultmann. Examples of the lasting impact of a single sermon are Jonathan *Edwards's *Sinners in the*

Hands of an Angry God (1741) and Martin Luther *King Jr.'s *I Have a Dream* (1963). See also *Preaching.

Homosexuality. See *Gay and lesbian interpretation.

Hopkins, Gerald Manley (1844–89). English Jesuit priest and poet. His poems, which are characterized by what he termed "sprung rhythm," an idiosyncratic use of language, and intense feeling, were not published until 1918, but had a profound impact on 20th-century poetry. In all his writings, including his most famous *The Wreck of the Deutschland* (1876) and *The Windhover: To Christ Our Lord* (1918), his frequent allusions to the Bible are often subtle and memorable.

Hosanna (Heb. *hosha'na*, "save!"; Gk. *hosanna*). Popular liturgical formula in both Jewish and Christian tradition derived from Ps. 118:25. In Jewish tradition *Hoshana Rabbah*, "the Great Hosanna," is the seventh day of the Feast of *Tabernacles marked by a procession carrying branches of palm, willow, and myrtle (Lev. 23:40; later known as the *lulab*), and singing Hoshana hymns. In Christian tradition "Hosanna to God in the highest" (Lat. *Hosanna in excelsis Deo*) and the palm branches, together with the *Benedictus (Ps. 118:26), are associated with Christ's entry into Jerusalem (Mark 11:9–10), celebrated on Palm Sunday (or "Hosanna Sunday") since the *Didache (10:6). In the *Mass the *Hosanna* and *Benedictus* are sung immediately after the *Sanctus. The palm branch, already a symbol of victory on Roman triumphal arches, became popular in Christian art, where it is carried by the martyrs in heaven (Rev. 7:9).

Hosea, book of. The first and longest of the twelve Minor Prophets. The prophet, apparently a contemporary of Amos, although neither refers to the other, addresses the people of Israel in the years leading up to the fall of Samaria in 721 B.C.E. The book begins with the story of his marriage to the unfaithful Gomer, or perhaps the vision of such a marriage as some have suggested, which he interprets as a parable of God's relationship with Israel (chaps. 1–3). The rest of the book consists of variations on the theme of Israel's apostasy despite God's enduring love for his people, and, unique among the 8th-century prophets, makes frequent use of Israelite tradition, including allusions to Adam, Jacob, the exodus, the Decalogue, and especially the years in the wilderness.

Hosea figures prominently in the NT, notably in Matthew (2:15; 9:13; 12:7), Paul (Rom. 9:25–26; 1 Cor. 15:15) and Revelation (6:16), and important Christian commentaries were written by *Jerome, *Theodore of Mopsuestia, *Andrew of St. Victor, and Albertus Magnus. A painting by Duccio di Buoninsegna (1311) shows Hosea carrying a scroll with the words "Out of Egypt have I called my son" (11:1), quoted by Matthew (2:15). From *Luther and *Calvin on, literary, historical, and philological issues became increasingly important for scholars, while recent commentators question the morality of the images of physical violence administered by a husband to his wife in Hosea. In Jewish tradition the beautiful final chapter, beginning "Return, O Israel," is the *haftarah for the Sabbath preceding *Yom Kippur, and the first Jewish settlement in Palestine, Petah Tikvah ("door of hope"), got its name from Hos. 2:15.

Hugh of St. Victor (1096–1141). First of the Victorine theologians at the Augustinian house in Paris (see *Andrew of St. Victor). His many writings, informed by contact with French Jewish scholarship and a revival of interest in Aristotelian philosophy, include the *Didaskalicon: De Studio Legendi* and works on Genesis, Judges, Psalms, Ecclesiastes, Lamentations, the Gospels, and

Paul. Although advocating a literal-historical approach as the first step in reading Scripture, he placed more emphasis on the search for a spiritual meaning, applicable to a life of pious devotion and meditation.

Huldah. A woman prophet like *Miriam and *Deborah. When consulted about the meaning of the book of the law discovered in the temple, she prophesied that the Lord would bring evil upon Jerusalem, but that the young king Josiah would die in peace before then and not witness the catastrophe (2 Kgs. 22:14–20). Josiah died in 609 B.C.E. and Jerusalem fell in 586. The rabbis speculate on why she was consulted in preference to her contemporary *Jeremiah, and record the tradition that she was also a school teacher (2 Kgs. 22:14 Tg). A double gate on the south of the temple area was known as the Huldah Gate (*m. Middot* 1:3).

Humor.   See *Comedy.

Hunt, William Holman (1827–1910). English painter, founding member of the *Pre-Raphaelite Brotherhood. His most famous painting, in Keble College Oxford, is the heavily symbolic *Light of the World* (1953–56) showing Christ standing with a lantern at an overgrown door with no handle, and the words "Behold, I stand at the door and knock" (Rev. 3:20). A visit to the Middle East inspired the striking image of *The Scapegoat* (1854) in a wilderness landscape (Lev. 16) and an oriental Jewish setting for *The Finding of Christ in the Temple* (1860; Luke 2:27). See *Pre-Raphaelites.

Hus, Jan (c. 1372–1415). Bohemian reformer, strongly influenced by the writings of John *Wycliffe, and burned at the stake for heresy. The first to preach in the vernacular, he revised and improved existing Czech versions of the Bible, as well as writing biblical commentaries and translating Wycliffe's writings. As an exegete he followed medieval methods, but as a reformer upholding the right of individual believers to read Scripture for themselves, he was 150 years ahead of his time. Today the Moravian Church in Europe and North America, formerly known as the Bohemian Brethren founded in 1458, has its roots in the teachings of Hus.

Hymns. The Psalms make up the largest book in the Hebrew Bible, which contains many other hymnic compositions known as "songs" (Gk. *ode*) such as the Song of the Sea (Exod. 15:1–18), the Song of Moses (Deut. 32:1–43), and the Song of Deborah (Judg. 5). In the NT there are references to hymn singing (Mark 14:16; Acts 16:25), and a number of hymns including the *Magnificat, *Benedictus, and *Nunc Dimittis in Luke 1–2 and, according to many scholars, the christological poems in Phil. 2:5–11 and Col. 1:15–20. The apocryphal *Odes of Solomon is probably an early collection of Christian hymns. Apart from contexts in which hymns were banned (e.g., by *Calvin), hymn writing has been an integral part of the history of Jewish and Christian worship since ancient times. Not infrequently, popular hymns brilliantly interpret and supplement the language and imagery of the Bible, which makes them an invaluable resource for biblical research.

Ibn Ezra, Abraham (1089–1164). Spanish poet, mathematician, grammarian, and biblical commentator. In 1140 he left Moorish Spain and traveled extensively in France, Italy, and England, where he continued his writing and disseminated his considerable learning, strongly indebted to the Arabs, to many of Europe's Jewish communities. His biblical commentaries, which (apart from Ezekiel, Proverbs, Ezra, Nehemiah,

and Chronicles that are no longer extant) are printed alongside those of *Rashi and *Kimhi in Rabbinic Bibles, are characterized by independent thinking and critical questioning, although broadly respectful of rabbinic tradition. He was among the first to notice anachronisms in the Pentateuch (e.g., Gen. 12:6), casting doubt on Mosaic authorship, and stylistic grounds for distinguishing Isa. 1–39 from Isa. 40–66.

Ichabod (Heb. "no glory"). The name given to the grandson of the aged priest Eli, born immediately after the death of his father Phineas in battle. Phineas's brother Hophni had also been killed, and Eli had died from shock at the news of the death of his two sons and the loss of the ark of God (1 Sam. 4:19–22). The name appears in Robert Browning's poem *Waring* (1842) and is elsewhere used in the sense of moral decline. Ichabod Crane is the main character in Washington Irving's short story *The Legend of Sleepy Hollow* (1820) and figures again in the Walt Disney cartoon *The Adventures of Ichabod and Mr. Toad* (1949).

Ichthys (Gk. ΙΧΘΥΣ "fish"). A Greek acronym for *Iesus Christos Theou Uios Soter*, "Jesus Christ, God's Son, Savior." Hence the frequency of the fish in Christian iconography (⌒×), although the symbolism of a newly baptized Christian swimming like a fish in the water of life has its own significance. See *Chi-Rho.

Icon. A small religious painting, usually on wood and often with a protective silver cover, showing the Virgin, Christ, or the saints, intended to be used as a focus for public and private devotion. Mentioned already by *Eusebius (c. 260–340) and illustrated by a few early examples from St. Catherine's Monastery on Mount Sinai, the production and veneration of icons was officially banned by Emperor Leo III in 726, and thousands of icons were destroyed in an iconoclastic outburst not dissimilar to attacks by the Reformers on Catholic churches in 16th- and 17th-century Europe. The end of the "iconoclastic controversy" in 843, still celebrated on the annual Feast of Orthodoxy, was marked by a huge increase in the production of icons and the permanent establishment of the icon as a central feature of the Eastern Orthodox tradition. For devotional reasons, the form and style of icon painting, although often very beautiful, followed rigid conventions, and like the language and music of the liturgy, has remained largely unchanged down to the present day. See *Byzantine art and architecture; *Idols.

Ideological interpretation. An approach to biblical interpretation deliberately aware of power relations and other sociopolitical factors operating both in the writing of a text and in its interpretation. At first primarily associated with *Marx and Engels (*The German Ideology*, 1846; ET 1947) and often treated with suspicion in traditional academic and ecclesiastical circles, there is now an increasing number of successful ideological studies of the Bible from José Porfirio Miranda's *Marx and the Bible* (ET 1974) and *Gottwald's *Tribes of Yahweh* (1979) to more recent works by *feminist, *postcolonial, *African American, and other writers.

Idols. Statues or images depicting animals, deities, or the like, set up as objects of worship. Although universally condemned in the Bible, from the Decalogue to Paul (2 Cor. 6:16), as associated with the religion of Israel's enemies and a threat to the unique character of YHWH, and violently destroyed by iconoclasts in various periods, the role of icons and statues in Christian worship has been common from ancient times. A change in attitude toward religions like Hinduism, in which idols have an important devotional function, raises questions on how biblical attacks on idolatry (e.g., Isa. 44:9–20), like those on witches and homosexuals, should be interpreted today. See *Icon.

Ignatius (c. 35–c. 107). Bishop of Antioch, arrested and taken to Rome, where he died as a martyr in the Colosseum. His seven letters, among them those to the Romans, the Ephesians, the Philadelphians, and Polycarp, were much quoted by the church fathers, and contain some of our earliest interpretations of the Gospels and Paul.

IHS. Derived from Greek ΙΗΣ (in uncials *IHC*), these are the first three letters of the name Iesous "Jesus," and a very frequent symbol in Christian iconography from the 4th century. For the non-Greek-speaking faithful, it came to be interpreted as an acronym of *Iesus Hominum Salvator* (Lat. "Jesus Savior of men"), *In Hoc Signo* (Lat. "in this sign"), and "In His Service."

Illustrated Bibles. Early illustrated mss of the Bible include the Vienna Genesis (6th century), the Codex Amiatinus with a striking picture of Ezra the scribe (7th century), and the Lindisfarne Gospels (8th century). The art of Bible illustration spread throughout early medieval Europe, and evolved in the 13th century into special pictorial Bibles such as the *Bible Moralisée* and the *Biblia Pauperum*, printed editions of which with woodcuts were popular in the 15th and 16th centuries. In Reformation Germany, with Luther's enthusiastic support, printed Bibles were frequently illustrated, while in Britain it was not until the late 17th century that the first illustrated English Bibles appear. By the mid-18th century the practice had become widespread, and many editions of the Bible, and especially *Family Bibles, contained detailed illustrations some by well-known artists. Modern illustrated editions frequently contain photographs of archaeological finds and the Holy Land as it is today, as well as selected examples of Christian art, both traditional and modern. Among famous artists who produced Bible illustrations are Hans Holbein, *Doré, *Rouault, and *Chagall. Jewish Bible illustration is very much less developed, but there are some illustrated Hebrew mss of parts of the Bible, and most editions of the *Passover *Haggadah are illustrated.

Image of God (Lat. *Imago Dei*). The point of resemblance between human beings, both male and female, and God according to the creation story (Gen. 1:26–27; 5:1), to be taken with being "like God" (Gen. 3:5, 22) later in the story, and "a little lower than God" in the Psalms (Ps. 8:5). The Bible uses two words: *tzelem*, "image," which elsewhere refers to physical resemblance (cf. Num. 33:52), and *demut*, "likeness," which is more abstract and appears to rule this out. Some believe it to be free will or reason or immortality, others superiority over the rest of creation. For the mystics it is what renders human beings capable of entering into union with God. In Christian tradition it was damaged in the *fall, and made perfect again in Christ (2 Cor. 4:4), although in Protestant theology, expressed most vigorously in modern times by *Barth, it was completely destroyed, leaving everything to the divine initiative.

Immanuel (Gk. *Emmanuel*). The name of a child referred to once in the Hebrew Bible (Isa. 7:14; cf. 8:8, 10) and once in the NT (Matt. 1:23). Like the two sons of Isaiah, Shear-jashub (Isa. 7:3) and Maher-shalal-hash-baz (8:1–4), the meaning of his name, "God is with us," is more important than his identity or that of the young woman who is his mother. The Greek version substitutes the word "virgin" (*parthenos*) for "young woman" (Heb. *'almah*), and interprets the verse as a prophecy of the miracu-

lous birth of a messianic savior. This is how Christians have understood the "Immanuel prophecy" from the beginning, making it one of the most fiercely disputed verses in the tragic history of Jewish-Christian relations. The term is never used as a messianic title in Jewish literature. In patristic discussion the verse was quoted as scriptural authority for the Virgin Birth and the incarnation ("God with us"), and in music it is best known for its appearance in the Advent hymn "O come, O come, Immanuel," which was the inspiration for James MacMillan's percussion concerto *Veni Veni Emmanuel* (1992).

Immortality. Not a central concept in the Bible, which develops the alternative notion of the *resurrection of the dead. The frequent picture in the Hebrew Bible of the continuing existence of the dead in *Sheol (Ps. 6:5; Isa. 14) has little to do with the hope of immortality. But it is referred to in connection with the tree of life (Gen. 3:22), once in Prov. 12:28, where a Hebrew word for "immortality" occurs (*al-mawet*; cf. Ugar. *bl mt*), and in a more developed form in the well-known passage about "the souls of the righteous" in Wis. 3. Enoch (Gen. 5:24) and Elijah (2 Kgs. 2:11) also achieve a form of immortality, but these are conspicuous exceptions.

Incarnation. Technical term for the entry of the divine into human form, in Christian theology that of the preexistent Son of God in the human form of Jesus of Nazareth in 1st-century Palestine. The belief is implied in the narratives of the Virgin Birth as well as in a number of Pauline passages that identify Christ as the "Wisdom of God" (1 Cor. 1:24), the "firstborn of all creation" (Col. 1:15), and as "emptying himself" (Phil. 2:7), but it is in John that Christ is clearly defined as "the Word made flesh" (1:14; cf. 6:62). There are some foreshadowings of this in the Apocrypha (Sir. 24:8–12; Wis. 18:15), but not until the Council of Chalcedon in 451 was the doctrine defined by the church against challenges from those who argued Jesus was not truly human or not truly divine, or that continuity between the two natures was not complete. The mystery of the incarnation, however, remains beyond any one definition, and its precise meaning and relationship to other doctrines (the fall, atonement, grace, the sacraments) have been continually debated. The modern quest for the historical Jesus raised questions for NT interpreters about the true nature of his humanity. An incarnational theology, with its roots in Kant and *existentialism, used it as a model for the involvement of God in human affairs, but two world wars and the *Holocaust rendered such idealism futile. See *Christology.

Inerrancy. The belief, common to many Jews and Muslims as well as Christians, that, because Scripture is "sacred" or divinely inspired, there can be no errors in it. The term itself was first coined in the 19th century as a response to the challenges of modern critical scholarship. Biblical references to the Mosaic authorship of the Pentateuch, the Decalogue being written "by the finger of God" (Exod. 31:18), and Jesus' respect for every "jot and tittle" of it (Matt. 5:18 AV; cf. Deut. 4:2; 12:32) lay the foundations for this, as does a tradition like Amos 7:14, which implies that the prophet (like Muhammad) was illiterate. Rabbinic tradition traced back not only the Written *Torah but also the *Talmud and *Midrash (the *Oral Torah) to *Sinai, and prescribed meticulous rules (e.g., involving counting words and letters) to ensure that no copy of the Torah had an error in it. On the other hand, there are traditions in the Bible about a normal writing process in the case of some texts (Jer. 36), as well as references to the human effort involved (2 Macc. 2:24–32), and it was soon appreciated that there were considerable variations in the versions used as Scripture by the church.

Modern *textual criticism and the acknowledgment that texts can have more than one meaning make the whole notion of inerrancy virtually impossible to apply to the Bible, although for *fundamentalists it still has a role to play.

Infancy Gospel of Thomas. A 2nd-century apocryphal work, extant in many versions. It contains stories of miracles performed by Jesus as a child that appear in the *Golden Legend*, the *Qur'an*, and elsewhere. See *Arabic Infancy Gospel*.

Inner-biblical interpretation. A method of interpreting the Bible, first identified by Michael Fishbane in *Biblical Interpretation in Ancient Israel* (1985), that uses quotations, references, and allusions to earlier texts in the later books. In contrast to much conventional historical-critical scholarship, it took seriously "later additions" and the later books of the Bible, such as Chronicles, as the earliest stage in the *reception history of the Bible and an important witness to the meaning of the texts, and was supported by an increase in scholarly interest in the sociopolitical history and *archaeology of the Second Temple period.

INRI. Acronym of Lat. *IESUS NAZARENUS REX IUDAEORUM*, "Jesus of Nazareth King of the Jews," frequent in paintings of the *crucifixion as the inscription above the cross. Sometimes the inscription is written in full in Hebrew, Greek, and Latin (John 19:19–20) (Fra *Angelico, *Holbein, *Rembrandt, *El Greco), or Aramaic, Greek, and Latin (van Dyck, *Rubens).

Inspiration. The influence of God, or in Christian doctrine more precisely, the Holy Spirit, on the process of speaking or writing what is then believed to be the *word of God or sacred Scripture. Biblical origins for the belief are to be found in accounts of the role of the Spirit of God in the prophetic experience (1 Sam. 10; Isa. 61:1; 2 Cor. 12), and in 2 Tim. 3:16, which states that "all scripture" is inspired. It is part of the doctrine of Scripture seen as an essential authority, on its own or alongside other ecclesiastical authorities. The notion is vague enough to permit debate on the proportion of divine activity to human in the biblical writers, as well as in many other inspired writers, artists, and musicians. See also *Inerrancy.

Intentional fallacy. A term coined by literary critics to highlight the problem of equating the meaning of a text with the original intention of its author. It has special relevance for biblical interpretation where little or nothing is known of the original authors or their universe of discourse, and has contributed to the shift of emphasis in the direction of *reader-response criticism and *reception history.

Interpretation, history of. A branch of biblical studies, which, beginning with *inner-biblical interpretation and *translation into the ancient versions as the earliest stages in the process, traces the origins and evolution of rabbinic and patristic methodology, the development of medieval philosophical and mystical approaches, through the Reformation and Enlightenment to modern critical scholarship and beyond. Important issues confronting the historian of biblical interpretation arise from the fact that the Bible functions as a source of authority within the religious institutions who hold it to be in some sense sacred, and its precise meaning therefore of more than mere academic interest. There were major disputes over the validity of the nonliteral, spiritual, or allegorical meanings of a text over against its historical or literal sense. Much of the church's anti-Jewish polemic stems from the polariza-

tion of Jewish and Christian interpretations: the Jews working with the Hebrew text, the Christians from the beginning with vernacular translations. No less significant was the Reformers' challenge to traditional Catholic interpretations based on the Latin *Vulgate, and their promotion of powerful alternatives, notably Luther's German Bible and the *Authorized Version. Then there was the crisis in the church caused by modern scientific approaches to the Bible, including *source criticism, *form criticism, and *redaction criticism, which not only questioned traditional interpretations but challenged the "truth" or historicity of many of the biblical narratives, including the Gospels. Finally in the postmodern period new reading strategies have been advocated that take account of sociopolitical, ideological, and literary-critical developments, including post-*Holocaust awareness, *Marxism, *feminism, *postcolonialism, *structuralism, and *reader-response criticism.

As early as 1974 Brevard *Childs already appreciated the value of what he called the history of exegesis in writing his commentary on Exodus. But it was not until the last decade of the 20th century that it began to take its place alongside conventional historical-critical research, as shown by the publication of two *Dictionaries of Biblical Interpretation* (Coggins and Houlden, 1990; Hayes, 1999) and a growing number of monographs on the "afterlives" of biblical texts, for example, Isaiah (John F. A. Sawyer, *The Fifth Gospel*, 1996), Jonah (Yvonne Sherwood, *A Biblical Text and Its Afterlives*, 2000), and Lamentations (Tod Linafelt, *Surviving Lamentations*, 2000). A distinction is often drawn between the history of interpretation, which is primarily concerned with the commentaries written by scholars like *Jerome, *Thomas Aquinas, *Luther, and *Gunkel, on the one hand, and *reception history or *Wirkungsgeschichte, which is more comprehensive and covers the Bible in art, music, literature, sermons, popular culture, and the like, on the other. Common to all these approaches, however, is the acknowledgment that the historical critics' narrow preoccupation with the text and its original meaning, particularly in its rejection of rabbinic, patristic, and medieval interpretations as "late" or inferior, obscured the value of centuries of interpretation, both as subjects for research in their own right and as aids to understanding the meaning of the Bible.

Intertextuality. The term was coined by the post-structuralist Julia Kristeva in the 1960s to stress the interdependence of literary texts, but it was T. S. *Eliot in "Tradition and the Individual Talent" (1919) who first formulated the notion of literature as a system of interrelated texts. In biblical interpretation it is employed to highlight the way in which one passage of Scripture illuminates another. One of the hermeneutical principles of *Hillel (1st century C.E.) was the use of one passage of Scripture to explain another. In some cases it may be a conscious allusion by one later writer to an earlier (Matt. 1:22–23 to Isa. 7:14). In others the relationship depends on the reader/interpreter making the connection, not on any historical dependence of one author on another. An example of this is the use of Ezek. 16:49 to explain what "rulers of Sodom" in Isa. 1:10 refers to, even though it is historically impossible that the 8th-century prophet could have known anything about Ezekiel, who lived at least a century and a half later. See *Holistic interpretation; *Inner-biblical interpretation.

Ipsissima verba. Latin for the "words actually spoken," for instance, by Isaiah or Jesus, the object of historical-critical research since the *Enlightenment. Recent research places more emphasis on the listener or reader who recorded the ipsissima verba and without whom they would have had no meaning at all. See *Reader-response criticism.

Irenaeus (c. 130–c. 200 C.E.). Authoritative theologian. Probably born in Asia Minor, where he heard Polycarp of Smyrna as a boy, he later moved to the West, where he became presbyter in Rome and later bishop of Lyons (c. 180 C.E.). He first traveled to Rome as presbyter with a letter urging toleration for Montanists and as bishop appealed for toleration of the Quartodeciman dating of Easter favored in Asia Minor, though his church followed the Roman practice. His two main works, *Against All Heresies* and the *Demonstration of the Apostolic Preaching*, show him to have been a devoted and experienced interpreter of Scripture, especially the OT. He insisted on the authority of the four canonical Gospels and Acts against the apocryphal writings favored by gnostics and against *Marcion's more limited *canon. His lasting contribution to Christian *iconography is his linking of the creatures in Rev. 4:7–8 (cf. Ezek. 1) to the four *evangelists.

Irony. A mode of writing in such a way as to invite the reader to recognize two or more levels of meaning in the same passage. The irony in Nathan's parable is made explicit in the words "Thou art the man" (2 Sam. 12 AV), while in the biblical stories of great men like Judah (Gen. 38), Sisera (Judg. 4–5), Samson (Judg. 13–16), and Holofernes (Judith) being outwitted or overpowered by women, it is left for the readers to enjoy. There is obvious irony in Job and Ecclesiastes, as well as in some of the parables of Jesus. Post-Holocaust interpreters of the book of Jonah, however, aware of the dilemma of a prophet who foresees the genocide of his people if he obeys God's command, should be cautious before too readily assuming it to be a study in irony. A full-scale study of irony in the Bible is that of Edwin Good (*Irony in the OT*, 2nd ed. 1981).

Isaac (Heb. *yitzhaq*). Favored son and heir of *Abraham, after the rejection of

Ishmael and his mother, *Hagar (Gen. 21; Rom. 9), but the least important of the three patriarchs. His name (from Heb. *tzahaq,* "laugh") recalls the story of his miraculous birth long after his mother Sarah had passed childbearing age (Gen. 17). While still a boy, he was victim of his father's decision to sacrifice him but survived (see *Akedah), and married Rebekah, by whom he had twins, Esau and Jacob. Tradition remembers him for his blessing of Jacob (Heb. 11:20), intended for Esau, the elder son, but acquired by deception (Gen. 27). Apart from the Akedah, Isaac appears rarely in art, *Raphael's painting in the Vatican showing Isaac and Rebekah making love (Gen. 26:8) being a rare exception.

Isaiah Apocalypse. A modern title given to Isa. 24–27 to highlight the distinctive language and imagery of the passage, which describes global disasters, the sun and moon going dark, the resurrection of the dead, and the defeat by YHWH of "*Leviathan . . . and the dragon that is in the sea." Parallels within the rest of the book of Isaiah are recognized, but it stands out from its immediate literary context as distinct and can probably be dated, along with *Joel, to the 4th century B.C.E., that is, to the latest stage in the composition of the book. See *Apocalyptic.

Isaiah, book of. The first of the *Major Prophets. In Jewish tradition Isaiah is the prophet of consolation, thanks to the seven "consolation readings" from chaps. 40–63 in the lectionary, and in modern times he provided *Zionism (even in its secular forms) with much of the language and imagery applied to organizations, settlements, and publications. He is frequently quoted, often by name, in the NT, and Christian interpreters found in their Greek and Latin versions of Isaiah *proof texts for almost every detail of Christ's life as well as for many doctrines and practices. *Jerome described Isaiah as

"more evangelist than prophet." Isaiah played a unique role in the history of Christian *anti-Semitism, both because of disputed interpretations of such passages as 7:14 (*Immanuel), and because of the violent invective addressed by Isaiah to Judah and the Judeans (e.g., 1:15; 65:2–3), which provided the church with scriptural authority for attacking the Jews. Isaiah's influence on the history of Western culture in general has been extensive. Images from Isaiah that were immensely productive in medieval Christian *art and architecture include the ox and the ass (1:3), the *Jesse tree (11:1–2), and the winepress (63:3). "Swords into plowshares" (2:4) and the "peaceable kingdom" (11:6–9) are popular in 19th- and 20th-century art. *Handel's *Messiah* (1741), *Mendelssohn's *Elijah* (1846), and *Brahms's *German Requiem* (1869) contain memorable settings of passages from Isaiah, as do many *hymns and other liturgical compositions. *Liberation theology has drawn heavily on Isaiah's visions of social justice (11:1–9; 16:3–5; 32:16–17), and *feminism on the female images of God in Isa. 40–66 (42:14; 49:15; 66:13).

*Eusebius, *Jerome, *Cyril of Alexandria, *Theodoret, *Thomas Aquinas, *Nicholas of Lyra, *Calvin, *Lowth, and *Gesenius all wrote commentaries on Isaiah, to which must be added *Luther's 1527–30 lectures. Modern scholars identify the earliest parts of the book (i.e., much of chaps. 1–12; 20; 28–31) as having been written against the background of the Assyrian invasions of the second half of the 8th century B.C.E. The prophet's words were probably first edited in the reign of Josiah (640–609), greatly expanded by the addition of *Deutero-Isaiah (chaps. 40–55) during the Babylonian *exile, and subsequently by other writings, of which perhaps the 4th-century *Isaiah Apocalypse (chaps. 24–27) was one of the last. Recent literary approaches to *Isaiah have focused on points of continuity between earlier chapters (1:5–6; 11:6) and later (53:4–5; 65:25), and on themes and images common to the whole book ("Holy One of

Israel," "daughter of *Zion,""justice"). In a postmodern age even passages like the four *Servant Songs are interpreted in their present literary context. See *Martyrdom and Ascension of Isaiah.

Ishmael, Rabbi (d. mid-2nd century C.E.). Important rabbinic authority, to whom are attributed the Thirteen Middot (exegetical principles) (cf. *Hillel), and the saying "the Torah speaks human language." To his disciples are attributed three halakhic *midrashim, *Mekhilta* on Exodus, *Sifre* on Numbers, and part of *Sifre* on Deuteronomy. See *Halakhah.

Isidore (c. 560–636). Archbishop of Seville. He devoted his encyclopedic knowledge to defending the church against barbarism and heresy, and to converting the Jews. His writings are for the most part textbooks and works of reference, including his hugely influential *Etymologiae* in 20 volumes, which covers grammar, rhetoric, mathematics, and medicine as well theology and ecclesiastical matters. In his exegetical works, notably *Quaestiones in Vetus Testamentum* and *In Libros Veteris et Novi Testamenti Proemia*, Isidore employs a developed allegorical or mystical method of exegesis, drawing heavily on the church fathers, especially *Augustine. Thus he provided medieval Christendom with a convenient digest of patristic tradition on the Bible.

Islamic interpretation. See *Muslim interpretation; *Qur'an.

Israel (Heb. *yisra'el*). Eponymous ancestor of the people of God. Originally called *Jacob, his name was changed to Israel ("for you have striven with God and with man and have prevailed" Gen. 32:28), so that his descendants are called the "children of Israel" (Exod. 1:1; Luke 1:16 AV), the *twelve tribes of Israel

(Gen. 49:28) and the Israelites (Gen. 32:32; Rom. 11:1). In an Egyptian text dated 1220 B.C.E. "Israel" refers to a foreign people living in Palestine, and some of the biblical stories of conquest and settlement by the "tribes of Israel" (Joshua-Judges) probably reflect conditions there in the succeeding two or three centuries. The short-lived but legendary "kingdom of Israel" under *David and *Solomon (cf. 1 Sam. 24:20) was followed by a long period in which "Israel" denoted the northern kingdom with its capital, from the 9th century, at Samaria (1 Kgs. 12:20), as opposed to *Judah in the south. With the fall of Samaria in 722 B.C.E. and particularly after the Babylonian exile, the Judeans were able to reappropriate the term and apply it to themselves as the people of God. In the Jewish liturgy it is the second word of the *Shema and is mentioned in five of the "Eighteen Blessings." See *Amidah.

Christians from the beginning also saw themselves as the "Israel of God" (Gal. 6:16), encouraged perhaps by Jesus' choice of twelve disciples corresponding to the twelve tribes of Israel (cf. Jas. 1:1), and the "New Israel" became a popular, though blatantly *supersessionist, term for the church. The *Samaritan minority to this day preserves the old northern interpretation of the term, while British Israelites also believe they are descended from the ten tribes of the northern kingdom. The name was chosen, not without controversy, for the Jewish State in 1948, and many Palestinian Christians still have problems with its biblical and liturgical use. See *Zionism.

J. One of the literary sources of the Pentateuch so called by *Astruc because it uses the name YHWH (French *Jahvé*). See *Documentary Hypothesis.

Jacob (Heb. *Ya'aqov*; Arab. *Ya'qub*). Younger son of Isaac, who cheated his elder brother *Esau out of his birthright and so became the third patriarch and father of the "sons of Israel." His name recalls the story of his birth when he grabbed his twin brother's heel (Heb. '*aqev*) (Gen. 25:25), but later in life, after wrestling with the angel, he received the name *Israel (32:22). He had twelve sons, by his two wives (Leah and Rachel) and their two handmaids (Gen. 35), and one daughter, Dinah. Of these his favorite, Rachel's son Joseph, died and was buried in Egypt, while the others, along with Joseph's two sons Manasseh and Ephraim, were the ancestors of the twelve tribes and explain the origin of the geographical names given to the regions in the land of Israel.

Many of the stories of Jacob are given an influential christological interpretation widely represented in Christian literature and art. They include his dream at Bethel, where he saw a ladder reaching up to heaven with angels ascending and descending on it (Gen. 28: cf. John 1:47–51; *Blake), his meeting with Rachel at "Jacob's well" (Gen. 29; cf. John 4; *Raphael), his wrestling with the angel (Gen. 32; Gauguin), and his role in the story of Joseph and his brothers (Gen. 37–50; *Rembrandt). In Jewish tradition Jacob represents the Jewish people, as frequently in the Psalms and the Prophets, and his rivalry with *Esau (and Edom) mirrors their relationship with *Rome and Christianity: Esau is the hunter and pragmatic man of action, while Jacob withdraws from the world and dwells in the "tents of the Torah" (Gen. 25:17). Jacob's blessing of the twelve tribes (together with that of Moses: Deut. 33) provided *Chagall with the inspiration for his famous twelve stained-glass windows in the Hadassah Hospital synagogue in Jerusalem.

James, Letter of. First of the Catholic Letters, traditionally but improbably attributed to James the brother of Jesus (Acts 15:13; Gal. 1:19). Although referred to by *Origen and *Clement of Alexandria, the letter was not accepted as canonical until the Council of Carthage in 397. A moral exhortation addressed to the Diaspora (1:1), it draws on the wisdom tradition, including Job, Proverbs, and Psalms, as well as the Decalogue and the Sermon on the Mount, and speaks of the "law of liberty" (2:12; cf. Ps. 119:96). There are full-length commentaries on James by *Bede, *Nicholas of Lyra, and *Calvin. Because it says "faith without works is dead," *Luther dismissed it as an "epistle of straw," but in modern times *liberation theologians and *postcolonial interpreters of the Bible have found inspiration in its option for the poor. See *Protoevangelium of James.

Japheth. One of the three sons of *Noah. See *Ham; *Shem.

JEDP. See *Documentary Hypothesis.

Jehovah's Witnesses. A *millenarian sect founded by Charles Taze Russell in Pittsburgh in 1872 under the name of the "International Bible Students' Association." Today there are around 6 million Jehovah's Witnesses worldwide. They have their own version of the Bible, published by the Watchtower Bible and Tract Society of New York in over 300 languages. Committed to the belief in the imminent advent of a messianic kingdom, they reject the authority of all existing forms of government, both secular and ecclesiastical. This subversive stance together with their persistent proselytizing has led to their suppression by some governments, notably that of Nazi Germany, under whom many died in the *Holocaust. They find in Scripture numerous references to contemporary history: the beast in Rev. 13, for example, is the Anglo-American world power. They are also noted for their opposition to blood transfusions (based on Acts 15:28–29), even when it is a matter of life and death, and their readiness, like

*Abraham and *Jephthah, to sacrifice their children for their beliefs.

Jephthah. Judge of Israel (Judg. 11–12). Having vowed on going forth to battle that if victorious he would sacrifice the first person he met on his way home, he kept his vow and sacrificed his own daughter. Though hailed in the NT as one of the great "men of faith" (Heb. 11:32), his action is condemned in *Midrash Rabbah* and by *Josephus, as well as by *Jerome, *Augustine, and many others, down to Phyllis Trible's *Texts of Terror* (1984). Jephthah inspired many writers, notably the Scottish humanist George Buchanan, whose Latin drama *Jephthes* (1554) was hugely influential throughout Europe. Compared with Agamemnon's daughter Iphigenia in Greek drama, and, like her, not infrequently saved from death at the last minute, Jephthah's daughter appears in oratorios by Carissimi (1650) and *Handel (1752), an opera by Montéclair (1732), and in paintings by *Blake, Dégas, Millais, Benjamin West, and others.

Jeremiah, book of. One of the *Major Prophets. His prophetic career in Jerusalem spanned the period from Josiah's reformation to the Babylonian exile when he went to Egypt. Most of the book is taken up with the prophet's condemnation of his people (and of other nations) and his predictions of imminent disaster, best known of which is perhaps the Temple Sermon (7:1–8:3), for which he was imprisoned as a traitor (cf. chap. 26). Hence the traditional view of Jeremiah as "prophet of doom" and author of Lamentations and Ps. 137 (LXX). The book contains several remarkable accounts of the prophetic experience such as the "visions" in chap. 1 and the so-called confessions in chaps. 11–20 ("O Lord, Thou hast deceived me," 20:7 AV). But there are also prophecies of hope, including his letter to the exiles (chap. 29) and the famous "new covenant" passage

(31:31–34); and the book, like 2 Kings, ends on a hopeful note with the release of the exiled king of Judah.

The prophet appears in Daniel (9:2), the Apocrypha (Sir. 49:6–7); 2 Macc. 15:12–16), and the NT (e.g., Matt. 16:14; cf. Heb. 8:8–12), but otherwise, apart from *Philo, the book does not play a major role in ancient Jewish and Christian tradition. Only *Origen, *Theodoret, and *Jerome wrote extensively on Jeremiah in the patristic period, and *Rabanus Maurus and *Thomas Aquinas in the Middle Ages. *Luther's *Preface* to Jeremiah (1532) is noted for its anti-Judaism, while *Calvin wrote a series of sermons on Jeremiah (1549) as well as a substantial commentary (1563). Modern historical-critical scholarship begins with *Duhm (1901) and reaches its climax with William McKane (2 vols. 1986, 1996). In literature, apart from Robert Burns's paraphrase of 15:10 and a Gerald Manley Hopkins sonnet beginning "Thou art indeed just, Lord" (12:1), Jeremiah is remembered more for his Lamentations than for anything in the prophetic book itself, as he is in Claus *Sluter's famous statue of him on the Well of Moses in Dijon (1395–1406), where the scroll in his hand bears the text beginning *O Vos Omnes* from Lam. 1:12. Since the 18th century the term jeremiad has been applied to laments and doom-laden sermons. There is also *Donatello's marble statue in Florence (1423–26), *Michelangelo's portrait of him in the *Sistine Chapel (1511), and *Jeremiah Lamenting the Destruction of Jerusalem* (Jer. 32–33) by *Rembrandt (1630). In music Leonard *Bernstein's *Jeremiah Symphony* (1942) is based on the books of Jeremiah and *Lamentations, and "Balm in Gilead" (Jer. 8:22) is a popular *African American spiritual. See *Lamentations, book of.

Jeremiah, Letter of. An apocryphal Greek composition, since Jerome often printed as the concluding chapter of *Baruch. Very different from the canonical letter of Jeremiah to the exiles (Jer. 29), it is a vitriolic and repetitive attack on idolatrous practices, including the role of women, and heavily dependent on passages from Isa. 40–46, Jer. 10:1–16, and some of the Psalms (e.g.,115:4–8; 135:15–18).

Jerome (Gk. *Hieronymos*) (c. 342–420). The most learned of the Latin Fathers, author of the *Vulgate and numerous biblical commentaries. He studied at Rome, Antioch, and as a hermit in the Syrian desert, where he learned Hebrew. From 386 he worked in Bethlehem on his OT translation, and despite official preference for the Greek *Septuagint, rejected the *Apocrypha and insisted that his Latin version should represent as much as possible of the original Hebrew. He wrote commentaries on all the Major and Minor Prophets except Jeremiah, which he failed to finish, and also on Genesis, Ecclesiastes, the Psalms, Matthew, Galatians, Ephesians, Titus, and Philemon. Christian artists often represent him with a lion at his feet, and anachronistically a cardinal's red hat on his head.

Jerusalem (Heb. *yerushalayim*, Arab. *Al-Quds*). The city in the Judean hill country that David made the capital of his kingdom and where the temple of Solomon was built on the site of the *Akedah (2 Chr. 3:1; Gen. 22). Known also as *Zion or the "daughter of Zion," it became the subject of extravagant beliefs and images. The city is invincible (Pss. 46; 48). The massed forces of the Assyrian king *Sennacherib could not conquer it, alone of all the cities of Judah (Isa. 36–37). It is from Zion that a new age of justice and peace will spread throughout the world (Isa. 2; Mic. 4). It is "the faithful city . . . the city of righteousness" (Isa. 1:21, 26), and "the holy city" (Isa. 52:1, Matt. 4:5).

When the city and temple lay in ruins after the Babylonian invasion of 586 B.C.E., prophecies about the creation of a new Jerusalem (Isa. 65:17–25) and a new temple (Ezek. 40–48) continued, and again after the destruction of Herod's Jerusalem and the Second Temple by the Romans in 70 C.E., there is the vision of a new Jerusalem coming down from heaven (Rev. 21:2). Despite Hadrian's attempt to remove all traces of Judaism from the city he renamed Aelia Capitolina in 131 C.E., Jews still recited the 15 "Songs of the Temple Steps" (Pss. 120–134) and prayed three times a day that God would return to a rebuilt Jerusalem. The tradition continued through the famous Zion poems of Judah Halevi (12th century) and 19th-20th-century *Zionism to the modern popular song *Yerushalayim shel zahab* ("Jerusalem of gold," 1967).

Although identifying and commemorating places mentioned in the Gospels, Christians have never felt the same physical attachment to the city of Jerusalem, dreaming perhaps more of the "Jerusalem above" (Gal. 4:26). For them the holy city is as often Rome as Jerusalem, and the Holy Land a place of pilgrimage rather than a homeland. The same is true of Muslim tradition, which, despite venerating the site of Muhammad's ascension to heaven within the sacred precinct, *al-haram al-sharif*, shifted the *qibla* (direction of prayer), in the Prophet's lifetime, from Jerusalem to Mecca. Apart from an impressive 10th-century B.C.E. structure to the south of the Old City (cf. 2 Sam. 5:9), and Hezekiah's tunnel with its famous inscription (cf. 2 Kgs. 20:20), little is left of preexilic Jerusalem. Archaeologists have been able to reconstruct Jerusalem as it was in the time of Christ, however, with a fair degree of precision, sometimes at the expense of Byzantine and Islamic levels.

Jesse tree. Popular image in medieval Christian iconography derived from Isa. 11:1–3. It shows the family tree of Jesus (cf. Matt. 1), starting with

David's father Jesse at the bottom (Ruth 4) and Mary or Jesus at the top, with ancestors arranged in the branches and sometimes surrounded by seven doves representing the seven gifts of the Spirit from v. 2. Famous examples are the "Jesse Windows" in Chartres Cathedral and Dorchester Abbey near Oxford. A frequent variation connects the wooden trunk of the tree with the cross as in the 16th-century Brougham Triptych in Carlisle Cathedral. The Jesse tree figures in the 15th-century German hymn *Es ist ein Ros' entsprungen,* and in a poem by Victor Hugo (1802–85) in which Boaz dreams of a tree with David singing at the bottom and Christ crucified at the top (*Booz endormi*).

Jesuits. Members of the Society of Jesus (SJ), a religious order founded in Paris in 1534 by the Spanish priest Ignatius Loyola. Noted for their spiritual discipline and the high level of their own education, they founded schools and universities in many parts of the world, and were active in combating Protestantism in Europe, and in their missionary activities especially in China, Japan, and Latin America, where they were the first to translate the Bible into many languages. Radical attitudes and methods led to their being suppressed throughout most of Europe from 1773 to 1814. Today they work mainly in higher education, but also actively campaign for human rights and social justice, and made a significant contribution to the *liberation theology movement. Notable Jesuit missionaries include Francis Xavier (Japan, India), Matteo Ricci (China), Roberto de Nobili (India), and Andrew Bobola (Eastern Europe), and among influential modern Jesuit scholars and writers are Gerald Manley *Hopkins, Teilhard de Chardin, Hans Urs von Balthasar, and Karl Rahner.

Jesus (Heb. *Yeshua,* Aramaic form of Joshua; Gk. *Iesous;* Arab. *'isa*). Jewish teacher, miracle worker, and founder of Christianity. Known as Jesus of Nazareth and Jesus Christ (Gk. *christos* = "Messiah"), he is rarely mentioned in the ancient Roman and rabbinic sources, and we are dependent almost entirely on the NT for details of his short life. Thanks to the profound effect he had on his followers from the beginning, numerous traditions grew up about his birth, early life, teaching, acts of healing, relations with the Jewish authorities, crucifixion, and resurrection from the dead. Of these, many are recounted in the language of the Psalms and Prophets, especially Isaiah, and may be apocryphal in the sense of not being based on what actually happened but prompted by the belief that Jesus was the promised Messiah. The church fathers clearly distinguished between the accounts in the four canonical Gospels and Paul on the one hand, and the many apocryphal documents like the *Gospel of Thomas* or the *Gospel of Judas,* which were rejected as noncanonical, on the other. Among such alternative versions of the story must be included the Muslim Jesus, son of Mary, as represented in the *Qur'an. For Christians and for Muslims, until modern times the historical Jesus was virtually identical with the Jesus of faith.

In addition to the messianic titles Christ, Son of David, and *Immanuel (Isa. 7:14), the two commonest terms applied to Jesus in the Gospels are "*Son of God" and "*Son of Man," both sounding rather strange in Greek and obviously translations from Hebrew or Aramaic. "Son of God" in Hebrew normally means a divine being, a member of the heavenly host (cf. Job 38:7), and this is what it probably means in many of its NT occurrences (e.g., Mark 1:1; 15:39), although the notion that he was merely an angel was in due course rejected (Heb. 1–2). Since occasionally the special relationship between God and his anointed king was envisaged as that of father and son (Ps. 2), and Jesus also addresses God as his father, the theological shift from a "son of God" to the one and only "Son of God" can be seen taking place already in the NT. Similarly the title "son of man" (Heb. *ben adam*; Aramaic *bar nasha*) normally means simply a human being, a member of the human race, but in the Gospels it is frequently applied to Jesus as the human being par excellence, the one who is to come, perhaps influenced by its occurrence in the apocalyptic visions of Daniel (7:13) and *1 Enoch* (37–71). It remained for the Greek theologians of the first four and a half centuries to work out the theological details of the relationship between the second person of the Trinity and the first, and that between the divine and human natures within the one person.

Apart from challenges from outside Christianity and the early acknowledgment of apparent inconsistencies in the NT accounts of the life of Jesus, it was not until Reimarus in the 18th century that the reliability of the Gospels as a historical record was seriously questioned and *The *Quest of the Historical Jesus*, as *Schweitzer called it (1906; ET 1910), really began. Despite many attempts to reconstruct his life as mythical savior, charismatic rabbi, or Marxist revolutionary, recent scholarship recognizes the limitations of a purely historical-critical approach and focuses more on the effect the Gospels have had on subsequent cultural, theological, and sociopolitical developments.

In art, from the 4th century Jesus is represented in a variety of forms ranging from a beardless young shepherd, like David or Orpheus, in the catacombs in Rome, to Christos Pantocrator on the domes and apses of Greek churches down to the present day. Throughout the Middle Ages conventional representations of scenes from his life appear in sculpture, stained glass, painting, and illuminated mss, addressed to a largely illiterate public. The Renaissance artists beginning with *Cimabue, Duccio, and Giotto (14th century) brought realism into Christian art, and from the 16th century on, with the spread of vernacular translations of the Bible, every detail of the narrative was interpreted in art, often clearly reflecting current social, political, and theological trends. Modern versions of the Gospels begin with 19th-century English images of "Gentle Jesus, meek and mild," and culminate in Kazantzakis's controversial novel *The Last Temptation of Christ* (ET 1960; film 1988), the popular musical *Jesus Christ Superstar* (1970), and Mel Gibson's violent film, *The Passion of the Christ* (2004). See *Christology; *Messiah.

Jewish interpretation.
The origins of rabbinic exegesis are probably to be traced, like those of patristic exegesis, to Hellenistic Greek scholarship, which flourished in the 3rd and 2nd centuries B.C.E. and whose goal was to interpret the works of Homer, Plato, Aristotle, and other classical writers. This had already been influential within Judaism, notably in the *Septuagint, the works of *Philo of Alexandria, and the NT, but rabbinic exegesis as we know it from the *Talmud and *Midrash was unique in that it was written in Hebrew or Aramaic and based exclusively on the original text. Neither the LXX nor the *Targum was ever subjected to the exegetical scrutiny that patristic scholars applied to their Greek, Latin, and other versions of Christian Scripture, to the virtual exclusion of the original Hebrew. The two traditions otherwise have much in common, including the recognition that texts have more than one meaning, and the distinction between a literal meaning (*peshat*), and a usually more significant nonliteral or homiletical meaning (*derash*). Another distinction of particular importance in rabbinic tradition is that between interpretations with a binding practical application in everyday life (*halakhah*) and more abstract poetic or theological interpretations (*aggadah*).

The rabbis devised a number of "principles of interpretation" (*middot*), of which the Thirteen Middot of Rabbi *Ishmael (2nd century C.E.) are the best known. These include such things as inference from *analogy, the importance of *context, and where two passages contradict each other, a third resolves it. Others not in Ishmael's list, although frequently used, are allegory, *wordplay, and *gematria. The earliest rabbinic commentaries are halakhic works on Exodus (*Mekhilta*), Leviticus (*Sifra*), Numbers (*Sifre*), and Deuteronomy (*Sifre*); and by the end of the talmudic period commentaries on the whole Pentateuch, the Five Scrolls, Jonah, and the Psalms, known collectively as *Midrash Rabbah* (*Genesis Rabbah*, etc.), had for the most part reached the form in which they have come down to us.

Alongside the rabbinic tradition, and in opposition to it, there have been various alternative methods of interpretation, such as those used by the Qumran sect (see *Pesher), the *Karaites, and the *mystics. But the rabbinic tradition prevailed in the works of the great medieval commentators, *Ibn Ezra, *Rashi, *Kimhi, and the rest, which are printed alongside the Hebrew text and the Targum in *rabbinic Bibles to this day. Since the *Haskalah, Jewish interpretation has been influenced by *historical-critical scholarship, although Orthodoxy has been slower to accept the insights of modern research than Christianity. In the 20th century new ways of reading the Bible evolved in response to the *Holocaust; and, after centuries of ignorance and anti-Jewish prejudice, the value of Jewish interpretations, ancient, medieval, and modern, has been increasingly appreciated by non-Jewish interpreters of both the Hebrew Bible and the NT. See *Allegorical interpretation.

Joachim of Fiore (c. 1135–1202). Italian mystic whose interpretations of Scripture, especially Psalms, the Gospels, and Revelation, were influential throughout medieval Europe. Said to have been inspired by a vision on Mount Tabor while traveling in the Holy Land, he understood the whole of history to be divided into three ages: the age of the Father, under the Law of the OT; the age of the Son, lived under the grace of the NT; and the age of the Holy Spirit, which proceeds from both the OT and the NT. His potentially subversive teachings about the imminent dawning of a new age and a "Spiritual Church" in an edition of his works known as the *Eternal Gospel* (1254) were much quoted by more radical successors such as the Spiritual Franciscans.

Job, book of. An extended literary treatment of the story of Job (Heb. *iyyov*; Arab. *Ayyub*), a legendary figure, proverbial for his righteousness (Ezek. 14:14; Sir. 49:9 Heb.) and patience (Jas. 5:11), who for no apparent reason suddenly suffered the loss of his entire family (except his wife), and fell victim to a disfiguring disease. His desperate attempts, and those of his "comforters," to find an explanation come to nothing, and in the end YHWH speaks to him "out of the whirlwind" (Job 38) and restores his fortunes. The brief but graphic prose narrative in chaps. 1–2 and 42:7–17 explains Job's sufferings as a test of his integrity engineered in heaven, unknown to him, by the "satan," one of YHWH's heavenly court. In the main part of the book (which is in verse), the comforters argue that no one is without sin (chap. 4) and thus Job must have sinned, maybe inadvertently, to have deserved such punishment (chap. 8), or else that his suffering has been sent to educate him (chaps. 32–37). Job in his agony suggests that perhaps God has made a mistake or even that suffering is a deliberate part of God's plan for the human beings he had created with such care (chap. 10).

Apart from the pseudepigraphical *Testament of Job* (1st century B.C.E.), a Targum of Job found at Qumran, and a number of allusions in the NT (Mark 10:27; Rev. 9:6), the book's impact does not appear much before *Augustine's *Adnotationes in Job* (399–404) and *Gregory the Great's influential *Moralia in Job*

(6th century), followed in the early Middle Ages by *Maimonides' parabolic reading in *Guide for the Perplexed* (book 3) and *Thomas Aquinas's *Literal Exposition*. *Calvin wrote a series of exegetical sermons on Job (1554–55), and in the 17th and 18th centuries there was a huge interest in the book evident in the numerous vernacular translations and major new studies like those of *Lowth (1753), *Herder (1782–83), and *Blake, whose 21 brilliant and original illustrations soon took on a life of their own. Many modern scholars, concerned to uncover the original form of the book and taking account of possible parallels in ancient Mesopotamian literature, have separated the prose prologue and epilogue from the poetic parts of the book and rejected as late additions the Elihu speeches (chaps. 32–37), the happy ending, and belief in life after death.

Job's huge impact on philosophy, theology, and psychology can be sampled in works by Kant, *Kierkegaard, *Jung, *Barth, *Gutiérrez, and many others, and on modern literature in Kafka's *The Trial* (1925), Robert Frost's *Masque of Reason* (1945), Archibald MacLeish's play *J.B.* (1956), Elie *Wiesel's *The Trial of God* (1956), and David Rosenberg's *Job Speaks* (1977). Several modern works have the title *Out of the Whirlwind* (Job 38:1), including a reader of *Holocaust literature by Albert Friedlander (1968) and a collection of essays on suffering by Rabbi J. B. Soloveitchik (2003). Artistic representations of Job appear already at Dura Europos (3rd century C.E.) and on the *sarcophagus of Junius Bassus (4th century, Rome), as well as in Islamic art from the 12th century. Sixteenth-century illustrations include Carpaccio's *Meditation on the Passion* (c. 1510) and Albrecht Dürer's *Job and His Wife* (c. 1510). In music, in addition to the famous aria in *Handel's *Messiah* (19:25), there are oratorios by Hubert Parry (1892) and Dallapiccola (1950), as well as a masque by *Vaughan Williams based on *Blake's illustrations, and choreographed by Ninette de Valois (1935).

Job, Testament of. See *Testament of Job.*

Joel, book of. The second of the *Minor Prophets. His position between Hosea and Amos suggests an 8th-century date, as does the threat of Assyrian invasion as background to his prophecies of imminent disaster and the coming of the *Day of the Lord. According to many modern scholars the apocalyptic imagery of the book, like that of the *Isaiah Apocalypse (Isa. 24–27), and perhaps also the mention of the Greeks (3:6), favor a much later date, probably 4th century B.C.E. Graphic images of swarming locusts, withering vines, earthquakes, the darkened sun, and the moon turned to blood, when men "beat their plowshares into swords" (cf. Isa. 2:4) and "the LORD roars from Zion" (cf. Amos 1:2), alternate with appeals for repentance and predictions that God will "restore the years that the locust has eaten" (Joel 2:25) and protect Jerusalem forever (2:32 [MT 3:5]).

These and other expressions appear throughout literature, but Joel's main contribution to Christian tradition is the promise that "I will pour out my spirit on all flesh: your sons and your daughters shall prophesy, your old men shall dream dreams" (2:28 [MT 3:1]), cited by Peter at Pentecost to explain the strange behavior of the disciples (Acts 2). In Jewish lectionaries Joel 2:15–27 ("Blow the trumpet in Zion; sanctify a fast") is the *haftarah for the Sabbath preceding *Yom Kippur along with Hos. 14:2–10 and Mic. 7:18–20.

Johannine Letters. Three of the *Catholic Letters, traditionally attributed, like the Fourth Gospel and Revelation, to "the beloved disciple" (John 13:23), although not all included in the *canon until the 4th century. Recurring terms like "light," darkness," "world," "truth," "love," and "abide" give the group a literary and thematic unity.

They exhort the readers to love one another as God loved them and as Christ commanded them, but also to deal firmly with "false prophets" and "deceivers" who do not believe, for example, in the true humanity of Christ.

The emphasis in 1 John on the relationship between faith and love made it a favorite text for Luther and other Reformers. Since the 17th century the traditional view on authorship has been rejected by most scholars on the grounds that the author describes himself as an "elder" (2 John 1; 3 John 1), together with other arguments, but numerous common themes and expressions throughout the "Johannine books" are universally acknowledged. That 2 John is the only NT writing addressed to a woman and her children has more recently prompted discussion of the implications of this for attitudes to women in the church, even though the usage itself may be a metaphor for the church in general.

John, Gospel of. The Fourth Gospel, since the 2nd century traditionally attributed to the disciple John the son of Zebedee, is considered the most spiritual or theological of the Gospels. While telling the same story, with considerable attention to geographical detail, for example, it differs significantly from the Synoptics. It begins with an account of how the eternal *Word (Gk. *logos*) of God "became flesh and dwelt among us" (AV), instead of a birth narrative. The miracles are presented as proofs of his divinity, not signs of the coming of the kingdom. Most of the incidents in Christ's life take place in *Jerusalem, not Galilee, and the chronology especially of the last days is different. His teaching is mainly in the form of lengthy discourses in which the unique "I am" sayings frequently appear: "I am the bread of life . . . the light of the world . . . the resurrection . . . the way, the truth, and the life." His Farewell Discourse at the *Last Supper is perhaps the most distinctive: in it he discusses his relationship with the Father,

his relationship with his disciples ("abide in me"), the coming of the Holy Spirit (the "Comforter"), and the ethical ideal of self-sacrifice (chaps. 13–16); then in the language of prayer he describes how his followers will one day share in his glory (chap. 17).

Johannine logos *Christology appealed to gnostic Christians, and it was to combat them and other heresies that early Christian writers, notably *Irenaeus, *Origen, and *Tertullian, wrote their own interpretations, which in turn influenced the development of orthodox Christian doctrine in the 4th and 5th centuries, when *Augustine and *Theodore of Mopsuestia were writing their commentaries. *Thomas Aquinas wrote the most influential medieval commentary, but it was the Reformers who saw John as the most important Gospel because it contains more of Jesus' words (*Luther) and can be used as a key to understanding the other three (*Calvin). With the *Enlightenment John's authenticity (*Herder) and historical reliability (*Reimarus) were questioned with fresh rigor, and new theories as to its origin put forward, including those involving a reassessment of the role in Christian origins of Hellenistic or Jewish *mysticism (Bousset, Harnack) and an oriental redeemer myth (*Bultmann). Twentieth-century scholars continued to wrestle with these and other similar historical-critical questions until new literary and social-scientific approaches focused instead on such issues as the dramatic or rhetorical power of the Gospel and the distinctive role of women.

In art the Fourth Evangelist is represented as sitting on the shoulders of Ezekiel, and, since Irenaeus, his symbol is the eagle because he "points to the gift of the Spirit hovering over the church." The image of the good shepherd, not original but given new poignancy in John 10:1–18 (cf. Heb. 13:20; 1 Pet. 5:4; 1 John 3:16) is familiar throughout the history of Christian iconography starting with numerous catacomb paintings and early sarcophagi. His image of "the Lamb of God (*Agnus Dei)* that takes away the sins of the world" (1:29, 36) is associated with John the Baptist in Christian art of all periods, and, as an integral part of the *Mass, has been set to music, often as a solo aria, by many of the greatest composers. "The Light of the World" (John 8:12; 9:5; cf. Matt. 5:14) is the theme of a painting by Holman *Hunt (1853–56) and an oratorio by *Elgar (1900). There are settings of the *St. John Passion* by *Schütz (1610), *Bach (1724), and Arvo *Pärt (1981).

John the Baptist.

A prophetic figure, living in the wilderness beside the Jordan and dressed in camel hair, who appears at the beginning of all four Gospels, preaching a once-and-for-all baptism of repentance and attracting a huge following among the people of Judea. Known as the "forerunner" (Gk. *prodromos*), "preparing the way of the Lord" (Isa. 40:3), he was identified with Elijah (Matt. 11:14), who, in rabbinic tradition, is herald of the messianic age (Mal. 4:5 [MT 3:23]). According to Josephus (*Ant.* 18.5.2) he was executed by Herod as a threat to law and order (cf. Mark 6). Connections between his form of ascetic apocalypticism and that of the nearby Qumran sect have been proposed despite obvious differences, and his precise relationship to Jesus, also known as the forerunner (Heb. 6:20), is not entirely clear. The Fourth Gospel omits any reference to baptizing Jesus with water, focusing instead on Jesus as the one who baptizes with the Holy Spirit (John 1:29–34).

The figure of John the Baptist is frequently represented in Christian art, usually with a lamb and a flag ("Behold the Lamb of God"). The scenes from his life most often represented are the baptism of Christ (*Piero della Francesca, *Perugino, El *Greco) and Salome with the head of John the Baptist (*Donatello, Fra Lippo Lippi, *Caravaggio), but there are also, especially in 15th- and 16th-century Italy, many paintings of John with his cousin Jesus as children, often with their moth-ers (*Leonardo da Vinci, *Madonna of the Rocks*). He is the subject of a medieval English *mystery play and a play by the Protestant John Bale (1495–1563), and his ascetic ideal figures prominently in literature (*Dante, *Chaucer, *Milton). He has a memorable aria in the rock opera *Jesus Christ Superstar* (1970).

Jonah, book of.

Fifth of the Minor Prophets. He is said to have lived in the northern kingdom in the 8th century (2 Kgs. 14:15), and foreseeing the terrible fate that was soon to befall his people at the hand of the Assyrians, refused to preach God's word in their capital, Nineveh. Rescued from the sea by a great fish sent by God, he went to Nineveh and gave them a chance to repent. God forgave them, and Jonah, pleading to be allowed to die rather than witness what was to happen, learns that God's love can extend even to Israel's most feared enemies if they repent. In Jewish tradition Jonah is read on the afternoon of *Yom Kippur both as a comment on the spiritual struggle of an individual reminiscent of *Elijah and *Jeremiah, and as a demonstration of God's willingness to accept repentance on the part of all his creatures, not just Israel. In the Gospels too "the sign of Jonah" is about repentance (Matt. 12; Luke 11).

The story is expanded with fanciful details in the *midrashim and interpreted as an allegory of the soul in the *Zohar. In the Qur'an Jonah (Arab. *Yunis*) is included among the prophets but criticized for his disobedience (37:139–48) and lack of faith (68:48–50). Among patristic and medieval Christian writers the prophet's name (Heb. *yona*, "dove") inspired discussion of the role of the Holy Spirit in the story, and many saw in the story the rejection of the Jews in favor of the Gentiles of Nineveh. *Luther and *Calvin by contrast focused on the inner struggles of the prophet. Modern critical scholars separate Jonah's psalm-like prayer from the belly of the fish from the prose narrative of the other chapters, and interpret the book, along with *Ruth, against the background of Jewish exclusivism in the time of *Ezra. There has been much discussion of its literary genre (allegory, parable, prophetic legend, wisdom story), while many have found parody, irony, and comedy in the book.

Numerous literary interpretations of Jonah include a verse paraphrase by Francis Quarles entitled *The Feast of Wormes* (1620), Father Mapple's sermon in Melville's *Moby Dick* (1851), plays by James Bridie (1932) and Laurence Housman (1942), and poems by Aldous Huxley (1917), A. M. Klein (1933), and Robert Frost (1947). In the artistic conventions of the *catacombs and *sarcophagi, Jonah was associated with death and resurrection, both his three days and three nights in the belly of a sea monster, ending with him being spewed out safely onto dry land (cf. Matt. 12:40), and the peaceful scene of him asleep under a tree, a symbol of repose after death. Later representations of the mouth of hell are sometimes derived from Jonah, and a painting by the Russian Jewish artist Eugene Abeshaus shows a *Holocaust survivor stepping out of the mouth of a whale onto the pier at Haifa (1978).

Joseph

1. (Arab. *Yusuf*). *Jacob's favorite son, born to *Rachel, who later died giving birth to Benjamin, the youngest of the twelve (Gen. 30; 35). Joseph's brothers resented the special "coat of many colors" given him by his father, and his dreams that he would one day rule over them. So they put him in a pit, sold him to some passing Midianite merchants, and reported back to their father that he had been killed by wild beasts, showing him Joseph's coat, which they had dipped in goat's blood, as evidence. Meanwhile Joseph was taken to Egypt and sold for twenty pieces of silver to Potiphar, captain of the pharaoh's guard, who was impressed with his abilities. When he rejected advances by Potiphar's wife, she had him imprisoned on false charges. But his fortunes eventually turned, as a result of his skill as an interpreter of dreams, and he was appointed to a high position in the pharaoh's government. He married Potiphar's daughter Aseneth, by whom he had two sons. Later reunited with his brothers, who had been forced by famine to leave Canaan, he arranged for them to live in Egypt in the employment of the pharaoh. This explains why the Hebrews were there at the beginning of the exodus story when "there arose a new king over Egypt who knew not Joseph" (Exod. 1:8).

No reference to these events has yet been discovered in contemporary Egyptian records, although there is evidence for a long period when unpopular West Semitic kings (Egyp. *hyksos*) ruled Egypt (c. 1800—1540 B.C.E.), and for the presence of Hebrew workers (Egyp. *'aperiw*; Akk. *Habiru*) in Egypt throughout much of the 2nd millennium B.C.E. Like the other patriarchal traditions the story of Joseph probably reflects later historical developments in the promised land: Joseph's two sons and heirs, Ephraim and Manasseh, for example, account for a very large part of northern Israel, "Ephraim" being occasionally used as an alternative for "Israel" (Isa. 7; Hos. 5). Joshua, Samuel, and Jeroboam, first king of the independent northern kingdom, were all Ephraimites.

The story of Joseph is briefly referred to in a psalm (105:16–23), the Apocrypha (Wis. 10:13–14; 1 Macc. 2:53), and the NT (Acts 7:9–16; Heb. 11:21–22), but there is an early Jewish elaboration of the story in *Joseph and Aseneth*, in which Aseneth converts to Judaism before Joseph will marry her, and the pharaoh's son, with the support of two of Joseph's brothers, tries to kill him and get her for himself. Josephus (*Ant.* 2.2–8) and the rabbis portray him as a model of moral virtue and physical beauty, while medieval Jewish sources, influenced by Arabic tradition, add further details to the story, including a touching account of Joseph weeping at his mother's tomb. The story is retold at some length in the Qur'an (sura 12), and later Muslim tradition tells how Joseph and Potiphar's widow, Zuleika, fell in love and got married. According to popular Arab tradition Joseph is credited with building some of Egypt's pyramids and obelisks.

Patristic and medieval Christian tradition stressed his chastity as in the Church of Notre Dame in Souillac, where his statue is paired with that of Isaiah (cf. Isa. 7:14). He is also very frequently seen as a type of Christ, cast into a pit, sold by Judah (Lat. *Judas*; Gen. 37:26–28), his bride Aseneth a type of the church, and his bloodstained coat ("many colored," LXX, AV; "richly embroidered," Vg; perhaps "long-sleeved," Gen. 37:3) interpreted as Christ's humanity, "put on" by him in the incarnation (John 1:14), and by his followers (Rom. 13:14; Gal. 3:27). This is the theme of George Herbert's poem "Joseph's Coat" (1633). Joseph inspired a number of successful works in literature and music, notably Henry Fielding's novel *The Adventures of Joseph Andrews* (1742) and *Handel's oratorio *Joseph and His Brethren* (1744), Thomas *Mann's four-volume classic *Joseph and His Brothers* (1933–44), and the rock opera *Joseph and the Amazing Technicolor Dreamcoat* (1968, 1972). There is a dramatic painting by *Velazquez of the sons showing Joseph's coat to their father (1630), numerous portrayals of Joseph with Potiphar's wife, including those of Guido Reni, *Raphael, *Rembrandt, *Tintoretto, *Blake, and *Chagall, and several episodes in the story illustrated together in one of *Ghiberti's magnificent bronze panels (1425–52) and an elaborate painting by Andrea del Sarto (1520).

2. (Arab. *Yusuf*). Husband of Mary the mother of Jesus, a carpenter (Matt. 13:55) and a "just man" (1:19). Three times guided by an angel in a dream, he first stood by Mary, despite the risk of scandal, and named their baby Jesus, then took his family to Egypt to escape the Massacre of the Innocents, and finally brought them back to Nazareth after Herod died (Matt. 1–2). He also ensured by his ancestry that Jesus was a "son of David" (Matt. 1:16) and went with Mary to Jerusalem for the presentation of Jesus at the temple, and to celebrate the *Passover when Jesus was twelve (Luke 2:22–52). After his prominent role in Jesus' childhood, he is not mentioned again. According to apocryphal tradition, in the *Protoevangelium of James* and elsewhere, he was much older than Mary and probably died before Jesus grew up.

The relationship between Joseph and Mary has prompted much discussion ranging from the suggestion that he suspected her of adultery and wanted to protect her from being stoned to death according to the law (*Augustine, *Milton), to scenes of reconciliation in which Mary forgives Joseph for his suspicions (York *Mystery Play), or Joseph like Hosea forgives his wife for her unfaithfulness (*Blake). His chief role in Christian tradition, however, is simply that of father in portraits of the Holy Family (*Mantegna, *Michelangelo, El *Greco), interpreted as one of the "Two Trinities" in a painting by Murillo (1675–82), and always present at the *Nativity, on their way to Egypt (Fra *Angelico, c. 1450; *Caravaggio, 1596–97; *Blake, 1799), and in the temple (*Giotto, 1320–25; *Rubens, 1612–14). His dreams, like those of the other Joseph, are also sometimes portrayed (Rembrandt, 1650–55), and he is the main character in the "Cherry Tree Carol," beginning "Joseph was an old man," and in a little 15th-century German musical drama *Joseph lieber, Joseph mein*, "Joseph dearest, Joseph mine," set to music by *Vaughan Williams.

Joseph and Aseneth. Pseudepigraphical work written in Greek probably in the 1st century B.C.E. or 1st century C.E. It is in the form of a romantic novel expanding the brief reference to Aseneth in the biblical story of Joseph (Gen. 41:45). Throughout the twists and turns of the story Joseph is represented as a model Jew, observing the dietary laws and resisting the advances of women in a Gentile society, although whether the author lived in Egypt or Palestine is not known. See *Joseph 1.

Josephus, Flavius (c. 37–100 C.E.). Jewish historian. Little is known of his life aside from his autobiography, but it seems likely that he was a well-educated Jew, from a priestly family, who on visiting Rome became an enthusiastic supporter of Roman culture. During the Jewish Revolt against Rome in 66–71 he at first fought with the Jews in Galilee, but then, strongly opposed to their growing fanaticism and the inevitability of defeat, joined the Romans. He accompanied Titus during the siege of Jerusalem, and was rewarded with Roman citizenship, a pension, and land by Emperor Vespasian. Seen as a traitor by his fellow Jews, he is not even mentioned in the *Talmud, but his writings were preserved by the early church and have been enormously influential as a unique record of events in 1st-century Palestine, even though he may not always be historically reliable and a famous mention of Jesus Christ, known as the *Testimonium Flavianum* (*Ant.* 18.63–64) is probably a Christian interpolation. His four works, the *Jewish War* (originally written in Aramaic), his *Life*, the *Jewish Antiquities*, and *Against Apion*, contain the fruits of Hellenistic and rabbinic scholarship as well as eyewitness accounts and meticulous topographical descriptions, which made him, for Christian and biblical scholars, one of the most popular of all the Greek historians.

Joshua, book of. First of the *Former Prophets. It tells the tale of Israel's settlement in the promised land from after the death of Moses to the death of his successor Joshua. The two main themes of the book, symbolized by the setting up of the twelve stones from the river Jordan at Gilgal (chap. 5), and the covenant ceremony at Shechem (chap. 24), are the organization of the people in their new land (chaps. 12–21), and the dangers posed by the existing inhabitants whose annihilation is described (chaps. 10–11), but was clearly not complete. Christian writers, seeing the connection between the names Joshua (Gk. *Iesous*) and Jesus, have often sought to spiritualize the battles and interpret rest in the promised land as heaven. Commentaries by Origen (c. 250) and Calvin (1563–64), both written toward the end of their lives, perhaps reflect their thoughts as death approaches. Modern critical scholars have recognized the "Deuteronomic style" of the book and seen it as the last book in a "*Hexateuch" (von *Rad) or part of a longer "*Deuteronomistic History" (*Noth). It has been at the heart of the modern debate about the origin and early history of Israel. On the one hand archaeologists, having identified some of the cities mentioned in the narrative, acknowledge serious chronological problems (e.g., Jericho was destroyed more than a century before Hazor); while on the other, many commentators argue that ideological factors in the conquest narrative obscure what was probably a more gradual process of settlement and assimilation.

In art famous interpretations of Joshua's exploits include the 5th-century mosaics in St. Maria Maggiore in Rome, *Ghiberti's baptistery door in Florence, and John Martin's *Joshua Commanding the Sun to Stand Still* (1816). There are also numerous paintings, medieval and modern, of Rahab and the spies. The rabbis say she was one of the four most beautiful women in the world and married to Joshua, while the fathers find in her a sign that even the most sinful can be redeemed. *Dante places her in paradise. Joshua is the subject of an oratorio by *Handel and the well-known American spiritual "Joshua fit the battle of Jericho."

Jubilees, book of. A Jewish work, probably written around the mid-2nd them, if "Iscariot" refers to his origins from the town "Kerioth" near Jerusalem, known as the one who betrayed Jesus to the authorities. With his 30 pieces of silver and his kiss, Judas is synonymous with treachery in all four canonical Gospels. Christian tradition for many centuries made the *anti-Semitic connection between Judas and "Jew," representing him in art, theater, and literature as a Jewish stereotype, and *Dante called that part of hell where Judas is placed *la Giudecca*, a name applied to Jewish ghettos throughout medieval Europe. In the 19th century D. F. *Strauss presented a more sympathetic account of the life of Judas, and many more recent interpreters of the Gospels have done the same, including Anthony Burgess, Robert Graves, and Nikos Kazantzakis. According to a gnostic *Gospel of Judas*, possibly the text mentioned by *Irenaeus (2nd century) and recently published from a badly damaged codex of unknown provenance, Jesus confided in him as the only one who understood him properly and whose "betrayal" was essential to his departure from the material world ruled by demonic powers.

Jude, Letter of.

Last of the *Catholic Letters, attributed either to one of the disciples, "not Iscariot" (John 14:22) or, according to *Origen and others, the brother of Jesus (Matt. 13:55). It is addressed simply "to those who are called," and is a general exhortation calling for steadfastness and condemning unspecified sinners to hellfire. Similar in style to 2 Peter, it contains a number of allusions to Scripture, both canonical and noncanonical (*1 Enoch*; *Assumption of Moses*), and a developed angelology (Zech. 3), and ends with a doxology reminiscent of Revelation (14:1–5). It is quoted by *Tertullian, *Clement of Alexandria, and *Origen, but not finally accepted as canonical until the 4th century. *Bede's commentary was influential in medieval Europe, but Luther regarded it, along with James and Reve-

lation, with contempt. Since then it has had little impact apart from Hardy's novel *Jude the Obscure* and the liturgical use of the final doxology in some Protestant churches. Jude is the patron saint of lost causes. See *Peter, Letters of.

Judges, book of

(Heb. *Shoftim*).   Seventh book of the Bible. It is a sequel to the book of *Joshua, but gives a very different account of the Israelites' settlement in Canaan. Here "they do evil in the sight of the LORD," meet with fierce opposition from the indigenous inhabitants, and are saved by a series of heroes known as "judges" who lead them to miraculous victories over the Moabites (Ehud), Canaanites (*Deborah and Jael), Midianites (*Gideon), Ammonites (*Jephthah), and Philistines (*Samson). A final section (chaps. 17–21), less well known, recounts further disturbing examples of evil and violence "when there was no king in Israel."

Their exploits are praised in the NT, along with those of David, Samuel, and the prophets (Heb. 11:32), but do not play a significant role in the patristic period. Where they do appear in early and medieval Christian art and literature (*Biblia Pauperum*), they are types of Christ (Samson) or the Virgin *Mary (Jael, Gideon's fleece). The scholarly commentaries of *Rabanus Maurus and *Hugh of St. Victor are notable exceptions. By contrast the rabbis and medieval Jewish commentators on Judges read the text closely and concluded, for example, that the actions of Jephthah, Gideon, and Samson were reprehensible. In the 17th century *Spinoza is one of the first to approach Judges from a historical-critical point of view, while in the next century *Voltaire uses the book (especially Jephthah) to prove that Judaism is a primitive and brutal religion. Modern scholars at first traced the pentateuchal sources J, E, and D in Judges, but later generally accepted the view that it forms part of a "*Deuteronomistic History" and, using the evidence of archaeology, sought to century B.C.E. It is included in the OT canon of the Ethiopian Orthodox Church and much valued by the Jews of Ethiopia (Falashas). In 50 sections, corresponding to the Jubilee of 7 x 7 years (Lev. 25), it is a commentary on Genesis and Exodus down to the institution of the *Passover, placing special emphasis on the laws concerning sacrifice, the Sabbath, intermarriage, and food. Its purpose is clearly to defend Jewish identity against the pressures of a Hellenistic environment. There is also a strong apocalyptic element in the many references to angels, demons, the imminent advent of the messianic kingdom, a new heaven and a new earth, and the promise of immortality after death. In addition to Ethiopic mss and numerous quotations in the Greek and Latin sources, fifteen fragments of the Hebrew original have been found at Qumran. The *Jubilees* calendar does not correspond to that of rabbinic tradition but is the same as that used by the Qumran community and *1 Enoch*, with which it has other literary and theological affinities.

Judah (Heb. *Yehuda*, Gk. *Ioudas*). Fourth son of Jacob, and eponymous ancestor of the Judeans, originally the people of Judah and subsequently the Jewish people. In biblical tradition he is remembered as the one responsible for selling his brother *Joseph to the Ishmaelites (Gen. 37:26–28) and for the encounter with his daughter-in-law *Tamar, but his name became synonymous with heroism and leadership (*Judas Maccabaeus, *Judith, Judah the Prince: see *Mishnah) and, on account of his most famous descendant King *David, messianic beliefs are associated with him from early times (cf. Gen. 49:10). The "Lion of Judah" (Gen. 49:9) has a messianic function in the NT (Rev. 5:5) and became a popular symbol in Jewish art (*Chagall 1960) as well as one of the titles of the Emperor of Ethiopia. In Christian tradition, however, the name often had *anti-Semitic overtones,

due in part to its association w Iscariot.

As a geographical term, Jud to the southern kingdom with i at *Jerusalem, as opposed to t dom of *Israel in the north, attested in contemporary extra sources as the name for the province established there after of the Babylonian Empire in 53. The history of the decline and fall kingdom of Judah is recounted in and Chronicles, and referred to re edly by the prophets (Isa. 3:8, 8:8 Roman times the term Judea referr the Jewish territory around Jerusa which expanded under Herod the C and was made into part of the prov of Syria in 6 C.E. After the unsucces. Jewish revolts of 66–70 and 132–135, Jewish population dwindled and province was renamed Syria Palestin

Judah Halevi (c. 1075–1141). Jewis poet and philosopher, friend of *Ibn Ezr After a life lived partly in Christia Spain, where he practiced medicine a the court of Alonso VI in Toledo, and then subsequently in Cordoba in the Muslim part of the peninsula, he decided to emigrate to Jerusalem, but got only as far as Alexandria, where he died. He wrote over a thousand poems, sacred and secular, characterized by brilliant use of the Hebrew language, mastery of poetic and musical patterns, and profound religious feeling. The best known are his passionate "Songs of Zion," unparalleled since the psalms of David. Shortly before he left Spain, all too familiar with the tensions between Christianity, Islam, and Judaism, he wrote an extremely influential philosophical treatise known as the *Book of Kuzari*, purporting to be a dialogue between a Jewish sage and the king of the Khazars, a convert to Judaism in the 8th century.

Judas Iscariot. One of the twelve disciples, perhaps the only Judean among distinguish fact from fiction in the narrative. More recent approaches apply a variety of new *literary-critical methods, or focus on sociopolitical and ideological issues raised by the narrative, such as the way women are depicted, especially those unnamed. Since the Renaissance the judges became very popular in literature, art, and music.

Judith, book of. Apocryphal work cited as scripture already in the 1st century C.E. and always very popular in the church, although its canonicity was questioned by *Jerome and others. Unlike *Esther, it was never part of Hebrew Scripture, although Jewish versions of the story exist and are sometimes associated with the Feast of *Hanukkah. It is written in Greek, although there may have been a Hebrew original now lost. Judith, an unmarried widow, who went forth with her maid to slay Holofernes, the Assyrian general, while all the Israelite menfolk watched from the city walls, is held up as a model of courage in Jewish tradition and by *Clement of Rome (1st century C.E.), but praised more for her chastity than her bravery by some of the church fathers. Others speak of her great beauty. Allegorical interpretations are developed by *Rabanus Maurus and, surprisingly, *Luther, who notes that the name of Judith's hometown, Bethulia, looks very like the Hebrew word for "virgin" (Heb. *betulah*). Modern scholars have sought to find a historical context for the story in the Persian period, or, perhaps more plausibly, the Maccabean period, and more recently applied literary and sociopolitical insights to analyze the gender tensions and ambiguities of one of the Bible's most successful narratives.

In Renaissance literature and art Judith stands for resistance to tyranny, as in Thomas Hudson's *Historie of Judith* (1584) and *Donatello's bronze statue of Judith and Holofernes, which was used as a symbol of civic liberty in Florence. The beheading of Holofernes was a favorite scene for painters of the 16th and 17th centuries, including *Caravaggio, *Cranach, Artemisia Gentileschi, and *Michelangelo (*Sistine Chapel). Many theatrical versions of the story exist, from a 15th-century Jewish play first staged in southern Italy, to Paolo Giacometti's *Giuditta* (1857) and Arnold Bennett's *Judith* (1919), which was set to music as an opera by Eugene Goossens (1929). Other musical settings include works by *Vivaldi (1716), Arne (1761), Parry (1888), and Honegger (1926), to which we might add *Mozart's early oratorio *La Betulia Liberata* (1771).

Jung, Carl (1875–1961). Swiss psychiatrist and psychoanalytical interpreter of the Bible. Brought up in a devout Christian environment dominated by his father, who was a Lutheran pastor, Jung was familiar with the Bible from an early age, and throughout his life used it as a source of insight and inspiration, ignoring traditional interpretations and current *historical-critical concerns in favor of his own often idiosyncratic analysis of *myths and *symbols. His works are rich in biblical phrases, images, and allusions, taken not only from Luther's Bible, especially the Gospel of John, but also from such extracanonical books as *1 Enoch* and the *Gospel of Peter*. In *Answer to Job* (1952; ET 1954), his only work devoted exclusively to a biblical text, he reveals the dark side of God and finds hope in the feminine figure of *Wisdom. See also *Psychological interpretation.

Justin Martyr (c. 100–165). Early Christian *apologist. Born in Nablus in Palestine, he first studied the Greek philosophers and then at the age of about 30 converted to Christianity. After a short period teaching in Ephesus, he moved to Rome and opened a Christian school, which counted *Tatian among its students, but was later denounced and, on refusing to take part in Roman sacrifice, he and some of his disciples were scourged and beheaded. Only two works by Justin are extant. The *Apology*, in two parts, the first addressed to Emperor Antoninus Pius (c. 155), the second to his son and successor, Marcus Aurelius (c. 161), upholds the uniqueness and superiority of Christianity over pagan philosophies. Without explaining or defending his method, he also illustrates in considerable detail how OT prophecies have been fulfilled in Christ. In the *Dialogue with Trypho the Jew* he argues that the *Law and the *covenant with the Jews are no longer binding, and that Christian interpretations of the OT (e.g., the *Immanuel prophecy in Isa. 7:14) are correct. His influence on later writers was considerable, and a number of later works were falsely ascribed to him.

Kabbalah (or **Qabbalah**; Heb. "received tradition"). System of Jewish *mysticism originating in the south of France in the 12th century C.E. Its roots can be traced to much earlier texts in which individuals speculate on what existed before creation (*Bereshit* *mysticism) and on Ezekiel's vision of the heavenly chariot (*Merkavah mysticism), or have visionary experiences of journeying to the heavenly palaces (*Hekhalot*). These are almost entirely extracanonical texts like *1 *Enoch*, and references in the *Talmud usually treat it as a dangerous and heretical phenomenon to be avoided, as in the story told of "the four who entered paradise": of the four only Rabbi *Akiva came back unhurt (*b. Hagigah* 15b). These mystical traditions survived on the margins of Judaism until the Middle Ages in works like *Sefer Yetzirah*, "Book of Creation," and the *Hekalot* literature.

Mysticism gained some degree of orthodox Jewish recognition with the appearance in the late 13th century of the *Zohar, the kabbalist's Bible, and the influence of the much-respected talmudist and biblical exegete *Nahmanides (1194–1270), who acknowledged the mystical

meaning of the Torah alongside the literal and allegorical meanings. An important stage in the subsequent development of kabbalistic philosophy is represented by Isaac Luria, the *Ari*, "Lion" (1534–72), whose ideas, collected by his disciples in a work known as the *Writings of Ari*, now take their place alongside the *Zohar*. Discredited in the eyes of Jewish orthodoxy by the messianic heresy of Shabbetai Zvi (1626–76), Kabbalah nevertheless remains an essential strand of Jewish tradition, not only in the *Hasidism founded by the Baal Shem Tov (1698–1750), but in the writings of many individuals, including *Buber (1878–1965), Gershom Scholem (1897–1982), *Heschel (1907–72), and Emil Fackenheim (1916–2003).

Fundamental to Kabbalah is the yearning to know an unknowable God through symbols, images, and feelings (cf. *Song of Songs). In the Zohar, "Book of Splendor" (Dan. 12:3), which is a mystical *midrash on the Torah, there are ten *sefirot*, "emanations, powers," between *En Sof* ("without end," utterly transcendent) and the world, described in biblical imagery as rivers, pillars, heavens, and the like and organized in patterns, such as a tree, a garden, and the primal man. Dynamic interactivity both between the *sefirot*, and between them and the created universe, is revealed in the Torah, and the more we know of it through study and contemplation, the nearer we come to knowledge and love of God (*devekut*, "cleaving [to God]"). Moreover, since all our actions interact with the *sefirot*, what we do on earth has cosmic implications and an impact on what goes on in heaven. Lurianic Kabbalah introduced new concepts partly in response to the expulsion of the Jews from Spain in 1492. From the notion of a god in exile and a creation shattered by the *sefirot*, there developed the idea of *tikkun*, "restoration, repair," and the existence of "sparks of the *Shekinah [God's presence]," which are everywhere but hidden from sight, each capable of being uncovered by an act of human kindness.

Kaddish (or **Qaddish**). Ancient and very popular Jewish *prayer, said in Aramaic, for the sanctification of God's name and the coming of the kingdom of heaven on earth. The opening words are from Ezek. 38:23 and the conclusion perhaps from Dan. 2:20. The *mourner's kaddish* is a longer version, including a reference to the resurrection of the dead, and is recited by a son or daughter of the deceased every Sabbath for eleven months after a death, and on the anniversary (Yiddish *yahrzeit)*. The *Kaddish de-rabbanan* ("Kaddish of the Rabbis") contains an additional prayer for the well-being of students of the Torah. Scholars have noted the similarities between the Kaddish and the 1st-century C.E. *Lord's Prayer *(Paternoster)* (Matt. 6:9–13).

Karaites (or **Qaraites**). A Jewish sect founded in Babylonia in the 8th century C.E. Like the Sadducees, they rejected the *Oral Torah in its entirety, and sought to get back to the literal meaning of Hebrew Scripture or *miqra* (*qara*, "to read aloud"), from which the name Karaite, "scripturist," is derived. For example, the prohibition in Exod. 23:19 refers literally to boiling a kid in its mother's milk and has nothing to do with a general ban on mixing meat with milk or milk products as it was interpreted in rabbinic Judaism. Defeated by *Saadia Gaon, champion of rabbinic tradition, in the 10th century, they were marginalized but survived in Egypt, Turkey, and parts of Europe. Today there are small Karaite synagogues in Israel and the United States, still with their own independent religious authority and institutions.

Kedushah (or **Qedushah**; Heb. "holiness"). Prayers proclaiming the holiness of God, especially the words sung in heaven by the seraphim in Isaiah's vision: "Holy, holy, holy, is the LORD of hosts . . ." (Isa. 6:3), and recited as part of the second of the "Eighteen Blessings." See *Amidah; *Sanctus.

Kerygma (Gk. "preaching"). NT Greek word used in the Gospels of the preaching of Jonah (Matt. 12:41), and by Paul of his own and his disciples' preaching as well as that of Jesus (Rom. 16:25). In some mss Mark's Gospel ends with a reference to "the sacred and imperishable kerygma of eternal salvation." Some modern scholars have used the term to distinguish redemptive preaching from a more didactic ministry (C. H. *Dodd), or to describe the demythologized crux of early Christianity (*Bultmann), and speak of "kerygmatic theology" (*Barth).

Ketiv. The Jewish scribes responsible for preserving the text of the Hebrew Bible drew a distinction between the *Ketiv*, "what is written," and the *Qere*, "what is read aloud," that is, how it should be pronounced. Because the Hebrew script exists independently of the systems of vocalization ("*pointing") invented later, it is possible to write the consonants of one word (K) with the pointing of another (Q). There are about a thousand cases of this in the MT, the consonants of the Qere being given in the margin. The best-known example is the *Tetragrammaton, the four consonants of the unpronounceable sacred name YHWH, written with the vowels of Adonai, "the Lord," because that is how it was to be pronounced. Similarly the names of the pagan deities Sakkuth (MT Sikkuth) and Kaiwan (MT Kiyyun) are written with the vowels of *shikkutz*, "abomination" (Amos 5:26). See *Manuscripts; *Masoretic Text.

Ketuvim (Heb. "Writings"). The third part of the Hebrew Bible (see *Tanakh)* containing three of the longest books (Psalms, Proverbs, and Job), five of the shortest (Song of Songs, Ruth, Lamentations, Ecclesiastes, and Esther), and four of the latest (Daniel, Ezra, Nehemiah, and Chronicles). It ends with the edict of Cyrus authorizing the rebuilding of the temple and the return of the Jews to Jerusalem. They are also known by the Greek term *Hagiographa, "sacred writings." There is a reference to "the law, the prophets, and the others that followed them" in the preface to Sirach (c. 130 B.C.E.), but precisely what books the third part contained at that time (probably not Daniel), and when the Writings reached the form they are in now, is unknown.

Kierkegaard, Søren (1813–55). Danish philosopher. Born into a wealthy and devout Lutheran family, he studied theology at the University of Copenhagen, graduating in 1840. In a series of intensely personal philosophical writings, especially *Philosophical Fragments* (1844) and *Concluding Unscientific Postscript* (1846), he attacked established Christian tradition, and developed what he called an "existential dialectic," essential to any serious discourse about God and discussed by philosophers ever since. His religious writings were no less significant, as the influence of *Christian Discourses* (1950) on *Barth and the Barthians demonstrates. In reading the Bible his experience of trying to identify with Jesus and the disciples made him look beyond current *historical-critical trends in biblical scholarship (e.g., D. F. *Strauss, *Life of Jesus*, 1835), to a more immediate encounter with the text as it stands. His famous study of Abraham's faith in Gen. 22 in the early philosophical work *Fear and Trembling* (1843), entitled from Phil. 2:12, is a monument to his spiritual struggle for self-awareness in the presence of God.

Kimhi (or **Qimhi**), **David** (c. 1160–1235). Jewish biblical commentator and Hebrew grammarian, also known by the acronym Radak (from Rabbi David Kimhi). He was born into a family of scholars who had emigrated from Spain to Narbonne in the south of France. His major work in Hebrew linguistics, entitled *Mikhlol* (*Summa*), comprises a gram-

mar and a lexicon ("The Book of Roots") usually printed separately, in which he provides a systematic digest of previous scholars' work, much of which was previously available only in Arabic. The two works were reprinted many times and translated into Latin for the benefit of Christian Hebraists. His commentaries on the Prophets (Joshua–Malachi) and part of the Writings (Psalms and Chronicles), printed in all rabbinic Bibles, supplement *Rashi on these books and have been widely used both by Jewish and Christian scholars. They are primarily concerned with the literal meaning of the text but make frequent use of traditional rabbinic interpretations.

King James' Authorized Version. See *Authorized Version.

King, Martin Luther, Jr. (1929–68). African American Baptist minister and civil rights activist. After gaining a PhD at Boston University, he became pastor of a church in Montgomery, Alabama, in 1954. A brilliant orator, he led the great march on Washington, DC, in 1963 where he made his famous "I have a dream" speech, and for the next five years his nonviolent campaign had a huge impact on American society, especially in the south. In 1964 he received the Nobel Peace Prize, and was assassinated in Memphis, Tennessee, in 1968, the day after his "I've been to the mountaintop" address (cf. Deut. 34). Brought up in the Baptist *fundamentalist tradition, he viewed the Bible as a unique source of inspiration and authority, but he also accepted the insights of modern *historical criticism, which for him made the exodus, the 8th-century prophets, and the Sermon on the Mount all the more relevant to the situation confronting him in 1960s America.

Kings, books of. In the Hebrew Bible, last of the Former Prophets, attributed to Jeremiah by the rabbis. In the Greek Bible Samuel and Kings are combined as 1, 2, 3, and 4 *Basileiai* ("Kingdoms"). They recount the history of the kingdoms of Israel and Judah from the death of David to the Babylonian exile, with a theological emphasis on the relationship between their fortunes and the behavior of their leaders. First Kings describes the building and dedication of Solomon's temple, the establishment of a separate northern kingdom of Israel (or Ephraim) with its capital at Samaria, and the exploits of the prophet Elijah. Second Kings covers the life of the prophet Elisha, and the decline and fall, first, at the hand of the Assyrians, of Israel under a series of evil kings, and then, despite the reforming efforts of Hezekiah and Josiah, of Jerusalem and Judah at the hands of the Babylonians. It ends optimistically, like the book of Jeremiah, with the release of King Jehoiachin from prison in Babylon.

Second Chronicles (4th century B.C.E.) is an interesting early reading of Kings, and there is also Josephus's version in his *Antiquities* (1st century C.E.). Kings is referred to many times in the NT, most memorably by Jesus in his Nazareth sermon (Luke 4). In the rabbinic and patristic literature there is much about Solomon, Elijah, and other characters in the narrative, but few scholars wrote works specially devoted to it. Commentaries by *Ephrem the Syrian (4th century) and *Theodoret (5th century) are exceptions. Medieval Christian commentaries include those of *Bede, *Rabanus Maurus, *Hugh of St. Victor, and *Nicholas of Lyra (who made good use of the commentaries of *Rashi and *Kimhi on the Hebrew text), and from the 17th century an increasing number of commentaries, including a remarkable one by the Spanish Jesuit G. Sanchez (1624). Modern *historical criticism has analyzed the Deuteronomistic elements in the style, structure, and theology of the text, and sought to reconstruct the history of the period with the benefit of archaeological discoveries, which include a good number of contemporary documents in Hebrew, Assyrian, and Babylonian. More recent studies of Kings highlight some of the ideological issues raised by the narrative, such as the attitude toward the northern kingdom and the role of women (Jezebel, Huldah).

The influence of 1 and 2 Kings on Western culture has been enormous. A significant number of passages from Kings appear in both Jewish and Christian lectionaries, including Solomon's prayer to be read at Sukkot (1 Kgs. 8), Josiah's discovery of the book of the covenant at *Passover (2 Kgs. 23), and verses from 1 Kgs. 1, set to music by *Handel as the anthem *Zadok the Priest* (1727), at the Anglican coronation ceremony. Elaborate developments of the traditions about Solomon and the *Queen of Sheba and of his miraculous throne (1 Kgs. 10:18–20) appear in Targum Sheni to the book of *Esther, while in Christian tradition the Queen of Sheba figures prominently in the *Legend of the True Cross*, exquisitely depicted in a series of frescoes by *Piero dell Francesca. Jezebel and her mother Athaliah appear in an oratorio by *Handel (1733) and in Racine's play *Athalie*, performed with incidental music by *Mendelssohn in 1845, who also wrote the oratorio *Elijah* (1846). The "Destruction of Sennacherib" (2 Kgs. 18–19) inspired both *Rubens and *Byron. Details about the Davidic ancestry of Jesus (Matt. 1) appearing in *Jesse trees all over medieval Europe, are derived from Kings.

Kohelet (or **Qohelet**).   See *Ecclesiastes.

Koine Greek. The language of Hellenistic education and culture superimposed by Alexander the Great and his successors on the peoples of Egypt, Palestine, Syria, and Asia Minor from the 3rd century B.C.E. It was a form of the Attic Greek used by Plato and Aristotle and was a good medium for philosophical and theological writing. It was the language in which much Jewish literature of the Second Temple period was written, including the *Septuagint, most of the apocryphal and pseudepigraphical literature, the works of *Philo and *Josephus, and the NT. The Jewish preference for Hebrew and Aramaic, however, prevailed and was a major factor in the schism with Christian writers for whom Greek was the main language of theology and who rarely returned to the Hebrew original. It is doubtful whether the church fathers could have formulated Christian doctrine in any other language. See *Greek; *Hellenism.

Koran.   See *Qur'an.

Kuhnau, Johann (1660–1722). German organist and composer. In 1682 he went to Leipzig, and eventually became organist and cantor in St. Thomas's Church, where *Bach succeeded him in 1723. Of special interest are his six "Biblical Sonatas" for harpsichord (1700), which are early examples of program music interpreting the stories of David and Goliath (1 Sam. 17), David healing Saul by his music (1 Sam. 16:23), Jacob's wedding (Gen. 29), the mortal sickness and recovery of Hezekiah (Isa. 38), Gideon, savior of Israel (Judg. 6–7), and the death and burial of Jacob (Gen. 49–50).

Kyrie eleison (Gk. "Lord, have mercy"; cf. Ps. 41:4, 10; Matt. 17:15). Early Christian prayer, which, along with *Christe eleison* ("Christ have mercy"), has been the first part of the Roman *Mass since the 9th century.

L.   In OT studies a primitive nomadic "Lay" source in the *Pentateuch proposed by Otto Eissfeldt to account for passages like Gen. 6:1–4, Exod. 4:1–9, and Num. 11:1–3, which he argued must be earlier than J and E. In NT Studies L is a Lukan source, postulated to account for passages occurring only in Luke.

Lamentations, book of (Heb. *Ekhah* "How . . . !" 1:1; Lat. *Threni*). In the Hebrew Bible, one of the Five Scrolls prescribed to be read on the fast of the 9th of Ab, commemorating the destruction of the temple. In the Christian Bible it comes immediately after *Jeremiah, to whom it was universally attributed, by both Jews and Christians, down to modern times. Current scholarship accepts the traditional date, but finds no evidence that Jeremiah was the author. Parallels in ancient Mesopotamian and Hellenistic literature have been adduced to help understand the meaning and purpose of the book. More recently scholars have turned to its afterlives in the laments of the Jewish poet Eleazar Kallir (6th century C.E.?), for example, and the post-Holocaust "literature of survival," and highlighted the element of a woman's protest especially in chaps. 1 and 2.

Jeremiah weeping over Jerusalem was interpreted as a type of Christ (*Dominus flevit*, Luke 19:41–44), and the reference to "the LORD's anointed" (Lam. 4:20) has been given various christological interpretations. John Donne's poetic translation (1549), however, influenced by a converted Jew, seeks to recreate the poems' original context. Since the early Middle Ages parts of Lamentations were sung at Mattins in Holy Week, and there are settings by *Tallis, *Palestrina and *Lassus. Modern musical interpreations include Leonard *Bernstein's *Jeremiah Symphony* (1942) in which verses from Lamentations are sung by a solo soprano (1:1–3; 4:14–15; 5:20–21), and a large-scale choral work entitled *Threni* (Lat. "Lamentations") by *Stravinsky (1958).

Langland, William.   See *Piers Plowman*.

Lassus, Orlande de (Ital. Orlando di Lasso) (1532–94). Flemish composer. Born in Mons, he visited Italy a number of times and served briefly as choirmaster in the Church of St. John Lateran in Rome (1553–54), but spent most of his life in the service of the duke of Bavaria in Munich. He was honored by Emperor Maximilian, the French king Charles IX, and Pope Gregory XIII. Among his 1,200 or so compositions, mainly religious, are four *Passions (one according to each Gospel), a *requiem, a set of spiritual madrigals entitled *Lagrime di San Pietro* ("The Tears of St. Peter"), and a marvelous setting of the *Penitential Psalms.

Last Supper. The final meal of Christ and the disciples in the upper room (Mark 14:15, cf. Acts 1:13) the evening before the crucifixion. It is the occasion of the institution of the *Eucharist according to the first three Gospels (also 1 Cor. 11:23–26), and of a long discourse by Jesus, preceded by his washing of the disciples' feet and followed by a prayer ("Father, the hour has come"), according to the Fourth (John 13–17). Many representations of the scene in art focus on the institution of the Eucharist, and the table appears to be empty apart from the chalice (Rosselli, 1481–82, *Poussin, 1640), while others portray a more or less sumptuous meal (*Signorelli, 1502; El *Greco, 1568). In fact the biblical accounts mention only bread and wine, although from early times a fish, symbol of Christ, occasionally appears on the table along with the bread and chalice. The presence of *Judas is referred to in all four Gospels. John's note that Jesus dismisses him from the room (13:29–30) is portrayed at *Chartres with the departing figure stealing a fish from the table, and *Leonardo da Vinci's celebrated *Last Supper* (Milan, 1498) depicts the psychological moment at which Christ announces that "one among you will betray me." All three of *Tintoretto's versions are even more dramatic, especially the last, painted shortly before he died (Venice, 1492–94), although the eucharistic meaning of the scene is always obvious. See *Maundy Thursday; *Passover.

Latin. Originally the language of Latium (modern *Lazio*) in central Italy and its main city Rome, but by the beginning of the Common Era it had eclipsed its competitors (mainly Etruscan and Greek) and was the chief language of administration and culture in Italy and the West. Monumental inscriptions in the famous Roman lettering and an ever increasing number of Latin-speakers appear throughout the Roman Empire including Syria, Palestine, and Egypt. In the beginning, however, Christian writers wrote in Greek, even in the West (e.g., Clement of Rome), and Latin was theologically the servant of Greek as the many Christian *loanwords illustrate (e.g., *evangelium*, *baptisma*, *Kyrie eleison).

The language of power eventually became the language of the church. Existing Latin words were given new meanings (e.g., *salus, fides, originale peccatum*), new words coined (*trinitas, consubstantialis*), and by the end of the 4th century Jerome's Latin version of the Bible, making use of earlier translations, had begun to replace all others in the Church of Rome. Church Latin became the exclusive lingua franca of European scholars and priests throughout the Middle Ages, until *Dante chose to write a major literary work in a language intended for ordinary people to understand, and the Reformers made it a priority to use the vernacular. Musical settings of the Mass or parts of it (e.g., *Agnus Dei), the Psalms (e.g., the Miserere), and numerous other biblical or medieval works (e.g., the Magnificat, *Carmina Burana*) are still normally performed in Latin, which is also still used by the Vatican as a means of international communication. See *Rome.

Latter Prophets. See *Nevi'im.

Law.   The laws revealed to *Moses and the Israelites at *Sinai are the constitution of the "kingdom of priests, a holy nation," created out of Hebrew slaves (Exod. 19:6), to equip them for their journey to the promised land. The biblical account is in two parts: the Sinai narrative from their first approach to the mountain accompanied by thunder and lightning (Exod. 19) to their departure in marching order (Num. 10); then in Deuteronomy, within sight of the promised land, Moses repeats the whole story of exodus and Sinai (Horeb) in his own words. The bulk of the legal material is divided into five law codes: the Decalogue (Exod. 20; Deut. 5), the book of the covenant (Exod. 21–23: cf. 24:7); the laws of the tabernacle (Exod. 25–40), the laws of Leviticus and the Deuteronomic code (Exod. 12–26). Many of the laws, usually described as statutes (Heb. *huqqim*) and ordinances (*mishpatim*), are repeated more than once, often in different forms, and cover every aspect of life from personal morality and social justice to eating habits and ritual purity.

Modern scholars have identified different types of material with parallels in the ancient Near East, and attempted to reconstruct their original date and function. The apodictic form ("thou shalt not …"), for example, appears to belong more to ethical instruction or the rhetoric of political treaties (covenant), than the casuistic ("if a thief is found …"), which is normal in language for use in lawcourts. The earliest material is probably to be found in the casuistic parts of the book of the covenant, while Leviticus, including what is known to modern writers as the Holiness Code (Lev. 17–26), in its present form is probably exilic or postexilic, although containing ancient traditions like the scapegoat ritual (Lev. 16). Obvious parallels in style and theology between Deuteronomy and Joshua–Kings have led to the widely held conclusion that it too belongs to the exilic period.

The rabbis interpreted the biblical laws, which according to their calculations amounted to 613 *mitzvot*, "commandments," with minute attention to detail, but argued that there are ethical principles that override most of them, such as the principle of saving life. In their preaching, like Jesus (Luke 10:27), they also reduced them to a few basic principles: according to David eleven (Ps. 15), Isaiah six (33:15), Micah three (6:8), and Habakkuk one (2:4) (*b. Makkot* 23b–24a). Paul's rejection of Jewish law was not because he believed it was wrong, but because he could not live up to it and had discovered an alternative (Rom. 7). After the *Talmud, the most famous compilations of Jewish law are the *Mishneh Torah* of *Maimonides (12th century) and Joseph Caro's *Shulhan Arukh* (16th century) to which may be added several important collections of *Responsa, both medieval and modern. See *Halakhah.

Law of Moses (Heb. *torat moshe*). The *Torah, first and most important part of the Hebrew Bible, also known as the Five Books of Moses or the *Pentateuch. It contains the "law of the LORD" (Exod. 13:9; 2 Kgs. 10:31) and other laws, but the term *torah*, sometimes translated "teaching, instruction" (Prov. 1:8), is not one of the normal terms for "*law." The Torah contains stories of creation, blessing, promise, hope, and much more, and in the Jewish liturgy corresponds to the Gospels.

Alongside the Written Torah at the heart of Judaism, there is the *Oral Torah (*Tora she-be'al pe*), that is, the teachings of the rabbis contained in *Talmud and *Midrash, without which the Bible is impossible to understand, and which are believed to go back in an unbroken chain to Sinai (*m. Abot* 1:1). The LXX translation *nomos*, "law," gave the Torah predominantly legalistic associations that the term itself does not have, and that led to the representation in art of the *synagogue as a blind woman clutching a tablet of the law rather than a Torah scroll, and of Moses as "lawgiver" rather than prophet.

Lazarus.

1. Brother of *Martha and Mary, who lived in Bethany and was brought back from the dead by Jesus after four days in the tomb (John 11). The narrative is full of graphic detail: the women's grief and anger that Jesus had not come sooner, the sympathy of the Jews, the weeping of Jesus, the moving of the stone, Jesus' prayer to his Father, his loud cry "Lazarus come forth!" and the appearance of Lazarus, stinking and tied up in cloths and bandages. The story takes place shortly before Christ's own passion and resurrection, and provides the context for his words "I am the resurrection and the life" (11:25). It also contains references to Caiaphas and the chief priests plotting to kill both Jesus (11:53) and Lazarus (12:10), and concludes with an account of how Jesus returned to Bethany the day before Palm Sunday and dined with Lazarus and his sisters once more (12:1–19).

Most patristic and medieval Christian commentators saw Lazarus as a type of Christ, freed from the bindings of mortality after suffering, dying, and being confined in a tomb, while since the Reformation *Luther, *Calvin, and others focus on evidence in the story for Jesus' true humanity, not only his grief and weeping, but also anxiety as he confronts death (11:33, 38). The raising of Lazarus is interpreted in some traditions, including the apocryphal *Gospel of Nicodemus, as Christ's victory over *Satan.

The question as to where Lazarus was during those four days is asked by Mary and the neighbors in Tennyson's *In Memoriam* (1849), and what happened to him in later life is the subject of much speculation, from the *Golden Legend* in which he is said to have been the first bishop of Larnaka in Cyprus, but is also associated with Marseilles and Autun in southern France, to Robert Browning's analysis of his state of mind at the age of 50 in his popular *Karshish* poem (1855). In Eugene O'Neill's play *Lazarus Laughed* (1925) his faith is tested by Jews, Greeks, and Romans till his death in a Roman amphitheater, while John Ford Noonan's play *Lazarus Was a Lady* (1970) and poems by Sylvia Plath (1965) and Thom Gunn (1983) explore some of the tragic life-and-death issues raised by the Lazarus story. In pictorial interpretations all the biblical details, often including the stench of the tomb, are faithfully portrayed as in paintings by *Giotto (1304–6), Sebastiano del Piombo (1517–19), *Caravaggio (1608–9), and *Rembrandt (1630). There are oratorios by *Schubert (unfinished) and several less well known composers including J. C. F. Bach (1773), Lorenzo Perosi (1898), and Franco Capuana (1920).

2. The poor man covered with sores in Jesus' parable (Luke 16:19–31), who became the patron saint of leprosy sufferers in the Middle Ages and gave his name to the *lazaretto*, a Christian institution established in Venice, Dubrovnik, Philadelphia, and elsewhere, for the care and isolation of immigrants with contagious diseases.

Leah.

Jacob's first wife and mother of six of his twelve sons, including Levi and *Judah, and his daughter *Dinah. Along with *Rachel, Jacob's second wife, the two sisters are revered as having built up Israel (Ruth 4:11), although Leah was less beautiful and "weak-eyed" (Gen. 29:16–17), understood by the rabbis to mean weak with copious weeping. Patristic commentators compare the worldly Leah to Martha and the more introspective Rachel to Mary as types of the two ways of Christian living (Luke 10:38–42), and this is how *Michelangelo depicts them (1545). Later references to Leah in *Shakespeare, Robert Browning, Thomas Hardy, and elsewhere highlight the rivalry between them and the greater desirability of Rachel. See *Tribes of Israel.

Lectionary.

Traditional Jewish lectionaries date from the early Middle Ages. The lectionary for weekly Sabbath readings divides the *Torah into 54 portions (*parashot*), beginning with Gen. 1:1–6:8 with a *haftarah (reading from the Prophets) from Isaiah (42:5–43:10), and ending with Deut. 33–34 with a haftarah from Joshua (1:1–18). The celebration at the completion of the annual cycle of *Torah readings is called *Simhat Torah*, "rejoicing of the law." Readings from the Torah, together with appropriate haftarot, are also prescribed for special Sabbaths, festivals, and other occasions, e.g., Lev. 16 and Jonah for *Yom Kippur.

Christian lectionaries modeled on the Jewish system date back to the 4th century C.E. and have been frequently modified. In the Catholic Church a new lectionary was published in 1969, implementing decisions taken at the Second Vatican Council, for example, to give more prominence to the OT. In the Anglican tradition a new Book of Common Prayer lectionary was issued in 1956 and with several subsequent revisions is still in use. Lectionaries, which are selective and frequently tailor the text to suit ethical or ecclesiastical principles (e.g., by omitting the last verse of Ps. 137 or the second half of 1 Tim. 2), play a significant role in determining which parts of the Bible are generally the best known and most preached upon. The variety of texts used by nonconformist preachers, free of the controls of any official lectionary, is therefore much wider.

Lent. A period of forty days fasting (Lat. *Quadragesima*) in preparation for *Easter, mentioned for the first time in the early 4th century. In the Western tradition it begins on Ash Wednesday and is preceded by a period of extravagant feasting known variously as Shrove Tuesday, Mardi Gras, or Carnival, memorably depicted in a painting by Pieter *Brueghel (1559). The English name Lent is derived from an Anglo-Saxon word for "spring," and the number 40 from the biblical traditions that Jesus fasted for 40 days and nights in the wilderness (Matt. 4:1–11), as did Elijah (1 Kgs. 19:8) and the citizens of Nineveh (Jonah 3:4). It was also the time spent by Moses with God on Mount Sinai (Exod. 24:18) and the amount of time it

rained on Noah in the ark (Gen. 7). Traditionally Lent is marked by special prayers and almsgiving as well as fasting, and the lectionaries reflect this by focusing on the true nature of fasting (Isa. 58:1–8, 8–14; Hos. 5:15–6:6; Ps. 51) and prayer (Matt. 6:7–15), on the one hand, and renewed commitment (Exod. 20:1–17; Deut. 30:10–20) and love for one another (Matt. 5:20–26; 23:1–12; 25:31–46), on the other. In the Western church *Alleluia and *Gloria are not sung during Lent.

Leonardo da Vinci (1452–1519). Italian artist, scientist, and inventor. Born in Tuscany he worked for a time in Milan, where he painted his most famous work, *The Last Supper* (1498), in the convent of Santa Maria delled Grazie, as well as two versions of the unique *Virgin of the Rocks*. He returned to Florence for a few years where he painted the *Mona Lisa* (1504), and then worked in France in the employment of the French king until his death. His paintings are very few but strikingly original. In the *Virgin and Child with St. Anne* (c. 1510), for example, Mary, sitting on her mother's knee, anxiously restrains the baby Jesus as he attempts to ride on a lamb, symbol of self-sacrifice to come. Nothing is known of Leonardo's personal faith, but his influence on subsequent artists including *Michelangelo and *Raphael, as well as on Christian tradition in general, has been immense.

Leprosy. Biblical "leprosy" (Heb. *tzara'at*) is now known to have had nothing to do with modern leprosy (Hansen's disease), which was not present in the ancient Near East before the 3rd century B.C.E. It seems to have been a disfiguring skin condition, probably similar to psoriasis, which was believed to produce ritual impurity in the sufferers and anyone they touched. The disastrous effect of the application of biblical language and attitudes toward people suffering from Hansen's disease, which is only mildly contagious but if untreated spreads throughout the body, starting with the face, cannot be overestimated.

Lesbian interpretation. See *Gay and lesbian interpretation.

Lessing, Gottfried Ephraim (1729–81). Enlightenment critic and playwright. From a Lutheran background, he rejected Christianity on the grounds that the accidents of history cannot be the proof of the truth of reason. His critical approach to the historicity of the Gospels was expressed in his edition of the *Reimarus fragments (1774–78) and in a study of the evangelists as "mere historians" (1788), where he argued for an Aramaic original underlying Matthew and used by Mark and Luke. His play *Nathan the Wise* (1779), about a saintly and enlightened Jew, modeled on his contemporary Moses *Mendelssohn (1729–86), is a powerful plea for religious tolerance.

Letters. See *Epistles.

Leviathan. Mythical sea monster representing the power of evil. Descriptions of YHWH's defeat of Leviathan "the twisting serpent and the dragon that is in the sea" (Isa. 27:1) are shared with other ancient Near Eastern creation myths (see *Ugarit), but in the Bible are applied to the creation of Israel in the exodus story (Ps. 74:13–14), and in particular to the parting of the Red Sea (Isa. 51:9–10). Leviathan appears twice in the book of Job, probably with the same meaning (3:8; 41) (although some commentators prefer the translation "crocodile" in chap. 41), and again in the apocryphal 2 Esdras, where he and *Behemoth emerge on the fifth day of creation (6:49–52).

Christian interpreters from *Origen and *Augustine use Leviathan and the *devil more or less interchangeably. *Calvin and others identify Leviathan as the pharaoh (Ps. 74:14) but also as a symbol of the power of evil in a more general sense, and this is how it used by *Hobbes, *Bunyan, *Blake, and other writers. In Herman *Melville's *Moby Dick* whales are routinely referred to as "leviathans," and the Israeli navy has given the name to one of its submarines. The monster is depicted on the Arch of Titus in Rome on the base of the Seven Branched Lamp (menorah) carried off in triumph from Jerusalem in 70 C.E. In Western Christian art it is a popular motif in scenes from the last judgment like those on the western façade of Rheims Cathedral (cf. Job 41:20) as well as in El *Greco's *Adoration of the Name of Jesus* (1576–79) and William *Blake's illustrations of Job.

Levinas,   Emmanuel (1906–95). Jewish philosopher. Born in Lithuania, he studied in Strasbourg and Freiburg, where he met *Heidegger. After World War II, which he spent in a German prisoner of war camp near Hanover, he completed his doctorate at the École Normale Israélite Orientale in Paris and taught at various institutions, including the Sorbonne, where he retired in 1979. In *Totality and Infinity* (1961) Levinas rejects Western imperialist thought that silences individual voices, and advocates instead the infinite realities experienced in face-to-face encounters with the otherness of God and fellow humans. His influence on *hermeneutics, *ethics, and sociopolitical thinking in general has already been considerable, but his profound new readings of the Bible, in which his philosophy and his knowledge of rabbinic thought are equally evident, have yet to become widely known.

Levites. Members of the priestly tribe of Levi, like *Moses and *Aaron. Although honored for their part in the *golden calf story (Exod. 32; Deut. 33:8–11) and valued as family priests (Judg. 17), their role in the *temple after the exile was restricted to providing music, acting as doorkeepers, and the like (Ezra 2:40–63). The book of Leviticus got its name from the Levites because it is mainly concerned with sacrifices and other rituals performed by the priests (although the Levites themselves are hardly ever mentioned). In modern Orthodox *synagogues, descendants of Levi still have certain privileges, including reading from the *Torah immediately after a *priest.

Leviticus, book of (Heb. *Vayyiqra*, "and he called," Lev. 1:1). The third of the Five Books of Moses, also known as *Torat Kohanim*, "the Priestly Torah," and in the LXX and Vg as Leviticus, "the Levitical book." In addition to ritual and ethical legislation, which includes the Day of Atonement (chap. 16) and the Jubilee (chap. 25), there is a narrative about the consecration of the priests (chaps. 8–10) and a concluding exhortation promising the people peace and prosperity if they obey the laws, but disease, famine, defeat, and destruction if they do not (chap. 26). It contains the verse "Love thy neighbor as thyself" (19:18 AV) and, because of its everyday vocabulary, was at one time considered the most suitable text for students of Hebrew to start with.

Alongside the *halakhic interpretations contained in the *Talmud and *Midrash (esp. *Sifra*), there are many examples of homiletical and nonliteral readings, including *Leviticus Rabbah* (5th century) and *Philo, who says that the ban on eating birds of prey (Lev. 11:13) is to teach us not to be domineering and rapacious, and regulations requiring a priest to be unblemished are about the human soul's search for perfection. In the NT Leviticus is interpreted as containing prefigurations of the sacrifice and priesthood of Christ (Heb. 7–10), and patristic commentators from *Origen to *Isidore of Seville continued this type of christological and allegorical tradition, not infrequently with an anti-Jewish motive. From the medieval period on there was more interest in the literal meaning of the text, and occasionally constructive dialogue between Christian interpreters (e.g., *Andrew of St. Victor) and their Jewish contemporaries (e.g., *Ibn Ezra).

Modern critical scholarship, while acknowledging that many of the detailed regulations and concepts are no doubt very ancient, have identified within Leviticus a distinct law code known as the Holiness Code (H), beginning like the other codes with laws concerning the killing of animals (chap. 17; cf. Deut. 12) and ending with blessings and curses (Lev. 26: cf. Deut. 27–28). It contains stylistic and thematic features very similar to Ezekiel, suggesting an exilic date earlier than the rest of the book, which seems to presuppose the existence of the rebuilt temple at Jerusalem. More recently with the application of social anthropology and new literary approaches attention has moved to the overall structure of the book and interpretations that highlight social justice and ecological concerns. In art Lev. 16 inspired Holman *Hunt's famous painting of the scapegoat who "hath borne our Griefs, and carried our Sorrows . . ." (Isa. 53:4 AV; 1854–55), while the Jubilee (Lev. 25), alluded to by Jesus in his Nazareth sermon (Luke 4), is a favorite among *liberation theologians and political activists concerned, for example, to tackle the problem of third world debt.

Lexicography.   See *Dictionaries and encyclopedias.

Liberalism.   Although its roots can be traced back to Renaissance humanism (*Erasmus) and the rationalism and political revolutions of the 18th century, the term is first used in relation to liberal Protestantism (*Schleiermacher, Ritschl, Harnack), liberal Judaism (C. G. Montefiore), and the British Liberal Party (Gladstone) in the 19th century. Critical of dogmatism and superstition, especially when they lead to intolerance and social injustice, liberalism encouraged the *historical-critical approach to the Bible at a time when the ecclesiastical hierarchies were opposed to it. In the 20th century, despite the efforts of Orthodox Judaism and Christian *fundamentalism, modern biblical studies, including such radical proposals as the *demythologization of the Gospels (*Bultmann), came to be widely recognized more as honest progress toward the truth than as a threat, even by the Catholic Church. Liberals then turned their attention more to ethical, social, and political issues than the study of the Bible. Liberalism's political descendant *liberation theology, however, saw a need for more radical innovation both in politics and in the study of the Bible.

Liberation theology.

A revolutionary theological movement, partly inspired by *Marxist interpretations of the Bible, that spread rapidly across Latin America in the wake of the Second Vatican Council (1962–65), which encouraged the study of the Bible in the vernacular and called for social justice throughout the world. With the blessing of the Conference of Latin American Bishops at a meeting in Medellin, Colombia, in 1968, churches and "base communities" throughout the continent found in the story of the exodus, the biblical laws protecting the poor, the prophets' visions of a new age of justice and peace, and the figure of Jesus Christ their "Liberator," the authority they needed to fight against poverty, oppression, and injustice. The movement spread to parts of Africa and Asia, where people were living in similar conditions and frequently encountered stubborn opposition from the established institutions. Academic leaders have been repeatedly silenced by the Vatican and their publications put on the Index. Their interpretation of the Bible (*Gutiérrez, Miranda, Boff, Sobrino), which is deliberately selective and biased in favor of the poor, combines the insights of ordinary uneducated people, applying the text to their own situation, with the results of modern critical scholarship. Fresh meanings are found for familiar passages: "everyone sits under his own vine" (Mic. 4:4) means everyone possesses a piece of land; while unfamiliar passages are rediscovered: thus an oracle against Moab is about justice for immigrants and refugees whom it mentions explicitly (Isa. 16:1–5), and the sin of Sodom is that "she had pride, surfeit of food, and prosperous ease, but did not aid the poor and needy" (Ezek. 16:49).

Libraries.

Despite ample evidence for temple and palace libraries in the ancient cities of Egypt, Mesopotamia, and elsewhere, no mention is made of any in Jerusalem, nor is there archaeological evidence from any of the sites in Palestine excavated so far, before the Second Temple period. The discovery of a "book of the law" in the temple during the reign of Josiah was exceptional (2 Kgs. 22:8). We can only speculate on the role of such insitutions, if any, in the process whereby the books of the Bible were written, copied, and stored in ancient Israel. The only reference to libraries in the Bible claims that both Nehemiah and Judas Maccabeus founded libraries in which they collected "the books about the kings and prophets, and the writings of David, and letters of kings about votive offerings" (2 Macc. 2:13). The 1st-century B.C.E. Greek author of 2 Maccabees was no doubt familiar with the huge library at Alexandria. During the following centuries magnificent libraries were built throughout the Greco-Roman world, such as those of Augustus and Marcus Aurelius in Rome, and of Celsus at Ephesus. Origen's library at Caesarea is another famous example, used later by Eusebius.

Libraries, both private collections and those in synagogues, monasteries, and other institutions, became the centers of learning. It was there that easy access to earlier works was possible.

Eusebius's ten-volume *History of the Church* (303–323 C.E.), for example, has quotations on almost every page from the works of authors of the 2nd and 3rd centuries, many of which are now lost, and it was normal for biblical commentators to refer to most if not all previous writings on each passage (see *Catena). On the other hand, libraries, like other institutions, are subject to ecclesiastical or political control, and this may have an effect on their contents and on the direction of scholarship, as when it was decided to burn all copies of the *Talmud in Paris in 1242 and in Rome in 1523.

Life of Adam and Eve.   First-century C.E. Jewish work, included in the *Pseudepigrapha. Also known as the *Books of Adam and Eve* and the *Apocalypse of Moses*, it continues the story of *Adam and *Eve from their expulsion from the garden of *Eden to their death. It tells of Adam's forty days' penance in the Jordan and Eve's in the freezing Tigris, and of the birth of Cain, Abel, Seth, and thirty other children. When Adam is near death, Eve and Seth journey to the gates of paradise to try to obtain a drop of life-giving oil from the tree of mercy, but fail.

Lilith.   A restless female demon (cf. Assyrian *lilitu*) in Jewish folklore responsible for marital problems and infant mortality. Said to have been Adam's first wife, she fled from the garden of Eden because she would not allow him to dominate her, and she has remained on the margins of society ever since. Outside Jewish tradition she appears in Goethe's *Faust* and poems by *Dante, Gabriel Rossetti, and Robert Browning, and there is a full-length allegorical novel about her by the Scottish minister George MacDonald (1895). She figures once in the *Dead Sea Scrolls in a list of "demons and howlers" (4Q510), and once in the Bible, where, rather surprisingly, she is described as resting peacefully toward the end of a passage about male violence and aggression (Isa. 34:14). A more positive image of Lilith as representing women's challenge to male domination, within marriage as well as in other institutions, is current among some Jewish feminists whose quarterly journal, published in New York since 1976, bears her name.

Linguistics.   The study of human language. The interpretation of a sacred text, written many centuries ago and in a language foreign to the vast majority of its readers, calls for a variety of linguistic strategies beginning with translation in the ancient world (see *Septuagint, *Targum) and culminating in modern scientific linguistics. The origin of the scientific study of the Hebrew language can be traced back to the work of the medieval Hebrew grammarians who, adapting Arab methods, produced the first Hebrew grammars and dictionaries. Christian scholars, never as committed to the study of the Hebrew original as their Jewish counterparts, did not seriously engage with Hebrew linguistics until the 16th century. Thereafter the dominance of *comparative philology for 300 years led to widespread and erroneous "*etymologizing" descriptions of Hebrew meaning, and also to the marginalization of the rabbinic, medieval, and Modern Hebrew data, which is closer in various obvious respects to Biblical Hebrew than Arabic, Babylonian, or *Ugaritic. The modern application of more sophisticated linguistic theory, which incidentally owes not a little to *missionaries working on Bible translation, shifts the emphasis away from historical linguistics toward subtler synchronic descriptions of the meaning of words and phrases, in the actual literary and social contexts in which they function. The application of sociolinguistics and pragmatics throws light on the way people use the language of Scripture and the effect it has had on others down the centuries, not least on women and the Jews. See *Semantics.

Literacy. Archaeological evidence for literacy in ancient Israel from around the 10th century B.C.E. suggests that we must take seriously the many references to *books (1 Kgs. 14:19) and writing (Exod. 24:4; Num. 17:2–3, Prov. 25:1) in the Bible, even if the tradition that *Moses wrote the *Pentateuch is rejected. The Hebrew *alphabetical writing system was far simpler to learn and use than Egyptian *hieroglyphics or Mesopotamian *cuneiform, and this is reflected in the variety and distribution of epigraphic material. On the one hand, from Samaria in the north and Arad in the south there are potsherds (*ostraca*) inscribed in a variety of fluent hands, and lengthy graffiti like the version of the story of *Balaam (Num. 22–24) on the plastered wall of a building at Tell Deir Alla. On the other, there are royal inscriptions written in stone like the Mesha inscription from Moab (cf. 2 Kgs. 3) and the Siloam inscription in Hezekiah's tunnel in Jerusalem. Moreover, the discovery of clay seals and bullae originally attached to papyrus mss proves that such documents did once exist in Palestine as they did, for example, in Egypt, where Jewish documents of the 6th–5th century B.C.E. have been found. Nothing of the kind has been found in Palestine earlier than the *Dead Sea Scrolls (1st century B.C.E.–1st century C.E.).

Jewish and Christian writers of the first centuries C.E. profited greatly from the spread of literacy in the Roman Empire, due to cheaper book production, a rapid increase in the number of *libraries, and the spread of a lingua franca, first *Greek in the East, then later *Latin in the West. There was some distrust of the written word expressed already by Plato, who favored spoken dialogue (*Phaedrus* 274f), as well as by Ecclesiastes (12:11–12) and Paul (2 Cor. 3:6). To this must be added the Jewish reverence for living debate, which is the preferred form of discourse in *Talmud and *Midrash, even though the *Oral Torah was eventually written down in 30 or 40 substantial volumes. But reading and writing, especially in Hebrew, have always been high on the agenda of Jewish educators, while the contribution of Christianity to the spread of literacy worldwide has been immense. Translation of Scripture into the vernacular was essential to the spread of Christianity from the beginning, and to this end missionaries devised new writing systems for Armenian (Mesrop), Russian (Cyril), and Gothic (Wulfilas), as well as for hundreds of modern spoken languages.

Literal meaning. The plain meaning of the text (Heb. *peshat*) as opposed to the allegorical or other nonliteral meanings (Heb. *derash*). From the Hellenistic period down to modern times it has been recognized that texts have more than one meaning, and most Jewish and Christian interpreters of the Bible have recommended the nonliteral meaning. There were rabbinic restrictions on overelaborate allegorizations, the Antiochenes like *Theodore of Mopsuestia rejected many traditional christological interpretations of the OT, and fundamentalists from the *Karaites to many modern evangelical Christians seek to "take the text literally." Rejection of nonliteral meanings in favor of the original meaning of the text, in its original language, was also a characteristic of biblical scholarship from the Protestant Reformers down to modern historical critics. More recently, with new literary approaches, together with disillusionment with the exclusive quest for originals, there has been fresh interest in how the Bible has been interpreted down the ages in ways very different from its literal meaning.

Literary criticism. The term is currently used to describe methods of analyzing and interpreting the meaning and structure of the books of the Bible, usually as whole literary units, as opposed to *historical criticism, which often got as far as *JEDP, three *Isaiahs, and the *Synoptic problem, but often neglected the Bible as literature. In addition to traditional methods of handling genre, plot, character, symbolism, irony, and a whole variety of rhetorical devices, modern literary criticism is informed by sociopolitical, psychological, and ideological insights, and by such notions as gender dynamics and the implied reader. One might add that such an approach has much in common with how readers and scholars of a precritical age read the Bible, and that consequently we have much to learn from their readings of the text. See *Reader-response criticism; *Reception history.

Liturgy.   Nothing certain is known of the liturgy used in the temples and sanctuaries of ancient Israel, although liturgical formulas like the one beginning "Arise, O LORD" (Num. 10:35–36; Ps. 132) may be very ancient, and some of the "Psalms of Zion" (e.g., 46; 48; 122) may have been used in pre-Davidic Jerusalem. For the Second Temple we have the detailed accounts of *Josephus and the *Mishnah, and there is little reason to doubt that the 15 "Songs of the Temple Steps" (Pss. 120–34) were sung there and that the threefold priestly blessing (Num. 6:24–26) was recited by the high priest on the Day of Atonement (cf. Sir. 50). The synagogue liturgy evolved independently of temple worship and consisted from the beginning of readings from the Torah and the Prophets (see *Lectionary), *Psalms, and prayers, including the *Shema, the *Amidah, and the *Kaddish. Many other prayers and hymns were added over the centuries, as well as passages from the Mishnah and *Talmud and secular compositions like *Leka dodi,* "Come my beloved," to welcome the Sabbath. Modern innovations since the *Haskalah* include the use in Reform synagogues of the vernacular and musical instruments, which are still prohibited in Orthodox Judaism.

The Christian liturgy originally had much in common with synagogue worship with readings from the Bible (Luke 4:16–20), psalms, hymns (Eph. 5:19) and prayers (1 Tim. 2:1), many like the *Sanctus (Isa. 6:3; cf. Rev. 4:8) at first probably the same in both church and synagogue. Biblical passages later found a new context in Christian worship, many of them known best by their Latin titles such as *Miserere (Ps. 51), *Magnificat (Luke 1:46–55), *Benedictus (Luke 1:68–79), *Nunc Dimittis (Luke 2:29–32), and *Dies Irae (Zeph. 1:15–16). Through the liturgy biblical texts, some of them obscure, were thus given a new meaning and currency they would not otherwise have had: the *Emitte Agnum,* "Send forth the Lamb" (Isa. 16:1 Vg), interpreted as a hymnic celebration of the Moabite ancestry of Jesus, is a striking example.

Lives of the Prophets.   A Jewish work, probably composed in Palestine in the 1st century C.E. It contains biographical details of the prophets, supplementing the biblical account with legendary material that became popular in later Jewish, Christian, and Muslim tradition. Special interest in geographical details, particularly where they were buried, perhaps suggests that the author, who shows a detailed knowledge of the topography of Jerusalem, was concerned to encourage the veneration of their tombs as pilgrimage sites.

Loanwords.   A number of loanwords have been identified in the Hebrew Bible, most of them easily explicable in terms of foreign influence. They include the words for "palace" (*hekal*) from Sumerian (*é.gal* via Babylonian), "flood" (*mabbul*) also from Babylonian, "helmet" (*qoba*) from Hittite, "horse" (*sus*) from Indo-Aryan, "papyrus" (*gome*) from Egyptian, and "law" (*dat*) from Persian via Aramaic. The influence of Biblical Hebrew on other languages, usually via Greek or Latin, can be seen in loanwords like "*Sabbath," "*Hosanna," "*Satan," and "Jubilee." Cases of semantic borrowing (*calque), that is, Greek words with Hebrew meanings, are also quite frequent in the LXX and NT, e.g., *kephale*, "head," in the sense of "leader, chief" (from Heb. *rosh*).

By far the most spectacular example is the influence of Hellenistic Greek on all the languages it came in contact with, which consequently have a disproportionate number of Greek loanwords. In Latin, for example, Greek words include *Genesis, Exodus, propheta, holocaustum, lepra, baptisma, evangelium*, and a host of others, and the same is true of Hebrew, Aramaic, Syriac, Coptic, and Arabic. Thus despite the efforts of *Jerome and others, it was the Greek Bible that had the greatest impact on Christianity, and on Western culture ever since. See *Semitisms.

Loisy, Alfred Firmin (1857–1940). French Catholic modernist biblical scholar. Excommunicated in 1908, he taught history of religions in the Collège de France for 20 years. His early works include studies of the religion of Israel and Babylonian parallels to Genesis, but it is for his historical-critical work on the NT and Christian origins that he is best remembered. A devout Catholic, he sought to show continuity between the teachings of Christ and the institution of the church, adopting a history of religions approach to the Gospels in which the role of *myth was central, and in his commentary on Galatians and elsewhere he was highly critical of the Pauline literature (not much of it by Paul himself) for its naive Protestant theology.

Lollards. A derogatory name, probably meaning "mumblers," given to the English followers of John *Wycliffe (c. 1330–84). Firmly committed to the belief that Scripture is the sole authority and that everyone should be allowed to read and interpret it for themselves, they opposed many Catholic doctrines and institutions, including the celibate priesthood and the pope. They were fiercely suppressed during Wycliffe's lifetime but survived through the 15th century, for the most part in secret and with little support from the ecclesiastical and political establishment, and contributed to the success of the English Reformation in the 16th. The Wycliffite English Bible was the work of the Lollards John Purvey and Nicholas of Hereford.

Lord (Heb. *adon*; Gk. *kyrios*; Lat. *dominus*). In the Hebrew Bible "Lord" is a term of respect used in addressing leaders (Num. 32:25), kings (1 Kgs. 1:17), and other men in positions of authority (Judg. 4:18). In religious discourse it is applied to YHWH, "the LORD" (Heb. *adonai*; see *Tetragrammaton). The common Hebrew word *baal*, "lord, husband" (Hos. 2:16 [MT 18]), is similarly applied to the Canaanite god *Baal (Judg. 8:33; cf. Babylonian *Bel*, "lord," Isa. 46:1). In Christian tradition the Greek term *Kyrios* (Lat. *Dominus*) as applied to Jesus acquired theological connotations related to belief in his divine nature (John 20:28: "My Lord and my God"), and OT passages originally about YHWH were applied to him (Isa. 33:22), although the distinction between the LORD (YHWH) and his anointed (*Messiah) could also be maintained (Ps. 110:1: cf. Mark 12:36). "Our Lord" came to be a euphemism in the church for the name Jesus, which, like YHWH, was for some too sacred to pronounce.

Lord's Prayer. The prayer beginning "Our Father" (Lat. *Paternoster*) recited by Jesus to the disciples (Matt. 6:9–13) when they asked him to teach them how to pray (Luke 11:1–4). It has obvious parallels with the *Kaddish, a very popular ancient Jewish prayer, and the opening parallels another Jewish prayer, of unknown origin, which begins "Our Father, our King" (*Avinu malkenu*; cf. Isa. 63:16; 64:8). Scholars disagree about some of the details, including the "daily bread" (or "bread for the morrow"), "from evil" (or "the evil one"), and the ending, which is not in all the best mss but appears already in the *Didache* and the Liturgy of John *Chrysostom. But it is clearly a prayer for the coming of the kingdom and for divine assistance in practical and ethical preparations for that day.

The earliest evidence for its use by Latin-speaking Christians is probably the famous *SATOR-AREPO* anagram square, discovered at Pompeii and therefore pre–79 C.E. when lava from nearby Vesuvius destroyed the town. It has held a central place in Christian private and public devotion since the 1st century. *Augustine compared its seven petitions to the seven gifts of the Spirit, and there are important commentaries on it by *Thomas Aquinas and Theresa of Avila. Musical settings include the last verse of the hymn "Now God be with us" (Ger. *Die Nacht ist kommen*) by the German reformer Petrus Herbert (1533–71), and a popular Caribbean arrangement with "Hallowed be thy Name" as a refrain.

Lorraine.   See *Claude Lorraine.

Lot.   Nephew of Abraham and incestuous ancestor of Moab and Ammon (Gen. 19:30–38). See *Sodom and Gomorrah.

Lower   criticism.   See   *Textual criticism.

Lowth, Robert (1710–87). Professor of poetry at Oxford and later bishop of London. His famous lectures on Hebrew poetry, first delivered in Latin and later translated into English (1787) and German (1793), were extremely popular both in his own lifetime and in the age of *romanticism after his death. He also wrote an eloquent commentary on the book of Isaiah including his own translation (1778; 2nd ed. 1779). He approached the Bible as a literary masterpiece, identifying prophetic inspiration with poetic genius, and was one of the first to analyze what he termed *parallelismus membrorum* in the structure of Hebrew *poetry.

Luke, Gospel of.   Third of the four canonical Gospels, dedicated like the book of *Acts to the Gentile Theophilus, and apparently written with a Gentile readership in mind. The Samaritans feature more positively in Luke (9:52; 17:16; Acts 8:25) than in the other Gospels (cf. Matt. 10:5), the number of disciples sent out by Jesus corresponds to the seventy nations of the world (Luke 10:1, 17; cf. *b. Sukkah* 55b), and some technical Jewish material present in the other Gospels does not appear in Luke (11:38–39; cf. Mark 7:1–23). The Acts of the Apostles, another work by the same author, himself a Gentile, begins in Jerusalem and ends in Rome. But this does not mean that the Gospel, despite its appeal to *Marcion, was in any way intended to be anti-Jewish. It begins and ends in the temple at Jerusalem. Jesus' circumcision is mentioned only by Luke (2:21). Jesus is throughout presented as the fulfillment of OT prophecy: the savior on the throne of his father David (1:32), "a light to lighten the Gentiles, and the glory of thy people Israel" (2:32 AV), his passion foretold in Isa. 53 (Luke 22:37). Even the twelve disciples are successors of the twelve tribes of Israel (22:30). Other distinctively Lukan themes are social justice (1:46–55; 4:16–30); a concern for the marginalized, especially widows, strangers, and lepers; and a special interest in the part played by the women in Jesus' life.

The Gospel was thought to have been written by Luke, the "beloved physician" (Col. 4:14) who also wrote the book of Acts. Luke accompanied Paul on two of his journeys (Acts 16:11; 20:6) and was with him in Rome (2 Tim. 4:11). The church fathers believed he was among the first Christians at Antioch, which figures prominently in Acts, and since *Origen he has been identified with "the brother who is famous among all the churches for his preaching of the gospel" (2 Cor. 8:16–24).

*Tertullian's *Against Marcion*, in which the full text is used to refute *Marcion's tendentiously abridged version, has been described as the earliest commentary on Luke. Influential allegorical interpretations include those of *Origen, *Augustine, and *Cyril of Alexandria, much quoted by medieval and Renaissance writers like *Bede, *Bonaventure, *Thomas Aquinas, and *Erasmus. Modern critics from *Reimarus (1774–78) on questioned the historicity of the Gospel and in particular the nature and reliability of Luke's sources. F. C. *Baur (1847) argued that there was more in Luke about the history of early Christianity than about the actual events of Christ's life, while Harnack (1908) and others discussed Luke's handling of Mark, Matthew, Q, or other earlier material so that the quest for the historical Jesus focused more on Mark and Matthew than on Luke. More recent literary-critical and socioanthropological approaches have returned to the study of the narrative as a whole and Luke's impact on his readers, ancient, medieval and modern.

In music and the liturgy the *Ave Maria, "Hail Mary" (Luke 1:28, 42), *Magnificat (1:46–55), and *Nunc Dimittis (2:29–32) all come from Luke, and there are passions according to Luke by *Schütz (1664) and *Penderecki (1966). Scenes only in Luke that have inspired writers and artists without number include the *annunciation, the *visitation, the babe in a manger, the *good Samaritan, the *prodigal son, and the road to Emmaus. His symbol, derived from the vision of the four creatures in Rev. 4:7 (cf. Ezek. 1:10), is the ox, and where the evangelists are depicted as seated on the shoulders of prophets (e.g., in a famous *Chartres stained-glass window), Luke's prophet is *Jeremiah, perhaps because in his gospel Jesus quotes Jeremiah's "new covenant" prophecy (Jer. 31:31; Luke 22:20). In Eastern Orthodox tradition he was believed to have been an artist himself and to have painted several icons of the virgin and child, while in Renaissance Florence the official guild of artists was the Accademia di San Luca, named after their patron saint.

Luther, Martin (1483–1546).

Founder of the German Reformation. After studying philosophy at Erfurt and training at an Augustinian monastery, where he was ordained priest in 1507, he was sent to teach at the newly founded University of Wittenberg in Saxony, where he was professor of Biblical Studies from 1512 until his death. His personal conviction that justification is by faith not works led him to attack ecclesiastical abuses in Rome and elsewhere, starting with his 95 Theses nailed to the church door in Wittenberg in 1517 and the publication of his treatise *On the Babylonian Captivity of the Church of God* in 1520. A papal bull was issued against him, which he burned, and he was excommunicated. Summoned to the Diet of Worms in 1521, he refused to recant and had to be spirited away to a castle in Wartburg for his own safety. It was during this period of seclusion that he produced perhaps his greatest work, his spectacularly successful German translation of the Bible, which was to play a crucial role in the Reformation but also marked a new stage in the development of the German language. By the time he returned to Wittenberg in 1522 his ideas had been enthusiastically accepted all over Germany. The concept of an independent national church was accepted at the Diet of Speyer in 1529, and the Augsburg Confession, first published two years later with Luther's approval, became with some modifications the standard of faith for the church that bears his name.

Combining a knowledge of Hebrew and Greek with a passionate conviction that understanding Scripture is about faith in Christ, Luther, like most patristic and medieval commentators before him, stressed the need to see beyond the "literal" meaning of the text to its "spiritual" meaning. On the *Immanuel prophecy (Isa. 7:14), he acknowledges that the original Hebrew does not have the word "virgin," but argues that it must refer to a virgin because otherwise it would not be a miracle. What is new in Luther's exegesis, apart from his brilliant use of the vernacular, is the emphasis on the divine initiative in Christ. This influenced his interpretation of the term "righteousness" wherever it occurs, for example, and led to his celebrated insertion of the word *allein*, "alone," in his translation of Rom. 3:28. His lectures on the Psalms (1513–15) and Isaiah (1527–30) and his commentary on Galatians (1535) are still widely used. He composed over 30 hymns, of which "Ein fest' Burg" ("A Mighty Fortress"), a paraphrase of Ps. 46, is one of the best known, first translated into English by Miles Coverdale (1539), and then by Thomas Carlisle (1831). Several portraits of Luther and one of his wife Katharina were painted by *Cranach, who lived in Wittenberg and was deeply influenced by Luther. His contemporary Dürer and Luther never met.

Luzzatto, Samuel David (1800–1865).

Italian theologian and biblical scholar, principal of the newly founded rabbinical seminary in Padua. In his numerous writings, which are in both Italian and Hebrew and had some influence on subsequent Jewish scholarship, he combines a respect for tradition, for example, the Mosaic authorship of the *Torah and a single author for *Isaiah, with a historical-critical sense that enabled him to emend the MT on occasion and apply modern philosophical and anthropological insights to the Bible. His works include commentaries on the Torah, the Major Prophets, Proverbs, and Job as well as grammars of Hebrew, Aramaic, and Syriac.

Maccabees, books of.

Four apocryphal works named after Judas Maccabeus, hero of the successful Jewish struggle against the Syrian king Antiochus IV Epiphanes in 168–164 B.C.E., but covering a much longer period. Written originally in Hebrew and modeled on Judges and Samuel–Kings, 1 Maccabees is an important source for the events of the Maccabean Revolt from the desecration of the temple (cf. Dan. 8:9–14; 11:29–35) and its rededication (Heb. *hanukkah) by Judas (1 Macc. 4), to the appointment of his nephew John Hyrcanus as high priest (135–104 B.C.E.). Second Maccabees retells the first part of the story in a much more homiletical style highlighting the role of God and the devotion of his people, notably the aged scribe Eleazar (2 Macc. 6), the mother and the seven martyred sons (chap. 7) and Judas himself (chaps. 8–15). Influenced by the book of Esther, 3 Maccabees tells of attempts by Ptolemy IV (221–205 B.C.E.), on each occasion thwarted by divine intervention, to enter the temple in Jerusalem and then to exterminate the Jews in Egypt, using elephants. Fourth Maccabees describes itself as a philosophical discussion of the two chief stories of courage and devotion told in 2 Maccabees, and concludes with a martyr's statement of faith in life after death.

All four books appear in some of the Greek mss of the Bible, but only 1 and 2 Maccabees were translated into Latin by *Jerome and have been considered canonical in all but the Protestant tradition. Judas Maccabeus is frequently interpreted as a type of Christ (Jerome, *Bede) or of militant evangelism (*Rabanus Maurus, *Luther), and was placed in paradise between Joshua and Charlemagne by *Dante (*Paradiso* 18:37–48). *Handel's oratorio *Judas Maccabaeus* (1747) was composed to celebrate the duke of Cumberland's victory at Culloden in 1746. The Jewish mother with her seven sons, known as the "Holy Maccabees" (2 Macc. 7; 4 Macc. 18), are frequently referred to in Christian tradition from Heb. 11:35, *Augustine, *Chartres Cathedral, and Luther down to a 19th-century painting in the Church of Santa Felicità in Florence. In Jewish tradition the books of Maccabees are rarely read, but at the annual festival of *Hanukkah the miracle of the oil used to light the temple lamp, recounted in the Talmud (*b. Shabbat* 21b), is celebrated as well as the victory itself over foreign aggression.

Magi. The "wise men [Gk. *magoi*] from the east" who were led by a star to Bethlehem to worship the newly born "king of the Jews," with gifts of gold, frankincense, and myrrh (Matt. 2:1–12). Although not stated in the Bible, *Tertullian already believed they were kings (cf. Isa. 60:1–7; Ps. 72:10–11) and *Origen that they were three in number, like the three wise kings who came to "comfort" Job (Job 2:11 LXX). Their names, Caspar, Melchior, and Balthasar, appear first in the 6th century, and their story is further elaborated in the influential *Golden Legend. As the first Gentiles to recognize the Messiah, they have played a prominent role in Christian theological and liturgical tradition from an early date, and the symbolism of three wealthy travelers from a distant land, guided by a star and bringing rich gifts to honor a baby in a stable, has inspired artists, writers, and musicians without number. Their meeting with Herod is also a popular theme in art and literature. The "Three Kings" are venerated at a shrine containing a richly decorated triple sarcophagus in Cologne Cathedral (c. 1180–1225). See *Epiphany; *Nativity; *Zoroastrianism.

Magnificat (Lat. "[My soul] doth magnify [the Lord]"). Latin title of the song of praise sung by Mary at her *visitation to Elizabeth (Luke 1:46–55), which was from early times an important part of morning worship in the Eastern church and of vespers in the Western church. It is clearly dependent on the Song of Hannah, the prophet Samuel's mother (1 Sam. 2), and some modern scholars have suggested it was originally sung by Elizabeth. Among notable musical settings of the Magnificat are those by *Vivaldi, *Bach, and *Vaughan Williams. Its revolutionary tone (Luke 1:51–53)

made it popular in the *liberation theology movement in Latin America, where in some countries it was banned for a time.

Maimonides (1135–1204). Greatest medieval Jewish philosopher, also known as Rambam (acronym for Rabbi Moses Ben Maimon). He was born in Spain but for most of his life lived in Cairo, where he was physician to Saladin and leader of the Jewish community. When he died, his body was taken to Palestine, where his grave in Tiberias is still a place of pilgrimage. In addition to *responsa, medical treatises, letters, and other works, he wrote a commentary on the *Mishnah, a massive code of Jewish law known as *Mishneh Torah* ("Recapitulation of the Law"; cf. Deut. 17:18), and his masterpiece, *Guide for the Perplexed* (*Moreh Nevukhim*), in which a major concern is to prove that the Bible and its traditional interpretations are compatible with Aristotelian philosophy. The whole of part 1 of this three-part work is devoted to discussing the meaning of biblical terms and selected passages (e.g., Gen. 3:5; Exod. 24:10). In his discussion of the Prophets and Job, to which he devotes considerable effort, he argues that many texts have two meanings, a literal historical meaning, and a more profound hidden meaning, which often accords better with spiritual and philosophical truth. The *Guide* was soon translated into Latin and much used by Christian writers, including *Thomas Aquinas. His "Thirteen Principles of the Faith," printed in Jewish prayer books, are sung in synagogues in the form of the 14th-century hymn beginning *Yigdal*, and in churches as "The God of Abraham Praise" (1770).

Major Prophets. *Isaiah, *Jeremiah, and *Ezekiel in the Hebrew Bible. In the Greek Bible, on which the Christian OT is based, *Daniel is classed as a Major Prophet, not one of the Writings (as in the Hebrew Bible), thereby creating, with the Book of the Twelve (Minor Prophets), a prophetic pentateuch like those of Moses and David (5 books of *Psalms).

Malachi, book of. Last of the twelve Minor Prophets. In many Christian Bibles it comes before the Gospels, where the prophecy beginning "Behold, I send my messenger" (3:1) is repeatedly cited (e.g., Mark 1:2). In Hebrew *malachi* simply means "my messenger" (cf. 3:1), and, as nothing at all is said about the author, the prophecies are considered by many to be anonymous. Some suggest that they were originally part of *Zechariah, made into a separate book to make up the number twelve, mentioned already in Sir. 49:10. There is a rabbinic tradition that Malachi was to be identified with Ezra the scribe, and that with Haggai, Zechariah, and Malachi the age of prophecy came to an end (*b. Megillah* 15a). The author's concerns include laxity in temple worship, foreign marriages, marital infidelity, and social injustice, which would fit a date in the early Second Temple period, c. 450 B.C.E.

The Jewish tradition that the messianic age will be heralded by the coming of Elijah finds scriptural authority in Malachi as does their belief in the continuing validity of Jewish law, against Christian claims, even when the Messiah comes (4:4–5 [MT 3:22–23]). The global perspective in 1:11 ("from the rising of the sun to its setting") has inspired many evangelical preachers and hymn writers, while *Handel's *Messiah* (1742) contains a memorable setting of 3:1–3, and "the sun of righteousness . . . risen with healing in its wings" (4:2) figures in Charles *Wesley's "Hark the herald angels sing" (1739).

Manasseh ben Israel (1604–57). Dutch rabbi and scholar. Born in Portugal, he grew up in Amsterdam, where he was appointed rabbi at the age of 18 and set up the first Jewish printing press. A brilliant teacher and orator, steeped in kabbalistic ideas and messianic hopes, he attracted the notice of Protestant scholars, not least the English Puritans, and in 1655 went to London, where his *Hope of Israel* (1650) and *Vindiciae Judaeorum* (1656) paved the way for the readmission of the Jews to England under Cromwell. His other publications, many of them written with a Gentile readership in mind, include a scriptural index to *Midrash Rabbah* (1628), *The Conciliator: A Reconcilement of Apparent Contradictions in Scripture* (4 parts, 1633–51; ET 1842; repr. 1972), and a short work on the statue of Nebuchadnezzar (Dan. 3), with four illustrations by *Rembrandt.

Manasseh, Prayer of. Short apocryphal work attributed to the evil king Manasseh (2 Kgs. 21:1–18), who is said to have "humbled himself before the God of his fathers" after being taken prisoner by the king of Assyria (2 Chr. 33:1–20). Apparently unknown to *Origen and *Jerome, but quoted by *Thomas Aquinas and included in the *Apocrypha of both Luther's German Bible and AV, it became a popular prayer in many Christian traditions but never found its way into Jewish worship. The most famous painting of repentant Manasseh among the ancestors of Christ (Matt. 1) is that of *Michelangelo on the ceiling of the *Sistine Chapel.

Manicheism. A syncretistic gnostic religion founded in southern Babylonia by a young teacher named Mani (c. 216–276 C.E.), who had broken away from the Jewish or Christian baptismal sect in which he grew up. It spread rapidly to Persia, north India, and China in the east, and west into Egypt, North Africa (where *Augustine was an adherent), and Europe, and flourished for a thousand years despite the efforts of the Christian, Muslim, and *Zoroastrian authorities to ban it. According to Manichean writings discovered in Chinese Turkestan and Egypt, the central myth is of a primeval conflict between the forces of light and the forces of darkness, during which sparks of light imprisoned in human bodies and elsewhere can be released by the special knowledge (Gk. *gnosis*) brought by Jesus, Buddha, the prophets, and Mani himself, who was believed to be an apostle of Jesus. The extent of its influence on Jewish *mysticism (see *Kabbalah) and some Christian heresies, such as the Albigensians in 12th-century Provence, is much debated.

Mann, Thomas (1875–1955). German novelist. Among his most successful works are *Buddenbrooks* (1901; ET 1924), *Death in Venice* (1913; ET 1925), *The Magic Mountain* (1924; ET 1953), for which he received the Nobel Prize for literature in 1929, and *Doctor Faustus* (1947; ET 1948). His four-volume novel *Joseph and His Brothers* (1933–43; ET 1948), was written during the Nazi era in Switzerland, where he made a series of anti-Hitler broadcasts, which later were published. Informed by an exhaustive study of Jewish and Christian interpretations, as well as by ancient Near Eastern history, cultural anthropology, and psychology (he greatly admired *Freud), it has been described as the greatest single commentary on the biblical story.

Mantegna, Andrea (c. 1431–1506). Italian Renaissance artist. He worked first in Padua, where he was influenced by *Donatello, and then for most of his life in Mantua. Mantegna's most distinctive paintings are characterized by a rather ominous light, even in the *Holy Family* (1495–1500, Dresden), and perspectives used to extraordinary effect in his famous *Lamentation over the Dead Christ* (c. 1490, Milan). Among his biblical scenes are the *Agony in the Garden* (c. 1459, National Gallery, London), *Circumcision of Christ* (1464, Uffizi, Florence), and *Judith and Holofernes* (1495, National Gallery, Washington, DC). One of his greatest surviving works, as well as the earliest, is the St. Zeno Altarpiece in Verona (1457–60).

Manuscripts. The earliest mss of the Hebrew Bible are the *Dead Sea Scrolls, which include at least fragments of every book in the Bible, except Esther and Nehemiah, as well as some noncanonical works such as Sirach and *Jubilees*. The earliest complete mss are the medieval codices, which, though 1,000 years later, are astonishingly close to the Dead Sea mss, except that marginal notes (*masora*) designed to make copying more accurate have been added, as well as an elaborate system of *pointing to indicate the correct punctuation, pronunciation, and cantillation. Known as the Masoretic Text, this was the standard for subsequent mss, one of the earliest of which, the St. Petersburg Codex (Codex Leningradensis), dated 1008 C.E., is now used in most printed editions of the Hebrew Bible. Manuscripts for liturgical use are still handwritten scrolls, written in unpointed Hebrew.

Well over 5,000 mss of the Greek Bible exist, mostly fragmentary, of which the oldest are 2nd-century C.E. papyrus fragments in Dublin, Manchester, and Ann Arbor, Michigan. The earliest complete mss, written in the uncial script, are Codex Sinaiticus (4th century) in the British Museum, and Codex Vaticanus (4th century) in Rome. Codex Bezae in Cambridge (5th century) represents a Western ms tradition and contains the Gospels in both Greek and Latin. Among the most important medieval mss of the NT, which are written in minuscule, are those in St. Petersburg (9th century), Paris (12th century), British Library (12th century), and Chicago (13th century). The oldest complete ms of the Latin Vulgate is Codex Amiatinus written in Northumbria soon after 700 C.E., and now in Florence, while there are mss of the Syriac, Coptic, Armenian, and other versions from the 5th century. See also *Books and book production; *Illustrated Bibles; *Paleography.

Maps. Many parts of the Bible, from the wanderings of the patriarchs and the geography of the promised land to descriptions of Solomon's temple and the new Jerusalem, can be illustrated and explained by the use of maps and plans. Maps are known to have existed from as early as the 2nd millennium B.C.E. and are referred to with increasing frequency in Hellenistic and Roman times. Some passages (e.g., Table of Nations in Gen. 10) were probably based on a map like the ancient Babylonian "map of the world," a copy of which survives dated c. 500 B.C.E. The earliest map of Palestine is the 6th-century C.E. Madeba mosaic on the floor of a Greek Orthodox church in Jordan. Some medieval and Renaissance mss contain maps of the world like the 13th-century *Mappa Mundi* in Hereford Cathedral, often with Jerusalem in the center, and the first printed map of Palestine is that of Gerardus Mercator (1512–94).

Since the 18th century, in the light of *archaeology and *historical criticism, Bibles and biblical atlases have been published with maps claiming to be of ever increasing accuracy. Still further refinement comes from the use of aerial and satellite photography, although access to such pictures of much of the Middle East is currently restricted for security reasons. Literary and sociolinguistic approaches to biblical interpretation, however, suggest that the geography of biblical narratives does not always correspond to modern reconstructions (e.g., the crossing of the Red Sea) and that the new maps may be less useful than older, more biblically accurate ones.

Marcion (died c. 160 C.E.). Heretical biblical interpreter. He was a wealthy shipowner born in Sinope on the coast of the Black Sea, and probably brought up as a Christian. He went to Rome in c. 140, and founded a breakaway sect that spread throughout the Roman Empire over the next century before being absorbed into *Manicheism. He insisted on a literal reading of the Jewish Scriptures, which demonstrated that their god was not the compassionate Father of Jesus. The warrior messiah taught by the Hebrew prophets had not yet come. Consequently, he argued that the true gospel revealed in Jesus had no connection to the prior covenants. He created an authoritative Christian Scripture comprising Luke's Gospel and ten epistles of Paul. Marcion's theology was condemned as heretical by the church and he was excommunicated in 144. He was the first to raise the issue of the canon of Scripture and the relation between Christianity and its Jewish roots. In part due to the influence of Marcion the church decided that the four Gospels and the OT are canonical, although they did not challenge Marcion's anti-Judaism with the same determination.

Mari. Present-day Tell Hariri, an important city on the Syria-Iraq border, founded c. 3000 B.C.E. and listed among the conquests of Sargon of Akkad (c. 2350) and the Babylonian king Hammurabi (1760). Excavations by French archaeologists in 1933–36 and 1951–56 revealed temples, palaces, and buildings of all kinds, and a royal archive of 20,000 cuneiform tablets written in Akkadian. References to Dan, Hazor, Ugarit, the Habiru, and the like, as well as a number of oracles delivered by court prophets, have been much quoted in discussions of the Bible in its original context.

Mark, Gospel of. Second and shortest of the four canonical Gospels. Jesus is introduced at the beginning as the "Messiah" (Gk. *christos*) and the "Son of God" (1:1; cf. 1:11), words echoed by the centurion who witnesses his death on the cross at the end (15:39), but there is no account of his miraculous birth. Picking up where the prophets left off (Mal. 3:1; Isa. 40:3), Mark begins with *John the Baptist, interpreted as "forerunner" of the messianic age; and after brief accounts of the baptism and temptation in the wilderness, Mark turns at once to the impact of his preaching and healing miracles on the disciples, the people of Galilee, and soon the whole country (3:7), beginning with the fishermen Simon Peter and Andrew.

The first half of the book is packed with incidents illustrating the authority (Gk. *exousia*) that Jesus exercises over physical and spiritual powers alike (1:22, 27; 2:10; 3:15), and proving that "the kingdom of God is at hand" (1:15). A quieter central section, which contains the transfiguration, tells how he confided in his disciples, with an ever increasing amount of detail as they journeyed toward Jerusalem, that he was the Messiah and that he would have to suffer and die, and so would his followers. The account of the entry into Jerusalem, the cleansing of the temple, the Last Supper, the trial, scourging, and crucifixion of Christ returns to the pace of the earlier chapters, and concludes rather abruptly with the scene of three women running away from the empty tomb, too afraid to tell anyone what they had seen. Some mss have brief accounts of the subsequent appearance of the risen Christ to Mary Magdalene and the disciples.

Commentaries on Mark are comparatively rare before modern times. *Origen wrote one that has not survived. *Jerome wrote ten homilies on Mark in which he comments on the different endings attested in the mss (c. 393), and *Augustine's Synoptic commentary includes Mark (c. 400), as do those of *Bede and *Calvin (1555). Modern scholars discount the testimony of Papias (c. 140) that the author was Peter's "interpreter" or Paul's companion John Mark (Acts 12), and also Augustine's view, widely accepted until the 19th century, that Matthew was the earliest Gospel. It is now universally believed that Mark is our earliest record of the life of Jesus, written probably in Rome about 40 years after his death, and used by Matthew and Luke as one of their principal sources. See *Synoptic problem. William Wrede's "messianic secret" (1901; ET 1971) shifted the emphasis from a quest for the historical Jesus, involving all the Gospels, to analyzing specific psychological and theological factors in Mark, and much subsequent research, applying the insights of literary criticism and ideological, sociopolitical, and materialist approaches, including *feminism and *liberation theology, has done the same.

In art the second evangelist is represented by the lion "roaring in the desert," a reference to Mark 1:3 according to *Irenaeus, and sits on the shoulders of Daniel. Paintings, musical settings, dramas, films, and literary reworkings of the life of Christ probably owe their inspiration more to the later Gospels than to Mark. But he is venerated as the first Orthodox Patriarch of Alexandria, a tradition referred to already by *Eusebius, and the first Coptic pope, as well as the patron saint of Venice, where St. Mark's Basilica is his best known legacy to Western culture. Mark's martyrdom is the subject of two paintings by *Tintoretto (1562–66), and *Donatello's statue of him (1411) prompted *Michelangelo to say, "If he really looked like that, one would believe everything he said in his Gospel."

Martha and Mary. The sisters of Lazarus in Bethany. Although Martha meets Jesus first when he comes to visit them on their brother's death, and it is to her that the words "I am the resurrection and the life" are addressed (John 11:21–27), it is Mary who is praised for listening to his teaching while Martha is gently rebuked for being anxious and troubled about domestic matters (Luke 10:38–42), and Mary who is remembered for her unworldly extravagance in anointing Jesus' feet to the dismay of Judas (John 12:1–8). Mary was traditionally merged with *Mary Magdalene. Christian commentators, including *Augustine, *Gregory the Great, and *Bernard of Clairvaux, have interpreted the two sisters, foreshadowed by two OT sisters *Leah and *Rachel, as models of two ways of Christian living, Martha's active life of serving others and Mary's contemplative life of prayer and devotion.

Modern uses of the two figures include Tina Beattie, *The Last Supper according to Martha and Mary* (2001), and Joanna Weaver, *Having a Mary Heart in a Martha World* (2007). In art the scene in the house of Lazarus is rare before the 16th century but then becomes frequent as in paintings by *Tintoretto (1580), Orazio Gentileschi (c. 1620), Vermeer (1654), Velazquez (1618), and *Blake (1805). See *Lazarus 1.

Martyrdom and Ascension of Isaiah.

An apocryphal work dating from the 1st century C.E., referred to by *Origen, *Jerome, and others. An Ethiopic version, clearly a Christian composition, consists of an account of the martyrdom of *Isaiah under Manasseh, who had him sawn asunder with a woodsaw, followed by his ascension to heaven, where he hears an account of the birth, life, death, and resurrection of Christ. The martyrdom tradition appears also in the *Talmud (*b. Yebamot* 49b). In the Middle Ages Isaiah is represented in Western Christian art with a saw as the symbol of his martyrdom, like St. Andrew with his cross and St. Catherine with her wheel.

Marx, Karl (1818–83).

German sociopolitical and economic theorist. Both his parents were Jews, but his father converted to Lutheranism and Marx was baptized when he was 6. Educated at the universities of Bonn and Berlin, he associated with the "young Hegelians" and briefly worked on a liberal newspaper in Cologne before moving in 1843 to Paris, where he met Engels. His famous *Communist Manifesto*, ending with the words "Workers of all lands unite!" was published in 1848, and the next year he moved to London, where he wrote the first volume of his greatest work, *Das Kapital* (1867), of which two more were published after his death. Marx did not acknowledge any influence from Jewish or Christian tradition, given his outpoken critique of religion in general and in

particular the notion that the poor have something to look forward to, but only after they are dead. Positive parallels can be found, however, in the appeals for social justice in the Bible and in the inspiration provided by its eschatological myth of a messianic age to come, in this world, according the rabbis, not the next. These and other revolutionary ideas have been thoroughly exploited in so-called Marxist interpretations of the Bible. See *Liberation theology.

Mary Magdalene.

A woman who had been healed of evil spirits (Luke 8:2), and who, with other women, was present at the crucifixion (Mark 15:40) and the empty tomb (John 20). In Mark and John she is the first person to meet the risen Christ and has played a central role in Christian tradition ever since, especially as a repentant sinner. The rabbis said she was a prostitute (*b. Shabbat* 104b). The church fathers identified her with the unnamed woman who washed Christ's feet (Luke 7), and also with Mary the sister of *Martha and *Lazarus in Bethany (Mark 14:3–9). The Eastern church claims she died and is buried at Ephesus, while in the West her tomb in Provence was a popular pilgrimage site in the Middle Ages. The Reformers, including Calvin, strongly opposed the Magdalene cult and argued that the three Marys were separate biblical characters.

Mary Magdalene remained an important model of humility and repentance, however, and continued to inspire poets and writers such as George *Herbert and John *Donne. More recently erotic elements in the story have been emphasized in the novels *The Last Temptation of Christ* by Nikos Kazantzakis (1951; ET 1960) and Dan Brown's *Da Vinci Code* (2003). She is a very frequent subject for painters and sculptors, whether clinging to the foot of the cross (Simone Martini, c. 1340) or mistaking the risen Christ for the gardener (Fra *Angelico, 1436–40; *Rembrandt, 1638). As a penitent sinner she is often depicted alone, seminude, in the desert, an alabaster flask of ointment and a symbolic skull by her side (El *Greco 1578–80; Canova, 1796).

Mary, the Virgin. The mother of Jesus, introduced by Matthew as fulfillment of the *Immanuel prophecy (1:23; cf. Isa. 7:14 LXX), and by Luke as the central character in the *nativity narrative. She then remains in the background for the most part until she appears at the foot of the cross (John 19:25) and after the resurrection with the disciples in the upper room (Acts 1:14). She does not appear to have had a central role in the church much before the Council of Ephesus in 451 at which she was given the title *Theotokos*, "Mother of God." Since then, despite objections from Protestant Reformers, including *Luther, for most Christians worldwide she has been raised to the level of Christ in prayer (Hail Mary, Angelus, rosary), practice (Lourdes, Fatima), and doctrine (*Assumption, Immaculate Conception).

In addition to her appearances in the NT itself, a *Life of the Virgin*, including scenes from the *Protoevangelium of James and other apocryphal works, appears frequently in art from mosaics in Santa Maria Maggiore in Rome (5th century), the Katholikon at Daphni (11th century) and St. Savior in Chora (now the Kaariye Mosque) in Istanbul (13th century) to Ghirlandaio (1486–90) and *Dürer (1509–11). OT prefigurations of Mary's virginity, depicted in the medieval *Biblia Pauperum* and elsewhere, include the burning bush (Exod. 3), Gideon's fleece (Judg. 6), the enclosed garden (*Hortus Conclusus*; Song 4:12 Vg), and the Closed Door (*Porta Clausa*; Ezek 44:2).

From as early as a 3rd-century *catacomb painting under the Church of St. Priscilla in Rome, the Madonna and Child has been perhaps the most frequent image of all in Christian iconography: from a 6th-century black Ethiopian woman and the elegant, bejewelled Madonnas of 16th-century Florence, to *Our Lady of the Victories* brandishing a Kalashnikov in 20th-century Mexico. There is also the late medieval *Pietà*, of which Michelangelo's statue in St. Peter's, Rome (1500), is the most famous example, in which Mary holds her dead son in her arms. Images inspired by festivals include the *Purification in the Temple* for Candlemas on February 2, the *Coronation of the Virgin* for the Feast of the Assumption (or Dormition) on August 15, and scenes with her mother St. Anne for the Immaculate Conception on December 8. The role of Mary in music and literature has been no less extensive.

Masaccio (1401–28). Greatest Italian painter of the early Renaissance. In his short life Masaccio, perhaps influenced by his older Florentine contemporary Brunelleschi, introduced sophisticated perspectives and a fresh realism into the way biblical scenes and characters are represented. Beside his beautiful *Madonna and Child with St. Anne* (1424–25) in the Uffizi and the stunning fresco of the *Trinity* in Santa Maria Novella, he is remembered best for his frescoes in the Brancacci Chapel in Santa Maria del Carmine, which include a poignant *Expulsion from Paradise*, and a graphic series of illustrations of the life of St. Peter mostly taken from Acts 2–5 and the *Golden Legend*, but including the fascinating *Tribute Money* from Matt. 17:24.

Masoretic Text. The standard text of the Hebrew Bible printed in most modern editions, and used by biblical scholars, both Jewish and non-Jewish. It is based on surviving mss from the 8th through the 11th centuries, notably the almost complete St. Petersburg Codex (Codex Leningradensis) dated 1008 C.E. These were produced according to the rules and conventions of scholars working in Babylonia and Tiberias known as "Masoretes," from Heb. *masora*, "tradition." They added marginal notes, known as the *masora magna* and the *masora parva*, designed to preserve the received text as accurately as possible, and devised systems of *pointing (*niqqud*) to ensure correct pronunciation and cantillation.

Mass. The main ritual in the Roman Catholic Church. It consists of five parts: *Kyrie, *Gloria, *Credo, *Sanctus (with *Hosanna and *Benedictus), and *Agnus Dei (with *Dona nobis pacem), which are all derived from the biblical texts except the creed (*Credo*). Music for High Mass (Low Mass is spoken) once consisted of plainsong melodies, which are still occasionally used, but since the 17th century there have been numerous settings, many of them performed as much in secular concert halls as in churches. These include popular masses by *Haydn, *Mozart, *Bach, *Beethoven, *Schubert, *Bruckner, and many others in traditional Latin, and Janacek's exciting Glagolitic Mass, for soloists, choir, and large orchestra, sung in Old Slavonic. See also *Requiem.

Materialist interpretation. An approach to biblical interpretation, influenced by *Marxism but not atheistic, that emphasizes economic and sociopolitical factors in the production of the Bible, its contents, and its contemporary application, particularly in the third world. For example, the effect of cheaper *book production on literacy and the spread of Christianity in the early Roman Empire has to be taken into account in discussions of the *canon. The Israelite settlement in Canaan (*Gottwald), the 8th-century prophets (Bernhard Lang), and Mark's Gospel (Fernando Belo) are read in the light of similar, better documented power struggles in our own world. See *Ideological interpretation; *Liberation theology.

Matthew, Gospel of. First of the four Gospels, and the most widely used and cited from the 2nd century on. Until modern times, it was believed to be the earliest and most complete account of the life of Christ. In Matthew Jesus' teaching is conveniently arranged in a "pentateuch" of five discourses (each ending "And when Jesus finished . . ."), ideal for catechetical instruction. In the early church it was believed to have been written in Antioch by Matthew the tax collector, one of the Twelve (Matt. 9:9), and to contain the actual words of Jesus. According to *Origen and *Jerome, who wrote major commentaries, and many others, it was originally written in Hebrew and addressed to the Jews. Unique to Matthew are the rabbinic expression "kingdom of heaven" and Jesus' special respect for "the law and the prophets" (5:17). Equally significant is the use, only in Matthew, of the word *ekklesia*, "church" (16:18).

Before 19th-century historical criticism, *Augustine's view that Mark was an abridged version of Matthew was widely accepted, although challenged by *Calvin and others, and few seriously doubted that Matthew was the earliest Gospel, closest to the Jewish origins of Christianity and historically the most reliable. Most biblical scholars now accept the priority of Mark, and the study of Matthew has moved toward *redaction criticism (e.g., how Matthew adapts Mark's account of the stilling of the tempest), and questions about the Gospel's distinctive narrative structure and theological themes, as well as its relationship to developments in post–70 C.E. rabbinic Judaism and other sociopolitical concerns.

Most films about Jesus owe a great deal to Matthew's Gospel, but Pasolini's *Il Vangelo secondo Matteo* (1964) stands out as the most serious attempt to illuminate the text. In art Matthew's symbol is the man (Rev. 4:7), because, according to Irenaeus, he emphasizes the human nature of Christ by beginning his Gospel with a genealogy. Many versions of the *Jesse tree also owe much to Matt. 1. There are paintings by Frans Hals, *Poussin, *Rembrandt, and others, but the finest is a series by *Caravaggio in Rome, in particular the wonderful *Calling of St. Matthew* based on 9:9 (1599–1600). In the Chartres tradition he sits on the shoulders of Isaiah, with whom he shares the responsibility for some of the church's bitterest anti-Jewish polemic. Only Matthew recounts the scene of Pontius *Pilate washing his hands and protesting his innocence, followed by the chilling words of the people: "His blood be on us and on our children" (27:24–25; cf. Isa. 1:15). From this *Tertullian deduces that Pilate was a Christian, and in Coptic tradition he became a martyr and saint venerated on June 25. Matthew's musical legacy is dominated by *Bach's *St. Matthew Passion* (1727).

Maundy Thursday. The Thursday of *Holy Week on which the institution of the *Eucharist is commemorated. The English name is derived from the Latin *mandatum novum*, "a new commandment (I give unto you, that you love one another)" (John 13:34), and footwashing (Lat. *pedilavium*, John 13:1–11) has been an important part of the Maundy Thursday ritual since the 4th century. A central element in the Catholic and Orthodox traditions is the Blessing of the Oils (*Chrism*), reflected in the Scripture readings used (Isa. 61:1–9; Ps. 89:20–27). See *Last Supper.

Meaning. Much of the biblical interpreter's task is taken up with defining the meaning of biblical words and phrases, both in the original Hebrew, Aramaic, or Greek, and in translation. By far the most frequent method in common parlance is to define the meaning of a term by its equivalent in another language: for example, *tzedek* means "righteousness." This is a very crude definition that, for example, ignores the fact that *tzedek* (unlike "righteousness") has a plural, and a very different semantic range requiring the translation "tri-

umph" in some contexts (Judg. 5:11). Definitions need much more data before an English equivalent is proposed: how does it differ from *mishpat*, "justice"? What other terms is it associated with? What happened to the term in later, much better documented Hebrew?

*Calque or semantic borrowing is a common feature of languages influenced by the Bible. The word "flesh," for example, in "All flesh shall see it together" (Isa. 40:5 AV; NRSV "people"), is an English word with a borrowed Biblical Hebrew meaning. Similarly there are many Greek words with Hebrew meanings in the LXX and NT, and in *Latin numerous words have borrowed Greek and Hebrew meanings. This phenomenon goes some way toward solving the problem of translation since "righteousness" may have borrowed some of the meaning of the Hebrew word it translates. See also *Original meaning; *Root meaning; *Semantics; *Semitisms.

Medicine. Attempts to explain some of the miraculous pregnancies, healing miracles, plagues, and the reasons why the meat of some animals may be eaten but not others, by modern medical science alone, have largely been abandoned, although studies of faith healing, alternative medicine, and tribal practices in many parts of the world may be relevant, not least in relation to various psychiatric conditions. The Bible for the most part explains disease as due to divine intervention (cf. Deut. 28:20–24). The skin disease that smites the prosperous Job (Job 2) and the Suffering Servant (Isa. 53; cf. 1:6) is undefined, but belongs to a category of conditions typically suffered by the poor (cf. Luke 16:19–31). A sharp distinction is drawn between the prophets as God's agents (2 Kgs. 4:8) and illegitimate "healers" (2 Chr. 16:12), although physicians were probably a normal part of the biblical world if rarely mentioned (Jer. 8:22), and their skill is highly praised by Ben Sira

(Sir. 38; c. 180 B.C.E.). Luke is said to have been a doctor (Col. 4:14). See *Leprosy.

Medieval interpretation. Early medieval scholars, both Jewish and Christian, drew heavily on the traditions they inherited from the talmudic and patristic period. In the Latin West *Augustine's theory of interpretation, promoted by *Gregory the Great, ensured that *allegorical and other nonliteral interpretations of the Bible flourished in the *art and architecture of the church as well as in the scholarly literature. Partly through the influence of Jewish scholars like *Rashi and *Maimonides, a few voices spoke up for the *literal meaning, for example, *Hugh of St. Victor in 12th-century Paris, *Thomas Aquinas, and the Franciscan *Nicholas of Lyra. But it was not until the Renaissance that thoroughgoing critical studies of the text, by scholars with a good knowledge of the original languages, can be said to have become the norm. Indeed, printed editions of the *Biblia Pauperum, a pictorial compendium of medieval interpretations, were still available in the 16th century, and both *Luther and *Calvin still cite with approval many traditional allegorical interpretations.

Megillot (Heb. "scrolls"). The five short books, grouped together among the *Ketuvim in the Hebrew Bible, to be read at festivals: Song of Songs at Pesah (*Passover), Ruth at Shavu'ot (Weeks or *Pentecost), Lamentations on the fast of Tish'ah be'av (Ninth of Ab) (cf. Jer. 39:2), Ecclesiastes at Sukkot (*Tabernacles), *Esther at Purim. The book of Esther is known as the "Megillah," and is the subject of a tractate of the Mishnah with that title.

Melanchthon, Philipp (1497–1560). Renaissance scholar and Protestant reformer. After studying Classics at Heidelberg and Tübingen, he became a colleague of *Luther at Wittenberg in 1518 and thereafter played a crucial role in the Reformation movement. He took part in the Leipzig Disputation (1519), the Diet of Speyer (1529), and the Colloquy of Marburg (1529), and is largely responsible for the Augsburg Confession (1530). His *Loci Communes* (1521) is the first systematic presentation of Reformation doctrine. In his commentaries on Romans (1522), Colossians (1527), and Matthew (1558) he approaches the text as he would Herodotus or Plato, applying literary, historical, and archaeological methods and discarding medieval nonliteral interpretations.

Melchizedek. King of Salem (Jerusalem, Ps. 76:2) and priest of God Most High (Heb. *El Elyon*), who offered Abraham bread and wine and blessed him after his defeat of the four kings (Gen. 14). He is mentioned again only once in the Hebrew Bible, where the king is addressed as "a priest forever after the order of Melchizedek" (Ps. 110:4), and once in the NT, where his mysterious origins and apparent immortality prompt comparison with Christ (Heb. 5–7). In a famous fragment from Qumran (11QMelch) he is, like the archangel Michael, a heavenly deliverer, and for *Philo he was an incarnation of the Logos. In rabbinic *midrash he was with Noah in the ark. Modern scholars have noted the recurring element—*zedek/-zadak/-zadok* in the names of kings and priests of Judah (Adonizedek, Zedekiah, Zadok, Jehozadak) as well as in the epithet "city of righteousness" (Heb. *tzedek*, Isa. 1:26), and suggest he was the ancestor of a hereditary priestly family there.

In Christian tradition his offering of bread and wine soon became a type of the *Eucharist, and in the liturgy he is often grouped with *Abel (Gen. 4:4) and *Abraham (22:15–18) as those whose sacrifices were acceptable to God. Melchizedek is a popular figure in Christian art from a mosaic (with Abel) in San Vitale in Ravenna (6th century) to a stained-glass window in *Chartres Cathedral and large-scale paintings by *Raphael (1518–19) and *Rubens (1625). In literature the good fortune of Melchizedek in not having "father or mother or genealogy" (Heb. 7:3) is occasionally cited by those troubled with family ties.

Mendelssohn, Moses (1729–86). German Jewish philosopher, often known as the "Father of the *Haskalah." Son of a poor Torah scribe and speaking only Yiddish, at the age of 14 he moved with his rabbi to Berlin, where he was befriended by *Lessing and others, and became a popular member of Berlin society, the first of many brilliant German Jews. Besides his main work *Jerusalem: or, On Religious Power and Judaism* (1783; ET 1838), a plea for Jewish emancipation and a powerful rationalist defense of the Jewish religion, he wrote commentaries on Ecclesiastes, Song of Songs, and Psalms, in which he displays a detailed critical knowledge both of the traditional Jewish sources and of contemporary non-Jewish scholarship. His famous five-volume *Bi'ur* ("Explanation") of the Torah, which contains a German translation in Hebrew characters and a commentary (1780–83), became very popular and was reprinted many times under the title *Sefer netivot ha-shalom* ("the book of the paths of peace," Prov. 3:17).

Merkavah mysticism. The Jewish mystical tradition derived from Ezekiel's vision of a heavenly chariot (Heb. *Merkavah*) (Ezek. 1), and developed in the *Hekhalot* literature and *3 Enoch*. The mystics, known as *yorde merkavah*, "riders in the the chariot," experienced visions of heaven, not unlike those of Isaiah (6), Paul (2 Cor. 12:1–10) and John of Patmos (Revelation), but much more extended and more terrifying. The *Mishnah prohibits discussion of Ezek. 1 unless a sage is present (*Hagigah* 2:1), and a mystical work entitled *Hekhalot Rabbati* (c. 5th century) was probably written, like a number of medieval Christian mystical texts, to prepare people for the experience. They needed to know the names of the angels guarding the entrance to each of the seven heavens or palaces (Heb. *hekhalot*); they had to have the courage to face Ezekiel's "holy creatures," gigantic and with hundreds of eyes, and his "wheels" like torches of light and the flames of burning coals; and they had to learn the words of the hymns they would sing when they reached the throne of glory. Some such hymns were discovered among the *Dead Sea Scrolls ("Songs of the Sabbath Sacrifice"), while others, like the 11th-century "Song of Glory" (*shir ha-kavod*), found their way into the synagogue liturgy. See *Mysticism.

Mesopotamian literature. The literature discovered in the area between the Tigris and Euphrates known today as Iraq, and neighboring countries, at Ur, *Babylon, *Nineveh, Nuzi, *Mari, and a host of other sites, some of them still being excavated. Mostly written on clay tablets between 3000 B.C.E. and around 100 B.C.E., it has survived in greater quantities than literature written on less durable materials, and includes writings of all kinds from hymns, letters, and legal documents to lengthy didactic and speculative literature, epics, and historical records. Of particular interest for biblical interpretation were the discoveries of the Law Code of Hammurabi, a "Babylonian Job" (*Ludlul bel nemeqi*), the official *Assyrian account of the military campaigns of *Sennacherib (2 Kgs. 18–19), and the edict of Cyrus (2 Chr. 36:22–23).

Messiaen, Olivier (1908–92). French organist and composer. Born in Avignon, he spent most of his life in Paris as organist and, from 1942, as professor at the Paris Conservatoire. Among his best-known compositions, which make use of birdsong, Asian rhythms, and new types of instruments, are the vast Turangalila Symphony (1946–48) and a work for organ entitled *Catalogue d'oiseaux* (1956–58), but the majority are religious or mystical. These include the apocalyptic works *Quattuor pour la fin du temps* ("Quartet for the end of time"), composed in a German prisoner of war camp in 1940, and *Couleurs de la Cité Céleste* ("Colors of the heavenly city") (1963), a work for piano and instrumental ensemble (including 4 trumpets and 4 trombones), inspired by verses from Revelation (4:3; 8:6; 9:1; 21:11, 19, 20). *La Transfiguration de Notre Seigneur Jésus-Christ* is a large-scale work for orchestra and 10-part choir (1969), and Messiaen also composed an opera, *Saint François d'Assise* (1983), and numerous organ works such as *La Nativité du Seigneur* (1935) and *Vingt regards sur l'Enfant Jésus* (1957).

Messiah.   The title meaning "expected Savior" is derived, by way of Latin (John 1:41 Vg), from the Heb. *mashiah*, "anointed." The Hebrew term is not normally used in a messianic sense in the Bible, where it refers most frequently to actual kings, including the non-Israelite Cyrus (Isa. 45:1), less often to priests (e.g., Lev. 4), and occasionally to prophets (Isa. 61:1). Already in Dan. 9:25–26 and Zech. 4:14, a messianic meaning can be detected, and this is a normal usage in the *Dead Sea Scrolls. The *Targum adds "the Messiah" in its Aramaic translation of Isa. 52:13, and in Midrash (Lam. Rab. 2.2) Bar Kokhba, leader of the Jewish Revolt in 130–35 C.E. was hailed as "King Messiah." In the early church, when the word *christos* appears in the Greek Bible, it was interpreted messianically, and references to the Messiah were found throughout Jewish Scripture, providing the inspiration and authority for some of the main Christian beliefs about Jesus. Finally, when the word *Christ* became more a personal name than a title, the terms *Messiah* and *messianic* became as much parts of Christian vocabulary as of Jewish. See *Christology.

Messianic secret.   A puzzling feature of the Gospel accounts of the life of Jesus, especially Mark, in which he tells the disciples and others to keep his messianic powers secret (Mark 5:43; 7:36). Related perhaps to the disciples' inability to understand him till after the resurrection, or to the gnostic notion that Jesus possessed esoteric knowledge communicated in parables that only initiates (like Judas, according to the *Gospel of Judas*) could understand, it was much discussed in 19th-century studies of the psychology of the historical Jesus. William Wrede's *Messianic Secret in the Gospels* (1901; ET 1971) broke new ground in the debate by arguing that the theme was a theological one designed to reconcile the early accounts of the life of Jesus with the author's postresurrection faith.

Metaphor.   A figure of speech in which language about one thing is directly applied to another in order to show points of similarity. It is frequent in the language of love ("Your eyes are doves," Song 4:1), worship ("The Lord is my shepherd," Ps. 23:1), instruction ("[Wisdom] is a tree of life to those who lay hold of her," Prov. 3:18), and polemic ("You brood of vipers!" Matt. 3:7). Like other nonliteral interpretations of the Bible (*allegorical, *christological), the identification and interpretation of metaphorical language sometimes raises crucial theological and philosophical questions, as in statements like "This is my blood of the covenant" (Mark 14:24) and the debate over how nonliteral metaphors like "Lord" and "Father" differ from the word "God" itself. See *Analogy; *Simile.

Metaphysical poets.   Originally a derogatory term, invented by Dr. Johnson, for a group of 17th-century English poets, including John *Donne and George *Herbert, whose writings are characterized by an elaborate, highly allusive, at times pedantic, style and deep religious feeling. Allusions to the language of the comparatively recent AV and the Book of Common Prayer are frequently original and constitute a fascinating and important chapter in the history of biblical interpretation.

Methodius.   See   *Cyril   and Methodius.

Micah, book of.   Sixth of the twelve Minor Prophets. Apparently a contemporary of *Isaiah (Mic. 1:1) and quoted by *Jeremiah (26:18), he preaches against injustice (Mic. 2:1–2) and the breakdown of society (7:5–6) and predicts divine judgment on both Samaria and Jerusalem (chaps. 1–3; 6:1–7:7). Like Isaiah he also promises future salvation in terms of a new age of justice and peace (4:1–4; cf. Isa. 2:1–3), new power to the daughter of Zion (Mic. 4:13), and the coming of a savior from Bethlehem (5:2; cf. Matt. 2:6). Micah also contains the vision of "every one sitting under their own vine and fig tree" (Mic. 4:4) and the most famous definition of true religion: "What does the Lord require of you but to do justice, love mercy, and walk humbly with your God?" (6:8).

Historical and textual critics have so far failed to reach agreement on when Micah was written, although most consider the book in its present form to be a 6th- or 5th-century B.C.E. work containing earlier material. The use of a variety of conventional literary forms (lament, oracle, cultic psalm) and images (Divine Warrior, women as victims) has been much discussed, as have the overall structure of the book and its relationship to Isaiah, Jeremiah, and Deuteronomy. Part of a commentary (*pesher) on Micah was found at Qumran in which Jerusalem is interpreted as the "Teacher of Righteousness" and Samaria as his adversary (on Mic. 1:5–6). Micah 7:18–20 is read in some Jewish traditions after *Jonah on

*Yom Kippur, and in Christian lectionaries during *Lent. Micah 5:2 is remembered in the Christmas carol "O Little Town of Bethlehem" (1868), and in a marble relief on the façade of Orvieto Cathedral (1310–30) showing the exaltation of Bethlehem (5:2) while God curses a woman representing Jerusalem (4:10). *Calvin preached twenty-eight hour-long sermons on Micah in Geneva between November 1550 and January 1551.

Michael.   One of the four *angels mentioned by name in the Bible. His name means "Who is like God?" (Heb. mi ka'el: cf. Exod. 15:11). In *Daniel he is "the great prince who has charge of your people" (12:1; cf. 10:13, 21), and in the War Scroll from Qumran he is the devil's chief adversary, as he is in 1 Enoch, the *Martyrdom and Ascension of Isaiah, and the NT (Jude 9; Rev. 12:7). In rabbinic tradition he is one of the four archangels, sometimes identified with Metatron, but also as the angel who fought with Jacob (Gen. 32:24–32) and the seraph that touched Isaiah's lips with a burning coal (Isa. 6:6–7). He is mentioned in the Qur'an (2:98) but never rivals *Gabriel in importance. In medieval Christian tradition St. Michael was considered patron saint of chivalry and is normally represented in art as a warrior (*Perugino, *Piero della Francesca), defeating "the dragon, that ancient serpent, who is the Devil" (Rev. 20:2) (*Dürer, Gerard David, Guido Reni, *Raphael). In *Milton's *Paradise Lost, he and Gabriel lead the war in heaven. In Orthodox tradition he is known as the Taxiarchos, "military commander," and in the Roman Mass for the Dead until 1970 his role as protector of souls, especially at the hour of death, was invoked in a special prayer. Numerous churches are dedicated to St. Michael or St. Michael and All Angels, many of them with impressive statues and stained-glass windows representing the archangel. A well-known modern example is Jacob Epstein's sculpture on the wall of Coventry Cathedral (1958).

Michaelis, Johann David (1717–91).
German Protestant scholar. As professor of oriental languages and theology at Göttingen from 1746 till his death, he published works on Hebrew, Arabic, and Syriac, as well as an influential *Introduction to the NT* (1750) and a work on Mosaic law in which he sought to interpret it in rational terms as the product of a primitive stage in human development. His massive annotated German translation of the OT was popular for a time.

Michelangelo Buonarroti (1475–1564).
Italian sculptor and painter. Brought up in Florence, in 1496 he came to the notice of a Roman cardinal who summoned him to Rome and commissioned his first great work, the uniquely successful marble *Pietà* now in St. Peter's (1497). After a short time back in Florence, where he sculpted his famous statue of *David* out of a gigantic block of marble, he returned to Rome in 1503 and was commissioned by Pope Julius II to design his tomb, a huge unfinished work in the Church of San Pietro in Vincoli, of which Michelangelo's *Moses* (1516) is the best-known feature. Meanwhile he was ordered to decorate the ceiling of the *Sistine Chapel (1508–12). No one before or since so brilliantly transformed biblical images like the *Creation of Adam* or the *Prophet Jeremiah* into exquisite works of art that have become part of everyday Western culture.

Back in Florence with a commission to design a façade for the Church of San Lorenzo, he went through a period of artistic inactivity, partly due to military events in which he was involved, and returned to Rome for good in 1534. It was then that he painted *The Last Judgment* (1536–41) on the wall behind the altar in the Sistine Chapel. This is painted in a style very different from all his earlier work, showing much less concern for beauty as an end in itself, as are the *Crucifixion of St. Peter* and the *Conversion of St. Paul* in the Capella Paolina in the Vatican, also from this later period

in his life (1545–50). In 1547 he was appointed architect of St. Peter's, where he worked loyally and for a small wage until his death.

Midrash (pl. midrashim).
A verse-by-verse rabbinic commentary on the Bible. The midrashic literature is divided into *halakhic and *haggadic according to its function. Halakhic midrashim derive laws (*halakhah*) from Exodus (*Mekhilta*), Leviticus (*Sifra*), Numbers (*Sifre*), and Deuteronomy (*Sifre*); while haggadic midrashim such as *Midrash Rabbah* on Genesis (*Genesis Rabbah*) and the other books of the Torah, as well as the Five Scrolls and Psalms, contain the rabbis' interpretations of the text for academic and homiletical purposes. The term *midrash* can also refer to the rabbinic method of biblical interpretation that involves looking beyond the literal meaning (*peshat*) for one or more non-literal meanings (*derash*). The verb *darash*, "to study," appears first in relation to Torah study in Ezra 7:10 (cf. Sir. 39:1–3), while in the *Talmud *bet midrash* is a school (cf. Sir. 51:23) and *darshan* is a preacher or interpreter of Scripture.

Millenarianism.
A belief held by some Christian groups, based on Rev. 20, that the saints will rule the earth for a period of a thousand years while Satan is chained in a bottomless pit. According to *Augustine and many influenced by him, Christ's victory over *Satan has already taken place so that the millennium, not literally 1,000 years, and the history of the church are coterminous. Many others, from Montanists (2nd century) and Anabaptists (16th century) to Seventh-day Adventists and Jehovah's Witnesses today, interpret Rev. 20 as referring to Christ's second coming and the millennium as still in the future. This partly depends on whether the millennium is understood to be in this world, like the messianic age in biblical and Jewish tradition, or in the world to come,

that is, after the Last Judgment (cf. Dan. 12:1–3; Rev. 20:11–14).

Milton, John (1608–74).   English poet. Born in London and educated at St. Paul's School and Christ's College Cambridge, Milton's earliest writings include paraphrases of Pss. 114 and 136. He considered taking holy orders but was violently opposed to many aspects of the church, and much of his writing consists of controversial pamphlets against episcopacy, on divorce, and in support of regicide and the Commonwealth. He became blind at the age of 43 and gradually withdrew from political life to devote himself to poetry. All his writings contain biblical quotations, and in his theological treatise *De Doctrina Christiana* (1655–61) he calls for an approach to Scripture that is informed by a knowledge of the original languages and context of the Bible, rejecting allegorical interpretations but retaining the importance of the analogy of faith. His epic masterpiece *Paradise Lost* was published in 1667, although he began work on it over thirty years before, and reflects his disillusionment with the restoration of the monarchy in 1660, which he saw as the triumph of evil. Its sequel *Paradise Regained* (1674) is about the temptations of Christ in the wilderness, and *Samson Agonistes* (1674) is a powerful study of the last days of a tragic hero, given autobiographical poignancy by the blindness of its author.

Minor Prophets.   The prophets, Hosea through Malachi, that make up the "Book of the Twelve," as opposed to the *Major Prophets.

Miqra (or **Mikra**).   A common rabbinic term for the Hebrew Bible, derived fom the verb *qara'*, "to read, recite" (cf. Qur'an). See *Rabbinic Bibles; *Tanakh.

Miracle Plays.   See *Mystery plays.

Miracles.   Biblical "signs and wonders" performed by a deity, usually but not always the God of Israel and his prophets. As well as God's prophets (e.g., *Elijah, *Elisha) and the disciples of Jesus (e.g., Acts 5:12), false prophets may perform signs and wonders too (e.g., Mark 13:22). They include all kinds of phenomena, from the plagues in Egypt, the turning back of the sun in the sky (Isa. 38:7–8), and the stilling of the tempest, to individual healing miracles and turning water into wine, and always it is the effect on the observer that is important, rather than any scientific aspects of the story. Some observers, like Pharaoh (Exod. 7:8–13), refuse to recognize God's hand in the miracle, while others, like *Miriam and *Moses, celebrate them in a song of triumph.

Modern scientific or rational explanations have been offered for some of the biblical miracles, for example, substituting a shallower "Reed Sea" (Heb. *yam suf*) for the Red Sea and positing an exceptional case of generosity among the five thousand (Mark 6:30–44). Literary-critical approaches have suggested that the miracles in the Gospels and Acts may be understood as episodes in the *myth of a cosmic struggle between good and evil, rather than accounts of what actually happened, or as mainly concerned with sociopolitical issues such as the *liberation of the poor and marginalized. There are traditions about charismatic miracle-working rabbis from Haninah ben Dosa in the time of Christ to modern *Hasidic masters, and there is a Hasidic saying that only a fool would believe that all the miracle stories about them are true.

Miriam (Vg *Maria*).   Sister of *Moses, traditionally identified with the unnamed sister who protected her brother when he was a baby (Exod. 2:1–10), and remembered as a prophet, musician (Exod. 15:20–21), and divinely appointed leader of Israel (Mic. 6:4). According to ancient Jewish tradition she prophesied, before Moses was born, that her mother would have a child who would save Israel. It is also said that she, like her brother, created a well for the Israelites in the wilderness that disappeared when she died. In Christian tradition her song of triumph, in which she recognizes God's hand in the crossing of the Red Sea (Exod. 15:21), foreshadows her namesake the Virgin Mary celebrating, with choirs of virgins in heaven, their safe passage through the sea of this world, and also *Mary Magdalene as the first witness of the resurrection (John 20:11–18). Others, seeking to reassess the role of women in the exodus story, argue that it was actually Miriam who composed the original militaristic Song of the Sea, like the songs of Deborah (Judg. 5) and Judith (Jdt. 16:1–3), and that her subsequent challenge to Moses' leadership, albeit unsuccessful (Num. 12), is evidence that one of the leaders of the exodus was indeed a woman.

Miserere (Lat. "Have mercy"). First word and frequent title of Ps. 51 (Vg 50). The popular setting by the 17th-century Italian composer Gregorio Allegri is said to have impressed the 14-year-old *Mozart so much that he wrote it down from memory after hearing it once. Verse 15 ("O Lord, open thou my lips . . .") is frequently used as a short prayer in its own right, and appears in the Jewish *Amidah.

Mishnah. A collection of rabbinic sayings, said to have been edited c. 200 C.E. by Judah the Prince, but many of them much more ancient. It is written in Hebrew and consists of 63 "tractates" arranged in six parts or "orders": agriculture, festivals, women, legal damages, sacrifice, ritual purity. It is thus not strictly a commentary on the *Torah but constantly refers to it and interprets it. Its contents are mainly halakhic, but not exclusively as the famous tractate known as *Pirqe Abot*, "the Sayings of the Fathers," proves. Both the Palestinian *Talmud and the Babylonian Talmud are running commentaries on the Mishnah, and together constitute the bulk of what is known collectively as the *Oral Torah. *Maimonides wrote a commentary on the Mishnah in Arabic c. 1160, and there are modern English translations by Herbert Danby (1933) and Jacob Neusner (1988).

Missionaries. The role of missionaries in the history of Christian biblical interpretation has been significant. From the very beginning the travels of *Paul, *Peter, and, if there is any truth in the legends, *Matthew, *Thomas, *Mark, and others as well, were aimed at interpreting Scripture and the life of Christ to those who did not understand it. The form in which the NT now exists owes much to that process. As Christianity spread, translations into Coptic, Armenian, Gothic, Slavonic, and countless other languages were undertaken on behalf of the church for the same reason, and it was often the missionaries who designed new writing systems and wrote the first grammars and dictionaries for languages not previously written down.

The same applies on a far grander scale to the missionary enterprise of the churches from the 16th century. Missionaries to China saw themselves fulfilling a prophecy about "the land of Sinim" (Isa. 49:12), and those working with the East India Trading Company applied the words of Isa. 60:9 to their work. Their imperialism and racial prejudice found plenty of scriptural authority in such passages as Mal. 1:11 and Isa. 54:2–3, regularly used in their pamphlets, sermons, and hymns. More recently *postcolonial interpreters have rejected that kind of biblical interpretation and sought to find biblical *authority for more enlightened attitudes toward different cultures.

Mithraism. The popular cult of the Persian sun-god Mithras, widespread throughout the Roman Empire until the 4th century C.E. It is based on the *myth that he slayed the bull out of which all human beings were created, and ascended to heaven, where he promises immortality to all who are initiated into his mysteries. Already by the end of the 2nd century C.E. *Tertullian noticed some striking similarities to Christianity, including baptism and the use of bread, water, and wine in the rituals, and believed the cult to be a devilish parody of Christianity. Some modern scholars have suggested that such similarities and the date of *Christmas, which falls on a Mithraic festival, prove Mithraic influence on early Christianity.

Monotheism. The belief in only one God. Explicit monotheism implies the denial that any other gods exist, and is comparatively rarely expressed in the Bible apart from Deuteronomy (4:35, 39; 32:39) and Isa. 45. The *Decalogue and the *Shema (Deut. 6:4) originally presupposed the existence of other gods and called for devotion to one God (henotheism), although frequently interpreted as referring to monotheism in Judaism and Christianity. Other passages given a monotheistic meaning by later, more philosophical readers include the LXX translation of "I AM THAT I AM" in Exod. 3:14 AV as "the one who exists" (Gk. *ho on*).

In *Maimonides' "Thirteen Principles of the Faith" the word used is *yahid*, "only" (Gk. *monos*), but this is not the word used in the Shema. The best example of explicit monotheism is the Muslim *shahada*, "There is no god but Allah . . . ," although the formula *allahu akbar*, which appears to mean "Allah is greater!" (comparative), has been cited as proof that explicit monotheism was not an essential part of early Islam either. The Christian doctrine of the *Trinity was devised by Greek theologians to protect the uniqueness of God (monotheism) as well as the divinity of Christ. See *Atheism.

Moses (Heb. *Moshe*; Arab. *Musa*). Prophet, teacher, and first leader of

Israel. Four of the five books of the *Pentateuch are devoted to his life story, from his birth and survival as a baby in the bulrushes to his death at the age of 120 on the hills overlooking the promised land. Moses led the Hebrews out of slavery in Egypt and at Sinai gave them their identity as "a kingdom of priests and a holy nation" (Exod. 19). The prophet with whom God spoke "face to face" (Exod. 34:11; cf. Deut. 34:10), he was the yardstick against which prophets (Deut. 18:15) and kings (2 Kgs. 23:25) were judged. Already in biblical tradition he was "unparalleled in all the signs and wonders he performed" (Deut. 34:10), and for *Philo he was "in all respects the greatest and most perfect of men." According to the 1st-century C.E. *Testament of Moses* he ascended miraculously to heaven (cf. Jude 9), and in the NT he appears in glory with *Elijah at the *transfiguration (Luke 9:28–36). References to him in the Bible outside Exodus-Deuteronomy are predominantly to the "*Torah of Moses" or the "book of the *law of Moses," and it is clear that from very early the Torah, both Written and *Oral, was believed to have been revealed to Moses at *Sinai. In the Gospels Mosaic authority is cited in legal discussions, and in the *Talmud there is a story that, when Moses once overheard Rabbi *Akiba discussing the Law with his disciples, he could not understand them, although they claimed Mosaic authority for what they were saying.

In Christian tradition comparisons with Jesus were made from the very beginning. In the *golden calf story Moses offers to die for his people (Exod. 32:32), while in Deuteronomy and perhaps in Isa. 40–55, like Jesus, he fulfills the role of the Suffering Servant bearing the sins of his people (Deut. 1:12; Isa. 53:4, 12; Matt. 8:17). His exceptional humility is referred to in Num. 12:3. Elsewhere in the NT a contrast is made between Moses, the servant to whom God entrusted his house, and Jesus, who was more like a son (Heb. 3:5–6), and between the old *covenant of Moses written on tablets of stone and Christ's new covenant in the hearts of believers. From Paul there grew up the belief that Moses actually placed a veil over the faces of the Jews (2 Cor. 3:12–15), so that when the *Messiah came, they could not recognize him. In Muslim tradition too he is sometimes accused of misleading the Jews.

No extrabiblical evidence has so far come to light to confirm the existence of Moses, and modern scholars have questioned the historicity of most of the biblical story, though his Egyptian name and his marriage to the daughter of a pagan priest are unlikely to have been invented. Since the historical criticism of the 18th century, belief in the Mosaic authorship of the Torah, known as the "Five Books of Moses," against all the evidence (e.g., anachronisms like Gen. 12:6b and abrupt changes of style), has been abandoned except within parts of Jewish Orthodoxy and conservative evangelical Christianity, although there has recently been scholarly interest in the Pentateuch as a single literary work.

Moses' extraordinary role in literature and Western culture in general, matched only by Jesus and the Virgin Mary, begins with Greek versions of the story by *Philo (*De Vita Mosis*), *Josephus (*Ant.* 2–4), and a little later, the influential *Life of Moses* by *Gregory of Nyssa. He is noted above all for his humility and his closeness to God, compared in some Christian traditions to the desert fathers. *Milton compares his 40 years in the wilderness with the temptations of Jesus. The Reformers stress his divinely sanctioned authority as lawgiver, and his hardness became for many, including John *Bunyan and William *Blake, his main characteristic to be countered by the love of Christ. Blake's retelling of the story in the *Book of Ahania* (1795) and the *Song of Los* (1795) makes Moses and religious legalism in general as oppressive as slavery in Egypt. The legends surrounding Moses' death inspired poems by George Eliot (1869), Rilke (1922), and Dietrich Bonhoeffer (1945), as well as Sigmund

*Freud's outrageous *Moses and Monotheism* (1939). In modern struggles against slavery, oppression, and social injustice, Moses the messianic leader has been used as a political symbol by post-*Holocaust Jewish writers like Sholem Asch (*Moses*, 1951), *African American preachers like Martin Luther *King Jr., and *liberation theologians like José Severino Croatto (*Exodus*, 1981).

Scenes from the life of Moses are frequently represented in art from the *Dura Europos frescoes (3rd century C.E.) and the Santa Maggiore mosaics in Rome (5th century) to the great series on the walls of the *Sistine Chapel, opposite and corresponding to the life of Christ. There are numerous paintings of the *Finding of Moses* (Veronese, *Poussin, Orazio Gentileschi), *Moses Striking the Rock* (*Tintoretto, Jordaens, Benjamin West), the *Golden Calf* (*Raphael, *Tintoretto, *Blake) and, less well known, *Moses Defending the Daughters of Jethro* (Rosso Fiorentino, Sebastiano Ricci). Famous statues of Moses, some of them with horns derived from a misreading of Exod. 34:30, include those of Claus *Sluter (Dijon, 1395–1403) and *Michelangelo (1513–16). Elsewhere, for example in paintings of the *transfiguration (Fra *Angelico), he has a halo. In film Moses is no less popular from Cecil B. DeMille's epic *The Ten Commandments* (1956) to the animated cartoon *Prince of Egypt* (1998), which adds some interesting haggadic details to the story, such as Moses' poignant compassion for his defeated "brother" Rameses at the end, a point made also in Rossini's opera *Mose in Egitto* (1818). In music there are also *Handel's *Israel in Egypt* (1739–38), Arnold Schönberg's unfinished masterpiece *Moses und Aron* (1930–32; first performed 1954), and the popular spiritual "Go down, Moses."

Moses, Assumption of.

A Jewish work, probably written in the 1st century C.E., purporting to contain the last words of Moses to Joshua before he died, and an account of his assumption to heaven. The first part, which foretells the history of Israel down to the end of the world, when "Satan shall be no more" (10:1), is known from a 6th-century Latin ms, the second only from a few Greek quotations. The work is alluded to in Acts 7:36, 2 Pet. 2:13, and Jude 9 as well as by the church fathers.

Moses, Testament of. See *Testament of Moses.*

Mozart, Wolfgang Amadeus (1756–91). Austrian composer. Born in Salzburg, he traveled from an early age throughout Austria and Germany, as well as to Paris, London, and Italy, where his musical genius was universally acclaimed. Despite financial problems and poor health, especially in his last years, his musical output as performer and composer was phenomenal, including 27 piano concertos, 41 symphonies, and over 20 operas. Apart from some exquisite examples in his motet *Exultate Jubilate* (Ps. 81; 1773), vespers (1779–80), and masses, Mozart's interpretations of biblical language are relatively few. They comprise an allegorical work on the first commandment, a passion cantata and a musical drama *La Betulia Liberata*, based on the book of Judith, all composed before he was 15, and the more mature *Davide Penitente* (1785), a cantata based on Ps. 51.

Muratorian Canon. A list of NT writings in an 8th-century ms discovered by the Italian scholar Muratori (1672–1750). Written in ungrammatical Latin and dating from the late 2nd century, it includes all the canonical books of the NT except Hebrews, James, and 1 and 2 Peter, and adds the Wisdom of Solomon and an early 2nd-century work known as the *Apocalypse of Peter.*

Music. Music is one of the first human inventions mentioned in the Bible (Gen. 4:21) and a special accomplishment of one of Israel's greatest leaders (1 Sam. 16:16–18; Ps. 151 [LXX]). Singing is a regular part of temple worship (1 Kgs. 10:12), as are musical instruments of various kinds (Ps. 150:3–5), and singing accompanies God's triumphs on earth (Exod. 15; Isa. 52:8) and in heaven (Rev. 14:2–3). There was singing at creation (Job 38:7) and there will be singing at the resurrection of the dead (Isa. 26:19). Jesus and the disciples sang hymns, probably the *Hallel Psalms (114–18), after the *Last Supper (Mark 14:26), and Paul encouraged his followers to sing "psalms and hymns and spiritual songs" (Eph. 5:19; Col. 3:16).

Despite the ban on musical instruments in the synagogue so long as there is no temple (cf. Ps. 137), the singing of the biblical Psalms and other poetic compositions remained an integral part of Jewish worship, and had a significant influence on the development of the Christian musical tradition, as had the system of musical notation used in the MT. Since the 18th century, organs and other musical instruments have become common in Reform and Liberal synagogues, and Jewish composers have written choral and orchestral works, including an oratorio *Isaiah the Prophet* by Alexandre Tansman (1951); *Samson Agonistes*, a ballet by the American Robert Starer (1961), and Leonard Bernstein's *Chichester Psalms* (1965).

Apart from a few voices of dissent, including those of *Augustine and *Calvin, singing hymns and performing musical works have been a central feature of Christian worship from famous hymns by *Ambrose, *Gregory the Great, Francis of Assisi, *Luther, George *Herbert, the Wesley brothers, and Cardinal Newman, to the medieval *Play of Daniel*, *Bach's two settings of the passion, *Bruckner's *Missa Solemnis*, and Benjamin *Britten's *Noyes Fludde*. The influence of the Reformation on the production of *hymns in the vernacular and explicit *paraphrases of biblical texts was profound, as was that of the Second

Vatican Council on the composition of simple popular settings of texts such as Isa. 43:1–7.

In addition to music specially written for performance in churches, there are innumerable highly successful oratorios, operas, and other works based on biblical themes, which are nowadays regularly performed to secular audiences. These often contain variations in the original plot (*Handel's *Jephthah*, 1752), innovative applications of biblical texts (Isa. 66:13 in *Brahm's *German Requiem*, 1869), and striking modern interpretations (Stravinsky's *Symphony of Psalms*, 1930). There are also some pieces written for instruments alone such as *Haydn's orchestral work *Seven Last Words* (1785), *Kuhnau's six remarkable *Bible Story Sonatas* for keyboard (1700), and *Messiaen's nine brilliant meditations for organ entitled *La Nativité du Seigneur* (1935). The marriage of the Bible with music, ranging from the sublime (Allegri's *Miserere*, Ps. 51) and the ceremonial (*Zadok the Priest*, 1 Kgs. 1:38–40) to the militaristic ("Mine eyes have seen the glory," Rev. 19:15) and subversive ("Go down, Moses," Exod. 5–10), is so much part of its *reception history as to make it almost impossible to separate them.

Muslim interpretation.

The Qur'an accepts the authority of the Bible, in particular the *Tawrah* (Torah) of Moses, the *Zabur* (Psalms) of David, and the *Injil* (Gospel) of Jesus (sura 3:1; 5:48–50), but also states that some of the traditions have been subject to human corruption (*tahrif*), which must be corrected (4:48; 5:18). Most important are the stories of the prophets, retold in the light of the final revelation to the prophet Muhammad: thus Muhammad's rejection by his people is reflected in the story of *Noah (sura 71); and *Abraham (*Ibrahim*) surrenders himself to God, as Muhammad is called to do (5:3), and becomes the first Muslim (2:131). Abraham establishes the Ka'aba at Mecca and the *qiblah* (the focus of Muslim daily prayer) is moved from Jerusalem to Mecca (2:142–45).

Muslim interpreters of the Qur'an continued the process of modifying and elaborating biblical traditions in ways sometimes also documented in the rabbinic and patristic literature. For example, the traditions in the Qur'an that Jesus ('*Isa*) created live birds out of clay (5:110) and was not really crucified—it only looked as though he was (4:156)—are found in gnostic texts. There are distinctive Muslim traditions about Enoch (*Idris*), *Job (*Ayyub*), *Hagar, Ishmael (*Isma'il*), the *Queen of Sheba (*Belkis*), *Jonah (*Yunis*), and many other biblical motifs. The tradition that *Adam and *Eve, after being expelled from *Eden and wandering alone for 200 years, met again on Mount Arafat near Mecca, accompanies the ritual of the Hajj.

Muslim scholars such as the Arab historian Al-Tabari (839–923) interpreted biblical texts as references to the spread of the descendants of Ishmael (Gen. 17:20) and the coming of the prophet Muhammad (Deut. 18:15). The Greek word *parakletos* "advocate, comforter" (John 14:26), read (perhaps in Syriac) as *periklutos* "praised," was likewise taken as a reference to the coming of *Ahmad*, "the praised one" (Muhammad), foretold by Jesus in the Qur'an (61:6). Sufi (mystical) interpretations of the "throne verse" (2:255) draw on Ezek. 1 and Rev. 4. From the 11th century, however, Muslims on the whole came to regard the Bible as "corrupted" and found enough material in the Qur'an and their own exegetical literature to be able to dispense with it entirely. Since then, with some exceptions, notably the Indian Muslim scholar Sir Sayyed Ahmad Khan (1817–98), who wrote commentaries on Gen. 1–11 and Matt. 1–5, published in Urdu, there has been little direct interest on the part of Muslims in the Bible. See *Qur'an.

Mystery cult.

A religious cult in which members undergo an initiation rite before being permitted to take part in its rituals and share its secret knowledge. There were a number of such cults in the Greco-Roman world associated with particular personalities such as Bacchus, Orpheus, Isis, and Mithras, or places, especially Eleusis near Athens. Apuleius (2nd century C.E.) gives a lively account of his initiation into the Isis cult (*Golden Ass* 11.2), and there is considerable archaeological and iconographical evidence for the cult of Mithras throughout the Roman Empire. Common to several of these cults was the belief that initiates can become one with their god or goddess who dies and rises again, and thus gain immortality. In many, women play a prominent role. There are obvious parallels with *Gnosticism and also with Christianity, where the word "mystery" is frequent already in the NT (Matt. 13:11), but attempts to trace significant historical connections have proved unconvincing. See *Mithraism.

Mystery plays. Medieval dramatizations of the Bible, originally associated with the "mysteries" of *Holy Week and Corpus Christi. Some were liturgical dramas, like the *passion plays, while others aimed to give a theatrical portrayal, in the space of one day, of the whole biblical story from creation to the day of judgment. The OT is covered only very sketchily, and nonbiblical material is often included such as the *harrowing of hell from the apocryphal *Gospel of Nicodemus*, and the legend of the True *Cross. The plays were performed once a year, often on large wagons, in the streets of many English cities, including York, Chester, Wakefield, and Coventry, and were exceedingly popular and influential for two hundred years. At the Reformation they were suppressed, but in the 20th century there has been a revival of interest and successful productions have been staged in York and elsewhere. See *Drama.

Mysticism. The religious phenomenon in which an individual experiences the divine in an immediate, often ecstatic way. In its most general sense it includes the experiences of Moses "whom the Lord knew face to face" (Deut. 34:10) and other biblical prophets (Isa. 6; Jer. 20), as well as Paul (2 Cor. 12) and other writers whose visions, spiritual turmoil, and journeys to heaven (Daniel, Enoch, Revelation) often correspond quite closely to the experiences of the better documented mystics of later Judaism, Christianity, and Islam. One of the nonliteral meanings of Scripture, according to both Jewish and Christian interpreters, is the mystical one recommended by some, seen as a danger by others. The rabbis repeatedly warn against unsupervised contemplation of the first few verses of Genesis or the book of Ezekiel. See *Kabbalah.

In Christian mysticism the immediacy of the experience is most often expressed in terms of love, divine and human, even erotic, probably because of Christ's striking use of the language of love, especially in the Fourth Gospel (John 13:34–35; 14–15; 21:15–17). The Song of Songs, interpreted allegorically, thus provided many mystics, including *Bernard of Clairvaux, Teresa of Avila, and John of the Cross, with the scriptural language and imagery they were looking for to describe the "mystic union" to which their lives of prayer and meditation were directed.

Myth. A story about gods and goddesses in another world and their interaction with events in this world. It was originally applied to Greek literature and avoided in discussions of the Bible, but from the 18th century, as parallels with Babylonian myths were discovered, scholars began to apply the term to biblical stories and distinguish between legends, sagas, history, and *myth. Since the pioneering work of Hermann *Gunkel, it is widely accepted that there are remnants of the Babylonian myth of a struggle between Bel/Marduk and the primeval monster Tiamat in many parts of the Bible including Gen. 1, several psalms (74; 89; 93), and Rev. 20. This was confirmed by evidence from *Ugarit of a similar mythical battle in Canaanite mythology between *Baal and "*Leviathan the fleeing . . . twisting serpent" (Isa. 27:1). Thus the biblical myth of YHWH's victory over chaos in Gen. 1 is an expression of faith in the power of Israel's God to overcome evil. His victory over dragons and sea monsters (Ps. 74:13), and over the Red Sea in particular (Isa. 51:9–10), shows how the myth can be applied to a historical event.

Another function of myth in the Bible is to explain how things are. The myth of God's conversations with *Adam and *Eve in the garden of *Eden, for example, tries to make sense of human free will (or sin) and the subservient role of women in society (Gen. 3), while the myth of God's heavenly court explains why a king of Israel died in battle (1 Kgs. 22) and why an innocent man suffered (Job 1–2). The biblical (and *Marxist) myth of a coming age of social justice is designed to give the oppressed something to work toward and hope for, as is the apocalyptic myth of a day of judgment when the wicked will be punished and the righteous rewarded. The process of *demythologization associated with *Bultmann and others in the 1950s and 1960s underestimated the social and political power of myth, and the work of structural anthropologists and literary critics since then has shown that the effectiveness of such myths, spiritually, emotionally, and politically, does not require a "primitive" mind. On the contrary, myths are often subtle, sophisticated, and profound, and provide a powerful medium for communities to express their religious beliefs.

Myth and ritual. The name of an approach to OT religion, derived from the title of a collection of essays edited by S. H. Hooke and published in 1933, in which British scholars explored the relationship between ancient Near Eastern rituals, in particular the annual Babylonian *Akitu* festival, and the Bible. Recently discovered *Ugaritic parallels were also cited. Language to accompany such rituals is certainly there in accounts of God's victory over primeval monsters, and the acclamation *YHWH malakh*, "the LORD is king" (Pss. 93:1; 97:1; 99:1), with which the ritual ends. Even though there is no evidence that the rituals themselves were ever practiced in Israel, the identification of a "myth and ritual" pattern in which the king plays a crucial role has thrown new light on many passages in the Bible, including some psalms (74; 93; 97), Davidic traditions (Isa. 9:6; Pss. 2; 45), and a variety of apocalyptic passages (Isa. 27:1; Rev. 20–21). See *Myth.

Naaman. Syrian military commander miraculously cured of "*leprosy" by the prophet *Elisha (2 Kgs. 5). Having heard of Elisha from a captured Israelite maid in the service of his wife, he traveled to Israel, but at first scorned the prophet's instructions to wash in the Jordan: "Are not Abana and Pharpar, the rivers of Damascus, better than the waters of Israel?" But when he eventually went down and dipped himself seven times in the Jordan, "his flesh came again like unto the flesh of a little child, and he was clean" (5:14 AV). His subsequent conversion to monotheism made him a model proselyte in rabbinic tradition, and he was also credited with being the man who "drew his bow at a venture" and killed King Ahaz in battle (1 Kgs. 22:34 AV). Jesus recalls the story in his sermon at Nazareth (Luke 4:27), which Christian commentators since *Irenaeus and *Tertullian interpret as illustrating the efficacy of baptism, while from the 18th century Naaman's humility and obedience became popular themes in evangelical sermons.

Nag Hammadi texts. A collection of over 50 papyrus texts, bound in 13 codices, discovered in 1945 in a sealed jar near the town of Nag Hammadi in Upper Egypt. Apart from a fragment of Plato's

Republic (588A–589B), a long tractate attributed to *Zoroaster, and several other gnostic works, they are all *apocryphal Christian texts, written in Coptic in the 4th century, and probably belonged to a heretical monastic community. Quotations from the NT are frequent, and many of the texts, including the well-known *Gospel of Thomas*, which is included in contemporary editions of Gospel parallels, add traditions about Jesus not found in the canonical Gospels. Of particular interest are numerous references to gnostic mythology, including the role of *Adam's third son Seth as heavenly savior. See *Gnosticism.

Nahmanides (1194–1270), Rabbi Moshe ben Nahman. Spanish scholar and mystic, also known by the acronym Ramban. Born in Gerona, he gained an international reputation as a talmudist and halakhic authority, but his knowledge of the Bible, philosophy, *Kabbalah, and *medicine won him widespread popularity far beyond the Jewish community. In his famous public disputation with the convert Pablo Christiani in Barcelona, he gained the respect of the Christian king, but he was later forced into exile by the *Dominicans. He traveled to Palestine and settled in Acre (1267), where he wrote his most original and influential work, *Commentary on the Torah*. In this he displays a detailed knowledge of *Rashi, *Ibn Ezra, *Maimonides, and other Jewish scholars, but breaks new ground by combining respect for the plain meaning of the text with a willingness to look for kabbalistic meanings where appropriate. He also wrote commentaries on Job and the Song of Songs.

Nahum, book of. Seventh book of the Minor Prophets, entitled "An oracle concerning Nineveh." Nothing is known of the author except that he came from a place called Elkosh and lived sometime before the fall of Nineveh in 612 B.C.E. (cf.

Tob. 14:4). His tomb is believed by some to be at Al-Qush, an ancient Jewish settlement 9 miles north of Nineveh in modern Iraq, though *Eusebius and *Jerome locate Elkosh in Galilee. In graphic images of lions, horses, chariots, earthquake, fire, and rape, he describes the destruction and humiliation of the Assyrians, while at the same time praising the Lord, "a stronghold in the day of trouble" (1:7), who is "restoring the majesty of Israel" (2:3). From ancient times the book has been interpreted as a call to faith in times of tyranny, literally as in the Nahum Commentary from Cave IV at Qumran (see *Pesher), or spiritually as in Jerome. *Luther in his *Lectures on Nahum* (1525) noted the significance of the prophet's name, "comfort" (cf. Isa. 40:1), and others have stressed that the book is about divine justice, not human revenge.

Modern discussions of the date of Nahum take account of parallels with the 8th-century prophets or with the book of *Jonah, and a reference to the city of Thebes (Nah. 3:8–9), which fell to the Assyrians in 663 B.C.E. The work was hailed as a poetic masterpiece by *Lowth (1763), and literary critics since then have observed the brilliant use of irony in 1:2–3 (cf. Exod. 34:6–7; Jonah 4:2), a possible acrostic in 1:3–7, the rapid succession of powerful images (unique in biblical literature), and the elegant literary structure of the book as a whole. Its impact on literature, music, and art, however, has been minimal.

Names. Personal names were chosen by a child's mother (Gen. 29:31–30:12; Luke 1:60) or father (Gen. 21:3; Matt. 1:21), often because they had some appropriate meaning or association. Compound names like *yesha'yahu* "Isaiah," for example, with the element -*yahu* "YHWH," or "Daniel," with the element -*el*, "God," have obvious religious significance, as has *Gideon's discarded Canaanite name Jerubbaal (Judg. 7:1). Names can be used to convey a theological message like *Immanuel, "God is with us" (Isa. 7:14), and a change of name is often highly significant as in the case of *Jacob/Israel (Gen. 32:28), *Zion/Hephzibah (Isa. 62:4), and Simon *Peter (Matt. 16:18).

In Hellenistic times the practice of Jews adopting Greek names like Jason, Alexander, and *Philo became widespread. In the absence of surnames in the modern sense individuals were known by their father's name (Isaiah ben Amoz, James the son of Zebedee) or by where they came from (Jesus of Nazareth) or by some other description (Honi the Circle-Drawer). A number of Jewish scholars are popularly known by acronyms (*Radak, *Rashi) or by Greek names with the suffix *-ides*, "son of" (*Maimonides, *Nahmanides).

Names of God. The Hebrew word *elohim*, "god(s)," is frequently used as a proper name, just as "God" is in English. But in addition Israel's *God has the unique personal name YHWH, corresponding to Babylon's Marduk, the Canaanites' Baal, and Greek Zeus. Probably pronounced "Yahweh," it was believed to be too sacred to be uttered except once a year by the high priest on *Yom Kippur. The four consonants (*Tetragrammaton) are pronounced *Adonai* or *elohim*, and they are translated into English as "the Lord" and "God," respectively. The two names appear already in the creation narrative (Gen. 1–3), where Elohim is used of God as creator of the universe, YHWH in his relations with humankind. The rabbis also observed that YHWH often refers to his compassionate attributes and Elohim to his justice. A third common but less distinctively Israelite word for God in the Hebrew Bible is El, known also from Canaanite mythology, with compounds like El Shaddai (Gen. 17:1). The Greek equivalents in the LXX and NT are *Kyrios*, "Lord," and *Theos*, "God."

Numerous other names and epithets are applied to God in the Bible, including "Mighty One of Jacob" (Gen. 49:24), "Our Father" (Isa. 63:16, Matt. 6:9), "Our King" (Ps. 47:6), and Abba, "Father" (Gal. 4:6). In Jewish tradition a variety of terms became popular as euphemisms for the Tetragrammaton, including *ha qadosh barukh hu*, "the Holy One Blessed Be He," and *ribbono shel olam*, "Master of the Universe," as well as *shekinah*, "Divine Presence," *shamayim*, "Heaven," *ha-maqom*, "the Place [i.e. the Omnipresent]," and simply *ha-shem*, "the Name." Many Christian traditions substitute "our Lord" and "our Lady" for the personal names Jesus and Mary, and practice bowing the head or genuflection when the sacred name of Jesus is uttered (Phil. 2:9). In Christian art, images of God, both Father and Son, are often accompanied by the Greek letters *A Ω*, "*Alpha and Omega" (Rev. 1:8; 22:13) or O ΩN (*Ho On*) "the one who is" (Exod. 3:14 LXX).

Narrative criticism. A method of interpreting biblical narratives, especially the Gospels, by applying standard literary-critical techniques. The term was coined in the 1970s as an antidote to *historical criticism, which had too often focused on questions of date, authorship, and sources at the expense of reading the text as it stands. It led to a reassessment of the role of the reader (see *Reader-response criticism), as opposed to the original author or redactor, and the value of *reception history.

Nathan. Court prophet who prophesies that *David's son will build a house of God and that his dynasty will endure forever (2 Sam. 7). He also plays a significant role in *Solomon's enthronement (1 Kgs. 1), but is remembered most for his parable of the rich man in which he accuses David of adultery with Bathsheba and the murder of her husband: "Thou art the man!" (2 Sam. 12:1–15 AV). The subsequent illness and death of their first child is predicted by Nathan, and David's repentance and soul searching are the subject of Ps. 51. The poor man's "little ewe lamb" in the parable has had an interesting afterlife in English literature, as have the dramatic words "Thou art the man," used as the title of a short story by Edgar Allan Poe (1844) and quoted to good effect by the Rev. Jabes Branderham in Emily Bronte's *Wuthering Heights* (1847).

Nathanael. One of the first disciples, described by Jesus as "an Israelite indeed in whom is no guile" (John 1:43–51 AV). He is remembered, like Thomas (20:24–29), as much for his doubts ("Can any good thing come out of Nazareth?") as for his confession of faith ("Rabbi, you are the Son of God. You are the King of Israel"). He is not mentioned in the Synoptic Gospels, but, since the 9th century, has been identified with *Bartholomew (Aram. *Bar Tolmai*, "son of Tolmai"). Both are associated with Philip (Matt. 10:3; John 1:45–46), and personal names like Nathanael Bartholomew are normal (cf. Simon Barjonah, Matt. 16:17; Joseph Barsabbas, Acts 1:23).

Nativity of Christ. The birth of Christ, celebrated at *Christmas. Luke's account contains the tradition about the census in the days of Caesar Augustus, which explains why Mary and Joseph were in Bethlehem of Judea at the time, and the detail that the birth was in a stable, heralded by a choir of angels that appeared to shepherds on a hillside nearby (Luke 2:1–20). Matthew tells how wise men from the east, led by a star, came to pay homage to the newly born "King of the Jews," bearing gifts of gold, frankincense, and myrrh and how the Holy Family had to flee to Egypt to escape Herod's Massacre of the Innocents (Matt. 2:1–12). The church fathers found OT authority for the story in Mic. 5:2; Num. 24:17; Isa. 60:3, 5, 6; Hos. 11:1 and elsewhere, and refer to details not in the Gospels, notably the presence of an ox and an ass, also in fulfillment of OT

prophecy (cf. Isa. 1:3; Hab. 3:2 LXX). Some of the earliest artistic representations of the scene show only the Holy Child and the two animals.

Before the Middle Ages detailed literary and artistic interpretations of the nativity are relatively rare, probably because of the pagan associations of Christmas. Earlier compositions like the popular hymn "Of the Father's love begotten" by Prudentius (348–c. 410), for example, and the 12th-century Advent Antiphon *Veni Immanuel*, "O come, O come Immanuel," have little to say on the nativity itself. It was Francis of Assisi who recognized the touching human and social symbolism of the scene in the stable, and, with his invention of the Christmas crib (Lat. *presepium*) in 1223, brought the nativity into the heart of Christian culture. Since then innumerable poets have been inspired by it from Dunbar, *Donne, and *Milton to Ezra Pound and T. S. *Eliot, and no biblical scene is more familar in Christian art from simple representations like that of Fra *Angelico (1441) and Gauguin's Tahitian version, to the splendid *Adoration of the Shepherds* by *Dürer (1504), *Poussin (1633), and many others, and the even more opulent *Adoration of the Magi* by Botticelli (1470–75), a scene far removed from the Franciscan interpretation of the story. The nativity of the Virgin *Mary and that of *John the Baptist are also celebrated and frequently depicted in Christian art.

Nehemiah, book of. One of the Writings (*Ketuvim) in the Hebrew Bible, closely associated with Ezra and Chronicles. In rabbinic tradition and the LXX it is part of a single book of Ezra (Esdras), while in the Vulgate and elsewhere, although it is a separate book, it is known as 2 Ezra. It begins and ends with Nehemiah's own personal account, punctuated with the prayer "Remember me, O my God, for good." As cupbearer to the Persian king Artaxerxes, he procured letters authorizing an expedition to Jerusalem, where he was appointed governor, oversaw the rebuilding of the city walls (chaps. 1–7), and "cleansed the city from everything foreign" with legislation on Sabbath trading and marriage (chaps. 12–13). The book also contains an important account of the reading of the *Torah by Ezra, the people's penitential response, and the celebration of the Feast of *Sukkot (chaps. 8–10). The rabbis interpreted 8:8 as the first reference to an Aramaic translation of the Torah (*Targum).

Ben Sira praises Nehemiah (Sir. 49:13), surprisingly omitting Ezra altogether. According to another apocryphal reference Nehemiah founded a library (2 Macc. 2:13), and in the Talmud (*b. Sanhedrin* 38a) he is identified with the messianic Zerubbabel (cf. Hag. 2; Sir. 49:13; 1 Esd. 4–6). Christian authors have interpreted his rebuilding of the walls of Jerusalem as working for the renewal of the church, as in a 17th-century work by the Puritan Jonathan Mitchell entitled *Nehemiah on the Wall* (1671) and the 20th-century American drama *Nehemiah the Builder* by Eleanor Wood Whitman (1926). The allusive language of prayer in Neh. 9 has had some influence on Christian literature, including the 19th-century hymn "Stand up and bless the Lord" (Neh. 9:5). See *Ezra, book of.

Nevi'im (Heb. "Prophets"). The second part of the Hebrew *Bible, made up of the "Former Prophets," Joshua, Judges, Samuel, and Kings; and the "Latter Prophets," which comprise the three "Major Prophets," Isaiah, Jeremiah, and Ezekiel, and the Book of the Twelve or "Minor Prophets," Hosea through Malachi.

New hermeneutic. A method of approaching the Bible, particularly the NT, in such a way as to recognize the power of language to change reality and create a "world," not just to communicate information. Invented in the 1950s by Ernst Fuchs and Gerhard Ebeling, students of *Bultmann, and informed as much by theological considerations as by *philosophy or literary and *linguistic theory, it seemed to provide a solution to the problem of bridging the 2,000-year gap between the time of Christ and today, and it proved successful in the interpretation of some texts, including the parables and the prologue to the Fourth Gospel. But it is unclear what role it can play alongside *reader-response criticism, structuralism, and other sociopolitical methods currently being developed.

Newton, Isaac (1642–1727). English mathematician. His early discoveries on differential calculus, gravity, and light refraction led to his appointment in 1669 as professor of mathematics at Cambridge, where he remained until 1699, when he was appointed Master of the Mint in London. Knighted in 1705, he led an active political life, twice serving as Member of Parliament, and also appears to have been a sincerely religious person, sharing some millenarian ideas with his contemporaries, and sought to express his belief in an omnipotent God, biblical prophecy, and a providential scheme in human history in terms similar to the laws of nature. His biblical writings, all published after his death, include works on biblical chronology, Daniel and Revelation, the cubit, and the authenticity of Trinitarian statements in the NT.

Newton, John (1725–1807). English evangelical clergyman. His early years were spent at sea, including a period as captain of a slave-trading ship, but he converted to Christianity, studied the biblical languages, and was appointed curate at Olney in Buckinghamshire, where he met the poet William *Cowper. Together they published a collection of hymns, *Olney Hymns* (1779), written mostly by Newton. He then moved to a parish in London, where he lived until his death. His hymns are mostly models of thoughtful and sometimes original biblical interpretation, the most famous being "Amazing Grace" (1 Chr. 16:17), popularized in the 1960s film *Alice's Restaurant* and in an arrangement for bagpipes. Others include "Glorious things of thee are spoken" (Ps. 87; cf. Isa. 33:20–21), "How sweet the name of Jesus sounds" (Song 1:3), and "Now may He who from the dead" (Heb. 13:20–22).

Nicholas of Lyra (c. 1270–1349).
*Franciscan scholar and biblical commentator. Born at Lyra near Evreux in Normandy, he studied in Paris and from 1319 served as provincial minister for northern France and later Burgundy. His five-volume commentary on the Bible, entitled *Postillae perpetuae in universam Sacram Scripturam*, printed in Rome 1471–72, was popular for many years. It displays a thorough knowledge not only of patristic and medieval Christian scholarship, but also of Hebrew and Jewish literature, including *Talmud, *Midrash, and "Rabbi Solomon" (*Rashi), whom he frequently quotes. He favored the literal meaning of the text, while not unappreciative of the spiritual and homiletical value of nonliteral interpretations, and often used his knowledge to differentiate between Jewish and Christian interpretations. His influence on *Luther is epitomized in the pun: *Si Lyra non lyrasset, Lutherus non saltasset*, "If [Nicholas of] Lyra had not played the lyre, Luther would not have danced."

Nicodemus. The learned rabbi who, according to the Gospel of John, went to Jesus by night to find out more about him (John 3), spoke up for him among his fellow Pharisees (7:45–52), and with Joseph of Arimathea prepared his body for burial (19:38–42). It is unlikely that he is identical, as some have suggested, with Nicodemon ben Gurion, a wealthy citizen of Jerusalem, mentioned several times in the *Talmud. The importance of Nicodemus as a Jewish convert and

bridge between the OT and the NT was appreciated by *Augustine, and his importance in patristic and medieval Christian tradition is further indicated by the existence of a Gospel attributed to him. In art Nicodemus features in paintings of the descent of Christ's body from the cross (*Rubens) and the entombment (Fra *Angelico, *Titian), although he is not always distinguishable from Joseph of Arimathea, while, in a striking marble *Pietà* by *Michelangelo in Florence (c. 1550), he takes the place of the Virgin Mary. Evangelical preachers found some of their favorite texts in Jesus' dialogue with Nicodemus about being "born again," "the wind bloweth where it listeth" (AV), "Moses lifted up the serpent . . . ," and "For God so loved the world. . . ." He is a prominent character in Sholem Asch's novel *The Nazarene* (1939), and in poems by Edwin Arlington Robinson (1932) and Howard Nemerov (1950). See *Gospel of Nicodemus*.

Nimrod. "A mighty hunter before the LORD" and founder of the great Assyrian cities of Nineveh and Calah (modern Nimrud) (Gen. 10:8–12; cf. Mic. 5:6). The name, probably derived from the Assyrian deity Ninurta (or Nimurta), to whom Calah was dedicated, is the title of the best-known of *Elgar's *Enigma Variations* (1899), and the name of a British maritime patrol aircraft in service since 1969. See *Babel, tower of.

Noah (Vg *Noe*). Righteous man, chosen with his three sons, *Shem, *Ham, and *Japheth, and their wives to survive the *flood, and ancestor of all the seventy nations of the world (Gen. 6–10). In the OT his righteousness is remembered as comparable with that of *Job and *Daniel (Ezek. 14) rather than that of *Abraham (Gen. 15:6), and "blameless in his generation" (Gen. 6:9) may imply that his righteousness was relative, especially in the light of the story of his

drunkenness (Gen. 9). In the NT, however, he takes his place alongside all the other models of faith (Heb. 11:7; cf. 2 Pet. 2:5). God's everlasting *covenant with Noah, with the rainbow as its sign, applies to the whole of humanity, although it can also be applied to his undying love for Israel (Isa. 54:9–10).

The rabbis identified seven "Noachian commandments," some derived directly from the Genesis story, some deduced from other passages about universal righteousness. They are normally said to consist of the prohibition of idolatry, adultery and incest, murder, blasphemy, robbery, eating meat torn from a living animal, and the demand for justice (*Midrash Gen. Rab.* 34:8). The righteous "sons of Noah" will have a share in the world to come. Ancient Christian interpreters saw Noah as a type of Christ, a second *Adam, and the *ark as the Virgin *Mary bearing the saving remnant in her womb. In the *Qur'an the story of the lonely prophet Noah's fight against wickedness and idolatry clearly mirrors Muhammad's own experience (sura 71).

In literature Noah is a very popular character whether as a type of Christ, builder of churches, space scientist, or inventer of wine. The drunkenness episode is also occasionally Christianized by seeing in Noah's vine a prefiguring of Christ, as in George *Herbert's poem *The Bunch of Grapes* (1633). There is a rare painting of this scene by *Michelangelo in the *Sistine Chapel. His shrewish wife is a popular, often comic character in some of the medieval *mystery plays, including the York Cycle. Parallels with flood stories from other cultures have frequently been noted, from *Philo's comparison between Noah and Deucalion in Greek mythology to modern scholars' citation of the ancient Gilgamesh Epic, in which Utnapishtim plays a role similar to that of Noah and the gods "crowd like flies" round him when they smell his sacrifice (Gen. 8:21).

Noli me tangere (Lat. "Do not touch me"). The words of the risen Christ to *Mary Magdalene when she met him in the garden (John 20:17 Vg). A popular subject for painters, the best-known include those by Fra *Angelico in San Marco, Florence (1440–41), *Titian in the National Gallery, London (c. 1515), *Rembrandt in Buckingham Palace (1638), and *Claude Lorraine in Frankfurt (1681). *Noli me tangere* is also the title of a powerful novel by the Filipino eye surgeon and world traveler José Rizal (1887; ET *The Social Cancer*, 1912), and a twelve hour and forty minute film by the French New Wave director Jacques Rivette (1971).

North American interpretation. Since the first European settlers began to colonize America, the Bible has played a central role in American public and private life. Even though it is absent from the Constitution and not taught in public schools, biblical phrases and images are still frequent in the media, in political discourse, and in everyday conversation, Catholic, Protestant, and Jewish, in many parts of the United States, not just the "Bible Belt." The 16th-century settlers' use of the book of *Joshua in discussions of how to treat the Native American population should be balanced against appeals for social justice from *Dominican priests like Bartolomé de las Casas quoting *Exodus and *Isaiah. In the *slavery debate, which lasted into the 19th century, both sides cited Scripture, and the Ten Commandments still retain an iconic presence in American ethical and political discourse. Many of the most popular works in American literature, from *Melville's *Moby Dick* (1851) and Stowe's *Uncle Tom's Cabin* (1852) to Faulkner's *Absalom, Absalom* (1936), Steinbeck's *East of Eden* (1952), and Potok's *The Chosen* (1967), contain frequent biblical references and allusions. It was in America that the first *Woman's Bible* was produced as well as the first blockbuster biblical epic films (e.g., *Ten Commandments*, 1956), where Martin Luther *King Jr. led his people up the mountain whence they could see the promised land (Deut. 34), and where you may find yourself behind a car with the sticker "In case of rapture (1 Thess. 4:17) this car will self-destruct."

In such a context biblical scholarship naturally flourished as the Society of Biblical Literature (SBL), founded in 1880 and now with a membership of over 8,000, testifies. SBL activities now include Asian hermeneutics, gender and sexuality, *postcolonialism, *semiotics, and other groundbreaking developments, which show how far American scholarship, and with it the scholarship of the English-speaking world, has progressed since the *Albright era and John Bright's ever popular *History of Israel* (1960). It is no longer universally assumed that German is the primary language of critical scholarship. See *African American interpretation.

Noth, Martin (1902–68). German OT scholar. Born in Dresden, he studied at Erlangen, Rostock, and Leipzig, and taught at the universities of Königsberg (1930–44) and Bonn (1945–64). For most of his life he was editor of *Zeitschrift des Deutschen Palästina-Vereins*, the German equivalent of the *Palestine Exploration Quarterly*, and instrumental in setting up the magisterial Biblischer Kommentar, Altes Testament, series. As well as commentaries on *Exodus* (1959; ET 1962), *Leviticus* (1962; ET 1965) and *Numbers* (1966; ET 1968), and a number of influential essays, his two best-known works in English are *The Deuteronomistic History* (1981; rev. 1991) and *The History of Israel* (1950; ET 1958; rev. 1962), which starts with the Israelite twelve-tribe system (amphictyonic league) in Canaan, proposed by him in 1930 in his earliest and most original work, *Das System der zwölf Stämme Israels*.

Numbers, book of (Heb. *Ba-midbar*, "In the wilderness," Num. 1:1). Fourth book of the *Pentateuch covering the Israelites' last few weeks at Sinai and most of their 40 years in the wilderness. "Numbers," translated from the LXX and Vg title, refers to the census in chap. 1 (cf. also chap. 26). As well as legislation on the Levites (chaps. 1–5), the nazirite (chap. 6), the red heifer (chap. 19), the festivals (chaps. 28–29), the boundaries of Canaan (chaps. 33–34), the cities of refuge (chap. 35) and other matters, the book contains some well-known narratives including the disobedience of *Miriam and Aaron (chap. 12), Korah's rebellion (chap. 16), and the *Balaam stories (chaps. 22–24). Numbers also contains the famous cry "Would that all the LORD's people were prophets" (11:29) and the threefold priestly blessing (6:24–26) (cf. Ps. 67:1; see *Tetragrammaton). The prayers beginning "Arise, O LORD . . . !" and "Return, O LORD . . . !" recited as the people of Israel set out from Sinai (10:35–36), accompany the procession of the Torah Scroll in synagogue worship. According to *Rashi the first of them is equal in importance, along with the first verse of Genesis, to a whole book of the Torah, giving a total of seven books corresponding to the seven pillars of wisdom (Prov. 9:1).

Ancient and medieval Christian writers also found plenty of material in Numbers for typological interpretations, such as Christ the Rock from which water flowed (Num. 20; cf. 1 Cor. 10:1–4), the Son of Man raised high on the cross like the bronze *serpent that gave life in the wilderness (Num. 21; cf. John 3:14), and a foreshadowing of the *Eucharist in the image of the two spies carrying their cluster of grapes on a pole (Num. 13:23). Nineteenth- and 20th-century pentateuchal criticism identified the sources J, E, and P in Numbers, probably spanning several centuries, as well as ancient songs (21:17–18, 27–30) and other poetic compositions (21:14–15), but concluded that it is dominated by the aims and interests of priests and Levites. The use of copper or bronze serpents in healing rituals (21:9) is well attested both in the discovery of a small 13th-century B.C.E. gilded copper serpent at Timna in the southern Negev, and later in the Hellenistic and Roman association of the serpent with Asclepius, the god of healing. The story is the subject of paintings by a number of artists, including *Michelangelo, *Tintoretto, and *Rubens. See also *Moses.

Nunc Dimittis (Lat. "Now lettest thou [thy servant] depart"). Latin title of the song of the aged Simeon when he held Jesus in his arms in the temple at Jerusalem (Luke 2:28–35). There may have been a deliberate wordplay in an original Hebrew version of v. 30 (Jesus = *yeshu'a*, "salvation"). The song soon found a place in the evening liturgy of most Christian traditions, east and west, and popular settings include those of Thomas *Tallis, Gustav Holst, and Geoffrey Burgon.

Obadiah.   Fourth of the twelve Minor Prophets and shortest book in the Bible (21 verses). Nothing is known of the author unless he is to be identified, as he is in rabbinic tradition, with an acquaintance of Elijah at King Ahab's court (1 Kgs. 18). The "vision of Obadiah" is about the crimes committed by Judah's neighbors, the Edomites, and the divine judgment that is to befall them when the "day of the LORD" comes. Graphic images focus on the rocky landscape of Edom, and on the family ties between *Esau (Edom) and *Jacob (Israel), which makes their hostility to Jerusalem all the more tragic. In a striking passage, unique in biblical prophecy, each of eight denunciations is introduced by the formula "You should not have . . ."

According to the rabbis Obadiah was an Edomite convert to Judaism, reflecting the later identification of Edom with the Church of Rome. Obadiah is rarely cited by the church fathers, *Augustine's messianic use of v. 21 in the *City of God* (18:31) being a conspicuous exception. The events alluded to in Obadiah are probably associated with the Babylonian invasions of the 6th century B.C.E. The first five verses are closely paralleled in Jeremiah (49:7–16), and there are references to Edom's anti-Judean role in that period elsewhere (Ps. 137:7; Lam. 4:18–22; Ezek. 25:12–14). Others have suggested a later date when Edom was finally occupied by the Nabatean Arabs (cf. 1 Macc. 5:25). Recent scholars, noting the position of Obadiah in the Book of the *Twelve, have suggested that it is grouped with *Joel and *Amos as a "Day of the Lord" prophecy, and followed by *Jonah as an antidote to its fierce xenophobia.

Odes of Solomon. A pseudepigraphical work containing 42 short hymns, known to us in Greek and Syriac versions. Probably Christian in origin, though possibly adaptations of originally Jewish compositions, they date from the 1st or 2nd century C.E. The words *gnosis* and *logos* are frequent, as are christological interpretations of the "Lady Wisdom" passages in Prov. 1–9. There is also the rare image of God as a mother with breasts. For the most part, however, the *Odes* are orthodox celebrations of life, far removed from gnostic pessimisim, and may have been associated with preparation for *baptism.

Old Testament.   The first part of the Christian *Bible containing the books of Jewish Scripture canonized by the church, but in a different order and supplemented by the *Apocrypha. The OT is thus not the same as the Hebrew Bible (*Tanakh) and, from the earliest Greek *mss down to modern editions, exists only in *translation. The term does not necessarily imply *supersessionism, but, before modern critical scholarship, Christian interpretations of the Greek or Latin OT were so completely different as to make constructive dialogue with Judaism virtually impossible. Even Christian Hebraists working on the OT frequently used their knowledge to refute Jewish claims. Calling it the "First Testament" or (inaccurately) the "Hebrew Bible" does not solve this problem.

Onesimus.   See *Philemon, Letter to.

Oracle.   Originally a form of divination in ancient Greece by which a deity or hero could be consulted, as at Delphi (Apollo), Dodona (Zeus), and the *Sibylline Oracles at Samos, Sardis, Cumae, and elsewhere. The AV, following the Vg, uses the word "oracle" (Lat. *oraculum*) for the "inner sanctuary" of the temple (1 Kgs. 6:5). But in most modern English versions the term "oracle" is most often a translation of the Hebrew word *massa*, "burden" (Isa. 13:1 AV), and is generally applied to a wide variety of prophetic utterances, including "salvation oracles" (Isa. 43:1–7) and "woe oracles" (Jer. 23:1–8). In the Roman Empire oracles would include divine communications such as those delivered to Mary (Luke 1:30–33) and Paul (2 Cor. 12:9) in the NT, and the widely consulted *Sibylline Oracles*. Oracular shrines still active at Antioch and elsewhere played a role in the persecution of Christianity and were officially abolished under Constantine after 325 C.E.

Oral Torah (Heb. *torah she-be'al-pe*).   The sayings and discussions that constitute the talmudic and midrashic literature of the first five centuries C.E. Much of this material is attributed to particular rabbis and is believed to have been handed down by word of mouth in a continuous chain of oral tradition that goes back, like the Five Books of Moses, to *Sinai. It is therefore as authoritative as the Written Torah: indeed, because it is much more extensive and deals in

greater detail with many issues only cursorily discussed in the Written Torah, it is considered in many cases even more authoritative. See *Torah.

Oral tradition.   The handing down of material by word of mouth without the necessity of written records. Evidence from preliterate societies around the world proves that it is possible to transmit in this way lengthy compositions of all kinds, virtually unchanged, for very long periods of time, but also that, even in literate societies, bards, priests, and others can perform extraordinary feats of memory. It is therefore difficult to distinguish oral compositions from material originally in written form, although the frequency of mnemonic conventions like rhyme, repetition, and acrostics in much biblical *poetry suggests an oral stage in its prehistory.

Writing is so frequently mentioned, however, from the Ten Commandments and the book of the covenant at Sinai (Exod. 20–24) to Hezekiah's scribes in Proverbs (25:1), the writing down of Jeremiah's prophecies (Jer. 36), and the work of Ezra the scribe (Neh. 8), that it is unlikely that oral tradition played a very significant role from at least the 10th century B.C.E. Some compositions, including ancient poems like the Song of Deborah (Judg. 5) and cultic compositions like most of the Psalms, probably existed for many years in oral form, but these were exceptions soon absorbed into what became a very literate religious tradition. It is thought that the words of Jesus were transmitted orally in some communities for a time, as were the sayings of the rabbis, before being committed to writing in the NT and the *Mishnah, repectively. See *Literacy; *Oral Torah.

Origen (c. 185–c. 254).   Theologian and first true Christian biblical scholar. Son of a martyr and himself victim of persecution in his later years, he succeeded *Clement as a Christian teacher in *Alexandria (c. 211–231), but was later forced to leave there and move to Palestine, where he established another famous school at Caesarea. In 553 he was condemned as a heretic, which partly explains why the Greek originals of most of his voluminous writings survive only in fragments or in unreliable Latin translations. His theological works include treatises on martyrdom, prayer, and the resurrection, and his eight books of *apologetic against the pagan philosopher Celsus (*Contra Celsum*).

He wrote commentaries on almost all the books of the Bible, as well as *scholia and many *homilies. His most original work of biblical scholarship was the *Hexapla. His contacts with Jewish scholars were probably not very close and his familiarity with rabbinic scholarship minimal. Dependent on Platonism, the methodology of *Philo, and some biblical precedents, Origen developed the *allegorical method of interpretation, by which the believer and the mystic can see beyond the literal meaning of a text to deeper truths within. Scripture has to be approached in a threefold manner (Prov. 22:20–21 LXX); it is like a living person consisting of body, soul, and spirit: the body or flesh of the text is the obvious, superficial level of interpretation that everyone can appreciate; the soul is its inner meaning open to believers; and the spirit of the text is its profoundest, mystical meaning, which only the chosen few can understand.

Original meaning. Ancient interpreters and translators assumed that a text has more than one valid meaning of which a nonliteral *allegorical or *mystical meaning may be the most relevant or important in a particular context. Modern *historical criticism, with its roots in early medieval Spain and France and increasingly refined during the *Renaissance and *Enlightenment, highlighted the "original meaning of the text" as the only valid goal of serious research. The term needs to be defined, however: Does it refer to the original meaning of separate units (e.g., *J or First *Isaiah or *Q) or of the text as it stands (Genesis, Isaiah, Mark)? Does it refer to what was in the authors' minds? Is that a practicable goal? Or does it refer to how they were understood by their original listeners or scribes? What is the context of the "original meaning" in that sense: Second Temple period Jerusalem, the early church? How does the "original meaning" differ from "the earliest we can reconstruct"? Why should the earliest necessarily be preferred? Disillusionment with the quest for originals, combined with a renewed interest in the many meanings discovered in the text by theologians, poets, painters, dramatists, and filmmakers (as well as historical critics) down the ages has opened the way to a more sensitive approach to the Bible in the many other contexts in which it has meaning, in addition to its original one.

Original sin. The doctrine that all human beings are by nature sinful. It appears already in Job (4:17–19), Psalms (143:2), and Sirach (25:24), but in Christian doctrine its biblical authority comes from Paul's interpretation of the story of *Adam and *Eve (Rom. 5:12; cf. 1 Tim. 2:14). Rabbinic interpretations focused on their discovery of human independence and free will, and developed instead the notion of an evil inclination (*yetzer ha-ra*) in everyone, in conflict with a good inclination (*yetzer ha-tov*), which may require the help of the Torah or a saint (*Tzaddik*) to prevail.

In Christian theology original sin is associated with concupiscence and thought of as a *fall from an original state of grace: only Christ and, according to Catholic doctrine, the Virgin Mary "full of grace," are without sin and can offer salvation through the sacraments of the church. The logical implications of the doctrine, not least for unbaptized babies and non-Christians throughout the world, have been the subject of theological debate from *Augustine and *Pelagius in the 5th century and the Reformers' elimination of human free will, to more liberal interpretations of the relevant biblical texts, informed by psychology and social anthropology. The reality of evil in the world, seen as the result of human sin, remains a central doctrine of both Christian and Jewish mystical tradition. See *Kabbalah.

Orthodox interpretation.

The Orthodox Church today comprises the four ancient patriarchates (Constantinople, Alexandria, Antioch, Jerusalem), five more recent patriarchates (Russia, Serbia, Rumania, Bulgaria, Georgia), and the Orthodox Churches of Cyprus, Greece, Albania, and some other countries. In the 5th and 6th centuries the Orthodox Church distanced itself on doctrinal grounds from the Nestorian churches in Asia and from the Coptic and Ethiopian churches in Africa. In the West the schism with the Latin (Roman) tradition is usually dated 1054, but goes back much earlier to insuperable theological, liturgical, and cultural differences. After the fall of Constantinople Russia became the largest of the Orthodox Churches, although Greek Orthodoxy also remains influential worldwide. Characteristic of Orthodox worship are prayers to the Mother of God and the saints, the veneration of *icons, and the use of archaic languages rather than the vernacular.

The Greek Bible, which includes the Prayer of *Manasseh, Psalm 151, and 3 *Maccabees as well as the OT *Apocrypha, has by and large been treated in the Orthodox Church more as an icon to be venerated than a text to be studied. The biblical commentaries of Oecumenius (6th century), for example, or Theophylactus (11th century), which are heavily dependent on the church fathers, especially John *Chrysostom, are exceptions, as is the great Byzantine scholar Photius (9th century), who was one of the very few to take account of the original Hebrew text. One effect of the Protestant Reformation in the West was that the Orthodox Churches tightened control on biblical interpretation, to the point where the faithful were officially prohibited from reading it in an albeit isolated pronouncement (1723). The modern period has seen new developments in biblical scholarship, especially in Greece, where a vernacular translation and a biblically oriented renewal movement called *Zoe* ("Life") have had some impact, although so far mainly within the academic community. The current search for a distinctively Orthodox hermeneutic was assisted by the "neo-Patristic" approach of the Russian theologian Georges Florovsky (1893–1979).

P.

Abbreviation for the "Priestly source" in 19th- and 20th-century discussions of the date and authorship of the *Pentateuch. See *Documentary Hypothesis.

Paleography.

The study of ancient and medieval mss on which our knowledge of the biblical texts is based. Paleographers familiar with varieties of Hebrew, Greek, or Latin handwriting can determine the date and provenance of a ms where a scribe's signature (colophon) is absent. They can also decipher the numerous abbreviations that evolved in particular schools and traditions, and have developed special technology to help piece together fragments that have become separated and to read *palimpsests, in which a ms has been reused and the older, overwritten text is usually the more interesting. See *Manuscripts; *Textual criticism.

Palestine.

The non-Jewish name, derived from the Hellenistic *Philistia* ("Philistine land"), given by Hadrian to the province of Judea after the Bar Kokhba Revolt (130–135 C.E.) (see *Judah). It is still widely used in *archaeology and biblical studies, although since the State of Israel was established in 1948 and the West Bank annexed in 1967, the term "Land of Israel" (*Eretz Yisra'el*) is often used as a synonym, without necessarily prejudging the issue of an independent Palestinian state.

Palestrina, Giovanni Pierluigi da

(1525–95). Italian composer. Born to wealthy parents in Palestrina, he sang in the choir of Santa Maria Maggiore in Rome till his voice broke, and then while still a teenager was appointed organist and choirmaster at the cathedral in his hometown, not far from Rome. His subsequent career was promoted by several popes, and took him from St. Peter's to San Giovanni in Laterano, back to Santa Maria Maggiore, and in 1566 to the key position of musical director of the newly established Roman Seminary. Here his productivity, his passion, and his command of counterpoint did much to achieve the Council of Trent's aim to rescue the Church from musical decadence, or worse the influence of Protestantism. He composed over 100 masses, five arrangements of *Lamentations, 35 *Magnificats, and 49 sacred madrigals, while his over 300 motets include many beautiful settings of biblical passages, including several from the *Song of Songs. He also composed many secular works, but no instrumental music.

Palimpsest.

A ms on which the original writing has been erased so that it could be used again. The practice was common when there was a shortage of writing materials, in 9th-century C.E. Europe, for example, and since the erasing process was rarely successful, many palimpsests contain valuable textual evidence for earlier ms traditions. Modern technology makes the task of reading the earlier ms easier. A 5th-century text of parts of the Greek Bible appears in a 12th-century palimpsest of works by *Ephrem the Syrian; and the earliest

surviving ms of *Jerome's *Vulgate, also dating to the 5th century, is a palimpsest overwritten with an 8th-century ms of a text by *Isidore of Seville. See *paleography.

Palm Sunday.

The Sunday before *Easter, the first Sunday of *Holy Week, also known as Passion Sunday, on which the entry of Christ into Jerusalem has been commemorated, since the 4th century at the latest, by the blessing of palm branches and a procession into church singing "*Hosanna" (John 12:13). In addition to the Gospel narratives and Ps. 22, readings include Isa. 50:4–7, Zech. 9:9–12, 1 Cor. 1:18–25, and Phil. 2:6–11, in which the theme is the weakness or folly of the way of the cross, although many Palm Sunday hymns place the emphasis more on Christ's ultimate triumph than on the passion, for example, "All glory, laud, and honor" (*Gloria, laus et honor*) by Theodulph of Orleans (c. 750–821).

Papias

(c. 60–130). Bishop of Hierapolis in Phrygia. His *Exposition of the Sayings of the Lord* is known to us only in fragments quoted by *Irenaeus, *Eusebius, and others. He believed that Matthew compiled a Hebrew version of the sayings of Jesus, later translated into Greek, and that Mark, Peter's "interpreter," started work on his Gospel in Rome near the end of Peter's life. The reliability of Papias was questioned already by Eusebius, but his evidence has been much quoted by modern NT scholars.

Parable.

In the Greek Bible the word *parabole*, from which Eng. "parable" is derived, corresponds to the Hebrew word *mashal*, "allusive or cryptic saying," and is applied to proverbs (Prov. 1:1; 10:1), allegories (Ezek. 17:2; Gal. 4:24) and riddles (Ps. 78:2; Matt. 13:35). Special training or knowledge is required to understand them, as they often contain secret teachings not available to everyone (e.g., Prov. 1:2–6; Eccl. 12:9; Matt. 13:11). At least 30 different parables are attributed to Jesus, all of them in the three Synoptic Gospels, and several of the best known ones (e.g., Ten Virgins, *Prodigal Son, *Good Samaritan) only in one.

From NT times down to the Middle Ages elaborate *allegorical interpretations were common (cf. Mark 4:13–20). *Origen saw the fall of *Adam in the "man who went down from Jerusalem (heaven) to Jericho (the world)," Christ as the Good Samaritan, the inn as the church, and the two denarii as the OT and NT. The Reformers, seeking the literal meaning, recovered theological and ethical teaching in the parables that had been obscured by allegorization. Modern commentators identify an eschatological element in some of the parables in Mark and Matthew, reflecting a belief in divine intervention in history, while in Luke the parables are powerful stories of real life in which repentance and social justice are prominent.

Paracelsus (1493–1541). A name coined for himself by the German alchemist and physician Theophrastus Bombastus von Hohenheim. Having studied medicine at several universities in Germany, Austria, and Switzerland, he became openly critical of existing theories and practices, and as an independent figure, traveling in Germany, Russia, and the Middle East, made a considerable contribution to the development of modern science and medicine. On a level with *Pico della Mirandola, *Erasmus, and other *Renaissance figures, and conversant with the *Corpus Hermeticum* and Jewish *kabbalah, he wrote many highly original commentaries on the Ten Commandments, Psalms, Daniel, Isaiah, Matthew, John, and most of the non-Pauline letters.

Paradise.   See *Eden.

Paradise Lost.   *Milton's epic masterpiece finished in 1667 but reflecting more than 30 years of the poet's controversial life in 17th-century England. Unparalleled in English literature but similar in scale and imaginative genius to *Dante's *Divina Commedia*, it begins with a description of *Satan and his court in hell (books 1–2). From heaven God sees Satan flying toward the world, but the *Son of God offers himself as a ransom (book 3). Meanwhile the biblical story of *Adam and *Eve and their *fall from grace is recounted, with the intervention of, first, *Raphael who tells Adam about the war in heaven (books 4–9), then the Son of God who intercedes for them (10–11), and finally, as they are being led out of paradise, the archangel *Michael who foretells the coming of the Messiah and the wicked state of the church until his second coming. Milton's brilliant use of the Bible, especially the apocalyptic language and imagery of the book of Revelation but also Isaiah, Daniel, and the Psalms, influenced the way we have read Genesis ever since. Famous illustrators of Milton include *Blake (1806), *Turner (1835), and *Doré (1866), and *Haydn's oratorio *Creation* (1798) contains some delightful musical interpretations of the happier parts of *Paradise Lost*. There is also an opera by the Polish composer *Penderecki with a libretto by Christopher Fry, first performed in Chicago in 1978.

Parallelism.   The most obvious structural characteristic of Biblical Hebrew *poetry, first identified as such by *Lowth. In synonymous parallelism the two verses in a couplet have the same meaning (Ps. 8:4), and in Hebrew often the same number of words. The second "rhyming" verse may modify the meaning in some way (Ps. 8:5) or simply echo the first by using a conventional word pair like father/mother (Prov. 1:8) or three/four (Prov. 30:18). Other common types of parallelism are antithetic parallelism (Prov. 1:7) and staircase parallelism

(Judg. 5:27; Ps. 93:3). Similar poetic techniques are found in ancient Assyrian, Babylonian, and *Ugaritic poetry. See *Word pairs.

Paraphrases, Scottish. In addition to the metrical versions of the Psalms, the General Assembly of the Church of Scotland in 1742 commissioned a collection of vernacular translations into English verse of other passages of Scripture, which came to be known as the Paraphrases and were eventually printed along with the Psalms. Over 66 passages were selected, half from the OT (e.g., Job 3:17–20; Isa. 53; Hos. 6:1–4) and half from the NT (e.g., John 3:14–19; 1 Cor. 15). Of these not all were successful (cf. Luke 15:13–25), but some found their way into Christian worship worldwide, including *O God of Bethel* (Gen. 28:20–22) and *While humble shepherds* (Luke 2:8–15).

Pardes. A Hebrew word meaning "paradise," sometimes used as an acronym for the four senses of Scripture: *peshat*, "literal," *remez*, "allegorical," *derash*, "homiletical," *sod*, "mystical." See *Jewish interpretation; *Quadriga.

Paronomasia. A type of *wordplay based on the similarity between two words or word forms. It is frequently used in the Hebrew Bible, especially in prophetic rhetoric: for example, "If you do not believe [*ta'aminu*], you will not stand firm [*te'amenu*]" (Isa. 7:9); when Jeremiah saw a rod of almond (*shaqed*), he was reassured that the Lord is awake (*shoqed*) (Jer. 1:11–12). Proper names are very often the object of wordplay, as for example, Isaac (Heb. *yitzhaq*; cf. *tzahaq*, "to laugh," Gen. 18:12–15) and Peter (Gk. *petros*; cf. *petra*, "rock," Matt. 16:18). Puns are almost impossible to translate but, for a reader who knows both Greek and Hebrew, there is probably one on the name Malta (Heb. *melita*, "escape") in Acts 28:1.

Parousia (Gk. "arrival"; Lat. *Adventus*). The return of Christ in glory, known also in English as the "second coming," and prepared for, along with *Christmas, in the liturgical season of *Advent. NT writers inspired by *apocalyptic eschatology and also by contemporary events, including the death of their *Messiah and later the destruction of Jerusalem, believed the Parousia to be imminent, and subsequent interpreters have found various methods of interpreting the texts when those expectations were not fulfilled. Some believe it is still imminent and "live every day as if it was their last" (cf. Eccl. 9:10; Matt. 6:34), while others have tried from time to time to determine the date of the Parousia (Dan. 12:11–13). There have been differing views on whether Christ will immediately sweep this world away forever when he comes (Rev. 21), or first establish a kingdom of justice and peace here on earth (Isa. 11:1–9), and on what is meant by the "rapture" in which the elect will be snatched up to heaven before the final cataclysm (1 Thess. 4:15).

The delay in the Parousia has been of central significance in modern biblical scholarship. On the one hand the *demythologization of apocalyptic language and imagery led many to dismiss it as virtually unintelligible to a modern reader, while on the other the insights of social anthropology (see *cognitive dissonance) and the evident power of eschatology to change lives whether in the Catholic Mass or a Marxist revolution, have encouraged a more positive evaluation of many of the NT texts in question. The Last Judgment is frequently represented in Christian literature and art, beginning with simple scenes of Jesus and the apostles seated as judges, sometimes with sheep and goats, awaiting judgment (6th century, St. Apollinare Nuovo, Ravenna; cf. Matt. 25), and later with all manner of terrifying variations on a grand scale (*Dante, *Giotto, *Signorelli, *Michelangelo, *Bosch). The "preparation" (Gk. *hetoimasia*) of Christ's judgment throne was a common motif in *Byzantine art. See also *Day of the Lord, *Millenarianism.

Pärt, Arvo (1935–). Estonian composer. At first influenced by Bartok, Prokofiev, and Shostakovich and restricted by Soviet control, he later experimented with atonality and serialism, but also for a time immersed himself in medieval and Renaissance religious music. One of his earliest works for orchestra, *Nekrolog* (1960), was dedicated to victims of the *Holocaust. Since 1982 he has lived in Berlin, where he describes his distinctive modern musical idiom as *tintinnabuli*, "the ringing of bells." Among his many increasingly popular settings of religious texts are the *St. John Passion, Berlin Mass, Nunc Dimittis, Magnificat, Te Deum,* several psalms (42; 51; 137), and the terrifying *Sarah Was Ninety Years Old* (Gen. 17:17).

Passion.   The events leading up to the crucifixion and burial of Jesus as recounted in the four Gospels and commemorated in processions along the Via Dolorosa (literally in Jerusalem or symbolically at *Stations of the *Cross represented in churches), the Tenebrae ("darkness") liturgy, Veneration of the Cross, and other special rituals. In Mark's Gospel Christ's passion is considerably more important than his *resurrection, while for Luke it anticipates the death of later martyrs, beginning with Stephen (Acts 6–7). In the Fourth Gospel Christ's death takes place on the eve of Passover, a day earlier than in the other Gospels, so that it becomes the ritual slaughter of a lamb that "takes away the sins of the world" (John 1:29). All four accounts cite details from the OT, including references to the mocking crowds (Ps. 22:7–8), his pierced side (Zech. 12:10), casting lots for his garments (Ps. 22:18), and the cry of dereliction on the cross (Ps. 22:1).

In medieval passion *iconography more graphic details from Scripture were added such as the pulling out of his hair (Isa. 50:6) and the wounding of his whole body "from the sole of his foot even to the head" (Isa. 1:6), and *anti-Semitism is common in the ugly depiction of Christ's Jewish tormentors. The "instruments of the passion" include the kiss of Judas, the cock that crew, the crown of thorns, whips, nails, hammer, ladder, reed and sponge, and the spear. Edwina Sandys's sculpture *Christa* (1975) in New York is a rare female reinterpretation of the passion. The passion of Christ is also the subject of numerous works of music, literature, film, and theater, from medieval *passion plays and *Bach's *St. Matthew Passion* (1729), to Nikos Kazantzakis's *Christ Recrucified* (1954; ET 1960) and Mel Gibson's controversial film *The Passion of the Christ* (2004). See *Sluter, Claus.

Passion plays.   Medieval *dramas depicting the trial, suffering, and death of Christ, originally part of the liturgy on Good Friday, but by the 12th century frequently performed outside the church, where they became increasingly elaborate and secularized productions. Comic characters like *Balaam and *Beelzebub were introduced, crude dramatic conventions evolved to represent the torture of Christ as sadistically as possible, and grotesque episodes were emphasized, like the death of Judas (Acts 1:18). Anti-Semitism was very common in the medieval passion plays. Despite attempts to ban them in the 16th and 17th centuries, they continued in some areas, notably Oberammergau in Bavaria, where they are still regularly performed, although in recent years in a revised form. Nikos Kazantzakis's novel *Christ Recrucified* (1954; ET 1960) is about a young man who plays Christ in a passion play performed in a contemporary Greek village. See *Mystery plays; *Theater.

Passover (Heb. *Pesach*).   Jewish festival, also known as the Feast of Unleavened Bread (Heb. *Matzot*: Exod. 23:25;

Mark 14:1, 12), celebrated in the spring in commemoration of the exodus (Exod. 12–15). The word recalls how the Lord "passed over" (Exod. 12:23; Heb. *pasah*, "limp") the houses marked with the blood of a lamb, where his people were celebrating their imminent freedom, and killed the firstborn of their Egyptian oppressors. The Seder meal is one of the most important family occasions in the Jewish year, and even some secular Jews still read the *Passover Haggadah ("How is this night different . . . ?" etc.), eat matzo, "unleavened bread," and bitter herbs, drink wine, and sing traditional Passover songs like *had gadya*, "one kid." Central to the Passover are the beliefs that it was all Jews, not only the ancestors, who were saved from slavery in the exodus, and that the *Messiah will come whatever happens. So an empty chair is prepared for *Elijah, forerunner of the Messiah. Many beautiful illustrated editions of the Passover Haggadah have been published from the Middle Ages till today.

In the Christian calendar *Easter often coincides with the Jewish Passover, and is called *Pascha* in Greek and Latin. Whether the *Last Supper was held on the night of the Passover or, as the Fourth Gospel says, the day before, there are parallels between it and the Seder, even though the NT writers (and probably Jesus himself) gave it an entirely new meaning: the head of the household's words, "This is the bread of affliction," correspond to Jesus' words, "This is my body broken for you"; cups of wine have symbolic significance; and at the end the participants sing together (Matt. 26:30). Paul refers to Christ as the Passover Lamb (1 Cor. 5:7) and the title "Lamb of God" (Lat. *Agnus Dei*), which first appears in the Fourth Gospel (John 1:29, 36; cf. Rev. 5:6, 12; 21–22), became one of Christianity's most enduring images in music, art, and liturgy.

Pastoral Epistles.   The three Pauline letters addressed to Timothy and Titus,

so called since the 18th century on account of their pastoral concerns. The young Timothy (1 Tim. 4:12; 2 Tim. 2:22) was one of Paul's closest friends (1 Cor. 4:17), and 1 Timothy for the most part deals frankly with practical issues such as the role of women ("she is to keep silent," 1 Tim. 2:8–15), and the behavior of bishops, deacons, widows, elders, slaves, and the rich (1 Tim. 3–6). He is also told to prevent the spread of false doctrine by certain persons whose "faith has been shipwrecked" (1 Tim. 1:19). Written from prison in Rome, 2 Timothy is more personal, making reference to Timothy's mother and grandmother, and pleading with Timothy to come soon to visit him, with his cloak, his books, and above all "the parchments" (2 Tim. 4:9–13), because "the time of his departure has come" (4:6). The Letter to Titus, written earlier while Paul was still a free man and Titus was in Crete, is concerned with discipline in church (chaps. 1–2) and state ("be submissive to rulers and authorities," 3:1).

Cited as Pauline by *Irenaeus (c. 180) and as canonical since *Tertullian and *Jerome, the Pastoral Letters have been widely used in relation to the organization of the church, although the terms "bishop" (*episkopos*), "elder" (*presbyteros*), and "deacon" (*diakonos*) have been interpreted in widely differing ways. Pauline authorship has been seriously questioned since *Schleiermacher, *Baur, and others who noted major differences in style and vocabulary, the absence of characteristic Pauline theology, and the difficulty of fitting the letters into what we know of Paul's life and ministry. The current scholarly consensus is that they were probably written pseudonymously, claiming Pauline authority, no later than 125 C.E.

Paternoster.   See *Lord's Prayer.

Patriarchs.   The three fathers (Heb. *Avot*) of the Jewish people, *Abraham,

*Isaac, and *Jacob, whose travels and exploits are recorded in the "patriarchal narratives" in Gen. 11–40. The term is used less frequently now as the importance of their wives, Sarah, *Rebekah, *Leah, and *Rachel, has been acknowledged. The discoveries of 19th- and 20th-century *archaeology at first sight appeared to provide historical evidence for placing some of the patriarchal narratives in the first part of the 2nd millennium B.C.E. Recent historians are more skeptical, but the impact of the patriarchal stories, such as the *Akedah, *Hagar and *Sarah, Jacob's ladder, and the *Joseph saga, on Judaism, Christianity, Islam, and culture worldwide can hardly be overestimated.

Patristic interpretation.   The interpretation of the Bible in the formative first six centuries of the Christian era. It was the church fathers, such as *Justin Martyr, *Origen, *Jerome, *Augustine, John *Chrysostom, and *Cyril of Alexandria, who fixed the canon of scripture and determined how it should be used to help define Christian doctrine, mainly in Greek, against Judaism and various heresies. In this period the Bible was translated into Syriac, Latin, Armenian, and other languages, mostly from the Greek, as the study of Hebrew among Christians was rare, Origen and Jerome being notable exceptions. The earliest extant mss of the Christian Bible, Codex Sinaiticus and Codex Vaticanus, come from this period.

Like the rabbis, the church fathers appreciated that texts have more than one meaning, nonliteral as well as literal, and encouraged *allegorical (often christological) interpretations of the OT, although some were opposed to excessive allegorization and stressed the value of the literal or historical meaning of the text (see *Antioch). Despite the efforts of the Reformers, historical critics, and others to get back to the original, the legacy of the church fathers is so central to Christian tradition, in the creeds

and the liturgy, as well as in Christian iconography, that it is impossible to separate the Suffering Servant (Isa. 53) from Christ or the ox and the ass (Isa. 1:3) from his manger.

Paul (died c. 65 C.E.).   "Apostle to the Gentiles," author of a large part of the NT, and main character in the book of Acts. A Jew, born in Tarsus with the name Saul, but a Roman citizen, he learned the trade of tentmaking and studied under Rabban Gamaliel ("the Elder") in Jerusalem, where he played a leading role in the persecution of Christians, including Stephen (Acts 8:1; 22:20). On the road to Damascus he had a vision of the risen Jesus ("Saul, Saul, why do you persecute me?" Acts 9:3–8), and, after temporary blindness, was converted to the new faith. After a short time with a disciple called Ananias in Damascus, where he was baptized and tried to preach in a synagogue, he had to leave the city and spent some time in Arabia. He returned to Damascus a second time but had to be rescued by night in a basket lowered from the city walls (Acts 9:23–25). He visited Jerusalem but again met with fierce opposition and returned to Tarsus, where he spent ten years in retirement.

His first missionary journey, on which he was accompanied by Barnabas and Mark, took him to Cyprus and southern Asia Minor. On his return to Antioch, the controversy with Peter on how Jewish law applies to Gentile converts was settled by a compromise at the first apostolic council in Jerusalem c. 50 C.E., and Paul from then on devoted himself mainly to working with Gentiles. On his second and third journeys he went to Asia Minor again (Galatia, Ephesus, Colosse) and Greece (Philippi, Thessalonica, Corinth), where he preached in the agora at Athens (Acts 17). His return to Jerusalem led to civic disturbances for which he was tried and found guilty before the Roman procurator in Caesarea. After two years in prison he appealed to Caesar and was taken to

Rome (via Malta, where he was ship-wrecked, Acts 27), and again imprisoned to be later executed under Nero. He was beheaded, it is said, at a place called Tre Fontane ("three springs") on the Via Appia, and is buried in the Basilica of St. Paul outside the Walls to the south of Rome.

Apocryphal writings about Paul include the *Acts of Paul, the *Apocalypse of Paul (based on 2 Cor. 12:2), and the "Letters of Paul and *Seneca," probably known to *Jerome and *Augustine, which contain a fictitious correspondence between Paul and his noble Stoic contemporary. From as early as the *sarcophagus of Junius Bassus (359 C.E.) and 5th-century mosaics in Ravenna, he is normally depicted in Christian art as short and bald, although *Donatello, *Raphael, and others give him a full head of hair. He is frequently represented in art with a sword, recalling both his martyrdom and his image of "the soldier of Christ" (Eph. 6:13–16). As providing the key to understanding the OT, he is also depicted removing the veil from over Moses' face (2 Cor. 3:12–16). Memorable paintings of the *Conversion of St. Paul* include those of Fra *Angelico (c. 1450), *Michelangelo (1542–1550), *Caravaggio (1601), *Brueghel (1567), and *Blake (1800).

Paul's impact on Christian theologians, especially *Augustine, John *Chrysostom, *Thomas Aquinas, *Luther, and *Barth, was profound and varied. Despite questions about the genuineness of some of his letters, beginning with *Hebrews, his teaching, particularly on women, the church, grace, justification by faith, the Eucharist, and the resurrection of the dead, has always been central to the history of Christianity. Recent scholarly reassessments of Paul stress his concern with immediate pastoral issues, rather than universal dogma, and his Jewish roots, although he is still widely considered to have been responsible for the schism between Judaism and Christianity. Much could also be said about his multifarious role in literature from Chaucer's *Canterbury Tales* (1387) and John *Bun-yan's *Pilgrim's Progress* (1678) to *The Apostle* (1943) by the Jewish writer Sholem Asch, and in music from well-known settings of verses from his letters in *Handel's *Messiah* (1742) and *Brahms's *German Requiem* (1868) to *Mendelssohn's oratorio *St. Paul* (1836).

Peace. In Hebrew (*shalom*) and Arabic (*salam*) "peace" is a greeting (1 Sam. 25:6) and refers as much to health and well-being (Isa. 53:5 AV) as to the absence of hostilities (1 Kgs. 4:24–25; Ps. 122). The "Prince of Peace" is a royal title (Isa. 9:6), and "peace" as a function of justice is a feature of the messianic age (Isa. 32:17; Luke 2:14). Greek *eirene* has a different meaning and is often avoided in the LXX (1 Sam. 25:6), but, under the influence of Hebrew, it does appear in NT greetings and blessings, accompanied by "grace" (Gal. 1:3) or "love" (Eph. 6:23), as also in the Latin liturgical formula *pax vobiscum*, "peace be with you" (Gen. 43:23 Vg). Other NT developments include the "God of peace" (Rom. 15:33) and the "peace of God which passeth all understanding" (Phil. 4:6 AV). Matthew contains both a blessing for the peacemakers (5:9) and a warning that armed conflict may be necessary (10:34). The dove that brought back an olive branch to Noah (Gen. 8:11) became a symbol of peace because, like the rainbow, it meant that God's "covenant of peace shall not be removed" (Isa. 54:9–10). See *War and Peace.

Pelagius (c. 354–425). British monk and heretic. Little is known about his life except that in Rome, Carthage, and Palestine his rejection of the notion of original sin and his belief in human responsibility and free will met with implacable ecclesiastical opposition. His treatise *On Nature* was robustly countered by *Augustine's *On Nature and Grace* and *Jerome's *Against the Pelagians*. Unlike his associate Celestius, who was condemned for heresy in 411, Pelagius at first survived two synods but was finally condemned, excommunicated, and expelled from Jerusalem in 418. The influence on medieval biblical scholarship of his commentary on Paul, probably through editions published under the names of Jerome ("Pseudo-Jerome") and Cassiodorus, was considerable, while many recent interpretations of Gen. 3, understood as a story of the discovery of free will rather than a fall from grace, could be described as openly Pelagian.

Penderecki, Krzysztof (1933–).

Polish composer. His avant-garde music has won widespread international acclaim, especially an early work entitled *Threnody to the Victims of Hiroshima* (1960), and has been featured in a number of films. In addition to four operas, eight symphonies, and other large-scale orchestral works, he composed many devoutly religious pieces, including a *Stabat Mater* (1962), *Magnificat* (1974), and the visceral *Canticum Canticorum Salomonis* ("Song of Solomon," 1973). He is perhaps best known for his *St. Luke Passion* (1966) and the *Polish Requiem* (1984), which had its origins in a commission for the Solidarity movement to commemorate those who died in the antigovernment riots in Gdansk in 1970, and was revised for performance after the death of the Polish pope John Paul II in 2006.

Penitential psalms. Seven psalms

that have had a special role in the Christian *liturgy, especially in *Lent, from early times. They comprise Pss. 6, 32, 38, 51 (*Miserere*), 102, 130 (*De profundis*), and 143, corresponding to the seven deadly sins, some say. They have been the subject of separate commentaries by a number of writers including *Gregory the Great (6th century), *Reuchlin (1512), and *Luther (1517), and set to music most notably by Orlande de *Lassus (c. 1559).

Pentateuch. The first five books of

the Bible, also known as the Five Books of Moses or the *Torah. The tradition of Mosaic authorship gives the work unique authority in Judaism, equivalent to the Gospels in Christianity, and from a literary standpoint focuses on the structural unity and dynamic of a prophet's vision, his eye undimmed, as he looks over the Jordan to the promised land (Deut. 34). The pentateuchal structure recurs in the book of Psalms, and, in Christian Bibles, the five prophetic books (four Major and the Book of the Twelve or Minor Prophets), and the five "Solomonic" wisdom books (Proverbs, Song of Songs, Ecclesiastes, Wisdom, and Sirach). See *Law of Moses.

Mosaic authorship was questioned already by *Ibn Ezra in the 12th century, and modern historical critics, notably *Wellhausen, identified a number of sources known by the symbols J, E, D, and P, whose date and authorship could then be examined. Thus the Pentateuch was seen as the result of a cumulative process reflecting social and political conditions in ancient Israel, for example, the time of David and Solomon (J), the northern kingdom in the 8th century (E), Josiah's Reformation in 621 (D), and the Babylonian exile (P). Numerous refinements have been proposed, but, while the general theory that the Pentateuch contains material from many different sources is still broadly accepted, recent scholarship is skeptical and less optimistic about our ability to unravel its complex literary texture, and has begun to focus once more on the final form of the text. See *Documentary Hypothesis.

Pentecost (Heb. *Shavu'ot*, "Weeks").

A major Jewish festival, originally associated with the barley harvest, seven weeks or fifty days (Gk. *penteconta*) after Passover (Lev. 23:15–22). It was later adapted to commemorate the giving of the *Torah at *Sinai because the Israelites arrived at Sinai fifty days after they left Egypt (Exod. 19:1), and associated with the book of *Ruth. In Christian tradition Pentecost, also popularly known as

Whitsunday, is the festival commemorating the descent of the Holy Spirit on the disciples (Acts 2), fifty days after the death of Christ at the time of the *Passover, and considered an appropriate time for baptisms. The miracle of the foreign languages that everyone can understand reverses the tower of *Babel story (Gen. 11), and fulfills the prophecy of Joel that a new age has dawned (2:28).

Evangelical preachers and commentators especially since the Reformation applied the story to the translation and distribution of the Bible, while the ecstatic nature of the disciples' experience (see *Glossolalia) provided scriptural authority and inspiration for enthusiastic and charismatic elements in the church, in particular the Pentecostal movement, which, from modest beginnings in Los Angeles in 1906, has spread worldwide. In art the scene is frequently represented, often with the Virgin Mary at the center, as in works by *Dürer, *Titian (c. 1550), and El *Greco (1596–1600), as well as in some early illuminated mss like the Rabbula Gospels (586, Florence) and the Shaftesbury Psalter (12th century, London). Others like the Pentecost Dome in St. Mark's Venice (12th century) anachronistically include Paul. There is an interesting theatrical interpretation of Pentecost in the Chester Cycle of Corpus Christi Plays.

Persia. The modern Islamic Republic of Iran. The Persian Empire at one time stretched from Egypt and parts of Greece in the west to India in the east, and in the Bible is remembered as a time of tolerance and security for minorities like the Jews, from the conquest of Babylon in 538 B.C.E. by *Cyrus (Isa. 45:1; 2 Chr. 36:22–23) to the conquest of Persia by Alexander the Great (333–323 B.C.E.). Persian, although now written in a form of the Arabic script, is not a Semitic language: it is Indo-European, like Greek, Latin, and Sanskrit. It left a significant mark on the Bible in words like *dat*, "law" (Esth. 1:13), and *paradeisos*, "paradise" (2 Cor. 12:4).

The influence of the ideas and images of the ancient Persian religion of the *Zoroastrians (modern Parsees), including dualism and angelology, can be seen in Daniel, Revelation, and other apocalyptic works, and the wise men from the east (Matt. 2) were probably Persian *magi (see also *Mithraism). The fictional book of *Esther, which tells of a Persian edict to eradicate the Jews, is the only biblical tradition openly critical of the Persian authorities.

Perugino, Pietro Vannucci (c. 1450–1523). Umbrian painter. He is best known for his paintings on the walls of the *Sistine Chapel: *Christ Giving the Keys to Peter*, and the *Baptism of Christ*, parallel to the circumcision of Moses' son in *Moses' Journey into Egypt*. He taught *Raphael, who worked with him on the Sala del Cambio in Perugia, and undertook numerous commissions in Florence and Umbria, most notably the Pazzi *Crucifixion* (1496), the deeply moving *Pietà* in the Uffizi, and the charming *Adoration of the Magi*, showing Lake Trasimeno in the background, in the Chapel of Santa Maria dei Bianchi in Città della Pieve, where he was born.

Peshat (pronounced *pshat*). In Jewish literature the plain or *literal meaning of the text, often contrasted with the homiletical *Derash.

Pesher. In the Hebrew Bible, a word for interpretation in general (Eccl. 8:1) or in particular of a dream (Dan. 4:6; 5:15, 25). At Qumran it refers to a type of commentary in which typically the biblical text is interpreted by reference to people and events in the contemporary experience of the community; for example, in a commentary on Hab. 2:4b, "interpreted this concerns [lit. "its *pesher* is"] all those who observe the law ... whom God will deliver . . . because of their suffering and their faith in the Teacher of Righteousness" (1QpHab 8). See *Jewish interpretation.

Peshitta. A translation of the Bible into *Syriac, a dialect of *Aramaic (see *Targum), probably originally produced for the benefit of the Jews of Syria and northern Mesopotamia in the 1st century C.E., but later monopolized by Christians, who added the NT by the 4th century C.E. This superseded Tatian's influential Syriac *Diatessaron (c. 160 C.E.) but originally did not contain Revelation, 2 Peter, 2 and 3 John, and Jude. For centuries the Peshitta was used by Christian communities throughout Western Asia and as far as India and China in the east, and is still used by the Assyrian Church and the Syrian Orthodox, mainly in Europe and the United States. For some it has special value as it preserves the words of their Savior as he would have spoken them originally in Aramaic.

Peter. Prince of the apostles. Simon Peter, a Galilean fisherman, nicknamed Cephas (Aramaic for "rock," Gk. *petra*; John 1:42) by Jesus, and his brother *Andrew were among the first of Jesus' disciples and Peter one of those closest to him. Simon's house in Capernaum served as a base for the movement (Mark 1:29–34). He was present at the raising of Jairus's daughter (Mark 5:37), walking on the water during a storm at sea (Matt. 14:28–31), and the transfiguration (Matt. 17:1–8), while his role in first recognizing Jesus as *Messiah at Caesarea Philippi led to his being appointed the "rock" on which the church would be founded (Matt. 16:18–19). His impetuous character is seen in his initial refusal to accept that Christ must suffer (Mark 8:32–33) or to allow Christ to wash his feet (John 13:6–10), and in his cutting off the ear of Malchus, the high priest's slave (John 18:10–11). On the night of Jesus' arrest and trial, three times he denied he was a disciple, but when the cock crowed he wept and was the first to hear from the women that the tomb was empty, and with them to be assured of Christ's resurrection. The Fourth Gospel ends with

a conversation on the shores of Galilee in which Peter three times declares his devotion to Jesus, and Jesus repeats three times "Feed my sheep."

In Acts Peter plays a leading role after the ascension and at Pentecost (Acts 2), and in the controversy about how Jewish law applies to Gentile converts. At first perplexed by a vision that appeared to say there was no distinction between clean and unclean food, he was later at odds with Paul, who claimed that Jewish law no longer applied (Gal. 2:11–14). Like Paul he is the subject of numerous apocryphal works, including the important *Apocalypse of Peter, the *Acts of Peter (2nd century), and the anti-Semitic *Gospel of Peter. But traditions about his *Quo Vadis* experience on the Via Appia, his crucifixion upside down, and burial in Rome go back to *Clement of Rome and *Irenaeus, if not to 1 Pet. 5:13, where "Babylon" most probably refers to Rome. His tomb in St. Peter's is now thought by many to be genuine. Peter was much cited in the patristic period as an ideal model for the church, but his role as the first bishop of Rome in an "apostolic succession" was not developed before the 5th century C.E. Since then his position within Catholic tradition as the first pope has never waned, despite the schism with the Orthodox Church, the Avignon Papacy, and the Reformation.

In art he is traditionally represented as taller and older than Paul, often with white hair, and carrying the "keys of the kingdom of heaven" given him by Christ (Matt. 16:19). *Christ Giving the Keys to St. Peter* is represented in a painting by *Perugino in the *Sistine Chapel and there is a life-size bronze statue in St. Peter's, the toes worn away by pilgrims' kisses. Many other scenes in the life of Peter have inspired artists, notably *Masaccio in a series of frescoes in Florence (1425–27) and *Raphael, whose tapestries in the Vatican include *The Miraculous Draught of Fishes* (Luke 5:1–11), the *Death of Ananias* (Acts 5), and *The Healing of the Lame Man at Solomon's*

Portico (Acts 5:12–16). Raphael also painted *The Liberation of St. Peter from Prison* (Acts 5; 1512), and there are some memorable paintings of the *Crucifixion of St. Peter* (*Giotto, 1328–31; *Michelangelo, 1542–50; Guido Reni, 1604–5), all in the Vatican. Peter also figures in Giotto's *Navicella* formerly in St. Peter's, now surviving only in copies (1305–13), *Christ Walking on the Water* (*Ghiberti, 1403–24), and the *Washing of the Feet* (*Tintoretto, 1560–65). *The Tears of St. Peter* (Luke 22:62) are the subject of a cycle of 20 spiritual madrigals by Orlande de *Lassus (1532–94) and a painting by El *Greco (1603–7). He was the subject of the 1959 Hollywood film *The Big Fisherman*, and has a colorful part also in *The Robe* (1953) and *Quo Vadis?* (1951).

Peter, Letters of. Two of the *Catholic Epistles in the NT. The first was written in Rome (referred to as "Babylon," 5:13) and addressed to Christian communities in Asia Minor. It is an eloquent exhortation to the faithful, full of biblical quotations and memorable phrases like "living stone," "love covers a multitude of sins," and "the devil prowls around like a roaring lion." It may have originally been written as a baptismal homily, in part at any rate (1:3–4:11). Doubts have been cast on Petrine authorship because the Greek style is not what one would expect from a Galilean fisherman, and the situation of persecution in Asia Minor (4:12) suggests an early-2nd-century date. The book was a favorite of *Luther and has had an impact on literature and church music disproportionate to its length. It also contains important *proof texts for the priesthood of all believers (2:5) and the *harrowing of hell (3:19; 4:6).

Second Peter is quite different in style and content. It is in the form of a letter but also contains elements of a farewell address like those of Moses (Deut. 33), Jesus (John 13–17), and Paul (Acts 20). Its early date and attribution to Peter were questioned already by *Jerome and since the Reformation generally rejected, mainly on account of references to Paul's writings as "scripture" (3:16) and to the delay of the *Parousia for more than a generation (3:3–4). Chapter 2 appears to be dependent on the book of *Jude. No biblical book is less quoted by the church fathers, and its subsequent role in the history of Christianity has been minimal, although *Bede wrote a commentary on it and *Luther spoke up for it.

Pharaoh. An Egyptian term meaning "Great House" (i.e., palace), it was first used as a royal title in Egypt in the 15th century B.C.E., and is a frequent *loanword in the Hebrew Bible as well as in Greek, Latin, and other versions and the Qur'an. Several pharaohs are mentioned in the Bible by name, including Shishak (945–924 B.C.E.; 1 Kgs. 14:25–26) and Neco (610–595 B.C.E.; 2 Kgs. 23:29–35), but it is the unnamed ones in the stories of *Abraham (Gen. 12), *Joseph (Gen. 40–47), and especially the exodus (Exod. 1–18) that have had the most influence in Jewish, Christian, and Muslim tradition. The pharaoh who "knew not Joseph" (Exod. 1:8), often identified as Rameses II (1279–1212 B.C.E.; cf. Exod. 1:11), is remembered as the oppressor who would not let God's people go free, and who was spectacularly punished, along with his country, by plagues and military disaster.

The rabbis were concerned about God's hardening of Pharaoh's heart (Exod. 7–10) and explained it as punishment for repeatedly refusing the opportunity to repent. He plays a more central role in early Christian writings, where he is interpreted as a type of the devil. Medieval and early modern writers portray him as a tyrant, drawing parallels with contemporary political figures such as Charles I (*Milton), Louis XIV (*Dryden), and Napoleon (Wordsworth). In Christian art Pharaoh's daughter is sympathetically portrayed by Hogarth, *Poussin, *Blake, *Chagall, and others, though it is for the death of his first-born (Alma-Tadema) and the destruction of his army in the Red Sea (John Martin) that he is bettered remembered. Some sympathy for him, however, is expressed in Cecil B. DeMille's *Ten Commandments* (1956) and in the more recent animated cartoon *Prince of Egypt* (1998).

Pharisees. According to Josephus and rabbinic usage, the Pharisees were distinct from the *Sadducees in that they accepted the authority of the *Oral Torah and believed in the resurrection of the dead. The term thus accurately describes both Paul (Phil. 3:5) and the rabbis whose teachings he studied and which are recorded in the *Talmud and *Midrash. Occasionally in the Talmud and very frequently in the NT, though not always (Luke 11:37; 14:1), the term itself, which probably means "separatists," is used in a derogatory sense of Jews who are legalistic and hypocritical, much as the term "Jesuitical" and indeed "Jew" can be used in Christian polemic.

Philemon, Letter to. Shortest of Paul's letters, written from prison to a member of the Christian community in or near Colosse (Col. 4:9, 17). It is an appeal to Philemon for leniency toward his runaway slave Onesimus, who has converted to Christianity and come to Paul for help. A bishop of Ephesus called Onesimus is mentioned by *Eusebius, and if this were the same person, it might explain how the letter gained its place in the canon despite its somewhat unedifying contents. It is rarely quoted in the patristic and medieval periods, not even by *Thomas Aquinas in his discussion of slavery, but *Luther and *Calvin use it as an illustration of Christian love. Modern scholars have discussed the date of Philemon and whether Paul was writing from Rome, the traditional view, or Caesarea (Acts 24–26). More recent literary and sociological analyses argue that the letter is addressed to a community

rather than an individual (1:2) and is about wider ethical and theological issues, beyond the immediate case of Onesimus. Bishop Onesimus is venerated as a saint by Catholics and Orthodox, and is the hero of a video game entitled *Onesimus: A Quest for Freedom.*

Philip. One of the twelve disciples, remembered for his role in bringing *Nathanael to Jesus (John 1:43–45) and in the feeding of the five thousand (John 6:5). At the *Last Supper it was his question that prompted Jesus' words, "He who has seen me has seen the Father" (John 14:8–9). He is said to have died, crucified as a martyr according to some, in Asia Minor. He was identified by *Eusebius and many others with another Philip, the evangelist whose missionary activities, notably the conversion of the Ethiopian eunuch whom he found reading Isa. 53, are recorded in Acts (8:5–13, 26–40). A gnostic *Gospel of Philip was discovered at *Nag Hammadi.

Philippians, Letter to. Sixth letter of *Paul, written in prison, probably in Rome, to the church at Philippi in northern Greece (Acts 16:12). In an unusually intimate and affectionate style, Paul thanks them for their gifts, gives them news of Timothy and Epaphroditus, as well as of his own life in prison, and exhorts them to "shine as lights in the world" (2:15) and "rejoice in the Lord" (3:1; 4:4). On a harsher note he attacks Judaizers, speaking as a "Hebrew of the Hebrews" himself (3:2–6). The letter also contains a short, difficult, but very significant christological passage about the humility of Christ, "who did not regard equality with God as something to be exploited, but emptied himself, taking the form of a servant" (2:5–11 NRSV). The passage has been cited in support of the doctrine of the true humanity of Christ, although Paul's use of the word "form" was used by Marcionites and gnostics to prove he only looked like a human being (Docetism). Modern critics have debated whether a "redeemer myth" underlying the passage had its roots in pagan gnostic religion, or is a development of Jewish traditions about *Adam (cf. *Philo), *Wisdom (Prov. 8:22; Sir. 24), and the Suffering *Servant in Isaiah (chap. 53). Nineteenth-century Lutheran theologians developed a kenotic theology of the incarnation based on this passage (Gk. *ekenose*, "emptied"), according to which Christ renounced all his divine powers so that his experience as a human being was real.

Quotations from Philippians are frequent in all periods of Christian literature, starting with *Clement of Rome (c. 96). The references to "bishops and deacons" (1:1) and genuflection "at the name of Jesus" (2:10) have been particularly influential in church history. The blessing beginning "The peace of God which passes all understanding" comes from 4:7, and Purcell's *Bell Anthem* (1682–85) is a beautiful setting of 4:4–7.

Philistines. One of several "sea peoples" known from contemporary Egyptian records and archaeological evidence to have invaded Asia Minor, Syria, Canaan, and Egypt in the 13th and 12th centuries B.C.E., and established themselves in cities on the coast of Palestine, including Ashkelon, Ashdod, Gath, and Gaza. The biblical stories of *Samson and Delilah (Judg. 13–16), *David and Goliath (1 Sam. 17), and other Israelite victories over the Philistines reflect the fact that the Israelites arrived in the area at around the same time. Defeated first by David (2 Sam. 5) and then the victims of subsequent Assyrian invasions, they were finally conquered and deported by the Babylonians in 604 B.C.E. (Jer. 47). Their name survives, however, in the word "Palestine," and despite their popular reputation for boorishness, their beautifully decorated pottery proves they were more cultured than their Hebrew contemporaries.

Philo of Alexandria (c. 25 B.C.E.–40 C.E.). Jewish Hellenistic philosopher and biblical scholar. Nothing is known of his life apart from the fact that he led a Jewish delegation to Rome to meet Emperor Caligula in 39–40 C.E. He knew very little Hebrew, if any, and wrote entirely in Greek, using the LXX version of the Bible. His knowledge of Greek philosophy, science, and literature was immense, and in most of his writings his aim is to reconcile Jewish tradition with Greek philosophy, especially Platonism. By using the allegorical methods of interpretation developed by Alexandrian scholars a century or so earlier, Philo attempted to remove from the biblical text suggestions that, for example, God could literally "walk in the garden" or "stretch out his hand," and to give rational, moral explanations for many of the laws, such as those banning the eating of eagles or shellfish and "boiling a kid in its mother's milk."

His exegetical works include a verse-by-verse commentary on most of Genesis and various treatises on creation (*De Opificio Mundi*), the life of Moses (*De Vita Mosis*), and the Ten Commandments (*De Decalogo*), as well as allegorical interpretations of the laws (*Legum Allegoriae*) and other subjects. He also wrote what appears to have been a commentary on the Sabbath lectionary in the form of questions and answers (*Quaestiones in Genesis*, etc.). His work had very little influence on rabbinic tradition, if any, and he is not referred to in Jewish literature until the 16th century. His influence on Christianity, however, both his Platonism and his *allegorical method of biblical interpretation, was immense, from *Clement of Alexandria, *Origen, and *Ambrose to the majority of biblical commentators down to the *Reformation period, when concern for the *literal meaning cast doubt on centuries of exegetical tradition. The so-called *Biblical Antiquities of Philo* has nothing to do with Philo (see *Pseudo-Philo).

Philology. The study of language and literature, especially the classics. See *Comparative philology.

Philosophy. Suspicion of human wisdom, and in particular Greek philosophy, goes back to Eccl. 12:12 (cf. Sir. 3:21–24) and Paul (1 Cor. 1:18–25; cf. Col. 2:8), and continues through *Tertullian ("What has Jerusalem in common with Athens?") and *Luther down to *Barth's commentary on *Romans (1919). But the role of philosophy in biblical interpretation has a long and distinguished history, starting with *Philo's apologetic rationalizations and allegorizations of the Torah (1st century C.E.) and the Alexandrian theologians *Clement and *Origen (2nd–3rd century). Neoplatonist idealism left its mark on *Jerome and *Augustine as well as on medieval theologians like *Bernard of Clairvaux and *Bonaventure; while Aristotelian philosophy, rediscovered in the Middle Ages by Jewish and Muslim philosophers, had a profound influence on *Thomas Aquinas and much of subsequent Western theology. Modern philosophers whose contribution to biblical interpretation has been significant include Kant, Hegel, *Kierkegaard, *Heidegger, and *Gadamer.

Phoenicians. A Semitic people living on the coast of what is now Syria and Lebanon. They are also referred to as Sidonians and Tyrians (1 Chr. 22:4) after two of their most famous cities, and occasionally as Canaanites (cf. Gen. 10:15–19). The Latin form "Punic" is applied to Hannibal and his wars with Rome. By the 6th century B.C.E. they had established important colonies in Asia Minor (Tarsus), Spain (Tarshish), North Africa (Carthage), and elsewhere, and their ships (Isa. 60:9) had circumnavigated Africa and reached the shores of Britain. They invented an alphabetical system of writing from which all Western *alphabets (Hebrew, Arabic, Greek, Roman, Cyrillic, etc.) are derived. Other lasting contributions to Western culture include purple dye (Jer. 10:9) and the "cedars of Lebanon" (Ps. 104:16).

Pico della Mirandola, Giovanni (1463–94). Italian philosopher and Hebraist. He studied at Bologna, Ferrara, and Padua, with visits to Florence and Paris, and got to know many leading Christian humanists as well as several Jewish scholars with whom he studied Hebrew and *Kabbalah, probably the first Christian scholar in the Renaissance to do so. In 1486 he challenged the church with 900 theses, for which he was condemned by the pope, and withdrew from public debate to spend the remaining few years of his short life in Florence. In 1489 he published a commentary on Gen. 1:1–27 entitled *Heptaplus*, and there are fragments of an unfinished commentary on Psalms. A true renaissance man, he devoted his brilliant mind to studying common ground between Plato and Aristotle, philosophy and religion, and Christianity and Judaism.

Piero della Francesca (c. 1420–92). Italian painter. Born in Sansepolcro in Tuscany, he worked in Florence, Urbino, Rome, and elsewhere until about 1475, when it seems he became blind and returned to his hometown. Among his pupils were *Perugino and *Signorelli. His most ambitious work is a series of exquisite frescoes in Arezzo depicting the *Legend of the True Cross* (1452–49), from the death of *Adam and the meeting of *Solomon and the *Queen of Sheba, to the victories of *Constantine and Heraclius. Among his most original paintings are the *Flagellation* (Urbino) with allusions to Ps. 2:2 and John 19:13, the stunning *Resurrection* (Sansepolcro), and a beautiful pregnant Madonna (Monterchi). His paintings show the influence of *Masaccio and Uccello, and are informed by a keen interest in mathematics, architecture, and theology.

Piers Plowman. One of the greatest poems of medieval England. It consists of a series of allegorical visions in which the narrator, on his search for truth and salvation, encounters characters like Lady Holy Church, Reason, the Seven Deadly Sins, Scripture, Conscience, and Piers the Plowman who comes closest to the Christian ideal. There are memorable descriptions of the *passion and the *harrowing of hell. The author was William Langland (c. 1330–1400), a contemporary of *Chaucer, probably in holy orders. His writing reveals detailed familiarity, often indirect, with biblical language and imagery, which he handles with rare imaginative power and a concern for social justice that appealed to the leaders of the Peasants' Revolt (1381) and the *Lollards.

Pietà (Ital. "pity, mercy"). A representation of the dead Christ accompanied by angels or, more often, the Virgin Mary, who holds his limp body on her knees. A development from more biblical scenes like the descent from the cross (Luke 23:53) and the lamentation (John 20:11), the *Pietà* became a frequent focus of devotion and meditation from the 15th century. *Michelangelo's marble *Pietà* in St. Peter's, Rome (1500), is probably the most famous, but there is a sculpture by *Donatello in London (1443) and paintings by *Bellini, *Perugino, El *Greco, *Delacroix, and many others.

Pilate, Pontius. Roman governor ("procurator") of Judea 26–36 C.E., under whom Jesus was crucified. His name appears on a stone inscription found at Caesarea in 1961. He is mentioned by Tacitus (*Annals* 15.44), and accused of anti-Jewish prejudice by *Philo and *Josephus. In the Gospels he is depicted as favorably disposed toward Jesus, so

that responsibility for Christ's death falls primarily on the Jews. In the Orthodox Church his wife Claudia Procla, who is believed to have converted to Christianity, is revered as a saint, while in Coptic tradition both he and his wife are saints. In Western tradition his importance is mainly as the historical context of the crucifixion in the Apostles' Creed ("suffered under Pontius Pilate").

Pilate's gesture of washing his hands is a frequent motif in literature from Lady Macbeth to John Proctor in Arthur Miller's *The Crucible* (1953), while references to his question "What is truth?" (John 18:38) are equally common, including the famous opening words of Francis Bacon's essay "On Truth": "'What is Truth?' said jesting Pilate" (1601). He is also remembered for his "What I have written, I have written" (John 19:22). In modern literature Pilate as a complex character in his own right is ubiquitous, from Mikhail Bulgakov's extraordinary novel attacking Stalinist bureaucracy *The Master and Margarita* (1938) to *The Pilate Tapes*, a series of witty poems by the New Zealander Vincent O'Sullivan (1986), and the English writer and journalist Ann Wroe's *Pontius Pilate* (2001), performed under the title *The Pilate Workshop* by the Royal Shakespeare Company in 2004. See *Acts of Pilate*.

Poetry, Hebrew. The distinction between Hebrew poetry and prose was largely ignored until modern times, mainly because it is so different from Western classical verse. Now that its techniques and structures are better understood, most printed editions of the Bible indicate that much of the Hebrew Bible is in verse, not only Psalms, Job, the Song of Songs, and the like, but also much of the prophetic books. There are also complete poems in narrative texts like the Blessing of Jacob (Gen. 49), the Song of the Sea (Exod. 15), and David's lament on the death of Saul (2 Sam. 1), as well as short pieces of verse like the Song of Miriam (Exod. 15:21) and the Song of the Well

(Num. 21:17–18). To these we may add some NT examples such as the canticles in Luke 1 and 2, although most of the original poetic form is lost in translation.

Hebrew verse is composed according to an ancient literary tradition, known to us from *Ugaritic texts of the 14th and 13th centuries B.C.E. and some other ancient Near Eastern parallels. In addition to parallelism and the use of conventional *word pairs, poetic style may involve alliteration (Isa. 24:17), onomatopoeia (Isa. 17:12), simile (Isa. 1:8), *metaphor (Ps. 18:2), chiasmus (Hab. 2:1), the refrain (Amos 4), and the *acrostic (Ps. 119). Most of these features are observable only in the original Hebrew, although the considerable rhetorical force of Hebrew poetry, whether in condemning injustice or promising new hope or praising God, is evident even in translation. See *Parallelism.

Pointing. In mss of the Hebrew Bible, a system of representing vowel sounds, accents, and musical notes, invented by the *Masoretes in the early Middle Ages to ensure the correct pronunciation of the sacred text. Scrolls for liturgical use, however, are traditionally still written in unpointed Hebrew, as is Modern Hebrew, where pointing is used only occasionally, for example, in the printing of poetry. Pointing systems were also devised for Syriac and Arabic, which are normally written without pointing, however, except for special purposes. See *Ketiv; *Qere.

Politics. Political leaders, institutions, and ideologies are seldom far from the center of attention in the Bible: from the prophets' attacks on the "rulers of Sodom" (Isa. 1:10; cf. Ezek. 16:49) and their eschatological myths about an age of justice and righteousness ruled over by a "Wonderful Counselor . . . Prince of Peace" (Isa. 9:2–7), to instructions to obey the king (Prov. 24:21) and all other political institutions as ordained by God

(Rom. 13:1), and to pay taxes (Matt. 22:19–21). These and many other biblical passages have inevitably played a significant role in politics, not only when church and state were one, but also in situations where the Bible has provided Christians with the authority and inspiration to challenge secular governments.

The process of selecting and interpreting texts from the Bible is complex and can be problematical, but the liberating modern critical insight that interpretation is never wholly unbiased has shifted the emphasis from what the text says to who is doing the interpreting and to what end, and above all from what it originally meant to what it has meant to those who believe it to be in some sense sacred and therefore authoritative, both today and in the past. For example, the Bible has been cited in support of *slavery (Eph. 6:5), tyrannicide (Jdt. 13:6–10), homophobia (Lev. 20:13), the gun lobby (Luke 22:36), white supremacy (Gen. 9:25–27), and the exploitation of the third world (Isa. 60:9; 66:20). But of course the political bias evident in the selection and interpretation of these examples can be set against the bias in favor of the poor, for instance, in the Law (Deut. 15:7–8), the Prophets (Isa. 11:4), and the Gospels (Luke 7:22), and the principle that all human beings are equal (Gen. 1–3), created by the same God (Job 31:15; Prov. 17:5). The decision on which is right or true or good is not based solely on the biblical evidence, but on whether you agree with slave traders, tyrannicides, and the like, or with the liberation theologians and their "option for the poor."

The Bible never played a more significant role in politics than it did in the 16th century, when, for example, not only the Peasants' Revolt of 1525 looked to Scripture for inspiration, especially the Apocalypse, but also *Luther's denunciation of it on the basis of texts like Rom. 13. *Anabaptist and other radical forms of Christianity in the 16th and 17th centuries were entirely founded on the vernacular Bible, as was Cromwell's Puritan Commonwealth. Black American musical interpretations of the exodus story, the promised land, and the "walls of Jericho tumblin' down" eventually had an effect on white American society, while radical Jewish settlers use some of the same texts to justify their occupation of Palestinian land. Two examples of a different kind are the Second Vatican Council document *Gaudium et Spes* (1965), which discusses in general terms the interaction between faith and politics, citing Scripture on every page, and the South African *Kairos* document (1985), which begins with a critique of Rom. 13:1–7, then turns to the beast that had "authority over every tribe and people and tongue and nation" (Rev. 13) and Peter's call to "obey God rather than men" (Acts 5:29 AV).

The influence of politics on the Bible in art can frequently be observed, as in late medieval stained-glass representations of the *Jesse tree (Isa. 11:1), which have a selection of French monarchs among its branches, and a 20th-century painting on the façade of a church in Lima showing Our Lady of the Victories brandishing a Kalashnikov. Wilfrid Owen's interpretation of the *Akedah (with *Britten's haunting setting of it in the *War Requiem*), was a powerful and subversive attack on political and military leaders during World War I, and there are several poignant post-Holocaust Jewish interpretations of *Esther and *Lamentations. See *Holocaust; *Ideological interpretation; *Liberation theology; *Postcolonialism.

Polyglot Bibles.   Printed Bibles containing the text in several languages, produced to meet the demand for the study of the Bible in its original languages. The oldest, printed in Spain in 1514–17, is the 6-volume Complutensian Polyglot, which has the text in Hebrew, Greek, and Latin, with *Targum Onqelos at the foot of the page in the Pentateuch. Even more ambitious was the London Polyglot of Brian Walton, also in six volumes, dedicated to Oliver Cromwell in 1655. In addition to the Hebrew Bible, the LXX, the OT *Apocrypha, the *targu-

mim, and the NT, it also contains the *Samaritan Pentateuch and Syriac and Arabic versions, all with Latin translations, and a volume of densely packed scholarly notes and comments.

Pontifical Biblical Commission.
A body set up by Pope Leo XIII in 1902 to safeguard Catholic tradition against aspects of modern biblical scholarship that seemed to undermine it. It continued to play a conservative role until Pius XII's encyclical *Divino afflante spiritu* of 1943, which encouraged Catholic biblical scholars to pursue more open-minded research. Since then, and also in the light of the Second Vatican Council document *Dei Verbum* (1965), the Commission, which now consists of twenty international biblical scholars, has published a dozen or so documents, including "The Historical Truth of the Gospels" (1964), "The Interpretation of the Bible in the Church" (1993), and "The Jewish People and Their Sacred Scriptures in the Christian Bible" (2001).

Pontius Pilate.   See *Pilate, Pontius.

Poole, Matthew (1624–79).   English biblical scholar. Born in York, he studied theology at Cambridge and served as rector in a London parish until his presbyterian beliefs forced him to flee to Amsterdam in 1678, where he died a year later. His *Synopsis Criticorum aliorumque Sacrae Scripturae interpretum* (5 vols., 1669–76) is a valuable compendium of 16th- and 17th-century biblical commentaries (Jewish, Protestant, and Catholic) on every book of the Bible. Today he is better known for a shorter commentary in English that is still in print under the title *Matthew Poole's Commentary on the Holy Bible* (3 vols., 1982).

Popular culture.   The Bible has been appropriated by the people to some extent in most periods of its *reception history, whether by gazing at stained-glass windows, singing hymns, listening to preachers, or reading it for themselves in the vernacular. But in today's world of globalization and mass media, popular culture differs from traditional art, music, and literature and has added a new dimension to biblical interpretation. In Monty Python's *Life of Brian* (1979), for example, slapstick comedy cannot conceal the serious satirization of hypocrisy and mindless institutions, while Homer and Marge throw new light on a familiar biblical text in the brilliant Adam and Eve episode of *The Simpsons* ("I'm sure God will let us return soon"; 1999). Very effective interpretations of biblical texts can be found in rock music, such as Pete Seeger's *Turn, Turn, Turn* on Eccl. 3:1–8 (1962) and Bob Dylan's *All along the Watchtower* on Isa. 21:5–9 (1967). The pop star Madonna included a controversial crucifixion scene in her 2006 "Confessions" tour. Scholarly research is increasingly being devoted to this phenomenon, but at the same time its other effect is to disseminate biblical themes and images, in modern guise, to the largest possible audience worldwide.

Postcolonialism. A late-twentieth-century term for cultures and ideologies free, or in the process of being freed, from Western imperial domination in Africa, Asia, and Latin America. Postcolonial interpretations of the Bible are critical of many of the assumptions and methodologies of white European scholars and missionaries, in particular their denigration of indigenous literatures and religions, whose voices are only now beginning to be heard. In a radical shift away from *historical criticism, biblical *archaeology, and Western cultural appropriation of the Bible, postcolonial interpreters in Latin America (Fernando Segovia), Africa (Musa Dube and Gerald O. West), India (R. S. Sugirtharajah), and Asia (Chung Hyun Kyung) seek to create for the first time serious alternatives

that are true both to the experiences of men and women emerging from colonial domination and to the dynamics of indigenous cultures.

The Bible-reading strategies adopted by "base communities" in Latin America, South Africa, Korea, the Philippines, and elsewhere in the 1970s and 1980s, and welcomed by many noted biblical scholars, illustrate the enormous effect such a shift can have, both on the participants themselves and on the course of history. Four volumes of Ernesto Cardenal's *Gospel in Solentiname* (ET 1976–82) contain numerous examples of the new method. In art biblical scenes in which the characters are not all white are now commonplace, as is the recognition that Jesus and his mother were Palestinian Jews, not blue-eyed blondes. A reading of some of the biblical stories through Canaanite eyes illustrates another type of postcolonial interpretation, as does the general observation that the ancient Near Eastern cultures described in the Bible are actually closer in many ways to some modern third world societies than to the world that most Western European Christians inhabit. See *African interpretation; *Asian interpretation; *Liberation theology.

Postilla. A medieval Latin word for a gloss or comment on a biblical text, most commonly applied to homilies or homiletical commentaries such as *Thomas Aquinas's *Postillae* on Job and the Psalms, and the influential *Postillae* of *Nicholas of Lyra on the whole Bible.

Postmodernism. The movement incorporates a critique of modernism and recommends new attitudes and methods. In relation to biblical interpretation it first of all challenges the assumption that there is one meaning, more or less accessible to modern *historical criticism. Not only has the scholarly quest for a single original meaning proved to have been more difficult than was at first anticipated, but texts manifestly have, and have had, more than one meaning, according to who is doing the interpreting: a Jew or a Christian, a Protestant or a Catholic, a white European female academic or a black African male novelist, an artist or an archaeologist, a poet or a sociologist. A postmodern commentary will allow many voices to be heard while acknowledging that some are relatively more beautiful or relevant or convincing than others.

Postmodernists question the hegemony of the guild of scholars and experts who would suppress some of these voices. While textual critics or Hebrew specialists might question the validity of an attempt to reconstruct the original meaning of a text, they have no right to pass any expert judgment on how it is interpreted in a Renaissance painting or a 19th-century English hymn or a Latin American base community. Similarly the assumption that serious biblical interpretation can properly be pursued only in commentaries and scholarly monographs has been challenged by serious studies of the Bible in film, popular culture, and the like, new psychoanalytical interpretations, and books like Stephen Moore's *God's Gym: Divine Male Bodies of the Bible* (1996).

The modern problem that there is an unbridgeable gap between the text of the Bible and its modern interpreters virtually disappears. As *Barth and others have said in another way, attributing the phenomenon to the activity of the Holy Spirit, a 21st-century reader can actually engage with the text in much the same way as its earliest readers, with or without the assistance of expert commentaries. The dynamic of the text and the immediacy of the encounter between text and reader are facts of history, as can be seen in its unparalleled effect on the history of Western culture, in all kinds of different contexts from the chapel to the battlefield, right down to the present. See *Ideological interpretation; *Popular culture.

Poussin,   Nicolas   (1594–1665). French classical painter. His early years were spent in France, but in 1624 he settled in Rome, where he remained till his death, apart from two unhappy years in Paris (1640–42) at the command of Louis XIII. His rich, colorful, but modestly proportioned landscapes and classical scenes were widely admired soon after his death and had a profound influence on many subsequent artists, especially in France. Notable among his many paintings of biblical subjects are *Hagar and the Angel* (Gen. 16), *The Finding of Moses* (Exod. 2), *The Judgment of Solomon* (1 Kgs. 4), *Esther before Ahasuerus* (Esth. 5:1–8 LXX), *The Ecstasy of Paul* (2 Cor. 12), *Landscape with St. John of Patmos* (Rev. 1; 1640), and the *Destruction of Jerusalem* (1639). His two series of the seven sacraments, of which less than half survive, contain the *Baptism of Christ*, the *Giving of the Keys to Peter* (ordination; Matt. 16:19), and two very different versions of the *Last Supper*. The four *Seasons* in the Louvre, painted during the last years of his life, allude to the garden of *Eden (*Spring*), *Ruth and Boaz (*Summer*), Joshua's spies (Num. 13:23) (*Autumn*), and the *flood story (*Winter*).

Prayer.   In the Hebrew Bible there are numerous prayers by individuals, including long, formal prayers like those of Solomon at the dedication of the temple (1 Kgs. 8) and Ezra on his return to Jerusalem from Babylon (Ezra 9). Some are in verse like those of Jonah (Jonah 2) and Habakkuk (Hab. 3) and many of the psalms, several times explicitly described as prayers in their titles (17, 86, 90). There are also many much shorter utterances like the prayers of Moses (Deut. 9:26–29), Samson (Judg. 15:18–19; 16:28), and Elijah (1 Kgs. 17:20–21). Even more informal are God's conversations with Abraham (Gen. 18) and Moses (Exod. 3), the very personal accusations of Job (Job 7, 10), and Jeremiah's confessions (Jer. 15–20; e.g., "O LORD, thou hast deceived me!" 20:7 AV).

In Jewish liturgical tradition all prayers (*tefillot*) are in the first person plural as are some of the psalms (44, 80, 90, 126). The temple was called the house of prayer (Isa. 56:7) and one of the three names for the *synagogue was "house of prayer." The three most important Jewish prayers are the *Shema, the *Amidah, and the *Kaddish, and from the 9th century these were included along with other material in the Jewish Daily Prayer Book (*Siddur*). The custom of wearing phylacteries (*tefillin*) has its origin in the Shema (Deut. 6:4–9). In Christian tradition the prayers of four women—Hannah (1 Sam. 2), Judith (9), Esther (Add. 14), and Mary (Luke 1)—are specially remembered, and several of the prayers in the Psalter have a signficiant role in the liturgy, including *O Lord Our Lord* (Ps. 8), the *Miserere (Ps. 51 [Vg 50]), and *De Profundis* (130 [Vg 129]). From the NT come the *Lord's Prayer, *Ave Maria (Luke 1:28, 42), *Magnificat, *Nunc Dimittis, and several benedictions (Phil. 4:7; Heb. 13:20–21).

Preaching. In the Hebrew Bible preaching and prophesying are synonymous (Ezek. 21:2; Amos 7:16), and the special vocabulary (e.g., Heb. *derash*; Gk. *kerygma*) does not appear till later. Preaching on the biblical text has always been a regular part of synagogue worship (Luke 4), and "preachers," who were not necessarily rabbis, are known as *darshanim*, their sermons (*derashot*) probably the origin of rabbinic *midrash. In Christian tradition too preaching has always been important whether as part of the liturgy or in a wider evangelical context. For John the Baptist, Jesus, Paul, and the disciples it was a major activity, to which the term "preaching the good news" (Gk. *evangelizo*), derived from passages like Isa. 52:7 and 61:1, was applied. In the 13th century the *Dominicans were established as the preaching order (*Ordo predicatorum*), while in Protestant tradition the term "preachers" came to be popularly applied to the clergy in general. Homiletics remains an essential part of the syllabus in Jewish and Christian seminaries. See also *Homilies; *Kerygma; *Prophecy.

Pre-Raphaelites. The Pre-Raphaelite Brotherhood (PRB) was founded in 1848 by three artists: William Holman *Hunt, his teacher John Everett Millais, and his fellow student Dante Gabriel Rossetti, partly in an effort to rescue religious art from stereotypes and superficiality. Derided by many but supported by John Ruskin, they attracted others to the cause, but after a few years went their separate ways. Millais's only contribution was his notorious *Carpenter's Shop* (1849), while Rossetti, after *The Girlhood of Mary Virgin* (1848–49) and *Ecce Ancilla Domini* (1849–50), turned his attention to subjects taken from *Dante and Arthurian legend.

Priest (Heb. *kohen*). In the Hebrew Bible priests are all descended from Levi, but only sons of Aaron officiated in the *temple, and are clearly distinguished from all other *Levites. In the Second Temple period many were *Sadducees (Heb. *tzedukim*), from aristocratic families descended in all probability from Zadok (Ezek. 44:15–16). Priestly families served in the temple on a weekly basis and received generous portions of animals and other produce offered in sacrifice. Their powerful mediating role between God and Israel led to the belief that they themselves were holy, and, even after the destruction of the temple in 70 C.E., when they no longer had a sacrificial function, this tradition survives. In Orthodox Judaism a priest (someone called *kohen* or Cohen) may not marry a divorcée or touch a dead body, and in the synagogue a Cohen is called to read first from the Torah and only he may pronounce the priestly blessing (Num. 6:22–27). The notion is also present in the description of Israel as "a kingdom of priests and a holy nation" (Exod. 19:6).

The person and work of Christ are seen as foreshadowed in the OT priesthood, especially as "high priest after the order of *Melchizedek" (Heb. 5) and in his high-priestly prayer in John 17, as are the frequent references in Christian tradition to altars and sacrificial rituals, and the image of the community of believers as "a holy priesthood" (1 Pet. 2:5). The term "priest" (Gk. *hiereus*; Lat. *sacerdos*) does not appear to have been applied to "elders of the church" (Acts 20:17), or "bishops and deacons" (Phil. 1:1), before the end of the 2nd century. The English term "priest" is ultimately derived from Gk. *presbyteros*, "elder."

Printing. Printing was first developed in Europe by Johannes Gutenberg in Mainz in the 1450s, and among the first printed books was the Gutenberg Bible (1455–56), an edition of the Latin Vulgate, designed to look as much like a medieval ms as possible. Before the end of the century Christian Bibles had also been printed in French, German, Czech, Italian, and other languages. The first Hebrew Bible was printed in 1488 by the Soncino Press in Bologna, and the first complete edition of the *Talmud, in the form still in use today, by the Christian printer Daniel Bomberg in Venice in 1500–1523. The role of printing on the spread of literacy and learning during and after the Renaissance and Reformation can hardly be overestimated. From being the private possessions of a few institutions and privileged members of society, books like the Bible and the Talmud, together with the works of classical and medieval writers, were soon available to everyone. Two hundred thousand copies of *Luther's Bible were produced in Wittenberg between 1534 and 1620. See *Books and book production.

Prodigal Son. The *parable of the younger son, welcomed home by his father after a life of debauchery, to the disgust of his obedient elder brother (Luke 15). In its original context, like the parables of the Lost Sheep and the Lost Coin, it is Jesus' answer to the Pharisees and the scribes who have criticized him for eating with sinners. But it is the image of the father's unconditional and disproportionate forgiveness of his son that most influenced subsequent liturgical and literary tradition. It became part of the church's teaching on repentance, particularly relevant on account of the words "Father, I have sinned," which appear twice in the parable, and then, especially from the 16th century, it was the subject of numerous plays, poems, novels, and works of art. Among the most famous paintings of the subject are those of *Dürer (c. 1496), *Rembrandt (c. 1662), and a series of six by Murillo (c. 1675), while in music there is an oratorio by Sullivan (1869), a ballet by Prokofiev (1929), *Britten's "Church Parable" (1968), and a song by the American folk-rock singer Jonatha Brooke entitled "Prodigal Daughter" (2007).

Proof text. A biblical text cited, usually out of context, in support of a doctrine, institution, or moral principle. The practice, which was already an established feature of rabbinic and patristic discourse, depends on general acceptance of the *authority of Scripture and on agreed methods of interpretation.

Prophecy. A phenomenon richly documented in the OT, both in historical narrative (*Balaam, *Deborah, *Elijah) and in the prophetic books (*Isaiah, *Jeremiah, *Amos), but also referred to as a "gift of the Spirit" in the NT (1 Cor. 12:10). There are two terms for "prophet" in Hebrew. The main one is *navi*, translated into Greek as *prophetes*, "speaker," and prophets describe their experience of "hearing" or "seeing" the *word of God, and being compelled to utter words that are not their own (Jer. 20:19), introduced by the formula "Thus says the LORD . . . ," "a burden (RSV "*oracle") of the LORD," or the like. The other term is *hoze* "seer," and they also tell of visions that enable them to predict the future, whether by seeing meaning in ordinary objects like an almond branch (Jer. 1) or by getting a glimpse into the workings of God's heavenly court (1 Kgs. 22; Isa. 6). This type of vision is elaborately developed after the end of the "age of prophecy" in many types of apocalyptic and mystical writing. Many of the prophets, including Elijah and Isaiah, could perform other miracles in addition to foretelling the future (1 Kgs. 17; Isa. 38:7–8). *Moses is the greatest of the prophets, "whom the LORD knew face to face" (Deut. 34:10) and the standard against which all others, whether attached to cultic institutions or as lonely individuals, are judged. In Christian tradition, beginning with the *Sermon on the Mount (Matt. 5–7), Jesus is a second Moses, and in Islam Muhammad is the last or the "Seal" of the prophets.

The historicity of the biblical stories about the prophets has been challenged since ancient times, but there is now general agreement that the prophetic experience was a historical reality, if not in every detail, and an important factor in determining the form and content of many biblical texts. Of particular significance are passages describing the effect that "behaving like a prophet" (Heb. *hitnabbe*) has on bystanders (Num. 11:25–29; 1 Sam. 10:6–13). Moreover, the phenomenon has parallels in other ancient Near Eastern cultures such as the royal court at *Mari, and in better documented modern contexts (e.g., shamanism). Alongside "woe oracles" against social injustice and predictions of national disaster (Amos 6), the prophets hold out hope in "fear not" prophecies of salvation and a coming messianic age of justice and peace to the ends of the earth (Isa. 43). Even if the words of the prophets are considered more prosaically to be the result of divine inspiration, on a par with other preachers or poets, ancient and modern, the impact of the biblical phenomenon on world religions and secular culture over 2,500 years is unique. See *Apocalyptic; *Mysticism.

Prophets, the. The second part of the Hebrew Bible. See *Nevi'im.

Protoevangelium of James. An apocryphal infancy narrative adding many details to the Gospel accounts, such as the names of the parents of *Mary, Joachim and Anne, who became popular in medieval Christian tradition. Written in Greek probably in the 2nd century, it was known as the *Gospel of James* until the 16th century, when a Latin translation was produced with the title *Protoevangelion Jacobi, fratris Domini* (1581).

Proverbs, book of (Heb. *mishle*). As the Hebrew title indicates (plural of *mashal*, "wise saying, fable, allegory"), the book of Proverbs contains more than proverbs. Like Deuteronomy, it begins with a homiletical prologue (chaps. 1–9) consisting of speeches by the teacher ("Hear, my son . . .") and *Wisdom, who is personified ("Come eat of my bread . . ."). A collection of proverbs makes up the main part of the book (chaps. 10–29), into which another piece of instruction described as "thirty sayings" ("my son, fear the Lord . . ."; 22:17–24:22) has been inserted. The book ends with an appendix containing the words of Agur and Lemuel (chaps. 30–31), including several sayings in the form "three things are too wonderful for me . . . ," and a poem in praise of the *eshet hayil*," woman of valor." It recommends Wisdom both as comprising practical skills of all kinds and as "the fear of the LORD," revealed in the *Torah.

Close ancient *Egyptian parallels, including the "Thirty Sayings of Amenemope" (22:20) and representations of the goddess Ma'at ("truth, justice") with an *ankh* ("life") in her right hand and a symbol of worldly power in her left

(Prov. 3:16), have shown how ancient many of these traditions are. Even more ancient are the Sumerian "Instructions of Shuruppak" from before 2500 B.C.E. References to the proverbial wisdom of *Solomon (1 Kgs. 3) and the "men of *Hezekiah" who are said to have copied some his proverbs (25:1) may therefore reflect some historical reality, even though the book in its present form was probably composed in the Second Temple period.

The influence of Proverbs on the language and literature of the world has been significant. It is frequently cited in rabbinic literature and there is a medieval *midrash. Various verses are commonly used in synagogue architecture, especially 3:18 ("She is a tree of life . . ."). Quotations are also common in the early church, beginning with Paul's reference to "heaping coals of fire" on the head of your enemy (Rom. 12:20; cf. Prov. 25:21–22), and both sides in the Arian controversy found scriptural authority in Prov. 8:22: Christ was "created" (Heb. qana; cf. Gen. 14:19) or "begotten, not made" (Heb. qana; cf. Gen. 4:1). The "seven pillars of wisdom" on which she built her house (Prov. 9:1) have been variously applied to the days of *creation, the gifts of the Spirit, the liberal arts, and the sacraments. *Rashi said they must refer to the seven books of the Torah (taking Gen. 1:1 and Num. 10:35–36 as equivalent to whole books); and T. E. Lawrence called his autobiography *The Seven Pillars of Wisdom* (1926), after the seven stations along the Hijaz railway line, which played a significant role in his life.

Psalms (Heb. *Tehillim*). First of the *Ketuvim, "Writings," third part of the Hebrew Bible, but in Christian Bibles grouped with the *Wisdom literature. Most of the psalms originally had a liturgical function, as the term *tehillim*, "praises," and many of their titles clearly indicate (6, 38, 75, 92, 100), but as they have come down to us, some of them, including the first and the longest, which

is the form of an *acrostic (119), have more in common with *Proverbs than anything cultic, while others are associated with incidents in the life of an individual (e.g., 3, 18, 51). Their present position between Job and Proverbs also suggests that their function is now as much to accompany study and private devotion as public worship. They are arranged in five books attributed to *David, thus comparing him with Moses and the Psalter with the Torah, while in Greek Bibles a short Ps. 151 celebrates the life of David in some detail. Other groupings include the Psalms of the Sons of Korah (42–49), the *Hallel Psalms (Heb. *hallel*, "praise) (113–118), and the 15 popular "Songs of the Temple Steps" (120–134). Some of the psalms are also attributed to *Moses (90), *Solomon (72, 127), *Adam (92, the Sabbath psalm according to the rabbis), and others. The book ends with five more hymns of praise (146–150).

In Jewish tradition the psalms have had deep significance both in the *synagogue and in the home, from "Out of the depths" (130) and "Who shall ascend the hill of the LORD?" (24) to the Hallel Psalms sung at the *Passover Seder, the Songs of *Zion (46, 48, 122, 126, 128), and popular Israeli arrangements of *Hinneh ma-tov uma-na'im* (133). The *Midrash Tehillim* is a medieval homiletical work, based on much earlier material, but occasionally referring to the experiences of the Jewish people in contemporary Europe. In Christian tradition the use of the psalms certainly goes back to Jesus and his disciples (Matt. 26:30), who often interpreted them messianically, and Psalms is quoted in the NT more than any other OT book, and at particularly significant moments (Matt. 22:41–46; Mark 15:33; Luke 19:38; Acts 1:16–20). There are commentaries by *Augustine, *Jerome, *Nicholas of Lyra, *Luther, *Calvin, and many others.

Modern scholars have sought to reconstruct the original cultic context for which some of the psalms were composed. *Gunkel, for example, identified individual laments (Ps. 22), royal psalms

(2, 110), community thanksgivings (67, 136), wisdom psalms (1, 119), and the like. An annual "enthronement of YHWH" ritual was proposed by some in which the defeat of evil, represented by *yam*, "sea," *nahar*, "flood," and other mythical creatures, was celebrated with the cry "The LORD reigns" (93, 96, 97, 99; cf. 74:12ff.; 89:9ff.), while others have suggested that a "salvation oracle," similar to those preserved in Isa. 43:1–7 and 44:2–8, was originally recited by a priest between a lament (Ps. 22:1–21) and a thanksgiving (Ps. 22:22–31; cf. Ps. 28).

The Psalter has always played a central role in the liturgies of the church, Eastern as well as Western, as well as in the private devotions of clergy and religious. But many psalms, especially in the Vg translation, have become familiar far beyond their use in Christian worship, including Monteverdi's *Beatus vir* (1), Allegri's *Miserere* (51), and Vivaldi's *Nisi Dominus* (127), as have settings by Kodaly (1923), *Stravinsky (1930), Leonard Bernstein (1965), and many others. There are also many memorable musical interpretations within works like *Mendelssohn's *St. Paul* (Ps. 51), *Verdi's *Nabucco* (Ps. 137), and *Brahms's *German Requiem* (Ps. 84). Metrical versions of the Psalms were produced in the 16th century, for the benefit of those who thought it was not appropriate to sing nonscriptural compositions in church, and the psalms in English have inspired a number of poets, notably *Milton (136), Addison (19), Burns (1), and *Coleridge (46). See *Paraphrases, Scottish.

Psalms of Solomon. Eighteen

psalms known to us in Greek and Syriac, probably originally composed in Hebrew around the mid-1st century B.C.E., and included together with the *Odes of Solomon* in the *Pseudepigrapha. The author(s), who may have belonged to Hasidic or Pharisaic circles, criticize the *Sadducees and refer to the death of Pompey in Egypt in 48 B.C.E. (2:30–31). The last two psalms are about the coming of a

Davidic messiah and the redemption of Jerusalem.

Pseudepigrapha. Writings attributed

to someone other than the actual author. The term is particularly applied to a number of pseudonymous Jewish works written between c. 200 B.C.E. and c. 100 C.E., but not included either in the Hebrew Bible or the OT *Apocrypha. They include the book of *Enoch, *Jubilees, the *Life of Adam and Eve, *Psalms of Solomon, *Martyrdom and Ascension of Isaiah, *Apocalypse of Baruch, *Sibylline Oracles, and the *Letter of *Aristeas. The testament, inspired by the Blessing of Jacob (Gen. 49) and the Blessing of Moses (Deut. 33), was also a favorite genre and, in addition to the *Testaments of the Twelve Patriarchs, there are *Testaments of Abraham, *Adam, *Moses, *Solomon and *Job. The relevance for biblical studies of these documents as source material for the study of varieties of Jewish tradition, previously neglected, is increasingly being appreciated by scholars, while their influence on subsequent Jewish, Christian, and Muslim tradition in literature, art, and music has sometimes been immense. There are English translations by R. H. Charles (1913) and J. H. Charlesworth (2 vols. 1983–85), and a critical edition is being prepared on the Internet: http://ocp.acadiau.ca.

Pseudo-Philo. The usual modern

name given to a work entitled *Liber antiquitatum biblicarum*, similar to *Josephus's *Antiquities of the Jews*, and falsely attributed to *Philo of Alexandria. Probably written, originally in Hebrew, in Palestine soon after 70 C.E., it consists of a free adaptation of the biblical story down to King Saul, and, like *Jubilees and the *Genesis Apocryphon*, contains some interesting variations, hitherto unknown or neglected.

Psychological interpretation. Psy-

chological analysis of biblical stories

and characters can be said to go back to rabbinic commentators who, for example, discussed how human beings choose between the *yetzer ha-tov* and the *yetzer ha-ra* (the good and evil inclinations), as well as to numerous patristic and medieval works on the soul (*De Anima*), influenced by Plato and Aristotle. But the application of depth psychology in the modern scientific sense only began in the 20th century with *Freud and *Jung. Although each devoted only one of his published works to the Bible, *Moses and Monotheism* (1939) and *Answer to Job* (1952; ET 1954) respectively, their influence was much wider, making interpreters aware of psychological factors operating in the stories and rituals (Freud) and seeking ways to enable them to apply their new readings of the text to their own lives and communities (Jung).

Since then psychological analysis has been used to throw light on such biblical phenomena as kinship laws, prophecy, demon possession, and healing miracles, as well as on the behavior of *Adam and *Eve, *Abraham, *David, *Jesus, *Paul, *Judas, and other key biblical characters. The notion of *cognitive dissonance was successfully applied to the Bible by Robert P. Carroll in *When Prophecy Failed* (1978), and Gerd Theissen's *Psychological Aspects of Pauline Theology* (ET 1987) is a thoroughgoing example. Under the influence of the French psychoanalyst Jacques Lacan (1901–81) and the Bulgarian-French feminist Julia Kristeva (1941–), future psychoanalytical approaches to the Bible are likely to focus more on language, or the absence and inadequacy of language, in relation to religious beliefs and institutions.

Purim. A minor Jewish festival commemorating the deliverance from Haman, who cast lots (Heb. *purim*) to decide on which day to destroy all the Jews in Persia. The story is told in the book of *Esther, known as the Scroll (*Megillah*), which is read in synagogues on the evening and the morning of Purim.

At the name of Haman it is customary for the congregation to shout and stamp their feet and wave rattles. In many places children dress up as Haman, Mordechai, and Queen Esther and perform a type of outdoor pageant. Some Reform Jews do not celebrate Purim because they consider it to be too nationalistic and based on a work of fiction.

Q. A hypothetical written source (Ger. *Quelle*) consisting of material common to both Matthew and Luke, mainly the words of Jesus. See *Synoptic problem.

Qabbalah.   See *Kabbalah.

Qaddish.   See *Kaddish.

Qaraites.   See *Karaites.

Qedushah.   See *Kedushah.

Qere.   An Aramaic term used by the *masoretes to distinguish between the consonantal text of the Hebrew Bible as it is "written" (*Ketiv*) and how it should be pronounced or "read" (*Qere*, from *qara*, "to read aloud"). See *Ketiv.

Qimhi.   See *Kimhi.

Qohelet.   See *Ecclesiastes.

Quadriga. The four senses of Scripture, compared by medieval writers to a chariot drawn by four horses (Lat. *quadriga*). See also *Pardes.

Queen of Sheba. Ruler of a kingdom in South Arabia and eastern Ethiopia (Isa. 45:14), who heard about *Solomon's legendary wealth and wisdom and came to visit him with "camels bearing spices, and much gold and precious stones" (1 Kgs. 10:1–13). He gave her "all she desired" (v. 13), which was understood in *Ethiopian tradition to include a son and heir named Menelek, ancestor of the Ethiopian royal dynasty. In both rabbinic and Muslim tradition, where she is known as Belkis, she is said to have had ugly hairy legs, exposed by the shining floor of Solomon's throne room. Medieval Christian commentators, who understood Solomon to be a type of Christ, saw her as prefiguring his bride the church, or, according to some, the Gentiles coming like the three wise men from afar to worship him. In a painting of the *Adoration of the Magi*, by Hieronymus *Bosch (c. 1510), Solomon and the Queen of Sheba are depicted on the collar of the second king. Other famous representations include a bronze relief by Lorenzo *Ghiberti on one of the baptistery doors in Florence (1425–52) and two exquisite scenes in *Piero della Francesca's *Legend of the True Cross* in Arezzo (1452–59). There are operas by Gounod (Paris, 1862) and Goldmark (Vienna, 1875), and a Hollywood film *Solomon and Sheba* (1959) starring Gina Lollobrigida.

Quest of the Historical Jesus.

The English title of Albert *Schweitzer's study of NT scholarship from *Reimarus to Wrede (1906; ET 1910), which became a catchword during most of the 20th century for scholarly attempts to separate historical facts from the beliefs and teachings of the early church and discover what really happened. Schweitzer's own somewhat psychoanalytical quest was challenged by the form critics' conclusion that we must rest content with the "Jesus of faith," but a "new quest" was inspired in the 1970s by a fresh look at the evidence for other 1st-century miracle-working rabbis, and since then the application of ever more sophisticated social-scientific theory suggests that the quest is not over yet.

Qumran. See *Dead Sea Scrolls.

Quotations in the New Testament.

A significant number of verses throughout all parts of the NT contain either direct quotations or clear allusions to the OT (usually LXX), especially Psalms and Isaiah. Some writers make the theological point that something in the present is a fulfillment of *prophecy (Matt. 4:14; 1 Cor. 15:54). Others use Scripture to provide *authority for a course of action (Luke 10:27; 2 Cor. 9:9) or a belief (Rom. 9:9–18; Heb. 10:5–7). Others simply use striking language and imagery from Scripture to express their feelings (Mark 15:34; Rev. 22:17). The effect depends on how familiar the readers or listeners are with the texts quoted. In his speech to an audience of Athenians, for example, Paul cites verses from Isaiah and Psalms that only his own followers would appreciate, but adds two from the Greek philosophers Epimenides and Aratus (Acts 17:22–34). There is one certain quotation from the *Pseudepigrapha in Jude 14–15 (1 Enoch 1:9) and a possible allusion to the *Martyrdom of Isaiah* in Heb. 11:37 (*Mart. Isa.* 5:11–14), while the apocryphal Wisdom of Solomon may be referred to in Heb. 1:3 (cf. Wis. 7:26).

Qur'an.

The sacred text of Muslims. It is believed to have existed in *Arabic in heaven before it was revealed, chapter by chapter, to the illiterate prophet Muhammad from 610 to 632 C.E., at first in Mecca and then, after the Hijrah in 622 C.E., in Medina. In the earliest passage he is instructed to recite it in the name of God (sura 96), and listeners wrote down what they heard on scraps of parchment, leather, stone, and other materials that were eventually collected and edited into one authorized text under the third caliph, Uthman (644–55 C.E.). The 114 chapters, known as suras, are arranged in order of length with the longest Medinan suras at the beginning and the shortest Meccan suras at the end, apart from the short "opening" sura (*Al Fatiha*). The Arabic verse in which it is written is eloquent, at times sublime, especially in some of the early apocalyptic suras, and sets it apart from any other Arabic compositions before or since. Muslims believe this "inimitability" (*I'jaz*) of the Qur'an is due to its divine origin and officially forbid translation into any other language.

Important parallels between the Qur'an and the *Torah include the belief that they both existed in heaven before being revealed to a prophet, the tradition that the public reading of the text should be in the original language, and the stories of *Abraham, *Joseph, *Moses, and others, albeit sometimes differently interpreted. Parallels with the NT are less significant, although some of the beliefs about Jesus and the Virgin Mary in the Qur'an are documented in noncanonical Christian literature such as the *Gospel of Thomas*. See *Muslim interpretation.

R. Abbreviation for "redactor," used by some literary critics for the editor responsible for combining earlier sources, such as J, E, D, and P, to produce the biblical text as we have it. See *Redaction criticism.

Rabanus Maurus (776 or 784–856). Abbot of the powerful Benedictine monastery of Fulda and archbishop of Mainz. A man of great learning and a prolific writer and poet, he devoted his life to promoting good scholarship among the monks and clergy of Germany, which earned him the title *praeceptor Germaniae*. His encyclopedic *De Rerum Natura* (also known as *De Universo*), based on Isidore of Seville's *Etymologiae*, was widely consulted throughout the Middle Ages. He wrote commentaries on most of the books of the Bible, as well as an interesting collection of allegories on Scripture, mainly drawn from the patristic literature. He is often credited with having written the hymn *Veni creator Spiritus.*

Rabbinic Bibles (Heb. *Miqra'ot Gedolot*). The first edition of the Rabbinic Bible, by the convert Felix Pratensis, was printed in Venice in 1517 by the Christian publisher David Bomberg, followed in 1525 by a second Bomberg edition, this time by the Talmudist Jacob ben Hayyim. This was used by the AV translators and became the standard for all subsequent editions down to the present day. Alongside the MT are printed the Aramaic *Targum and the commentaries of *Rashi, *Nahmanides, *Ibn Ezra, *Kimhi, and others where available. Since 1992 the volumes of a completely new edition being produced at Bar Ilan University have begun to appear, but a complete ET is not yet available.

Rabbinic interpretation. See *Jewish interpretation.

Rachel. One of the "mothers of Israel" (Gen. 29–50), *Jacob's second wife and mother of his favored sons *Joseph and Benjamin. She died in childbirth (Gen. 35:16–20), and her tomb near Bethlehem is still venerated by pilgrims. As "mother of Israel" she is described as weeping for her children in exile (Jer. 31:15) as well as for the children slaughtered by Herod (Matt. 2:17–18). Patristic interpreters from *Augustine on contrast Rachel, like *Lazarus's sister Mary, interested in eternal things, with *Leah, the more domestic "laboring" wife like *Martha (Luke 10:38–42). Her romantic encounter with Jacob at the well (Gen. 29) is a favorite subject of painters, including *Raphael (1518–19), as is the hiding of the idols from her father, Laban (*Tiepolo, 1726–29).

Rad, Gerhard von (1901–71). German OT scholar. Born in Nuremberg, he studied at Erlangen and Tübingen, and taught at Leipzig (1930–34), Jena (1934–45), Göttingen (1945–49), and Heidelberg (1949–67), where he inspired a whole generation of scholars and preachers. His studies of Deuteronomy contain some original insights on a "historical creed" (26:5–6) and the "holy war," while his two-volume *Old Testament Theology* (1957–60; ET 1962–65) is noted for its analysis of *Heilsgeschichte* (*salvation history) and important discussions of the role of the prophets in the Christian Bible. He also wrote a much used commentary on *Genesis* (1953; ET 1960) and a study of *Wisdom in Israel* (1970; ET 1972).

Radak.   See *Kimhi, David.

Rambam.   See *Maimonides.

Ramban.   See *Nahmanides.

Raphael (Raffaele Sanzio) (1483–1520). One of the greatest Italian Renaissance painters. Born in Urbino, he worked industriously with *Perugino and Pinturicchio, then moved to Florence. By 1509, when he went to Rome, he had painted many of his best-loved works, such as the *Sposalizio* ("Betrothal of the Virgin"; 1504), the *Madonna of the Goldfinch* (1506), and the *Holy Family with a Lamb* (1507). In Rome, in the employment of Julius II and Leo X, he produced three large-scale works: the paintings on the walls and ceilings of the Stanze in the Vatican (including the *Judgment of Solomon* and the *Liberation of St. Peter*), a series of scenes from the book of Acts depicted on tapestries for the *Sistine Chapel, and the Loggia frescoes showing 52 scenes from the OT known as "Raphael's Bible." His artistic genius combined with a strong devotional sense (he is said to have had a vision of the Virgin) can be seen especially in his numerous paintings of the Madonna,

from the early *Madonna with the Book* (1504) to the late *Holy Family below the Oak* (1518), and reached its peak in his later works such as the *Vision of Ezekiel* (1518) and the unfinished *Transfiguration* (1518–20, Vatican).

Rashbam (c. 1080–1174). Acronym for Rabbi Shmuel ben Meir, French biblical and talmudic scholar. He was a grandson of *Rashi and wrote commentaries on the Torah, Judges, Prophets, Psalms, Job, Song of Songs, and Ecclesiastes, of which his Torah Commentary (beginning at chap. 18) is printed in *Rabbinic Bibles. He aimed at expounding the literal meaning of the text, even more so than his grandfather, with whom he occasionally disagreed.

Rashi (1040–1105). Acronym for Rabbi Shlomo Yitzhaqi ("ben Isaac"), greatest of the medieval Jewish commentators. He was born in Troyes and was appointed rabbi there after studying for a time in Germany. His commentaries take pride of place in most complete editions of both the Bible and the Babylonian *Talmud. His biblical commentary was used by *Andrew of St. Victor and *Nicholas of Lyra in Paris, and has been translated into Latin (17th century) and several other modern European languages. It is particularly valuable as a compendium of material from the *targumim, *Talmud, *Midrash, and other earlier sources, but he also had a keen interest in the *peshat or "plain meaning" of the text.

Ras Shamra.   See *Ugaritic.

Rastafarianism.   A messianic cult originating in Jamaica in 1930 when Ras Tafari was crowned emperor of *Ethiopia and given the titles Haile Selassie (Ethiopic for "power of the Trinity"), King of kings, and Lion of the tribe of

*Judah (Rev. 5:5), in apparent fulfillment of a prophecy made earlier in the century by Marcus Mosiah Garvey. Rastafarian practices are derived from the Bible, especially from Nazirite tradition (Judg. 13:4–5), including long hair ("dreadlocks"), abstaining from strong drink (Lev. 21:5; Num. 6:5), a special vegetarian diet (*Ital*) avoiding shellfish (Lev. 11:10), pork (cf. Lev. 11:7) and other meat (Num. 6:6, "a dead body"), and smoking cannabis (*ganja*; Gen. 3:18b; Prov. 15:17; Rev. 22:2). Biblical teaching about exile in Babylon is applied to Jamaica, the United States, and Western culture in general, and a special role is given to Africa, in particular Ethiopia, in the history of salvation (cf. 1 Kgs. 10:1–13; Pss. 68:31; 87:4–6). Reggae lyrics, including those of their most famous exponent, Bob Marley, often contain poignant uses of biblical language and imagery.

Reader-response criticism. An approach to literature focusing more on the assumptions and reactions of the reader or implied reader than on the author. It arises from the observation that "the bare text is mute"; that is, a text has no meaning until someone reads it. The problem that there might then be as many meanings as there are readers is partially addressed in the notions of an "interpretive community" (Stanley Fish, *Is There a Text in This Class?* 1980) and an "aesthetic of reception" (Hans Robert Jauss, ET 1982), while numerous examples of feminist, Marxist, postcolonial, and other readings of the Bible, in which the readers' presuppositions are declared, prove its value as an exegetical method and amply illustrate how the same text can and does have different meanings in different contexts. See *Reception history; *Wirkungsgeschichte*.

Rebekah (Heb. *Rivka*). One of the "mothers of Israel" (Gen. 24–27), wife of *Isaac and mother of the twins *Esau and *Jacob. Isaac and Rebekah became hus-

band and wife after the death of his mother *Sarah (24:67). The blessing of Rebekah (24:60), just before she put on her veil and met Isaac for the first time, is recited at Jewish wedding ceremonies. In patristic and medieval commentaries she is a type of the church, adorned as a bride with heavenly virtues (*Ambrose), and favoring Jacob, that is, the righteous people of God, over the wicked Esau (*Rabanus Maurus). Commentators from John *Chrysostom to *Thomas Aquinas defended her deception of Isaac (Gen. 27), either on the grounds that it was for the best, or by arguing that if one interprets Jacob's lie in a mystical or figurative sense, then it is not a lie. Modern writers referring to the "stolen blessing" are less sympathetic. There are some famous paintings of Rebekah's encounter with Abraham's servant Eliezer at the well (Gen. 24), including those by Murillo (1650) and *Poussin (1648).

Reception history. The history of how a book or a passage or a word has been contextualized and interpreted down the centuries in different parts of the world. Recent interest in this aspect of biblical studies, embodied in the Blackwell Bible Commentary series (2004–), is due partly to disillusionment with the historical-critical quest for a single original meaning, and partly to the impact of the social sciences and new methods of *literary criticism (see *Reader-response criticism). Its value, both as a source of information on the history of communities in which the Bible was influential and as a treasure-house of interpretations of biblical texts for modern commentators to exploit, can hardly be overestimated. See *Context; *Wirkungsgeschichte*.

Redaction criticism. An approach to the study of biblical texts concerned with the editorial process by which originally separate units or sources were combined into the literary form in which we now have them. Alongside the study of *JEDP, for example, redaction criticism focused on the aims and interests of the redactor (*R) or editor of the whole *Pentateuch, while in NT scholarship from the 1950s questions about the theological concerns of the evangelists began to replace or at any rate supplement traditional *form criticism and *source criticism. In the narrowest sense of the term, redaction criticism differs from other literary approaches to the final form of the text in its preference for the notion of redactor or editor rather than author, and in consequence interest in more of a scissors-and-paste activity rather than a creative process. Most redaction critics, however, would minimize the distinction between redactor and author, and concentrate on what the final shape of the text tells us about its theological perspective as well as its date and authorship. Franz Rosenzweig observed that, in the case of the Torah, the letter R (for redactor) might equally stand for *Rabbenu*, "our teacher," one of the commonest rabbinic titles for *Moses, thereby giving new meaning to the traditional belief in the Mosaic authorship of the Pentateuch.

Reformation. A major religious movement closely related to developments in the study and use of the Bible, beginning with the English philosopher John *Wycliffe (c. 1330–84) and the Czech preacher Jan *Hus (c. 1372–1415) and culminating in the break with Catholicism led by *Luther, *Zwingli, *Calvin, Henry VIII, John Knox, and others in the 16th century. Central to Protestant teaching was belief in the supremacy of the Bible (*sola scriptura*), studied in the original languages instead of the Latin of the *Vulgate, and made available to everyone, thanks largely to the invention of *printing, in vernacular *translations, and the impact of this on how the Bible was interpreted was immediate and irreversible. The new church leaders rejected the *Apocrypha, placed more emphasis

on the literal or historical meaning of Scripture, and challenged traditional efforts to find scriptural authority for the sacraments and other Catholic doctrines. Some found in Scripture eschatological visions of catastrophe and redemption that supported the creation of radical breakaway sects; others used Scripture to impose puritanical ideals on their followers. Some prohibited the singing of all *hymns except metrical versions of the Psalms and other *paraphrases of Scripture.

The Bible's direct influence on Protestant cultures in Europe, America, and elsewhere reached its height in the 17th century, but its legacy remains profound to this day despite the challenges of *historical criticism, secularism, and globalization. Parts of Judaism also experienced a reformation under the influence of the European *Enlightenment or *Haskalah*.

Reimarus, Hermann Samuel (1694–1768). German biblical scholar. His famous *Wolfenbüttel Fragments*, in which he rejects all miracles and accuses biblical writers of deliberate deception, was published posthumously by Lessing (1774–78) and caused a sensation in Germany. Later analyzed by *Strauss (1862) and *Schweitzer (1906; ET 1910), Reimarus is considered by many to have been the chief pioneer of modern *biblical criticism.

Rembrandt, Harmenszoon van Rijn (1606–69). Dutch Protestant painter. His early works on biblical themes include *Belshazzar's Feast* (c. 1635) and the dramatic *Blinding of Samson* (1636) in which his remarkable skill in handling light and dark is already evident. But it was after the tragedy of his wife Saskia's death in 1642, his bankruptcy in 1656, and a scandal that brought him into conflict with the church that he produced his most profoundly spiritual interpretations of biblical characters and situations, including many relating to the passion. Some of the most strikingly original are *David and Uriah* (1665), *Adoration of the Shepherds* (1646), **Peter Denying Christ* (1660), *Supper at Emmaus* (1648), and **Prodigal Son* (1669).

Renaissance (Ital. *rinascimento*, "rebirth"). The revival of art and literature, particularly in 15th- and 16th-century Italy, created by the rediscovery of classical models and the influence of humanist scholarship. A move away from the formalism of Byzantine iconography toward greater realism is evident already in the works of *Cimabue, Duccio, and above all *Giotto in the 14th century, but it was with *Masaccio, *Brunelleschi, Fra *Angelico, and others in 15th-century Florence that the Renaissance was truly established, culminating in the works of *Leonardo, *Raphael, and *Michelangelo in the High Renaissance of the early 16th century. It spread to other parts of Italy, especially Venice (*Titian, *Tintoretto), and to Germany (*Bosch, *Dürer, *Cranach, *Grünewald), the Netherlands (van *Eyck), and England (Holbein). At the same time the work of Renaissance humanists studying Greek, Latin, and Hebrew literature, such as *Pico della Mirandola, *Reuchlin, and *Erasmus, had a significant effect on the study of Scripture, evident not only in the new vernacular translations but also in the way painters and sculptors represented biblical themes.

Reproaches (Lat. *Improperia*). Twelve short texts adapted from the OT, in which Christ on the cross rebukes the Jews for sending him to his death. Beginning "My people, what did I do to you?" (Lat. *Popule meus, quid tibi feci?*), they contrast what God did for them with what they have done to him: for example, "I led you out of Egypt, you prepared a cross for me; I opened the sea before you, you opened my side with a spear; I gave you a royal scepter, you gave me a crown of thorns." Each verse is followed by a refrain in Latin and Greek, *Sanctus Deus, Hagios Ischyros . . . eleison emas, miserere nobis*, "Holy God, holy and strong . . . have mercy on us." Their origin is obscure but they are known to have been popular in the Western church from the 12th century. Traditionally sung during the Veneration of the Cross on Good Friday, they have been set to music by many composers, including Vittoria and *Palestrina, but are rarely performed today because of the risk of a blatantly anti-Semitic interpretation.

Requiem. The traditional Roman Catholic *Mass for the dead, so called from its opening words, *Requiem aeternam dona eis, Domine* ("Eternal rest grant them, O Lord"). The text and structure are similar to the ordinary Mass with the addition of this introduction, the *Dies Irae, and the omission of the *Gloria and the *Credo. Of the numerous musical settings of the Latin text, those by *Mozart, *Berlioz, *Verdi, and Fauré are among the best known, while *Brahms's *German Requiem* is based on passages from *Luther's Bible, and *Britten's *War Requiem* incorporates poems by Wilfred Owen.

Responsa. The answers given down the centuries by rabbis in response to questions on *halakhah. The earliest collections of responsa were made in 10th-century C.E. Babylonia with the authority of the heads of the two great Jewish communities at Sura and Pumbeditha. Important orthodox responsa, from those of *Maimonides and *Rashi down to Moshe Feinstein (1895–1986), are now accessible on the Internet, while those of the Reform rabbi Solomon Freehof (1892–1990) are also well known.

Resurrection (Gk. *anastasis*). The resurrection of the dead, although explicitly rejected in a number of OT texts (Isa. 38:16–19; Job 14:7–12; Ps. 88), has been a central belief for most readers of the Bible, Jews and Christians, for well over 2,000 years. While *Sadducees rejected the belief (Matt. 22:23), the *Pharisaic interpretation of many passages (e.g., Job 19:25; Pss. 1:5; 17:15; 73:24; Isa. 26:19; 60:20) is the one that prevailed. It is associated with the belief that God's judgment will ultimately triumph, if not in this world, then in the next (Dan. 12). There are two famous passages in the Apocrypha about the resurrection of martyrs (Wis. 3:1–9; 2 Macc. 7), and a rabbinic tradition that *Isaac actually died and rose again from the dead "on the third day" (Gen. 22:4). The miraculous powers of *prophets and miracle workers include bringing people back from the dead (*Elijah, *Lazarus).

The resurrection of Jesus, in some ways perhaps less theologically significant than the crucifixion and actually omitted from one of the four Gospels (Mark 16:8), was attested, according to the other three Gospels and Paul (1 Cor. 15:3ff.), by the evidence of the disciples who visited the empty tomb and many others who claimed to have seen the risen Christ in Jerusalem, Galilee, and elsewhere. The historical reliability of this testimony cannot be proved, but was not seriously challenged by Christian scholars until modern times. Despite inconsistencies in the Gospel accounts and the absence of external corroboration, however, the empty tomb is still venerated in Jerusalem and the resurrection celebrated on *Easter Sunday in all forms of Christianity worldwide.

Among representations of the resurrection in art and music may be mentioned the striking painting by *Piero della Francesca of Jesus stepping out of the tomb (c. 1460), paintings by Fra *Angelico (1440–41) and *Rembrandt (1638) of his meeting with Mary Magdalene in the garden (John 20:11–18), Duccio's Doubting Thomas (1308–11; John 20:24–29), and *Bach's choral setting of "Et resurrexit" in the Credo of his B Minor Mass (1748). Mahler's second symphony, known as the Resurrection (1895), contains settings of two 19th-century German poems, and Tolstoy's novel with the same title (1899) is a thinly veiled attack on Russian Orthodoxy. See *Easter.

Reuchlin, Johannes (1455–1522). German humanist whose Hebrew learning made a significant contribution to 16th-century study of the OT in the original language. In addition to an elementary introduction to Hebrew grammar (1506), a study of the *penitential psalms in Hebrew (1512), and a treatise on Hebrew accents (1518), he also published two works on *Kabbalah. His defense of Jewish literature against the *Dominicans' campaign to destroy it resulted in a heresy trial in which he was found guilty.

Revelation, book of.   The last book in the Christian Bible, also known as the Apocalypse (Gk. "Revelation") of John. It is described as a "prophecy" (1:3; 22:18–19) revealed to John on the Lord's Day in a series of visionary experiences on the Greek island of Patmos. After a short section made up of letters addressed to the seven churches in major cities of nearby Asia Minor (chaps. 2–3), it consists of a series of visions beginning with God on his heavenly throne (chap. 4) and the opening of the seven seals (chaps. 5–11), and ending, after war in heaven (chap. 12) and the destruction of "Babylon the Great" (chaps. 13–18), with final victory over Satan and Death (chaps. 19–20) and the creation of a new heaven and a new earth. At that moment the new Jerusalem comes down out of heaven "like a bride adorned for her husband" and the throne of God and the Lamb replace the temple (chaps. 21–22). Like other apocalyptic works, the book is full of extraordinary images such as the four winged creatures beside God's throne (cf. Ezek. 1), beasts rising out of the sea (Rev. 13), "the dragon . . . that ancient serpent called the Devil and

Satan" (chap. 20), and the scarlet woman called Babylon, "drunk with the blood of the saints" (chap. 17).

The symbolism of these images and of the numbers and patterns present throughout the book have been interpreted and applied in many different contexts, from *Augustine's City of God and the revolutionary eschatology of *Joachim of Fiore and others in the Middle Ages, to Protestant attacks on *Rome, romantic appropriations of the text by visionaries like William *Blake, and the use of apocalyptic discourse in 20th-century *liberation theology. Modern interpreters, under the shadow of the *Holocaust, the threat of nuclear annihilation, and continuing global poverty and disease, see the radical language and imagery of Revelation as an attempt to confront the problem of evil and suffering in the world and find comfort in mystical or eschatological answers where human efforts fail.

The tradition that the author was John the evangelist goes back to *Papias and *Justin Martyr (2nd century C.E.), although this was already questioned by Eastern fathers such as Dionysius of Alexandria and John *Chrysostom on the basis of stylistic differences between it and the Gospel, and the book was at first excluded from the *canon in the Eastern church. However, parallels between the Fourth Gospel and Revelation, notably the use of "*Word of God" and "Lamb of God" as titles of Christ, suggest a Johannine tradition common to both, although differences in style make common authorship very unlikely. *Babylon is clearly a coded reference to Rome, and persecution of the churches in Asia Minor under Domitian (81–96) provides the most likely original context for the book, despite the tempting *gematria that identifies 666, the number of the beast (13:18), with Emperor Nero (37–68).

The influence of Revelation on literature and the arts has been immense, especially the many passages made familiar from the liturgy. In music well-known examples include "Worthy is the Lamb" (Rev. 4:11) and the Hallelujah Chorus (19:6, 16) from *Handel's Messiah (1742), the ending of *Brahms's German Requiem (1867; Rev. 4:11; 14:13), and *Walton's Belshazzar's Feast (1931; Rev. 18–19). To these could be added numerous hymns such as "Holy, Holy, Holy" (4:4–10), "Mine eyes have seen the glory" (14:17–20), and "O what their joy and their glory must be" (Quanta qualia), based on chaps. 21–22. In art images from the Apocalypse are ubiquitous. The four winged creatures representing the *evangelists are among the commonest (4:6–8), as are the four horsemen (chap. 6), the archangel Michael fighting with the dragon (chap. 12), and the new Jerusalem (chaps. 21–22). Many representations of the Last Judgment draw heavily on chap. 20. There are famous paintings of St. John on Patmos (1:9) by *Giotto (1320), Botticelli (1490–92), Hieronymus *Bosch (1504–5), and Velazquez (1618). *Dürer's woodcuts illustrating the Apocalypse (1492) became very influential not least because they were available in printed form. Many films owe their inspiration to the Apocalypse, of which special mention might be made of Ingmar Bergman's classic The Seventh Seal (1957). See *Apocalyptic; *Millenarianism.

Rewritten Bible.   A term used since the 1980s to describe literature, such as Deuteronomy and the books of Chronicles, that retell biblical narratives for a different readership and purpose. It is particularly applied to Jewish literature of the Second Temple period, when it appears to have been a popular literary genre, and includes the *Genesis Apocryphon and the Temple Scroll from Qumran, the book of *Jubilees, the *Martyrdrom and Ascension of Isaiah, and parts of *Sirach (chaps. 44–49) and 1 *Enoch (chaps. 6–11). Josephus's Antiquities from the last part of the 1st century C.E. may also be included. Characteristic of such "rewriting" are the filling in of explanatory details not in the original, the updating of legal material, the omission of incidents damaging to the great biblical characters, and the insertion of contemporary beliefs such as the *resurrection of the dead.

Rhetorical criticism. An approach to the study of texts originally based on the methods advocated by Aristotle, Cicero, and other classical writers, whose chief objective was to train public speakers. Applied to biblical literature it incorporates also the insights of modern *literary criticism and the social sciences. The aim is to explore the dynamic relationship between writer and reader (or listener) by systematically asking why a literary unit is structured in a particular way, what stylistic techniques have been used, for what purpose, and addressed to whom. The *feminist critique of the stories of *Hagar and of *Jephthah's daughter would be a well-known example of the application of rhetorical criticism to the OT, while the rhetorical analysis of some of Paul's letters has been especially productive in NT studies. The main contribution of rhetorical criticism to biblical studies has been to shift the emphasis away from narrow *historical criticism to the meaning of the texts as they stand, and it has provided a transition to other methods, including discourse analysis, *reader-response criticism, and *ideological interpretation.

Ricoeur, Paul (1913–2005). French philosopher. Brought up on the Bible by Protestant grandparents, he studied under Gabriel Marcel at the Sorbonne and, as a prisoner of war, read Husserl, *Heidegger, and other German philosophers. He was professor first at Strasbourg, then in Paris, where he worked with *Levinas and taught *Derrida, before moving to Chicago, where he held appointments both in the Divinity School and the philosophy department. His influence on current biblical studies,

through his lectures and publications, including *The Symbolism of Evil* (ET 1967), *The Conflict of Interpretations* (1974), *Essays on Biblical Interpretation* (1980), and *Figuring the Sacred: Religion, Narrative, and Imagination* (ET 1995), is evident in postmodern attempts to relate the language of biblical texts, particularly the NT, to other modes of discourse, especially sociopolitical and philosophical.

Romans, Letter to the. Canonically the first and longest of Paul's letters, written in Corinth c. 57 C.E. It is the only one addressed to a Christian community he had not himself founded (15:20). Paul begins with a formal greeting, which includes a summary of what he is going to say in the letter, citing Hab. 2:4: "The righteous shall live by faith" (1:1–17). In three sections, each ending with a memorable vision (8:35–39), doxology (11:33–36), or blessing (15:13), Paul maintains that only through faith in the redeeming work of Christ can humankind be saved from sin and its consequences. The first section focuses on Abraham's faith as a model for all believers, Gentile and Jew alike (chap. 4), and on the death and resurrection of Christ in which they share through baptism, so that "nothing will be able to separate us from the love of God" (8:39). In an emotional discussion of the destiny of the Jews, "my own brethren" (9:3), Paul, frequently quoting Isaiah, who "cries out concerning Israel" (9:27), accepts that it must be God's will that they have rejected Christ, but that it must also be his will to save them, "for who has known the mind of the Lord?" (11:34). In the third section he turns to the practicalities of life in a Christian community, as members of the body of Christ, living in the last days: for "the night is far gone and the day is it hand" (13:12). Citing Proverbs and Leviticus, he calls for generosity, respect for those in authority, and above all love of one's neighbor. The letter finishes with a personal message to over twenty Christian men and women known to Paul in Rome (15:14–16:27).

Romans has played a crucial role in theological controversy and church history from the *Pelagian controversy and the *Reformation down to *Barth's epoch-making commentary (1919; ET 1933) and more recent discussions of relations between the church and the Jewish people. *Augustine's interpretation of Romans (esp. 5:12) dominated Christian teaching on original sin and predestination down to Peter Abelard, *Thomas Aquinas, and others in the Middle Ages. *Luther's reading of 7:14–25 (*simul iustus et peccator*, "at the same time righteous and a sinner") provided the basis for his doctrine of justification by faith alone, while Paul's analysis of the power of the Spirit in chap. 8 inspired evangelical revivalists like John Wesley. Verses from chap. 8 are set to music in two of *Bach's motets (vv. 1–2, 8–11, and 8:26–27) and in *Handel's *Messiah* (vv. 31, 33–34). *Historical-critical attempts since F. C. *Baur to locate Romans in a particular situation (e.g., a phase in Paul's relations with Jerusalem or a spiritual crisis in his own life) have so far been largely unsuccessful.

Romanticism. A popular term applied to developments in philosophy, literature, and the arts at the end of the 18th century as a reaction, not unrelated to the French Revolution, against the cut-and-dried cerebral conclusions of the European *Enlightenment. For many, like *Goethe and Shelley, it involved the rejection of traditional· dogmatic Christianity as well, but for Christian romantics, like *Coleridge and Wordsworth, it consisted in a fresh appreciation of the divine beauty of nature and the truth of the human imagination. *Schleiermacher's definition of religion in terms of human feelings is a lasting example of the influence of romanticism on philosophical theology. Although many of the romantics, like Chopin, Wagner, and Puccini, had little time for the Bible, typical romantic interpretations of Scripture can be found in the poetry of *Blake and

*Byron, paintings by *Turner, *Delacroix, and Holman *Hunt, and numerous settings by *Brahms, *Mendelssohn, and *Verdi. The influence of romanticism on biblical scholarship, however, was minimal until the late 20th century when *reader-response criticism, *reception history, and other methodologies led to a heightened awareness of subjective and emotional factors involved in the interpretive process, both in our own day and in the ancient and medieval religious contexts in which the many meanings of the biblical text were first so richly explored and can still bring tears to our eyes.

Rome. Capital of the Roman Republic until the time of Augustus, and then of the Roman Empire, though no longer the location of the imperial court from the 3rd century until its fall in 476 C.E. Already a world power by the 3rd century B.C.E., Rome's military might is epitomized by the destruction of the cities of Carthage in North Africa and Corinth in central Greece, both in 146 B.C.E., and of Jerusalem in 70 C.E. No less impressive are the architectural and engineering achievements of ancient Rome, evident to this day in their walls, roads, aqueducts, villas, and bathhouses, and the legacy of Roman law worldwide. Roman poets, orators, philosophers, and historians, generously supported by the emperors, especially Augustus (27 B.C.E.–4 C.E.) and the Antonines (138–180), preserved the heritage of Classical Greece, not only by using Greek models for much of their own writing, but by collecting and editing classical literature and even transporting whole libraries from Greece to Italy.

*Paul is said to have preached freely to large crowds of Jews and Gentiles in Rome for a period of two years (Acts 28:23–31), and his letters to the Colossians and Timothy may have been written from prison in Rome, as was 1 Peter. Revelation 17–18 depicts Rome's imperial and commercial power as a whore

seated on the city's well-known seven hills. The tradition that Paul and *Peter died as martyrs in Rome goes back to the late 1st century. In addition to their tombs, venerated as early as the 2nd century C.E., there is evidence in the catacombs and early church buildings for a substantial Christian community by the end of the 3rd century. When *Constantine legalized Christianity c. 313 C.E., he provided an official residence for the pope, believed to be the apostolic successor of Peter, the first bishop of Rome, and ensured that this would be the capital of Western Christendom until the Reformation. The language of the Bible, the *liturgy, and theological discourse in the Catholic Church was *Latin, the language of ancient Rome, and for most Christians the epithet "Holy City" came to be applied more often to Rome, the "Eternal City," than to *Jerusalem.

Rome and the Romans are rarely mentioned by name in the Bible apart from Pontius *Pilate and Paul's connections with the city (Rom. 16; Acts 18:1–4; 22:25–29). But from an early date many other passages were understood, by both Jews and Christians, to refer to Rome. The term *Kittim* refers to the Romans in Daniel's vision (11:30; cf. Num. 24:24) and in the *Dead Sea Scrolls. In rabbinic tradition *Esau and the Edomites are normally identified with the Romans, not least because they had appointed the Edomite (Idumean) Herod as king of Judea (40–4 B.C.E.), and later with the Christians so that prophecies like that of *Obadiah had particular relevance in the Middle Ages. Christians in the aftermath of periodic persecution at the hands of the Romans interpreted the "whore of Babylon" (Rev. 17) as Rome and calculated by *gematria that the beast was Emperor Nero (Rev. 13:18). But 1,400 years later *Perugino's official painting of "Christ handing the keys to St. Peter" in the *Sistine Chapel shows two of Rome's triumphal arches in the background and Jesus giving instruction on paying tribute to Caesar (Luke 20:21–25). By contrast, the Reformers,

including *Luther, viewed Babylon in the Bible as Rome and interpreted the "Babylonian captivity" (e.g., Ps. 137) as a reference to the Roman papacy's attack on the true church of Christ. See *Seneca; *Sibylline Oracles*; *Virgil.

Root meaning. The meaning of a word derived from its *etymology. Thus some say the root meaning of the word *hoshia* ("to save") is "to give room to" (cf. Arab. *wasi'a*, "to be spacious"). Apart from the fact that the etymology proposed here is incorrect, the problem is that a word's root may have little or nothing to do with its current usage (e.g., the word *syringe* comes from Gk. *syrinx*, "flute"). The synchronic evidence from actual usage shows that the notion of "giving room to" someone in distress does occur in the Bible but not in connection with the verb *hoshia* (e.g., Gen. 26:22; Pss. 4:1; 119:32, 45, 96). A particular author may make use of "root meanings," as in the case of names like "Israel" (Gen. 30:29) and "Moses" (Exod. 2:10), and a passage like Isa. 7:9, where the Hebrew words for "believe" and "establish" have the same root. Since the publication of *Barr's *Semantics of Biblical Language* (1961), the use of root meanings in scholarly writings is rare, and etymological data are best ignored, as in the Sheffield *Dictionary of Classical Hebrew* (1993–).

Rosenzweig, Franz (1886–1929). German Jewish existentialist thinker. Brought up in an assimilated family, he at first considered converting to Christianity; but in 1913, in an Orthodox synagogue on *Yom Kippur, he discovered his Jewishness and devoted the rest of his life to the study and practice of Judaism. His major work, *The Star of Redemption* (1921; ET 1971), the first parts of which were written on postcards while on military service (1917–18), emphasizes the continuous nature of revelation through experience in the world and in the liturgy, and has been popular in both Orthodox and Reform Judaism. With his friend *Buber he worked on a German translation of the Bible until his untimely death from a muscular degenerative disease that had afflicted him since 1922.

Rossi, Azariah dei (1513–78). Italian Jewish scholar. He studied medicine at Mantua but also Greek, Latin, and Italian as well as history and archaeology. His great work, *Me'or Einayim* (Heb. "Light of the Eyes," Mantua 1573–75), contains scientific surveys of Jewish history, archaeology, and chronology in which he criticizes some of the *allegorical interpretations of *Philo and questions the historicity of traditional *aggadah. His ideas and conclusions were treated with suspicion by Jewish traditionalists but much quoted by Christian Hebraists, including *Buxtorf and *Lowth. He also wrote a Hebrew translation of the *Letter of *Aristeas* and a description of the earthquake from which he and his wife miraculously escaped in Ferrara in 1571.

Rouault, Georges (1871–1958). French painter and engraver. Trained initially as an apprentice to a stained-glass artist and later a member of the *Fauves* (Matisse, Derain), he was motivated by a deep religious faith and a concern for human suffering and social injustice, which made him, according to many, the most important religious artist of the 20th century. His greatest work is the *Miserere*, a series of 58 engravings on human suffering and Christian faith, completed shortly after World War II, that include profound and emotive interpretations of familiar verses from the Bible (Isa. 53:7; John 11:25; 13:34; Ps. 130:1; Rom. 6:3; Phil. 2:8), as well as from Horace, *Virgil, Lucan, Plautus, Pascal, and others.

Rubens, Peter Paul (1577–1640). Flemish painter and diplomat. After completing his studies in Antwerp and Venice, where he was much influenced by the Italian *Renaissance painters, his travels took him to Madrid, Paris, London, and Cologne as well as his native Antwerp. He was a man of great erudition and sensitivity whose many representations of biblical scenes and characters are often of great beauty and power. Notable among his best-known paintings are *Samson and Delilah* (1609), *Judith with the Head of Holofernes* (c. 1616), *Feast of Herod* (1633), and, perhaps his greatest achievement, the *Raising of the Cross*, *Descent from the Cross*, and *Resurrection* on the altarpiece of Antwerp Cathedral (1610–14).

Ruth, book of. One of the Five *Scrolls in the Hebrew Bible, read at the Festival of Shavuot (*Pentecost), because this is the festival at which the giving of the *Law is commemorated and Ruth the Moabitess is seen as the ideal convert who took upon herself the *Torah as the Israelites did at *Sinai. In the Christian Bible Ruth comes between *Judges, when "there was no king in Israel," and *Samuel, which tells the life story of her great-grandson King *David (cf. Matt. 1:5–6). The book tells the touching story of Naomi, widowed in Moab with two sons married to Moabite women. The two sons also die and Naomi is distraught. But the wife of one of them, Ruth, decides to devote her life to her ("where you go I will go . . . your people shall be my people, and your God my God," Ruth 1:16), and returns with her to Bethlehem. It is harvest time. Out in the fields and at the threshing floor, Ruth meets the wealthy Boaz, a kinsman of Naomi's husband, and with Naomi's help they are married and celebrate the birth of a son and heir.

Rabbinic tradition attributes the book of Ruth to Samuel, and an early date is not impossible. Many, especially Christian scholars, have argued for a postexilic date and interpreted the idealization of a Moabite woman in the ancestry of

*David as polemic against the exclusivist teaching of *Ezra and *Nehemiah on foreign marriages (Neh. 13:23–31), but the style and pathos of the book make this highly unlikely. More recent attention focuses on the literary merits of the work and on the unusually sensitive treatment of the plight of single women in ancient rural society.

In rabbinic tradition as well as Christian, including *Dante (*Paradiso* 32.10–24) and *Blake (*Jerusalem* 62.11), Ruth is one of the "mothers of Israel," beside Sarah, Rebekah, Bathsheba, and others. Elsewhere in English poetry she is mentioned alongside Martha's sister Mary (Luke 10) in *Milton's *Sonnet IX* (1645), and in Keats's *Ode to a Nightingale* the birdsong recalls homesick Ruth "in tears amid the alien corn" (1819). In art there are paintings by *Rembrandt (1645) and *Poussin (1660–64), and a series of five lithographs by *Chagall (1960). See also *Jesse tree.

Saadia Gaon (882–942). Saadia ben Joseph, biblical scholar, talmudist, and philosopher, was gaon (head) of the Academy of Sura in Babylonia. Although best known for *Emunot ve-De'ot* (1880; ET *Books of Beliefs and Opinions*, 1948), a philosophical work written in Arabic and later translated into Hebrew, Saadia's translation of the Bible into Arabic broke new ground in its use of *philology, and his Hebrew grammar and lexicon made a significant contribution to medieval Jewish *linguistics. Against the *Karaites he stressed the importance of human reason in the process of interpreting the *Torah.

Sabbath (Heb. *shabbat*). Unique Jewish festival celebrated every seventh day, involving rest (Heb. *shabat*) from all forms of work and traced back to God's resting after the six days of creation (Gen. 2:1–3; Exod. 20:8–11). Elsewhere its origin and purpose are derived from the experiences of the Israelites in Egypt and the need for everyone, including servants and domestic animals, to have a regular day of rest (Deut. 5:12–15). Preparations for the coming of the Sabbath ("the bride") include the lighting of two candles at home, and there is a special Sabbath meal at home on Friday evening. Public worship on Saturday morning includes the reading of the prescribed weekly parashah ("portion") of the *Torah, and on Saturday evening the end of the Sabbath is marked by a ceremony known as Havdalah (Heb. "division") celebrating the division between sacred and profane.

The fundamental importance of this Jewish institution can be gauged by the strict legislation surrounding it in the Bible (Exod. 35:1–3) and the *Talmud (it is the only feast day to have two tractates devoted to it, *Shabbat* and *Eruvin*), and by the story that in the Maccabean period people were willing to die rather profane the Sabbath (1 Macc. 2:32–41). The rabbis later argued, as did Jesus (Matt. 12; Mark 3:1–5), that the saving of life takes precedence over Sabbath law. Still strictly observed by Orthodox Jews, the Sabbath laws are interpreted more leniently in the Liberal and Reform traditions, while outside Judaism its spiritual and social value has been acknowledged universally, even though Christians, apart from Seventh-day Adventists, transferred its benefits to Sunday (Lat. *Dominica*, "the Lord's Day"; cf. Acts 20:7). The principle was extended to the sabbatical year and the jubilee after seven sabbaticals (Lev. 25).

Sacrifice. An offering made to a deity. In some traditions the offering is seen as food for the god (cf. Lev. 3:11, 16); in others as a gift to express thanks or remorse in the hope that it will elicit a favorable response (Lev. 4:27–31); in others as a means of involving priest, worshiper, and deity in a communal celebration (Lev. 7:11–18). The English term *sacrifice* (as in "self-sacrifice") implies that the ritual is concerned less with the effect on the deity than on the worshipers, required to give up something dear to them or valued by them. In the Hebrew Bible sacrifices by individuals that have had a significant influence on later discussion include the sacrifices of *Cain and *Abel (Gen. 4), *Abraham (Gen. 22), and *Jephthah (Judg. 11), and the notion of self-sacrifice appears in connection with *Moses (Exod. 32:32; Deut. 1:9) and the Suffering Servant (Isa. 53:10). The elaborate system described in the *Torah, defining the terminology and prescribing different sacrifices for particular occasions, classes of worshipers, and the like, presumably reflects current practice in the *temple at Jerusalem. Some of the prophets' polemic, like that of Isaiah (66:1–4; cf. Amos 5:21–27) and Jeremiah (7:21–22), seems to go beyond attacks on abuses of the system to challenge the system itself, and with the destruction of the Second Temple in 70 C.E. the system came to an end in Judaism and will be resumed only when it is rebuilt.

In Christianity, by contrast, sacrifice remained a fundamental motif, evident in the centrality of the altar in church architecture, the church's teaching on martyrdom and self-sacrifice, and the interpretation of the death of Christ as the sacrifice of a lamb, especially in the Fourth Gospel and Revelation, and of his *blood as redemptive (Heb. 9:22). The church fathers believed the *Eucharist was in some sense a sacrifice, and this has been the official doctrine of the Catholic Church since the Council of Trent, although rejected by the Reformers as undermining the uniqueness of the once-for-all sacrifice of Christ on the cross. Sacrifice has played a central role in Christian art and literature, from innumerable paintings of the sacrifice of *Isaac prefiguring the crucifixion, to George *Herbert's poignant soliloquy concluding "my woe, man's weal" (The Sacrifice, 1633).

Sadducees (Heb. tzedukim). A Jewish sect, listed by *Josephus alongside *Pharisees and *Essenes (Ant. 13.5.9). From wealthy families of priestly lineage, they were traditionalists who rejected the *Oral Torah, the *resurrection of the dead, and other popular beliefs (Matt. 22:23). When the *temple was destroyed, they lost their authority to the Pharisees and to what came to be known as *rabbinic Judaism. Their name suggests they claimed descent from King David's priest Zadok (1 Kgs. 1), according to Ezekiel the only true priestly family (Ezek. 40–48; cf. Sir. 51:29), but there is no corroboration of this in the ancient sources. See *Karaites; *Melchizedek.

Salvation history (Ger. Heilsgeschichte). A term coined in the 19th century when optimism about the quest for what actually happened was at its height, and later associated particularly with Gerhard von *Rad (OT Theology, 2 vols., ET 1962–65). It was applied by some to the saving events themselves, such as the exodus and the resurrection (Oscar Cullmann), by others to the biblical account of those events (von Rad), and by others to the readers' existential participation in the events (*Bultmann), and is perhaps best avoided.

Samaritan. A dialect of *Aramaic still used by the Samaritan community at Nablus (ancient Shechem). It is written in a distinctive form of the Old Hebrew script. The bulk of the Samaritan Scriptures, which include their own Chronicles and exegetical works such as the Memar Marqa, cannot be dated much before early medieval times, though they may contain ancient material. The Samaritan *Pentateuch, an important witness to the text of the Hebrew Bible, dates back to the 4th century B.C.E., and is actually in Hebrew, written in the Samaritan script.

Samson (Heb. shimshon). Biblical hero from the tribe of Dan and last judge of Israel (Judg. 13–16). His story is full of action and memorable images, from his miraculous birth and early exploits to his betrayal by the harlot Delilah, his blindness, and his final feat of supernatural strength in which he wreaks vengeance on the Philistines. Unlike the other judges, he acts throughout as an individual rather than as a leader, and dies alone in enemy territory, illustrating the meaning of the verse "in those days there was no king in Israel: every man did what was right in his own eyes" (Judg. 17:6; 21:25). Modern scholars, noting the connection between his name and the sun (Heb. *shemesh*), have suggested that the cutting of his hair that led to his blindness may, in an original solar myth, have referred to the disappearance of the sun's rays in an eclipse.

In the early church Samson was remembered, like the other judges, for his faith (Heb. 11:32), but also as a type of Christ, his arms stretched out between the two pillars where he died, for example, prefiguring Christ on the cross. Later interpreters especially in the Middle Ages, including Peter Abelard and *Chaucer, turned their attention to Delilah, like *Eve the source of evil and wholly responsible for Samson's downfall. *Renaissance writers saw him above all as a repentant sinner, his blindness bringing him closer to God, and it is this character during the agony of his last few hours that is the hero of *Milton's great poetic drama *Samson Agonistes* (1671). In art there are many famous representations of the Samson story, including a relief on the Fontana Maggiore in Perugia (1278) and a woodcut by Dürer (c. 1498) showing his fight with the lion, four dramatic paintings by *Rembrandt (1635–41), *Samson and Delilah* by *Rubens (1609–10), and *Samson Destroys the Temple* by *Chagall (1957). Samson is also the subject of an oratorio by *Handel, based on Milton (1743), an opera by Saint-Saëns (1877), and a Cecil B. DeMille blockbuster, *Samson and Delilah* (1949).

Samuel, books of. Originally one book attributed in part, according to rabbinic tradition, to the prophet Samuel, who plays a key role in the first book. In the LXX 1 and 2 Samuel are combined with 1 and 2 *Kings in a single four-part work entitled the "Books of the Reigns." First Samuel begins with the story of Samuel's birth and how he came to be a prophet of the Lord and leader of Israel. Against the threat of the *Philistines he anoints first *Saul and then *David as kings of Israel, and the rest of the book is taken up with an account of their exploits up to the death of both Samuel and Saul. Second Samuel tells of David's conquest of *Jerusalem, his marriage to *Bathsheba, and the birth of Solomon, but ends with the conspiracy of his son *Absalom and a terrible plague, leaving the death of David and the establishment of his dynasty till the first two chapters of 1 Kings.

The ambivalence of the two main characters, Saul and David, is striking and is related to the ambivalent attitude toward the institution of the monarchy itself (1 Sam. 8). The narrative is packed with action (the capture of the ark, David and Goliath, the witch at Endor), colorful characters (the priest Eli and his two sons, Jonathan, Michal, Abigail, the prophet Nathan) and a variety of other material, including four poems: Hannah's prayer, which became the basis for the Virgin Mary's *Magnificat (1 Sam. 2; cf. Luke 1); David's lament over Saul ("How are the mighty fallen!" 2 Sam. 1); David's song of deliverance (cf. 2 Sam. 22 = Ps. 18), and his last words, "the oracle of the man who was raised on high" (2 Sam. 23). Modern scholarship identifies different sources, such as local legends about the ark and Jerusalem, and an early "Succession Narrative" (2 Sam. 9–20; 1 Kgs. 1–2), possibly written in part during the reign of David. The influence of Deuteronomic style and theology is evident throughout and suggests to many that 1 and 2 Samuel are part of a larger *Deuteronomistic History running from Joshua through Kings.

The story of the child Samuel at Shiloh is depicted in art by Edward

Burne-Jones, Joshua Reynolds, and others, and given a contemporary interpretation in Rudy Wiebe's "The Vietnam Call of Samuel Reimer" (in *The Blue Mountains of China*, 1970). Samuel's comments on sacrifice are echoed in the NT (1 Sam. 15:22; cf. Mark 12:33) and his critique of monarchy (1 Sam. 8) has been cited in the context of constitutional controversy (e.g., by Henry Fielding, Thomas Paine, S. T. *Coleridge). In the 18th century his memorable description of David as "a man after God's own heart" (1 Sam. 13:14; cf. Acts 13:22) became the ironic title of an anonymous attack on Christianity, quoted with approval by *Voltaire.

Sanctus (Lat. "Holy"; Gk. *Trisagion*; Heb. **kedushah*).   Latin title of the hymn beginning "Holy, Holy Holy," sung by the seraphim in Isaiah's vision (Isa. 6:3) and by the four living creatures in *Revelation (4:8). From ancient times it has been an important part of Jewish and Christian *liturgy in which heavenly and earthly worshipers are believed to join forces. It is a hymn praising the "LORD of hosts" (Lat. *Dominus Deus Sabaoth*) in the sense of creator of "the heavens and the earth and all their host" (cf. Gen. 2:1; Isa. 45:12). Combined with the *Benedictus and the *Hosanna, it has been sung as the fourth part of the Roman Catholic *Mass since the 6th century, and memorably set to music by *Bach, *Mozart, *Beethoven, *Verdi, *Britten, and many others.

Sarah.   First of the "mothers of Israel." Wife and half-sister (apparently; see Gen. 20:12) of *Abraham, she was childless until her old age when she miraculously conceived and bore *Isaac, half-brother of Ishmael, the concubine *Hagar's son, whom she subsequently sent away into the wilderness. She died immediately after the "binding of Isaac" (*Akedah; Gen. 23:2), and was buried in what became the family tomb in Hebron, venerated to this day. In rabbinic tradition she is the most beautiful woman

that ever lived, a better prophet than Abraham, and the only woman to have been addressed directly by God rather than by an angel. Her behavior toward Hagar and Ishmael is justified because she had seen Ishmael engaging in immoral acts. She was strongly opposed to Abraham's determination to sacrifice Isaac and is said to have died of grief before they returned.

Her role in the stories of the encounter with the king of Egypt (Gen. 12) and the visit of the angels to Abraham's tent by the oaks of Mamre (Gen. 18) are popular in Muslim tradition (cf. Qur'an 11:74). In Christian tradition Paul's *allegory in which she is the freedom of Christ, the new covenant, and "Jerusalem above" (Gal. 4) was followed by many ancient and medieval Christian writers, some of whom also saw in her a type of the Virgin Mary, her laughter a temporary lapse (Gen. 18:9–15).

Sarcophagus.   An ancient type of coffin usually made of terra-cotta, stone, or marble, and often richly decorated. Typical of the 2nd millennium B.C.E. are anthropomorphic sarcophagi used by the Egyptians, Philistines, and others, and the sarcophagus of Ahiram of Byblos (c. 10th century B.C.E.) is famous for a lengthy inscription in the ancient Phoenician script. The giant iron bedstead of the legendary King Og of Bashan, which "you could still see in Rabbath Ammon" (Deut. 3:11), may have been a sarcophagus. From the 2nd century C.E. wealthy Roman families normally buried their dead in sarcophagi, and some of the many that have been preserved may be Christian, although explicitly Christian images and symbols are rare. After *Constantine, however, there are some important examples of Christian iconography, of which the most outstanding is that of Iunius Bassus, prefect of Rome, who died in 359 C.E. His sarcophagus has ten intricate sculptures showing Adam and Eve, the sacrifice of Isaac, Job and Daniel from the OT, echoed by four scenes from Christ's passion, Peter's arrest, and Paul on his way to martyrdom. See *Rome.

Satan.   One of the names of the *devil. The Hebrew word means "adversary" (1 Kgs. 11:14) and in the Hebrew Bible can refer to a member of God's heavenly court, charged with testing Job's faith (Job 1–2; cf. Zech. 3:1–2). But elsewhere he assumes a more independent evil character, in opposition to God (1 Chr. 21:1; cf. 2 Sam. 24:1), and with the development of more elaborate angelology is identified with the "prince of demons" (Mark 3:22). The personal name "Satan" became a frequent *loanword in Latin, while Greek preferred the translation *diabolos,* "accuser," from which the English word "devil" is derived.

Saul (Heb. *sha'ul*).   First king of Israel, anointed reluctantly by Samuel at the wish of the people (1 Sam. 10). When his military achievements were overshadowed by David's ("Saul has slain his thousands and David his ten thousands," 1 Sam. 18:7), he was consumed by jealousy and depression, and, although spared twice by David, died ignominiously in battle along with his son Jonathan (1 Sam. 31). Christian tradition, from the church fathers to the Reformers, unanimously condemn him for his arrogance and disobedience, as does *Milton, for whom he is the archetype of a bad king, comparable to Charles I.

The rabbis were more favorably disposed toward him, some even arguing that he was morally superior to David, and sympathy with him as a tragic hero characterizes most of his frequent appearances in literature, music, and art. Of these *Byron's four *Hebrew Melodies* on Saul (1816), Browning's dramatic monologue *Saul* (1845), and André Gide's gay interpretation of the story in the drama *Saul* (1906; first performed 1922) are representative examples. In music there are *Handel's oratorio

(1739), with its popular "Dead March," and a four-act opera by Carl Nielsen (1902), while in art best known is *Rembrandt's painting *David Playing His Harp before Saul* (1650–60).

Scapegoat (Heb. *azazel*).   The goat selected to be sent away into the wilderness "bearing the sins of the people" in the annual ritual of the Day of Atonement or *Yom Kippur (Lev. 16). The other goat was sacrificed. The English term comes via Greek and Latin from a folk *etymology of Heb. *azazel* (Lev. 16:8; cf. *'ez,* "goat"; *azal,* "went away"). Azazel was believed by the rabbis to have been the ancient name of a precipitous region near Jerusalem, where the scapegoat was sent to its death. It is also frequently understood to be a name for the devil (*1 Enoch* 8–10) despite the theological problem raised by the notion of making an offering to the devil (Lev. 16:8). Modern scholars have suggested Azazel might originally have been a Babylonian deity.

There is an elaborate account of the ritual in *Mishnah *Yoma,* and a brief reference to it in Hebrews, although not to the scapegoat itself (Heb. 13:11–13). The saving work of Christ is more often compared to that of a lamb (John 1:29) or the Suffering Servant (Matt. 8:17) than a goat, and although the term "scapegoat" has become all too familiar in accounts of the persecution of the Jews and other minority groups, the actual biblical image has never played a significant role in European culture, Holman *Hunt's famous painting (1854) being a conspicuous exception.

Schleiermacher, Friedrich (1768–1834).   German Protestant theologian and philosopher. His major work, which earned him the title "father of modern theology," was a study in dogmatics entitled *The Christian Faith* (2 vols. 1821–22; ET 1928). An accomplished biblical critic and author of a life of Jesus, works on Paul and Luke, and an NT introduction, Schleiermacher was much more than a dogmatic theologian. With the romantics and against the rationalists, he argued that religious experience, which is a fundamental part of human existence, must inform and inspire the enterprise of interpreting the NT, the only means we have of getting to know Christ. He faced the historical problem that the texts were written nearly 2,000 years ago for a very different readership, and evolved a hermeneutics designed to take account of this, maintaining that modern interpreters must never forget that the text they are studying is part of sacred Scripture. At the same time their task is to get as near as they can, by good *linguistics, psychology, and historical method, to the mind of the individual author. His influence down to our own time, even on those who disagree with his conclusions, has been considerable.

Scholia.   Notes written in the margins of mss, ranging from brief jottings to lengthy commentaries. The system seems to have been invented in Hellenistic *Alexandria and was taken over by Christian and Jewish scholars. Unlike glosses, which are often mere paraphrases of the text, scholia frequently consist of quotations from earlier scholars, and occasionally preserve valuable material otherwise unknown. See *Catena.

Schubert, Franz (1797–1828).   Austrian composer. Already playing piano, violin, and organ at the age of 9, he studied under Salieri and taught briefly at his father's school, but devoted his short life to composing, most notably over 600 lieder, living all his life in Vienna and never holding any official position. His works on biblical themes, in addition to masses and settings of the *Magnificat, *Stabat Mater dolorosa, and two *psalms (23; 92), include Miriam's *Song of Triumph* (Exod. 15; 1828) and an unfinished oratorio, *Lazarus, or the Celebration of the Resurrection* (John 11:1–14).

Schürer, Emil (1844–1910).   German NT scholar, influenced by *Schleiermacher, *Baur, and Ritschl. His lifetime achievement was to produce the first comprehensive study of the Jewish background to the NT entitled *History of the Jewish People in the Time of Jesus Christ* (2nd Ger. ed. 1886–87; ET 5 vols., 1890–91). Employing the full range of Jewish sources, including recently discovered papyri, rabbinic literature, the *Pseudepigrapha, archaeological evidence, and numismatics, he produced a systematic account, in three parts, of the political history, culture, and religion of the Jews from the Maccabean period down to the end of the Bar Kokhba Revolt (135 C.E.). Criticized for its Christian bias, the unevenness of his knowledge of the Jewish sources, and the omission of Greco-Roman material, it nonetheless inaugurated a new era in NT studies, and thanks to the magisterial revised English edition by the Oxford historians Geza Vermes, Fergus Millar, and Martin Goodman (1973–87), it remains the best reference work available.

Schütz, Heinrich (1585–1672).   German composer. He studied with Gabrieli in Venice and did much to promote Italian music in Germany. Of his many settings of biblical texts in Latin and German, precursors of many better known 18th-century compositions, the best known are his *Psalms of David* (1619, 1628, 1661), the *Christmas Oratorio* (1664), his passions according to Luke (1664), Matthew (1665), and John (1666), and his final work, entitled *Swan Song*, which consists of 12 motets concluding with the *Magnificat* (1671).

Schweitzer, Albert (1875–1965). German theologian, medical missionary, and musicologist. Born in Alsace, he studied theology in Strasbourg, Berlin, and Paris, and published two controversial works on the life and teaching of Jesus (see *Quest of the Historical Jesus*), and another on Paul, before deciding to give up his academic career in 1913 and work as a medical missionary at Lambaréné in French Equatorial Africa. He continued to write, not only his memoirs but also a work on Christian ethics (1923; ET *Philosophy of Civilization* 1950) and a study of Paul's mysticism (1930; ET 1931), and was awarded the Nobel Peace Prize in 1953. His interpretation of the NT was colored as much by his "thoroughgoing eschatology" as by his efforts to integrate his scholarship with life as a Christian in the 20th century, and, despite opposition from the academic world, he had considerable influence on European and American Protestant theology.

Scribe (Heb. *sofer*).   A term applied in the Bible to those with writing skills (Ps. 45:1), but much more frequently to government officials (2 Sam. 8:17) and scholars (Sir. 39:24). Thus while Baruch's role as Jeremiah's amanuensis was primarily one of writing and reading (Jer. 36), Ezra, "a scribe skilled in the law of Moses" (7:7), was also an expert in interpreting and teaching the *Torah. The authority claimed by the scribes was challenged by the prophet Jeremiah (8:8) and by Jesus, who groups them with the Pharisees (Matt. 23). Their association with chief priests and elders in the Gospels (Mark 11:27) confirms their role in the Jewish hierarchy, but precisely how they were related to other groups is uncertain. In rabbinic tradition and all subsequent Jewish history, where handwritten scrolls are essential in synagogue worship, the skill of the scribe as artist and meticulous copyist is highly valued. See *Masoretic Text; *Writing.

Scrolls.   See *Megillot.

Seder Olam Rabbah (Heb. "the order of the world").   A rabbinic history of the world from creation down to the Bar

Kokhba Revolt (132–35 C.E.). Traditionally attributed to Rabbi Yosé (ben Halafta), a major figure in 2nd-century rabbinic debates, *Seder Olam* is quoted already in the *Talmud and frequently in *Rashi and most subsequent discussions of biblical *chronology.

Semantics.   A branch of modern *linguistics concerned with *meaning. Philosophers, exegetes, and philologists since ancient times have devised strategies to define, explain, and translate words and phrases for different purposes. Modern semantics heightens scholars' awareness of the problems involved and suggests new methods and terminology. The importance of *context was appreciated already by the rabbis and early church fathers who understood that a word or passage could have more than one meaning, depending on its context (literal/historical, homiletical, christological, allegorical, or the like). But the modern distinction between *diachronic* and *synchronic* approaches added a new precision, particularly in relationship to the misuse of historical or etymological data (diachronic) in definitions of words as they are used in a particular context (synchronic) (see *Root meaning). The distinction is also of fundamental importance in defining the precise *contextualization* of a passage before attempting to describe its meaning. "I know that my Redeemer liveth" (Job 19:25 AV) has a different meaning in the (early medieval) MT, in *Handel's *Messiah* (1742), and in modern reconstructions of its original context.

The notion of a word's *associative field* has proved useful in word definitions and lexicography. Kinship terms and color names were among the first examples of associative field studies, but now there are numerous others including biblical words for salvation, purity, fear, truth, and grace. By arranging vocabulary in sets of words of related meaning instead of in the usual arbitrary alphabetical order, semantic distinctions between synonyms and other semantic relations can be studied to a higher degree of precision. The distinction between *transparent* and *opaque* words can be valuable both in word definition and in the discussion of style and the use of literary devices. The transparent word *demut*, "likeness" (cf. *damah*, "to be like"), for example, explains the more opaque word *tzelem*, "image," in Gen. 1:26. The *semantic range* of one word, systematically compared with that of another, in the same language or another, is also a valuable method of defining meaning: thus Heb. *hayah*, "to be, happen," and *tzedek*, "righteousness, triumph," have a very different semantic range from their nearest equivalents in Greek, Latin, or English. See *Barr, James.

Semiotics. The science of signs (Gk. *semeion*, "sign"). Discussion of the nature and function of signs, including words, gestures, images, symptoms, and the like, how they are produced and how they are interpreted, can be found in ancient philosophical, theological, and medical literature, and *Augustine already recognized the link between the theory of signs and language. Modern semiotic theory, as applied to language and literature in particular, stresses the arbitrary nature of the relationship between a sign and what the sign stands for, and consequently the need to know something about who interprets it, how and in what social context, before anything at all can be said about what it means.

Words and images operate in language communities where their behavior is informed and controlled by social conventions without which communication would be impossible. In biblical studies the *parables have been analyzed on semiotic principles to help explain why they have multiple meanings, the conclusion being that they have had multiple readers, each with their own set of conventional codes and structures by means of which they interpret the signs. Similarly the meaning of the

controversial "*Immanuel sign" in Isa. 7:14 can be analyzed by reference to its reception in 8th-century B.C.E. Jerusalem, the early church, rabbinic Judaism, and medieval Christian iconography. The work of Umberto Eco, professor of semiotics in Bologna, and others, by comparing the career of a biblical text in society to that of advertisements, war memorials, film icons, musical catchphrases, and birdsong, encourages interpreters to see their role as much more than philologists and literary critics. See *Reader-response criticism; *Reception history.

Semitic languages. The group of historically related languages comprising East Semitic (Akkadian, Babylonian, Assyrian), Northwest Semitic (*Hebrew, *Aramaic, *Ugaritic, *Phoenician/Punic, Maltese) and Southwest Semitic (Arabic, Ethiopic, Amharic, Epigraphic South Arabian). The name, derived from Noah's son *Shem, was coined in 1781 by A. L. Schloetzer, and since then attempts have been made to reconstruct "Proto-Semitic" and to locate its region of origin. The Semitic languages are now known to belong to a larger group known as Afro-Asiatic (or Hamito-Semitic), which includes ancient Egyptian and Coptic, Berber-Lybian, Chadic (e.g., Hausa), and Cushitic (e.g., Somali). Since the most conspicuous speakers of a Semitic language in Europe were the Jews, the term *anti-Semitism was coined in the 19th century as an ethnic synonym for *anti-Judaism*.

Semitisms. Words and expressions, especially in NT Greek, showing signs of the influence of either Hebrew or Aramaic. These include both actual Aramaic *loanwords like *abba* (Rom. 8:15) and *maranatha* (1 Cor. 16:22), and Greek words or phrases with Hebrew or Aramaic meanings like "son of man" (Matt. 9:6; 10:23) and "it came to pass" (Luke 2:1, 15, 46 AV) (see *Calque). There has been much discussion as to whether these reflect the direct influence of Aramaic on the NT writers or whether the Semitisms were already accepted in the Greek they were using. They are present in all parts of the NT but more frequent in Mark and John than in Matthew, Luke, and Acts. If *dikaios*, "just," in Matt. 1:19 is an example, then Joseph was a "virtuous" man (Heb. *tzaddiq*), concerned as much with Mary's well-being as with legal matters.

Seneca, Lucius Annaeus (c. 4 B.C.E.–65 C.E.). Roman writer and philosopher. Born in Spain and educated in *Rome, he was for a time Nero's tutor and exercised some influence in politics until, accused of conspiracy, he was forced by Nero to commit suicide. He wrote ten tragedies that were popular in Shakespearean England, and his Stoic philosophy appealed to many Christian writers, including *Tertullian, *Jerome, and *Augustine. There is an apocryphal correspondence between Seneca and *Paul and a famous painting of his death by Jacques-Louis David (1773).

Sennacherib. Assyrian king (705–681 B.C.E.) who led the invasion of Judah in 701. The biblical account describes the destruction of his army by the angel of the Lord and his retreat to Nineveh, where he was murdered by his sons (Isa. 36–37), although contemporary records and the account in 2 Kings suggest that Sennacherib withdrew only because *Hezekiah capitulated and paid a huge tribute of gold and silver stripped from the temple (2 Kgs. 18:13ff.). Nevertheless the escape of Jerusalem, the only city in the region to do so, became one of the legends of Zion immortalized not only in the Bible itself (Isa. 37:21–35; cf. Ps. 48), but in *Byron's famous poem *Sennacherib* (1915–16) and an opera by Mussorgsky (1867). See *Assyria.

Sensus plenior (Lat. "the fuller meaning"). A 20th-century term current in Catholic theological debate up to the Second Vatican Council in 1965. Like other ancient and medieval nonliteral meanings, the *sensus plenior* referred primarily to christological interpretations of the OT, explained as the consequence of divine intervention, unknown to the original authors (cf. Rom. 15:4). Since then reconstructions of the historical meaning of the text (e.g., in *liberation theology) have to some extent shifted the focus of interpretation away from nonliteral meanings, although recent emphasis on *reception history and *reader-response criticism may go some way to rehabilitating it.

Septuagint (LXX). Originally a Greek translation of the *Pentateuch produced, according to the *Letter of *Aristeas*, for the Jews living in *Egypt during the reign of Ptolemy II Philadelphus (285–246 B.C.E.). Named after the seventy-two scholars who, according to legend, independently produced identical versions, it was hailed in Egypt as an important landmark in the history of the Jews, but was later treated with suspicion in the *Talmud. The rest of the Hebrew Bible was later translated into Greek and additional books added to it (see *Apocrypha) to form the Greek OT, nowadays widely referred to as the LXX. Other Jewish versions were made including those of *Aquila, *Symmachus, and *Theodotion, but it was the Christian church that adopted the LXX as Scripture, already combined with the NT in our earliest complete mss of the Bible. The influence of the LXX on the church, to the detriment of the Hebrew original, was immense from OT quotations in the NT to the Latin Vg and the formulations of Christian doctrine in the 4th and 5th centuries. For textual critics it provides a witness to the Hebrew original much earlier than the MT, although not always as reliable. See *Hexapla; *Manuscripts; *Translation.

Sermon on the Mount. Discourse delivered by Jesus on a hill in Galilee, containing the *Beatitudes, the *Lord's Prayer, and much of his most important ethical and religious teaching: "turn the other cheek . . . consider the lilies of the field . . . knock and it shall be opened unto you" (Matt. 5–7). It seems intended to represent Jesus as a new Moses on a new Mount Sinai. In it Jesus repeatedly refers to Scripture, both in his intention to fulfill the law and the prophets (5:17) and in his new commandments, which are contrasted with the old ones ("you have heard . . . but I say unto you . . ."). Some of the material appears in the Sermon on the Plain (Luke 6:20–49), or elsewhere in Luke's Gospel (e.g., the *Lord's Prayer in Matt. 6:9–13 and Luke 11:2–4). Since the 4th century or earlier, the traditional site has been venerated on what is called the Mount of the Beatitudes near Capernaum.

Important commentaries were written by John *Chrysostom and *Augustine (who first gave Matt. 5–7 its title), Peter Lombard, *Luther, and *Calvin. Among modern interpreters some read it as ethical teaching relevant only in a world about to come to an end (*Schweitzer), others take it literally as a manifesto for socialism and nonviolence (Tolstoy), and others understand it figuratively as a call for total obedience to Christ (Bonhoeffer). Jewish commentators have stressed the overlap between the teaching of Jesus and rabbinic literature, some to encourage dialogue (C. G. Montefiore), others to detract from the originality of Christianity (Gerald Friedlander 1911). The scene is depicted on a wall of the *Sistine Chapel, judiciously placed opposite *The Tables of the Law and the Golden Calf* (1481–82).

Sermons. See *Homilies; *Preaching.

Serpent. The wisdom and healing powers of serpents were proverbial (Matt. 10:16; Num. 21:4–9; John 3:14–15), and the appearance of a serpent in the garden of *Eden initiated the process whereby men and women became like God "knowing good and evil" (Gen. 3:22). The wisdom of the wise can be an evil (Isa. 5:21; Jer. 9:23–24), and Christian interpretations of the Genesis story as the "*fall" stress the disobedience of *Adam and *Eve, God's anger, and the origin of human suffering and death (Rom. 5:14; 1 Cor. 15:22). In ancient Near Eastern mythology "*Leviathan the twisting serpent" (Isa. 27:1; Ps. 74:14) was also a symbol of primeval chaos, identified with the *devil and *Satan (Rev. 20:2), and in Christian art its defeat is depicted both as a triumph of physical might (cf. Isa. 27:1) and as a victory won by the Virgin Mary with her heel on the serpent's head (cf. Gen. 3:15).

Servant Songs. Four passages in Deutero-Isaiah (42:1–4; 49:1–6; 50:4–9; 52:13–53:12), identifed by the German scholar Bernhard *Duhm (1892) as by a different author and about a distinct individual. The theory was widely accepted both by scholars and in the church, where the identity of the Servant was hotly debated, to the exclusion of other issues, for the best part of a century, theories ranging from *Moses, Jehoiachin, and *Deutero-Isaiah himself to an unnamed rabbi of the Maccabean period and Jesus. More recently the four songs have been examined in their context alongside other references to the Servant of the Lord (e.g., 41:8–9; 44:1–5), and similar passages about "the daughter of Zion" (e.g., 40:9; 49:14–15; 54; 60:1–9; 66:7–14.), in which the stories of the two characters mirror the fate of the people addressed. Beautiful christological interpretations of the Servant ("a light to the nations," 49:6; "wounded for our transgressions," 53:4) have dominated Christian tradition since the beginning, while Jewish interpreters appreciated better how these powerful texts can have more than one meaning, referring to the life of the *Messiah in some contexts (42:1 Tg; 52:13 Tg), and the history of the Jewish people in others (49:3).

Seven Words of the Savior on the Cross.
Words taken from the four Gospels (Luke 23:34; 23:43; John 19:26–27; Matt. 27:46; John 19:28, 30; Luke 23:46) as a focus for meditation and devotion in Holy Week, especially during the three-hour service on *Good Friday. There is an oratorio on the *Seven Last Words* by *Schütz (1645), both a choral work and a string quartet by *Haydn (1787), and a cantata by James MacMillan (1993).

Sexuality.
In the Genesis account of creation procreation is encouraged by God ("be fruitful and multiply," Gen. 1:28), and relations between the sexes subsequently discussed in some detail (Gen. 2:18–24; 3:16; 4:1). In the laws, adultery, incest, and homosexuality are all treated as serious offenses against the sanctity of marriage (Exod. 20:14; Lev. 20), although divorce (by the husband) is permitted (Deut. 24:1–2). There are cautionary tales about male masturbation (Gen. 38:8–10), homosexuality (Gen. 19:1–12), prostitutes (Prov. 7), foreign marriages (Ezra 10), and lust (Rom. 1:24; cf. Matt. 5:27), and while the temple was still functioning in Jerusalem, discharges of semen and menstrual blood were considered unclean, requiring special purification rituals (Lev. 15). Rabbinic tradition devotes much space to these laws, even though some were no longer relevant after the destruction of the temple in 70 C.E.

Christian interpreters have tended to overemphasize the sexual element in some biblical passages to the exclusion of other matters (Gen. 3; Isa. 1:10; cf. Ezek. 16:49), and maintain that laws in Leviticus on sexual matters are still valid while others, for example, the dietary laws, are not. Nowadays most would find unacceptable biblical teaching on homosexuality (Lev. 18:22; 20:13; 1 Cor. 6:9–10), the subordination of women in marriage (Gen. 3:16; Sir. 25:26; 26:14; 1 Tim. 2:11–15), and the frequency of images of the sexual abuse of women (e.g., Judg. 19; Isa. 47). But the Bible also celebrates erotic love (*Song of Songs), the love of two men for each other (2 Sam. 1:26) and the strength and independence of women, whether married (*Eve, *Sarah, *Rebekah) or single (Naomi, *Judith). See *Feminism; *Gay and lesbian interpretations.

Sforno, Obadiah (c. 1470–1550).
Italian humanist and biblical commentator. After studying in Rome, where he taught Hebrew to *Reuchlin, he became head of a rabbinic college in Bologna. His commentary on the *Torah, printed in *Rabbinic Bibles, is characterized by the application of Renaissance science and humanist values. In his comments on the tower of *Babel story he makes an obvious reference to the dome of St. Peter's, completed in 1546. He also wrote commentaries on Jonah, Habakkuk, Zechariah, Psalms, the Song of Songs, and Ecclesiastes.

Shakespeare, William (1564–1616).
Much research has been devoted to Shakespeare and the Bible and, like a number of other mysteries surrounding his life, the results remain controversial. Educated probably at the local grammar school and brought up in a churchgoing family, Shakespeare would have been thoroughly familiar with biblical language and imagery both from the Book of Common Prayer and from one or other of the English Bible versions in use at the time. Almost every play has numerous biblical quotations or allusions, although some of these may already have been current in the literary English he was using. Parallels have also been noted between *The Tempest* and Genesis, *Henry V* and Exodus, *Macbeth* and parts of Judges, *King Lear* and Job, etc. Although none of his plays is on a biblical theme, and it is not always certain that he was deliberately alluding to the Bible, many biblical commentators have found in Shakespeare illuminating parallels, if not actual reworkings, of

verses such as Isa. 45:8 ("The quality of mercy . . . droppeth as the gentle rain from heaven," *Merchant of Venice* 4.1.183) and Job 10:8–13 ("As flies to wanton boys are we to the gods: they kill us for their sport," *King Lear* 4.1.30).

Shammai. Prominent rabbi in the time of Christ, contemporary of *Hillel. Disputes between the "House of Shammai" (*Bet Shammai)* and the "House of Hillel" (*Bet Hillel*) are frequent in the *Talmud and usually conclude with the rejection of the more rigorous ruling of Shammai. He is described as "bad-tempered" in the Talmud, although the saying "Welcome everyone with a cheerful countenance" is also attributed to him (*m. Abot* 1:15).

Shavuot. See *Pentecost.

Sheba. See *Queen of Sheba.

Shekinah. God's "presence," which dwells (Heb. *shakan*) in the *tabernacle (Heb. *mishkan*) (Exod. 25:8) and the *temple (1 Kgs. 8:12; Ps. 132:14; Ezek. 43:7). The noun does not appear in the Hebrew Bible but is frequent in rabbinic literature, where it functions like the Memra as a kind of intermediary. It is present when two people discuss the *Torah (*m. Abot* 3:3) and when ten people pray together (*Abot* 3:9). Its light is brighter than the brightest sun (*b. Sanhedrin* 39a) and shines on the saints in heaven (*b. Berakhot* 17a). The similarity of the Hebrew word to Gk. *skene*, "tent, tabernacle," may have influenced the choice of this word as a translation of *mishkan*, "dwelling place," suggesting a temporary structure (John 1:14; Heb. 8:2; Rev. 21:3), whereas the Hebrew word is semantically closer to "being at home" (cf. *shekenim*, "neighbors," Ruth 4:17; Jer. 6:21). (See *Anthropomorphism.)

Shem. Eldest son of *Noah, and ancestor of the Hebrews as well as the Assyrians (Ashur), Syrians (Aram), and South Arabians (Sheba) (Gen. 10:21–31). He and his brother *Japheth, ancestor of the Persians (Madai), Greeks (Javan), and Europeans (Ashkenaz), receive Noah's blessing, while the youngest son, *Ham, ancestor of the Egyptians and the Canaanites, is cursed and condemned to a life of slavery for his part in the story of Noah's drunkenness (Gen. 9:20–27). See *Semitic languages.

Shema (Heb. "hear"). The Jewish declaration of faith, recited morning and evening every day. It consists of the passage beginning "Hear, O Israel, the Lord your God is one" (Deut. 6:4–9) together with Deut. 11:13–21 and Num. 15:37–41. These passages refer to the custom of wearing the *tallit* ("prayer shawl"), and tefillin ("phylacteries"), which contain the complete text written on a tiny parchment scroll, and to the mezuzah on the doorpost of every Jewish house, which contains the first two passages. The Shema also contains the command to "love your God with all your heart and soul and might" and to "teach your children diligently." It was described by Jesus as the first commandment (Mark 12:29), and it is said to have been on Rabbi Akiba's lips as he died a martyr's death. The poetic preface to Primo Levi's post-*Holocaust novel *If This Is a Man* (1947; ET 1960) is a paraphrase of the Shema.

Sheol (AV "the grave"). The shadowy abode of the dead also known in the Hebrew Bible as the Pit (Isa. 38:17–18) and in the NT as Abaddon (Rev. 9:11) or Hades (Luke 16:23 NRSV) or Gehenna (Matt. 5:27–30; RSV "hell"). In Isaiah's satirical lament over the death of the king of Babylon, the ghosts of Sheol are excited by his arrival (Isa. 14:9–11), but more often Sheol is depicted as a place of dust (Job 17:16) where people are forgotten (Ps. 6:5) and have no further contact with God (Isa. 38:18). An alternative view of life after death appears in Dan. 12:1–3, and this was accepted, with some exceptions (notably the *Sadducees), in Christianity, Judaism, and Islam. See *Resurrection.

Shlomo ben Isaac, Rabbi. See *Rashi.

Sibylline Oracles. A collection of sacred Greek writings attributed to sibyls or women prophets, named after places associated with them, for example, the Delphic and Phrygian sibyls. The books were housed in *Rome, first in the temple of Jupiter and then later under Augustus in the temple of Apollo, and consulted on the authority of the Senate in times of crisis. The Rome copies were destroyed by fire in 83 B.C.E. and a commission set up to collect new copies from other parts of the world. Like *Virgil's Fourth Eclogue, which foretells the coming of a messianic age, the *Sibylline Oracles* were appropriated by Jews and Christians, who edited them, adding explicitly Jewish and Christian material, and increased their number to a total of fifteen, of which three are missing. The sibyls then took their place alongside the prophets in Christian tradition, as on the ceiling of the *Sistine Chapel, where there are seven prophets and five sibyls (Delphic, Cumaean, Libyan, Persian, and Erythrean), and in the *Dies Irae: *teste David cum Sibylla* ("as both David and the Sibyl witness").

Signorelli, Luca (c. 1445–1523). Italian artist. Born in Cortona in Tuscany, he worked mainly in Rome, Florence, and Siena, and the huge painting on the walls of the *Sistine Chapel showing the last days of Moses is also usually attributed to him. But he is best known for his decoration of the Chapel of San Brizio in Orvieto Cathedral (1499–1502). This shows the *Preaching of Anti-Christ* (modeled perhaps on the fanatical Florentine preacher Savanorola) and the *Last Judgment* in six extraordinarily crowded scenes based quite literally on passages like Mark 13 and Rev. 20, with allusions to the *Dies Irae, the *Golden Legend*, and other medieval traditions. His style is characterized by attention to anatomical detail and suggestions of violent action.

Simon, Richard (1638–1712).   French biblical scholar. Educated at the *Jesuit school in Rouen and the Sorbonne in Paris, he studied Hebrew, Syriac, and Arabic and defended the Jews when one of their leaders was burned at the stake in Metz in 1670. His most important work was a *Critical History of the OT* (1678), in which he among other things rejects the Mosaic authorship of the *Pentateuch. It was censored by the Catholic hierarchy in France but published in the Netherlands (1680) and later in an English translation in London (1682), where it influenced the poet John *Dryden, the philosopher John Locke, and others. Later scholars, including *Michaelis and *Herder, described him as the founder of OT criticism.

Sinai.   Desert region between the Red Sea and Palestine, where the Hebrews' 40 years in the wilderness began. Mount Sinai, traditionally located on Jebel Musa in the south, was where they stopped on the fiftieth day of their wanderings and received the *Torah from God (see *Pentecost). The Sinai narrative begins with thunder and lightning, earthquake, fire, smoke, and a trumpet blast when they arrive (Exod. 19), and concludes when they leave, in an orderly procession led by the ark of the covenant, on their journey to the promised land (Num. 10). As well as the details of the law itself, including the *Decalogue, it contains an account of the covenant ceremony (Exod. 24), the *golden calf episode (chap. 32), and the building of the *tabernacle (chaps. 35–40). Known also as Horeb, especially in Deuteronomy, it was also the scene of Moses' burning bush experience (Exod. 3) and thought of as the original dwelling of YHWH (Deut. 33:2; Judg. 5:4–5).

In rabbinic tradition *Torah mi-sinai,* "the law from Sinai," refers to the Oral Law, believed to have been given to Moses at the same time as the Written Torah (see *Oral Torah), and Sinai comes to mean authoritative tradition so that a feminist critique of Judaism can be entitled *Standing again at Sinai* (Judith Plaskow, 1990). Paul uses it to refer to the old *covenant (Gal. 4:24–25), while *Gregory of Nyssa interprets it as an allegory for the knowledge of God, depending on the faith of those who seek to climb it. Famous representations of Mount Sinai in art include an enameled miniature on the *Verdun Altar (1181), where it is connected with the flames of the Holy Spirit at Pentecost (1181), and two early paintings by El *Greco, perhaps influenced by *Byzantine iconography (1568–72). In the valley below Jebel Musa stands the ancient Monastery of St. Catherine, which since 1575 has held a special place in the Greek Orthodox Church, and holds an important collection of *icons and *manuscripts, of which the priceless Codex Sinaiticus, now in the British Museum, was once part.

Sirach (Ecclesiasticus).   Popular Christian name for the apocryphal work properly entitled the "Wisdom of Jesus (Jeshua) ben Sira." In the Greek Bible it is known as *Sirachides* ("son of Sirach") from which its Christian name Sirach is derived. In Latin it has been known since the 3rd century as the book of Ecclesiasticus. Heavily dependent on Proverbs and Ecclesiastes, it is in the form of an instruction in which an old man passes on the fruits of his experience and learning to his son (2:1; 4:1; 51:13–30). It contains proverbs and a variety of other types of material, much of it arranged thematically in sections on free will (15:11–20), women (chaps. 25–26), the ideal scholar (chaps. 38–39), and the like. Wisdom, identified with the Torah, is personified in several passages, notably chap. 24, and there are a number of references to the finality of death (e.g., chap. 41). Unusual in the OT wisdom tradition, the history of Israel is celebrated in a lengthy hymn, beginning with Enoch and Noah and ending with Nehemiah and a recent high priest (chaps. 44–50). The book ends with a hymn of thanksgiving and a piece of conventional autobiography (chap. 51).

Written in Hebrew, probably in Jerusalem c. 180 B.C.E. and, according to the prologue, translated into Greek by the author's grandson in Egypt c. 132 B.C.E., it has played a significant role in both Jewish and Christian tradition. Copies of the Hebrew text were found at Qumran, Masada, and the *Cairo Genizah, and it is respected and quoted, although not as Scripture, in Jewish literature, ancient, medieval, and modern. In Christian tradition it is quoted as Scripture by patristic writers, and, although *Jerome questioned its canonicity, it was included in all Greek and Latin mss of the Bible and not considered apocryphal until the Reformation. In church lectionaries readings from Sirach include chap. 24 on the Virgin Mary ("Wisdom speaks her own praises"), 27:30–28:7 on brotherly love, and 44:1–14 on *All Saints' Day ("Let us now praise famous men"), while the author's misogyny (e.g., 25:16–26) and priestly bias (45:6–26, 50:1–24) have also been much commented on.

Sistine Chapel.   A chapel, alleged to be of the same dimensions as Solomon's temple, built for Pope Sixtus IV (1471–84) in the Vatican. It is best known for its ceiling painted by *Michelangelo

(1508–12). This is a work of exquisite imaginative genius on a gigantic scale, consisting of a narrative sequence of nine biblical scenes, starting above the altar, from *creation to the drunkenness of *Noah after the *flood, with the creation of *Eve as the center point. It is surrounded by a series of seven prophets and five sibyls, and at a lower level above the windows, by a series depicting the ancestors of Christ (Matt. 1). In the four corners are the stories of *David and Goliath, *Moses and the brazen serpent, *Esther's victory over Haman, and *Judith's over Holofernes. On the wall behind the altar is *The Last Judgment* also by Michelangelo (1536–41) but painted more than 20 years after the ceiling and in a very different style. It depicts Christ in the center surrounded by the whole human race, either rising toward paradise or sinking toward the gaping mouth of hell, all depicted in vivid, often grotesque images, some of them derived from *Dante.

The walls are decorated with two cycles of huge frescoes designed by *Perugino, assisted by Botticelli, Pinturicchio, *Signorelli, and others, and depict scenes from the life of Moses on one side, corresponding *typologically to scenes from the life of Jesus on the other (1481–82). Perugino's *Handing over the Keys* is one of the most memorable and typifies the ecclesiastical theme of the whole series. Below these paintings, and completing the extraordinary coverage of the whole Bible, were hung tapestries depicting scenes from the Acts of the Apostles, designed by Perugino's pupil *Raphael and woven in Brussels (1515–19). Seven of Raphael's cartoons, drawn to scale, are in the Victoria and Albert Museum, London, while the tapestries themselves are in the Vatican Museums.

Slavery. Both the Hebrew term *eved* and the Gk. *doulos* have a wider semantic range than either "slave" or "servant," but it is clear that slavery was an accepted institution in the biblical world. There is detailed legislation in Exodus (21:1–11), Leviticus (25:39–55), and Deuteronomy (15:12–18; 23:15–16), and many references throughout the Bible, both OT and NT. Legislation about the treatment of slaves is clearly influenced by the exodus story: "Remember that you were a slave in the land of Egypt" (Deut. 15:15; cf. Lev. 25:42, 55). Regulations for the release of slaves is the subject of the first law in the book of the covenant (Exod. 21:1–11), and an escaped slave is to be protected and not returned to his master (Deut. 23:15–16.; cf. Philemon). Although for baptized Christians there is "neither slave nor free" (Gal. 3:28; 1 Cor. 12:13), master-slave relations are often referred to in the NT (e.g., Eph. 6:5–7; 1 Tim. 6:1–2), and applied to the status of Christians before God (Rom. 1:1; Phil. 1:1; cf. Mark 10:42–45), as well as to the *Son of God himself, who "took the form of a slave" (Phil. 2:7).

Slavery became less widespread in the centuries following *Constantine, although legislation modifying the status of slaves rather than abolishing it was passed by Justinian in the 6th century. *Augustine, *Thomas Aquinas, and others argued that slavery was a result of the fall. From the 16th century European settlers in America reduced thousands of Native Americans, and later Africans, to slavery, supported by Christian interpreters of the Bible, citing the conquest of *Canaan (Deut. 20), the mark of *Cain (Gen. 4), and the curse of *Ham (Gen. 9:25–27) as scriptural authority for their actions. Counterarguments from Scripture based on the prophets' call for justice and mercy (Mic. 6:8), Jesus' condemnation of materialism and greed (Matt. 6:25–33), and the notion of a God who is biased in favor of the poor and needy (Isa. 10:1–2) eventually prevailed and slavery was officially abolished in the 19th century; but these perspectives are still needed to combat continuing "body trafficking" and the exploitation of children and the vulnerable. See *Liberation theology.

Sluter, Claus (c. 1350–1405). Flemish sculptor. His most famous piece of biblical interpretation is on the hexagonal *Moses Well* in Dijon, which shows six prophets carrying scrolls foretelling Christ's *passion: Moses (Exod. 29:39), David (Ps. 22:16), Isaiah (53:7), Jeremiah (Lam. 1:12), Daniel (9:26), and Zechariah (11:12).

Smith, William Robertson (1846–94). Scottish theologian and orientalist. His brilliant application of historical criticism, seen first in the article on "Bible" in the *Encyclopaedia Britannica* (1875), led to a charge of heresy in his church and removal from the chair of Hebrew and Old Testament exegesis at Aberdeen (1881). As professor of Arabic at Cambridge, as well as university librarian and editor of the *Encyclopaedia Britannica*, he continued his pioneering work with *The Old Testament in the Jewish Church* (1881), *The Prophets of Israel* (1882), and *Lectures on the Religion of the Semites* (1889) until his early death. His concern to get at what the prophets were saying to their own people and apply it to contemporary religious experience, alongside his groundbreaking studies of the sociology of ancient Semitic religion, left its mark on biblical scholarship to this day, even though some of his ideas (e.g., on totemism and communion sacrifice) have been rejected.

Sociology. The study of social patterns and institutions. The term was coined by the French philosopher Auguste Comte (1798–1857) and first successfully applied to biblical studies by W. Robertson Smith in *The Religion of the Semites* (1889). More recently there have been many important sociological studies of biblical subjects, informed by both *archaeology and contemporary socioeconomic, political, and psychological research. These include the settlement of the "tribes of YHWH" in Canaan (N. K. *Gottwald), the reign of David (J. W.

Flanagan), OT prophecy (R. R. Wilson, R. P. Carroll), apocalypticism (P. Hanson), the "first urban Christians" (W. A. Meeks, H. C. Kee), property and riches in the early church (M. Hengel, G. Theissen), Mark's Gospel (V. Robbins, C. Myers), and women (B. J. Brooten, E. A. Clark). Many of these and similar studies have revolutionized our way of approaching the Bible even if, in some cases, lack of evidence makes the sociologists' task extremely difficult.

Sodom and Gomorrah. The names of two legendary "cities of the plain," traditionally identified with the desolate wasteland south of the Dead Sea, and said to have been utterly destroyed by fire and brimstone because of their wickedness (Gen. 18–19). The biblical story tells how *Abraham interceded for them, arguing that they should be saved if ten righteous men could be found there, and how his nephew Lot and his family fled from Sodom just in time, though his wife looked back and was turned into a pillar of salt. The homosexuality of the Sodomites is implied in the story (Gen. 19:5) and produced the offensive term *sodomy*, though the sin of Sodom is defined very differently in Ezek. 16:49. In art the destruction of Sodom and Gomorrah inspired dramatic paintings by *Dürer, *Turner (1805), John Martin (1852), and others; but the role of Lot and his wife and daughters in the story is much more frequent, from a 4th-century Christian *sarcophagus to works by *Raphael, *Rembrandt, *Rubens, Velazquez, *Delacroix, and *Dali.

Solomon (Heb. *Shlomo*; Arab. *Suleyman*). King of Israel, son of David and Bathsheba, also called Jedidiah, "beloved of the LORD" (2 Sam. 12:25; cf. Ps. 127:2). Remembered as one who "excelled all the kings of the earth in riches and wisdom" (1 Kgs. 10:23), his reign was a time of unparalleled peace and prosperity when the *temple was built and good relations established with Tyre, Egypt, and, thanks to a visit from the *Queen of Sheba, parts of southern Arabia and eastern Ethiopia. His many marriages to foreign women and support for their religions, however, incurred divine displeasure; and when he died his kingdom split into two parts, Israel in the north and Judah in the south. In the NT his glory is less than that of "the lilies of the field" (Matt. 6:29) and his wisdom excelled by that of Christ (Matt. 12:42).

There are impressive archaeological remains of 10th-century B.C.E. Solomonic cities at Hazor, Megiddo, and Gezer (1 Kgs. 9:15), but any trace of the First Temple at Jerusalem has yet been found, and "Solomon's mines" at Timna in the southern Negev date from an earlier period. Scholarly attempts have been made to reconstruct a "Solomonic enlightenment" supported by evidence for *literacy activity, international contacts, and internal peace, and close parallels to *Proverbs such as the Egyptian Instruction of Amenemope make an early origin for important parts of the Israelite wisdom tradition possible, but scholars are nearly unanimous in giving a postexilic date to most of the Solomonic literature as it has come down to us.

There are innumerable legends in Jewish midrash about Solomon, such as his ability to understand the speech of birds and animals; his magic carpet, which enabled him to breakfast in Damascus and dine in Media; his huge hippodrome rivaling that of the Roman emperors; above all his magnificent throne and how it was usurped by the demon Asmodeus. Solomon's seal was a magic amulet prized by Jews and Christians alike. The Qur'an elaborates the stories of his liaison with the Queen of Sheba (27:16–45), his warhorses (38:30–31), and his death (34:13), and makes him a devout follower of Allah. Early Christian tradition saw Christ prefigured in Solomon as king and judge, and as riding on an ass (1 Kgs. 1:38). He came to be proverbial for the wisdom of

both philosopher (*Dante) and magician (*Luther), and increasingly remembered for his famous words from Ecclesiastes, "All is vanity" (W. M. Thackeray 1847–48). In art an early fresco showing Solomon on his throne appears at Dura Europos (3rd century C.E.) and there are paintings of his dream at Gibeon (1 Kgs. 3:3–15) (Giordano, *Chagall), the *Judgment of Solomon* (1 Kgs. 3:16–28) (*Raphael, *Poussin, *Blake), and the visit of the Queen of Sheba (*Piero della Francesca, *Tintoretto, Holbein).

Solomon, Testament of.   See *Testament of Solomon.

Son of God.   In the Hebrew Bible "sons of God" (Heb. *bene elohim*) are "divine beings, angels, members of the heavenly court" (Gen. 6:1–4; Job 1:6; 38:7), just as the "children of Israel" (*bene yisra'el*, Exod. 15:1) are "Israelites," and the "daughters of Israel" (*benot yisra'el*; Judg. 11:40) are "Israelite women." In NT Greek the term *huioi theou* is applied to "angels" (Luke 20:36) or "saints" (Matt. 5:9; cf. Wis. 8:7). The singular "son of God" does not occur in the OT, but appears in the Apocrypha (cf. 2 Esd. 7:28) and the *Dead Sea Scrolls as a messianic title, and is frequently applied to Christ in the NT. At an early stage it may have been intended to indicate that he was a divine agent like *Michael and *Melchizedek, or raised to divine status after his death like a Roman emperor (Mark 15:39). There are already in the NT references to his preexistence (John 1:1–14; Phil. 2:5–11), however, and to a unique relationship between divine Father and Son (John 14; Gal. 4:4–6), providing scriptural authority for the church's doctrine of the second person of the Trinity as both "*Son of Man" and "Son of God."

Son of Man.   A common term in Hebrew (*ben adam*) and Aramaic (*bar nasha*), somewhat awkwardly translated

into Greek and other languages. It normally means a member of the human race ("son of Adam," Ps. 8:4; Isa. 51:12), and is used repeatedly by God to address the prophet Ezekiel (cf. "O man," Mic. 6:8). Its application to a messianic figure in Daniel, where it distinguishes him from the four great beasts (Dan. 7:13), and the Similitudes of *1 Enoch* (e.g., chap. 46), suggests that the term, especially in Greek, is allusive and would normally refer to something more than "an ordinary human being." The "Son of Man" appears in explicitly apocalyptic contexts in the NT (Mark 13:26; Rev. 14:14), but also in passages where his humanity is at issue (Matt. 17:22), and scholars are not agreed on the significance of its application to Jesus. Some say it always refers to a messianic figure, while others argue that Jesus may have originally used the term (in Aramaic) in the sense of "me, a mere mortal." Patristic scholars found in the NT titles "Son of God" and "Son of Man" ideal scriptural authority for their doctrine of the two natures of Christ. George *Herbert, in his sonnet *The Son*, celebrates the wordplay by which "we give one only name / To parents' issue and the sun's bright star . . . We him in glory call, The Son of Man." *Jesus: The Son of Man* was a best-seller by the Lebanese American Khalil Gibran (1928), and more recently the film *Son of Man* (2006) is a life of Jesus set in South Africa. Very different is René Magritte's famous surrealist self-portrait entitled *The Son of Man* (1964).

Song of Songs (or Song of Solomon; Heb. *shir ha-shirim*, "Song of Songs"; Lat. *Cantica Canticorum*; "Canticles"). A short collection of love poems attributed to Solomon and included in the Hebrew Bible as one of the Five Scrolls. Its place in the *canon, despite its erotic imagery and the absence of any reference to Israel or God, was strongly defended by Rabbi *Akiba, who said, "All the world is not worth the day on which it was written" (*m. Yadayim* 3:5), on the grounds that it is

an expression of God's love for his people. It is the scroll prescribed to be read at *Passover, celebrating God's redemption of Israel.

Ancient and medieval Christian commentators, who similarly applied it to the relationship between God and the soul or Christ and the church, include *Origen, *Jerome, *Gregory the Great, the Venerable *Bede, and particularly *Bernard of Clairvaux, whose eighty-six homilies on the first two chapters were influential within the monastic tradition. Some also advocated a mariological interpretation which led to its use at feasts of the Virgin. Some of the Reformers, including *Calvin, favored a literal interpretation of human love as inspired and blessed by God, while their Catholic contemporaries John of the Cross and Teresa of Avila, continuing the allegorical tradition, applied the poem to their experience of mystical union with Christ. Modern scholars cite parallels from ancient and more modern Near Eastern wedding poetry and understand the book as a celebration of human love, perhaps a commentary on Gen. 1–3 (*Barth, *Trible).

The language and images of the Song have inspired many artists and composers. There are paintings by *Chagall and *Dali, black Madonnas are often inscribed with the words "I am black but comely" (Song 1:5 AV), and the enclosed garden (*hortus conclusus*, 4:12) is frequent as a symbol of Mary's virginity (e.g., Fra *Angelico's *Annunciation*). In Monteverdi's *Vespers* (1610) verses from the Song alternate with Psalms, and *Vaughan Williams's choral work *Flos Campi* ("Flower of the Field"; 1925) was inspired by 2:1. "My beloved is mine" (2:16), set to music by *Britten (*Canticles*, 1947), is also a popular song in many languages, including the original Hebrew (*Dodi li*). One of Toni Morrison's most successful novels is *The Song of Solomon* (1977), and *Love Is Strong as Death* (8:6) is the title of a study of bereavement (J. D. Freeman and P. White, 1999) and an autobiographical novel by a former Catholic priest (William F. Powers, 2006).

Song of the Three Children. One of the additions to the book of *Daniel, after 3:23 in the LXX and Vg, included in the OT *Apocrypha. It contains the Prayer of *Azariah, one of the three young men (Dan. 1:7) thrown into the fiery furnace by Nebuchadnezzar, and the hymn sung by them during their ordeal ("Bless the Lord . . . for he has delivered us from the burning fiery furnace," v. 66). Part of it became the canticle known in Latin as the *Benedicite, "Bless (the Lord)," beginning, in the English version printed in the Book of Common Prayer, "O all ye works of the Lord, bless ye the Lord" (35–68). The three figures appear in early Christian art, sometimes dressed as Persians and prefiguring the three wise men.

Sortes Biblicae. A means of divination whereby an oracular answer could be received by selecting a page and verse of the Bible at random. The same procedure was used with Homer's *Iliad* (*Sortes Homericae*), Virgil's *Aeneid* (*Sortes Virgilianae*), and the Qur'an (*Sortes Koranicae*). Although banned by the church, a number of mss of the Bible, including the 5th-century Codex Bezae, contain evidence that the practice was widespread. It appears to have influenced *Augustine's discovery of Rom. 13:13–14, which changed his life (*Confessions* 8.12). Citing Prov. 16:30, John Wesley and others have used sacred Scripture in this way to find out God's will.

Source criticism. A major branch of modern *historical criticism concerned to identify and analyze literary sources used by the biblical authors. The method was applied first and most elaborately to the *Pentateuch when inconsistencies, anachronisms, and variations in style made Mosaic authorship virtually impossible, and the search for alternative author(s) necessary. Two sources were identified by *Astruc in 1753, one using the name Elohim for God (Gen. 1), the other YHWH (Gen. 3), and subsequent scholars, notably *Wellhausen, developed the four-source (JEDP) hypothesis, each assigned a date, author, and original context that were then further refined. The method has been applied to many other texts, including the Gospels; for example, Matthew and Luke can be shown to be using two sources: Q, containing the sayings of Jesus, and Mark. Recent scholarship, aware of the risk of fragmenting the text and neglecting its meaning, focuses on authorship, the redaction process and the relationship between the sources. See *Documentary Hypothesis; *Redaction criticism; *Synoptic problem.

Speculum humanae salvationis (Lat. "Mirror of Human Salvation"). A popular medieval source book. It was composed c. 1324 by Ludolph of Saxony, a *Dominican friar, and is known to us from 350 mss, 70 of them illustrated, and several early printed editions. Four illustrations accompany each of the 40 NT subjects, one of them depicting the scene itself, the other three containing types or antecedents. These are taken not only from the OT, as in the *Biblia Pauperum*, but also from Jewish and pagan sources, thereby proclaiming that the whole of human history, not just the biblical story, is *salvation history, embraced within God's plan.

Spencer, Stanley (1891–1959). English painter. His paintings were often controversial, and it was not until after two world wars, which inform much of his work that he was made a Royal Academician and knighted. Among his paintings are several representations of the resurrection, one set in the churchyard at Cookham, Berkshire, where he lived (1924–27), and another in a shipbuilding yard at Port Glasgow on the

Clyde, where he worked for a time (1950). Others on biblical themes include *The Sword of the Lord and Gideon* (Judg. 7:18), *Man Goeth to His Long Home* (Eccl. 12:5), *Joachim among the Shepherds* (based on *Giotto from the apocryphal life of *Mary), the *Centurion's Servant* (Luke 7), and *Christ Carrying the Cross* (1920).

Spinoza, Baruch (Benedict de)

(1632–77). Dutch Jewish philosopher. His radical views on the Bible and religion in general led to his being placed under the ban (*herem*) by the Jewish community in Amsterdam in 1656. He moved to Rijnsburg, Voorburg (1662–69), where he published a treatise on Descartes (1663), and later to the Hague (1670–77), where his *Tractatus Theologico-Politicus* was published anonymously in 1670. In this he advocated a scientific approach to biblical interpretation that anticipated much of what came to be known as *historical criticism. He stressed the importance of reconstructing the original literary and social context as accurately as possible, examining the process of canonization, and seeking rational explanations for miracles. He argued that the whole narrative from Genesis through Kings was the work of Ezra, whose ethical and political aims and interests are evident throughout. In his major work, the *Ethics*, published posthumously in 1677, he advocates a thoroughgoing pantheism, rejecting the notion of a personal God and an immortal soul. His influence as one of the great 17th-century rationalists on philosophers like *Hegel and *Schleiermacher and literary critics like Goethe and *Coleridge was considerable.

Spiritual meaning.

The deeper nonliteral meaning of Scripture, advocated by most early Christian commentators, following Paul's famous dictum: "the letter killeth but the spirit giveth life" (2 Cor. 3:6 AV). The notion was applied particularly to texts concerning circumcision, dietary laws, sacrifice, and the like, which the Jews took literally, although many Jewish writers from *Philo on were equally well aware of the distinction between *literal and nonliteral meanings.

Spurgeon, Charles Haddon

(1834–92). English Baptist preacher. As pastor in Southwark, London, from 1854, his sermons were so popular that a new church, known as the Metropolitan Tabernacle, seating 5,000, was built for him. He disapproved of his church's modest acceptance of new *historical-critical methods of biblical exegesis and resigned from the Baptist Union in 1887, but his sermons, published in 50 volumes and translated into many languages, remain popular to this day.

Stabat Mater dolorosa

(Lat. "The mother stood grieving"). A popular medieval Latin hymn describing the suffering of *Mary the mother of Jesus at the crucifixion. The only explicit biblical reference is to the words of Simeon to Mary in the temple: "a sword will pierce your soul also" (Luke 2:35). Its author is unknown but it is frequently attributed to Jacopone da Todi (d. 1306). It found its way into the liturgy in the later Middle Ages, and has been set to music by numerous composers, including *Palestrina, Pergolesi, *Haydn, *Verdi, Rossini, Poulenc, and Arvo *Pärt (1985).

Stainer, John

(1840–1901). English composer. Born in London and first employed as an organist at the age of 16, he was appointed organist at Magdalen College Oxford in 1860 and St. Paul's Cathedral London in 1872. He was knighted by Queen Victoria in 1888 and became professor of music at Oxford in 1889. Among his numerous compositions are two cantatas, *The Daughter of Jairus* (1878) and *St. Mary Magdalen* (1887), and two oratorios, *Gideon* (1865) and, his best-known work, *The Crucifixion* (1887), which includes the chorus "God so loved the world" (John 3:16), especially popular in *African American churches. He also composed many anthems such as "And Jacob was left alone" (Gen. 32:24), "How beautiful upon the mountains" (Isa. 52:7) and "What are these that are arrayed in white robes?" (Rev. 7:13).

Stanton, Elizabeth Cady (1815–1902). American Presbyterian social reformer. Active in the antislavery movement and first president of the National Women's Suffrage Association, she coauthored a *History of Woman Suffrage* (3 vols., 1887) and wrote an autobiography entitled *Eighty Years and More: Reminiscences 1815–1897* (1898). Her *Woman's Bible* in two volumes (1895, 1898; repr. 1974) contains only passages specifically about women and passages in which they are conspicuous by their exclusion (about one-tenth of the canon) with a brief commentary. It is witty and incisive, the first serious attempt to tackle the issue, but rejected by the church and biblical scholars until the 1990s. The title of *The Women's Bible Commentary* (ed. C. Newsom and S. Ringe, 1992; 2nd ed. 1998), however, was a conscious tribute to her pioneering work. See *Feminism; *Womanism.

Stations of the Cross. A sequence of 14 stopping places along the "Way of the Cross" (Lat. *Via Crucis*), the route taken by Jesus from Pilate's house to the Holy Sepulchre. From the Middle Ages, at the instigation of the *Franciscans, who had custody of the holy sites in Jerusalem, the route was identified and followed by Christian pilgrims in an annual act of devotion on *Good Friday. The custom spread to Europe in the 15th century and the 14 "Stations" officially listed by a Franciscan c. 1720. Now they can be seen in all Catholic churches, often designed by distinguished painters and

sculptors (*Tiepolo, Eric Gill, André Girard). They are: (1) Christ is condemned to death (Luke 23:24), (2) he receives the cross (John 19:17), (3) he falls for the first time, (4) he meets his mother, (5) Simon of Cyrene is made to help him (Luke 23:26), (6) Veronica wipes Christ's face, (7) he falls a second time, (8) he meets the women of Jerusalem (Luke 23:27–31), (9) he falls a third time, (10) he is stripped of his garments, (11) he is nailed to the cross, (12) he dies on the cross, (13) his body is taken down from the cross and laid in the arms of Mary (*Pietà*), (14) his body is laid in the tomb. Some of these scenes, particlarly (4), (6), and (13), are not in the canonical Gospels and are derived from apocryphal works such as the *Acts of Pilate. An alternative scriptural sequence was created in 1991 by Pope John Paul II and since then celebrated annually in the Colosseum in Rome.

Steinbeck, John (1902–68). American novelist. His novel *The Grapes of Wrath* (1939), which was made into a successful Hollywood film in 1940, is a study of poverty and social injustice in the United States and a powerful indictment of capitalism that earned him the Pulitzer Prize. His other novels, especially *East of Eden* (1952), a 1917 version of the *Cain and *Abel story, also made into a film starring James Dean, have been much studied for their use of biblical language and imagery. He was awarded the Nobel Prize for Literature in 1962.

Strauss, David Friedrich (1808–74). German theologian. A student of *Baur and influenced by *Schleiermacher and Hegel, his most famous work is a *Life of Jesus* (1835–36), translated into English by George Eliot (3 vols. 1846), in which he denies the historicity of everything supernatural in the Gospels. This led to his dismissal from his teaching post at Tübingen. His history of Christian doctrine from the beginning to Hegel, published in 1840–41, was equally devastating, but his brilliant critique of Schleiermacher, *The Christ of Faith and the Jesus of History* (1865; ET 1977), may be said to have inaugurated the era of modern NT criticism.

Stravinsky, Igor (1882–1971). Russian composer. Studied with Rimsky-Korsakov and, for Diaghilev, composed the ballets *Firebird* (1910), *Petrushka* (1911), and *Rite of Spring* (1913), which made his name in the West. He became a French citizen in 1934 but in 1939 moved to the United States, where he spent the rest of his life. His interpretations of biblical themes include an apocalyptic musical play *Flood* (1962), a cantata *Babel* (1944), a sacred ballad *Abraham and Isaac* (1963), and his best-known choral work *Symphony of Psalms* (1933) based on Pss. 38:13–14; 39:2–4; and 150.

Structuralism. An interdisciplinary methodology concerned with surface structures in a text as opposed to questions about authorship and historical context. Evolving from the writings of the linguist Ferdinand de Saussure, the anthropologist Claude Lévi-Strauss, and the Russian folklorist Vladimir Propp, its application to the Bible by Edmund Leach, Roland *Barthes, and others opened a new chapter in the history of interpretation. By analyzing the tensions or binary oppositions between elements within a text, and, at a deeper level, between it and another text (e.g., a biblical story and a classical myth), insights into its meaning emerge that had been concealed by earlier *allegorical, *historical-critical, or other methods. Despite its shortcomings as an independent or self-contained methodology, its influence on biblical studies has been significant and beneficial. See *Anthropology; *Postmodernism; *Semiotics.

Supersessionism. The claim that Judaism has been superseded by Christianity, in particular that the old *covenant made with the Jews at *Sinai (Exod. 19–24) has been cancelled by a new covenant (Luke 22:20; 2 Cor. 3:6), and the old *Israel replaced by the church as the "New Israel." A major factor in the history of Christian *anti-Semitism from the beginning, it influenced attitudes toward the OT, rejected by *Marcion, read in translation and interpreted christologically by most Christian interpreters, and "dejudaized" by Hitler, but more seriously it affected Christian perceptions of the Jews and Judaism as not only inferior, but heretical and a challenge to the church's authority. In modern times, especially since World War II, the rich variety, truth, and value of Jewish traditions alongside those of Christianity and Islam have been increasingly appreciated by non-Jewish scholars, and the church hierarchies have gone some way toward recognizing the dangerous errors of supersessionism.

Susanna. Apocryphal addition to the book of *Daniel, appearing as chap. 13 in the LXX and Vg. It tells the story of how Daniel came to the rescue of a beautiful and virtuous young woman, falsely accused of adultery and condemned to death by two elders whose advances she had rejected. The story became popular in Christian tradition as an allegory of the soul saved from the *devil, and there are many paintings of *Susanna and the Elders* from 3rd-century *catacombs to the Renaissance masters Veronese (1560), Van Dyck (1618), and *Rubens (1635–38). *Handel composed an oratorio *Susanna* (1749), and there is a famous allusion to the story in the *Merchant of Venice* ("A Daniel come to judgment!").

Swedenborg, Emanuel (1688–1772). Swedish scientist and mystic. After a successful career as a scientist, at the age of 55 he experienced a supernatural call to found the "New Church" within the existing institutions, but distinct from them in its teaching. He studied Scripture, applying his own scientific/mystical exegetical method and redefined the OT *canon as the Pentateuch, Joshua, Judges, Samuel, Kings, Psalms, and the Prophets, and the NT as the Four Gospels and Revelation. His numerous publications, some in Latin, include *Heaven and Hell* (1758), *Divine Love and Wisdom* (1763), and *The Apocalypse Revealed* (1766), and were widely read in his own day, referred to by Kant, *Blake, *Coleridge, and others. The Church of the New Jerusalem was founded in London in 1787 and today has a membership of around 40,000 Swedenborgians worldwide.

Symbol.   The importance of symbols in biblical interpretation has frequently been neglected partly because of suspicion of images in general (cf. Exod. 20:4–6; Isa. 44:9–20), and partly because of historical concerns that focus on exodus, exile, resurrection, and the like as facts rather than on their significance as symbols. While the fantastic symbolism of *Ezekiel, *Daniel, and *Revelation has always been appreciated, as have the menorah, the hand of God, the dove, the *fish, and other traditional symbols in Jewish and Christian *art and architecture, reading the Bible as primarily symbolic has always been controversial. In the early church Alexandrian *allegorical interpretations were challenged by the Antiochenes, who favored a more literal reading of the text. The Reformers fiercely rejected medieval symbolism, associated with Rome, in favor of a historical interpretation; and in modern times those who read Scripture symbolically, like *Blake, *Bultmann, and Austen Farrer, have been treated with extreme caution by many because they seem to question the historicity of the Bible. More recently the work of structural anthropologists, literary critics, semioticians, and others have heightened awareness of the issue and shown how the recognition of symbols is an essential part of the reading process—

which alone explains the impact of the Bible on 2,000 years of literature, art, and music. See *Anthropology; *Attributes; *Emblem; *Semiotics.

Symmachus   (2nd century C.E.). Author of a Greek translation of the Hebrew Bible. Like *Aquila and *Theodotion, he was probably a Jewish proselyte. His version is in a readable style and sacrifices verbal accuracy to theological or literary acceptability. *Anthropomorphisms in the Hebrew text, for example, are often absent from Symmachus's Greek. It was in the fourth column of *Origen's *Hexapla.

Synagogue.   Greek term, corresponding to Heb. *bet ha-knesset,* for the building where Jews assembled (Gk. *synago;* cf. Joel 2:15–16) for worship and instruction. Known also as *bet ha-midrash,* "house of instruction" (cf. Sir. 51:23) and in Yiddish as *shul,* "school," its origins are obscure. It has been suggested that the institution goes back to the Babylonian exile, but in that case it would be strange that it is not mentioned explicitly in the Hebrew Bible. The meeting of elders at Ezekiel's house (Ezek. 14) could be the beginnings of some kind of synagogue. The *Talmud interprets "the small [or temporary] sanctuary" in Ezek. 11:16 and "the meeting places of God" in Ps. 74:8 as references to synagogues in foreign lands. Synagogue inscriptions dating from the 3rd century B.C.E. have been found in Egypt, and 1st century B.C.E.–1st century C.E. synagogues have been identified in Delos in Greece and at Masada, Gamla, and elsewhere in Israel. Synagogues are mentioned frequently in the NT, and, according to a reference in the Talmud (*b. Ketuvot* 105a) there were 394 in Jerusalem when it was destroyed in 70 C.E. By the 7th century we have hundreds of synagogue inscriptions and synagogue remains, often beautifully decorated (*Dura Europos, Beth Alpha, Gaza, Mopsuestia), from all over the world.

Synagogue worship was never seen as a substitute for *temple worship. Prayers for the rebuilding of the temple are still recited daily, and, along with the ban on animal sacrifice, the use of a menorah and musical instruments is also forbidden in orthodox synagogues because of their association with the temple. The main architectural features of a traditional synagogue are the *ark containing the Torah and other *scrolls in the wall nearest Jerusalem, the *bimah*, "reader's platform," a woman's gallery, a chair for the president, and a genizah or storeroom for damaged or heretical mss. Larger synagogues may also contain a library, a law court, and accommodation for guests. Hebrew texts frequently displayed in synagogue architecture include the *Decalogue, Gen. 28:17, Isa. 26:2, and Prov. 3:18, and verses from Num. 10 are recited when the Torah scroll is brought out of the ark ("Arise, O LORD . . . ," v. 35) and returned ("Return, O LORD . . . ," v. 36).

Synoptic problem.

The literary-critical problem of explaining the relationship of the three Synoptic Gospels, *Matthew, *Mark, and *Luke, which clearly have much in common over against the Fourth Gospel, but also significant divergences. The most common view, the "Two-Source Theory," is that Mark is the oldest Gospel and Matthew and Luke later used Mark and *Q as their main sources. Among other current theories is the proposal, originally put forward in the 18th century, that Matthew was written first, followed by Luke, and finally Mark, in which material from Matthew and Luke is conflated. Much recent scholarship focuses on each of the Gospels as a literary work in its own right, rather than as part of a Synoptic problem, but analyzing the process whereby each reached its present unique form can throw light both on historical questions and on the meaning of particular texts.

Syriac.

A dialect of *Aramaic used mainly by Christians in Syria, Iraq, and other parts of Western Asia to this day. The Syriac script, like Arabic, is a cursive development from the Hebrew alphabet. A vast body of Syriac literature survives, mainly from the 5th–10th centuries, but including the *Peshitta and the works of the 4th-century scholars Aphrahat and *Ephrem. Interesting and important in their own right, Syriac exegetical traditions, themselves much influenced by the school of *Antioch, also influenced Armenian, Coptic, and Ethiopian Christianity in the east as well as, to a lesser extent, Byzantine and Latin tradition farther west.

Tabernacle

(Heb. *mishkan*). Portable sanctuary built by the Israelites at *Sinai (Exod. 25–30) and carried in front of them as they journeyed toward the promised land (Num. 10:33–36). Also known as the "tent of meeting," it was believed to be the "dwelling place" (Heb. *mishkan*) of God (Exod. 25:8–9), represented by a cloud overhead, and access to it was strictly controlled by the priests. The innermost sanctuary or "Holy of Holies" contained only the *ark (*aron*) of the covenant, a box containing the Ten Commandments, covered by a lid known as the mercy seat (*kapporet*) and adorned by two cherubim whose outstretched wings touched over the ark. This room could be entered only once a year by the high priest on *Yom Kippur (Exod. 30:10; Lev. 16). It was separated by an embroidered curtain or veil (*parokhet*) from the main part of the building, in which stood the seven-branched golden lamp (*menorah*), the altar of incense, and the table of the showbread. This was surrounded by a courtyard in which were the main altar, where animal sacrifices were burnt, and a bronze basin for washing (Exod. 30:18). The structure was 30 by 10 cubits (about 15m by 5m) and the courtyard 100 by 50 cubits (about 50m by 25m).

This concept of a mobile sanctuary with the ark of the covenant at its center, and signs that God was with his people in the wilderness, had obvious relevance when the *temple of Solomon was destroyed in 586, and for Jews in the Diaspora after the destruction of the Second Temple in 70 C.E. The ark (now containing the *Torah Scroll) is the focal point of the *synagogue, and Yom Kippur remains the holiest day in the Jewish year. Scholars have suggested that the elaborate description in Exodus was written after 586 B.C.E. as a kind of spiritual reconstruction of the temple, which at the time lay in ruins at Jerusalem, and that the original wilderness shrine was actually a much smaller and simpler structure, perhaps similar to those attested among some modern nomad tribes.

In Christian tradition the tabernacle, built according to a heavenly pattern (Exod. 25:40; Heb. 8–9), foreshadows Christ, who "tabernacles among us" (John 1:14). As containing in its Holy of Holies the Word made flesh (John 1:14), "tabernacle" also became the normal term for the ornamental receptacle of the Blessed Sacrament, placed on the high altar or sometimes in a separate chapel.

Tabernacles, Feast of (Heb. Sukkot).

Also known as "Booths," the autumnal feast celebrating the end of the fruit harvest, and commemorating the period spent by the Israelites in the wilderness when they lived in flimsy huts or "booths" (Heb. *sukkot*). Branches of palm (Heb. *lulav*), myrtle, and willow are waved and citrus fruit carried in procession round the *synagogue. On the eighth day, known as the "rejoicing of the law" (Heb. *simhat torah*), the annual cycle of readings from the *Torah is completed. The book of *Ecclesiastes (Kohelet) was assigned to be read at this feast, and the *Hallel Psalms (113–118) sung, whence the liturgical term "*Hosanna!" associated with the seventh day especially, is derived (118:25). Some of the traditions associated with the Jewish festival have been transferred to *Palm Sunday in Christian tradition (cf. John 12:13).

Tallis, Thomas (c. 1505–85). English

composer. As organist at the Chapel Royal in London, Canterbury Cathedral, and elsewhere, he received support from both Queen Mary and Queen Elizabeth, and composed many successful liturgical works, in English as well as Latin, which earned him the title "father of English cathedral music." Among these are two settings of *Lamentations* and a Christmas Mass, entitled *Puer natus est nobis* (Isa. 9:6). Of his over 40 motets, such as *Audivi vocem* (Jer. 40:10; Matt. 25:6) and *In jejunio et fletu* (Joel 2:12–13), perhaps the most wonderful is his forty-part motet *Spem in alium*, a setting of words based on Jdt. 9:19 and 6:15.

Talmud (Heb. "teaching"). The title

given to the two vast collections of rabbinic teaching, known as the *Oral Torah, which claims at least equal authority with that of the Five Books of Moses or Written Torah. They are known as "Yerushalmi," that is, the Jerusalem or Palestinian Talmud, completed c. 400 C.E. in Palestine, and "Bavli" or the Babylonian Talmud, completed c. 500 C.E. in Babylon. Written mainly in *Aramaic, they are in the form of commentaries on the *Mishnah, each passage of Mishnah being followed by what is known as the *Gemara* (Aram. "completion"), which contains arguments and debates on a great variety of topics (not always relevant to the Mishnah under discussion), as well as stories from the lives of the rabbis, popular legends, science, and folklore. Bavli is more complete than Yerushalmi, and, although later, contains early and authoritative material. Copies of the Talmud were confiscated and destroyed by the church authorities in Paris (1242), Rome (1553), and elsewhere because of alleged anti-Christian passages. Complete translations into German, English, and other European languages have made the Talmud more accessible to contemporary readers. Ancient historians, NT scholars, and others have found it to be a largely untapped source of information on social, political, and religious conditions in the later Roman Empire.

Tamar. Daughter-in-law of Judah whose two sons died leaving her a childless widow (Gen. 38). By disguising herself as a harlot she tricked her father-in-law into committing incest with her (Lev. 18:15), thereby ensuring Judah's line of descent to *David and the *Messiah, for which she is remembered (Ruth 4:12; 1 Chr. 2:4; Matt. 1:3). Parallels with the Joseph story (Gen. 38:5–11: cf. 49:8; 38:27–30: cf. 41:50–52) and with Tamar's less fortunate namesake (2 Sam. 13), as well as possible allusions in Jacob's Blessing (49:8–12), have been much discussed, but her courageous role in the history of Israel's origins has had surprisingly little impact. The meeting of Tamar and Judah inspired a number of painters, including *Tintoretto, *Rembrandt, *Delacroix, and *Chagall.

Tanakh. A popular acronym for the Hebrew Bible, standing for the Law (*Torah), the Prophets (*Nevi'im) and the Writings (*Ketuvim). Cf. *Miqra.

Targum. A translation of the Hebrew Bible into another language, especially *Aramaic. The custom of providing an Aramaic translation of the Bible in *synagogue worship probably goes back to early in the Second Temple period (according to rabbinic tradition the time of Ezra; cf. Neh. 8:7–8), when Hebrew ceased to be the spoken language of most Jews. An official targum of the *Torah, known as Targum Onqelos, was eventually produced in Babylonia c. 100 C.E., and is still printed in all *Rabbinic Bibles. Other targumim of the Torah include Targum Yerushalmi (or "Pseudo-Jonathan") and Targum Neofiti from Palestine, and Targum Jonathan of the Prophets. There are also a number of fragmentary targumim, including those discovered in the *Cairo Genizah and among the *Dead Sea Scrolls.

Targum Onqelos is more literal than the others, but all have a tendency to modify the original to fit later considera-tions, by removing anthropomorphisms, for example, in a sentence like "the LORD came down to see the city" (Gen. 11:5). Paraphrasing is very common; the famous Targum Sheni of Esther, which contains an elaborate description of Solomon's throne, is an extreme example. The value of the targumim for biblical interpretation has been much discussed. Do they provide evidence for how Jesus and Paul understood Jewish Scripture? How early is the messianic reading of the *Servant of the Lord in the Targum of Isaiah (42:1; 52:13)?

Tatian (120–173 C.E.). Christian apologist. Born in Assyria and schooled in Greek philosophy, he converted to Christianity in Rome, where he was a student of *Justin Martyr. He subsequently returned to the East, where he published a robust defense of Christianity, fiercely condemning Greek culture as evil (*Oratio ad Graecos*). Despite the influence of his other more famous work, the *Diatessaron*, a harmony of the four Gospels, his views were criticized by Western theologians, including *Irenaeus, *Tertullian, and *Origen, as well as by the Syriac Church.

Tavener, John (1944–). English composer. His early works include the cantatas *Cain and Abel* (1965) and *The Whale* (1968), based on the story of Jonah. As a member of the Russian Orthodox Church and attracted to *mysticism, especially Sufism, he is best known for his settings of the Orthodox liturgy (e.g., *Trisagion*) and more recently *The Beautiful Names* (2007), a choral meditation on the 99 names of God in the Qur'an, sung in Arabic.

Taw. Last letter in the Hebrew alphabet. Shaped like a *cross in the ancient script, the mark, written in ink on the foreheads of the righteous (Ezek. 9:3–6), was identified as the sign of the cross in

Christian tradition. The "Tau Cross" in Christian iconography, however, particularly associated with Francis of Assisi, is derived from the Greek letter *tau* (τ).

Te Deum (laudamus) (Lat. "[We praise] thee, O God"). A Latin hymn traditionally attributed to *Ambrose on the occasion of *Augustine's baptism, but almost certainly much earlier. It follows the pattern of the Apostles' Creed, drawing on Isaiah's vision of worship in heaven (Isa. 6) and the language of praise from the Psalms, to celebrate the Christian faith and pray for God's mercy. Among many well-known settings of the Latin original are those of *Haydn, Berlioz, *Bruckner, and Kodaly, while English versions for occasions of national thanksgiving were composed by *Handel (1743) and William *Walton (1953).

Temple. The First Temple at Jerusalem, normally referred to as the "house of the LORD" (Heb. *bet YHWH*), was built by *Solomon (1 Kgs. 6–7) on Mount Moriah, where Abraham had sacrificed a ram in place of his son Isaac (Gen. 22) and David had built an altar (2 Chr. 3:1). It contained the "*ark of the Lord," the menorah, the bronze *serpent, and other relics of the wilderness period, and was the center of Judean worship until its destruction by the Babylonians in 586 B.C.E. (2 Kgs. 25). While the temple at Jerusalem lay in ruins, *Ezekiel imagined a new temple, filled with the glory of the Lord, with life-giving water pouring from under its threshold (chaps. 40–48). The Second Temple, built in the days of Haggai and Zechariah immediately after the exile (Ezra 6:14–15), and massively reconstructed by Herod the Great (40–4 B.C.E.) and his descendants, became in the absence of the monarchy a more powerful centralized institution, politically and economically, under the control of a wealthy hereditary priesthood. After it was destroyed by the Romans in 70 C.E., it remained an endur-

ing symbol of Jewish hope, and prayers for the rebuilding of the temple are still said daily in synagogues worldwide.

The *Temple Scroll* from Qumran (2nd century B.C.E.) and a large part of the *Mishnah are devoted to detailed discussions of the structure and rituals of the Second Temple, and there is a lengthy account in Josephus (*Ant.* 15.11). Jesus, following a well-established prophetic tradition, condemns aspects of temple worship (Matt. 21:12–13; cf. Jer. 7:11) and correctly predicts its destruction (Mark 13:2). Even though Jesus himself may not have envisaged Judaism without a temple, early Christians soon saw the church as the new temple (Eph. 2:19–22), from which Gentiles and women would no longer be excluded (1 Pet. 2:5). At the crucifixion the veil of the temple was rent (Matt. 27:51) and in the new Jerusalem there would be no temple because "its temple is the Lord God . . . and the Lamb" (Rev. 21:22). *Augustine, *Calvin, and many others continued this line of interpretation, but many also, including *Bede, *Nicholas of Lyra, and Isaac *Newton, as well as *Rashi, *Maimonides, and other medieval Jewish scholars, attempted detailed historical descriptions of the temple, in the belief that it would one day have to be rebuilt when the Messiah comes. The Knights Templar, founded in 1118 to protect Christian pilgrims, took their name from Solomon's temple.

A celebrated example of the role of the temple in literature is George *Herbert's collection of poems entitled *The Temple* (1633), perhaps in three parts corresponding to the porch (Heb. *ulam*), the temple (Heb. *hekal*), and the Holy of Holies (Heb. *devir*) of Solomon's temple. Another example of a very different kind is William *Blake's recurring use of negative references to the temple as a clumsy human institution interfering with the immediacy of true religious experience. In art fanciful Christian representations of the temple appear frequently in scenes from the life of Christ, such as *Perugino's *Christ Handing the Keys to Peter* in the

*Sistine Chapel (1481). A more ancient and perhaps more accurate recollection of the façade of the Second Temple is represented in a fresco at Dura Europos (3rd century C.E.), while the temple treasures being carried off triumphantly by Roman soldiers are depicted on the Arch of Titus in Rome (1st century C.E.).

No trace of Solomon's temple survives, although ancient parallels to its plan, decoration, and furnishings have been discovered in Phoenicia, Cyprus, and Palestine. Since 1967 archaeologists have discovered substantial areas of Herodian masonry, in addition to the Western Wall, depicted on the Madeba Map (6th century C.E.) and venerated by Jews since the Middle Ages. Today the beautiful Umayyad Dome of the Rock (Mosque of Omar) (685–91 C.E.) stands on the site of the temple, known to Muslims as the "sacred precinct" (Arab. *haram al-sharif*), where Muhammad's heavenly journey began (Qur'an 17:1).

Ten Commandments.   See
*Decalogue.

Tertullian, Quintus Septimius Florens (c. 160–220). Father of Latin theology. Born and educated in Carthage, he converted to Christianity in Rome and then returned to Carthage, where he later became an advocate of the apocalyptic Montanist sect. His works, which are mostly polemical (e.g., *Adversus Judaeos*; *Adversus Marcionem*), display brilliant rhetorical skills as well as a preference for the literal or historical meaning of Scripture, which he quotes and discusses frequently. He believed the church to be the only true interpreter of the Bible and argued against *Marcion for the unity of OT and NT. His only systematic commentary is on the *Lord's Prayer in his treatise *On Prayer*. Although he may have worked with the Greek Bible, he wrote mainly in Latin and had a profound effect on the language of the Western church.

Testament of Abraham.   A 1st-century C.E. pseudepigraphical Jewish work, probably originally written in Greek in Egypt. It tells how the archangel *Michael comes to take Abraham's soul to *paradise, but Abraham refuses to die and is transported in a chariot to see the whole world. Michael also shows him the gates of paradise and the fate of the wicked and the righteous after death. When Death finally comes to him as he lies in bed and tricks him, the angels come and take his soul to heaven (cf. Luke 16:22).

Testament of Adam.   A pseudepigraphical work, known from 6th-century C.E. Syriac and Arabic mss. Probably Jewish in origin with Christian additions, it contains *Adam's last words to his son Seth in which he foretells the coming of Christ and the end of the world. Noteworthy are Christ's words to Adam: "Be not sorrowful . . . I will come down into thy house, I will dwell in thy flesh, for thy sake I will be born as a child."

Testament of Job.   Pseudepigraphical Jewish work of the 1st century B.C.E. or 1st century C.E., surviving in Greek and Coptic mss, and listed among apocryphal texts by the church at the end of the 5th century. It expands the biblical narrative about *Job, giving a more prominent role to his wife, for example, and portraying *Satan in a more favorable light. It also provides early evidence for mystical practices, speaking in tongues, and other Christian phenomena rarely referred to in mainstream Christian tradition.

Testament of Moses.   A pseudepigraphical work also known as the *Assumption of Moses*, although the one extant Latin ms of the work (6th century) contains no mention of his being taken up to heaven (cf. Jude 9). It comprises *Moses' last words to Joshua in which he

reveals, in conventional apocalyptic style, all that is to happen from his death until the end of the world, which for the author, probably a contemporary of Christ, was imminent. His Pharisaic beliefs can be seen in his respect for the Maccabean martyrs (9:1–7; cf. 2 Macc. 6–7) and opposition to the politicization of Judaism.

Testament of Solomon. Pseudepigraphical Jewish text of uncertain date and origin, known only from 15th-century mss and possible references in earlier literature. Probably written in the 1st to 3rd centuries C.E., it is one of the oldest magical texts attributed to *Solomon, and tells how he used a magic ring ("Solomon's seal"), given him by the archangel *Michael, to control the numerous demons that threatened the building of the temple at Jerusalem.

Testaments of the Twelve Patriarchs. A pseudepigraphical work modeled on the last words of *Jacob (Gen. 49) and *Moses (Deut. 33). It contains a wide variety of material including apocalyptic (*T. Levi*) and ethical teaching (*T. Gad*). It was compiled as a single Christian document by c. 200 C.E. but contains earlier Jewish material, possibly from originally separate testaments. Known to the NT writers, especially Paul, who frequently alludes to the *Testaments* (e.g., Rom. 1:32; cf. *T. Asher* 6:2), but rarely cited in the early church, it was widely studied in the Middle Ages, and its date and authorship have been much debated since then. The discovery at Qumran of *Testaments of Levi, Judah,* and other patriarchs in Hebrew and Aramaic, although not themselves the actual sources of the work, make a Jewish origin likely, at least for the genre.

Testimonia. Collections of *proof texts such as the 1st-century B.C.E. *Messianic Anthology* found at Qumran (4Q175). This contains passages from the *Torah predicting the coming of a prophet (Deut. 18:18–19), a royal *messiah (Num. 24:15–17), and a priestly messiah (Deut. 33:8–11). The first Christians had to find scriptural authority for their beliefs (Luke 24:27; Acts 17:2), and it may be that the "words of the Lord" (Acts 20:35) and the "parchments" (2 Tim. 4:13) originally included such *testimonia* as aides-mémoire before the Gospels were available, although no certain evidence of this practice has so far been discovered. See also *Florilegium.

Tetragrammaton. The four Hebrew consonants *YHWH* (יהוה) representing the sacred name of God. In Jewish history down to the present day it has had unique religious significance. In the alphabetical numerical system, for example, the forms *YH* (= 15) and *YW* (= 16) are avoided. Mention is made in the *Talmud of amulets with the Tetragrammaton inscribed on them (*b. Shabbat* 115b) and the use of the *Name in magic formulae is well documented in the Middle Ages. In the *Kabbalah it plays a crucial role, both as a focus of meditation and as in instrument of creation. The Name was believed to be too sacred to utter (cf. Lev. 24:11) except once a year by the high priest on *Yom Kippur when he emerged from the Holy of Holies and pronounced the threefold blessing (Num. 6:24–26; Sir. 50:1–21). There are many cautionary tales about the danger of the Name, including one that, during his martyrdom at the hands of Manasseh, *Isaiah pronounced it in desperation and was swallowed by a tree, which was then sawn in two (cf. Heb. 11:37).

In the *Dead Sea Scrolls the Tetragrammaton is sometimes written in a special ancient Hebrew script, and in some Greek mss it is rendered ΠΙΠΙ in an attempt to represent the Hebrew letters in Greek. On the basis of references in the patristic literature, where it is written in Greek letters as *IABE* or the like, it is thought to have been pronounced

"Yahweh" (Ger. *Jahweh*). In the Hebrew Bible, where it occurs over 5,000 times, it is conventionally pronounced *Adonai* "the LORD" (Gen. 2:4), or *elohim*, "God" (Gen. 15:2), and this is how it is translated into English. The consonants *YHWH* or *JHVH* (*Ketiv) written with the vowels of Adonai (*Qere) produced the hybrid English form *Jehovah*.

The meaning of the name is given in the burning bush story as "the one who is" ("I AM," Exod. 3:14), but the Hebrew verb *hayah*, "to be," has a different semantic range from its English or Greek equivalents, and "the one who is" in this context probably suggests "the one who acts [or intervenes] in history." Some scholars have suggested the name is causative in form and means "he who causes to be" or "creates." The Greek interpretation of the name, *ho on*, the "one who exists" (Exod. 3:14 LXX), is more philosophical, implying that no other gods exist, and thus explicit monotheism. The three Greek letters give the name a Trinitarian form in which it frequently appears in Greek iconography, applied to Christ as well as God the Father. See *INRI.

Textual criticism (lower criticism).

The critical study of a text known only from ms copies, with a view to determining what the original author wrote. In the case of a sacred text like the Bible, copied religiously by specially trained scribes, errors are rare but inevitable, as variations between ms traditions and the ancient versions testify. As early as the 2nd century C.E. the scribes responsible for copying the Hebrew Bible devised a system of textual criticism involving marking doubtful forms and noting corrections in the margin (Heb. *masora*), although many of these were motivated by theological rather than text-critical concerns. For example, the sentence "YHWH remained standing before Abraham" was considered irreverent (cf. Gen. 19:27 AV) and changed to "Abraham still stood before YHWH."

The success of these scribes can be seen in that the surviving mss of the MT show very little variation. Modern text critics, however, have found evidence of a more ancient pre-Masoretic textual tradition in the LXX and other ancient Greek versions, as well as, more recently, in the *Dead Sea Scrolls, which are a thousand years older than the Masoretic mss. Three critical editions of the Hebrew Bible are currently available: the *Hebrew University Bible* (Jerusalem, 1997–), the *Biblia Hebraica Quinta* (Stuttgart, 2004), and the *Biblia Qumranica* (Tübingen, 2005–).

NT textual criticism, unlike OT textual criticism and classical philology, has a bewildering quantity and variety of material to work with. There are papyrus mss going back to the beginning of the 2nd century C.E., not long after the later books of the NT were written, and parchment codices from the 4th century on, totaling well over 5,000 mss. There are also mss of ancient translations of the NT into Latin, Syriac, and Coptic, as well as versions in Armenian, Arabic, and other languages, to which must be added the vast number of quotations in the patristic literature. From the time of *Constantine efforts were made to standardize the text, and by the 9th century a standard Byzantine text had been established. From the 16th century printed editions of the Greek text, by *Erasmus and others, appeared, but it was not until the discovery of Codex Sinaiticus and the work of Tischendorff, Westcott, and Hort in the 19th century that modern NT textual criticism originated. Twentieth-century critical editions of the Greek NT include Eberhard Nestlé (Württemberg, 1898), Alexander Souter (Oxford, 1910; 2nd ed. 1947), and Nestlé-Aland (Württemberg, 1993), culminating in the *Editio Critica Major* (ECM; Münster, 1997–).

Textual critics identified various types of common scribal errors like dittography (writing the same letter or word twice), haplography (omitting a repeated letter or word), and confusing two letters that look alike. They also created a set of rules, for example, "Where there are two readings, the more difficult reading is to be preferred." With the tools of textual criticism it is possible to evaluate the reliability of one ms against another, but also to emend the text where it is problematical and to find meanings considered historically or theologically more appropriate. See *Ketiv; *Manuscripts; *Masoretic Text; *Qere.

Theater. See *Drama.

Thecla. Follower of Paul, not mentioned in the Bible, but said to have been equal to the apostles. A saint in both Catholic and Orthodox tradition, she was venerated particularly at Iconium (modern Konya; Acts 14:1). There is a huge painting by *Tiepolo of *Saint Thecla interceding for the plague stricken* in Este Cathedral near Padua (1759). See *Acts of Paul*.

Theodore of Mopsuestia (c. 350–428). Antiochene theologian and influential biblical exegete. He studied with John *Chrysostom in *Antioch before being appointed bishop of Mopsuestia in 392. Because of his role in the rise of Nestorianism, he was condemned as a heretic at the Second Council of Constantinople in 553 with the result that only fragments of his writings have survived apart from commentaries on Paul's Letters and John's Gospel. His approach to Scripture derived from a background in literary criticism and may be described as historical, showing a keen interest in the original context of each text, as well as in etymological and textual matters. Critics of the *Alexandrian school accused him of treating the text literally, like the Jews, and ignoring the deeper allegorical meanings that make Scripture come alive in its Christian context. In some cases, however, usually on the authority of the NT, he

identified a fuller sense (*sensus plenior*), as in his discussion of the Suffering *Servant and *Jonah as prefiguring Jesus.

Theodoret of Cyrrhus (c. 393–466). Antiochene theologian and exegete. As bishop of Cyrrhus in Syria and personal friend of Nestorius, he became involved in christological controversy, and attended the councils of Ephesus (431) and Chalcedon (451). His writings against *Cyril of Alexandria were eventually condemned by the church, but his commentaries on Paul and most of the OT, in which the influence of *Theodore of Mopsuestia is evident, were recognized as models of the Antiochene method.

Theodotion (2nd century C.E.). Author of a Greek translation of the Hebrew Bible. Like *Aquila and *Symmachus, he was probably a Jewish proselyte. His version appears to have been modeled on the *LXX rather than translated directly from the Hebrew. It was used by *Origen to fill in gaps in the LXX version of *Job and *Jeremiah, and, in the case of the book of *Daniel, Theodotion's Greek was preferred by the church to the LXX from the 4th century on.

Thessalonians, Letters to. Two letters written by Paul from Corinth to the Christians of Thessalonica in northern Greece, where he had recently made many converts, including "a great many of the devout Greeks and not a few of the leading women" (Acts 17:4). The first letter, noticeably affectionate in tone and obviously proud of the new young community, regrets being forced to leave them so suddenly (2:17) and exhorts them to live exemplary lives, appropriate to God's holy people, that will earn the respect of outsiders (4:9–12). He also addresses the bereaved, assuring them that, when the Lord comes again, "the dead in Christ will rise first" and be taken up to heaven along with those who are alive (4:13–18). Second Thessalonians also deals with the second coming, and advises those who appear to have abandoned ordinary life out of apocalyptic enthusiasm that they should not be too anxious or excited because first the antichrist ("the lawless one"), restrained for the moment, must come and take his seat in the temple before the "Lord Jesus slays him with the breath of his mouth" (2:1–12).

The two letters are frequently cited in Christian literature from as early as the *Didache (late 1st century C.E.), and appear in *Marcion's *canon (2nd century C.E.). There are commentaries by John *Chrysostom, *Theodore of Mopsuestia, *Jerome, *Rabanus Maurus, Peter Lombard, *Thomas Aquinas, and *Calvin. Modern scholars now generally accept that 1 Thessalonians is Paul's earliest letter, written c. 51 C.E., and also the authenticity of 2 Thessalonians, although this has been questioned on the grounds that the eschatology and some of the vocabulary differ in the two letters. The identity of the "restrainer" (neuter in v. 6; masculine in v. 7) has been much discussed: traditionally understood to be the archangel *Michael as in other apocalyptic literature (Dan. 12; Rev. 12), he or it is identified by some as the church or the Roman Empire. The doctrine of the rapture, embraced by some millennial sects today especially in the United States, finds its most specific scriptural expression in 1 Thessalonians (4:15–17), as does the title of the 1972 rapturist film *A Thief in the Night* (1 Thess. 5:2).

Lord and my God" (John 20:28), and is present at the scene of the miraculous catch of fish (John 21) and the ascension (Acts 1). According to an early tradition he went as a missionary to the Parthians and founded the Assyrian Church in Iraq, but farther east the Syrian Christians of Kerala believe Thomas brought Christianity to India, where he died as a martyr and was buried at Mylapore, now a district of Chennai (Madras). In 394 his remains were taken to Edessa, the center of the Syriac-speaking church, and in 1228 to Ortona in Italy, where they are still venerated. See also *Acts of Thomas; *Gospel of Thomas; *Infancy Gospel of Thomas.

The church fathers contrasted Jesus' words to Thomas ("Put forth your finger . . .") with those to *Mary Magdalene in the garden ("Do not touch me"), and held him up as a model of faith (John 20:29). He became a popular character in medieval *mystery plays, where some of the apocryphal legends, including those about his Indian connection, make their appearance. In art Doubting Thomas is frequently depicted: a bronze sculpture by Verrocchio in Florence (1483) and paintings by *Caravaggio (1603), *Rubens (1615), and *Rembrandt (1634) are among the best known. There is a tradition that the Virgin gave him her girdle, now venerated in Prato Cathedral near Florence, and this is represented in a number of paintings of The *Assumption with St. Thomas Receiving the Girdle, in the National Gallery, London, the Vatican, and elsewhere.

Thomas (Heb. *te'om*, "twin"; Gk. *Didymus*; cf. John 11:16). One of the twelve disciples, identified in the Syrian tradition with Judas (not Iscariot) (John 14:22). He is briefly referred to in the *Synoptic Gospels, but in the Fourth Gospel offers to die with Jesus (John 11:16) and is associated with the saying "I am the way, the truth, and the life" (John 14:6). After initial disbelief, Thomas addresses the risen Jesus as "My

Thomas Aquinas (c. 1225–74). *Dominican philosopher and theologian. He studied and taught mainly in Paris (1252–56, 1268–72) and the Dominican priories in Naples and Orvieto. His greatest achievement is the *Summa Theologica*, which, along with his other works, was given authoritative status in later Roman Catholic theology (1879). He wrote important commentaries on the four Gospels (*Catena Aurea*, "the Golden Chain"), Epistles, Isaiah, Jeremiah, Psalms, and Job, as well as on some of the works of Aristotle. He sought to use Scripture to establish sound Christian doctrine and was not unsympathetic to some traditional allegorization, but at the same time placed great emphasis on the literal meaning of the text. In his commentary on *Job, Thomas broke with medieval tradition and was the first to interpret the dialogue between Job and his comforters as a serious discussion of divine providence.

Tiepolo, Giambattista (1696–1770).
Italian artist. Last of the great Venetian painters, his rococo style gave a fresh, often somewhat remote interpretation to familiar biblical scenes as in his early frescoes such as the *Sacrifice of Isaac*, *Jacob's Dream*, and the *Judgment of Solomon* (1726–29). Many of his subjects are apocryphal, like the *Martyrdom of St. Bartholemew*, the *Education of the Virgin*, and the *Discovery of the True Cross* (c. 1745), but his *Angel Helping Hagar*, the *Nativity*, *Rest on the Flight to Egypt*, and *Christ Carrying the Cross* are strikingly original.

Timothy, Letters to.   See *Pastoral Epistles.

Tintoretto, Jacopo Robusti (1518–94).
Venetian painter. Perhaps a pupil of *Titian but influenced more by *Michelangelo, Tintoretto lived most of his life in Venice and worked almost exclusively on biblical and religious subjects. Many of his paintings are huge and filled with ordinary people and movement, often giving the subject a fresh and distinctive interpretation, as in the early *Christ Washing the Disciples' Feet* (c. 1547), the *Marriage at Cana* (1561), and his final painting of the *Last Supper*, completed shortly before he died. His decoration of the Scuola Grande di San Rocco in Venice, on which he worked with a large team of assistants for over 20 years, contains an elaborate iconographical scheme, like the one in the *Sistine Chapel, covering episodes from the OT and the NT. In the Albergo (or council chamber) are paintings depicting, on one wall, Christ before Pilate and Christ carrying the cross up a steep Calvary (1566–67) with a brilliant *Ecce Homo* (John 19:5) above the door between them, and on the wall opposite a vast Crucifixion scene (over 5m by 12m). The great Upper Hall has thirteen scenes from the OT on the ceiling and ten from the Gospels on the walls. On the walls of the Lower Hall are eight scenes from the life of the Virgin Mary, including a strikingly original *Annunciation* and the *Circumcision* of her son.

Titian (Tiziano Vecellio) (c. 1488–1576).
Venetian painter. After some years studying with *Bellini and working as assistant to Giorgione, his famous *Assumption of the Virgin* (1516–18), which dramatically shows his appreciation of the genius of *Michelangelo and *Raphael, established him as a great painter in his own right, and his subsequent career is marked by commissions from Emperor Charles V, Pope Paul III, King Philip of Spain, and many others. In addition to great paintings of mythological subjects such as *Bacchus and Ariadne* (1520–22), Titian's wide-ranging religious works have a sensual realism and originality that appeal to the intellect as much as the soul. Typical are his beautiful paintings of the biblical women from the early *Gypsy Madonna* (c. 1510) and *Noli me tangere* (John 20:17; 1511–1512) to the *Presentation of the Virgin at the Temple* (1534–1538), *Annunciation* (1562–1564), and a *Penitent Mary Magdalene* (1567). Striking examples of Titian's fresh approach to familar subjects are his *Cain and Abel*, *David and Goliath*, and *The Sacrifice of Isaac* (1542–1544), now in the Church of Santa Maria della Salute in Venice, and paintings of the *Supper at Emmaus* (c. 1530), and *St. John the*

Evangelist on Patmos (c. 1547). Among a number of extraordinarily poignant scenes from the life of Christ are *Ecce Homo* (1548), the *Entombment* (1559), and two paintings done in the last years of his life, the *Crowning with Thorns* and *Pietà*.

Titus, Letter to.   See *Pastoral Epistles.

Tobit, book of.   First book of the OT *Apocrypha. It tells the story of the pious Jew Tobit, an official in the Assyrian government of *Sennacherib at Nineveh, and his son Tobias. Tobit is aged, blind, and poor. So his son travels to Media to recover a debt owed to him, and, with the help of the angel Raphael, rescues his kinswoman Sarah from the demon Asmodeus, marries her, returns with the money, and heals his father's blindness. After his parents die, Tobias and his family return to Media, where with great joy they receive the news that Nineveh has been destroyed. Filled with echoes of biblical narratives (Isaac and Rebekah, Joseph, Job) and prophecies (Isaiah, Jeremiah, Ezekiel, Amos, Nahum) as well as Jewish folklore (Asmodeus, *Ahikar), the book seeks to promote the best of Jewish ethical and religious tradition, including almsgiving, burial of the dead, and steadfast faith that will ultimately be rewarded. Parallels with *Sirach (c. 180 B.C.E.) and the discovery of Hebrew and Aramaic fragments of the book at Qumran suggest a late 3rd century B.C.E. date for its original composition, probably in Aramaic. Like *Judith, the book did not find its way into the Jewish *canon, although the existence of medieval Hebrew mss prove its continuing use among Jews. But it has been extremely popular in the church since the 1st century. There are commentaries by *Bede and *Nicholas of Lyra, and it is regularly quoted in discussions of asceticism (12:8), marriage (11:5–15), and Christian living in general (chap. 4). Readings from Tobit, especially Tobias's wedding prayer (8:5–8) and Tobit's "prayer of rejoicing" (chap. 13), appear in many lectionaries.

Tobias and the Angel is the title of a play by James Bridie (1930) and a novel by the American writer Frank Yerby (1975), while there is a remarkable new reading of the story in Salley Vickers's novel *Miss Garnet's Angel* (2000). There is also a church opera by the British composer Jonathan Dove (1999). In art Tobias, accompanied by the angel and usually with his dog (11:4), inspired many artists, notably *Rembrandt (1637); Filippino Lippi, who painted the young Tobias twice, once with three angels (1475–1480, 1485); *Raphael, who shows Tobias presenting the Madonna with the fish (cf. Tob. 6:1–8) (1512–1514); and an unusual painting by Domenico Feti in the Hermitage, St. Petersburg, of Tobias healing his father's blindness (Tob. 11).

Torah.   The first and most sacred part of the Hebrew Bible, also known as the Five Books of Moses or the *Pentateuch, believed to have been given to Israel, along with the *Oral Torah, at *Sinai. The term has been translated since the LXX as "law" (Gk. *nomos*) to stress its authority as a rule of life for all Jews, and this has influenced outsiders' perceptions of Judaism. But the Torah contains much more than law, especially in Genesis and the first half of Exodus. The Hebrew word *torah* normally means "instruction" or "teaching" in general, and Moses' "vision" (Deut. 34) of a world in which divine intervention on behalf of the weak culminates in the establishment of a people, equipped with all they need to survive as they journey toward the promised land, comes much closer to gospel than law.

Reading the weekly portion of the Torah (parashah) is the focal point of public worship. The Torah Scroll, with silver finials, wrapped in an embroidered mantle and wearing a silver crown and decorative breastplate, is ceremoniously carried in procession from the holy *ark (*aron ha-qodesh*) to the *bimah* (elevated platform). The "Rejoicing of the Torah" (*simhat torah*) on the eighth day of *Sukkot marks the end of the annual reading cycle (Deut. 33–34) and the start of the next (Gen. 1:1–6:8). In Jewish tradition the Torah is celebrated in many biblical passages, such as Proverbs, where she is identified with Wisdom (e.g., 3:18; 4:9; 6:22); the Song of Songs, where she is God's bride (1:15); and Ps. 119, where every letter of the Hebrew alphabet joins in her praise. According to the *Midrash the Torah was created before the world (cf. Prov. 8:22), given by God to Israel against the advice of his angels, and intercedes for them now that the *temple is destroyed (*Esther Rab.* 7:13). The rabbis say that the Torah is greater than kingship and the priesthood (*m. Abot* 6:6), and that where two or three discuss it together, the divine presence (*Shekinah) rests among them (*Abot* 3:2–6). See *Synagogue.

Tosefta (Aram. "addition"). A compilation of rabbinic sayings and discussions, probably from the same period as the *Mishnah (c. 200 C.E.), and arranged in the same six orders. Little is known about its date and authorship, or about its precise relationship to the Mishnah and *Talmud, which are usually given pride of place among rabbis and scholars alike.

Tradition history or **Tradition Criticism** (Ger. *Traditionsgeschichte*). An approach to the study of texts concerned with the origin of traditions, whether single words ("Hebrew," *kyrios*) or beliefs (divine kingship, *resurrection), and the process whereby they were handed down or adapted to the form in which we have them now. It was partly a reaction against some of the mechanistic excesses of the historical critics who focused exclusively on literary sources (e.g., *JEDP), but also a recognition that real-life situations were involved at every stage in the transmission process. Attention switched from the date of a tradition to its *Sitz im Leben* ("setting in life"), in the cult, in the royal palace, in the lawcourt, or the like, which could be reconstructed with a new degree of precision from available archaeological and social-scientific data.

The method was applied with some success to Genesis and the Psalms (*Gunkel), while a critical analysis of the association of *oral traditions (e.g., the names of God) with individual tribes or sanctuaries brought great benefit to OT study. NT scholars on the whole have found the method on its own less productive, perhaps because the timescale is so much shorter. Tradition criticism, along with *form criticism, *source criticism, and *redaction criticism, remains in the biblical scholars' toolbox, but it is less used than it used to be as a result of current literary and sociopolitical interest in the text as it stands, and in its *reception history.

Transfiguration (Gk. *metamorphosis*). The transfiguration of Christ was when "his face shone and his garments became white as light," *Moses and *Elijah appeared and talked with him, a bright cloud overshadowed them, and a voice from the cloud said, "This is my beloved Son . . ." (Matt. 17:1–8). Peter, James, and John witnessed the event, and it is referred to in 2 Pet. 1:17–18. Allusions to the *Sinai tradition (Exod. 34:29; 24:15–18) indicate that Jesus is here portrayed as a new Moses (Deut. 18:15; Acts 3:22–23), but the incident also reveals his divine nature shortly after Peter's confession at Caesarea Philippi (Matt. 16), and anticipates his *ascension (Acts 1:9).

The "high mountain" where it took place (Matt. 17:1) is traditionally identified (since *Origen) as Mount Tabor in Lower Galilee, and a Church of the Transfiguration has existed there since Byzantine times. The Feast of the Transfiguration has been celebrated on August 6, especially in the Eastern churches, since 1457 in commemoration of a victory over the Turks on that day the previous year. In the West it has been less significant. Its influence on English literature has been slight, Edwin Muir's poem (1949) being a conspicuous exception, but there are many fine paintings of the subject including those by Fra *Angelico (1440–1441), *Bellini (1455, 1487), Botticelli (1500), David (1520), *Raphael (1518–1520), *Blake (c. 1800), and *Dali (1964–1967). *Messiaen composed a large-scale choral work, *La transfiguration de notre seigneur Jésus-Christ* (1969).

Translation.   The first biblical translations were into *Aramaic (*Targum) and *Greek (*Septuagint) during the Second Temple period for the benefit of Jews whose everyday language was no longer Hebrew. But although the Targum remains an important text alongside the MT, and many famous Jewish translations of the Hebrew Bible have been made, from *Saadia's Arabic version and the German versions of Moses *Mendelssohn and Martin *Buber–Franz *Rosenzweig, to the New Jewish Publication Society English version (1962; 2nd ed. 1985), translation has never replaced the original in the way it has done throughout the history of Christianity. From the beginning the *missionary enterprise of the church appreciated the need to communicate with people in as many languages as possible (Acts 2:5–13), and Greek, Syriac, and Latin versions of their sacred texts or parts of them were probably in circulation by the end of the 2nd century C.E., followed soon after by Coptic, Armenian, Ethiopic, Arabic, Irish, Gothic, and Russian. Many of these versions became sacred texts in their own right, like Jerome's Latin *Vulgate, which in the West replaced all other versions until the late Middle Ages. Apart from a few scholars like *Nicholas of Lyra and *Pico della Mirandola, no one knew very much about the original Hebrew of the OT.

Thanks to the courage and vision of scholars and reformers like *Wycliffe, *Hus, *Luther, and *Tyndale, and the invention of the *printing press, vernacular translations of the Bible, many from the original Hebrew and Greek, became widely available by the 16th century. At the same time the church's missionary enterprise that followed the discovery of America in 1492 and rapidly spread to India and East Asia prompted translations of the Gospels into Chinese, Japanese, and some of the Native American languages by the mid-17th century. The creation of the *Bible Societies in the 19th and 20th centuries ensured that this process continued, and today there are translations of the Bible available in over 2,000 languages.

The first complete translation of the Bible into English, made from the Latin Vulgate, was that of John Wycliffe (1380–82), not replaced until the 16th century when several printed versions were produced including those of William Tyndale, Miles *Coverdale, and the *Geneva Bible, culminating in the publication of King James's *Authorized Version (1611) and the Catholic *Douay-Reims Bible (1609–10). The 20th century has seen a proliferation of English versions including *The Complete Bible: An American Translation* (1939), *Revised Standard Version* (1952), *New English Bible* (1970; rev. as *Revised English Bible*, 1989), *New International Version* (1978), *Good News Bible* (1976), and *New Jerusalem Bible* (1985). Some of these use inclusive language while remaining true to the original (e.g., "let us make human beings in our image"). Others introduce the latest archaeological or comparative linguistic theories without regard to style or tradition: "she broke wind" (Judg. 1:14 NEB) for "she dismounted" (REB) is an extreme example, but "the valley of deepest darkness" (Ps. 23:4 REB) for the "valley of the shadow of death" (AV; cf. MT) is not. See *Authority; *Meaning; *Semantics.

Tribes of Israel.   The twelve tribes of Israel make their first appearance at the end of the book of *Genesis where they receive the blessing of Jacob on his deathbed (Gen. 49:28). The book of *Exodus tells how they are transformed into a "kingdom of priests and a holy nation" at *Sinai (Exod. 19:6), symbolized by a ring of twelve standing stones (Exod. 24:4; cf. Josh. 4:19–24), and their names engraved on Aaron's breastplate (Exod. 28:21; cf. Ps. 133:2). See *Aaron. At the end of the *Torah they receive the blessing of *Moses (Deut. 33), and then the book of *Joshua relates how they settled in the regions of the promised land that bear their names.

Most of the patriarchal narratives in Genesis are about Jacob, whose name was changed to Israel (Gen. 32), and his sons ("the sons of Israel"), but especially about *Judah, from whom the Davidic *Messiah would come (Gen. 49:10) as well as the terms "Judean" and "Jew," and about *Joseph, whose two sons Ephraim and Manasseh account for the major part of the northern kingdom (Israel), including Bethel, Shechem, and Samaria. Benjamin, Jacob's favored youngest son by Rachel, who was also Joseph's mother, was the ancestor of Saul, and on his land was the city of Jerusalem. Levi plays a minor role in Genesis (chap. 34) but stands out from the rest in the *golden calf story (Exod. 32), and as ancestor of Moses, Aaron, and all the hereditary priestly families (Deut. 33:8–11), whose descendants, called Cohen ("priest"), Levi, Levin, Lewinsky, or the like, to this day have a special role in Jewish public worship. The Levites possessed no land.

To get behind the complexities of the biblical narrative, modern scholars have sought to identify localized tribal traditions underlying some of the stories. Some have noted parallels with twelve-tribe amphictyonic leagues in ancient Greece and elsewhere (*Noth), while others have applied new socioanthropological and ideological insights to the "conquest" or "settlement" narratives with interesting results (Mendenhall, *Gottwald). More recently attention has switched to the literary subtleties of the stories themselves and how they have been handled, both within the Bible (Ps. 80; Jer. 31:15) and down the centuries. The twelve tribes left their mark on NT tradition (Matt. 19:28; Rev. 7), and today they are perhaps best represented in *Chagall's famous stained-glass windows in the Hadassah Hospital in Jerusalem (1962). There remains to be mentioned the endless speculation in certain quarters about the fate of the "lost tribes of Israel" and who if any can rightfully claim to be their descendants.

Trinity. The doctrine of the Trinity, God in three persons, Father, Son, and Holy Spirit, was worked out against various heresies by the church fathers, especially *Athanasius and *Augustine, and given its most complete expression by *Thomas Aquinas. The doctrine itself is not biblical, but finding scriptural authority for it was an essential part of the process. The three mysterious men addressed as "My lord" by Abraham (Gen. 18) are frequently cited in Trinitarian discourse, as are the creation of men and women "in our image" (Gen. 1:26), the threefold priestly blessing (Num. 6:24–26), the *Sanctus in Isaiah's vision (Isa. 6; cf. Rev. 4:8), and the three persons referred to in passages about the *Servant of the Lord (Isa. 42:1; 61:1; cf. Matt. 3:16–17; John 1:32–34). Solomon praises God for sending both Wisdom (Christ) and his Holy Spirit from on high (Wis. 9:17). A Trinitarian formula occurs in relation to baptism at the end of Matthew's Gospel (where "the name" of the three persons is singular: 28:19), and in the grace at the end of 2 Corinthians (cf. 1 Pet. 1:2), while in the Fourth Gospel the interrelationship of the three persons, Father, Son, and Holy Spirit (Paraclete), is dealt with in some detail (John 14:12–31).

In art the Trinity is often represented by the Father in heaven, above the crucified Christ, with the Dove between them (Botticelli, 1491–93; *Signorelli, 1510). It is also often represented by Abraham's three visitors, especially in Russian *iconography: indeed, wherever they appear, as on *Ghiberti's bronze doors on the Baptistery in Florence (1525–52), they were no doubt interpreted in this way by many. Both *Raphael in his famous *Disputation of the Holy Sacrament* in the Vatican (1509–11) and Dürer in the *Adoration of the Trinity* (1511) show OT kings and prophets acknowledging God in three persons. Despite historical-critical reservations about such Christian interpretations of Scripture, Isaiah's vision gave the church its most familiar Trinitarian expression in the Sanctus and inspired several popular hymns, including Bishop Reginald Heber's timeless "Holy, Holy, Holy, Lord God Almighty."

Trisagion (Gk. "thrice holy"). See *Kedushah; *Sanctus.

Turner, Joseph Mallord William

(1775–1851).   English painter. His beautiful early watercolors of English landscapes and architecture are already innovative, but it was his fascination with sunlight, waves, clouds, and towering mountains in the later oil paintings like *Hannibal Crossing the Alps* (1812), *The Eruption of Vesuvius* (1817), *The Fighting Téméraire* (1839), and *The Slave Ship* (1840), that established him as truly revolutionary and forerunner of the impressionists. Among his biblical paintings, most distinctive are scenes from the OT such as the deluge (1805, 1815, 1843), Jacob's ladder (1830), the fifth and tenth plagues of Egypt (1800–02), and the burning fiery furnace (1832), but he also painted two dramatic illustrations of the Apocalypse: death on a pale horse (Rev. 6:8; 1825) and the angel in the sun (Rev. 19:17; 1846).

Twelve, Book of the.

The twelve Minor Prophets, considered as a book that together with the four Major Prophets (Isaiah, Jeremiah, Ezekiel, and Daniel) in the Christian Bible constitute a prophetic pentateuch. The traditional order of the Twelve appears to be chronological: the first six (Hosea–Micah) prophesied in the second half of the 8th century under the threat of Assyrian invasion; the next three (Nahum, Habakkuk, and Zephaniah) at the end of the 7th century when the Assyrian Empire came to an end with the destruction of Nineveh; and the last three (Haggai, Zechariah, and Malachi) in the early years of the Second Temple period (521 B.C.E.–70 C.E.). Attempts have been made to identify a literary or thematic structure in the book as a whole. In the LXX, for example, the first six are in a different order, ending with Jonah, which then provides a link with Nahum, the other prophet of Nineveh. But most studies treat each book separately, apart from Haggai and Zechariah, the two prophets who helped to rebuild the temple (Ezra 5).

Tyndale, William

(1494–1536). English reformer and translator of the Bible. He studied at Oxford and Cambridge, but when his plan to translate the Bible into English received no support from the church in London, he traveled to Germany, where the first part of his translation was printed in 1525. He was condemned as a heretic in 1536 and burned at the stake at Vilvoorde near Brussels. His translations of the NT, the Pentateuch, and Jonah were printed during his lifetime, and he left Joshua–2 Chronicles in ms form. He worked from the original Hebrew and Greek, although dependent too on Luther's new German version (1522) and the Vulgate, and added explanatory notes where he thought necessary. His English is clear and direct, and had a significant influence on subsequent English versions, including the *Authorized Version.

Typology.

A systematic arrangement of material according to type, in biblical studies applied to literature and art: Isaac carrying the firewood on his back (Gen. 22:6), Samson carrying the city gates of Gaza on his back (Judg. 16:3), and Jesus carrying the cross on his back (John 19:17). From the beginning, Christian interpreters used typology both to make sense of the life, death, and resurrection of Christ and to give new meaning to the OT. Other examples are Jonah's three days and three nights in the belly of a whale (Matt. 12:39–41), "a priest forever after the order of Melchizedek" (Heb. 7), and the miraculous rock that provided water in the wilderness (1 Cor. 10). Popular types of the Virgin Mary are the burning bush (Exod. 3), Gideon's fleece (Judg. 6:36–40), and the "garden locked, the fountain sealed" in the Song of Songs (4:12); and types of the church include Noah's ark (1 Pet. 3:18–22), the twelve tribes (Jas. 1:1), "Mount Zion, the city of the living God" (Heb. 12:22), and the temple of Solomon.

Such typologies are the basis of the illustrations in the *Biblia Pauperum* and the *Speculum humanae salvationis*, and of many other iconographical schemes, including the *Verdun Altar and the *Sistine Chapel, as well as a fundamental part of Christian exegetical tradition as it has developed over the centuries. Unlike *allegory, typology retains and exploits the meaning of the original OT story as well as its Christian application, and has therefore come under less criticism from those scholars and interpreters who favor the literal or original meaning of the text.

Ugaritic. A Northwest Semitic language, closely related to Hebrew, known to us since the discovery in 1929 of a large collection of documents, written in a *cuneiform *alphabet, in the city of Ugarit (modern Ras Shamra) on the coast of Syria, which flourished c. 1400–1200 B.C.E. Ugaritic literature, which is mostly in verse, is similar in style and structure to Biblical Hebrew *poetry. Many words, *word pairs, and phrases are common to both literatures, such as "rider of the clouds" (cf. Ps. 68:4), *al-mawet*, "immortality" (Prov. 12:28 AV; Ugar. *blmt*), and "the sun was ashamed," a reference to a solar eclipse (Isa. 24:23). The biblical myth of a battle between the deity and "Sea" (*yam*; Ps. 89:9; Matt. 8:23–26), "Flood" (*nahar*; Ps. 93), "Leviathan the twisting fleeing serpent" (Isa. 27:1), and other monsters of the deep (Ps. 74:12–14; Rev. 20) has exact parallels in Ugaritic. In the NT Beelzebul, "prince Baal" (Matt. 12:24) is attested in Ugaritic and some of the traditions associated with the death and resurrection of *Baal and the role of his powerful sister, the Virgin Anat, have also left their mark on early Christianity.

Ulfilas (Wulfila) (c. 311–c. 382). Translator of the Bible into Gothic. Born in Visigothic Dacia (modern Rumania), he went to Constantinople, where in 341 C.E., he was consecrated bishop of the Goths, who were at that time Arians. He is said to have translated the whole Bible, except for 1 and 2 Kings, whose warlike stories he feared might have a bad effect on the already bellicose Goths. For his translation he invented a special script derived from the Greek and Latin alphabets, and introduced some *loanwords like *aiwangeljo* (Gk. *euangelion*). Only about half of the Gospels, fragments of the Pauline Letters, and three chapters of the book of Nehemiah have survived in 5th-century mss.

Urim and Thummim. A means of divination associated with the priesthood in ancient Israel (Exod. 28:30; Deut. 33:8). It probably involved the casting of lots to gain a yes/no answer to a question (cf. 1 Sam. 14:41), but the Urim and Thummim were no longer in existence in the Second Temple period, and nothing is known of the original meaning of the two terms. The rabbis and *Josephus connected them with the twelve jewels on the high priest's breastplate that "shone" (cf. Heb. *or*, "light") and revealed the "truth" (cf. Heb. *tam*, "perfect"). Christian tradition, going back to the LXX and Vulgate, translates the terms "Manifestation and Truth" or "Light and Truth," although George *Herbert in his poem "Aaron," a short meditation on Christ as high priest, has "Light and perfections in the breast" (*The Temple*, 1688). "Urim and Thummim" appears in Hebrew on the crest of Yale University with the Latin translation *Lux et Veritas*, "Light and Truth."

Ussher, James (1581–1656). Irish Anglican archbishop. A learned scholar and historian, he published many works on various topics in Latin and English, and lived the last part of his life in England, where he was given a state funeral by Oliver Cromwell in Westminster Abbey. He is best known for his biblical chronology, printed in the margins of many Bibles, according to which the creation of the world took place on October 23, 4004 B.C.E., and Christ's birth was exactly 1,000 years after the completion of Solomon's *temple.

Vaughan Williams, Ralph (1872–1958). English composer. Son of a clergyman, he studied at Cambridge, the Royal College of Music in London, and then with Max Bruch in Berlin and the young Ravel in Paris. An active member of the Folk Song Society and editor of the *English Hymnal* (1907), his compositions include many secular works as well as motets, a Mass in G, a *Magnificat, and other music for the Anglican liturgy. Other works on specifically biblical themes include *Flos Campi* (Song 2:1; 1925), *Job*, a masque based on *Blake's illustrations (1931), and five variations on the folk song *Dives and Lazarus* (Luke 16:19–31), scored for strings and harps (1939).

Venite (Lat. "Come!"). The first word and Latin title of Ps. 95 (Vg 94). Since the Rule of St. Benedict (c. 540) the *Venite* has been a familiar element in the morning liturgy in many Christian traditions, up to and including the Anglican Book of Common Prayer. Some recent editions omit the somewhat harsh final verses. In Jewish tradition it is the first of five psalms (95–99) sung at the weekly service for the Inauguration of the *Sabbath on Friday evening.

Verbal inspiration. The belief that every word of a sacred text like the Bible is inspired by God. Some interpret this to mean that the text is infallible, having been dictated verbatim by God to his prophet, for example, *Moses in the case of the *Torah. The role of the human agent in the process would then be entirely passive, although according to rabbinic legend, Moses occasionally argued with God. The tradition that Muhammad was illiterate (cf. Amos 7:14) stresses the divine origin of the *Qur'an still more explicitly. Others, less concerned about literal inerrancy, have understood verbal inspiration differently, more akin to the way in which poets and artists are inspired, while still maintaining a belief in the unique authority of the Bible. For many the role of the interpreter, whether the church or the individual inspired by the "inner testimony of the Holy Spirit" (*Calvin), was as crucial as that of the original author.

The challenge posed by modern *historical criticism, which seriously questioned the truth and accuracy of the Bible, was handled in different ways. In the Catholic Church the First Vatican Council in 1870 reiterated the doctrine of verbal inspiration and the inerrancy of Scripture, and it was not until 1943 that the encyclical *Divino afflante spiritu* opened the way for a more liberal approach to biblical studies, later confirmed in the Second Vatican Council (1962–65). Some Orthodox Jews and some evangelical Christians, however, still tenaciously adhere to the Mosaic authorship of the Pentateuch and similar precritical beliefs. Within Islam too the belief that the Qur'an is the actual speech of God (Arab. *kalam allah*) can be interpreted as implying either that it is the only source of authority (*sunna*), or that some human interpreters, such as the ayatollahs, have authority as well (*shia*). See *Literal meaning; *Pontifical Biblical Commission; *Word of God.

Verdi, Giuseppe (1813–1901). Italian composer. Son of an innkeeper and employed as an organist at the age of 9, he started composing in 1828 and three years later moved to Milan, where his first opera *Oberto* was performed at La Scala in 1939. He soon became an international celebrity with almost annual successes like *Rigoletto*, *Il Trovatore*, *La Traviata*, *Simon Boccanegra*, *Don Carlos*, and *Aida*, culminating in *Otello* and *Falstaff*, the two Shakespearean masterpieces composed toward the end of his long life. Of his operas, only one, *Nabucco* (Nebuchadnezzar; 1842), has a biblical theme, but he also composed a *Te Deum, two popular arrangements of *Ave Maria, a well-known Paternoster, and a setting of a passage from *Dante's *Paradiso* beginning "Vergine madre figlia del tuo Figlio" (1898), as well as his famous *Requiem* (1874). The crowds at his funeral sang the chorus of the Hebrew slaves from *Nabucco* (cf. Ps. 137).

Verdun Altar. A richly decorated feature of Klosterneuburg Abbey near Vienna. It is mainly the work of the 12th-century French artist Nicholas of Verdun, whose 45 enameled panels, showing scenes from the OT and the NT, constitute one of the most elaborate examples of iconographical *typology.

Virgil, Publius Vergilius Maro (70–19 B.C.E.). Roman poet. Born in Mantua, he studied rhetoric and politics in Milan and *Rome, and philosophy with the Epicurean Siron at Parthenope

near Naples. His ten pastoral *Eclogues*, the four *Georgics*, and especially the *Aeneid*, which became a national epic, celebrating the history of Rome down to the reign of Emperor Augustus, greatly influenced all later Latin writers, including many Christians. The Fourth Eclogue, which describes a golden age to be inaugurated by the return of a virgin and the birth of a male child, was interpreted, like some of the *Sibylline Oracles*, as containing a prophecy of the Virgin Birth. Despite strong opposition from the church fathers, including *Jerome and *Augustine, Virgil became a much respected and studied figure in the church for many centuries, his name changed from Vergilius to Virgilius and his association with Parthenope (Gk. *parthenos*, "virgin") given new significance. He is *Dante's guide through the *Inferno* and *Purgatorio*, although not permitted to enter *Paradise*, and appears occasionally in Christian art alongside the kings and prophets of the OT.

Virgin Mary. See *Mary, the Virgin.

Visitation. The visit of *Mary, sixth months pregnant, to her cousin Elizabeth, at which Elizabeth said, "Blessed art thou amongst women . . ." (see *Ave Maria), and Mary sang the *Magnificat (Luke 1:39–56). Celebrated as a feast day since medieval times, it has been a popular subject for *icon painters and Western artists including Fra *Angelico, *Giotto, *Tintoretto, and *Rubens, who places it alongside the *Descent from the Cross* in his famous altarpiece for Antwerp Cathedral (1612–14). The traditional site of the visitation is venerated at Ein Kerem near Jerusalem. In Greek Orthodox tradition it is known as *ho aspasmos*, "the embrace (of Mary and Elizabeth)."

Vivaldi, Antonio (1678–1741). Italian composer. Son of a violinist at St. Mark's Venice, he was ordained priest ("the red-haired priest") in 1703, but devoted his life more to music than to the church. His most important compositions were instrumental, including over 230 violin concertos, of which the *Four Seasons* is the best known; but he also composed a number of oratorios and operas, of which the Latin oratorio *Juditha* is the only one on a biblical subject. Among his sacred choral works are a number of settings of the *Gloria, *Magnificat, *Stabat Mater dolorosa, and several psalms (110, 113, 127).

Voltaire (François-Marie Arouet)

(1694–1778).   French writer. He quickly rejected his *Jesuit upbringing, and his bitter attacks on the political and ecclesiastical establishment led to imprisonment more than once and exile in London, Berlin, and elsewhere in Europe, where he became an international figure. He was welcomed back to Paris at the age of 84 in 1778 just before he died, although it was not until after the revolution in 1789 that his remains were reinterred in the Pantheon. His complete works, which include plays (*Oedipe, Mahomet, Irene*), short stories (*Candide*), treatises, letters, and a *Dictionnaire philosophique portatif* (1764; ET 1765), take up more than 250 volumes, and of these a considerable number are witty satirical criticisms of Christianity and the Bible. Making full use of the results of modern scholarship, in particular a critical interest in apocryphal texts, he questions the truth and historicity of much of the Bible, especially everything miraculous, and bitterly ridicules images like that of a Davidic *Messiah "who breathes nothing but blood" (Isa. 63:1–6; Ps. 137:9) and the religious intolerance implied by the notion of a chosen people. He was the first to make available this kind of critical questioning to ordinary people outside the academic world, but it took over a century for it to be taken seriously by the establishment.

Vulgate.

The Latin version of the Bible made by *Jerome (c. 382–400 C.E.) that became, after some revisions (e.g., by Alcuin of York, 8th century), the official text of Scripture in the Western church. Based on Greek mss of the NT and, in the later editions, Origen's *Hexapla for the OT, it was a significant linguistic achievement, not recognized at first and occasionally idiosyncratic, but an essential element in all subsequent biblical research, alongside the *Septuagint, *Targum, and *Peshitta.

The oldest complete ms of the Vulgate is Codex Amiatinus (c. 690–700), and the first printed edition was the famous Gutenberg Bible (1456). Challenged by the Reformers seeking to get back behind it to the original meaning, it was declared the only authorized Latin text in the Catholic Church at the Council of Trent (1546) and remained so until a new Latin version was produced in 1979, by which time vernacular versions had already replaced it in the liturgy.

Walton, William (1902–83).   English

composer. Born in Lancashire, he studied at Oxford, where he was a choral scholar, and lived most of his life in London. During World War II he composed music for official films and was knighted in 1951. Among his most successful works are two Coronation Marches (1937, 1953), two symphonies, and concertos for piano, viola, violin, and cello, as well as *Façade* (1923), and the incidental music for the film *Henry V* (1944). In addition to some church music, Walton arranged a selection of pieces from *Bach cantatas as a ballet entitled *The Wise Virgins* (1940; cf. Matt. 25), and his own cantata *Belshazzar's Feast* (1931) is a brilliant musical interpretation of passages from Isaiah (13:6; 39:7), Daniel (chap. 5), Psalms (81; 137), and Revelation (18:2).

War and Peace.   Wars and military

images take up a disproportionately

large space in biblical narrative and poetry. They appear first in the patriarchal period (Gen. 14:13–16) and, with few exceptions like the book of *Ruth and the *Song of Songs, are rarely absent; and when we think of the "wars and rumors of wars" in the Gospels (Mark 13:7) and the "war in heaven" in Revelation (12:7), this does not apply only to the OT. The Preacher acknowledges that "there is a time for war and a time for peace" (Eccl. 3:8). Explicit legislation on military engagement is given in the *Torah (Deut. 20), and *Thomas Aquinas cites Paul (Rom. 13:4) and Psalms (82:4) in his famous discussion of the doctrine of a "just war," and a variety of other texts in his instructions about fighting on the *Sabbath (1 Macc. 2:41; John 7:23) and the role of priests in war (Matt. 26:52; 2 Cor. 10:4) (*Summa Theologica* 2b.40).

Despite his teaching on turning the other cheek (Matt. 5:38–42), Jesus advises his followers to arm themselves against dangers on the road (Luke 22:36), employs a proverbial comment about how kings decide whether to wage war (Luke 14:31), and stresses that the peace he offers is not of this world (John 14:27): "I have not come to bring peace, but a sword" (Matt. 10:34; Luke 12:51). In many cases victory or defeat in battle is attributed to divine intervention, not military superiority: the story of Gideon's 300 explicitly warns against Israel boasting that "My own hand saved me" (Judg. 7:2; cf. Ps. 33:16). It is thus God who defeats the Egyptians (Exod. 15), the Assyrians (Isa. 37; Nahum), and the Babylonians (Daniel); and the image of God as a successful "man of war" (Exod. 15:3; Isa. 42:13) and a "mighty hero" (Ps. 24:8; 45:3) is perhaps the most bellicose aspect of the biblical tradition. The Davidic *Messiah is no less warlike (Ps. 89:19), and in the final battle even the Lamb wins a military victory (Rev. 17:14). The frequent title "Lord of hosts [Heb. *sabaoth*, "armies"]," however, came to refer more

to the creation of the heavens and the earth than military might (Gen. 2:1; Isa. 40:26; 45:12; see *Sanctus).

Yet it is the "swords into plowshares" passage, repeated twice in the Bible (Isa. 2:4; Mic. 4:3), that had the greatest impact on 20th-century readers. Quoted by Gorbachev when the Russian army withdrew from Afghanistan in 1989, and depicted in a huge bronze statue outside the United Nations building in New York, it has also appeared in the title of at least twenty publications since the 1980s. There are other important visions of a coming age of justice and peace in the Bible (Isa. 11:1–9; 16:3–5; 32), and the "Mighty God" title in one case appears alongside the "Prince of Peace" (Isa. 9:6), and in another beside the image of God as a mother (42:13–14). Of many 20th-century works on "war and the pity of war," perhaps the most effective use of a biblical text is Wilfred Owen's military retelling of the *Akedah (Gen. 22).

The situation for Jewish interpreters of the Hebrew Bible has changed since the establishment of the State of Israel in 1948, now the most powerful military presence in the Middle East. On the one hand Jewish religious radicals cite the Bible to defend Israel's right to live on the West Bank, giving biblical names to their settlements and justifying the use of force if necessary. On the other hand, the "swords into plowshares" verse is inscribed, in Hebrew and Arabic, on a "monument of peace" set up in Jerusalem after the Six Day War in 1967, and when Prime Minister Rabin shook hands with the Palestinian leader Yasser Arafat in Washington, DC, in 1993 he quoted Isaiah: "Peace, peace to the far and the near, says the Lord" (Isa. 57:19). See *Peace.

Watts, Isaac (1674–1748). English hymn writer. Born and brought up in Southampton, he refused a normal university education in favor of a Dissenting Academy, where he became tutor and later pastor of an Independent parish in London. From 1712 till his death, he suffered from ill health and devoted most of his time to writing theological and lyrical works. He wrote over 600 hymns, which earned him a DD from Edinburgh University and rare praise from Dr. Johnson. They include "Jesus shall reign where'er the sun" (Ps. 72), "O God our help in ages past" (Ps. 90), and "When I survey the wondrous cross" (Gal. 6:14), according to Matthew Arnold, "the finest hymn in the English language."

Weber, Max (1864–1920). German sociologist. He studied law at Heidelberg, taking lectures in economics, medieval history, and theology there, and then in Berlin and Göttingen. He was professor of economics for eight years at Freiburg but suffered a serious breakdown on the death of his father in 1897. He had no regular teaching commitments until 1917 when he gave a series of lectures on sociology in Vienna. In 1919 he accepted a professorship at Munich but was forced to leave by right-wing student protests and died the following year. He wrote on the sociology of politics and government, on the religions of China and India, and on economics. But his most famous essay, *The Protestant Ethic and the Spirit of Capitalism* (1904; ET 1930), and his study of *Ancient Judaism* (1917–19; ET 1952) were never followed up with further studies of the Bible, Christian origins, and Islam as he would have wished. But his theory that social structures and rituals are governed by shared ideas (e.g., *Zion) and beliefs (e.g., in, life after death), as well as economic factors such as the destruction of the *temple and the authority of individual charismatic leaders like *Moses and *Elijah, laid the foundation of modern sociology of religion.

Weeks, Feast of.   See Pentecost.

Wellhausen, Julius (1844–1918). Biblical scholar and orientalist. Born in Hameln, he studied theology at Göttingen and was professor of OT at Greifswald for ten years. A devout Christian, he felt that his historical-critical teaching was inappropriate in a theological faculty, and resigned to become eventually professor of *Semitic languages at Marburg (1885–92) and Göttingen (1892–1913). He published significant studies of Muhammad and pre-Islamic Arabia (1889), and of the NT and Christian origins, including his early study of the Pharisees and Sadducees (1874; ET 2001) and works on the Gospels (1903–8) and Acts (1914). But it was for his analysis of the sources (JEDP) and composition of the *Pentateuch, especially as published in the *Prolegomena to the History of Israel* (1883; ET 1885) that his name became a byword among Christians worldwide. Building on the earlier documentary theories of *Astruc, W. M. L. De Wette, and K. H. Graf, he observed that there are few traces of "Mosaic law" either in Joshua–Kings or in the prophetic books and concluded that "the law is later than the prophets." This had implications not only for the date and authorship of the sources, which worried fundamentalists, but also for the history of Israelite and Jewish religion, to which he devoted a later study (1894) and which according to many reinforced Christian prejudices about postexilic Judaism.

Wesley, Charles (1707–88). English hymn writer. Born in Epworth and educated in London and Oxford, he was ordained in 1735 and, after some years as an itinerant preacher, including a brief spell in North America with his brother John, settled first in Bristol and then in London. He wrote well over 5,000 hymns, most of them topical and ephemeral, but many are still sung by Christians of all denominations, including "Hark the herald angels sing," "Love divine, all loves excelling," "Rejoice, the

Lord is king," and "Jesus, Lover of my soul." Less familiar but exegetically interesting is "Come, O thou traveller unknown" (Gen. 32).

Whitsuntide.   See *Pentecost.

Wiesel, Elie (1928–).   Jewish *Holocaust survivor, novelist, and political activist. After the war he lived in France, where he became a close friend of the novelist François Mauriac and published his first novel *Night* (*La Nuit*) in 1955 (ET 1960). In that year he moved to New York, where he has continued to publish widely, and was awarded the Nobel Prize for Literature in 1986. His writings are informed by his nine months as a teenager in Auschwitz and characterized by frequent and consistent denunciations of violence and racism worldwide. His post-*Holocaust handling of biblical themes, such as *Cain and Abel, the *Akedah, *Jacob at Peniel, and *Job, in his novels (*The Town beyond the Wall*, 1962; *Beggar in Jerusalem*, 1970) and plays (*The Trial of God*, 1979) as well as in studies like *Messengers of God* (1976) and *Sages and Dreamers* (1991), is often poignant, original, and theologically challenging.

Wirkungsgeschichte.   A term invented by *Gadamer to denote the process whereby a text has an "effect" or "impact" (Ger. *Wirkung*) on its readers. See *Reader-response criticism; *Reception history.

Wisdom (Heb. *hokhmah*; Gk. *sophia*; Lat. *sapientia*).   In the Bible wisdom is a powerful commodity recommended as a "tree of life" (Prov. 3:18), a source of riches and honor (8:18), fundamental to a just society (Prov. 8:15; Isa. 11:1), and active in human history from the very beginning (Wis. 10). It can also be an evil condemned by the prophets (Isa. 5:21; Jer. 8:8), and this ambivalence is reflected in the story of the serpent (cf. Matt. 10:16) through whom *Adam and *Eve became like God, "knowing good and evil" (Gen. 3:22), but were also cursed because that same wisdom, acquired by disobedience, would lead to murder (Gen. 4), global wickedness (Gen. 6), and the tower of *Babel (Gen. 11).

In Jewish tradition "the fear of the Lord" was seen as an essential element in wisdom from as early as Job (28:28) and Proverbs (1:7; 9:10; cf. Sir. 1), and Wisdom was identified with the *Torah (Ps. 119; Sir. 24). For Christians she was identified with Christ, present like a master craftsman at creation (Prov. 8:22–31), and calling on them to "come eat of my bread and drink of the wine I have mixed" (Prov. 9:5). For Paul Christ is "the power of God and the wisdom of God" (1 Cor. 1:24), and he was celebrated as Divine Wisdom (*Hagia Sophia*) by the church fathers and in the church that stood on the site of the Ayasofya Mosque in Istanbul till 1453. Some Greek writers used the masculine word *logos*, "Word, reason," instead of the feminine *sophia*, and this introduced philosophical ideas not present in the Hebrew (John 1). There have also been theologians since *Irenaeus (2nd century C.E.) who identified biblical Wisdom with the Holy Spirit (cf. Isa.11:1), implying that one person of the Trinity was female. Some modern scholars have noted parallels between the personification of Wisdom in Proverbs, almost a goddess in some passages (Prov. 1:28), and the Egyptian goddess Ma'at ("truth, order"), depicted with the *ankh* ("life") symbol in one hand and a symbol of power in the other (cf. Prov. 3:16), or with the Greek goddess of love, Aphrodite, to whom a seven-pillared temple was dedicated in Cyprus (Prov. 9:1).

Wisdom literature.   A modern term for the books of *Job, *Proverbs, *Ecclesiastes, and the *Song of Songs, grouped together with *Psalms, in Christian Bibles, between the historical books (Genesis–Esther) and the Prophets. To these are normally added "Wisdom psalms" (e.g., 1, 34, 37, 49, 78, 127) and the apocryphal books of *Wisdom of Solomon and *Sirach. Apart from Job, Sirach, and the Psalms (except Pss. 72:1; 127:1) these are traditionally attributed to Solomon (cf. 1 Kgs. 10:23–24). The Wisdom literature contains collections of wise sayings (Heb. *meshalim*) and practical teaching on coping with life, but it also addresses the question of why the righteous suffer and the wicked prosper and celebrates the beauty of human love.

The occurrence of similar literary patterns and themes elsewhere in the Bible (e.g., the *Joseph story, *Deuteronomy, *Tobit, *Sermon on the Mount) suggests that the term should not be applied too rigidly. The present position of the book of Psalms between Job and Proverbs perhaps indicates that their role is as much to accompany private devotion and reflection as public worship, whatever their origin. Close parallels in Egyptian and Mesopotamian literature, such as the "Thirty Sayings of Amenemope" (cf. Prov. 22:17–24:22) and a "Babylonian Job," prove that many of the conventions and motifs in these books go back long before Solomon, even if there are indications that they mostly reached their present form in the Second Temple period.

Wisdom of Jesus ben Sira. See *Sirach.

Wisdom of Solomon. Apocryphal work placed after Job in the LXX and after the Song of Songs in the Vulgate. It is written in Greek and has a fourfold rhetorical structure. A prologue addresses the rulers of the earth and recommends righteousness, identified with *wisdom, as the only way to immortality (1:1–6:11). Depiction of the "wicked" conspiring to put the righteous "son of God" to death (2:10–24)

reassures readers that the righteous will have eternal life (3:1–9). The author (*Solomon) then praises wisdom (6:12–9:18), recalling how he "became enamored of her beauty" and prayed for her (cf. 1 Kgs. 4), and received all his knowledge, skill, and virtue from her. Next the role of Wisdom in the whole of history from the beginning down to the exodus is celebrated in such a way as to highlight the difference between true religion and idolatry (chaps. 10–15), and then the final part of the book, in a powerful retelling of the *Passover story, shows how God destroys the wicked and saves his people (chaps. 16–19).

Clearly influenced by Hellenistic style and philosophical ideas, such as the four cardinal virtues (8:7) and the "immortal soul" (8:19), the book was probably written in the 1st century B.C.E. It has been suggested that the last part might have been a kind of Passover *haggadah for the Jews of *Alexandria. Although it is not quoted in the NT, its direct influence can probably be seen in passages like Rom. 9:21–23 (cf. Wis. 12:12–18), Eph. 6:11–17 (cf. Wis. 5:17–20), and John 17:3 (cf. Wis. 15:3) as well as the Passion Narrative. *Ambrose and *Augustine wrote homilies on Wisdom, both lost, and there are commentaries by *Rabanus Maurus, *Anselm, *Nicholas of Lyra, and others. Two passages are commonly prescribed to be read at Catholic funerals (3:1–9; 4:7–15), of which one, beginning "The souls of the righteous (are in the hand of God)" (Lat. *Justorum animae*; 3:1) has been set to music by *Lassus, *Byrd, Stanford, and others, as well as by *Brahms in his *German Requiem* (1869).

Womanism. A movement originating in the writings of the African American writer Alice Walker, citing the black folk expression "you acting womanish," i.e., outrageous, audacious, grown up (vs. "girlish"), and exploiting the wit and wisdom of the black mother-daughter relationship. Brought up on the Bible, often the only book in the house and the

one that for centuries expressed their own dreams of social justice and freedom from *slavery, womanists are reluctant to abandon it despite its abuse by their oppressors. Building on earlier feminist and sociopolitical studies, they read the stories of *Sarah and *Hagar, the *Queen of Sheba, Gomer, the Ethiopian eunuch, and others with fresh critical attention to how the combined issues of race, gender, and poverty influence the interpreter and affect the lives of their people. See *Feminism; *Sexuality.

Woman's Bible.

Woman's Bible. See *Stanton, Elizabeth Cady.

Word of God.

Word of God. A means of communication, not always verbal, between heaven and earth. The "words of God" are communicated to *Moses on *Sinai (Exod. 20:1), and the Ten Commandments are properly known as the "Ten Words" (Gk. *Dekalogos*). Prophetic utterances are usually introduced by formulas like "Hear the word of the LORD" and "The word of the LORD came to me," implying their heavenly origin and divine authority (cf. Jer. 23:18). The prophetic "word" (Heb. *dabar*, "word, matter, event") is occasionally visible as well as audible: "the word that Isaiah son of Amoz saw concerning Judah and Jerusalem" (Isa. 2:1). Jesus and his disciples preached the "word of God" (Luke 5:1; Acts 4:31).

In the Bible the heavens and the earth are created by God's command (Ps. 33:6; cf. Gen. 1:3, 6, 9) and his people delivered from destruction by his word (Ps. 107:20; cf. Wis. 15:18). This led to personification in both Jewish and Christian tradition. In Jewish tradition, beginning with the *Targum (esp. Yerushalmi), Aramaic *Memra*, "the Word (of God)," replaces the divine name, especially in contexts considered theologically inappropriate, e.g., "the Memra repented" (Gen. 6:6 Tg) (see *Shekinah). But it can also be a divine agent or mediator in its own right (Exod. 20:1 Tg). The Greek translation **logos*, "word," introduced philosophical ideas not present in the Hebrew, and in Christianity led to a "Logos Christology" first described in the prologue to the Fourth Gospel: "the Word became flesh" (Gk. *ho logos sarx egeneto*, John 1:14). According to this all forms of divine-human communication are concentrated in the person of Jesus Christ, a doctrine of revelation of which the liturgical and theological implications were worked out, in Greek, during the first four centuries C.E. Creation by the word occurs also in the *Qur'an (2:117; 6:73) and "the Word of God" (Arab. *kalimat allah*) is a title given to Jesus (3:34; 4:169).

The term is applied to Scripture already in the NT (Mark 7:13), but other passages were also interpreted as references to the Bible, notably Isa. 40:8, cited in 1 Pet. 1:25, which became a favorite slogan of Luther's followers: "the word of God endures forever" (*Verbum Dei manet in aeternum*). The verse features memorably also in *Brahms's *German Requiem*. It is normal in many Christian liturgies to introduce readings from Scripture with the words "Hear the word of God as it is written in . . ." "This is the Word of God," or the like, although there is theological controversy on precisely what it means in terms of divine authority. In Islam the Qur'an is believed to be the uncreated "speech of God" (*kalam allah*). See *Authority; *Verbal inspiration.

Word pairs.

Word pairs. Two words of related meaning, such as synonyms (wilderness//desert, Isa. 40:3), opposites (right//left, Prov. 3:16), correlatives (blind//deaf, Isa. 35:5), and metaphors (honey//oil, Prov. 5:3). Recent research has shown that Hebrew *poetry shared with the *Ugaritic literary tradition a stock of such word pairs, which had a similar function to that of the conventional formulae used in Greek epic poetry ("rosy-fingered dawn," "grey-eyed Athene") and point to an original oral tradition. This has important exegetical implications: the first term in a word pair, for example, is normally the main one so that sometimes nothing new is said about the second (Prov. 1:8). See *Parallelism.

Writing.   See *Alphabet; *Literacy.

Writings. The third part of the Hebrew Bible. See *Ketuvim.

Wycliffe, John (c. 1330–84). English religious reformer. Born in Yorkshire, he studied theology and philosophy at Oxford, where he was appointed Master of Balliol in 1360 and received his doctorate in 1371. He published over 40 works, including several on the role of the Bible in the church. Much influenced by his reading of *Augustine, John *Chrysostom, and *Bonaventure, he argued that the correct interpretation of Scripture depended as much on the spiritual life and virtue of the individual interpreter as on church dogma, and called for a vernacular translation of the whole Bible (including the *Apocrypha) so that all members of the church could have access to it. His works were condemned as heretical in 1428, and in the same year his bones were dug up by the church authorities and burned. The translation of the Vulgate into English, known as the Wycliffite Bible, which Wycliffe undoubtedly inspired even though it was done by his disciples Nicholas of Hereford and John Purvey, was officially banned in 1415, but 100 mss survived and printed editions were published in 1731 and 1850. Through his supporters known derisively as Lollards ("mumblers") and the Bohemian reformer Jan *Hus, his influence on the European Reformation was considerable.

YHWH.   See *Tetragrammaton.

Yahwist (Fr. *Jahviste*). The name given to the hypothetical author of the J source, coined by the French scholar *Astruc. See *Documentary Hypothesis; *Pentateuch.

Yerushalmi (Heb. "of Jerusalem"). The Palestinian *Talmud.

Yom Kippur (Heb. "Day of Atonement"). The great Jewish fast held annually on the 10th of Tishri, that is, ten days after Rosh Ha-Shanah (New Year's Day) and five days before Sukkot (*Tabernacles) (Lev. 23:23–43). Leviticus 16 contains a description of the ritual in which one goat is sacrificed to YHWH and another, the "*scapegoat," sent away to Azazel in the wilderness, bearing the sins of the community (Lev. 16:20–22; cf. Isa. 53:12). In the Second Temple period this was the one day in the year on which the high priest entered the Holy of Holies, and when he came out he blessed the people in the words of the priestly blessing: "The LORD bless you and keep you . . ." (Num. 6:24–26), for once pronouncing the *Tetragrammaton. The significance of this liturgical moment can be gauged from the poetic description in Sir. 50. The *Mishnah tractate *Yoma* (c. 200 C.E.) gives a vivid and practical account of how things were done before the *temple was destroyed.

Today Yom Kippur is the holiest day of the year, widely observed by fasting and public worship, as a day of repentance and spiritual renewal. The haunting *Kol Nidre*, "all vows," with its note of remorse and triumph, which has been set to music by Bruch (1881), Arnold Schönberg (1938), and others, is traditionally sung on the night of Yom Kippur. Isaiah 57:14–58:14 is read at the morning service ("Is not this the fast that I choose . . . to let the oppressed go free?"), and the book of *Jonah in the afternoon because it is about God's willingness to forgive repentant sinners. Only sins against God can be atoned for, however;

sins against one's neighbor have to be set right first on the human level. See *Rosenzweig, Franz.

Zechariah, book of. Eleventh of the twelve Minor Prophets. Haggai and Zechariah are mentioned together in connection with the rebuilding of the temple at Jerusalem after the exile (Ezra 6:11) in the early years of the reign of the great Persian king Darius (522–486 B.C.E.) (Zech. 1:1; 7:1). The first part of the book (chaps. 1–8) contains a series of visions filled with angels (including *Satan), horses, chariots, horns, mountains, and other images, and tells of two anointed leaders, a king (Zerubbabel) and a priest (Joshua), and a time when Jerusalem will once again be called "the city of truth" (AV), with boys and girls playing in the streets and the world acknowledging that it is God's dwelling place. The second part of the book (chaps. 9–14) has no visions, no angels, no dates, and no mention of the rebuilding of the temple. It contains instead prophecies about the violent defeat of Judah's enemies, reminiscent of other oracles against the foreign nations (cf. Isa. 13–20; Jer. 46–51), and shows none of the optimism present in the early chapters. The last chapter begins with a description of the *Day of the Lord when the Mount of Olives will be split in two and Jerusalem, raised on high, will dwell in security.

Scholars generally agree that chaps. 9–14 ("Deutero-Zechariah") come from a later period than 1–8, and have suggested that the mention of Greece (9:13) and a possible reference to the famous siege of Tyre by Alexander the Great in 332 B.C.E. (9:2–3) point to a period late in the 4th century, to which Isa. 24–27, Joel, and other early *apocalyptic writings probably also belong. The book as a whole is filled with allusions to earlier prophecy (e.g., 1:3, 14; 2:2; 8:3; 14:5) but also anticipates later apocalyptic style, especially in chaps. 9–14. The similarity between the "oracles" in chaps. 9–11 and 12–14, and the anonymous "oracle" now attributed to *Malachi (Heb. "my messenger") has prompted the suggestion that Malachi was originally part of the book of Zechariah.

Zechariah has played a significant role in both Jewish and Christian tradition. Two passages appear in the Jewish lectionary, one at *Hanukkah because of the reference to the golden menorah (2:10–4:7) and one at *Sukkot (14:1–21). "On that day the LORD will be one and his name one" (14:9) has special significance (cf. Deut. 6:4) and concludes one of the great Jewish prayers, the *Alenu*, with which every synagogue service ends. Zechariah 9:9 heralds the coming of the *Messiah both in Jewish *midrash (*Gen. Rab.* 56:2) and the NT (Matt. 21:5), while the concept of a suffering savior in Zech. 12:10 also appears both in the *Talmud (*b. Sukkah* 52a) and the Fourth Gospel (John 19:37). Christians from the beginning found in Zechariah detailed allusions to the life of Christ that earned him a place with the *Major Prophets in Christian iconography (see Claus *Sluter; *Sistine Chapel): "humble and riding on an ass" (9:9), "the thirty pieces of silver" (11:12), the piercing of his side (12:10), and the wounds in his hands (13:6 Vg). In music best known is the soprano aria "Rejoice greatly, O daughter of Zion" (9:9), in *Handel's *Messiah* (1742), but Zechariah is also responsible for William *Cowper's hymn "There is a fountain filled with blood" (13:1; 1771).

Zephaniah, book of. Ninth of the twelve *Minor Prophets. Grouped with *Nahum and *Habakkuk, the book is traditionally associated with Jeremiah "in the days of Josiah" (1:1). It contains descriptions of the terrifying "*Day of the Lord," and a series of withering attacks on the nations of the world, including Judah (3:1–7), softened by calls to "Seek the LORD" (2:3) and "Wait for me, says the LORD" (3:8), and by a final celebration of the day when Jerusalem's fortunes will be restored (3:14–20). The style is allusive and at times ambiguous; for example, the Hebrew words describing the city as "rebellious, defiled, and oppressing" could equally well mean "respected, redeemed, the dove" (3:1), although the context makes clear that it refers not to Nineveh, as the prophet's Judean audience might have wished, but to Jerusalem (cf. 3:4–5).

Allusions to Zephaniah in the NT include two in Revelation (6:17; cf. Zeph. 1:14–18; 14:5; cf. 3:13) and one in the Gospels (John 12:13–15; cf. Zeph. 3:16–17; Zech. 9:9); and the church fathers, including *Theodore of Mopsuestia, *Jerome, and *Augustine, found references to the *resurrection (3:8), *Pentecost (3:9), and the kingdom of Christ (3:12). The Reformers saw themselves and the true church as the remnant envisaged by Zephaniah in a world dominated by evil and idolatrous powers (3:11–13). Modern scholars have focused on the original historical context of the book, noting, for example, that the prominent reference to idolatry in Judah (1:4–6) must have been before Josiah's reformation in 621, and suggesting that the death of the last mighty Assyrian king Ashurbanipal in 627 might have contributed to Zephaniah's eschatology. More recently Zephaniah's concern for the poor (3:12) attracted the attention of *liberation theologians, and the reference to Cushi (Heb. "Ethiopian," Jer. 23:13) among his ancestors (Zeph. 1:1) has provided *Africans and *African Americans with evidence that one of the biblical prophets was black. But it was Zephaniah's horrifying *Day of the Lord imagery, especially in 1:14–18 (Vg), that left its deepest impression on Christian tradition, through the medieval *Dies Irae hymn.

Zionism. In the Bible Zion is a poetic name for *Jerusalem, surrounded by ancient mythical images (Pss. 46; 48; 125), personified as a beautiful courageous young woman (Isa. 37:22; 52:1–2), and the focus of extravagant hopes for the future (Isa. 2:2–5; Mic. 4:1–4). Since the

Jews in Babylon remembered Zion and vowed never to forget her (Ps. 137), Zion has remained a symbol of hope for Diaspora Jews worldwide. The "Songs of Zion" of *Judah Halevi (d. 1141) are a poignant medieval example, and although the founder of modern Zionism, Theodor Herzl (1860–1904), did not himself make much use of biblical language and imagery in his writings, the pioneers and politicians who sought to realize his dream certainly did. One of the earliest Zionist organizations, Bilu, took its name (an acronym) from Isa. 2:5 and its motto from 60:22a. The first Jewish agricultural school in *Palestine (1870) was called Miqveh Yisrael ("hope of Israel," Jer. 14:8), the first colony (1878) Petah Tikvah ("door of hope," Hos. 2:15), and the first town Tel Aviv (1909) (Ezek. 3:15). A disproportionate number of modern Israeli place names are biblical, like Rishon LeTzion ("first to Zion," Isa. 41:27), Rehovot ("room to live," Gen. 26:22), Rosh Pinah ("cornerstone," Ps. 118:22), and Ayelet Ha-Shahar ("the hind of the dawn," Ps. 22:1 MT).

Such a celebration of the restoration of Zion's fortunes, reminiscent of Ps. 126 ("we were like those who dream"), sung as part of grace after meals on the *Sabbath and festivals, is bitterly opposed by many, especially some ultraorthodox Jews who claim returning to Zion before the *Messiah comes is blasphemy, and by the Palestinians, whose land has been overrun by foreigners. For Palestinian Christians many parts of the Bible that celebrate the destruction of Egyptians, for example, and sing the praises of Zion and *Israel, are virtually unusable in the present political climate. If all sides could focus on the internationalization of Jerusalem, Zion might become once again a symbol of peace and justice for all nations.

Zohar (Heb. "splendor"). The main work of the *Kabbalah, written in a somewhat artificial *Aramaic probably in 13th-century Spain by Moses de Leon, but in the form and style of a rabbinic work purporting to be, like the *Mishnah, from the 2nd century C.E. The title "Book of Splendor" comes from Dan. 12:3, where it refers to the shining of the wise in the world to come. It is a midrashic commentary on the *Pentateuch containing an unrivaled variety of daring concepts, images, and interpretations, fundamental to Kabbalah, but also fascinating and often moving in themselves. It eventually became the third sacred text of Judaism alongside the Bible and the *Talmud, for several centuries rivaling even *Maimonides' *Guide for the Perplexed*, and influencing non-Jewish humanists like *Pico della Mirandola and Johannes *Reuchlin, until the 18th-century *Haskalah* (*Enlightenment) when it was rejected as superstitious. It remains canonical in *Hasidic Judaism, however, and respected even by those unsympathetic to its mystical teachings.

Zoroastrianism. The religion founded by the prophet Zoroaster (Zarathustra), probably c. 1000 B.C.E. in northern Iran, and known from his seventeen hymns (*Gathas*) and the voluminous *Avesta*, composed in the 4th century C.E. under the Sassanians, but incorporating much ancient material. The religious leaders were known as the *magi. Victims of persecution in the Muslim world, especially Iran, many Zoroastrians settled in India where they are known as Parsees ("Persians"), as they are also in Europe, the United States, and elsewhere. The supreme deity is Ahura Mazda, "Wise Lord," who created everything that is good, opposed to Angra Mainyu (Ahriman), "hostile spirit," who invaded the world and brought into it death and evil spirits. Human beings are engaged in a cosmic struggle, in the sense that every good deed helps Ahura Mazda, and can look forward to a day when the righteous are rewarded, the wicked punished, and the whole cosmos regenerated.

Some of the colorful *eschatology, angelology, and demonology of the magi probably appears in the Bible (*Daniel, *Revelation) and through the *apocalyptic traditions influenced Judaism, Christianity, and Islam. The "wise men [Gk. *magoi*] from the east" may have been Zoroastrians (Matt. 2:1). Zoroastrian dualism, which claims that the power of evil appears in history at times to be a match for the power of good, is also there in *midrash, *Kabbalah, and much 20th-century literature, although explicitly denied in the Bible (Isa. 45:6–7) and officially condemned as heretical by all three religions. Zoroaster appears in discussion with Ptolemy in *The School of Athens* by *Raphael (1509), as Sarastro, the stern moralist, in *Mozart's *Magic Flute* (1791); and as Zarathustra in the title role of Nietzsche's attack on Christianity (1883–91; ET 1961), which in turn inspired Richard Strauss's symphonic poem *Also Sprach Zarathustra* (1896), popularized as the theme music for the film *2001: A Space Odyssey* (1968).

Zwingli, Ulrich (Huldreich) (1484–1531).   Swiss reformer. He studied theology in Bern, Vienna, and Basel, where he met *Erasmus. In 1518 he went to Zurich, where his popular lectures and polemical sermons contributed much to the success of the Swiss Reformation. He remained there until his death in battle as a military chaplain. His commentaries on Genesis (1527), Exodus (1527), and Isaiah (1529), as well as other writings on the Bible, including *The Clarity and Certainty of the Word of God* (1522), are characterized by a concern for what he called "the natural sense" of Scripture. He advocated careful study of the original languages and an appreciation of rhetorical devices that often point beyond the literal meaning of the text. Against *Luther he argued that in the sentence "This is my body" (Matt. 26:26) the verb "is" should not be understood literally, but as "signifies." His beautifully illustrated German translation of the Bible, the "Zurich Bible," was published before Luther's.

Further Reference

Ackroyd, P. R., et al., eds. *Cambridge History of the Bible.* 3 vols. Cambridge: Cambridge University Press, 1963–70.

Aichele, G., et al. *The Postmodern Bible (The Bible and Culture Collective).* Ed. E. Castelli, S. D. Moore, G. A. Phillips, and R. M. Schwartz. New Haven: Yale University Press, 1995.

Barton, J., and J. Muddiman, eds. *The Oxford Bible Commentary.* Oxford: Oxford University Press, 2001.

Berlin, A., and M. Z. Brettler, eds. *The Jewish Study Bible.* Oxford: Oxford University Press, 2004.

Carmi, T., ed. *The Penguin Book of Hebrew Verse.* New York: Viking, 1981.

Coggins, R., and J. L. Houlden, eds. *A Dictionary of Biblical Interpretation.* Rev. ed. Philadelphia: Trinity Press International, 2003.

Cross, F. L., and E. A. Livingstone, eds. *Oxford Dictionary of the Christian Church.* 4th ed. Oxford: Oxford University Press, 1974.

Glassé, C., ed. *The New Encyclopedia of Islam.* Walnut Creek, Calif.: AltaMira Press, 2001.

Hastings, A., A. Mason, and H. Pyper, eds. *The Oxford Companion to Christian Thought.* Oxford: Oxford University Press, 2000.

Hayes, J. H., ed. *Dictionary of Biblical Interpretation.* 2 vols. Nashville: Abingdon, 1999.

Hornblower, S., and A. Spawforth, eds. *The Oxford Classical Dictionary.* 3rd ed. Oxford: Oxford University Press, 1996.

Jacobs, L. *The Jewish Religion: A Companion.* Oxford: Oxford University Press, 1995.

Jeffrey, D. L., ed. *Dictionary of Biblical Tradition in English Literature.* Grand Rapids: Eerdmans, 1992. Useful selections from English poetry can be found at http://rpo.library.utoronto.ca/display/index.cfm and http://www.americanpoems.com.

Kennedy, M., ed. *The Oxford Dictionary of Music.* Rev. ed. Oxford: Oxford University Press, 2006. Choral music scores, with translations, biblical references and a great deal of information, can be accessed at http://www.cpdl.org/wiki/index.php/Main_Page.

Klauck, H. J., B. McGinnn, P. Mendes Flohr, et al., eds. *The Encyclopedia of the Bible and Its Reception.* Berlin: de Gruyter, forthcoming. http://www.degruyter.de/cont/fb/th/thEbrEn.cfm.

Murray, P. and L., eds. *Oxford Companion to Christian Art and Architecture.* Oxford: Oxford University Press 1996. A large selection of art works with some background information can be viewed at http://www.wga.hu/index.html; another useful site is http://www.biblical-art.com.

Newsom, C. A., and S. H. Ringe, eds. *Women's Bible Commentary, with Apocrypha.* 2nd ed. Louisville: Westminster John Knox, 1998.

Rogerson, J. W., and J. M. Lieu, eds. *Oxford Handbook of Biblical Studies.* Oxford: Oxford University Press, 2006.

Sawyer, J. F. A., D. Gunn, J. Kovacs and C. C. Rowland, eds. Blackwell Bible Commentaries. Oxford: Blackwell, 2004– . Commentaries on all the books of the Bible with the emphasis on reception history. http://www.bbibcomm.net

Sawyer, J. F. A., and J. M. Y. Simpson, eds. *Concise Encyclopedia of Language and Religion.* Amsterdam: Elsevier, 2001.

Vanhoozer, K. J., ed. *Dictionary for Theological Interpretation of the Bible.* Grand Rapids: Baker, 2005.

West, G. O., and M. W. Dube, eds. *The Bible in Africa.* Leiden: Brill, 2000.

Index of Biblical References

References to biblical topics are included even where chapter and verse are not given in the text: for example, Cain (Gen. 4), Merkavah (Ezek. 1), annunciation (Luke 1:26–32).